Rebellion

Britain's First Stuart Kings, 1567–1642

TIM HARRIS

OXFORD
UNIVERSITY PRESS

OXFORD

UNIVERSITY PRESS

Great Clarendon Street, Oxford, OX2 6DP,
United Kingdom

Oxford University Press is a department of the University of Oxford.
It furthers the University's objective of excellence in research, scholarship,
and education by publishing worldwide. Oxford is a registered trade mark of
Oxford University Press in the UK and in certain other countries

First Edition published in 2014

Impression: 1

Published in the United States of America by Oxford University Press
198 Madison Avenue, New York, NY 10016, United States of America

British Library Cataloguing in Publication Data
Data available

Library of Congress Control Number: 2013940851

ISBN 978-0-19-920900-2

Printed in Italy by
L.E.G.O. S.p.A.—Lavis TN

For Beth

ACKNOWLEDGEMENTS

When working on this book, I have been fortunate to receive advice and feedback from numerous friends and colleagues who have expertise in the field. John Cramsie, David Cressy, Lori Anne Ferrell, Ken Fincham, Jonathan Israel, Peter Lake, Jason McElligott, Anthony Milton, Micheál Ó Siochrú, David Smith, Nigel Smith, Allan Macinnes, David and Joyce Ransome, Kevin Sharpe, and Stephen Taylor all read various chapters in draft and/or answered questions about specific interpretative issues. David and Joyce read the whole lot, very closely, and saved me from numerous small errors and careless slips. I owe them a tremendous amount—for this and for many other things—and I cannot thank them enough. Kevin was reading some of my draft chapters right up until his final illness. He will be sorely missed and I am hugely disappointed that he did not live long enough to see the end result. The historiography of early Stuart Britain and Ireland is vast and sophisticated, and although I have endeavoured wherever possible to root my findings in my own reading of the primary sources, in a work of this nature I have inevitably drawn extensively on the published work of others who have furrowed this field before me. I remain heavily indebted to their scholarship, as I have tried to acknowledge in the endnotes.

I also need to thank my students at Brown. Keara Kelly served as my undergraduate research assistant at an early stage of this project, sponsored by a grant from the Office of Dean of the College at Brown. Various draft chapters were inflicted upon my undergraduates and graduate students, as compulsory assigned readings in their courses. Some of my PhD students read the whole lot in draft, believing (rightly or wrongly) it might give them an edge in prelims. To all of them I owe a lot, perhaps more than they recognize.

The research and writing of this book would not have been possible without the generous support of a number of institutions and foundations. I am grateful to the Andrew W. Mellon Foundation for funding two periods of extended research leave—first at the Folger Shakespeare Library in Washington DC (2006–7) and then at the Institute for Advanced Study in Princeton (2011–12). I would also like to thank the Wardens and Fellows of Merton College, Oxford, for electing me a visiting fellow for the Trinity Term 2008 and the Master and Fellows of Emmanuel College, Cambridge, for making me a Senior Visitor at the College during the Easter Term and summer of 2012. In addition, I was privileged to be a fellow at the Cogut Humanities Center at Brown University for the Spring Semester of 2009 and a Visiting Research Fellow at the Long Room Hub at Trinity College Dublin during the late spring and early summer of 2011. I found all these experiences incredibly rewarding and enjoyable; hopefully this book testifies in some measure to how productive my time at these various institutions proved to be. Stephen Carroll at Trinity gave me many useful tips and leads about sources during my stay in Dublin, while Ben Kiernan (an expert on modern-day Cambodia) was always ready, either in the Hub or over a pint in a nearby pub, to discuss atrocity literature. A special mention needs also to go to my cohort of early modernists at the Folger, the Institute for Advanced Study, Oxford, Cambridge, and Trinity Dublin (both faculty and graduate students)—you know who you are—for their intellectual support and companionship, and being willing to listen as I began to shape some of my ideas for this book. Oxford University Press proved to be incredibly supportive throughout this whole process; in particular I would like to thank Luciana O'Flaherty, Matthew Cotton, Emma Barber, Anna Silva, Phil Henderson, Frances Topp, and the anonymous reader for the Press. As always, I am heavily indebted to my agent Clare Alexander, who encouraged me in my ideas for this book and helped me formulate the original book proposal and place this project with the Press. As Clare and OUP will know, this is not quite the book I originally intended to write. I hope they feel it has its merits nevertheless.

Last but not least I have to thank my family, all of them now in England—parents, siblings, in-laws—who did the things that family are good at, just being there when you need them. My children—Victoria and James—had fled the nest before I started work on this project, so it is not that they had to live with it in quite the same way they lived with my previous books, but for the fact that they relocated to Cambridge, England, which became the family base for much of the time while I was researching and writing. My wife Beth ended up being dragged everywhere with me—Oxford, Cambridge, Washington, Princeton. I like to think she enjoyed herself, wherever I took her. She did not complain, at least, and was even still willing at the end to help check footnotes. I owe her a lot, not least for being there with me.

CONTENTS

CONTENTS

LIST OF PLATES

CONVENTIONS AND STYLE

In quoting from original sources, I have extended contemporary contractions but otherwise adhered to the original spelling and capitalization, though I have very occasionally provided modern punctuation to assist in readability. (In particular I have inserted apostrophes to indicate the possessive.) Dates are in old style, although with the new year taken as having started on 1 January (rather than 25 March, as it did at the time). Works cited were published in London, unless otherwise stated. To save space, I have cited only the main titles of secondary works, omitting the subtitles (unless the subtitle is crucial to giving the reader some idea of what the book is about). Because of the ready availability of printed sources online, I have quoted from the original publication whenever possible, even when a work is available in a modern anthology. These days it is usually quicker and easier for scholars to check a reference by logging in to Early English Books Online than by making a trip to the nearest research library. I have made an exception, however, with regard to more philosophical works, when there is a definitive modern edition. Thus, for example, I quote the original pamphlet of James I's speech to parliament of 21 March 1610, but quote from the Sommerville edition of James's *Trew Law of Free Monarchies*—Johann P. Sommerville, ed., *King James VI and I: Political Writings* (Cambridge, 1994)—even though the speech of 21 March 1610 is also in the Sommerville edition. I have invariably quoted from the original State Papers for England, which are now available online, because the calendars are incomplete. The calendars for the Irish State Papers, however, are much fuller, and so I have quoted them unless I have uncovered additional information in original.

Up until 1971, British currency was in pounds (£), shillings (*s.*) and pence (*d.*). There were 12 pence to a shilling and 20 shillings to the pound (one shilling was worth five new pence). An English pound was worth twelve Scottish pounds. A mark was two-thirds of a pound, i.e. 13*s.* 4*d.* (67 new pence).

Map 1. England: counties

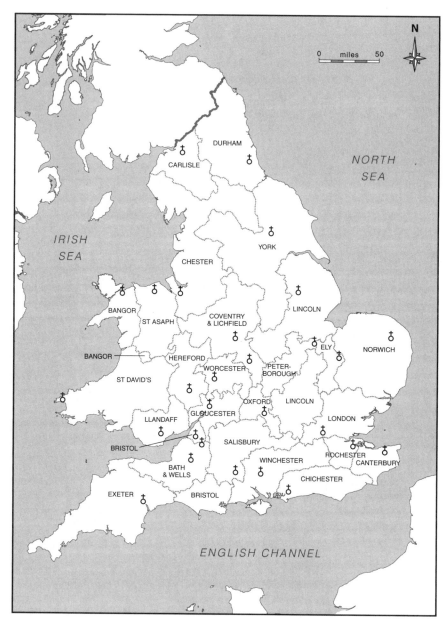

Map 2. England: dioceses

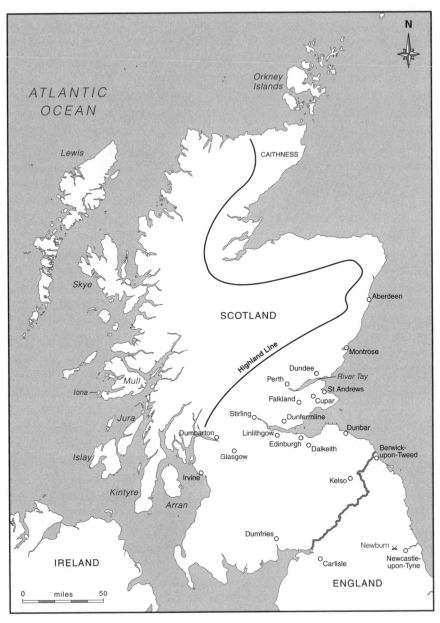

Map 3. Scotland

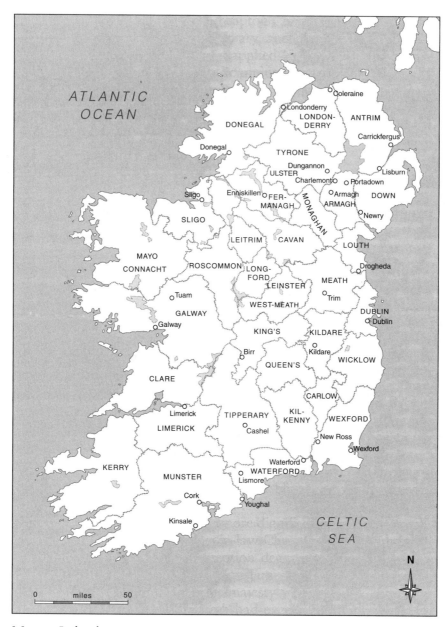

Map 4. Ireland

Prologue

On 1 April 1603 James VI of Scotland began his long march south from Edinburgh to London to take up his inheritance as James I of England. Now thirty-six, and having been king of Scotland almost his entire life, it was a moment he had been eagerly anticipating. Scotland was a comparatively poor country and James's period of rule had been testing, to say the least. He had come to the throne at the age of thirteen months, after his mother, Mary Queen of Scots, had been ousted in a Protestant coup, and he came to reign over a country where the predominant Presbyterian interest of the lowlands did not welcome royal attempts to govern the Kirk and where much of the Highlands and the Borders with England were not yet fully subordinated to the government of the crown. He had been kidnapped as a boy and held captive by a noble faction, had battled to bolster the authority of the Scottish crown when he assumed the reins of government himself upon reaching the age of majority, and had narrowly escaped an assassination attempt a few years before acceding to the English throne. James described his Scottish subjects as a 'barbarouse and stiffe nekkit people', as he put it in a letter to Sir Robert Cecil shortly before his accession; 'Saint george', he thought, 'surelie rydes upon a touardlie rydding horse', whereas in Scotland he found himself 'daunting a wylde unruelie coalte'.[1] England seemed to have much to offer. It had a more developed centralized state than Scotland, five times the population (which increased the fiscal, commercial, and military potential of the state), a better climate for agriculture, and a terrain more favourable to internal trade and communications. Perhaps most appealingly, the revenues of the English crown were over twenty times those of the Scottish crown.[2]

A dynastic contingency, one of those accidents of succession that not infrequently befall hereditary monarchies, had resulted in James Stuart becoming heir to the childless Elizabeth Tudor, the 'Virgin Queen of Blessed Memory', who had died on 24 March 1603. Indeed it is ironic that, for all Henry VIII's efforts to secure the future of the Tudor dynasty—including six wives and a new religion—it should be the descendants of Henry's elder sister, Margaret, who had married into the (then still Catholic) Scottish royal family, who would provide the rulers of England in the seventeenth century. Yet while we think of James as the first Stuart monarch of England—and thus a Scot from a long line of Scottish kings—he was always keen to emphasize his descent from Henry VII, the founder of the Tudor dynasty. And just as Henry VII had ended the Wars of the Roses and united the houses of Lancaster and York, so James saw his destiny as being to bring about a union of Scotland and England and an end to centuries of hostilities between the two kingdoms.

If James was looking forward to taking up his English inheritance, his English subjects appear to have been looking forward to him. Elizabeth had grown 'very covetous in her old days', and 'the people' were said to have been 'generally weary of an old woman's government'.[3] More importantly, James's accession produced a final, and seemingly satisfactory, resolution to one of the most pressing and sensitive problems of Elizabeth's reign, namely, who would succeed the Virgin Queen? For a long time, Elizabeth's heir had been the Catholic Mary Queen of Scots, until she was eventually executed by the English state in 1587. With Elizabeth ever reluctant to name her successor, a disputed succession with interference by European superpowers seemed a genuine possibility—an alarming prospect given the heated intensity of confessional strife across Europe and with England still at war with Catholic Spain. In 1595 the English Jesuit Robert Persons had predicted that the succession could not possibly be settled 'without some warr'.[4] Yet in the end, James VI and I was to inherit 'more peaceably', as the Scottish Presbyterian minister James Melville put it, than the king 'him selff or any uthir could haiff expectit'.[5] Furthermore, James had two sons and a daughter—Henry Frederick (b.1594), Elizabeth (b.1596), and Charles (b.1600)—the first English monarch already to have heirs at the time of his accession since Henry IV in 1399.

England was not without its own problems, however. Although the English crown was wealthier than the Scottish, it was not wealthy. Inflation over the sixteenth century had hit royal revenues badly, a fact obscured only temporarily by the sudden injection of cash provided by the sale of monastic lands after the Reformation. Elizabeth had been forced to be frugal for much of her reign; she could more easily afford to be so since she had neither spouse nor children to support. James had both, and he had to take on not just the debt left by Elizabeth (in itself not that significant) but a system of financing royal government that had come to be woefully inadequate in an inflationary era and an age of warfare between the rival confessional powers of Europe. Furthermore, England had slipped into a severe economic crisis in the 1580s and 1590s—decades which saw harvest failure, cattle disease, renewed outbreaks of the bubonic plague, rising unemployment, and soaring prices. Greater poverty for those at the lower levels of society had led inevitably not only to increased mortality but also to a rise in crime: felony prosecutions increased dramatically in the last decade of Elizabeth's reign, while in Oxfordshire in 1596 there were plans laid for a rebellion against the evil of enclosure.[6] In addition, England was religiously divided. Although convinced Catholics were by now a small and declining minority, Protestants were split between the 'hotter sort' who adhered to a more bibliocentric faith (typically styled 'Puritans' by their enemies) and those who preferred the more ceremonial forms of worship associated with strict adherence to the Book of Common Prayer and the Thirty-Nine Articles. Indeed, Elizabeth had faced a major challenge in the 1580s from an organized Presbyterian movement, with support in parliament, demanding fundamental reforms in the Church.

Any ruler of England also had to work with the English parliament, a bicameral legislature of Lords and Commons which was responsible for granting taxation and enacting legislation and which seemed to be growing more self-confident as an institution. Despite the overriding expectation that consensus politics would be the norm, the precise nature of the constitutional relationship between the crown and parliament was ill-defined and serious tensions often arose. Moreover, inflation had steadily eroded the value of the forty-shilling freehold, the qualification for the franchise in the counties, which meant that the elected chamber, the House of Commons, was coming to be representative of a broader cross-section of the population.[7] Nor was it only opinion in parliament that an English monarch had to worry about. Given that the crown lacked a professional civil service, in order to get its policies enforced it was dependent upon the cooperation of the unpaid agents of government in the localities: not just the nobility, gentry, and merchants, who served as Lord and Deputy Lieutenants, justices of the peace, and civic magistrates in the counties and towns, but also men of middling and even humbler status who served as trial jurors and local officeholders, whose support could not necessarily be taken for granted but who needed to be persuaded that government initiatives deserved to be enforced. If policies proved particularly unpalatable, people at the local level might take matters into their own hands by engaging in various forms of passive and active resistance—from noncompliance, through to petitioning, riot, and even rebellion. Opinion 'out-of-doors' could not easily be ignored.

James VI not only became king of England in 1603; he also became king of Ireland. It had been Pope Adrian IV in 1155 who had originally granted Ireland to the kings of England, so that they could bring Roman Christianity to the country, 'subject that people to laws', and 'root out...vice'.[8] England's real claim to rule Ireland, though, was based on conquest, which began under Henry II in 1169. Originally a feudal dependency of the English crown, in 1541 Ireland was raised by Henry VIII to the status of a kingdom, with the Irish crown vested in the king of England, his heirs and successors. Government in Ireland was based on the English model, with a legislature of Lords and Commons representing borough corporations and counties and a Lord Lieutenant or Lord Deputy serving as the king's viceroy—although Poynings' Law of 1494 had established that the Irish parliament could not enact legislation unless it had first been approved by the king and privy council in England. Yet the English conquest of Ireland remained incomplete until 1603. English influence waxed and waned in the Middle Ages, but was strongest in the area around Dublin (known as the Pale), although there was also an English presence in the provinces of Leinster and Munster and in a number of coastal towns and cities; the provinces of Connacht and Ulster, by contrast, remained effectively outside English control. A problematic ethnic divide, between the descendants of the original Anglo-Norman conquerors (Old English) and the indigenous Gaelic Irish (ancient Irish)—a situation further confused by intermarriage (the mixed Irish, or Old English who had assumed Irish ways and manners and thus 'degenerated', that is 'unpeopled' themselves)—was further complicated after the Reformation by a messy religious one.[9] Neither Henry VIII's nor Elizabeth's attempts to export the English Reformation to Ireland had met with much success, leaving the Old English and Gaelic Irish (and thus also the mixed Irish) firmly entrenched in their Roman Catholicism, necessitating a further influx of (new) English to rule in the name of the Protestant monarchy of England. The result was heightened resentment among the conquered and Catholic peoples of Ireland and an increasing propensity for these peoples to look to violence. In 1593 the Gaelic Irish of Ulster launched a rebellion against the crown of England—known as Tyrone's rebellion, after Hugh O'Neill, earl of Tyrone assumed leadership in 1595—which received backing from the king of Spain and took the best part of a decade to put down.[10]

James VI and I was to inherit all these problems, to add to the ones that he already had in Scotland. He had come to the Scottish throne in the wake of a revolution which had seen parliament carry out a reformation in the Kirk, overthrowing Catholicism and replacing it with Presbyterianism, and oust his mother from the throne. During the lengthy royal minority that followed, the authority of the Scottish crown was further eroded. At least in Scotland, or so it used to be thought, the crown had the advantage of enjoying greater independence from parliament. The electorate was small, making parliament less susceptible to the pressures of public opinion, while the king could raise taxes and even legislate through the more informal Conventions of Estates, which could meet without the forty-days summons required for a parliament. Furthermore, the Scottish parliament was unicameral, sessions were short, and its legislative agenda was managed by a select-steering committee known as the Lords of the Articles, which presented legislation for approval on the last day of the session with little debate in the full parliament. The Lords of the Articles came to comprise eight representatives of the four estates of clergy, nobility, shire, and burgh commissioners, plus eight officers of state—making 40 in total—the original logic being to make sure that the different estates had equal representation given that they sat in the same chamber. However, in the early seventeenth century the system developed whereby the bishops elected the nobility and the nobility elected the bishops, and then the representatives from these two estates together elected the shire and burgh representatives. Since bishops were royal appointees, this in theory gave the crown considerable control over the composition of the Articles.

In fact this traditional view of the Scottish parliament is misleading. It was not until 1606 that the clerical estate was made up predominantly of crown nominees (the bishops), and although this system of election might have been used in 1607 the first explicit reference to its use is not until 1609. Moreover, Scottish members of parliament did not just idle away their time as the Lords of the Articles deliberated; they met in separate committees of the estates and had continual contact with their representatives on the Articles, while members (and indeed non-members) could petition the Articles to make proposals or to protest about their proceedings. Thus the reason why there tended to be little debate when the final programme of legislation was put before parliament was because this programme had already been extensively discussed, debated, and amended. Initially at least, then, the Articles were as much a tool of parliament as it was of the crown. It was not that James VI inherited a system in which parliament was subservient and easy-to-manage; rather, both James and his successor Charles I faced the task of trying to make the Scottish parliament more subservient to the royal will.[11]

If this multiple-kingdom inheritance was not enough to worry about, James faced a testing international situation when he acceded to the throne of England—and Ireland—in 1603. Europe was in flux. The Reformation and concomitant Counter-Reformation had unleashed a wave of religious warfare across the continent: in the German-speaking lands of central Europe, in the Low Countries, and in France.[12] At the same time a military revolution had made the cost of fighting wars increasingly expensive, as armies became larger, military technology improved, and wars became more difficult to win (and thus much longer).[13] The English monarchy could ill afford to get involved in European entanglements; yet it also found it difficult to stay out of them. Elizabeth did get drawn into a war against Habsburg Spain from 1585 onwards, in defence of Protestants in the Low Countries who were in revolt against Habsburg rule, into the civil war in France (1589–95) in support of the French Protestants (Huguenots, as they were called), and faced a major rebellion in Ireland in the 1590s. The cost of the warfare that concluded the last eighteen years of Elizabeth's reign was around £4.5 million.[14]

Managing this problematic inheritance posed major challenges. James needed to improve the condition of royal finances. He had to try to bring the ecclesiastical establishments in his three kingdoms into closer harmony with each other, especially in an age which had yet to accept the principle of religious pluralism and where the existence of schism in the Church had proved so destabilizing to many European polities. He needed to make sure that his control over all his territories was secure, especially given that he ruled Ireland and Scotland (after 1603) as an absentee monarch. And he had to negotiate the complex power dynamics that existed in his separate kingdoms, being careful not to upset too many people—or too many of the people that counted—and that he kept enough of the right sort of people on his side. James achieved a great deal: he brought bishops and ceremonies back into the Scottish Kirk, he promoted Protestant plantations in Ireland (the plantation of Ulster dates from his reign), he seemed to bring relative harmony to the English Church. But he also faced major difficulties and encountered many problems along the way: he fell out with his English parliaments, he struggled to get a grip on royal finances, European affairs seemed to conspire against his goal of being the peacemaker of Europe, and he upset many in both Scotland and Ireland.

James VI and I just about got by. His son Charles I, who came to the throne in 1625, soon ran into difficulties—so much so that he decided to rule for an extended period without calling a parliament in England between 1629 and 1640. The various initiatives Charles pursued in Church and state were to prove deeply controversial and ultimately provoked rebellions in all three of his kingdoms. The first to rise were the Covenanters in Scotland (1638–40). They were followed by the Catholics of Ireland (1641). Then finally in 1642 England erupted in civil war.

The result was a catastrophe for the Stuart monarchy. The wars that followed were to end in defeat for the crown and unleash a revolution that was to see the disestablishment of the Church of England and the abolition of episcopacy in England (1646), the trial and execution of Charles I for treason (January 1649), and the abolition of kingship and the House of Lords (March 1649). Scotland and Ireland, who refused to accept the outcome of this revolution, were to lose their independence as they were eventually subdued—or conquered—by Oliver Cromwell by 1651. And this all came at a huge price in terms of human suffering and misery. In the period 1640–52 about 100,000 men died in battle in England and Scotland, and a further 140,000 of war-related disease and starvation. If we include Ireland, the total death toll rises to 540,000, or some 7 per cent of the population of the three kingdoms. England lost 3 per cent of its population, Scotland 6 per cent, and Ireland, by a conservative estimate, some 15–20 per cent. To put these figures in perspective, in the First World War British military fatalities were only 1.6 per cent of the population. During the period 1640–52 there were at least a further 120,000 wounded but not killed. Some 11,000 homes were destroyed in towns and villages in England and Wales alone, and a further 150–200 country houses, to the total cost of £1.5 million. Across the three kingdoms as a whole, the cost of damage to residential property was in the region of £2.2 million.[15]

* * *

The purpose of this book is to explore why things went so disastrously wrong for the early Stuart monarchy. Why did it prove impossible to

hold this multiple-kingdom inheritance together? Was this inheritance unmanageable, or inherently unstable, meaning that some sort
of major cataclysm was bound eventually to come? Or were the
problems that arose due to the failings of the particular men in
charge? Was it the case, as has sometimes been alleged, that Charles I
was not up to the job, or did the way that James chose to address his
problems end up exacerbating them, making the inheritance more
difficult for his son to manage? Or were the early Stuarts, perhaps,
just unlucky? This book is in part a study of what James and Charles—
and those they appointed to act in their name—were trying to achieve
and the extent to which they were or were not successful. Yet it also
looks more broadly at the social contexts in which politics operated.
It seeks to uncover the experiences, concerns, and aspirations of
ordinary men and women who lived under Stuart rule, what impact
government policy had upon their lives, whether they welcomed or
resented government initiatives, and why some of them were provoked ultimately to rebel. It combines high politics with low politics,
politics in-doors (at court and in parliament) with politics out-of-
doors (whether in the form of public celebrations, riots and demonstrations, alehouse talk, mass petitioning, or popular uprisings). It
endeavours to give appropriate balance to developments in all three
kingdoms, affording due weight to Scottish and Irish affairs as well
as those in England and Wales. Since Wales, a principality rather than
a separate kingdom, had been fully incorporated—politically, admin-
istratively, legally, and ecclesiastically—into the English state since
1536, with representation in the English parliament and dioceses
within the Church of England, discussion of developments in Wales
will be incorporated into the sections on England.

Although one objective of this book is to shed light on the origins
and causes of the civil war that broke out in 1642, it is not as such a
study of the origins of the English Civil War. It is certainly not written
backwards, from the vantage of 1642, with material selected in order
to highlight why the early Stuart monarchy was ultimately to fail. It
is a study of the kingship of James VI and I and Charles I up until
1642. The aim is to understand why they did what they did, what
problems they were seeking to address or issues they were attempting
to solve, why they thought it made sense to make the choices they
did, and what the consequences were of the initiatives they chose to
pursue. History may show that one or both of them fell short, but
they did not set out to fail; they thought they were acting in the best
interests not only of the monarchy but also of their kingdoms and of

the peoples over whom they ruled. They were doing their best to fulfil what they understood to be their divinely ordained duty of good kingship.

I have chosen to call this book *Rebellion*, which requires an explanation. For scholars of an earlier generation, choosing to embrace the term rebellion rather than revolution to describe the troubles that befell the three kingdoms in the 1640s could be an interpretative statement, a siding with Revisionist historians against Whigs and Marxists, or alternatively a political statement, indicating a sympathy for Charles I (rebellions, by definition, are illegitimate uprisings; revolution, as used in the seventeenth century, carried more neutral overtones, and even—by the time of the Glorious Revolution—positive ones, as the mechanism whereby good people could deliver themselves from tyranny).[16] Neither is my intention here. This book is chronologically framed by rebellions. It opens with rebellion—in Scotland against Mary Queen of Scots and in Ireland against Elizabeth—and it finishes with the rebellions in Scotland, Ireland, and England between 1638 and 1642. Nor do I intend to imply that I do not believe there was a revolution in mid-seventeenth-century Britain and Ireland; I most certainly do. But my account stops before that revolution (or those revolutions) and I do not believe that the rebellions of 1638–42 were launched in order to bring about the revolution that ultimately transpired; that is to say, they were not launched in order to bring about the sort of settlement in Church and state across the three kingdoms that was established after the regicide of 1649 and the final subduing of Scotland and Ireland in 1651.

Some qualification is necessary, however. Neither the Scottish Covenanters, nor the Irish Catholics, nor the English parliamentarians who showed themselves ready in the last resort to use violent force in their opposition to the government of Charles I would have seen themselves as rebels. They saw themselves as loyal subjects of the crown seeking to achieve a redress of their grievances: the Scots proceeded at first by way of petitioning, the English by working for reform through parliament, whereas the Irish insurgents of 1641 claimed to be acting with Charles I's approval. It was Charles, in fact, who declared war on his Scottish subjects and then his English subjects; I do not think the English parliamentarians would have gone to war with Charles unless Charles had declared war on them, though of course Charles saw it differently and believed that his Scottish and then his English subjects had left him no option but to use military force to suppress his political and religious opponents in

9

these two kingdoms because they were already, in effect, in rebellion against him.

If there is reason to question whether it is correct to style the Scots, the English, and even the Irish who rose up against Charles I as rebels, there is also reason to question whether it is wrong to label them revolutionaries. It is true that the Scottish Covenanters saw themselves as acting to defend their true religion in opposition to the innovations introduced under James VI and I and Charles I and were looking to put the clock back, to 1581, to return to an older system rather than to establish a new; but in justifying their opposition to Charles I, and their decision ultimately to use force, they did embrace a revolutionary ideology, and they did end up effecting a revolution in Church and state between 1638 and 1641. The Catholics of Ireland who rose in 1641—despite professing loyalty to the crown, and despite seeking to gain through force reforms which they had been promised but repeatedly denied—in reality never had the support of the crown for their actions; and although initially the objectives of the leaders of the uprising might have been fairly limited (to seize the strongholds of the country so as to be able to negotiate with the government from a position of strength), the Irish rebellion quickly turned into an attempt to overthrow the English plantation of Ireland, with considerable violence perpetrated against English and Protestant settlers (though there was violence on both sides, it should be stressed), actions which could certainly be deemed revolutionary. In England the opponents of Charles I saw themselves as trying to defend rights that had been infringed by the crown, as trying to reform the state and not (initially) as trying to remodel it. However, there was a radicalization process over time. Many of those who had supported the reforms in 1640–1 were to become royalists in 1642. And they became royalists because they thought those who continued to press for further reform in Church and state were going too far, threatening to reduce the English king to a doge of Venice (in effect make England a republic) and destroy the Church of England through root and branch reform. In short, those who became royalists in 1641–2 did so because in essence they thought their opponents were promoting a revolution in Church and state.

I

·················

'How to Reigne Well'

*One of the Ancients said formerly, That then a Prince was truly King,
when he was truly Just; and that the truly Just Man governed himself
according to the Laws.*

Hinc Illae Lachrymae (1692), 212.

'The knowledge how to Reigne well', recorded Roger Whitley in his
commonplace book sometime in the later seventeenth century, 'is
the most difficult of all others': 'to obey well, makes a state happy',
but this in turn depended 'on the Prince's commanding well, and
that on a Prince's wisdome'.[1] Born in North Wales in 1618 and educated at Christ Church, Oxford before entering Gray's Inn in the
late 1630s, Whitley was to fight for Charles I in the civil war,
although he was to side with the Whigs under Charles II and support the Williamite revolution of 1688–9 which resulted in the
overthrow of James II.[2] Witnessing, as he did, two revolutions during his lifetime—Whitley was to die in 1697—he belonged to a generation which had cause to think long and hard about what
constituted wisdom in a prince and what limits, if any, there were
on a subject's duty to obey if a prince fell short in the difficult task
of commanding well.

So what did it take to 'reigne well' at this time? How was a king
supposed to rule and what was expected of him? How much power
did he have—and what, if any, were the limitations on his authority?
Earlier generations of historians tended to see the revolution of the
mid-seventeenth century as the result of a fundamental constitutional
conflict between a Stuart monarchy, which was bent on strengthening
the powers of the crown and even determined to make itself absolute,
and parliament, which set itself up as the protector of the people's
liberties against the threat of royal tyranny. Few would accept such a

view today. The idea that the early Stuarts tried to claim new powers for the crown or acted beyond the limits of their acknowledged authority, or that there was a basic ideological cleavage between those who supported the absolutist pretensions of the crown and those who championed parliamentary sovereignty, has been called into serious question. Indeed, many scholars would now insist that there was considerable political and constitutional consensus up until the eve of the Civil War and that conflict, when it arose, was more often than not the result of factional rivalries or even of misunderstandings, rather than being ideologically driven.[3] Others, however, feel that this emphasis on consensus has gone too far, and would point to the existence of multiple competing constitutional discourses in early Stuart England, insisting that conflict, when it arose, shows that rival political actors did harbour quite distinct ideological outlooks.[4]

It seems to have been the case that there was a broadly accepted, albeit rather loose, ideological consensus over basic ideals. The king was expected to rule and his powers were recognized to be extensive. He was also expected to rule well, which in turn meant promoting the welfare of his people, adhering to the rule of law, taking good counsel, and working through parliament when appropriate. About this all were agreed. However, what this meant in practice could be interpreted in different ways, lending support to the views both of those who saw the English monarchy as unlimited and of those who saw the crown as operating under certain constraints. When things were running smoothly, it was possible for people to live with ambiguity and for the consensus to be sustained. When tensions arose, different political actors might seek to describe the constitutional framework in varying ways, so as to justify the course of political action they deemed it necessary to take. Those in dispute tended to think they were working from commonly shared assumptions about how the political system operated. They certainly tended to argue that they bought into (what they represented as being) these commonly shared assumptions. But it is readily apparent that people held somewhat different assumptions about the nature of the English constitution and the extent and limitations of the powers of the crown.

God's Lieutenant

James VI and I had an exalted view of monarchy. In his *Trew Law of Free Monarchies*, published originally in Scotland in 1598 and reprinted in London in April 1603 shortly after his accession to the

English throne, he articulated a view of divinely ordained monarchy where the king, as God's lieutenant upon earth, sat upon God's throne and was accountable to none but God.[5] It was a view he repeated in a speech to parliament on 21 March 1610. 'The State of Monarchie', he proclaimed, was 'the supremest thing upon earth. For Kings are not onely God's Lieutenants upon earth, and sit upon God's throne, but even by God himselfe they are called Gods.' 'God hath power to create, or destroy, make, or unmake at his pleasure, to give life, or send death, to judge all, and to be judged nor accomptable to none', he continued; 'And the like power have Kings: they make and unmake their subjects: they have power...of life, and of death: Judges over all their subjects, and in all causes, and yet accomptable to none but God onely.'[6]

To a modern reader such views might seem extreme. To contemporaries, however, the idea that the monarch ruled by divine right and had God-like powers was entirely conventional. The Tudors had embraced it. In a meeting with the clergy at Baynard's Castle in 1514, Henry VIII had proclaimed that 'kings of England...never had any superior but God only'. The preamble to Henry's Act in Restraint of Appeals of 1533, which launched England's break with Rome, articulated a theory of imperial kingship in which the 'realm of England' was defined as 'an empire' ruled by a king 'furnished by...Almighty God with plenary, whole, and entire power, pre-eminence, authority, prerogative and jurisdiction'.[7] The theory of divine-right monarchy was frequently articulated from the pulpit. David Owen, preaching in 1610, claimed that 'Kings have their authoritie from God, and are his Vicegerents on earth, to execute justice and judgement for him'.[8] This was because it said so in the Bible. Romans 13:1 states that 'the powers that be are ordained of God', whereas Psalm 82 has God say of kings: 'I have said, Ye are Gods.' It was a view that was generally shared by those who served in the House of Commons. Upon accepting his nomination as Speaker of the House on 7 April 1614, Ranulph Crew acknowledged that James was 'the image and representation of God upon earth, for kings be gods upon earth, sitting there upon God's throne to administer justice and judgment unto his people'.[9] Even outspoken critics of crown policy agreed. The Puritan pamphleteer and critic of Jacobean foreign policy Thomas Scott accepted not only that kings were 'like Gods' and were 'God's substitute' but also that James was 'called a God upon Earth by God himselfe'.[10] Sir Edward Coke, the lawyer MP who framed parliament's Petition of Right of 1628, believed that the king 'is over us the

Lord's annointed...next under Christ Jesus our supreame Governour'.[11] The Scottish Covenanter Alexander Henderson, when justifying Scottish resistance to Charles I in 1639, nevertheless conceded that the king was 'God's Deputie and Vice-gerent' and that 'God hath given him power and authority to command and governe'.[12] Even John Pym, the man who was to lead parliament to war against Charles I in 1642, acknowledged in the Commons in 1621 that the king was God's agent on earth and thought that monarchy was 'the perfectest State of Government'.[13]

James VI and I's claim that the king was 'accountable to none but God only' was also widely accepted. Henry of Bracton, the much-respected medieval jurist, had written that the king was subject to no man; if the king committed any wrong, God would be his revenger. This reflected the basic truism that the king could not be tried in a court of law: he could not be subjected to a trial by his peers because as king he had no peers. According to the warden of All Souls College, Oxford, Richard Mocket, writing in defence of the oath of allegiance in 1615, kings were 'subject onely unto God' because 'no mortall man' could 'punish them by any judiciall sentence'.[14] Similarly the Puritan Thomas Scott could argue that because God set Caesar 'to arbitrate indifferently betwixt party and party', to enable him to 'do this freely' and 'without feare', God 'set him above all, exempted him from all other Judges but himselfe, and the Lawes'; it was an 'authority' which Scott went on to describe as 'absolute'.[15]

The king was absolute because he was above the law or *ab legibus solutus*. He was also absolute in the sense that his power was full or complete. He thus did not share his sovereignty with any other individual or body. Since the break with Rome in the 1530s, which had removed papal pretensions to exercise spiritual jurisdiction in England, the king of England no longer shared his sovereignty with the pope. Hence why many 'hotter' Protestants were happy to acknowledge that the English king was absolute, subject to no other earthly power.[16] Prior to his accession to the English throne, James had insisted kings of Scotland were 'absolute' in order to refute English pretensions to suzerainty over Scotland; indeed, the English had sought to justify Elizabeth's right to execute Mary Queen of Scots in 1587 in part on the grounds that 'the Scottish Queene was no absolute Queene, but...was inferior to the crowne of England'.[17] Nor did the king share his sovereignty with parliament.[18] Thus at the beginning of the seventeenth century the claim that the monarch was absolute was conventional. One commentator, writing of Elizabeth I in

1601, asserted that the queen was 'so absolute a Soveraigne, and so soveraigne an Empresse' that she 'truly meriteth the true title of Caesar'.[19] When James visited Berwick in 1604, the town's recorder proclaimed him as 'the first soule, and absolute Monarche, of all the Bryttishe Islandes'.[20]

The king had considerable power. He settled all questions of policy, both foreign and domestic. He appointed and dismissed at will all officers of state—counsellors, judges, and justices of the peace. He could summon, prorogue and dismiss parliament as and when he pleased, and parliament could enact no legislation without the king's consent. The role of the people was to obey. To quote the Elizabethan homily on obedience, it was 'an intolerable ignorance, madnesse, and wickednesse for subjects to make any murmuring, rebellion, resistance, or withstanding, commotion, or insurrection against their most deare and most dread Sovereigne Lord and King, ordeined and appointed of God's goodnes for their commodity, peace, and quietnesse'.[21] Nor did it matter how well the king ruled. 'The duety of the Subject is always to be obedient', justice of the peace Richard Crompton proclaimed at the Staffordshire sessions in 1588; 'Heere is no exception of Turke nor Infidell, of the wicked and ungodlie Prince, more then of the Christian and vertuous King'.[22]

This did not mean, however, that there were no limits on the king. There were certain expectations as to how the king should use his power. According to the royalist champion John Maxwell, writing from Civil War Oxford in 1644, although 'the power of all Monarchs' was '*Legibus soluta*, subject to no over-ruling power of man', it would be wrong to think that kings were 'free from the direction of, and obligation to the Law of God, nature, and common equitie'.[23] Since kings were 'gods upon the earth', it was expected that kings should follow the 'example of God', and rule in a God-like way.[24] 'You must doe God's worke', preached William Laud to Charles I in 1625, which was 'to preserve, and beare up...the Earth, and the people'.[25] The mirror of princes literature of the Middle Ages had promoted the view that the ideal prince would have the following virtues: justice, mercy, temperance, prudence, moderation, chastity, diligence, courage, piety, and wisdom.[26] There was thus broad agreement that the king was both absolute and expected to rule according to law. As one Middle Temple lawyer put it in 1579, the commonly articulated view that 'the King by his Prerogative is above his laws', if 'rightly understood', was 'not amisse spoken'; however, to say that the king was 'soe superior over his lawes and Acts of Parliament' that he was 'not bound to governe by the same', but could govern 'at his will and pleasure', was 'repugnant to the...politick state of Government' established in England and also contrary 'to the rule of Equitie and Common reason', since what could 'be more...seeming to equitie then the Prince to be bound by his owne law'.[27]

James VI and I held similar views. In his *Trew Law* he insisted that God had installed kings to 'minister Justice and Judgement to the people', 'advance the good, and punish the evill', 'establish good Lawes', and 'procure obedience to the same'. Indeed, the king was 'a naturall Father to all his Lieges', and as the father had a 'fatherly duty...to care for the nourishing, education and vertuous government of his children', so was the king 'bound to care for all his subjects'.[28] In his *Basilikon Doron*, an advice manual on how to be a good king written for his son Henry in 1598, James insisted that although the king was ordained of God and accountable to none but God, he was nevertheless 'ordained for his people, having received from God a burthen of government, whereof he must be countable'. This distinguished a good king from a tyrant, who by contrast believed 'his people ordeined for him'. 'A good king', James continued, would govern by executing good laws and 'protect his people' by 'force of armes'.[29] Likewise, James acknowledged that he was obliged to rule according to law in his speech of 21 March 1610. As 'Kingdomes began to be setled in civilitie and policie', he explained, 'Kings set downe their mindes by Lawes', and the king became '*Lex loquens* [a speaking law]', after a sort, binding himselfe by a double othe to the observation of the fundamentall Lawes of his Kingdome: Tacitly, as by being a King, and so bound to protect aswel the people, as the Lawes of his kingdome; And Expresly, by his othe at his Coronation'. 'So', James concluded, 'every just King in a setled kingdome' was 'bound to observe that paction made to his people by his Lawes, in framing his government agreeable thereunto' and 'leaves to be a King, and degenerates into a Tyrant, assoone as hee leaves off to rule according to his Lawes'.[30]

Rulers, then, were supposed to rule according to the law and for the good of their people. Queen Elizabeth, in her famous Golden Speech to parliament in 1601, had emphasized her willingness to venture her life for the good and safety of her subjects.[31] James thought a king should employ 'all his studie and paines, to procure and maintaine' the 'well-fare and peace of his people'; he even went so far as to have the motto 'salus populi suprema lex' (the welfare of the people is the supreme law) inscribed on some of his Scottish coins.[32] Promoting the welfare of the people involved protecting their liberties, properties, and religion. As Charles I put it in a royal declaration published in 1640: 'as for the Libertie of the people...no king in the World shall be more carefull to maintain them in The Propertie of their Goods, Libertie of their Persons, and true Religion, then I shall be'.[33] That it was a widely held assumption that kings were expected to rule for the welfare of their people is confirmed by various sayings and dicta recorded by Roger Whitley in his commonplace book: 'A Good Prince, esteems nothing comparable, to the safety of his People'; a prince's 'subjects should be Governed, not Tyrannised, and they should...be able to call what they have, their owne, Preserving Propriety and Liberty'; 'the Liberty of the People' consists 'in Enjoying the fruites of their Labors, their Goods, Possessions, Estates and personall Liberty, according to the knowne Lawes of the Land'.[34]

Although expected to rule according to law, the king did possess certain extra-legal powers. These were in essence emergency powers, allowing the king to act above the law by dint of his prerogative when following the letter of the law would be inequitable or to the public peril.[35] As James's Attorney General for Ireland Sir John Davies put it: 'the King doth exercise a double power, viz an absolute power...when he doth use Prerogatives onely, which is not bound by the positive Law; and an ordinary power of Jurisdiction, which doth co-operate with the Law, and whereby he doth minister Justice to the people, according to the prescript rule of the positive Law'.[36] The king could in certain circumstances seize his subjects' property if the public welfare necessitated it. For example, if London were on fire he could destroy a house in order to create a fire break to stop the fire spreading from roof to roof, even though that house was someone's personal property, since the greater good required such action. Likewise, he could impose certain emergency levies at times of national danger, say to ward off invasion by a foreign armada if there was not time to wait for parliament to meet and grant subsidies.[37] He could also issue dispensations from the law, when strict enforcement would result in a palpable injustice. This was, of course, the logic behind the royal pardon. The king could not, however, issue dispensations for something that was wrong in itself (against the moral law of God), only for something that had been made criminal by statute.[38] Although the king's prerogatives were arbitrary, in the sense that they were beyond the law, it was assumed that in the normal manner of things the king would not rule arbitrarily and there were certain accepted assumptions concerning how his prerogatives should be deployed—with the emphasis again being on the welfare of the people. Thus Lord Chief Baron Sir Thomas Fleming stated in 1606 that the king's power was 'double, ordinary and absolute': his ordinary power was 'for the execution of civil justice', where the king enforced that which could not be changed without parliament; his 'absolute power' was that which 'applied to the general benefit of the people' or 'salus populi', but was not to be 'executed to private use, to the benefit of any particular person'.[39]

It was a commonplace of the age that it was 'the Cheifest Duty of a Prince, to administer the Lawes justly'.[40] Indeed, in his coronation oath the king swore that in 'all his Judgments' he would 'minister Equity, Right, and Justice'.[41] The royal chaplain Thomas Scot (not to be confused with the Puritan pamphleteer of the same name) elaborated upon the theme of justice in a sermon delivered before King James in 1616. A champion of divine-right royal absolutism and a staunch anti-Puritan, Scot claimed that the virtues looked for in a king were 'Justice, Equity, Clemency, and Discretion'. 'Justice upholdeth the seat of Kings', he pronounced, although 'Equity, Discretion, and Clemencie' must 'alwaies attend upon Justice'. By contrast, 'cruelty, and over-much severity', which Scot thought stemmed from an 'effeminate disposition of the minde', were to be 'discommended and prohibited in a Magistrate': when men in authority ruled 'by rigour and oppression' it made 'the people', who otherwise would be obedient, 'mutinous and clamorous'. Scot therefore advised that kings not be too severe in enforcing the letter of the law: 'Lawes must bee sharpely enacted, but the penalties of Lawes must not be so straightly exacted', for 'a Magistrate like a Physician should never use extreame medicins but for extreame diseases'; 'the people will be best ruled', he concluded, 'when they are mildly governed'.[42] James himself agreed. In his *Basilikon Doron* he had written that kings should 'Use Justice, but with such moderation as it turne not in Tyrannie'; and along with justice he urged 'Clemencie, Magnanimitie, Liberalitie, Constancie, Humilitie, and all other Princely vertues'.[43]

None of what has been said so far placed any practical limits on the powers of the crown. The expectation may have been that the king should rule according to law and for the benefit of the people, and that he should administer the laws justly, but he could not be held accountable to any human agency if he did not. He would, however, be held accountable to God, and we should not underestimate the power that the ultimate threat of divine retribution held for contemporaries as a check on tyranny. As Laud put it in a sermon to parliament in June 1625, 'even Kings themselves...have need to looke to their waies. For God is over them with *Ego iudicabo*, I will one day call for an account.'[44] One also needs to recognize that the corporal metaphor contemporaries employed to describe how their political system operated made it difficult to conceive why any king should want to abuse his power. For the king was the head of the body politic, and by hurting other parts of that body he was only hurting himself. As James said in his speech of 21 March 1610, 'it were an idle head that would in place of physicke so poyson or phlebotomize the body as might breede a dangerous distemper or destruction thereof'.[45] According to John Dove, preaching at St Paul's Cross in 1606, 'The welthe and strengthe of the people is the welthe and strengthe of the Kinge, and the soundnes of the hedd dependeth upon the soundness of the inferiour members, by which the hedd is caryed, for the hedd bareth not them, but they bare up it'.[46] The conclusion was the same when the metaphor used was that of the ship of state. 'A wicked king is like a crazed ship', one early seventeenth-century diarist recalled having read, 'which drowens both selfe and all that are in it'.[47]

Ambiguities

If there was broad agreement over the nature of monarchical authority at the very general level, ambiguities nevertheless abounded. If the king ruled by divine right and was absolute, but was still obliged to rule according to law, did the king ultimately control the law or the law the king? A medieval constitutionalist tradition seemed to suggest that the king was constrained by the law. Bracton had gone so far as to insist that the king of England was 'under God and the law, because the law makes the king'.[48] In 1215 rebellious barons had imposed a charter of liberties on King John—Magna Carta—to ensure that the king governed not by his 'will' but by the law of the land (*lex terrae*), by which was understood law made with the 'counsel and consent' of the barons. Magna Carta was confirmed several times over the course of the thirteenth and fourteenth centuries and established the principle that no Englishman was to be imprisoned or dispossessed of their property except by due process of law, and was frequently invoked to abridge the jurisdiction of the prerogative courts. The depositions of Edward II (1327) and Richard II (1399)—both technically forced abdications—seemed to imply that parliament could hold a king accountable for his misrule. In the fifteenth century the common lawyer Sir John Fortescue developed the view that England was a limited or constitutional monarchy (*dominium politicum et regale*): although the king was above the law in the sense that he was not subject to anyone, he nevertheless could not make law by dint of his prerogative since legislation required the assent of the realm expressed in parliament.[49]

Medieval constitutionalism, however, was undermined by the Tudor understanding of imperial kingship. Henry VIII saw the king as 'under God but not the law, because the king makes the law'.[50] By the early seventeenth century many theorists took the line that the laws were made by the king, albeit at the request of his people in parliament, but not by parliament itself. The fact that no bill could become law until it received the royal assent and that only the king, as chief executive, had the power to give any new legislation the force of law, meant for them that the king was ultimately law-maker. This was James VI and I's view. In his *Trew Law* he wrote that because kings 'in Scotland were...before any Parliaments were holden', then it followed that 'the kings were the authors and makers of the Lawes, and not the Lawes of the kings'.[51] But he clearly thought the same applied to England. In his speech of 21 March 1610 he explained that the laws were 'properly made by the King onely': it was the people who asked, but it was the king who granted. Nevertheless it is significant that in a speech championing divine-right monarchy James emphasized the king's obligation not only to rule according to law but also to observe 'that paction made to his people by his Lawes', hinting at a quasi-contractual element within the English constitution.[52]

What hinted most at some form of contractual element within the constitution was the oath kings took at their coronation to uphold 'the Laws and approved Customes of the Realm'. The oath contained the proviso that the king should uphold those laws and customs that were 'not prejudicial to his Crown' and that he should put out 'evil Laws and Customes' and do his utmost to preserve all the 'Lands, Honours, and Dignities, Rights and Freedomes, of the Crown of England', so one might question what limits this actually placed on the crown.[53] One author in 1639, seeking to refute the resistance theories of the Scots who had risen in rebellion against the crown, insisted that no mutual contract was made between the king and the people at the coronation, but rather the king, 'of his owne accord', merely promised 'to discharge honestly and faithfully that charge, which God hath committed and entrusted him with', citing James VI and I's *Trew Law* in support.[54] This was certainly a widely accepted reading. In April 1603, shortly after the accession of James VI and I, John Manningham recorded in his diary the view of the barrister John Hawarde that if a prince 'voluntarily promise to see the lawes of God and nature performed, this is no condicion to restrayne him selfe, but an honourable promise of endeavour to discharge his duty'.[55] Yet James's views could be read in different ways. Citing James's speech of 21 March 1610, a parliamentarian pamphleteer of 1647 concluded both that 'every King of England' was 'bound expresly by his Oath at his Coronation to be a just King, in observing his solemne Covenant made with his People', and that even if the king 'at his Coronation did take no Oath at all', nevertheless 'his very being a King' implied 'as much as an Oath' and obliged him 'to protect as well the People, as the Lawes of his Kingdome'.[56] James himself seemed to get into a tangle when writing about the coronation oath in his *Trew Law*. At first he appeared to deny that a contract was made between the king and the people, or at least such a contract as contained 'a clause irritant' that if the king broke his side of the bargain the people were no longer obliged to keep their part; however, he proceeded to discuss the king's promise made at his coronation to exercise 'honorably and trewly' the duty of his office as if it were a contract, writing of 'this contract... betwixt the king and his people', although he insisted that God (not the people) was 'the onely Judge betwixt the two parties contractors'.[57]

Even if one believed the king controlled the law and merely bound himself by laws which were of his own making, this nevertheless left the king bound by the law in some respect. James's Attorney General and Lord Chancellor Francis Bacon, while acknowledging that one of the principal jobs of the sovereign was to be 'a Lawgiver' and to give 'their subjects good laws', was nevertheless adamant that this did not mean that the laws were 'but cobwebs': 'for certain it is', Bacon stressed, 'that good laws are some bridle to bad princes, and as a very wall about government'.[58] The king's discretionary powers—which allowed him to act outside or beyond the law in times of emergency—were nevertheless limited by law. The king could not issue pardons or dispensations that jeopardized the interests or property rights of his subjects; he could not dispense an individual from a law that allowed a third party to collect a fine by way of compensation. Moreover, the way government functioned in practice was supposed to afford subjects security for their liberties and properties. Judges, when they were appointed to office, took an oath not only to maintain all prerogatives of the king but also to administer justice equally to all people.[59] Not that we should cast the judges' obligation to uphold justice as some form of check on the crown; it was perceived as being in the best interests of the crown that they did so precisely because it was the king's ultimate responsibility to see that justice was upheld. As Lord Keeper Finch put it in a speech delivered at the inauguration of two new judges in Common Pleas in January 1640: the king 'will expect an accompt from you for hee desires Justice to bee done to his people...And if you should doe injustice you will make the king to be tearmed a king of Injustice, for an unjust Judge doth cast a reproach upon the king himselfe.'[60]

Kings obviously could not do and know everything themselves, and so they needed to take counsel. Indeed, the fact that for more than fifty-five years prior to James's accession England had been ruled first by a boy king and then by two women had served to encourage a conciliar view of royal government. In 1558 the Scottish Reformer John Knox, in a polemic directed at Mary Tudor, Mary Queen of Scots, and Mary of Guise, had infamously blasted female rule as 'repugnant to nature, contumely to God'.[61] When Elizabeth came to the throne later that year, Protestant Englishmen of course now had a ruler with whom they were happy, but they still faced the problem of how to justify her right to rule. One strategy was to see it as providential— Elizabeth had been chosen by God. But theorists also sought to argue that Elizabeth was supposed to rule with the advice of godly men— either godly counsellors or godly members of parliament (MPs).[62] Furthermore, James had himself acceded to the throne in Scotland in 1567 as a thirteen-month-old minor after a coup that had resulted in the deposition of his mother, Mary Queen of Scots, leaving royal government in the hands of competing noble factions around the king. James's subsequent assertion of the absolute nature of the monarchy in both Scotland and England was in part an attempt to reassert the authority of the crown in both kingdoms after a period when that authority had seemingly been significantly diminished.

Even when the realm was under the rule of an adult, male king, the king still had to take advice, and he was not supposed to choose 'yes men' who would simply endorse his point of view. Given that kings were God's lieutenants on earth, it followed that their counsellors should be 'such as are of God'. It was especially important not to have as counsellors people who would flatter princes, praise things that were not praiseworthy, or palliate a king's vices.[63] The Puritan pamphleteer Thomas Scott, condemning flatterers, believed that a land was happy when it had 'good, wise, faithfull, and bold Servants' who would 'advise boldly and truly upon everie occasion', for what could be worse than for a prince to 'be in danger, and none about him dare tell him so'.[64] James believed that 'the wisdome of a kinge' was to be 'cheifely seene of his officers' and it was vital 'not to Choose them that hee affects most, but to use every man accordinge to his proper fittnes'.[65] Indeed, it was a common saying of the time that 'The greatest treasure a Kinge can enjoy, is a wise man nere him'.[66] Yet the obligation to take counsel did not necessarily serve to undermine the theory of royal absolutism; in many respects it served to reinforce it. For if a king was absolute and thus could not be held accountable for his actions, nevertheless those who ruled in the king's name could be. This was the logic of the axiom 'the king could do no wrong'. It did not mean that the king was free to do wrong unchecked, but rather that if wrong were done in the name of the crown his ministers were to blame. As the author of a manuscript tract on government, writing in the 1620s, put it: the way for kings 'to wynne Love, and Trust', was in 'all Actions to proceed Justlye', and 'yf any thinge bee done, not Justiffyeable, or unfit to bee allowed, As often tymes it happeneth', then they were 'to lay the Blame upon the Minister, which must be performed with soe great shewe of Revenge, and dissimulation, by reproveinge and punisheinge the ministers'.[67]

The question of counsel leads inevitably to a consideration of the role of parliament. On the surface it seems to have been quite limited. Parliaments had no existence independent of the crown: the king determined when they should meet, and how long they should meet for. Members of parliament could offer advice to the king about affairs relating to their own localities, but they were not supposed to advise the king about national affairs unless he specifically asked for advice. Although the king enacted legislation through parliament, parliamentary bills could not become law without the royal assent. It is true that there was a well accepted principle that the king could not tax his subjects without their consent being given through parliament, and this could give parliament some leverage against the crown if it chose to withhold supply until grievances were redressed. Nevertheless, it was an expectation that parliament would vote taxes when asked.[68] As John Dove preached at St Paul's Cross in 1606, because the king administered justice to his subjects and maintained the common peace and wealth of the land, 'wee muste be forwarde in all contributions and payments which maye serve for the mayntenance of the regall estate of the Kinge…All payments which be for good purposes…we muste in Christian duetye yelde unto.'[69]

Some scholars have downplayed the significance of early Stuart parliaments, even questioning whether regular parliaments were deemed necessary or desirable. Whereas in the fifteenth century only once did three years or more elapse without the calling of a parliament, following the accession of the Tudors in 1485 parliaments met much less frequently: under Elizabeth they sat on average only once every three and a half years and then for a mere ten or eleven weeks at a time.[70] The meeting of parliaments meant that the merchants and gentry had to forsake their businesses and estates to be resident in London to attend parliamentary business; and the summoning of parliaments invariably meant the imposition of new taxation, which was hardly likely to be welcome to the country at large. If so, then the long intermissions in parliaments in England under James (1614–21) and Charles (1629–40) were not necessarily unwelcome. Indeed Lord Treasurer Salisbury, in detailing James's desperate need for money before the Lords in February 1610, thought he was offering words of comfort when he concluded by saying he hoped 'we shall not need to have often parliaments'.[71]

Such a view, however, fails to do justice to the value that many contemporaries placed on the role of parliament within the constitution. Parliament was an ancient institution—indeed, some claimed that parliaments pre-dated the Norman Conquest of 1066 and originated in Anglo-Saxon times—and was seen by some commentators as a defender of English liberties guaranteed by the ancient constitution. There were even laws from Edward III's reign in the fourteenth century stipulating that parliaments should meet every year. Medieval parliaments had also developed the process of impeachment, whereby parliament could hold royal ministers accountable for misdeeds committed in the name of the crown.[72] It is true that there had been no impeachments under the Tudors and that the laws requiring annual parliaments had not been observed. Royal apologists disputed the antiquity of parliaments and the notion of an ancient constitution, insisting (historically more correctly) that it was kings who had first called parliaments into being and that therefore (somewhat more questionably) that parliaments must be subordinate to the crown. Nevertheless, several developments had served to enhance the prestige of parliament during the sixteenth century. The Tudors had achieved their great revolutions in the Church—the Henrician break with Rome, the Edwardian Reformation, the Marian Counter-Reformation, and the Elizabethan settlement—by working through parliament. As Henry VIII had put it in June 1535, papal authority had been abolished by the 'advice, consultation, consent and agreement...of the bishops... nobles...commons...assembled in our high court of Parliament, and by auctority of the same'.[73] Most agreed that the crown was stronger—and could achieve much more—when king and parliament worked together. The Venetian ambassador Alvise Contarini offered some perceptive insights into the nature and role of the English parliament in a series of observations he made during the course of 1626. 'The institution of Parliament', he wrote on one occasion, 'was very ancient', and 'although the king was absolute', he nevertheless 'submitted to the rule of the laws, and to the counsels and deliberations of his people, so as to be more readily supported'. On another occasion he stated that while 'in every department of the Government the king can do whatever he pleases, yet, with regard to money, he requires the assent of his subjects, with whom, so long as he is agreed, no sovereign in the world can obtain more solid supply'. Indeed, 'former sovereigns', Contarini continued, 'when united with the Parliament, disposed not merely of the fortunes of their subjects but of their consciences as well, having thrice made the majority of them change even the religion in which they had been reared and educated'.[74]

The House of Commons was also valued as the representative of the people. Not that the Commons was representative by modern-day standards. One had to own 40 shillings worth of freehold land to vote in county elections, while there was some sort of property qualification for the franchise in most borough constituencies. Nevertheless, as a result of inflation during the sixteenth century, the franchise was not as restrictive as it once had been, and it has been estimated that perhaps has many as 27–40 per cent of adult males had the right to vote by 1640.[75] Moreover, the logic behind counties and borough corporations sending two members to Westminster was so that they could inform the centre of the concerns of their localities, concerns about which those at the centre would be unaware (and thus unable to address satisfactorily) unless so informed by these local representatives. As James explained in his speech at the opening session of the 1621 Parliament, 'The House of Commons is called, for that they best know the particular estate of the country; and if the king shall ask their advice, can best tell what is amiss, as being most sensible of it'.[76] Parliaments were thus prized as a point of contact between the centre and localities, and for this reason regular meetings were deemed essential, even if the parliamentary sessions themselves need not last long. Hence a Civil War royalist like Roger Whitley, while at times critical of parliaments in his post-Restoration writings, nevertheless accepted that parliaments were 'good Phisicke, to Cure the distempers, of the Body Politique, which cheifly grow in Intervalls of them'. But they were 'an ill constant Dyet', he thought, which was why Queen Elizabeth, 'who knew well the Constitution of the Nation', called them frequently, but continued them 'for a short tyme'.[77] And although few questioned that the king alone could determine when, and for how long, parliament should sit, and most would have agreed that there were times when parliaments were unnecessary, nevertheless it was expected that the king should call a parliament if circumstances warranted one.

It was thus even possible to describe England as a mixed monarchy. In 1559, at the beginning of Elizabeth's reign, John Aylmer observed that 'The regiment of England is not a mere Monarchie... nor a mere Oligarchie nor Democracie, but a rule mixte of all these... to be sene in the parliament house'. To Aylmer, the monarch was one of the three estates, and Aylmer vested sovereignty in the three estates acting in parliament, rather than in the king acting alone. Sir Thomas Smith, writing in the early 1560s, concluded that 'The most high and absolute power of the realme of Englande' was 'in the Parliament'.[78] Such views ran counter to the idea that the crown was absolute and thus were denounced by apologists for the crown. Certainly James VI and I regarded himself as sovereign and as not being one of the three estates, which in his view comprised the lords spiritual, lords temporal, and commons. The point to emphasize is that alternative ways of describing the constitutional set-up were available: England's particular brand of monarchy was such that it could be perceived in different ways. Indeed, it could be perceived in different ways by the same people at different times. The lawyer and constitutional scholar John Selden, a man who was to side with parliament at the time of the Civil War, in a tract first published in 1610 could describe the three estates as being 'the King, the Lords and the Commons'. In the 1640s, by contrast, Selden could observe that 'The king [was] not one of the three Estates, as some would have it'.[79]

Because the crown lacked a professional bureaucracy, local government was run by amateurs. At the top level the counties were administered by Lord Lieutenants, deputy-lieutenants, and justices of the peace, who were appointed by the crown and drawn primarily from the landed elite (the titular nobility and the gentry). The Lord Lieutenants and their deputies were in control of the local militias, and the justices of the peace presided over the county quarter sessions and typically served as presentment jurymen at the twice-yearly assizes, the courts which tried more serious offences and which were presided over by circuit judges sent out from Westminster. But there were other county offices too—the sheriff, appointed for one year, who empanelled jurors; the coroner, who investigated cases of violent death; the presentment and trial jurymen who presented and heard offences at quarter sessions; and those who served in the county militias. At the parish level, in both town and countryside, there was a host of local offices, from the churchwardens, overseers of the poor, and parish constable, to lesser officers such as scavengers, beadles, sextons, clerks, nightwatchmen, and surveyors of the highways. Most who held such offices were elected and served for a limited term (one or two years) by a system of rotation. Given that there were nearly 10,000 parishes in England and Wales, and assuming that each parish had one constable, two churchwardens, and two overseers of the poor, there must have been at least 50,000 officeholders in any one year—excluding the lesser offices and those who served in the militias or as jurymen. Perhaps one-twentieth of the adult male population annually held some form of local office; and if offices were rotated and people served for only one year, then in theory in any given ten-year period as much as one half of the adult male population might have held some sort of local office. It is true that one was supposed to be a householder of independent means to serve, and some positions carried considerable prestige, so it tended to be the 'better sort' or the more prosperous middling sort who ran the parishes. But some offices were burdensome and unpopular—not everyone relished serving as village constable and having to inform on the sins of one's neighbours—and there are examples of people elected to lesser offices hiring paid substitutes to serve in their stead. As a result, people from fairly low down the social scale could be in the front line of law enforcement in their capacity as constables, beadles, and nightwatchmen. In short, ordinary people played an important role in governing their own communities, and the central government could find it very difficult to get those at the local level to enforce unpopular policies and initiatives, unless pressure could be brought to bear to persuade or compel local officeholders to do their duty or else some measure could be devised to sidestep the local agents of law enforcement.[80]

It was the corporate towns that were most independent of royal authority. Between 1520 and 1670 the proportion of the population of England that lived in towns rose from 5.5 per cent to 13.5 per cent.[81] The number of incorporated cities and boroughs in England rose from 38 in 1500 to 181 by 1640 (there were a further 14 in Wales). With a charter of incorporation—a gift of the crown—came the right to self government, and most civic constitutions saw power shared, in classical republican fashion, between the one, the few, and the many: a fixed-term mayor, normally elected in some way; a select group of aldermen or senior burgesses who served, as it were, as senators, usually appointed for life, with the initial appointment typically being by co-option but often involving some sort of electoral element; and a broader group of common councilmen, the elected representatives of the freemen or citizens, who again served for a fixed term but who could submit themselves for re-election. Many corporate boroughs had the right to empanel their own jurymen (or to elect a sheriff and under-sheriff to do so), to supply their own justices of the peace, and to convene their own borough courts to handle minor legal infractions. The larger cities (such as Bristol, Norwich, and York) were able to incorporate as counties, which gave them the right to appoint their own militias and hold their own assizes. A Venetian visitor observed in 1557 that England, in matters of justice, was not 'like other kingdoms and Christian provinces, governed by civil and imperial laws, but by municipalities, almost like a republic'.[82] Furthermore, office-holding was regarded as a duty and an obligation, and the importance of public service was underpinned by a civic humanist (Ciceronian) ethos that stressed the role of virtuous citizens working for the better good of the commonwealth. Contemporaries saw England as being filled with semi-autonomous city commonwealths or civic palatinates. In 1600 Thomas Wilson, writing to insist that English cities should be free from royal interference, claimed that 'every citty' was, 'as it were, a Comon Wealth among themselves'.[83] Commonwealth, of course, was simply the English form of the Latin *res publica*.

In short, England was a monarchy filled with little commonwealths and quasi-republics—not just the cities and corporate towns, but also village republics, and gentry republics. Indeed, Sir Thomas Smith titled his famous study of 'the manner of government or policie of the realm of England' (written in 1562–5 although not published until 1583) *De Republica Anglorum*—literally, 'on the republic of England' (though perhaps best translated as 'on the commonwealth of England').

Because it was seen as the monarch's duty to rule for the common good (or common wealth), it was quite appropriate to style the realm of England a commonwealth. James VI and I was happy to do so, even though he regarded himself as absolute; it was not until after the interregnum of 1649–60 that the word commonwealth developed negative connotations. All areas of England, it should be stressed, were ultimately under the crown's control. Corporate boroughs, for instance, were single persons at law (by dint of their incorporation) but still subjects of the crown. But England was a monarchy in which there were many citizens concealed within its subjects, and one in which many of its inhabitants were used to participating, to some degree, in the process of government at the local level. It also had a political culture which invited people to think of the responsibilities of those in government—whether lesser magistrates or superior magistrates—in ways in tune with classical republican ways of thinking.[84]

This in turn raises the question more broadly of what role ordinary subjects might have been afforded in politics. The standard government line was that they had no role. The justice of the peace Richard Crompton, when pondering in a speech to the Staffordshire sessions in 1588 whether 'it were lawfull for the Subject, to enter into the examinations of causes or matters appertayning to the Prince and soveraigne Governour', reminded his listeners that it was not.[85] James VI and I was adamant that the people were not to be drawn into the *arcana imperii* (the secrets of the state): the people should trust the king to do what was right.[86] Yet again the reality never quite matched the rhetoric. Even though those in power might not have wanted ordinary people to reflect on how they exercised power, in practice early modern monarchs found that the best way of keeping their subjects on their side was to try to persuade the people that they were, indeed, exercising their power appropriately. Thus both the Tudors and the Stuarts found it necessary to sell themselves to their subjects, to project an image of majesty through appropriately staged processions and royal rituals, to explain their policies through proclamations, declarations, pamphlets, and sermons, and to encourage public commemoration of state accomplishments (battle victories, deliveries from conspiracies) through bonfire celebrations and firework displays. The idea that the people were supposed to be kept out of the *arcana imperii* is belied by the fact that the reigning monarchs themselves at times found it necessary to draw their subjects into the examinations of causes of matters appertaining to the prince and sovereign governor.[87]

Let us recap, then. The king, though absolute and not accountable to his subjects, was supposed to rule according to law and God would punish him if he did not. He had sworn an oath to rule according to law, and he ruled through ministers and judges who were obliged to uphold the law and who could be held accountable if they did not. The king was also supposed to rule for the benefit of his subjects and to take good counsel. Although kings did not share their power with parliaments, it was expected that the king, when appropriate, would rule through parliament, and parliament was valued for its conciliar role and as a guarantor of the people's liberties. All of this meant that the English king, although absolute, was not as absolute as the kings of France and Spain, who could make law on their own, 'without further approbation of the common wealth'.[88] As Sir Thomas Overbury put it in 1609, the French monarchy under Henri IV was 'most absolute because the kinge theire not only makes Peace and Warr, Calls and dissolves Parliamente, pardoneth, naturilizeth, innobleth, names the valewe of money, presseth to the warre, but even makes Lawes imposes taxes at his pleasure and all this hee doth alone'.[89]

Furthermore, it was possible to describe the political system that existed in England in different ways. One could characterize it either as an absolute monarchy or as a limited monarchy. One could see it as a mixed polity or alternatively deny that it was mixed. One could even choose to emphasize quasi-republican features of the constitution, not to assert that England was in essence a republic, but to emphasize that government was supposed to be conducted for the common good or common wealth and that those who served in government were supposed to be motivated by civic mindedness and not self-interest. The English monarchy was certainly one that depended upon widespread participation in the process of governing at the local level and where many communities—especially corporate towns—enjoyed considerable rights of self government.

This is not to suggest that the political nation in England was split into rigid ideological camps, divided between absolutists and constitutionalists, and certainly not between monarchists and republicans (there were virtually no out-and-out republicans in England prior to the Civil War). There was, as has been argued here, a broad, if somewhat loose consensus over what the constitutional framework was in England, a set of assumptions about the powers of the monarchy that most could quite happily embrace as long as people did not push too hard for clearer definitions. It tended to be moments of political conflict or crisis that prompted people to search for definition, or the need to justify a particular course of action that led some to empha-size one of the available discourses at the expense of another: the king can do this because he is absolute, or alternatively, the king can-not do this because although he is absolute he is also obliged to rule according to law. A final point to recognize is that protagonists often adopted a particular ideological stance for polemical advantage; they might choose to clothe themselves in the rhetoric of their political opponents for tactical reasons. What might appear at first glance to be contemporary descriptions of the constitutional set-up were often, in fact, nothing of the sort, but rather arguments constructed with the deliberate aim of undermining the position of one's political oppo-nents. Hence why critics of both James VI and I and Charles I were willing to acknowledge that the king was absolute, ruled by divine right, and was the father of his people, in order to lend greater plausi-bility to their arguments about why they thought royal power was being exercised inappropriately. Hence also why Charles, on the eve of the Civil War, was prepared to acknowledge that England had a mixed monarchy, with the king being one of three estates, in order to deny the validity of the reforms being pressed by parliament to limit the power of the crown further.

Providing for the Safety of Body and Soul

So far we have focused on the constitutional position of the crown, and seen that one of the most basic expectations of a king was that he should uphold justice and the rule of law. He also had certain other fundamental responsibilities. One was to protect his people, by military means if necessary. It was the king's prerogative to determine all matters of foreign policy and the king was the nation's leader in war. It was not, however, the expectation in England that the king should seek to achieve glory for his nation through the pursuit of military conquests. There had, for sure, been a Renaissance ideal of the king as a noble warrior, which Henry VIII had bought into to a certain extent. Yet peace, it must be stressed, was seen as a positive ideal, and normally preferable to war—and in an age of bloody con-fessional strife on the Continent, the terrible cost (both financial and human) of being sucked into avoidable and unproductive military conflicts with neighbouring states was apparent for all to see. As one author put it in 1621, at the time of James's negotiations over a mar-riage alliance with Spain, those who wanted 'warr for warr's sake not for peace, favour not the things which are of God', for 'hee is the God of peace and love'.[90] Or as one clergyman preaching at Oxford in the 1630s put it: 'they Erre who Terme Warr an Exercise of Manhood rather then Inhumanity. Nay it is such a Spectacle of Cruelty wherin alone mankind exceeds the Rage of Savage Beasts.'[91] Even those who believed that England should be armed ready for war, and not be afraid of engaging in a just war, nevertheless agreed that peace was 'the best of earthly blessings given unto mortality: more safe then any warre: more secure then any victory: more glorious then all triumphs'.[92] It is true that the early Stuarts were often criticized for pursuing a pacific foreign policy. Yet the main thrust of the attack was the perceived failure to secure either the national interest or the international Protestant interest.[93] It was not that pacificism in and of itself was seen as indefensible: the readiness of panegyrists to celebrate James VI and I's desire to be the peacemaker of all Europe speaks to the contrary.

There was also a widespread consensus that it was the English monarch's responsibility to uphold the true religion. The preamble to the Thirty-Nine Articles of 1563 had stated that it was the crown's duty 'to conserve and maintain the Church...in the unity of the True religion, and in the Bond of Peace'.[94] Elizabethan writers had made the point time and time again. In 1585 Thomas Bilson wrote that 'in delivering the sworde to Princes', God had charged them to maintain 'true religion' as well as minister 'civil justice'; a king, as God's lieutenant, 'above all thinges' was to defend God's holy Church 'from wronges'.[95] Similarly, in 1588 Richard Some observed that it was the prince's 'duetie' to provide not just 'for the safetie of the bodies' of his subjects, but also 'for the safetie of the[ir] soules', and 'True religion' was 'the foode of the soule'.[96] James VI and I agreed that it was 'the chiefest of all Kingly dueties' to 'settle the affaires of Religion, and the service of God'.[97]

The king's responsibility to uphold true religion meant that he should not tolerate schism or heresy. It was widely believed that diversity of opinions caused turbulence, that schism destabilized the state, and that heresy was a cancer or gangrene that would destroy the body politic if not cut out. It was a way of thinking that dated back to the founding fathers of the Church and had been reinforced during the Middle Ages. Its veracity seemed only to be confirmed by the European wars of religion that had followed in the wake of the Reformation.[98] The trouble was that England's long-drawn-out process of Reformation in the sixteenth century had seen the emergence of a country where different styles of religious practice and outlook had come to flourish.

Roman Catholicism was firmly on the defensive by the end of the sixteenth century. Initially, Elizabeth had been careful not to make martyrs out of adherents to the old faith when she restored Protestantism following her accession in 1558: the old Marian bishops, who refused to conform, were placed under house arrest (there were to be no burnings at the stake as with the Protestant bishops Cranmer, Latimer, and Ridley under Mary Tudor); under the 1559 Act of Uniformity the fine for non-attendance at church was a mere 12d. (5p in modern currency); and although one could be punished with death for a second refusal to take the oath of allegiance, Elizabeth made sure that the oath was never tendered a second time. However, conspiracies by militant Catholic minorities (such as the rebellion of northern Catholic earls in 1569 and the Ridolfi plot of 1571, both in favour of Mary Queen of Scots, and a further spate of plotting in the 1580s), the papal bull *Regnans in Excelsis* of 1570 declaring Elizabeth a heretic and excommunicated and releasing all her subjects from any allegiance to her, and the arrival—from the mid-1570s—of seminary priests trained on the Continent (joined by the Jesuits from 1580) on a mission to reconvert the English (and thus seemingly, by implication, to dislodge them from allegiance to their sovereign) prompted the government to take stern action. In response to *Regnans in Excelsis*, in 1571 it was made a treasonous offence to call the queen a heretic. In 1581 parliament increased recusancy fines to £20 per month (once convicted, the recusant had to go on paying the fine until he conformed) and made it treason for anyone claiming the power to absolve subjects from allegiance to the queen or attempting to withdraw men from obedience to the state. In the following year the queen and privy council took the drastic step of issuing a proclamation declaring that all seminarists and Jesuits were *ipso facto* traitors and making it a capital felony for lay people to harbour or relieve them, a measure that was subsequently confirmed by statute in 1585. Nevertheless, the penal laws were selectively enforced. Although a total of 124 seminary priests were executed between 1577 and 1603, the capital legislation was seldom applied to the laity. And while some high-profile Catholic landowners were financially ruined by cumulative recusancy fines, most were not pursued with vigour. The aim was to make an example of a few prominent individuals and potential troublemakers as a way of cowing the rest into obedience. The result was that Catholicism survived, but as the religion of a small minority:

out-and-out recusants perhaps constituted only 2 per cent of the population by the end of Elizabeth's reign, although there was probably a fairly large (albeit indeterminable) number of church papists, those who attended the services of the Church of England without ever being fully won over to its doctrines. A combination of evangelical preaching and print and jingoistic propaganda—in the wake of the massacre of Protestants in Paris on St Bartholomew's Day in 1572, England's war in alliance with the Protestant Dutch against Catholic Spain from 1585, and the failed invasion of England by the Spanish Armada in 1588—meant that the majority of English people became vehemently anti-Catholic and hostile to all manifestations of popery.[99]

Yet if England, by 1603, was an overwhelmingly Protestant—and anti-Catholic—nation, different Protestant groups disagreed over what constituted true religion, as England split between those who were happy with the Elizabethan settlement in the Church—the Act of Uniformity and Book of Common Prayer of 1559 and the Thirty-Nine Articles of 1563—and those who saw the need to purify the Church further (who came to be known by the name of 'Puritans', originally a term of abuse). Some put emphasis on preaching and reading scripture, others more on a strict adherence to the ceremonies prescribed by the prayer book (which included kneeling for communion, the use of the cross in baptism, and the provision that ministers should wear a surplice). Elizabeth's own brand of Protestantism was idiosyncratic: she favoured a sacrament-centred style of piety, was suspicious of excessive preaching, and had a very un-Protestant taste for elaborate church music. Her first generation of Church leaders, however, were largely Marian exiles who had studied at the reformed centres on the Continent and who took her Church in a decidedly Calvinist direction; indeed some of them, like Edmund Grindal (consecutively bishop of London and archbishop of York and then of Canterbury), were not unsympathetic to the demands of moderate Puritans. The Elizabethan Church did face a challenge in the 1570s and 1580s from an English Presbyterian movement, led first by Thomas Cartwright and then John Field, who called for the abolition of offensive ceremonies and the outlawing of episcopacy, although most English Puritans thought their position too extreme. However, from the 1580s a second generation of more conservative and disciplinarian clerics rose to prominence in the English Church—the highest profile being John Whitgift, archbishop of Canterbury from 1583 to 1604—who took a much tougher line on all forms of

Puritan dissent. Upon his translation to Canterbury, Whitgift demanded that all the clergy subscribe three articles: the first acknowledging the royal supremacy (by itself hardly controversial), the second and third declaring that the Book of Common Prayer and the Thirty-Nine Articles contained nothing contrary to the word of God. Many who had no desire to cause trouble in the Church found they could not subscribe to such a far-reaching declaration. Whitgift promptly suspended some 300 to 400 ministers, which threatened to rend the Church in two; under pressure from the government, he allowed doubtful ministers to subscribe with qualifications. The subscription campaign gave a temporary spur to the Presbyterians, who managed to introduce into parliament in 1587 a bill to replace the Book of Common Prayer with the Geneva Book of Discipline. But Field died in 1588 and without his organizational genius the English Presbyterian movement was never the same. The intemperate Marprelate tracts of 1588–9, with their vitriolic attacks on the established Church, provoked a backlash, fuelled by a clever propaganda campaign sponsored by Whitgift and his chaplain Richard Bancroft, canon of Westminster, and by 1592 the English Presbyterian movement had been driven underground.[100]

Despite his anti-Puritanism, Whitgift was a doctrinal Calvinist. However, the supposed 'Calvinist' consensus of the Elizabethan Church, if such a consensus had ever genuinely existed, was showing signs of fragmenting by the end of Elizabeth's reign. The 1590s saw the rise of a group of avant-garde conformists, men such as Lancelot Andrewes (royal chaplain, canon of St Paul's, and master of Pembroke College, Cambridge) and Samuel Harsnett (another Pembroke don), who challenged the Calvinist doctrine of predestination, placed a greater emphasis on ceremonialism, and called for the beautification of churches.[101] Whitgift had to discipline Harsnett for preaching against predestination at St Paul's Cross in August 1584, and in a dispute over predestination that had originated at Cambridge in 1595 Whitgift intervened to draw up nine articles—known as the Lambeth Articles—vindicating the Calvinist position. Elizabeth was angry, however, when she learned that the Articles had been compiled and discussed without her authority, and immediately ordered Whitgift to suppress them. For Whitgift, the Lambeth Articles said nothing new but merely clarified the existing position of the Church; Elizabeth's hostility was rooted in a concern for the royal prerogative, though she was also suspicious of Calvinists. Her opposition left it unclear where the Church stood on the issue, making it possible in the long run for both Calvinists and anti-Calvinists to represent themselves as in conformity with the principles of the Elizabethan Church.[102]

England had a small group of separatists, or Brownists as they tended to be called, after the Cambridge graduate and early separatist leader Robert Browne, but persecution forced many of these into exile in the Low Countries in the 1580s. Protestant separatists could also be caught under the anti-Catholic legislation, either for failure to attend church services or for challenging the royal supremacy. Indeed, in 1593 the government enacted further legislation against recusants that specifically included seditious sectaries, stipulating that convicted separatists who failed to conform should abjure the realm or be punished as traitors. The anti-separatist legislation had the effect not only of stigmatizing radical Puritans in the public eye as dangerous political subversives, but also of associating them with papists. In 1593 the Protestant separatists and religious controversialists Henry Barrow, John Greenwood, and John Penry were sentenced to death for writing against the royal supremacy under the terms of the 1581 legislation originally aimed at Catholics.[103]

In short, post-Reformation England was a religiously pluralistic society that found it difficult to accept religious pluralism.[104] It was not that England's rulers embraced a policy of zero tolerance of religious difference. Elizabeth famously proclaimed she had 'no desire to make windows into men's souls', while James frequently proclaimed his belief that consciences could not be forced. The government's official line was that it was against persecuting people for their religious beliefs. That was something Roman Catholics did; persecution was a popish principle. Loyalty was the issue. 'No man, either in my time, or in the late Queene's', James wrote in 1609, 'ever died here for his conscience... if he breake not out into some outward act, expresly against the words of the Law; or plot not some unlawfull or dangerous practise or attempt'.[105] It was a widely believed position (at least by English Protestants): as one poet somewhat inelegantly put it in the immediate aftermath of the Gunpowder Plot of 1605, 'But nere t'was read that Catholicke | for Conscience lost his breath: | But for Conspiracies gainst Kings | drag'd to immediate death'.[106] Yet it was not always an easy distinction to sustain—especially in the broader context of the Counter-Reformation European wars of religion, where the state's enemies were its religious enemies. The archdeacon of Ely, Robert Tynley, preaching at St Paul's Cross in 1608 on the anniversary of the Catholic Gunpowder Plot, after first charging Catholics with perverting 'the lawfull subjection of people to their Sovereignes' went on to insist that 'lib-ertie of Conscience' could not be allowed not only because 'Popish Doctrine' was 'pernicious...to States and Kingdomes' but also because 'light' and 'darkenes' could not breathe the same air nor 'the puritie of the Gospell have any agreement with Popish Superstition'.[107] As William Laud, Charles's archbishop of Canterbury from 1633, put it in a sermon preached towards the end of James's reign: the peace of the Church 'must not be broken in any corner', for 'a sedition, or a schisme in a corner, in a Conventicle, (which is the place where they are usually hatched) will fire all if it bee suffered'.[108] It was a view shared by most English Protestants, with the exception of a handful of separatists. One observer, who was critical of Charles's attempts to impose uniformity in the Church in the 1630s, nevertheless acknowledged in the secrecy of his own commonplace book that any state or kingdom that admitted of 'two Religions' would never prosper, 'because a house devided against it selfe can-not stand, and diversitie in religion, breadeth the worst bloode in a state that can be, for from this diversitie in Religion, ariseth warrs, tumoults, Sedission, and massaker, unto the ruine of most famous States'.[109]

The promotion of true religion was seen as essential to the smooth running of society and government. As Romans 13 taught, subjects were obliged to obey the divinely ordained powers-that-be not just out of fear, but for conscience sake. For James 'the principles of sound religion' were 'the foundation of true and sincere obedience'.[110] The Cornish MP Sir John Eliot, who was to be serially imprisoned in the Tower (where he eventually died in 1632) for his opposition to the Caroline government in the late 1620s, encapsulated the thinking of most contemporaries well when he said in parliament in June 1625: 'Religion is the touchstone of all actions...Religion it is that keeps the subject in obedience, as being taught by God to honour his vice-gerents...Where there is division in religion, as it does wrong divin-ity, it makes distractions amongst men and so dissolves all ties and obligations, civil and natural, the observation of heaven being more powerful than either policy or blood.'[111] 'From the happinesse and quiet of Religion', one ultra-royalist explained in 1644, 'issueth forth necessarily the happines and quiet of the Civil State'; for 'Religion and the feare of God, and nothing else', he continued, 'teacheth Kings how to rule, and Subjects how to obey...it teacheth our reverence, service, and obedience'. In short, 'Religion' was 'the nurse of the quiet of State and Common-wealth'.[112]

Yet if imposing the true religion was seen as an essential—and necessary—duty of kings, doing so in a kingdom in which there was no consensus over what constituted the true religion was bound to provoke discontent. It could even raise concerns that the king was acting tyrannically by imposing on his subjects a religion which was not the true one; it could certainly raise doubts as to whether that king was fulfilling his divinely ordained function. The situation becomes more complicated once Scotland and Ireland are added to the mix. In Scotland, the Reformation had seen the establishment of a Presbyterian Kirk which in terms of liturgy and Church government was significantly different from the episcopalian Church in England, and where not the king but Jesus Christ was head of the Kirk; for Presbyterian Scots, for a king to seek to impose his vision of true religion by dint of his own royal authority was to set himself up in competition with Christ, or in other words as an anti-Christ. In Ireland a failed Reformation had left the vast majority of the population Roman Catholic, who did not think that the religion which English kings saw it as their duty to impose was indeed the true one.[113]

Religion was to prove a minefield for the early Stuarts. The danger was that the more seriously one took one's responsibility to promote the true religion, the greater the risk of provoking further problems. Left untreated, however, the cancer of religious heterodoxy and schism seemed likely to undermine the health of the body politic.

How to Respond to Tyranny

Finally, then, what could one do if the king did not rule according to the law, misused his prerogatives, did not rule justly, or failed to provide for the safety of the bodies and souls of his subjects? The conventional teaching of the Church was that one 'must rather obey God then man'.[114] If the king asked you to do something that was against the moral law of God, you should not comply. Nevertheless, you could not actively resist, and you had to accept punishment for noncompliance. One's only recourse against tyrants was prayers and tears. It was a view accepted by conformists and nonconformists alike. Thus the Puritan Thomas Scott, in a work published in Amsterdam in 1623, could urge that if 'thy conscience tells thee, the Religion commanded by the King, or some ceremony used in the Church according to the Lawes established, is...contrary to the truth', it was 'better to obay God then man' and 'not to doe what is commanded by man'; nevertheless, 'thou art to suffer what is injoyned by him...submitting thy will to God's holy ordinance, and obaying the Magistrate for conscience sake'.[115]

Again, the reality was somewhat more complicated. Both the Bible and history taught that in practice people often did resist. Moreover, the sixteenth-century wars of religion had seen the development of legitimations of resistance to tyrannical rulers, by both Catholics and Protestants. In the British context, justifications of resistance had been articulated in the mid-sixteenth century by opponents of the regimes of Mary Tudor and Mary Queen of Scots.[116] That was precisely why pro-government propagandists preached non-resistance, of course. James made the contemporary agenda quite explicit in his *Trew Law*, condemning the 'seditious preachers in these daies of whatsoever religion'—he was thinking particularly of Scotland and France—who took it upon themselves 'to stir up rebellion under cloake of religion', and referring to 'the unhappy iniquitie of the time' which had seen 'treasonable attempts' often meet with 'good successe'.[117]

Yet although champions of royal absolutism decried resistance and said that it could never be legitimate, they did at times see fit to offer the reminder that tyranny could well prompt subjects to rebel, as a way of reinforcing the point that kings should not rule tyrannically. Preaching in 1610, David Owen insisted that 'God hath forbidden Christian subjects to resist', who were to endure tyranny with patience. Nevertheless, Owen conceded that God did sometimes 'permit rebels...to prevaile against Kings' who showed contempt for the law and neglected their duty.[118] Moreover, although the Christian's response to tyranny could only be prayers and tears, what was the point of all those prayers and tears if not to try to persuade God to do something about the problem? Just as God might punish people for their sins by visiting a tyrant upon them, He would also come to their rescue if they showed themselves duly penitent.[119] 'God doth never leave violence, Injustice, or Cruelty unpunish'd', Roger Whitley recorded in his commonplace book; 'God disposeth of the Affections of his subjects, as he meanes to raise, or Ruine theire Princes'.[120] As always, James VI and I's own reflections on this issue are perceptive and revealing. God, he insisted in his *Trew Law*, 'as the great Judge may justly punish his Deputie, and for his rebellion against him, stir up his rebels to meet him with the like'. These rebels would still be playing 'the divel's part'. Yet in concluding his discussion of non-resistance, James explained that he did not think 'by the force and argument of this...discourse so to perswade the people, that none will hereafter be raised up, and rebell against wicked Princes'.[121]

The view that tyranny was likely to provoke rebellion appears to have been widespread. One man recorded in his commonplace book *c.*1625 the saying from Tacitus that 'Tyrannie is a violent rule against the lawes and customes; which causeth rebellion, which is an insurrection against the prince to pluck him from his throne'.[122] Another, writing in about 1698 (his views undoubtedly coloured by the revolutions of the seventeenth century), saw fit to recall how Machiavelli, despite regarding 'risings in arms and clandestine conspiracies' as 'the greatest crime that can be committed among men', nevertheless saw them as likely to occur 'as often as Princes Tyrannize', since it was 'impossible, that Humane Nature...can support with Patience and Submission, the greatest Cruelty and injustice'.[123] Thus ironically the biggest check on tyranny was the threat of rebellion, even though rebellion was deemed illegitimate. Asked once at dinner 'whether there could be no Case in which Defensive Arms were Lawful' Dr Alexander Colville, the principal of St Mary's College at the University of St Andrews in Scotland, replied: 'It was fit for the People to believe them unlawful, and for Kings to believe them lawful.'[124] The Arminian cleric Peter Studley, writing in 1635 during Charles I's 'personal rule', observed that 'no man living in the world doth naturally...love the person of a Tyrant'.[125] As Roger Whitley recorded in his commonplace book, 'That Prince, who is not Loved, cannot be well obeyed'.[126]

What further complicated matters was that Tudor and Stuart monarchs, by their foreign policy decisions, seemed to acknowledge that there could be circumstances in which rebellion against one's sovereign was legitimate. Elizabeth, for example, had supported the rebellious Dutch in their efforts to throw off Spanish rule. Charles I was to support the rebellious Huguenots in France in the late 1620s. Even the Church's teachings on non-resistance appeared to have their limits. John Jewel, the man who composed the Elizabethan homily against resistance, nevertheless excused the Scots for rising against Mary Queen of Scots and praised Luther, Melanchthon, and French Protestants for resisting oppression.[127]

Finally, we might suggest that the ideology of legitimation in which the Stuarts clothed themselves—the 'public transcript' that it was their duty to uphold the law and rule for the welfare of their people—in turn opened up 'the possibilities of (legitimate) resistance' through the exploitation of contradictions inherent in that transcript that allowed it be criticized in its own terms.[128] We see this in crowd protest. The London weavers who rioted in 1595 to protest against alien workers taking their jobs, for example, justified their actions by proclaiming that 'Every Christian Kinge and Queene is sworne to maintaine the good estate of the Commonwealth and welfare of the people'.[129] Time and again opponents of the Stuarts over the course of the seventeenth century were to claim that it was legitimate to oppose government initiatives, if those in power were not acting in accordance with the law or for the benefit of the people. In making such claims, it was possible for those engaged in acts of opposition to represent their actions as being in accordance with consensual norms and values.

James VI and I

James VI of Scotland, 1567–1603

James VI and I was born at Edinburgh Castle on the morning of 19 June 1566. The son of Mary Queen of Scots and her second husband, Henry Stewart, Lord Darnley, he was baptized on 17 December in a magnificent ceremony in the Chapel Royal of Stirling Castle according to the rites of the Catholic Church—the last great public Catholic ceremony in sixteenth-century Scotland. His mother, the widow of Francis II of France and briefly queen of France herself in 1559–60, christened him Charles James—James because the traditional name of kings of Scotland, Charles after the present king of France, Mary's brother-in-law Charles IX, who was James's godfather. It was Mary who Frenchified the spelling of the family name to Stuart. James became king of Scotland on 24 July 1567, following his mother's forced abdication, and was crowned five days later in a Protestant ceremony, with the fiery Scottish reformer John Knox preaching the coronation sermon. He was just thirteen months old. For a Scottish sovereign to inherit the throne at such a tender age was in itself not that unusual: every Scottish monarch since 1406 had come to the throne as a minor, while James's grandfather James V had been a mere eighteen months old and his mother just seven days. What *was* unusual was the fact that the previous monarch was still alive and claiming to be the rightful sovereign. James was never to see his mother again. Imprisoned first in Loch Leven Castle, Mary escaped at the beginning of May 1568 and, after a failed attempt to recapture her throne by force, fled to England, where she was to remain captive for the rest of her life. She was to be executed by the English state in 1587.

The conventional image of the man who was to rule England as James I from 1603 to 1625 was for long an unflattering one: a boorish, ungainly, lazy, and cowardly Scot, who was given to alcoholic excess, rarely washed or changed his clothes, and had blatantly homosexual relationships. It is a gross caricature, and deeply unfair, deriving in large part from a vicious lampoon penned by the disgruntled ex-courtier Sir Anthony Weldon. Weldon's James is indeed a creepy figure: a man of 'timerous disposition', with large eyes 'ever rowling after any stranger' who came into his presence, a tongue 'too large for his mouth' (which 'made him speake full in the mouth...and drinke verey uncomely, as if eating his drinke, which came out into the cup of each side his mouth'), and legs so weak that he had to prop himself up by leaning on other men's shoulders, his fingers all the while 'fidling about his codpiece'.[1] As with all caricatures, however, through all the distortions and misrepresentations it contained hints of elements of truth.

The derogatory remarks about James's way of talking most likely reflect an English difficulty with his thick Scottish accent. According to Francis Bacon, the king's speech was 'swift and cursory, and in the full dialect of his country'.[2] Yet James was regarded as an excellent public speaker. When Lord Keeper Williams had to deputize for James at the opening of the second session of the 1621 parliament, the judge Sir Richard Hutton observed how it was difficult to speak for the king, 'who was the most absolute Orator'.[3] James was also learned and highly intelligent. His early education was supervised by the great Scottish humanist and historian (and champion of resistance theory) George Buchanan, and by the Greek scholar Peter Young. Buchanan was a harsh and unsympathetic master, not averse to giving his charge a beating from time to time. The young James was terrified of him, grew up to despise him, and continued to have nightmares about Buchanan until the end of his reign[4]—although he did in later life express pride in having been taught by a man of such academic distinction. James was good at his studies and came to develop a love of learning and a passion for scholarship that was exceptional among kings at the time. The French envoy the Marquis de Fontenay observed in 1584 how James 'grasps and understands quickly...judges carefully and with reasonable discourses' and was 'learned in many languages, sciences, and affairs of state'.[5] As an adult James wrote poetry and also works of philosophy, in which he outlined his own theories of kingship. In 1603 an English courtier reported that 'the King is of sharpest witt and invencion, redie and pithie speche, an exceeding good memorie' and that 'his lerning and religious virtues' had 'extolled him above all princes in the world'.[6] On one occasion, following a tour of the Bodleian Library in Oxford, James reputedly said that if he were not king he would have liked to have been a don.[7] The Jacobean bishop William Barlow, writing of James's performance in debate with the Puritans at the Hampton Court Conference of 1604, described the king as 'a Living Library, and a walking Study'.[8] Not everyone agreed with how James applied his intelligence, however. Weldon thought James 'crafty and cunning in petty things'. Henri IV of France supposedly dubbed him 'the wisest foole in Christendome': 'wise in small things, but a foole in weighty affaires'.[9]

The adult James was a man of middling stature, 'rather tall than low, well set and somewhat plump, of a ruddy Complexion' and with 'light brown' hair, and a 'very thin' beard.[10] But he carried himself awkwardly. Having spent his early years holed up in dark Scottish castles, deprived of sunlight, he may have had rickets as a very young boy. He was certainly slow to walk and remained somewhat unsure on his feet for the rest of his life. He probably also suffered from mild cerebral palsy, which gave him the characteristic irregular writhing movements.[11] Contemporaries commented upon the 'unwildines or weaknes in his Limbs', which made 'his carriage ungainly, his steps erratic and vagabond'. Hence why, when 'walking amongst his nobles', he was often seen 'to lean upon their shoulders', although this was interpreted as a sign of royal favour. James himself admitted in 1584 that he was 'of a Feeble Body' and could 'not Labour long at Business', since it made him ill. Fontenay found the teenage king 'too Lazy', and although he thought this 'excusable in so young Age', worried that if it were allowed to continue it might harden 'into a Habit'. Fontenay also found James's manners 'rude and very uncivil, both in speaking, eating, clothes, games and conversation in the company of women'.[12] Even sympathetic writers acknowledged James to be 'much given to swearing', and 'not so careful of his carriage as he might be'.[13] Weldon reckoned him 'the greatest blasphemer in the world', who could 'sweare faster than speak'.[14]

Nor did James keep one of the more dignified courts in the world. When he entertained his brother-in-law Christian IV of Denmark at Theobalds in July 1606, the reception degenerated into a drunken shambles.[15] It has thus been said that James failed to be majestic, or to project an appropriate image of majesty to his people—something at which his predecessor Elizabeth had excelled.[16] Writing in 1607, the Venetian ambassador observed that James did 'not caress the people nor make them that good cheer the late Queen did, whereby she won their loves'; instead, he seemed rather to regard them with 'contempt and dislike'.[17] Similarly, one anonymous English author remarked how James did not 'delight in Popular salutation' and that 'the poorer sorte' contrasted this with 'the manner of their late

Queene', who 'would often speake Kyndlye to the Multitude', and urged James to find some way to 'satisfye their Zealous Affections', or else 'the poore Rascalls...wilbee Angrye with you'.[18] James preferred hunting trips to the pomp and ceremony of formal royal progresses, and the 'great flocks of people' that turned out to try to catch a glimpse of their monarch clearly caused him anxiety. On one occasion he protested that he wished he could make 'an inhibition that while hee hunted his Deere the people should not hunt him'.[19] He was certainly thought by some to put hunting before his people: c.1611–12 a man from Faversham in Kent supposedly said that it was a 'pitty that ever this King came to the crowne of England, for he hath more regard of his dogs then he hath of his subjects or common wealth'.[20] Yet it would be wrong to paint a picture of a king who preferred sport to statecraft. James's councillors always went with him on his hunting trips, during which he spent much of his time 'in State contrivances', while his regular forays into the countryside of southern England enabled him to mix with the leaders of local society in a relaxed and informal manner, helping to foster loyalty in the process. He would also visit the principal towns in the locality, often touching for the King's Evil. He himself did not believe in the thaumaturgical power of kings, knowing it to be 'a Device, to ingrandize the Vertue of Kings, when Miracles were in fashion'; but he saw the wisdom in letting his subjects believe in it, and how it could help cement popular belief in his divine right to rule.[21]

'By nature' James was said to be 'placid' and 'averse from cruelty', loving 'quiet and repose' and having 'no inclination to war'.[22] His desire was to be the peacemaker of all Europe, taking as his motto 'Beati Pacifici' (Blessed are the Peacemakers).[23] Sir John Oglander, who was knighted by James at Royston in 1615 and who rose to be deputy governor of Portsmouth and then of the Isle of Wight, described him as 'the most cowardly man' he ever knew. The Spanish ambassador in 1604 thought James 'as timid as a woman'. Certainly his years in Scotland left James with a fear of kidnap and assassination, and he always slept surrounded by three other beds, and he wore a padded doublet that was supposed to be 'pistol-proof'.[24] According to one late seventeenth-century historian, James had such 'a Natural Aversion to Arms' that 'he could not indure the sight of a naked Sword'.[25] It is a charge that is undoubtedly unfair: as king of Scotland James was to lead an army in battle six times before succeeding to the English throne.[26] Yet it was an impression that came to stick. His supposed fear of all things military even became the subject of jokes. James 'allwayes esteem'd Soldiers the Worst of Men', one contemporary wrote, so that when a certain lord, newly returned from the wars abroad, 'desir'd the honor to kiss his Majestie's hands, the King told him, That he fear'd he would bite it, and therefore bad that he should be mufled'.[27]

James also had homosexual leanings. One contemporary commented that the king chose his favourites on the basis of their 'handsomnesse', and that 'the love the King shewed was as amorously convayed, as if he had mistaken their Sex, and thought them Ladies'. Some of his leading favourites were more than happy to try to oblige the king by labouring to resemble women 'in the effeminatenesse of their dressings'.[28] Sir John Oglander noted that James 'loved young men, his favourites, better than women, loving them beyond the love of men to women', and claimed he had never seen 'any fond husband make so much or so great dalliance over his beautiful spouse' as he had 'seen King James over his favourites, especially the Duke of Buckingham'.[29] James fondled and kissed his male favourites in public, he wrote love letters to them, and he also shared his bed with them. It is unclear the extent to which James's relationships with his favourites were physical—sodomy was not just a sin but a capital felony, one of those crimes, James wrote in his *Basilikon Doron*, 'ye are bound in conscience never to forgive'—although on balance the available evidence strongly hints that they were, even if that physical activity stopped short of anal intercourse. James, of course, also condemned drinking and swearing, but that did not stop him from indulging in both. The diarist Sir Simonds D'Ewes, writing in 1622 at the time of Buckingham's ascendancy, recalls discussing 'the sinne of sodomye' with a close friend and expressing his fear that it was so widespread in London that 'wee could not but expect some horrible punishment for it'—'especially', D'Ewes continued, 'it being, as wee had probable cause to feare, a sinne in the prince [i.e. king]'.[30]

Despite his fondness for attractive young men, James fulfilled his kingly responsibility of securing the succession. In August 1589, at the age of twenty-three, he was married to the fourteen-year-old Danish princess, Anne or Anna (b. 12 December 1574), second daughter of Frederick II, king of Denmark and Norway, one of the wealthier kingdoms in Europe at this time. The marriage—which was conducted by proxy in the great hall of the royal palace at Kronborg in Denmark—brought with it a dowry of £150,000 Scots and access to valuable trading concessions for Scottish merchant ships passing through Øresund (the strait that separates the Danish island of Zealand from the Swedish mainland). Anne eventually set sail for Scotland on 5 September, but her flotilla encountered heavy storms and after two weeks at sea was forced to take refuge in the southern fjords of Norway. Learning of his new bride's distress, James, against the objections of his advisors, set sail to rescue her, and they were married in person at the bishop's palace in Upslo (not far from modern-day Oslo) on 23 November. From there they returned to Kronborg on 21 January 1590 and finally back to Scotland in the spring, landing safely at Leith to a formal state reception on 1 May. Anne was soon pregnant, although she was still very young, and she miscarried in mid-September, three months short of her sixteenth birthday. Her first child—Henry—was born at Stirling Castle on 19 February 1594, and she was to give birth to six more children over the next few years (with further miscarriages in between), testifying to the intimacy that she enjoyed with her husband at this time. Of these, only two were to survive infancy: Elizabeth (b.19 August 1596) and Charles (b.19 November 1600).[31] Nevertheless, it would be wrong to think of James as being bisexual, as we would understand the term. (Contemporaries, of course, lacked the concept.) James showed no interest in women, either before his arranged marriage to Anne or after, and he never had any mistresses. As Sir John Oglander observed, 'He was the chastest prince for women that ever was, for he would often swear that he had never known any other woman than his wife.'[32]

Raised a Lutheran, in the mid-1590s Anne converted to Catholicism, which she found more congenial than the Scottish brand of Calvinism. She practised her Catholic faith in private, however: although she refused to take the Anglican communion at her English coronation in 1604, as queen of England she attended Protestant services and sermons and maintained Protestant chaplains and preachers. A well-educated woman and a talented linguist, she became a powerful patron of the arts, helping to promote a number of architectural projects and playing a significant role in the development of the court masque. Yet she grew more distant from James as time went by. The trust between the pair first appears to have been broken when James insisted that she hand over their first-born, Henry, to be raised by the earl of Mar and Mar's mother at Stirling, James feeling that for security reasons it would be best if he and his heir did not live under the same roof. Although Anne continued to be a significant figure in Scottish court politics in the 1590s and early 1600s, her influence with her husband declined after 1603.[33]

* * *

James ruled Scotland for nearly thirty-six years before coming to the English throne, and in order to understand James the king of England we have to start with James the king of Scotland. His experiences north of the border were crucially formative, helping not only to mould his political personality but also to shape his political outlook. Out of necessity he became a reforming king. He was not afraid to be confrontational or to take on powerful interests. Yet he also learned a certain political pragmatism, how to read a political situation, and to appreciate which battles he could win, which he had to win, and which were not worth fighting too hard for.

James faced a daunting prospect when he eventually assumed personal responsibility for government following his lengthy minority. The decade of his birth had witnessed two revolutions. A Protestant coup of 1560, while Mary Queen of Scots was in France, saw the Scottish parliament introduce a Protestant Confession of Faith, outlaw the mass and papal jurisdiction, and commission what became the *First Book of Discipline*, a document heavily influenced by Genevan ideas. A second revolution in 1567 saw Mary deposed and a new parliament ratify the reforming legislation of 1560 and pass an Act requiring all Scottish monarchs in future to swear an oath at their coronation promising to protect the true religion. Civil war (1567–73) and years of factional fighting followed, as different noble factions sought to gain control of the crown, using their respective parliaments to strike at their opponents. The first regent of the infant James's reign, the earl of Moray, was assassinated in 1570, as was the second, the earl of Lennox, in 1571. The fourth, the earl of Morton, was overthrown in a coup in 1578 and executed in 1581.

Illustrative of the chaos of these years is the confusion over when James's personal rule might be said to have begun. James first accepted the nominal reins of government in 12 March 1578, three months short of his twelfth birthday, following the downfall of Morton. He followed this with a spectacular state entry into Edinburgh in October 1579 and a progress through Fife and Angus in June 1580. However, during these years the government was effectively run by James's first 'favourite', Esmé Stuart, a Frenchman of Scottish descent who was created earl and subsequently duke of Lennox. Lennox soon made enemies. His French and Catholic background raised suspicions about his true political and religious agenda, even though he converted to Protestantism, while James's open displays of affection for him led to allegations that Lennox had drawn the young king 'to carnal lust'. On 22 August 1582 a group of ultra-Protestant notables abducted the young king and held him captive in Ruthven Castle (now Huntingtower Castle) just outside Perth, seized control of the government, and ordered Lennox to leave the country. James escaped from the Ruthven Raid lords in June 1583 and declared his intention to be 'universal king' (that is, above faction), though in fact control of the government was to pass into the hands of the man who helped engineer his escape, fellow detainee James Stewart, who became earl of Arran. It was only with the overthrow of Arran in November 1585 that James's personal rule as king of Scotland effectively began, by which time the king was in his twentieth year.[34]

The lengthy and chaotic royal minority had revealed the degree to which the crown had become powerless in the face of noble conspiracy. It had led to a revival of resistance theory in Scotland as Buchanan penned defences of Mary's deposition.[35] It had created religious rifts, both within the political elite and among the population at large, as Scotland began the transition to becoming a Protestant country. And it had seen the rise of the General Assembly of the Kirk, which, in the absence of an adult monarch, tended to act as if it were the sovereign authority in the state with regard to ecclesiastical affairs.

When James finally assumed responsibility for running the government, therefore, much work needed to be done to reassert the authority of the crown in Scotland. As James himself complained to Fontenay, the power of the great lords had increased because, for more than forty years, they had had only women and little children to govern them, or else traitorous and greedy regents.[36] A manuscript treatise on 'The Generall State of the Scottish Comon wealthe', dating from the latter part of the sixteenth century, identified the weaknesses of the Scottish monarchy as being the crown's lack of financial resources, its lack of independence from parliament, 'contentions and jealousies' between the prince and an over-mighty nobility (with their hereditary offices and jurisdictions, especially in the Highlands), a weak middle class, and an impoverished lower class of tillers and husbandmen who were 'ever apte for faction and tumulte'.[37] It is not known whether James ever saw this treatise, but he clearly recognized the problems himself. In his *Basilikon Doron* of 1598—the 'how-to-rule' manual he wrote for his eldest son Henry—he advised his successor to 'hold no Parliaments, but for necessitie of new Lawes'; censure the oppressions committed 'by the greatest ranke'; 'embrace the quarrel of the poore and distressed'; increase royal control over the Highlands and Borderlands; tackle the problem of 'heritable Shirefdomes and Regalities'; keep the nobility in line by teaching them 'to keepe your lawes'; encourage trade and industry; and stop the seditions of 'the common people' (who, he felt, had a tendency 'to judge and speake rashly of their Prince'). James also included a long section on the Church, in part a reaction to his own problems in dealing with the Scottish Presbyterians. Thus *Basilikon Doron* complains how during 'the reformation of Religion in Scotland...many things were inordinately done by popular tumult and rebellion' and warns Henry to 'take heede' of the Puritans ('verie pestes in the Church and Common-weale') and as a 'preservative against their poison' to promote 'the godly, learned and modest men of the ministerie...to Bishoprickes and Benefices'. 'Hate no man more then a proude Puritane', James exhorted; 'represse the vaine Puritane' and 'banish their conceited paritie' (Scottish Presbyterianism), since this 'can neither stand with the order of the Church nor the peace of a Commonweale and well ruled Monarchie'. James also advised his heir to 'suffer no conventions nor meetings among Church-men [i.e. General Assemblies of the Kirk], but by your knowledge and permission'.[38]

If the problems were readily identifiable, they were less easily solved. The first step for James upon assuming control of the government was to try to recover royal estates alienated during his minority. Scotland had been so used to royal minorities during the fifteenth and sixteenth centuries that the practice had developed of allowing monarchs who had come to the throne as a minor to revoke alienations made during their minority, so long as they did so before they reached the age of twenty-five. James actually issued three revocations. The first was in 1581, when as a fourteen-year-old he revoked all grants made by his regents. The second, in 1584, ratified that of 1581 with minor alterations. The third, which came in 1587, when James turned twenty-one, was more extensive, revoking not just all grants made during his minority but also those by Mary Queen of Scots before his coronation and any alienations of rents, lands, or heritages by any of his predecessors to the prejudice of the crown.[39]

James sought to tame the Scottish nobility. He intervened personally to reconcile disputes between feuding families, and finally in 1598 he secured the passage of an Act whereby the nobility agreed that their feuds would be submitted to the justice of the royal courts.[40] He brought men of lesser status into the royal administration, appointing the lawyer Sir John Maitland of Thirlestane as his Lord Chancellor in 1587, the most powerful man in Scotland after the king, who steadily built up an effective bureaucracy drawing upon the lairds, urban lawyers, and younger sons of the great houses loyal to the crown. James had no desire to rid himself of the nobility, but thought they should be maintained at court, and endeavoured to tie them to the crown through gifts and pensions and other forms of patronage. He challenged the near monopoly of criminal justice exercised by lords of the regality by reviving justice ayres and authorizing lairds to hold quarter sessions on the English model. Such initiatives did not totally solve the problem. Many nobles were concerned about what they saw as an erosion of their privileges, and two dissident earls—the Catholic Huntly and the Protestant Bothwell—showed they were still willing to use violence to challenge the authority of the crown. However, the defeat of their rebellions in 1594–5 and their subsequent exile (Bothwell's permanent, Huntly was reprieved in 1597) seemed to show that the crown could no longer be held to ransom by disgruntled aristocrats.[41]

James took a close interest in parliament, determined to work with it in order to carry out reforms in Kirk and state—in part to further the idea of Scotland being an integrated body politic rather than a country in which authority was exercised by autonomous noble factions, in part so that he could raise much-needed revenues. James attended his first parliament in 1578 and was present at all eleven meetings of parliament prior to his accession to the English crown in 1603. In order to ensure the crown was better informed of local grievances and also to broaden the base of consent for taxation, in 1587, on reaching the age of majority, he revived defunct legislation from 1428 allowing lairds (lesser landowners below the ranks of the titular nobility) to sit in parliament as shire representatives.[42] Then in 1594 he secured an Act whereby before public business could be introduced into parliament it should be submitted three weeks in advance to be vetted by a committee comprising four members of each estate, though in fact this system was never put into operation.[43]

James's reign saw a dramatic increase in both the scale and frequency of parliamentary taxation. Whereas the highest sum asked for during the Morton regency had been £12,000 Scots, £40,000 Scots was demanded in 1581 (under Lennox), while in 1588 and in 1594 the sums were £100,000 Scots—on the former occasion to meet the costs of the forthcoming royal marriage, on the latter of Prince Henry's baptism. Taxes could in addition be raised outside of full parliaments via Conventions of Estates and James also developed a more efficient system of tax collection, while other means of improving the health of royal finances included raising customs on trade and a debasement of the Scottish currency. Such increases were not without their political cost, and although an upswing in trade in the 1570s and rising prosperity for the landowning and mercantile classes had temporarily made the increased fiscal exactions tolerable, as the economy subsequently deteriorated there was pressure for the king to curb his own prodigality. In 1596 James appointed an eight-man commission known as the Octavians, headed by the conformist Catholic Alexander Seton, earl of Dunfermline, to reform royal finances. They set about revising the customs rates, investigating traditional revenues of the crown, and cutting back royal expenditure (including noble pensions), but their economies upset courtiers and nobles whose perks were hit, while the Kirk saw in the commission an unwelcome Catholic presence at the centre of government. The political costs were too high and James disbanded the commission at the beginning of 1597. The next year, in a cynical move, James declared the crown bankrupt, defaulting on his debts to his bankers but enabling him to survive until 1603, when the removal of the court to England eased the financial burden on the Scottish crown.[44]

James also wanted to assert greater royal control over the Kirk. Unlike England, where the Reformation had been instituted by the crown, in Scotland it had been instituted against the crown, and James's lengthy royal minority had meant that the newly reformed Kirk had been able to develop with remarkably little interference from secular authorities. Yet although a faction was to emerge within the Kirk, led by the theology professor Andrew Melville, which insisted that the kingdom of Christ and the temporal kingdom were separate and independent, with the latter having no right to interfere with the former, this was not the principle on which the Scottish Reformation was established. The Reformation had been an act of state, legislated for by parliament, and the Confession of Faith had granted to the civil authority the conservation of religion and the suppression of idolatry. And although the reformed Kirk was to develop a Calvinist system of Church courts, from the General Assembly at the top down to the kirk session at the parish level, for the time being bishops remained, albeit with lesser powers than their English counterparts and considerable lack of clarity over what their role should be.

In 1572 the Concordat of Leith, negotiated between representatives of the Kirk and the crown, allowed for a reformed episcopate appointed by the crown but accountable to the General Assembly. But the form of episcopacy that developed provoked the hostility of the General Assemblies of the later 1570s, in large part because the regent Morton made appointments without consulting the Kirk. Following Morton's fall came the inevitable backlash. A *Second Book of Discipline* in 1578 called for the end of episcopal power in Scotland and was more insistent on the separation of the two kingdoms (although still allowing the civil magistrates a role in defending and upholding the Kirk), while two years later the General Assembly declared episcopacy unscriptural. At the beginning of 1581 Lennox, to convince people that his conversion to Protestantism was sincere, published a new Confession of Faith—the King's Confession, though frequently referred to as the Negative Confession, because of its fierce condemnation of popery. Subscribed by the king and his household on 28 January, in March the crown ordered ministers to urge their parishioners to subscribe it. Approved by the General Assembly in April, the Confession expressed abhorrence of 'all kynd of Papistrie', especially 'the wsurped authoritie of that Romane Antichrist'—i.e. the pope—and 'his worldie monarchie, and wicked hierarchie'. The wording was ambiguous, though Presbyterians assumed that this hierarchy included 'the degree and superiority of bishops'.[45] The same year saw the establishment of thirteen presbyteries or local church courts, mainly in the east and the lowlands, which were intended as a model for what was to be introduced elsewhere. However, in 1584, as part of the effort to restore royal authority following the Ruthven Raid, Arran steered a series of measures through parliament asserting royal authority over all estates, 'alsweill spiritual as temporall'. Styled the 'Black Acts' by the Kirk, they stipulated that no one was to assemble without the king's permission, that bishops should make presentations to benefices and have the power to deprive unworthy ministers, and that all clergymen and schoolmasters should confirm in writing their submission to the king's majesty and to bishops or other ministers appointed by him. (In effect they established the royal supremacy in Scotland.) Although the Black Acts did not address the question of whether bishops should sit in parliament, it was assumed that they should and they continued to do so.[46]

As James embarked on his personal reign, he found it necessary to tread cautiously with regard to the Kirk, in an effort to build up support as he pursued reforms in other areas. In 1585, as a conciliatory gesture, he denied that he wanted to set himself up as head of the Kirk, although he continued to defend bishops as sanctioned by the Bible and the early Church. At the General Assembly of 1586 a compromise was reached whereby the king was allowed to honour ministers with the title of bishops, but the old dioceses were abolished and replaced by smaller provinces, and the bishops were not to have exclusive powers of visitation, which instead were to be exercised by commissioners of visitation subject to provincial synods and the General Assembly. As part of the compromise the number of presbyteries was expanded to fifty-one, and they were given the power to ensure that preaching was pure and discipline maintained and to administer poor relief. The commissioners and bishops were to moderate the synods and presbyteries in which they resided. The king was granted a role in the convocation of General Assemblies and it was acknowledged that they met with his authority, though at the same time it was stipulated that General Assemblies should meet annually.[47]

The settlement of 1586 promised to establish a mixed polity, retaining episcopacy within Presbyterianism and a limited royal supremacy. But James failed to appoint any new bishops: his one nominee, Robert Pont, declined the offer of the bishopric of Caithness in 1587 on the General Assembly's advice. Desperately short of money, that same year James agreed to an Act of Annexations transferring ecclesiastical lands inalienably to the crown. The measure in effect made any prospect of the revival of diocesan episcopacy in the future extremely difficult (it would have to be undone), though by stripping the assets of the Kirk it also upset the General Assembly. James was later to regret his decision; in his *Basilikon Doron* he advised his heir to annul what he described as 'that vile acte'. It is not clear, however, that James was unhappy at the time with the direction in which the Kirk was moving. In August 1590, in part provoked by a recent sermon preached at St Paul's Cross in London by Richard Bancroft (then canon of Westminster) attacking Scottish Presbyterianism, he gave a speech to the General Assembly at Edinburgh in which he praised God that he was 'King in such a Kirk, the sincerest Kirk in the world'—better than the Kirk of Geneva, which he condemned for celebrating Easter and Christmas, and certainly better than 'our neighbour Kirk of England', whose service was 'ane evill said messe in English'. Urging those present 'to stand to your purity, and to exhort the people to do the like', he concluded by promising to 'maintain the same' for as long as he was king. The speech was received by fifteen minutes of rejoicing.[48]

Tensions came to a head again in 1592, however, when the General Assembly demanded tougher measures against Catholics and the repeal of the Black Acts and Act of Annexation. James was furious, but needing to win back support he agreed to the passage of what later became known as the Golden Act in the parliament that met at

Edinburgh in June of that year. This ratified the Presbyterian system of ecclesiastical government and allowed no place for an episcopate, and in the process it overturned a number of the Black Acts, though crucially not the first one, asserting the royal supremacy over spiritual as well as temporal matters. Moreover, the fact that all this was done by parliament set a precedent for the civil authority legislating on ecclesiastical matters, while the Act also gave the crown the right to name when and where General Assemblies should meet. To emphasize the point, upon the dissolution of parliament the privy council immediately issued a proclamation stipulating the date and place of the next General Assembly. Episcopacy by now had largely atrophied; when the archbishop of St Andrews, Patrick Adamson, who towards the end of his life suffered from bulimia, died in February 1592, he was not replaced. Nevertheless, the king had ensured that he maintained some degree of control over the Kirk.[49]

Despite the passage of the Golden Act, the Kirk continued to be anxious about the king's leniency towards Catholics and the presence of supposed crypto-Catholics at court. James in turn was becoming increasingly concerned about the stridency of Presbyterian attacks. Things came to a head in 1596 with the setting up of the eight-man treasury commission headed by the conformist papist Dunfermline. In September 1596 some commissioners of the General Assembly and various other ministers met in Cupar and decided to send a delegation to the king at Falkland Palace in County Fife, led by Andrew Melville, to urge that 'the dangerous indevours' of 'the Papist Lords' might be prevented. When James expressed his anger both at their commission and at the fact that they had met without his consent, Melville tugged the king's sleeve and called him 'God's sillie [weak] vassall', reminding him that there were 'twa Kings and twa Kingdomes in Scotland', that James was a 'subject' to 'Chryst Jesus the King, and his kingdome the Kirk', of whose kingdom James was 'nocht a king, nor a lord, nor a heid, bot a member', and that those to whom Christ had committed the government of the Kirk had 'sufficient powar of him' to convene and assemble. Then in October David Black, a minister from St Andrews, delivered a defamatory sermon criticizing James, Queen Anne, and Queen Elizabeth of England, and condemning 'all Kingis' as 'the devillis childrene'. Summoned to appear before the privy council, Black insisted that he could be held accountable only by a Church court for what he had said from the pulpit, and was backed by the commissioners of the General Assembly. James banished the commissioners from the capital and the council found Black guilty on 9 December. On 17 December a riot broke out in the capital when James rejected a petition from Edinburgh ministers calling for the removal of crypto-Catholics from the king's counsels, and James had to flee to Linlithgow and take the privy council with him.[50]

The events of late 1596 convinced James it was time to take greater control over the Kirk and help explain the hostility towards the Scottish 'Puritans' he was to express in his *Basilikon Doron*. James made a point of attending every General Assembly from 1597 until his departure for England in 1603, to emphasize the fact that as king he wielded both swords, civil and ecclesiastical. He banned from attending those ministers whom he expected to be troublesome, and brought pressure to bear on those who did attend to vote the way he wanted them to. He asserted royal control over the times when the General Assembly should meet: he prorogued the meeting of 1599 until a new scheme of parliamentary representation for the Kirk had been agreed, which he wanted the General Assembly to ratify. Just like parliaments, General Assemblies were to meet only when summoned by the king. In March 1600 a General Assembly which met at Montrose approved a scheme whereby the king could choose commissioners to sit in parliament from a pool of nominees provided by each provincial synod.[51] Having persuaded the Kirk to agree to the principle of ecclesiastical representation in parliament, James summoned a convention of commissioners from the various synods to meet at Holyrood the following October and got it to consent to the appointment of three bishops to sit in the parliament which met that November. The Kirk refused to acknowledge the authority of the convention and denied the legitimacy of the appointments. Nevertheless, James had got his way and the bishops were back. By 1605, only three of the thirteen Scottish bishoprics remained to be filled.

James also made a start at addressing the problems of lawlessness in the Borders and the Highlands. The signing of a defensive league between England and Scotland in July 1586, whereby both countries agreed to provide each other with aid in the face of an invasion of either homeland, required that James step up border security. In September 1586 a Convention of Estates voted £15,000 Scots to establish a force of men to police the Anglo-Scottish frontier.[52] The following spring James went on a justice ayre to Dumfries, the first of what was to be a series of personal demonstrations of royal authority in the Borders. In 1587 parliament passed a General Band requiring both Border and Highland chiefs to find surety for the good behaviour of their tenants and clansmen and to present themselves before the king at Edinburgh every year, although for the time being the legislation proved impossible to enforce in the Highlands.[53] In 1590 a council for the Borders and Highlands, a subcommittee of the privy council, was set up, and although it met regularly for only a year and a half, it did at least push the full council into giving more sustained attention to these areas. It was not until the later 1590s that James began to give the Highlands serious attention, the main incentive being to try to make the area contribute more to the royal coffers. Although a series of planned royal visits to the Highlands never materialized, James did send his deputy Colonel William Steward to Kintyre, where the great Highland chief Angus MacDonald of Dunyveg made a submission in person and agreed to pay more rent. In December 1597 parliament passed an Act threatening Highland chiefs with forfeiture of their land if they did not submit a valid title to the Exchequer within five months, a Scottish version of the policy of surrender and regrant which had been used by Tudor monarchs in Ireland.[54] Few if any met the deadline, but the initiative did provide a legal basis for action against Highland chiefs at a later date, should the government feel determined to act (as it was to do after James VI had become king of England). The government also experimented with a policy of plantation in the Western Isles, focusing on Lewis, with the idea that colonists from the Lowlands would help bring civilization to what James regarded as one of the most barbaric parts of the realm and also foster the economic development of the area. The enterprise soon ran into difficulties in the face of local opposition, while for would-be settlers the risks were too high and the returns too uncertain; the significance lay mostly in the precedent it set for the strategy that James was later to take in Ulster.[55]

One last attempt to capture the king occurred in August 1600 in a mysterious episode known as the Gowrie conspiracy. On the morning of 5 August Alexander Ruthven, the younger brother of the earl of Gowrie, came to James at Falkland Palace to tell him that a strange man had been seized in the fields near Gowrie House in Perth carrying a pot full of gold coins. James decided to make haste to Perth to see this man and his treasure for himself. When he arrived at Gowrie House, he was treated to an early afternoon meal, after which Alexander showed James upstairs to his room. According to James, once inside Alexander locked the door behind them, grabbed a dagger, and threatened to kill him in revenge for the execution of William Ruthven sixteen years earlier. James thrust his head out of a window shouting treason and murder, and began to grapple with his assailant. Various members of the royal party, who were milling around in the grounds, rushed inside to help the king. In the meantime James's attendant made his way up to the room by another stairway and stabbed Alexander, whom the king pushed down the stairs. Finding his brother dead, the earl rushed into the chamber brandishing two swords, though on seeing the king he dropped his weapons, and was killed immediately.

The truth behind the incident is difficult to establish, since we have only James's word to go on. The strange man with the pot of gold was never found. It has been suggested that James fabricated the plot to rid himself of a troublesome family who had a history of disaffection and to whom he owed a considerable amount of money, and even that Alexander's ire had been prompted by the fact that the king had made a sexual advance to him, although there is no evidence to support either of these claims. Given James's alleged aversion to edged weapons, it seems unlikely that he had set out for Perth with the deliberate intent to kill the Ruthvens. Whatever the truth, on 15 November parliament declared the Ruthvens posthumously guilty of treason, which resulted in their property being forfeited to the crown and the disinheritance of their heirs, and established 5 August as an annual day of thanksgiving for delivery from the conspiracy.[56]

* * *

James VI has usually been seen as a highly successful king of Scotland prior to his accession to the English throne in 1603.[57] Given the scale of the problems confronting him, and the crisis of authority the Scottish monarchy faced, there can be no doubting his very real achievements. By 1603 he had strengthened the position of the crown vis-à-vis the nobility, parliament, and the Kirk; he had begun the process of bringing the Highlands and the Borders more firmly under the rule of law; and he had improved the financial position of the monarchy. Acknowledging James's successes, however, should not mislead us into thinking that he had solved all the problems he had set out to tackle. The job was as yet incomplete and there was still much work to be done. Although James was to claim in his farewell address delivered in the High Kirk of St Giles on 3 April 1603 that he had 'settled both Kirk and Kingdome, in that estate which he mynded not to alter in any wayes, his subjects living in peace',[58] he was well aware that further alterations would be necessary. Becoming king of England afforded him the opportunity to be more aggressive in his pursuit of reform in Scotland, insulated from his Scottish subjects as he now was both by distance and greater prestige, and enabled him to pursue measures that he would not have been able to contemplate while solely king of the Scots because the political costs would have been too high. Yet if James had felt hampered by practical realities in Scotland, and in that sense thought that becoming king of England would be liberating, his experience of ruling Scotland—where he needed to tread carefully, know how to bargain and negotiate, and recognize when it was necessary to hold back—taught him invaluable skills. Perhaps the greatest testimony to what he had achieved in Scotland is the fact that after 1603 he was able to rule the kingdom as an absentee monarch.

3

A Stranger in the Land

'Now the corner-stone is laid of the mightiest monarchy in Europe.' So wrote Francis Bacon to James I upon his accession to the English crown in March 1603.[1] Bacon was alluding to how the uniting of the crown of Scotland with that of England (and also of Ireland) had created a new multiple monarchy with the potential to establish itself as a powerhouse in Europe. It was overly optimistic but, of course, it was not a disinterested assessment: Bacon had been frustrated in his ambitions for high legal office under Elizabeth and was trying to ingratiate himself with the new monarch in the hope of preferment. He was knighted shortly afterwards and was later to rise to be Solicitor General, Attorney General, Lord Keeper, and Lord Chancellor and be promoted to the peerage as Baron Verulam and Viscount St Alban.[2]

Not everyone would have agreed with Bacon's assessment. Bartholomew Ward, a tailor from Littlebury in Essex, did not like the idea of 'a forreyne Kinge' and thought 'theare weare as wise men in England to bee Kinge as the Kinge of Scotts'.[3] The English candidate with the best claim was Edward Seymour, Viscount Beauchamp, the son of the earl of Hertford and Lady Catherine Grey (the sister of England's nine-day queen, Lady Jane Grey). Thomas Browne, a yeoman from Buntingford in Hertfordshire, believed that the earl of Hertford 'was readye in the weste Cuntrye with thirtie thousand men to withstand the King's comynge into England' and promised 'that whilst hee the said Thomas lived, a Scott shold not weare the Crowne of England'.[4] There were rumours of Catholic disaffection. One man allegedly predicted that if the new king did not grant toleration to Catholics 'he should not live longe'.[5] As Elizabeth's last days approached, the government took the precautionary step of placing suspect Catholic gentry under restraint.[6] Protestant separatists were another cause for concern. Coggeshall labourer John Trapps was indicted at the Essex quarter sessions in July 1603 for allegedly maintaining that the English bishops were 'Antichristians' and that the Church of England as now established in England was 'not the trewe Church'.[7] Some were even predicting the downfall of the monarchy. Maidstone labourer Richard Hartropp, upset at having 'a strange kinge come out of another land with a companye of spanielles followinge him', was indicted at the Kent quarter sessions that same month for predicting that James would likely be killed 'before Michaelmas daye nexte' and that within four years of the king's death 'theare shalbee noe kinge in England'.[8]

The government was decidedly jittery, and understandably so. England and Scotland had not always been on the best of terms, England was just coming out of a nine-year war with Catholic Ireland and was still at war with Spain, whereas it was feared that Scotland's 'auld' ally France might seek to stir up trouble between the English and Scots in order to exploit a potentially contentious succession to its own advantage. The feeling that the succession would not pass without incident was widespread. When Elizabeth fell terminally ill in mid-March 1603, many Londoners and nobles began stocking up on armour, munitions, and victuals, fearful of what might happen. Yet when the queen died and James was proclaimed in the capital on 24 March, 'all things' were 'very quiet'. There was 'no tumult...noe disorder in the city', while at night Londoners celebrated with bonfires and bells. Overall the people seemed 'well satisfied', looking forward in expectation 'of a flourishing common wealth'.[9] Whatever sadness Elizabeth's death 'bequeathed to all England', wrote one contemporary, 'was amply paralleled with the hopes conceived of the virtues of her famous Successour'.[10] The French ambassador observed that 'the satisfaction [was] universal among the English', as it was also among the Scots, despite the 'rooted and ancient hostility of the English to the Scottish'.[11]

The English made their joy known as James made his long progress south from the Scottish to the English capital. When James reached Berwick-upon-Tweed on 6 April, 'the common people seemed so overwrapt with his presence', it was said, 'that they omitted nothing...to express loyall dutie and heartie affection; kneeling, shouting, crying "Welcome" and "God save King James".' 'Great were the rejoicings, and loud and hearty the acclamations', as James made his way from Berwick to London; and when he finally reached the outskirts of London on 7 May, such were 'the multitudes of people in highwayes, fieldes, medowes, closes and on trees' who had come out to greet him, 'that they covered the beautie of the fieldes'.[12] Commenting

64

on the smoothness of the transition, Bacon observed 'with what wonderful still and calm this wheel is turned round'.[13]

Despite evidence of some disaffection, then, the vast majority of English people looked to the accession of James I with an air of optimism, glad that the issue of the succession had finally been peacefully settled and hoping that the new king would prove good not only for the country but also for themselves. As James journeyed south, he was presented with numerous petitions from various groups pleading their cause, among them Catholics and Puritans, and even the poor hoping for an end to monopolies and a reduction in 'impositions, polings, and payments'.[14] When welcoming the new king on his entry to the City of London in May 1603, the Middle Temple lawyer Richard Martin—in a speech that had been vetted by Elizabeth's leading courtier Robert Cecil—observed how the English looked to James not just 'for an admirable goodnesse' but also for a 'particular redresse'. James, Martin observed, had already demonstrated his prudence in Scotland, where he had reduced 'those things to order in Church and Commonwealth which the tumultuous times' of his 'infancy had there put out of square'. Ireland would now require his 'justice', after 'the miseries...of Civil Wars'. And England, Martin hoped, 'would be the schoole' where the king, 'a most skillfull and faithful Physitian', would practise his 'temperance and moderation' in addressing 'our true griefes'—including 'unjust monopolies, delays in justice...corruption in the church' and 'the exploitation of the poor by heavy taxation'.[15]

There was a lot for James to do when he acceded to the English throne. He had to sort out the relationship between the two independent kingdoms of Scotland and England in the new multiple monarchy: there had been a union of the crowns, but should the union go further than this and what sort of union should it be? He had to fix problems in the Church and tackle the legacy of religious division bequeathed by England's ongoing process of Reformation. He had to improve the crown's financial situation, but do so in a way that would not create unnecessary burdens on the poor or stifle economic growth. And he had to work out a viable—and affordable—foreign policy for an under-resourced crown in an age of confessional strife across Europe. Moreover, he faced the challenge of doing all this for a multiple-monarchy where the constituent kingdoms (and their respective populations) did not necessarily share the same priorities.

* * *

Although James had already acquired considerable experience as a king in Scotland, England was a different proposition. By his own admission, it took quite a while for him to find his feet: 'being heere a stranger in government', he later recalled, he resolved 'to keepe silence seven yeeres, and learn myself the Lawes of this Kingdome'[16]— a statement which while overestimating his ability to remain silent nevertheless conveys a sense of the king's own appreciation of the daunting nature of the challenges that lay before him.

To ensure a smooth transition in government, James issued a proc-lamation upon leaving Scotland on 5 April confirming all existing officeholders in their positions, at both the local and central level, including all fourteen of Elizabeth's privy councillors.[17] He retained Thomas Sackville, Lord Buckhurst, as Lord Treasurer, elevating him in the peerage to earl of Dorset in March 1604. Most significantly, he continued Robert Cecil as Secretary of State, creating him Baron Cecil of Essendon in August 1603, Viscount Cranborne the following year, and earl of Salisbury in 1605. He did, however, also promote a number of men who had been out of favour with the previous regime: Henry Percy, earl of Northumberland, banished from court under Elizabeth for keeping up a secret correspondence with James when king of Scotland; Thomas Howard, soon to be created earl of Suffolk, the son of the late duke of Norfolk, who had been executed in 1572 for conspiring to marry Mary Queen of Scots; and Norfolk's brother, the crypto-Catholic Henry Howard, created earl of Northampton, who had also been in correspondence with James prior to Elizabeth's death. And he inevitably wanted to keep some of his trusted Scottish advisors close to him. Thus he appointed five Scots to the privy coun-cil, which caused some suspicion among the English, although these appointments were more symbolic than real, since the governments, and thus privy councils, of both England and Scotland were to remain separate. Where the Scots made real headway was in the royal house-hold. Over the course of James's reign the Scots captured over 40 per cent of the higher court offices, largely concentrated in the bedcham-ber, the privy chamber, the queen's household, and the households of the two princes—leading to complaints that James 'filled every corner of the Court with theis beggarly "blew caps"'.[18] One manuscript piece complained that there was such partiality at court towards the Scots that the English felt 'much disgraced', denied access to the king's person and left 'unrewarded' for their service to the state.[19]

The coronation of James and Anne took place on 25 July, although a renewed outbreak of the plague in London and the south-east meant that there could be no formal royal entry into the City; Londoners had to be content with catching a glimpse of their new sovereigns as they travelled by barge from Westminster Abbey back to Whitehall after the ceremony was concluded.[20] There was some discussion beforehand as to whether the service itself should be scaled down. This was to be the first thoroughgoing Protestant coronation in England—both Edward VI and Elizabeth had been crowned by Catholic bishops—and James had concerns about being anointed, being 'against priestly benedictions', although in the end he did agree to go with tradition. The ceremony itself highlighted certain of the ambiguities inherent in the crown's constitutional position. The bishop of Winchester, Thomas Bilson, preached on Romans 13, 'the powers that be are ordained of God', to emphasize the divinely ordained nature of monarchy and condemn any form of active resistance, even to tyranny. (Although God was to be obeyed before man, only passive disobedience was allowed.) Bilson even went so far as to argue that 'all that is ours, both goods and lands', 'must bee subject', and that kings 'should have...their affaires both of peace and war supported by the goods and lands of their subjects'—seemingly implying that subjects had no absolute property rights and undermining the principle of consent to taxation, although Bilson insisted that since kings had sufficient lands and revenues 'to maintain their Royall estate', they had typically not 'fleeced their people...nor expected taxes oftner' than necessary. Yet Bilson also emphasized that kings had responsibilities: to do God's will, execute justice, take 'care of true Religion', and conserve the 'publike and private peace', under pain of punishment from God.[21] During the ceremony itself, of course, James took an oath promising to uphold the laws and customs of the realm.

The Hampton Court Conference

The last three royal successions in England had all brought with them a significant transformation in the religious policy of the government—Edward VI in 1547 with his thoroughgoing evangelical Reformation, Mary in 1553 with her Catholic Counter-Reformation, Elizabeth in 1558 with her Protestant restoration. Although Elizabeth had done much to consolidate the position of Protestantism and the Church of England during her long reign, excluded religious groups predictably hoped that this latest change at the top would lead to an amelioration of their plight. Since the 1580s there had been increased persecution of Catholics, and since the 1590s of Protestant separatists (still a tiny minority in England), and both Catholics and separatists hoped for some degree of toleration. Advanced Protestants, or Puritans as they tended to be called—those who saw themselves as part of the Church of England but were disappointed with the conservatism of the Eliza-bethan religious settlement—saw the accession of a king from Pres-byterian Scotland as an opportunity to press for further reform in the Church (although they were far from supporting liberty of conscience for either Catholics or Protestant separatists). Catholics were opti-mistic because James was the son of a Catholic queen, and many were eager to testify their loyalty to the new regime: the Wiltshire Catholic Baron Arundell of Wardour had James proclaimed in Shaftes-bury, he later boasted, 'eight days before any neighbour town durst do the like'. Indeed, through such highly public displays Catholics hoped to show that they were more loyal than some Protestants. When the Northamptonshire recusant Sir Thomas Tresham took it upon himself to proclaim James outside the mayor's house in North-ampton, he seized the opportunity to lecture the town officials and local gentry on the subject's duty to give unqualified obedience to their rightful king, which prompted one local Puritan preacher to pronounce that James should be acknowledged only if he proved 'sound in religion'.[22]

James was opposed to persecuting people purely for their religious beliefs, and informed Northumberland at the very start of his reign that he would not persecute any who gave 'an outward obedience to the law'.[23] It is true that in his *Basilikon Doron* James had called Puritans the 'verie pestes in the Church and Common-Weale'. How-ever, in his preface to the English edition, published just two days after Elizabeth's death, he explained that he had been referring 'onely to that vile sect amongst the Anabaptistes, called the Family of love', and 'such brain-sicke and headie Preachers' who agreed with 'the generall rule of all Anabaptists, in the contempt of the civill Magis-trate'; he did not mean those who preferred 'the single forme of poli-cie in our [the Scottish] Church' to 'the many Ceremonies in the Church of England' (that is, the English Presbyterians), or those who were persuaded 'that their Bishops smell of a Papall supremacie' or 'that the Surplise, the cornerd cap, and such like' were 'the outward badges of Popish errors' (mainstream English Puritans). Indeed, he claimed to love 'equally' the 'learned and grave men of either of these opinions', so long as they were content to live 'soberly and quietly with their owne opinions' and did not resist authority, break the law, or stir up 'rebellion or schisme'. He even encouraged them to press their case 'by patience, and well grounded reasons' to persuade others 'to like of their judgements'.[24]

As James journeyed south into England, the Puritans presented him with their 'Millenary Petition'—so called because the petition claimed to have the support of 'more than a thousand...subjects and ministers'—pressing their case for reform. Professing loyalty to the crown and denying that they aimed at 'a popular parity in the Church', they called for minor changes: the abolition of the use of the sign of the cross in baptism and of baptism by women (that is, midwives, because it implied adherence to the popish view that an infant who died before baptism would not be granted salvation); doing away with the ring in marriage, wearing the cap and the surplice, and bowing at the name of Jesus; a stricter observance of the Sabbath, the establishment of a preaching ministry, and an end to non-residency and pluralism; and the redress of abuses in the administration of excommunication. They concluded by asking for a 'conference among the learned' to resolve these issues.[25] The Catholics presented a petition assuring James of their 'devoted' allegiance, reminding him of their sufferings on behalf of his mother, Mary Queen of Scots, pointing to the good effects of toleration in France, and pleading for 'the free use of [their] Religion, yf not in publicke Churches, at the lest in private howses'.[26] James purportedly told them 'he would not use extremity, yf they continued in duty like subjects'.[27] Others, however, called for 'a uniformyty in true Religion without disturbance of Papistes or Puritanes'.[28] It was clear that he would have trouble pleasing all groups.

With the crown short of money, James allowed the fines levied on Catholics for non-attendance at church under the Elizabethan recusancy laws to be collected in May. For English Catholics it was a bitter setback, which prompted some more desperate types to consider other ways of obtaining redress. The secular priest William Watson concocted a scheme to seize the king on Midsummer Day and hold him hostage in the Tower until he granted full Catholic toleration. But Watson and his small band of conspirators failed to secure any show of support, midsummer came and went, and Watson fled to the West Country. In the end it was two leading Catholic clerics—George Blackwell, the pope's appointment as Catholic Archpriest of England, and the Jesuit Henry Garnett—who exposed the conspiracy to the government, hoping to save face for the English Catholic community.

Government investigations into the 'Bye Plot', as it became known, revealed that one of the conspirators—George Brooke—was the younger brother of William Brooke, 10th Baron Cobham, Elizabeth's Lord Warden of the Cinque Ports, a man who was known to be disappointed at being passed by for favour under the new regime. Cobham was brought in for questioning but denied any involvement; however, George then alleged that Cobham had been negotiating for 600,000 crowns from Spain 'to assiste and furnish a second action for the surprise of his majesty'—the first mention of what was to become known as the 'Main Plot'. The government also decided to interrogate Cobham's friend Sir Walter Ralegh, another out-of-favour Elizabethan; believing that Ralegh had turned against him, Cobham in a fit of pique denounced Ralegh, accusing him of conspiring with the ambassador from the Spanish Netherlands to procure Spanish support to overthrow James and to place Lady Arabella Stuart (the great-great-granddaughter of Henry VII and a Catholic) on the throne. Cobham later retracted his testimony, though in a subsequent confession he did provide a more convincing account of Ralegh's treasonous correspondence with the ambassador. Watson and two other Bye Plotters were convicted of treason and duly executed. Ralegh and Cobham, together with the Bye Plotter Sir Griffin Markham, were brought to the steps of the scaffold but at the very last minute had their sentences commuted to life imprisonment.[29]

Despite such intrigues, James remained willing to turn a blind eye to Catholics who were loyal, and for the remainder of 1603 chose not to enforce the recusancy fines. The result was predictable: large numbers of people stayed away from church, especially in the north of England, where Catholicism remained strong, and petitions began to circulate in favour of formal toleration for Catholics. However, James did not wish to see the number of Catholics increase and had no sympathy for those who sought to proselytize or to encourage subjects to put loyalty to the pope before that to the king. Hence on 22 February 1604, with Protestant opinion in the country growing alarmed at the apparent growth of popery, he issued a proclamation commanding all Jesuits and other Catholic clergy to depart the realm by 19 March, the day that parliament was due to meet.[30]

James decided to follow up on the Puritan suggestion for a conference, announcing one would be held at Hampton Court in January 1604. Yet the chances of meaningful reform already appeared to be receding. There was no overhaul of ecclesiastical personnel: James left the Church in the hands of the men who had run it under Elizabeth, with the ageing Whitgift still at Canterbury and Bancroft at London, both of whom, while theologically Calvinist, were stridently anti-Puritan. On 24 October James issued a proclamation stating that he thought the established Church in England agreed 'to the worde of God, and the forme of the Primitive Church'. Although he acknowledged that it was worth reviewing whether any 'Corruptions' had been brought in over time, he clearly did not wish to see any major change, and wrote to Whitgift a few days later urging him to ensure that 'all men' be made 'to conform themselves' and that any 'new forms not prescribed by authority' introduced into 'the celebration of divine service' be 'severally repressed'.[31]

The Puritans were not allowed to send their own delegates to Hampton Court. Instead, the choice was made by the privy council, who, following the recommendations of the bishops, invited four moderate Puritans to attend: Dr John Reynolds (an Oxford theologian), Laurence Chaderton (the first master of Emmanuel College, Cambridge), Thomas Sparke (a former archdeacon), and John Knewstub (the rector of Cockfield in Suffolk). The conference opened on 14 January, with the crucial debate taking place on the 16th, when James gave the Puritans the chance to make their case against Church ceremonies. If they could show any to be against the word of God, he promised, he would remove them; if not, 'he would never take them away', since 'he came not...to make innovations, but to confirm, whatever he found lawfully established'. By all accounts the Puritans argued their case 'weakly'; James told them that if a student of theirs had performed so poorly they would have caned his 'buttocks'—alluding here, no doubt, to how he had been treated by his own tutor.[32] When Reynolds suggested that bishops should exercise jurisdiction jointly with his 'Presbyteri' (the pastors and ministers of the Church), James—fearing that Reynolds had 'a Scottish Presbytery' in mind—angrily retorted that Presbyterianism agreed 'as well...with Monarchy, as God, and the Divell' and proclaimed 'No Bishop, no King'.[33] Having to his mind won the debate, James was willing to offer certain concessions: he agreed to limit pluralism, provide the means for a full preaching ministry, abolish lay baptism, issue a new catechism, amend faulty translations in the prayer book, and provide a new, authorized translation of the Bible. In exchange, however, he wanted all ministers to subscribe to Whitgift's Three Articles of 1583 acknowledging the royal supremacy, that the Book of Common Prayer contained nothing contrary to the word of God, and that the Thirty-Nine Articles of 1563 were agreeable to the word of God. Moreover, he rejected Reynolds's proposal to modify the Thirty-Nine Articles to incorporate the position on predestination upheld by the Lambeth Articles of 1595.[34]

A revised Prayer Book appeared in February 1604, differing little from its Elizabethan predecessor save for the stipulation against lay baptism and an additional section on the catechism.[35] In March James issued a proclamation demanding conformity to the prayer book and that offenders be punished 'according to the Lawes of the Realme heretofore established'.[36] A new Bible—The King James Bible or Authorized Version—appeared in 1611, now the best-known, best-selling, most published, and most widely distributed book in the English language. Although it had been Reynolds who had proposed the idea at Hampton Court, James had long wanted a new translation.[37] The most popular English language version then in use was the Geneva Bible, which had not only translated certain key terms so as to lend support for Presbyterianism over episcopacy but which also contained marginalia suggesting that God sanctioned resistance to ungodly monarchs. Bancroft, who succeeded Whitgift as archbishop in March 1604, oversaw the whole project: the marginalia went, and the Authorized Version translated 'ecclesia' as 'Church' rather than the Genevan 'congregation' and 'presbyteros' as 'priest' rather than 'elder'.[38] The working out of the rest of the recommendations from Hampton Court would have to await the meeting of parliament and of Convocation.

The Parliament of 1604 and the Form of Apology and Satisfaction

Because the plague was raging in London—over 25,000 lost their lives to the disease in the City and liberties alone in the first year of the reign[39]—James had to delay the meeting of parliament until 19 March 1604. The government did little to influence the elections, although James did issue a proclamation in January urging voters to choose experienced men, not to elect bankrupts or outlaws, and to avoid those 'either noted for their superstitious blyndness one way, or for their turbulent humours other waies'. As the Venetian ambassador recognized, it was an exhortation not to elect Catholics or Puritans. To ensure some degree of government oversight, James stipulated that all returns were to be brought to Chancery, with any made contrary to his proclamation 'to be rejected as unlawfull'.[40]

Just before parliament opened, James decided to make his much-delayed coronation procession through London. He took up residence at the Tower on 13 March, where the chaplain William Hubbock delivered a Latin oration—subsequently published in English—calling on James to unite his realms: 'one king, one people, one law'. The procession itself took place two days later. Huge crowds lined the streets as James rode slowly through the capital past seven arches with various pageants representing him as a god-like figure, the champion of peace and plenty, faith and justice, the heir to ancient kingdoms, and the emperor of a new Britain.[41]

James developed the themes raised by Hubbock in his speech at the opening of parliament on the 19th, which he delivered again three days later because not everyone had been present on the opening day, and which he subsequently had printed. Thanking the people of England for the warm reception they had given him upon his accession, he addressed three broad areas: peace, religion, and the law. He wanted to maintain 'Peace abroad with all foreign Neighbours', which he said would promote trade and commerce. Yet he also wanted 'Peace within', and here his new subjects were blessed, James boasted, since inward peace was annexed to his own person in two ways: first, as the lineal descendant of Henry VII, who had united the houses of Lancaster and York and ended the Wars of the Roses, and secondly as king of Scotland and England, who in his person brought about 'the Union of Two ancient and famous Kingdoms'. God clearly wanted the two kingdoms united, James proclaimed, since there were no natural borders between the two countries, they shared the same language and religion, and they possessed a 'Similitude of Manners'. 'What God hath conjoined', James implored, 'let no Man separate. I am the Husband, and all the whole Isle is My lawful Wife.'

Turning to ecclesiastical affairs, James observed that although he found 'but One Religion…publickly allowed, and by the Law maintained', which was the one that he professed, there was 'another Sort of Religion', that of the 'Papists', and there were also 'Puritans and Novelists', whom he described as 'a private Sect, lurking within the Bowels of the Nation'. James stated that he acknowledged 'the Roman Church to be our Mother Church', albeit 'with some Infirmities and Corruptions', even going so far as to say that he would be willing to meet the Catholics 'in the Midst' in 'a general Christian Union in Religion' if they abandoned these corruptions, and insisted that he was against 'Persecution…in Matters of Conscience'; he therefore recommended that parliament find some way of relaxing the penal laws against peaceful Catholics, although the Catholic clergy should not be allowed to stay in the country if they continued to uphold the papal supremacy and the pope's right to depose heretical rulers. As for 'the Puritans and Novelists', however, who differed with those of the established Church not 'in Points of Religion' but 'in their confused Form of Policy, and Parity', since they were 'ever discontented with the present Government, and impatient to suffer any Superiority', they could not 'be suffered in any well-governed Commonwealth'.

With regard to the making of laws, James promised that he would always prefer the well-being of the 'Commonwealth' to his own 'privates Ends', this being how 'a lawful King' differed 'from a Tyrant'. He urged parliament not 'to seek the making of too many Laws', since 'the Execution of good Laws' was 'far more profitable' than burdening 'Men's Memories with the Making of too many of them', and he reminded members that both he and they sat on God's thrones and were 'answerable to God, for the due Execution of our Offices'. He then proceeded to emphasize the responsibilities he had as king towards his subjects. The difference between 'a rightful King, and an usurping Tyrant', he amplified, was that whereas the tyrant believed his kingdom and people were 'only ordained for Satisfaction of his Desires', the 'righteous and just King' acknowledged himself 'to be ordained for the Procuring of the Wealth and Prosperity of his People'. James promised that his subjects' welfare would always be his 'greatest Care': for, 'as the Head is ordained for the Body, and not the Body for the Head; so must a righteous King know himself to be ordained for his People, and not his People for him'.[42]

The session got off to an inauspicious start. After returning from hearing the king's speech on the 22nd, the Commons raised the issue of a disputed election return for Buckinghamshire, where Sir John Fortescue, a long-serving privy councillor who was now in his seventies, had been vying for the first county seat with Sir Francis Goodwin, a leading member of the local gentry and a former MP himself. On the day of the election, the county bench recommended that Fortescue be returned, a decision that Goodwin publicly endorsed; however, the electors called for Goodwin, Fortescue therefore withdrew, and the electoral writ was returned to Chancery naming Goodwin and Sir William Fleetwood as knights for the shire. The problem was that the sheriff noted on the writ that Goodwin was an outlaw, so the clerk for the crown refused to accept Goodwin's return, issued a second writ for a fresh election, and Fortescue was now returned alongside Fleetwood.

It was unclear whether Goodwin was still technically an outlaw, since his outlawry had been for debts which he had since paid and for which he had been discharged by his creditors; there were even suggestions that some of the evidence might have been tampered with by the court. The real issue at stake, however, turned on whether Chancery or the Commons had jurisdiction over disputed elections. The Commons claimed it as one of their privileges, being concerned about setting a precedent of allowing the king and council to void an electoral return: as one member warned, 'a Chancellor may call a Parliament of what Persons he will, by this Course'. James insisted that he had no personal stake in whether Goodwin or Fortescue was returned but had simply followed the advice of the judges and ordered the Commons to discuss the matter with them, adding that while he did not intend 'to impeach any Privilege', they should remember that 'they derived all Matters of Privilege from him' and 'they should not be turned against him'. The Commons hastened to draw up a 'Humble Answer' to the king, defending their position, but a furious James replied that he 'commanded, as an absolute King', that they confer with the judges. This 'Thunderbolt', as one member called it, stunned the Commons, who decided to petition the king asking to be allowed to explain their case to him in person. The outcome of the meeting was a compromise: the Commons agreed that both Goodwin and Fortescue should be debarred and a new election ordered, and James in turn recognized the Commons as a judge (though not the sole judge) of election returns.[43]

James also ran into difficulties over his hoped-for union between Scotland and England. He had been pushing the issue ever since he came to the throne. The silver medal minted to commemorate his accession hailed him as 'the Emperor of the whole Island of Britain' and his coronation medal as 'Caesar Augustus of Britain'.[44] Shortly after his arrival in England he had issued a proclamation, ostensibly aimed at preserving peace on the borders between the two kingdoms, claiming that since 'all the best disposed Subjects' of both his realms desired that the Union 'should bee perfected', he would soon bring this about with the advice of the parliaments of both kingdoms, and that all his subjects were henceforth to 'esteeme both the two Realmes as presently united, and as one Realm and Kingdome'.[45] The question of union was raised formally in the upper house by Lord Chancellor Ellesmere on 14 April, and the Lords proposed a conference with the Commons to discuss the king's desire that England and Scotland be renamed Great Britain and commissioners be appointed to address the question of the different laws, rites, customs, and usages of the two kingdoms.[46] The Commons proved less enthusiastic than James had hoped, insisting that even the change of name was no simple matter. The laws of England were English laws, Sir Edwin Sandys pointed out; by taking away the name of England, 'we take away the Maxims of the Law', while an English parliament could not 'make any Laws to bind Britannia'.[47] The Lords agreed to check with the judges, who confirmed that the name could not 'be altered now without Prejudice to the State'.[48] Frustrated, James chastised the Commons for not embracing the matter more willingly, and warned them not to be transported by 'a few giddie Headis'.[49] The Commons resented the accusation, protesting that they neither had been, nor intended to be, 'led away by any giddiness whatsoever', but they did agree to appoint commissioners to discuss the Union, on condition that their recommendations would be advisory only and have to come back to parliament for approval. MPs were further angered when the bishop of Bristol, John Thornborough, published a *Discourse* arguing the 'urgent Necessity of the desired happy Union', which they felt cast aspersions on the proceedings of the Commons. Thornborough, in the end, was forced to make a public apology in the Lords.[50]

In his January proclamation, James had stated that he was calling parliament so that he could redress his subjects' grievances.[51] On the first full day of business, therefore, MPs fell to discussing what grievances needed to be redressed. The way was led by Sir Robert Wroth, who raised the issues of wardship (the ancient feudal right of the crown to manage the estates of a tenant-in-chief who was a minor[52]), purveyance (the right of the crown to buy provisions and services for the royal household at below market prices), monopolies, dispensations from the penal statutes, the transportation of ordnance to foreign countries, and abuses of the Exchequer. He was followed by Sir Edward Montagu, who added his concerns about the burden of the commissary courts, the suspension of Puritan ministers, and depopulating enclosures.[53] Although the Commons set up two committees to look into these grievances, little progress was made. A bill against monopolies made it through the Commons but did not get past the Lords. Wardship and purveyance had long been grievances which even the government wanted to address; indeed, Cecil himself had probably encouraged Wroth to raise the issue in the Commons in the first place.[54] But James would need some form of compensation, the Lords and Commons could not agree what level of compensation was appropriate, while both the Board of the Green Cloth (who oversaw purveyance) and the Masters of the Court of Wards denied the existence of abuses. In the end Cecil, who had been willing to bargain for the abolition of both purveyance and wardship, withdrew the offer.[55] Parliament did, though, pass a measure against enclosure, a re-enactment of an Elizabethan statute of 1598 against converting tillage into pasture.[56]

In a controversial move, James agreed to the setting up of a conference between the Lords and Commons for the reformation of ecclesiastical grievances. Convocation, the Church's deliberative body, normally expected to possess exclusive jurisdiction in matters of religion, and indeed James had only recently licensed Convocation to draw up a new code of canons (discussed below). James seems to have thought that Church and parliament would work together in a spirit of cooperation; instead, he just provoked a row, with Convocation threatening to make a formal protest to the king if the bishops, who sat in the Lords, continued to confer with the Commons about religious matters. On the agenda for the joint conference were proposals that ministers should be required to subscribe only to the Thirty-Nine Articles, that pluralism and non-residency be eradicated, that the educational qualifications and stipends of ministers be improved, and that ministers who dutifully performed their functions should not be punished for failing to use the sign of the cross in baptism or to wear the surplice. It was a programme that testified to the Puritan sympathies of many who sat in the Commons, but which had little support in the Lords: the bills against pluralists and to provide for a learned ministry stalled in the upper house. All was not quite lost, however. James needed money, and although initially he had not pressed for a subsidy, because the four subsidies granted by Elizabeth's last parliament in 1601 were still being collected and he did not want to risk alienating the Commons by asking for more as he pursued his desired union of the realms, with the union having run into difficulties there was no longer the same reason for caution. James therefore approached Sir Francis Hastings, the chairman of the Commons' committee for religion, to sound out the House about the possibility of granting a subsidy, seemingly promising in return to listen favourably to the Commons' concerns over religion. Yet although the Commons approved a petition to the king on 13 June urging him to amend the canons, on 19 June it declined to vote any subsidies. James therefore refused to receive the petition, and the next day authorized Bancroft to proceed with the canons.[57]

Increasingly irritated with the attitude of the lower house, James summoned members to Whitehall on 30 May and gave them a stern talking to. (Unfortunately, no copy of the speech survives). Stung by this rebuke, the Commons decided to appoint a committee to draw up a document explaining their 'Actions and Intentions'. The Form of Apology and Satisfaction, as it was known, came before the lower house on 20 June. Written in the name of the Commons as a whole, it defended 'the privileges' of the House, which the Commons claimed were not held by grace of the king but were their 'right and due inheritance'; stipulated that the Commons was the sole judge of election returns; and insisted on the freedom of elections, freedom of speech, and the freedom of MPs from arrest. It said that they had particular cause to 'watch over [their] privileges', since 'the prerogatives of princes may easily and do daily grow', and 'the privileges of the subject...once lost' were not easily recovered without 'much disquiet'—an allusion to the growth of royal absolutism on the Continent. 'If good kings were immortal', there would be no need 'to strive so for privilege'; but the same God who had given them a wise and religious king sometimes permitted 'hypocrites and tyrants in his displeasure and for the sins of the people', and 'hence the desire of rights, liberties, and privileges'. It urged the need to reform certain ecclesiastical abuses and to furnish the land with a 'learned, religious, and godly ministry' and—in an allusion to concurrent proceedings in Convocation to reform canon law—emphasized that James would be 'misinformed' if anyone tried to convince him that 'the Kings of England have any absolute power in themselves either to alter Religion...or to make any laws concerning the same' other than 'by consent of Parliament'. It also reiterated the Commons' concerns about purveyance and wardship, stating a willingness to offer the crown compensation if these were abolished.[58]

The Commons never formally adopted the Apology, seemingly because of disagreement over the wording—too extreme for some, not strong enough for others—and it was never presented to the king. It would be wrong, however, to be too dismissive of its significance. The fact that the Commons had asked for it to be drawn up in the first place suggests that the Apology addressed what were genuine concerns of the House. It was not forgotten, and was frequently quoted in later parliaments.[59] James certainly knew of it. Frustrated, he decided to prorogue parliament on 7 July, complaining that although in Scotland he 'ruled amongst men not of the best temper', his proposals had at least been respected, whereas in England people

seemed determined 'to find faults with [his] propositions'.[60] On 20
October he issued a proclamation changing his royal style to King of
Great Britain, 'as a signification of that, which in part [was] already
done' and a 'Prefiguration of that, which is to be done hereafter'—
though it included a proviso excluding this new title from any legal
proceedings or instruments, and in practice the name change was
ignored by the English.[61]

James did at least achieve some success with regard to establishing
'outward Peace'. Since 1585 England had been at war with Spain, in
support of the United Provinces in their revolt against Habsburg rule.
As king of Scotland, however, James had had no quarrel with Spain
and was eager to bring the war to an end, which was a drain on government finances, impeded trade, and encouraged privateering (little
better than piracy to James's mind). The peace should more correctly
be seen as the final chapter in Elizabethan foreign policy: Cecil was
the true architect and had long been working for peace, although
Spanish support for the rebellion in Ireland and continued Spanish
backing for the pretensions to the English throne of the Infanta-Arch-
duchess Isabella, the daughter of Philip II and a direct descendant of
John of Gaunt, delayed the prospect of ending the war until there
was peace in Ireland and the English succession had been secured.
Shortly after coming to the throne, James declared a ceasefire at sea.[62]
Some MPs were suspicious of James's motives, given the king's professed desire both to relax the laws against Catholics and to clamp
down on Puritan nonconformity. Others felt the government was
selling out the Dutch. A number of tracts circulated warning that if
the English abandoned the Dutch, they would be forced to seek the
protection of the French, which would be worse for England than if
the Dutch submitted to Spain, since the French would gain control of
the shipping of the Low Countries. In fact, James had been eager to
bring the Dutch to the negotiating table, but the Dutch would send
an envoy only if he were recognized as the representative of an independent nation, which Spain refused to do. In the end, therefore, only
the Spanish and the English were party to the Treaty of London of 18
August 1604; hostilities between Spain and the United Provinces continued until 1609. The treaty guaranteed the right of English merchants to trade with Spain and the Spanish Netherlands, without
harassment from the Inquisition. There was, however, no mention of
toleration for English Catholics; Philip III of Spain was content with
verbal assurances from James that they would escape persecution for
their beliefs.[63] Nevertheless, the English public seemed not particularly

impressed. There were no public celebrations. Indeed, in the City of London the proclamation of the peace was apparently 'received in sullen silence', broken here and there by exclamations of 'God preserve our good neighbours in Holland and Zealand', while many of the London churches offered prayers for the success of the Dutch as they continued their struggles alone against Spain.[64]

Peace gave a stimulus to overseas trade and the expansion of oceanic commerce. In particular, it allowed the English to turn their attention once again to the New World, following Sir Walter Ralegh's explorations under Elizabeth and the failed attempt in the 1580s to establish a colony at Roanoke Island, in what is now North Carolina but which at the time was styled Virginia. The English needed to act if they were not to lose out to not just the Spanish but now also the French in the Americas: the expedition of the French explorer Samuel de Champlain had led to the establishment of a French settlement at Port Royal, Acadia (in what is now Nova Scotia) in 1605, while in 1608 Champlain was to found Quebec City. In 1606 James set up two joint stock companies to develop settlements on the Atlantic coast of North America: the Plymouth Company, which was to occupy territory between the 45th and 38th parallels, and the Virginia Company, which was to settle the area between the 41st and the 34th parallels (with neither to develop settlements within 100 miles of each other). In 1607 the Plymouth Company established a colony at Popham on the Kennebec River in what is now Maine, but the fierce winter discouraged settlers and it was abandoned after a year. In May 1607 the Virginia Company established a settlement at Jamestown, and despite a shaky start this was to survive.[65]

The Canons of 1604 and the Subscription Campaign

As parliament sat, James ordered Convocation—the Church's deliberative body—to prepare a definitive code of canons. There was a need for action: English ecclesiastical law had become confused in the aftermath of Henry VIII's break with Rome and it was no longer clear which ancient canons were still in force. Yet providing a clear definition of the laws and beliefs of the Church would also help establish, as Bancroft put, whether the Puritans were 'joined with them or severed from them'.[66] The new canons, in essence little more than a codification of existing laws and practices, sanctioned the use of the new prayer book and made it an offence punishable by excommunication to impugn the royal supremacy, the rites and ceremonies of the Church or its hierarchy, or to attend conventicles. They also enjoined kneeling at communion, bowing at the name of Jesus, using the sign of the cross in baptism, and wearing the surplice; condemned various Puritan practices, such as private fasts and prophesyings; and required all ministers to subscribe to the Three Articles, as James had called for at the Hampton Court Conference.[67] It was clear that many Puritans would have difficulty conforming to a Church thus defined. MPs complained that Whitgift's Three Articles had not been sanctioned by parliament and tried to block publication of the canons.[68] James, however, was determined to enforce subscription. On 16 July 1604 he issued a proclamation giving ministers until 30 November to subscribe under pain of deprivation.[69]

The policy proved bitterly divisive. The archbishop of York, Matthew Hutton, questioned the wisdom of going after Puritans rather than Catholics, when the latter, he claimed, had lately 'growne mightily in number, courage and insolence'. Although he disliked the Puritans' 'fantasticall zeale', at least they agreed with the Church 'in substance of religion', differing only 'in Ceremonies and accidents', and for 'the most parte love[d] his Majestie'. Cecil disagreed: such were 'the turbulent humours of some that dreame of nothing but of a newe Hyrarchye directly opposite to the state of a Monarchie' that indulging such men would be 'the high waye to break all bounds of unity, to nourish scisme in the Church, and finally to destroy both Church and Common wealth'. Bancroft explained to the bishops that James's inclination was to show 'clemencie'; but those who 'refused to yield their obedience and conformitie' did so out of 'a factious desire of innovation', and if they suffered as a result it was due 'to their own obstinacie'.[70]

Local Puritans rallied to the defence of their ministers. In November 1604 over 200 local yeomen delivered a petition to the king at Royston begging him not to enforce subscription, since this would deprive them of a ministry. The tone was said to be 'partly supplicatory, partly minatory', and although James responded to the petitioners cordially—he promised that if they sent ten of their 'wisest' to discuss the matter he would instruct his council 'to give them honest satisfaction'—he was deeply alarmed. He told Cecil that he had 'daily more and more cause to hate and abhor that sect, enemies to all kings', and ordered him to have the ringleaders arrested and examined. The council found the petition to be 'sedition with roots spreading far wider than was supposed'; the Venetian ambassador reported that James 'took it to be almost an act of rebellion' and could not 'tolerate the presence in his kingdom' of those 'who refuse[d] to recognize authority, be it spiritual or temporal'.[71]

Further petitions against subscription followed over the next weeks and months—from Warwickshire, Leicestershire, Lincolnshire, the corporation of Northampton, and Northamptonshire—and rumours began to spread that while persecuting the Puritans James was intending to grant Catholics toleration. The petitioning campaign showed that Puritans had supporters in high places. The Northamptonshire petition, which was delivered on 9 February 1605, was signed by forty-five local gentry and presented to the king by the county MP Sir Edward Montagu, a keen patron of godly ministers who had raised the issue of religious grievances in the 1604 session of parliament, and whose brothers James and Henry were dean of the Chapel Royal and Recorder of London respectively (Henry later became earl of Manchester); it had been drawn up by Sir Francis Hastings, brother to two earls of Huntingdon and great-uncle of the current earl, who hailed from Leicestershire but now sat as MP for Somerset. Equally worrying for the government was the Northamptonshire petitioners' claim that support for the Puritan ministers ran into the 'thousands'. James summoned Montagu and Hastings before the council to answer for their actions, stripped them of their offices, and ordered them to depart into the country. In the meantime the judges confirmed the king's right to make law for the Church by dint of the royal supremacy, thereby upholding the legality both of the canons (even though they had not been confirmed by parliament) and of the deprivations (even though these had resulted in ministers being stripped of their freehold property without trial at common law).[72] One pamphlet appeal to parliament alleged that the deprivations were contrary 'both to Charta Magna, and also to many statutes'; it was 'also against reason', it continued, that 'the basest Cobler and Tinker' could not be ejected from his freehold 'but by a Jury of 12 men', while 'the ministers and Ambassadors of Christ Jesus, in the matters of eternall life', could be cast out of theirs, 'by one man only, and not only without any Jury, but also without any complaint or accusation against them'.[73] Yet as government spokesmen were quick to point out, Magna Carta did not apply to ecclesiastical jurisdiction and ecclesiastical offences had never been subject to trial by jury; moreover, 'the Refractarie Ministers' were not prosecuted for 'sober executing their Ministeriall function', but 'for giddie innovation and noveltie, for faction, schisme and impugning the Magistrate's auctority, or disturbing the peace and quietnesse of the Church'.[74]

The English Puritans were not the dangerous political subversives James feared them to be. They were at pains to represent themselves as 'loyal and true-hearted subjects' who, like the king, were opposed to 'papisme...Brownism, and all other schismatical and heretical opinions' (to quote the words of the Northamptonshire petition).[75] James's reaction was conditioned by his difficult dealings with the Scottish Presbyterians, not helped by reports that the English ministers were said to be 'in close relations with the Puritans of Scotland'; if the English Puritans had not been able to achieve as much power and influence as had the Scottish Presbyterians, James appears to have believed, it was because Elizabeth had suppressed them.[76] Yet although James might have overreacted, his fears were not totally unfounded. The Puritans were well organized and well connected, and they were trying to orchestrate a campaign of noncompliance, hoping that if enough ministers refused to subscribe the government would have to back down.[77] There was some localized trouble. In the parish of Enborne, Berkshire, the parson Robert Brooke tried to stir his parishioners up against the prayer book, refusing to use it and preaching against it, 'saying the papists doe now rejoyce that wee use as they use' and that 'divers good men had sought to reverse the...booke of Canons'. Then on 20 February 1605 the doors of his church were found broken open, the prayer book and canons having been taken out of the church chest, torn to pieces, and scattered in the seat where the service was usually read—although it transpired that Brooke himself had staged the incident and his parishioners reacted by reporting Brooke to the authorities.[78] At about the same time a minor cleric named Thomas Bywater, who had contacts with both London and Northamptonshire Puritans, was imprisoned in the Tower for distributing a libel, which reached the king at Ware, condemning the 'persecution of the Puritans' as 'unjust and injudicious', praising 'the virtues' of Queen Elizabeth, and accusing James of neglecting the government of the country and thinking 'of nothing but the chase and his own pleasures'.[79]

In the end, the vast majority of ministers did subscribe, although only after much heart-wrenching. Between seventy-three and eighty-three did not, about one per cent of the ministry, and lost their livings as a result. The worst-hit diocese was Peterborough (which included the Puritan stronghold of Northamptonshire), where sixteen ministers were deprived (6 per cent of the ministry), followed by London, which saw thirteen deprivations, and Norwich, which saw nine.[80] James appears to have believed that he had succeeded in separating the moderates from the radicals and driving the latter out of the Church.[81] If the framers of the Millenary Petition were correct in boasting that over 1,000 ministers supported their call for reform—and other sources seem to confirm that perhaps 10 per cent of the clerical personnel of England could be considered as some shade or other of Puritan at this time—then the vast majority of Puritans seemingly remained within the Church. Yet it is not clear that the deprivations targeted only hard-core radicals, since in practice beneficed clergy (who tended to be more moderate in their Puritanism) were more vulnerable than stipendiary lecturers or donative curates. Moreover, there was considerable lay sympathy for the plight of the godly ministers, and a number of testators set aside funds in their wills for the support of those who had been deprived or silenced.[82] In the wake of the clampdown, a number of separatists—those who had already 'cut themselves from the Communion' of the Church—opted for voluntary exile, planting themselves 'in divers towns of the Low Countries'. It was hardly out of sight out of mind, however, since they took advantage of the freedom they had there to publish 'many dangerous Books and Pamphlets in English' upholding 'their Anabaptisticall Opinions...to the Slander of the Ecclesiastical Government' in England.[83]

The Gunpowder Plot and the Failure of Union

The tightening-up on Puritan dissent at a time when James was calling for a relaxation of the laws against Catholics proved a cause of concern among MPs. Parliament pressed for further anti-Catholic legislation, and although James was reluctant to agree to any measure that might endanger the peace with Spain, he did in the end bow to pressure to pass a bill confirming all existing laws against recusants.[84] Moreover, in his conflict with the Puritans over the subscription campaign, James found it necessary to deny publicly that he was soft on Catholics and to proclaim that he wanted the recusancy laws strictly enforced. It was a statement that was seized upon by Attorney General Egerton, who in his pre-circuit speech to the assize judges in Star Chamber on 13 February 1605 exhorted judges to increased diligence against recusants.[85] At the end of March the Venetian ambassador was to complain how 'the persecution of Catholics' was 'vigorously conducted': 'all suspect houses', he observed, were searched, and 'if crosses or anything indicating the Catholic religion' discovered the owner was imprisoned, while the search for priests was also 'keen', with all those found 'imprisoned and threatened with execution'.[86]

With formal toleration for Catholics looking as far off as ever, and with the international Catholic powers seemingly having abandoned the English Catholic community following the peace of 1604, a few desperadoes were willing to contemplate extreme measures. What materialized was a plot to blow up the king, the young Prince Henry, and leading members of the government at the opening of parliament on 5 November 1605.

The origins of the Gunpowder Plot in fact date back to 1603, when an English Catholic gentleman named Robert Catesby began discussing with his friend Thomas Percy the possibility of assassinating the new king. By the spring of 1604 the conspiracy had widened to include Catesby's cousin Thomas Winter, a man named John Wright, and a deeply Scotophobic mercenary who had recently returned from the Low Countries called Guy Fawkes. The gunpowdering of Westminster Hall was supposed to be a prelude to a popular rebellion to be launched in the Midlands, during which the conspirators would seize Prince Charles and Princess Elizabeth and install the latter on throne. Practical planning began in May 1604 when the conspirators rented a house that backed onto the parliament building and set about trying to build a tunnel between the two. It was not until after ten months of futile labour that they discovered that the house next door had a cellar that ran directly under the parliament building. The conspirators therefore rented that house instead, knocked down the cellar wall, and began moving into the relevant chamber some twenty barrels of gunpowder. The plot was leaked to the government in an anonymous letter sent to Baron Monteagle in late October, and Fawkes was arrested after a search of the House of Lords late on the night of 4 November; upon examination, he was to boast that he would have blown both James and his Scottish courtiers back to Scotland.[87] The government encouraged Londoners to celebrate deliverance from the plot with bonfires on the night of 5 November, starting a tradition that has survived to the present day: Chamberlain observed that the City witnessed 'great ringing and as great store of bonfires as ever I thincke was seene'. Most of the conspirators fled London when they learned of the plot's discovery. The sheriff of Worcester's men caught up with them at Holbeach House in

Staffordshire, and in the ensuing battle Catesby and a number of others were killed. Eight survivors were brought to London and alongside Fawkes were hanged, drawn, and quartered for treason.[88]

The revelations did much to fuel and further reinforce anti-Catholic sentiment in England. Pamphleteers rushed to denounce the Gunpowder Plot as the latest in a long line of Catholic conspiracies against the Protestant states of Europe, conjuring up graphic images of Catholic atrocity—the sacking of cities, deflowering of virgins, and slaughtering of innocents. Recalling the horrors of the St Bartholomew's Day massacre in France, one poet rhymed, 'There Papists tossed harmeles babes, | upon their speares sharpe point: | Then did their wombs eviscerate, | and teare them joynt from joynt', and invited readers to imagine 'dismembered corps' and 'dissevered' limbs lying 'mangled every where' had the plot to blow up parliament succeeded.[89] One Puritan writer, celebrating God's 'goodnes towards the whole land' in delivering England from 'the late most bloudie, horrible, unnaturall and monstrous conspiracy of the Papists', noted that 'our deliverance' was all the greater because 'the mischeife plotted against us' was not just 'bodily' but also 'spirituall', with the aim of reducing all our posterity 'to the former bondage of popish blindnes, superstition, and Idolatry, so to have perished everlastingly'.[90] The Church of England cleric and anti-Puritan controversialist Oliver Ormerod warned in 1606 how the 'Jesuites and Seminarie Priests' had sought to ensnare 'many a seely soule in this land' and 'set the marke of that Antichristian beast in theire forheades' and 'the Cursed seeds of sedition in theyr heartes'. For Ormerod, Catholics were as bad as, if not worse than, the Turks, and at heart pagans.[91] Gabriel Powel, despite writing against Puritans in other works, insisted that the Puritans were nowhere near 'as dangerous enemies unto the State, as the Papistes', recalling how the Elizabethan bishop of London John Aylmer had once said that if he were 'amongst ten thousand Precisians' he might fear for his bishopric, but if he 'were in the company but of one Papist' he might 'justly fear for his life': 'The one would cut my coate', but 'the other my throate'.[92]

Some, however, used the occasion of the plot to take a swipe at radical Protestants. In his speech before parliament on 9 November, the king himself reminded those present that there had been threats against his life from Protestants as well as Catholics (even though he abstained from using confessional labels), recalling in a clear allusion to the Gowrie conspiracy how in the kingdom of his birth God had delivered him 'from the very Brink of Death, from the Point of the

Dagger'.[93] The bishop of Rochester, William Barlow, preaching at St Paul's Cross the following day in condemnation of 'the inhumane crueltie', 'brutish immanitie', 'divelish brutishnes', and 'hyperdiabolicall divelishnes' of the Gunpowder Plot, warned that there were 'some amongst us' (i.e. in England) who came 'very neare to the same dangerous position' of the Catholics in making 'Religion the stawking-horse for Treasons', and recalled how Scotland had bred the likes of Knox and Buchanan, those 'two fiery spirites of that Church and Nation where they lived'.[94]

Salisbury managed to exploit the loyalist reaction in the aftermath of the Gunpowder Plot to induce parliament to make a grant of taxation worth nearly £400,000 in 1606.[95] In addition, parliament passed a measure entitling the king to seize two-thirds of the estates of Catholic recusants instead of taking the monetary fine of £20 per month (thereby undermining the ability of wealthy English Catholics to sustain priests and centres of Catholic worship)—legislation which also introduced a new oath of allegiance commanding Catholics to acknowledge James as lawful king, renounce the pope's deposing power, and to denounce as 'impious and heretical' the 'damnable doctrine' that excommunicated or deprived princes 'may be deposed or murdered by their subjects'.[96] The government insisted that the oath was designed merely as a test of civil obedience, and many English Catholics, encouraged by the English archpriest George Blackwell, were willing to take it. Yet to some it appeared that the oath, by blurring the boundaries between excommunication, the deposing power, and tyrannicide, was endeavouring to trick Catholics who disapproved of the last into renouncing central aspects of Roman doctrine. The new pope, Paul V, condemned the oath as heretical and issued two breves urging English Catholics not to take it, while Cardinal Bellarmine wrote a letter to Blackwell in September 1607 reproving him for taking the oath. James took it upon himself to respond to Bellarmine in kind, first with his *Apologie for the Oath of Allegiance*, published anonymously in early 1608, subsequently translated into Latin and French, and republished in 1609 prefaced with a lengthy *Premonition* to European monarchs.[97]

James thought it possible to distinguish between moderates and extremists, 'betweene Papists of quiet disposition, and in all other things good Subjects', and 'such other Papists as in their hearts maintained the like violent bloody Maximes' of the Gunpowder plotters.[98] It was a distinction that few of his Protestant subjects shared. Parliament probably supported the oath of allegiance in the belief that

Catholics would refuse to take it and thus unveil themselves as intrinsically disloyal. Calvinist conformist divines likewise preached that the Catholic religion was inherently treasonous. Robert Tynley, archdeacon of Ely, preaching at St Paul's Cross on 5 November 1608, held that 'to bee a Rebell and a Traitor, be all one with a Catholike'; 'this Religion' perverted 'lawful subjection'.[99] John King, dean of Christ Church and future bishop of London, preaching at Whitehall that same day, believed the world was divided into two sorts of men, the wicked and the righteous, and that 'cruelty' was the 'ensigne and badge' of the Catholic Church and the pope 'a homeborne Turke'.[100] Indeed, for many it was the prospect that some Catholics might actually take the oath that was alarming; better for the state to have open and professed recusancy. Only avant-garde conformists sympathized with James's attempt to distinguish the moderates from the extremists; Lancelot Andrewes, for example, in his defence of the oath of allegiance took care to emphasize that the oath did not attack all forms of popery.[101]

What, then, of the fate of actual English Catholics? The sources are patchy and thus the evidence ambiguous. The oath of allegiance was imposed unevenly, though more rigorously than sometimes thought, and was used as an incentive to persuade Catholics to conform to the established Church, not simply as a civil test of loyalty. In 1607 two priests sentenced to death were offered a reprieve if they took the oath; one did and saved his life. There was no systematic clampdown in the aftermath of the Gunpowder Plot. In Middlesex the years 1606–7 saw a dramatic rise in the number of convictions for recusancy; nevertheless fines totalling some £28,000 remained unpaid, suggesting that the government was not hell bent on destroying the recusant community. However, the assassination of Henri IV of France by a Catholic fanatic in mid-May 1610 sent shivers down the spine of the English establishment and prompted a crackdown on Catholic recusancy in England. In response, on 2 June James issued a proclamation calling for 'the due execution of all former Lawes against Recusants', the disarming of all Catholics, and the administration of the oath of allegiance, and ordering priests and Jesuits to leave the realm under pain of death—recalling the 'evil behaviour' of Catholics at home 'and the devilish and unnaturall murder of the late French King' in justification.[102] The proclamation was followed by legislation extending the range of people who could be required to take the oath, no longer just recusants or suspected recusants, but all subjects. In July Archbishop Bancroft issued instructions to his bishops asking them to report the exact number of recusants in their respective dioceses. There were soon reports of prisons being filled with those who refused to take the oath, while in December a further two priests were executed—one for an attack on the bishop of London, George Abbot, the other for not having departed the realm after having been banished five times. Concern about international Catholic conspiracy was a factor behind James's decision to appoint the stridently anti-Catholic Abbot to succeed Bancroft at Canterbury in February 1611—a surprise to many since Abbot was the most recent elevation to the episcopal bench. (At forty-eight Abbot was the youngest archbishop of Canterbury since Thomas Cranmer, the man whom Henry VIII had appointed to oversee the break with Rome back in 1532.) The government's enthusiasm for administering the oath continued over the next few years, motivated by a combination of security and financial concerns; by 1615 Jesuits were to claim that Lord Chief Justice Coke had so far ordered 16,000 Catholics to take it.[103] Over the course of the reign as a whole, the government was to execute a total of twenty-five recusants (of whom twenty were priests), a disturbing figure to be sure but far less than the 189 who were put to death in the period 1570–1603.[104]

The preoccupation with the Gunpowder Plot meant that the question of the Union was not discussed again until the third session of parliament, which began in November 1606.[105] In his speech from the throne on the 18th, James said that he esteemed Scotland and England 'as Two Brothers' that had 'equal Parts of his Affections' and should be subject 'to One Rule and to One Law', and called for the abolition of all hostile laws, for freedom of trade, and for the naturalization of Scots born prior to his accession to the English crown.[106] His goals were fully spelled out in 'The Instrument for the Union' that had been drawn up by the English and the Scottish commissioners, and which was introduced into parliament on 20 November 1606.[107] Yet the Commons proved unenthusiastic. The only model for perfect union the English understood was that of Wales, which was a conquered country. Sandys thought the Scots would have to submit themselves to the English and subject themselves to English law, something which the Scots would clearly never accept. The English warmed to the idea of free trade; again the Scots objected, well aware there would not be a level playing field. Yet MPs were deeply opposed to the idea that both the English and the Scots should enjoy a common citizenship. The issue here centred around whether the king or the law was the ultimate seat of authority. James thought his subjects owed their allegiance personally to him, and that since he was king in both kingdoms his subjects in both kingdoms possessed the same legal rights. Most MPs took the view that since England and Scotland had different legal systems, James's Scottish subjects could not enjoy the same rights at law in England as did his English subjects.[108] Behind the legal arguments, however, lay an undercurrent of national antipathy. 'God hath made People apt for every Country,' Nicholas Fuller declared in the Commons on 14 February 1607; 'some for a cold, some for a hot Climate, and the several Countries he hath fitted to their several Natures and Qualities.' If a man owned two pastures, 'the One Pasture bare, the other fertile and good', Fuller continued, he would not pull down the hedge that divided them, for if he did 'the Cattle will rush in in Multitudes'; it would not be good 'to mingle Two Swarms of Bees under one Hive, upon the sudden'.[109] Christopher Piggott had been even less discreet in a speech he had delivered the previous day: 'Let us not join murderers, thieves, and the roguish Scots with the well-deserving Scots,' he implored; 'They have not suffered above two kings to die in their beds, these 200 years.' Although they waited a few days, MPs realized they could not let such 'invective against the Scotts and Scottish nation' go unpunished, and dispatched Piggott to the Tower.[110]

Parliament did, after much heated discussion, eventually pass a bill to remove hostile laws. However, none of the other proposals of the commissioners made it into law. The prospect of union was dead. The legal status of those born in Scotland after James had succeeded to the English throne, however, was clarified by the ruling given in Calvin's Case in 1608, when Lord Chancellor Ellesmere concluded that 'these Post-nati' were, 'by their Birthright', 'liege subjects to the King; and capable of estates of Inheritance, and freehold lands in England'.[111]

* * *

It had been a shaky start to the reign. As a foreigner and newcomer, James had often been unsure of himself, and had frequently misread situations because he was making judgements on the basis of his experiences in Scotland. He had failed to achieve what he most wanted, namely union between England and Scotland; he had had a significant misunderstanding with the House of Commons in the first session of his very first parliament; and he had initiated a drive for conformity in the Church which had seen large numbers of godly ministers suspended from or deprived of their livings. There had been a number of foiled Catholic plots against the new regime, including a major terrorist conspiracy aimed at blowing up the king and key members of the royal family and government. The country was also suffering, having been hit by a devastating renewed outbreak of the plague, while inflation was still high and the economy, although beginning to pick up after the peace with Spain, continued to show signs of fragility.

A jarring reminder of the depth of socio-economic tensions in certain parts of the country occurred in the spring of 1607. From late April through to June a series of disturbances broke out across the agrarian heartland of England, starting in Northamptonshire but spreading to Leicestershire, Warwickshire, and other Midland counties, as angry crowds—who styled themselves 'levellers' and 'diggers'—rose to pull down enclosures. The Midland Rising, as it has become known, mobilized thousands of people, across an extensive geographical area (both urban and rural). The insurgents were well organized, being led by a tinker from Desborough, Northamptonshire, named John Reynolds but who went by the title 'Captain Pouch', and produced their own manifestoes. Their anger was directed against those landlords who continued to convert arable to pasture, in violation of the government's anti-enclosure legislation of 1604—'encroaching tyrants which would grind our flesh on the whetstone of poverty', as the Warwickshire diggers put it, enclosure being held responsible (in the eyes of the poor) not only for driving people off the land but also for forcing up the price of grain. At Newton in Northamptonshire a bloody pitched battle broke out as a makeshift force of cavalry and infantry assembled by the local gentry, having failed to persuade the crowds to dissolve peacefully, charged the rebel camp, killing some forty to fifty and injuring many others. Several more of the rebels were executed, either summarily under martial law, or under the terms of a special judicial commission convened at Northampton on 21 June. The government had escaped a major scare, though at the price of slaughtering dozens of its subjects. The Midlands had indeed suffered deeply. In Northamptonshire alone, in excess of 27,000 acres had been enclosed, resulting in the destruction of some 350 farms and the eviction of close to 1,500 people. Dearth did inevitably follow depopulation; the year following the rising there was a serious shortage of corn, caused (it was believed) in part by producers holding back grain from the market in the hope of forcing prices even higher and in part by enclosure.

Yet although the enclosure rioters expressed a degree of class hatred against tyrannical landlords who pursued private gain at the expense of the poor, they protested their loyalty and allegiance to the king, whom they expected to be sympathetic to their plight. And although the crown's priority was the restoration of law and order, it did temper justice with mercy. In August 1607 James set up a royal commission to investigate the scale of illegal enclosure and depopulation across the Midlands; armed with its findings, over the course of 1608 the government brought a series of successful actions in Star Chamber against leading Midlands gentry found guilty of violating the law. In June 1608, with corn prices now 30 per cent higher than they had been a year earlier, the crown intervened to regulate the grain market by issuing the Elizabethan dearth orders.[112]

4

....

Settling the Affairs of Religion

In a proclamation issued at the beginning of March 1604 calling for conformity to the Book of Common Prayer, James identified the settling of 'the affaires of Religion' as 'the chiefest of all Kingly dueties'.[1] Even allowing for a certain amount of rhetorical posturing, there is no doubting that he took his obligation to promote the service of God seriously, and his handling of religious matters is normally seen as one of the Jacobean success stories. No one should minimize the problems he faced. The Church he inherited was torn, between those who were happy with the Elizabethan settlement of 1559–63 and those who wanted further reform. Within both camps there were those with more moderate and others with more radical leanings— ultra ceremonialists or avant-garde conformists at one extreme, and radical Puritans at the other. There were also those—Catholics—who remained outside the Church and others—Protestant separatists— who opted not to be part of it. As we have seen, the various competing groups all had their own expectations of the new monarch, and James not only initially disappointed the Catholics but also managed to get himself embroiled in major confrontation with the Puritans at the start of his reign, resulting in the deprivation of about 1 per cent of the ministry. Yet despite this sticky start, over the course of his reign as a whole James seems to have done a reasonably good job at keeping religious tensions in check.

James's strategy for managing the Church, it is normally argued, was to isolate the radicals—both Catholic and Puritan extremists— and hold the religious centre together within a Church that was broadly Calvinist. Scholars have written of a 'Calvinist consensus' in the Jacobean Church and even of a 'Jacobean consensus'.[2] James himself, we have been reminded, was a Calvinist who was committed to a preaching ministry and his Church was run by Calvinists. Although he did give bishoprics to a few anti-Calvinists, or Arminians as they tended to be called—those who prioritized ceremonies

over preaching and who denied the Calvinist doctrine of predestination—
he never gave them real power within the Church.[3] When the Dutch
Reformed Church held a synod at Dort in 1618 to discuss the rise of
Arminianism, James instructed the delegates he sent to attend to support the anti-Arminian majority. While James could be harsh on religious extremists who were politically disloyal, he had no desire, so he
said, to persecute those with tender consciences if they remained
loyal. After the initial wave of persecution at the beginning of his
reign, he appears to have been not too concerned about Puritan nonconformity: four-fifths of those clergy who lost their livings under
James were deprived between December 1604 and December 1606.
James sought to manage the clergy, it has been claimed, through subscription rather than the enforcement of ceremonial uniformity: one
had to subscribe to the Three Articles to be admitted to the ministry,
but the authorities tended to turn a blind eye to what ministers did
after that, unless there were flagrant abuses. In this way a delicate
peace was maintained within the Church, one that admittedly began
to show signs of cracking by the early 1620s, but one which was not
shattered until the reign of Charles I and the rise to dominance within
the Church of the Arminian faction.[4]

While there is much to be said for this view, it needs qualification.
To speak of a consensus risks being misleading, since it seems to
imply a lack of conflict or disagreement.[5] It is better to talk of a Jacobean balancing act, with James seeking to incorporate different interests within the Church as a way of containing conflict. Such an
approach enabled James to keep his options open and to play different factions off against each other, but did little to resolve the underlying religious tensions both within the Church and across English
society more generally. Ultimately, the balancing act proved impossible to sustain. It is also oversimplified to suggest that the basic religious cleavage in early Stuart England was between Calvinists and
anti-Calvinists, between those who believed in predestination and
those who believed in universal redemption. People disagreed over
more than the soteriology of grace; indeed, one may wonder how
many people truly fully grasped the finer points of dispute. For many
of the laity, how one was expected or allowed to worship—attitudes
towards the liturgy and the role of preaching—could be just as important: perhaps more so, since it affected more immediately how one
experienced the religion being upheld by the established Church.
Furthermore, James's own religious views were more complex than
often represented. The idea that he was broadly tolerant needs to be

qualified by the fact that at times he appeared quite intolerant and even helped propagate arguments for religious intolerance, while the notion that he was not that concerned about ceremonial conformity (so long as people remained loyal) is belied by the fact that both in England and in Scotland his regime did, at times, show itself very concerned about ceremonial conformity. It is vital to understand the true nature of the Jacobean Church, and James's policies for the Church, if we are to understand the Caroline Church—how it could be possible for Charles not only to perceive why his vision for the Church could be an appropriate way of addressing the religious problems that (he believed) he faced but also how it could be possible for him to address those problems in the way that he did. To put it another way, we cannot understand the stridently anti-Puritan nature of the Caroline Church without appreciating the strident anti-Puritanism that already existed in Jacobean England, and we cannot understand the Arminian turn which the Church was to take under Charles without appreciating that Arminians had already achieved a platform in the Church under James.

* * *

James may have been raised in Calvinist Scotland, but he was a moderate Calvinist at best. In his *Basilikon Doron* he came close to endorsing the view that human works were meritorious and he had little sympathy for the speculative (non-biblically-sanctioned) predestinarianism of Puritan evangelicals, or for the view that God's grace, once given, could never be extinguished. At the Hampton Court Conference he had rejected the proposal made by Reynolds to modify the Thirty-Nine Articles to include the unequivocally Calvinist statement on predestination embodied in the Lambeth Articles of 1595 and supported John Overall when attacked by Reynolds for maintaining that salvation was contingent upon repentance.[6] He disliked the Dutch Arminians in large part because of their opposition to a prayer book and Church hierarchy; in other words, he feared them for the same reason that he feared the English Puritans.[7] All in all, his desire to be *rex pacificus* led him to back the promotion of closer relations among the major Christian Churches—English, Calvinist, Lutheran, Catholic, and Greek Orthodox—in the hope of easing the religious tensions that threatened the peace of Europe.[8]

James was an ardent champion of episcopacy. He believed in *iure divino* episcopacy and his support of the institution was intrinsically tied up with his fear of Puritan parity. In his *Premonition* of 1609

James defended bishops as 'an Apostolike institution, and so the ordinance of God', contrary to the views of both the Puritans and the Jesuits: indeed, he thought that Jesuits were 'nothing but Puritan-papists'.[9] Unlike Elizabeth, James did not leave sees vacant for extended periods as a way of easing pressure on the Exchequer: rarely was a diocese without a bishop for more than a few months. James also believed that bishops had an important role to play in the secular administration. All three of his archbishops of Canterbury—Whitgift, Bancroft, and Abbot—served on the privy council, as did four other bishops (Bilson, Andrewes, Montagu, and Williams); he increased the episcopal presence in Star Chamber (by the middle of his reign two or three bishops were regularly in attendance); and almost all of his bishops had seats on the magisterial bench. James had no qualms about considering bishops for high office: in 1618 he made Abbot first commissioner of the Treasury, and in 1621 he appointed John Williams of Lincoln Lord Keeper.[10]

Over the course of his reign James created an episcopal bench that represented a broad range of opinion, reflecting the diversity that already existed in the Church—though not among the episcopate—at the time of his accession. Although the Elizabethan Church had been broadly Calvinist in doctrine and emphasized preaching over sacraments, there had been tensions: between those who wanted further reform and those who did not; between those who sympathized with the godly and those who urged the need for a harsher stance towards the Puritans. The 1590s had seen the rise of a group of avant-garde conformists, which included the likes of Lancelot Andrewes (dean of Westminster from 1601) and Samuel Harsnett (appointed archdeacon of Essex shortly before Elizabeth's death), who challenged the Calvinist doctrine of predestination, placed a greater emphasis on ceremonialism, and even called for the beautification of churches. Elizabeth herself had favoured a sacrament-centred style of piety: in the Chapel Royal choristers would sing to the accompaniment of organ music and clergy wearing the full medieval vestments would bow towards a richly adorned communion table which was placed altarwise at the east end. In Westminster Abbey the services were modelled on the Chapel Royal, and the communion table was likewise placed altarwise.[11]

James opted to embrace this diversity—a calculated balancing act to ensure that no one faction in the Church felt excluded and to provide him with a spectrum of advice, as well as to afford him greatest room for manoeuvre. Among James's episcopal appointees there were

Calvinists and anti-Calvinists, anti-Puritans and those who were less strident in their opposition to Puritan nonconformity, ardent ceremonialists (both Calvinist and Arminian), and staunch anti-Catholics. Calvinists held the most important sees. Both of the men James appointed to the see of Canterbury were Calvinists: Bancroft (translated 1604), and Abbot (translated 1611), the latter decidedly indulgent towards Puritan nonconformity. So was James's appointee to the archbishopric of York, Tobias Matthew (translated 1606), an active preacher and a hounder of Catholic recusants in the northern province. The clergyman to whom James was closest in his early years was James Montagu, another committed Calvinist albeit a staunch defender of episcopacy, whom James made a royal chaplain and then dean of the Chapel Royal in 1603, bishop of Bath and Wells in 1608, and finally bishop of Winchester in 1616. Another prominent Jacobean Calvinist was Thomas Morton, appointed a royal chaplain in 1606, dean of Gloucester in 1607, bishop of Chester in 1616, and bishop of Coventry and Lichfield in 1619. James's first four appointees to the bishopric of London were all Calvinists: Richard Vaughan (1604), Thomas Ravis (1607), George Abbot (1610), and John King (1611–21), with all but Ravis somewhat sympathetic towards Puritan nonconformity.

Yet James also promoted Arminians. He made Andrewes bishop of Chichester (1605), Ely (1609), and Winchester (1618; confirmed February 1619), and Harsnett bishop of Chichester (1609) and of Norwich (1619). He enjoyed the company of Richard Neile, another associate of Andrewes, whom he made dean of Westminster in 1605 when Andrewes moved to Chichester, and then successively bishop of Rochester (1608), Coventry and Lichfield (1610), Lincoln (1614), and Durham (1617). Other Arminians and avant-garde conformists also found favour: John Overall, appointed bishop of Coventry and Lichfield (1614) and subsequently Norwich (1618); George Montaigne (or Mountain), dean of Westminster (1610), bishop of Lincoln (1617) and of London (1621); and John Buckeridge, bishop of Rochester (1611). James was, however, reluctant to promote the man who was to emerge as the most controversial Arminian churchman of the age—William Laud. Ordained in 1601, Laud got his first rectorship in 1609 (at West Tilbury, Essex), became Master of St John's, Oxford in 1611 (where he oversaw the beautifying of the chapel), and then subsequently a prebendary of Lincoln (1614), archdeacon of Huntingdon (1615), and dean of Gloucester (1616). But it was not until 1621 that James made Laud a bishop, appointing him to the poor and remote Welsh see of St David's, and then only at the bidding of the royal favourite, the marquess of Buckingham. James, in fact, warned Buckingham that Laud had 'a restless spirit' and could not see 'when matters are well', but loved 'to toss and change and bring things to a pitch of reformation floating in his own brain'.[12] Moreover, when James advanced Arminians, he sometimes compensated by filling their old position with a Calvinist. Thus when James moved Harsnett from Chichester to Norwich in 1619, he replaced him with the Calvinist George Carleton of Llandaff. Nevertheless, the trend is clear. At the time of James's accession there were at most two bishops who could possibly be categorized as avant-garde conformists or proto-Arminians: John Young of Rochester (who died in 1605) and Thomas Dove of Peterborough (appointed because he had impressed Elizabeth by his preaching; only later did his sympathy for proto-Arminians emerge). By 1611 there were five, by 1617 seven, and by 1619 eight—out of a total episcopal bench of twenty-four (excluding the two archbishops).[13]

Even so, by 1620 there were still twice as many Calvinists as Arminians, while of the five most important sees—Canterbury, York, London, Winchester, and Durham—only two (London and Winchester) had Arminian bishops. Yet we also need to consider the question of lived experience, what the balance in the Church would have looked like to those on the ground. James sometimes gave 'Puritan areas' sympathetic bishops, as he did the diocese of London, for example, between 1604 and 1621—with the exception of Thomas Ravis, bishop between 1607 and 1609, a Calvinist who was nevertheless rabidly anti-nonconformist. However, James sometimes appointed noted Arminians and strident ceremonial conformists to oversee notorious nonconformist areas. What would the Jacobean Church have looked like to Leicestershire Puritans from 1614, one might wonder, when their diocesan at Lincoln was first Neile (1614–17) and then Montaigne (1617–21) or to East Anglian Puritans from 1618, whose diocesans were first Overall (1618–19) and then Harsnett (1619–29)?

Diversity on the bench meant that there was no theological consensus. Theological disagreements became particularly intense following Abbot's appointment in 1611. From about this time Neile began to gather around him staunch anti-Calvinists like Buckeridge, Laud, Andrewes, and Overall (the forerunner of what was to be known as the Durham-house group following Neile's elevation to Durham in 1617), with the respective pro- and anti-Calvinist groupings endeavouring to manipulate James by exploiting his fears both of popery and of Puritanism: the Neile group accused Abbot of being inclined to Puritanism himself, while Abbot charged the Arminians with having popish leanings.[14] Yet the split between Calvinists and anti-Calvinists was not the only source of disagreement. Calvinists themselves were divided, between those who wanted to uphold ceremonial conformity and those who took a more relaxed attitude. Indeed, given that Puritans were themselves Calvinists, it often made tactical sense for the government to employ Calvinist conformists to write anti-Puritan polemic. A case in point here is the Oxford-trained cleric Gabriel Powell, who was chaplain to Bishop Vaughan of London and rector of the crown living of Chellesworth, Suffolk, from 1606. Theologically staunchly Calvinist and a zealous anti-papist (who had written works denouncing popery and the Roman Church as the 'synagogue of Antichrist'), Powell was also a key government apologist in the campaign at the beginning of the reign to clamp down on Puritan nonconformity. James's first archbishop of Canterbury, the staunchly Calvinist Richard Bancroft, was also, of course, a noted anti-Puritan.[15]

It is probably fair to say that James did not want to allow himself to be under the sway of any one particular faction in the Church (and in this he certainly differed from his son). Moreover, he always made it clear who was in charge and bishops ignored royal policy at their peril. James could at times reprimand those bishops whom he felt were too indulgent of Puritan nonconformity. Yet he also refused to bow to pleas of the Arminians for more rigorous discipline.[16] And although he became more dependent upon the Arminians towards the end of his reign, which encouraged some clergy to be bolder about preaching the doctrine of universal redemption before the king, he continued to make clear his distaste for such views. For example, when Edward Simpson of Trinity College, Cambridge, preaching before the king at Royston in November 1617, 'fell upon a point of Arminius's doctrine touching universalitie of grace', James was so 'displeased' that he asked the heads of the Cambridge colleges to examine Simpson's sermon; when they returned 'a favourable censure', acknowledging that certain things preached were allowable, James then ordered the heads of houses to attend him in Newmarket, where, after a detailed discussion, it was decided that Simpson should be made 'to retract what he had saide, in the same place', when the king returned there after Christmas.[17]

How, then, should we characterize the Jacobean regime's stance on Puritanism? The main drive against clerical nonconformity took place between 1604 and 1609, when as we have seen between seventy-three and eighty-three ministers were deprived of their livings for refusing to subscribe to the Three Articles in the aftermath of the Hampton Court Conference (the vast majority of them in the period 1604–6). After 1609, the diocese of Lincoln (under Barlow) saw a brief flurry of deprivations in 1611–12, as likewise did Chester (under Morton) in 1616–18—on both occasions the local bishop was in essence trying to complete the unfinished business of 1604–6. Those clergy who were prepared to affirm their loyalty to the regime by subscribing tended to be given much slack. It was a policy that in practice sanctioned a considerable degree of occasional nonconformity at the parish level. Undoubtedly the Arminian bishops were unhappy with the extent to which Puritans seemed to be indulged, and from the second decade of the reign we find them asking searching questions about nonconformist practices in their visitation articles. But the small number of nonconformists presented, and the mildness of the punishments administered, suggest that they were well aware that a harder line would not win royal approval. There were occasional crackdowns on Puritan preaching. For example in 1611 Neile, when at Coventry and Lichfield, managed to get James's approval for the silencing of the Puritan lecturer Arthur Hildersham at Burton-upon-Trent, by pointing to Hildersham's connections with the local anti-Trinitarian Edward Wightman (Wightman was soon to earn the distinction of being the last person to be burned at the stake for heresy), and for shutting down the local Puritan lectures. Neile also appears to have discouraged ministers from preaching twice in one day. Barlow at Lincoln suspended three lectureships between 1608 and 1613 and refused to allow a fourth to be established, while Harsnett took action against nonconformist preaching. Yet for the majority of James's reign—with the exception of 1604–6—it appears that the regime was not particularly tough on Puritanism.[18]

Having said that, there is no doubt that James had a deeply ingrained suspicion of Puritans. This was conditioned by his dealings with the Scottish Presbyterians in the 1590s and it translated into a concern about English Puritans in the early years of his reign in England. As a newcomer to England, James doubtless at first misunderstood the nature of English Puritanism, and it is normally suggested that his views moderated as he became more familiar with political and religious realities in his new kingdom. Yet his fear of Puritanism never went away. In his *Premonition* of 1609 he stressed that he had always been 'an enemy to that confused Anarchie, or paritie of the

Puritanes' and reiterated his allegation in his *Basilikon Doron* that he 'found greater honesty with the highland and border theeves, then with that sort of people'.[19] Speaking in parliament in 1610 in reaction to MPs' attempts to dispute the king's right to levy impositions by dint of the prerogative, James revealed his prejudices by proclaiming that only 'papists and puritans' ever sought to impose limitations on the monarchy.[20] James's anti-Puritanism revived with a vengeance after the outbreak of the Thirty Years War in Europe in 1618, when the Puritans emerged as outspoken critics of his pacific foreign policy. While it is often claimed that James distinguished between moderate and radical Puritans, he did not always do so consistently, and he certainly adopted a tougher line on more mainstream Puritanism towards the end of his reign. Nor was the distinction between moderates and radicals always easy to sustain. James's concern, it has been said, was with those who were disloyal, who refused to obey royal authority. Yet to many conformist Protestants, and certainly to most upholders of prayer book ceremonialism, any form of Puritan nonconformity was a defiance of royal authority, an affront to the royal supremacy by dint of which the king was to determine what practices were legitimate in the Church. The confusion in James's own mind is seen in his last-ditch attempt at damage limitation in the English edition of his *Basilikon Doron* by qualifying what he had previously written against Puritans: although he now claimed to have been referring only to radical separatists, his remarks reveal that he was not quite sure if he did mean just these or in fact any 'heady preacher' who sought to undermine the authority of the civil magistrate.[21]

A number of authors sought to exploit the king's sensitivities concerning potential Puritan radicalism. The most aggressive anti-Puritan polemic was published towards the beginning of the reign, at the time of the subscription campaign, some of it part of the government's attempt to justify why it was taking a tough line. It nevertheless reveals a mindset that some embraced and a discourse of anti-Puritanism that had already been forged and was in the public domain. Writing in 1604, seemingly at Archbishop Whitgift's prompting, the vicar of Sittingbourne in Kent, William Covell, proclaimed that there was nothing 'more fatal to the prosperitie of God's Church than the violent nourishing of *contention* within her Bowells', 'nothing safer to a Kingdome than that the Religion professed be but only one', and 'few things of greater advantage' for 'the safetie of all states...than the severitie of Justice in the strict execution of penall lawes'. 'Banish all Heretikes from Christ's fold,' Covell urged James; 'discover those

Anabaptists who stirre up contentions to hinder Religion'; these 'Anabaptists' did now petition and 'hope for favour' (an allusion which suggests that by 'Anabaptists' he meant Puritans more generally), but now was 'the time to make and execute lawes against them'. This would not be persecution but 'deserved punishment', for these were 'more daungerous than other Heretikes, because they are transformed into the shapes of some amongst us'.[22] William Wilkes, writing in defence of James's drive towards uniformity in 1605 (in a work published with a preface by the king), characterized a refusal to conform to the ceremonies of the Church as 'wicked and ungodly rebellion'. History showed what 'many fearefull miseries...both Church and common-weale' had 'sustained, by the restlesse affections of disagreeing mindes in matters of this kinde', since 'a continuing distance of Ceremonies' occasioned 'continuall hatred', which was 'the mother of sedition', 'tumult', 'insurrection', and 'ruine'. Wilkes therefore exhorted both civil and ecclesiastical authorities to enforce the laws against nonconformists and explicitly denounced toleration: 'To submit the publick constitutions of State, to the instabilitie of private fancie, no pollicie did ever tolerate', and it was 'better with moderate severitie to correct them which disturbe the Peace of the Church with unhallowed contentions, then by suffering inconformitie unto good lawes to give passage unto confusion'. It is important to note that although Wilkes stressed the necessity of obedience to kings, his emphasis was on the rule of law. Indeed, he explicitly linked obedience to the law with freedom and liberty: 'If you will bee free, obaye the Lawe: If you take awaye the Lawe, you take away libertie, we therefore obaye the Lawe that wee may be free.'[23]

In a lengthy and vitriolic attack of 1605, the Suffolk rector Oliver Ormerod lambasted English Puritans not only for corrupting true religion but also for undermining the authority of the crown and stirring up the masses against the state. Ormerod was particularly concerned about the intrinsically anti-monarchical nature of Puritanism. 'Their chiefest writers', he claimed (alluding to Continental Calvinist and Scottish Presbyterian resistance theorists), had 'blazed and divulged abroad, that Christian Soveraignes ought not to be called heads...of the particular and visible Churches within their Dominions'; that 'they ought not to medle with the making of Lawes, orders, and ceremonies for the Church'; that 'all Princes ought to submit themselves under the yoake' of 'their discipline' and that those who 'shal dissanul the same' were 'God's enemie, and to be held unworthy to raigne above his people'.[24] Even moderate forms of Puritan dissent showed a lack of respect both for divinely sanctioned royal authority and for God. The Puritan habit of calling extraordinary fasts, 'without the knowledge and authorizement of the Magistrate', for example, was 'a minishing of his [the Magistrate's] authoritie', since the king alone, as head of the church, had the right to call such fasts.[25] Likewise, the Puritan refusal to observe the ceremonies of the Church was implicitly a challenge to the crown's authority, since human laws in matters indifferent to salvation, which had been 'received by a whole Church', bound people in 'conscience, by vertue of the general commaundement of God, which ordaineth the Magistrate's authority'. Yet 'our Puritanes', Ormerod continued, 'thinke, that a Christian man's libertie is to live as hee list…our Sectaries thinke it servitude…to submitte…to the yoake of humane obedience in thinges indifferent'.[26] Worse still, the Puritans were stirring up the masses to disobedience, amazing 'the vulgar' and frightening 'the multitude' through their 'strange manner of preaching', thereby distracting 'millions of the vulgar sort from their love and liking of the present state'.[27]

In lashing out at the Puritans, Ormerod compared them to the radical Anabaptist movement in Germany at the time of the Peasants' War of 1524–6. Yet he also sought to stigmatize English Puritans by accusing them of popery. It was true that the Puritans claimed to be against all things that smacked of popery, but 'in defacing and depraving of this Church of England', they joined with the Catholics 'against us': just 'as there was a day when Herod and Pilate were made friends', so too there is a day 'when Papist and Puritanes are made friends'. Not only did both Puritans and Papists criticize the established Church, they both also denied the royal supremacy. 'By this you may see, that our Sectaries doe shake hands both with the Anabaptists and the Papists…and doe al jointly oppugne the Prince's authoritie in causes ecclesiasticall'.[28] Although Ormerod recognized that James had laboured continually since his accession to quench the Puritans' 'raging heate', it was vital, he thought, that James keep the Puritan flames from 'kindling again': 'For as a fire that is kept downe, if it breake forth againe, doth burne more fiercely: so these fiery spirits…if they breake foorth again, they will rage more furiously.'[29] Ormerod clearly thought his views were in line with royal policy, citing approvingly James's proclamation in favour of uniformity at the beginning of his reign, the fact that at the Hampton Court Conference James found that there was no cause why any change should be made to the Church, and the *Basilikon Doron* wherein James had described Puritans as worse than 'highland or border theeves'.[30]

James allowed a number of clergymen to preach sermons at court—and subsequently to publish those sermons—outlining exactly why Puritans (even moderate Puritans) should not be indulged. Preaching at court in 1606 on the anniversary of James's accession, royal chaplain Anthony Maxey urged that conformity was necessary to preserve order, to prevent popular upheaval and 'revolution', to guard against being infected by Presbyterian practices north of the border, and to maintain the authority of the crown. The 'common people', Maxey continued, were 'soone stird up, quickly led awry'; it therefore betrayed 'a vaine and proud spirit for any, especially men of religion and understanding, to...seeke to win unto themselves the applause of common people', since 'the braine-sicke humour of the multitude' was 'subject and pliable to every change and revolution'. It was not many years ago, Maxey recalled, alluding to the Puritan challenge to the Elizabethan Church settlement in the 1580s, that 'divers personages of great credit and countenance...invegled many weake men, young divines, trades-men, artificers, and such like' to cry out 'for the Geneva discipline, and Scottish reformation in the Church'. The result was disastrous: 'the ignorant multitude once stirred up, the whole land was in sects, and tumults, the state was troubled, the Prince was disobeyed, [and] good lawes were neglected'.[31]

Maxey went so far as to predict that if any form of nonconformity were permitted, civil war would ultimately ensue. 'A rent or schisme in the Church', he claimed, was like 'a great breach in the Sea', there being 'almost nothing able to close it up againe, Howsoever at the first it seemes of small reckning'. The German Peasants' War started with 'a small sparke', but it quickly raised 'such a flame'. 'The base multitude' seized temples, 'cities were set on fire, banishment and proscription inflicted upon the innocent, and at length a butchery massaker made of fiftie thousand people slaine at one time, and an hundred thousand Christians murdered at an other'. Although 'they began with the Bishops and Clergie,...they ended with the deposing of civill Magistrates and destruction of the people'. Maxey immediately leapt to a comparison with the Puritan movement under Elizabeth. 'The contentions...in our Church' were 'at the first...a little sparke'; but 'from this sparke, as from Hydra, what a number of poysoned heades sprong up: Anabaptists, Brownists, Puritaines, Catharists, Atheists, the familie of love, and such like'. These groups challenged the Church ceremonies established by Edward VI and ratified under Elizabeth, they condemned the Church government as 'utterly unlawfull and Antichristian', they demanded that the Book of

Common Prayer be abolished, and they claimed 'That all the Ceremonies of our Church were Popish' and should 'be swept away', that bishops were 'an Antichristian and divellish hierarchy', and that 'reformation of Religion' belonged 'to the commonaltie: and that the people [were] better then the King, and of greater authoritie'. In short, 'the most dangerous heresies' had at first 'beene raised of a small matter, and seemed nothing, but in the ende they have shadowed the face of the Church, and caused immesurable bloudshed'. Indeed, 'the greatest Monarchies, and most flourishing Kingdomes of the world', Maxey intoned, 'have never received such fearefull blowes, and unexpected down-fals by open and forraine enemies, as they have done by stealing innovations and secret treasons, first, raised by sects and heresies, in religion': recall the 'blooudy massakers of France', the 'wearisome broiles of Flanders', and the 'high indignities offered heretofore in Scotland, to our most worthy and religious King James' by those of the 'presbiteriall discipline'.[32]

Sermons preached at court did not necessarily reflect James's own opinions. Just as James appointed clergy of differing viewpoints to the episcopal bench, so he was happy for the court pulpit to be a site of debate, where preachers could argue for their own preferred style of piety.[33] It was part of James's balancing-act strategy for the Church and left him considerable room for manoeuvre, since he never firmly identified himself with any one position. Nevertheless, James gave clerics with strong anti-Puritan views a highly visible platform, and he allowed the logic of the case against Puritan nonconformity to be articulated in the highly prominent media of pulpit and press. It might have been a way of keeping Puritans in check by reminding them that there were those who were eager to take a tougher line than the king himself. Yet it risked encouraging anti-Puritan bigotry at the ground level. One pamphleteer, writing in support of the deprived ministers in 1606, lamented 'what division and contention there hath been betwixt the ministers of the word in this kingdom', especially what had been said 'by the conformable part in . . . reproch of the other': 'most bitter invective sermons, private raylings, and publicke disgracefull bookes' against 'those whom they call Puritan, precise, scismaticall, and refractary ministers'. As a result of this 'contention among the ministers', there had been 'no lesse dissention and alienation of minds and hartes, betwixt other of his Majestie's subjects', and such 'discord and contention', our author predicted, could not 'but be daungerous for King and kingdome'.[34]

Moreover, James at times openly embraced the language of anti-Puritanism in his own writings and public speeches. We have noted his *Basilikon Doron* and his speeches to parliament in 1604 and 1610 already. James returned to the theme of anti-Puritanism in his *Meditation upon the Lord's Prayer* of 1619. This *Meditation* had been prompted by the fact that James felt the nation's 'zeale to prayer' was 'quite dried and cooled', something he blamed on 'the Puritans', who would 'have us hunt for hearing of Sermons without ceasing, but as little prayer as yee wil'. Here James collapsed any distinction between moderate and radical Puritans: he saw 'the very rebellious Brownists' as acting in 'imitation of their fathers, the English Puritans', whom they merely strove 'to outgoe in zeale': 'For our Puritans wil say no set prayer...prescribed by their mother the Church', just as 'the Brownists' refused to say the Lord's Prayer. In case anyone thought he wronged 'our Puritans, in calling them the Brownists' fathers', James proceeded to explain in further detail how the Brownists founded 'their totall separation' 'upon our Puritans' grounds'. 'Our Puritans' were 'adverse to the governement of Bishops, calling it an Antichristian government' and they 'quarrell with all the Ceremonies of our Church, that agree not with their taste, because the Church of Rome doth use them'; the Brownists merely 'boldly' put into practice what the Puritans 'doe teach, but dare not perform'. Indeed, 'our Puritans', James said, were 'the founders and fathers' not only 'to the Brownists' but also of 'all these innumerable Sects of new Heresies, that now swarme in Amsterdam'. 'Trust not to that private spirit or holy ghost which our Puritans glory in,' James implored his readers, 'for then a little fiery zeale will make thee turne Separatist, and then proceed still on from Brownist to some one Sect or other of Anabaptist, and from one of these to another, then to become a Judaized Traskite, and in the ende a profane Familist.' (We may wonder where this assertion leaves James's attempt in his preface to the English edition of the *Basilikon Doron* to distinguish between English Puritans and the members of the Family of Love.) 'Letting slippe the holde of the true Church' and trusting 'to the private spirit of Reformation according to our Puritans' doctrine', James was adamant, would cause us to 'slide by degrees into the Chaos, filthy sinke and farrago of al horrible heresies, whereof hell is the just reward'.[35]

What, then, of James's personal style of piety? How did he worship, and what forms of worship did he encourage in his churches? James kept both the Chapel Royal and Westminster Abbey the way Elizabeth had left them. He approved of images, believing there was the world of difference between worshipping an idol and looking at pictures depicting scenes from the Bible. When Neile became dean of Westminster Abbey in 1605, Neile refurbished the choir, donated communion plate worth some £40, installed a new organ, and provided cloths of gold for the altar.[36] What was done where depended on who was in charge, and it would be naïve to assume they were invariably carrying out the will of the king. Neile, for instance, probably owed his deanship to the influence of Cecil and Bancroft, rather than being hand-picked by James himself—although James clearly soon took to Neile and was keen to advance him further when opportunity subsequently arose.[37]

James's reign saw a movement towards the re-edification of parish churches. It was certainly the case that work needed to be done. The uncertainties created by the religious upheavals of the sixteenth century—with successive rulers stripping churches, re-adorning them, and stripping them again—and then by a childless queen who would not name her successor, had left parishioners reluctant to invest, and many churches were in a desperate condition for lack of routine maintenance. With James secure on the throne and England's religious future more settled, the rebuilding could now begin. London led the way—at least sixteen London churches were repaired in the first decade of the seventeenth century—although there was also rebuilding in the provinces. There is no reason to suppose that Puritans were opposed, in principle, to re-edification; even if they saw the church simply as a building where they heard the word of God, they still did not want the roof collapsing on them as they were listening to the preacher. Nevertheless, several of the renovated churches were 'somewhat beautified', with religious imagery, stained-glass windows, and church plate. In 1620 James issued a royal commission for rebuilding St Paul's Cathedral in the heart of London—St Paul's had been badly damaged by fire in 1561 and still not properly fixed—hiring the classical architect Inigo Jones to carry out the work. Financial difficulties as the country drifted towards war with Spain, however, meant that nothing had been done by the time of James's death.[38]

In the majority of English churches—even the renovated ones—the communion table was placed not at the east end (the site of the altar in pre-Reformation days), but east–west in the chancel, and communicants often knelt around all four sides to receive communion. In fact, the Elizabethan injunctions of 1559 had stated that the communion table should stand at the site of the altar, and only be moved into the chancel at the time of the Eucharist, but to keep moving the table was too much bother, and the injunction was honoured more often in the breach. The canons of 1604, rather than clarifying the situation, had added to the ambiguity by stating merely that the communion table was to be placed in the church or chancel so that the minister 'may be more conveniently heard of the communicants in his prayer and ministration, and the communicants also more conveniently...communicate with the said minister'; they said nothing about where the communion table was to be at other times. Some of the avant-garde conformists favoured positioning the communion table altarwise. William Laud, following his installation as dean of Gloucester in December 1616, not only moved the Cathedral's communion table to the east end, justifying his action by appeal to the Elizabethan injunctions, but also instructed his prebendaries to bow to it. It was an initiative that caused some consternation in the city. In mid-February 1617 a libel was found in St Michael's, Gloucester protesting that 'the removing of the Communion Table' in the Cathedral 'savoured of superstition, that it was translated from a communion table to a high Altar, and that worship and obeisance was now made unto it'; what made matters worse was that the curate and the parish clerk read the libel out, so that everyone in the city was soon talking about it.[39] However, high altars were not yet the norm for cathedrals. When James journeyed to and from Scotland in 1617, three of the five cathedrals he visited—Durham, Carlisle, and Chester—did not have altarwise tables, while the situation at the other two, Lincoln and York, is unclear. Durham did reposition its altar table later that year, however, following the death of Bishop William James and his replacement by Neile, and in 1620 Neile had the wooden table replaced by a stone altar. When Harsnett moved to Norwich in 1619 he instructed at least eight of the city's churches to move their communion tables to the east end.[40]

It has been said that James was not too concerned about ceremonial conformity, so long as people did not wilfully disobey or challenge royal authority. Nevertheless, James promoted within his Church many men who were quite keen on ceremonial conformity and his own actions and statements as king suggest that he did believe in the importance of ceremonies. He defended ceremonies at Hampton Court, and they were enshrined in the canons. The court pulpit thundered with sermons in support of ceremonies in the 1610s. At Easter in 1614 Andrewes preached on the text 'At the Name of Jesus, every knee should bow' (Philippians 2:10), while on 1 September 1616

Maxey complained how most worshippers were 'like Elephants...they have no joynts in their knees, they talk, whisper, and gaze about, without any kind of bodily reverence'. In 1618 Buckeridge preached that 'not onely the inward devotion and prostration of our soules...but also the outward prostration and kneeling of our bodies' was 'required at our hands', indeed was a 'duetie in divine worship', and the king must 'compel all men to enter into God's house' and 'joyne together, not onely in *unitate*, in the unitie and substance of Religion, and worship of God, but also *in uniformitate*, in uniformite of outward order and ceremony of God's service'.[41] Of course we face the same dilemma concerning the extent to which court sermons reflected, or influenced, royal policy; the week after Neile's Easter sermon of 1614, Norwich Spackman preached at Whitehall that God 'will not have a bended knee, but an upright heart...not prostrated bodies but humbled soules'.[42] Yet James certainly wanted his Scottish subjects to have a bended knee; he first suggested to a Scottish General Assembly in 1616 that the Kirk prescribe kneeling for communion, a policy initiative which eventually bore fruit with the Five Articles of Perth of 1618.[43] In 1618 both the Calvinist Morton and the Arminian Buckeridge published works as part of a Jacobean propaganda offensive in defence of ceremonies.[44] James contributed to this campaign himself with his *Meditation upon the...XXVII Chapter of St Matthew* of 1620, where he insisted that God taught that we were 'to worship him and his onely Sonne as well with our bodies...as with our soules' and condemned 'our foolish superstitious Puritanes, that refuse to kneele at the receiving of the blessed Sacrament'.[45]

To what extent, then, did the Jacobean regime push for ceremonial uniformity? Practices varied considerably from place to place and time to time, depending on who was in charge at the local level and what sorts of initiatives they felt willing—or able—to undertake. There is a considerable amount of evidence from the church court records, however, to belie the notion that the Jacobean regime was indifferent to ceremonial conformity. In 1605 the inhabitants of Oldham in Lancashire were collectively charged with not kneeling at communion; in nearby Manchester in 1622 some twenty-four parishioners were presented for refusing to kneel.[46] In 1611 John Bradford of Thurlaston, Leicestershire, was excommunicated for refusing to kneel. Sixty-three parishioners of All Saints, Northampton refused to kneel for communion at Easter 1614 in protest against the installation of the new conformist vicar, David Owen, in succession to the Puritan preacher Robert Catelin; at Ashby-de-la-Zouch, Leicestershire, the following year, the vicar rejected 100 parishioners who would not kneel.[47] Sometimes prosecutions were undertaken by private individuals or members of the congregation who were displeased with their minister's actions or angry with the Puritans in their midst.[48] Sometimes an enforcement drive was initiated by a ceremonialist divine. When Neile moved to Lincoln in 1614, he bore down heavily on over sixty ministers for nonconformity, among them a young John Cotton of Boston who was later to make a name for himself in New England.[49] On occasion a ceremonialist might find local circumstances conspired against an effective enforcement campaign. Robert Sibthorpe found it difficult to enforce conformity in his respective livings of St Giles and then St Sepulchre in the notoriously Puritan town of Northampton in the 1610s; he had far fewer problems, however, when he moved to nearby Brackley in 1622.[50] Yet the prosecution for ceremonial nonconformity under James was not insignificant. One study of the court records for the archdeaconry of Nottinghamshire has revealed that there were eighteen citations for not kneeling at communion between 1605 and 1617, compared to just fourteen between 1630 and 1642 (during what is normally thought of as being the more repressive regime of Charles I). In the same archdeaconry there were forty citations for sermon gadding or unlicensed preaching between 1605 and 1610, the same number as in 1630–40.[51]

Ecclesiastical court records show that the laity and the clergy did not always get along. The vast majority of conflicts were relatively minor—a reflection, perhaps, of a generalized but low-intensity anticlericalism. Yet it was the Puritan clergy who were the most confrontational. Indeed, they saw it as their responsibility to be so: for Jesus had said that he 'came not to send peace, but a sword...to set a man at variance against his father, and the daughter against her mother, and the daughter in law against her mother in law'.[52] William Perkins, the great Elizabethan Puritan theologian, had urged the godly to 'separate and withdraw' themselves 'from all ungodly and unlawfull societies of men', for 'their society is not of God but of the devil, and they that are of this society, can not be of the holy communion of Saints'.[53] Parishioners did not always enjoy listening to moralizing sermons. They certainly did not relish being singled out for their personal sins in front of the whole congregation, as could sometimes happen.[54] Yet some parishioners also resented Puritan ministers playing fast and loose with the prayer book service, refusing to wear the surplice, or allowing people to stand for communion. Godly parishioners, on the other hand, might resent conformist clergymen who were unedifying preachers, but who nevertheless forced them to kneel for communion or tried to baptize their children with the sign of the cross.

Tensions between the godly and the profane, between conformists and nonconformists, have been documented for the England of the 1580s and 1590s, and by the late Elizabethan period a powerful, negative stereotype of the censorious, hypocritical, and inherently disloyal Puritan had already begun to emerge, fuelled by sermon, print, and stage.[55] It was a stereotype that some people readily bought into. In 1598, when some of the parishioners of Mapperton, Dorset, petitioned against their nonconformist curate and his supporters, they complained about how the 'puritans' went about 'to steal away the hearts of the people by their stained reformations, and also to deprive our queen of her due obedience, backbiting their superiors and condemning their brethren, disquieting the Church and abusing the office of godly preaching'.[56] So entrenched had the view of the hypocritical Puritan become by 1602 that not only were Puritans called hypocrites, one diarist observed, but a hypocrite was called 'a puritan'.[57]

There is no reason to believe that such tensions were becoming more pronounced under James. They certainly did persist, however, and further reinforce the point that Jacobean England was not a con-sensual religious society. In Dorset in the summer and early autumn of 1606 three libels circulated condemning the Puritans for being not only kill-joys—'All honest recreations and merriments they blame'—but also disloyal: 'For what our king commands, that they do deny, | Yea praying, kneeling and standing all these they defy.'[58] A similar libel, supposedly from a 'plaine Protestante to the precise Puritan', was composed in Cheshire about the same time (though it is unclear whether it circulated). 'I confesse my selfe to be sinfull, wheras thou Hipocrite takest vpon thee to be sinlesse, Thou thankest god thou art not as I am an open synner, And I thank god I am not as thou art a secret Desembler', it opens, and goes on to condemn Puritans not only for hypocrisy and disloyalty to the crown, but for being socially divisive, uncharitable towards the poor, lacking in mercy, and ene-mies to popular culture. 'So god loue me as I hate a Puritane,' our author proclaimed; 'the verie name is so odiouse to my eares.'[59] You will find the Puritan 'Proud and Ambitious | Unchaste Avaritious... Ignorant and hatefull | Awdacious Ungratefull', one early seventeenth-century manuscript poem claimed: 'A formall hypocrite...A loathsome animall'.[60] Indeed, there are numerous anti-Puritan libels from the Jacobean period, most of them the product of local squabbles between Puritan and anti-Puritan factions. At Nottingham, where a libel of 1618 denounced the 'Pure secte that sprang from hell' who 'leave the Church to Conventicle', the clash centred around rival factions within the local government: the libellers were a former mayor, local clergy, a goldsmith, and some ancient gentry; the libelled, another former mayor and his son (a zealous clergyman), a local parson, a draper, and a respectable local woman. At Stratford in 1619–20 there were a series of libels against the Puritans who ran the town government and controlled the local pulpit: 'these men...keepe the pooer in awe', one read; 'O lord doe then revenge the poor, I and their right again to them restore, I have these hypocrites mischeife bread', for if 'their minister...continue longe' and 'not make amends for this wronge, he shall never gett the people's love'. Some communities saw clashes over maypoles. Stratford did in September 1620, when the authorities' decision to take down a maypole erected at the town fair provoked a riot as a crowd of some forty or so gathered to set it up again. When John Band tried to cut down the maypole erected in the churchyard at East Brent, Somerset, in 1615, a crowd of women and children tried to stop him, and he had to draw his sword to frighten them away.[61]

James did try to alleviate some of the tensions by coming out in support of popular pastimes on Sundays and holidays. As he journeyed through Lancashire in August 1617 on his way back from Scotland, the inhabitants of Myerscough presented him with a petition complaining that the Lancashire JPs had issued orders against lawful recreations on the Sabbath. Lancashire was an unusual county: it had a strong Puritan presence, but it also contained many Catholic recusants, and for many years the local authorities had been struggling in their efforts to enforce regular church attendance. In August 1616 the local magistrates at the Lancaster assizes had therefore issued a series of orders designed to compel Sunday observance: most of these related to not working on the Sabbath, though the seventh order stipulated that there be 'no pipinge, Dancinge, bowlinge, beare or bull baitinge or any other profanation upon any Saboth Day in any parte of the Day: or upon any festival day in tyme of Devine service'. What irked James was the fact that local JPs had taken it upon themselves to change the law of the land; he also believed that Puritan rigour was counterproductive and most likely driving people away from church. He therefore had the local bishop, Morton of

Chester, draft a declaration to be read in Lancashire parish churches outlining what recreations would be allowed on a Sunday.

In many respects, James's 'Declaration...Concerning Lawfull Sports' of 1617 (or Book of Sports, as it is typically known) was a conventional sabbatarian document. It prohibited bearbaiting, bull-baiting, interludes, and bowling, because these were already forbidden by law, ordered parish officials to present any who used lawful recreations before divine service had ended, and debarred recusants completely from engaging in such sports; but it stipulated that 'no lawful Recreation' should be barred after divine service, on the grounds that 'the common and meane sorte of people' needed exercise to 'make theire bodies more able for warrs' and would otherwise just head straight for the alehouse after church and engage in 'idle and discontented speeches'. In his preface, however, James chose to attack the 'puritanes and precise people' for trying to stop lawful recreations in Lancashire, while later in the document he urged the bishop of the diocese either to make 'all the puritans and precisions...to conforme [them] selves or to leave the Cuntrie according to the lawes of our Kingdome and Canons of our Church'. In 1618 James reissued the Book of Sports, with minor alterations—'May-games, Whitsun-ales and Morris-dances; and the setting up of Maypoles and other sports therewith used' were added to the list of lawful recreations—and made it national, ordering the clergy throughout the country to read the declaration in their parish churches.[62]

If the Book of Sports was intended to defuse local tensions, it backfired. In some areas champions of Sunday sports appealed to it as a way of legitimizing their hostility to local Puritans. At Allbriton in Staffordshire in November 1618, for example, a group with 'drums and guns' gathered outside a church while parishioners were attending evening prayers, 'shot off their pieces, and cried, "Come out, ye Puritans, come out".' At Lea Marston in Warwickshire that same month several people came to church wearing 'fools coats', stayed for a while, but then left before the service was over and rushed off to the local alehouse where they 'tabred and danced the whole time'.[63] What eased tensions was the fact that few bishops seemed interested in trying to enforce the Book of Sports. Indeed, Abbot prohibited his clergy from reading it and persuaded the king to withdraw his order that it be read in church.[64] This, of course, meant that things were back to square one. In 1624 Susan Kent of Wylye, Wiltshire, complained that her vicar's moralizing, preaching, and catechizing did not leave enough time for dancing on Sunday afternoons, as allowed by the

Book of Sports, protesting: 'We had a good parson here before but now we have a puritan.'[65]

* * *

What then, finally, to make of the Jacobean Church? Consensus is surely the wrong word to use to describe the religious complexion of England in the early seventeenth century. There were significant differences of opinion—not only about how to worship and about how salvation was attained, but also how far conformity should be enforced and also about the sort of threat those who chose not to conform were perceived to pose. We are left with a king who can be read (and could during his reign be read) in different ways. A case can be made that he was broadly tolerant, concerned more about obedience to royal authority than strict conformity, that he embraced competing theological different factions within the Church while sustaining the Elizabethan vision for the Church, which was broadly Calvinist if not as committedly predestinarian as some of its Calvinist clerics would have desired. On the other hand, a case could be made that it was he who undermined the previous Calvinist near-monopoly of the Church by promoting Arminians and avant-garde conformists, that he put into positions of authority in the Church men who were often far from tolerant of Puritanism and were keen to enforce ceremonial conformity, and that his regime (and indeed the king himself) helped to perpetuate and further promote a rhetoric of anti-Puritanism that was to fuel religious rivalries and bigotry at the local level.

None of what has been said necessarily detracts from James's achievement. Given the tricky nature of his religious inheritance, one could argue that he did a masterful job in keeping things together in the way that he did. There was to be no repeat of the Presbyterian challenge to the Church that Elizabeth had faced in the 1580s, and there was not to be the crisis in the Church that was to confront Charles by the end of the 1630s. From this perspective, one might suggest that the Jacobean balancing act in the Church—delicate though that balance might have been—was a striking success. James might have bumbled along at times, made mistakes at others; he might initially have let his Scottish experiences colour his reading of the situation in England; he might have been given to the occasional overblown rhetorical outburst lambasting the Puritans. But he never quite put his rhetoric into practice, and despite an initial wave of persecution and sporadic subsequent conformity drives in particular locations, by and large there was considerable flexibility in the

Jacobean Church. This proved to be a regime that showed a willingness to indulge difference, a readiness (on occasion) to turn a blind eye.[66] Having said that, it is clear that James did not solve any of the religious problems that he inherited. At best he contained them. Some of the policies he pursued may well have exacerbated them.

5

One Good Steward Would Put All in Order

The English courtier and writer Sir John Harington, observing at the time of James's accession how 'England...of Late is bankrupt grown', punned that 'one good STEWARD would put All in Order'.[1] England was not quite bankrupt in 1603. Elizabeth had died with debts of around £420,000, but much of this was covered by the triple subsidy voted by Elizabeth's last parliament in 1601 that was still being collected. Nevertheless, royal revenues had declined dramatically over the course of the sixteenth century, due to the failure to update the valuations of crown lands, wardships, customs, and subsidies in an inflationary era. By 1602 it has been estimated that the crown's ordinary revenue—at £357,617—was 40 per cent less in real terms than it had been when Henry VII died in 1509. The fact that the propertied classes were allowed to evaluate their own net worth for taxation purposes led to serious underassessment, and as men dropped off the subsidy books (either through death or impoverishment) they were not fully replaced by those who had inherited wealth or were rising in society. Whereas at the beginning of Elizabeth's reign a single parliamentary subsidy had brought in over £137,000, by 1588–9 it was worth just £105,000 and by 1601 a mere £76,000. Furthermore, the military revolution that was sweeping across Europe was resulting in longer and more expensive wars, making it increasingly difficult for governments to raise by consent the levels of taxation necessary to win them—which explains why the new system of warfare created pressure for constitutional change across Europe and led to erosion of the traditional system of representative estates in many European monarchies. The Elizabethan regime had just about got by thanks to the sale of monastic lands, but now those lands had run out.[2] Harington was correct, then, to point to a serious problem. However, his optimism was to prove misplaced; whereas Elizabeth had shown a keen awareness of the financial limitations of the English crown, James proved not to be the good steward hoped for and soon piled up the debts.

* * *

MPs found it difficult to understand how James could be short of money, given that there was now 'no war with Spain, no war in Holland, no army on the Scottish border'.[3] Not all the problems were of James's own making. He had expenses Elizabeth did not. He was married with children: the setting up of a separate establishment for Prince Henry, for example, cost £25,000 per year. As a king of Scotland who resided (and was expected to reside) full-time in England, he had to have some Scottish advisors at court, and these had to be compensated. Removing the royal family from Scotland alone cost £10,000, Elizabeth's funeral £20,000, his royal entry into London a further £10,000, and entertaining royal ambassadors £40,000, while he needed to re-equip the royal wardrobe with appropriate attire for himself and his male servants after half a century of female rule. Securing the peace in Ireland and on the Continent also cost money: he spent £600,000 on the army in Ireland in the first five years of his reign and £26,000 per year maintaining English garrisons in a number of Dutch towns. Nor did MPs fully appreciate the extent to which the real value of royal revenues was being eroded by inflation. What they did notice was James's extravagance. Whereas in 1603 pensions, fees, and annuities for crown officials cost in total £27,900, by 1608 the cost had risen to over £48,000, by 1614 it was just short of £105,000, and by 1616–17 £116,000. In 1607, at a time when his own debts were mounting, James gave £44,000 to three courtiers—Viscount Haddington, Lord Hay, and the earl of Montgomery (the first two Scots)—to pay off their debts. James's generosity towards his Scottish courtiers caused particular resentment: 'The Scotchmen are but beggars yet, | Although their begginge was not small', penned one wit; 'But now a Parliament doth sitte, | A subsidy shall pay for all'. By 1610 James had given his Scottish followers some £90,000 in gifts and more than £10,000 in pensions.[4]

There were three ways of improving the king's financial position: by increasing the yield from traditional sources of revenue, introducing economies, or acquiring new sources of income. Better management could have increased the revenues from crown lands; despite widespread alienations under the Tudors, the crown estate at the beginning of the seventeenth century still had potential for revenue augmentation. Yet the crown appeared to believe that reform would be impractical, and preferred to reward courtiers and officials with grants of crown lands under favourable leases rather than risk alienating existing clients and tenants by making them pay a fair market rent. In the meantime, it continued to sell land to raise cash: between 1603 and 1613, James raised £681,953 through the sale of lands with an antiquated (below market value) annual rental of £26,809, a short-term gain for a long-term loss.[5] In 1604 Lord Treasurer Dorset introduced a new book of rates, bringing the customs valuations in line with inflation, and in addition leased out the collection of customs for a seven-year period for an annual fee of £112,400 (increased to £120,000 in 1607). The Great Farm, as it was called, was so successful that it was renewed in 1611 for £136,000 p.a. and in 1614 for £140,000 p.a.[6]

The king could try to milk more from feudal dues, such as purveyance and wardship, though this would be unpopular. There were complaints already by November 1605 that 'the people' were 'more heavily burdened than under the late Queen', since the king spent so much time in the country, where local farmers were 'obliged to furnish beasts and waggons for transporting the Court from place to place' and 'forced to supply provisions at low prices'; Elizabeth had at least 'insisted that her officers should requisition no more than necessary, but now', the Venetian ambassador observed, 'the officers exact twice as much as is required and sell the surplus at high prices...enriching themselves and ruining the peasants'.[7] Two bills against purveyance were introduced in 1606, but purveyance was too valuable to the crown, and both were rejected.[8] Elizabeth's Lord Treasurer Burghley had realized that wardship was resented, and had made no attempt to increase its yield in line with inflation: in fact, the income from this source fell from £20,000 to £14,000 over the course of the reign. But Salisbury (who was appointed Lord Treasurer in May 1608) felt he had no option but to insist on a realistic valuation of the properties; by his death in 1612 wardships were bringing in over £23,000 and by the end of the reign nearly £40,000.[9]

The government also tried to raise more money by imposing an extra duty on luxury goods. Impositions—as they were called—had been levied in the past, but usually as a short-term, emergency measure, and their legal status remained unclear. In 1606 a Levant merchant named John Bate refused to pay the duty on his imported currants on the grounds that it had not been sanctioned by parliament. Bate's Case came before the Court of Exchequer, where Chief

Baron Fleming ruled in favour of impositions on the basis that they fell within the king's 'absolute power'. 'All customs', Fleming argued, were 'but the effects and issues of trade and commerce with foreign nations', and 'all commerce and affairs with foreigners' were 'made by the absolute power of the king'. With regard to whether the king could tax a subject's goods without consent of parliament, Fleming adjudged that this was 'not here the question', since this impost was 'not upon a subject' but 'upon Bates as a merchant' who imported goods into England, and that 'at the time when the impost was imposed...they were the goods of the Venetians', neither 'the goods of a subject nor within the land'.[10] It was a questionable distinction, since importers passed on the costs of any duties imposed to the English consumer. Moreover, armed with the precedent, in 1608 the government issued a new book of rates levying impositions on a broader range of luxury goods, including now exports as well as imports. By 1610 impositions were bringing in a total of £70,000 per year, a not inconsiderable sum when one considers that over the course of his reign James received a total of only £900,000 in parliamentary grants (an average of just £41,000 per year).[11]

Such efforts were not enough to fix the problem, however. Even with the parliamentary grant of 1606 worth £400,000, expenditure was outstripping income. By 1608 the public debt had risen to over £1,000,000, and although Salisbury succeeded in getting this down to £300,000 by 1610, there was an annual deficit of £50,000. Moreover, both the debt and the deficit looked set to increase, because of the need for a separate establishment for Prince Henry upon his investiture as Prince of Wales and because there was the possibility of a war in Cleves.[12] What was needed was not just an additional grant of supply, but a radical restructuring of the way the monarchy was financed.

The Great Contract

Salisbury proposed sacrificing certain prerogative revenues in return for an annual grant of parliamentary taxation. He and his colleagues at the Exchequer worked out the basics of their scheme over the summer and autumn of 1609 and were finally ready to put the idea of the Great Contract, as it became known, before parliament when it reconvened in February 1610. Salisbury documented the crown's desperate need for money in a speech before the Lords on the 14th, explaining that the king's payments exceeded receipts by £200,000, and that the government was asking therefore for 'both money and revenue', to 'put the King out of debt' and to 'have sufficient supply to maintain and support his…annual charge'. At a conference of both Houses the following day, Salisbury offered a detailed review of the crown's debts, revenues, and expenditures before urging parliament 'to consider of some such supply as may make this state both safe and happy', promising in return to grant them 'any reasonable request for the public good'. It was left to the Chancellor of the Exchequer Sir Julius Caesar to clarify in the Commons on the 20th that the king wanted a grant of taxation worth £600,000, to clear his debts, and an annual revenue of £200,000, while Salisbury pressed the same case in the Lords four days later.[13]

The Commons jumped quickly to discuss their grievances. They fixed at first on the recent publication of a legal textbook called *The Interpreter* by the Regius Professor of Civil Law at Cambridge University, Dr John Cowell.[14] The work had appeared in 1607 and was not a philosophical treatise but an extensive legal dictionary. However, under the headings 'King', 'Parlament', 'Praerogative of the King', and 'Subsidie' Cowell had written that the king was 'above the Law by his absolute power' and 'might make lawes of himselfe', that the liberties of the subject were not rights but privileges held at the king's discretion, and that subsidies were a tribute paid to the king in return for him graciously allowing his subjects to participate in the legislative process.[15] What was worrying was that such ideas appeared to have the backing of those in high places. Cowell had dedicated his book to Archbishop Bancroft, while Salisbury's former chaplain Samuel Harsnett, now bishop of Chichester, had recently preached a sermon at Whitehall arguing that Christ's injunction 'Render unto Caesar' meant that subsidies were not gifts but duties. Most disturbingly, James himself was reported to have said certain things over dinner in derogation of the common law, 'highly extolling the Civill Law before it' and approving of Cowell's book.[16]

The government, eager for parliament not to get distracted from the main task of sorting out the crown's finances, rushed to condemn *The Interpreter*—though not the theory of royal absolutism. Thus Salisbury told the Lords on the morning of 8 March that although, by 'the law of this realm', James had 'as absolute power as ever any monarch in this kingdom', the king did not wish his power to be discussed and took exception to Cowell's book. That afternoon Salisbury informed the Commons that James thought Cowell had been 'too bold with the common laws of the realm' and that it was 'absurd' to suggest 'that the king may take subsidies without the consent of his people'; nevertheless, Salisbury insisted, James took himself 'to be beholding to no elective power', since he derived his 'greatness from the loins of his ancestors, from the law of nature, of nations, and from the laws of the realm'.[17]

James clarified his own position in a speech to parliament on 21 March, which was subsequently published by the king's printer. It was a brilliant attempt at damage limitation. Acknowledging that he had made some indiscreet observations in private over dinner, he proclaimed that he greatly admired the common law, had no intention of changing 'the ancient forme of this State...by the absolute power of a King', and condemned Cowell's *Interpreter*. It was true, he continued, that kings ruled by divine right and had god-like powers, but in settled kingdoms kings set down their minds by laws and were obliged to rule according to these laws, as they promised to do at their coronation. Referring to Harsnett's recent sermon, James insisted that what the bishop had said 'of a King's power in *Abstracto*' was 'most true in Divinitie', although if he [James] had been in his place, after speaking 'as a Divine' about 'what was due by the Subjects to their Kings in generall', he would have 'concluded as an Englishman' and exhorted his subjects 'to consider how to helpe such a King as now they had', 'in a setled state of a Kingdome', 'according to the ancient forme, and order established in this Kingdome'. James nevertheless remained adamant that it was 'Sedition in Subjects, to dispute what a King may do in the height of his power', and he would not allow his 'power to be disputed upon'.[18] One contemporary reported that the king's speech was 'to the great Contentment of all Parties', especially the conclusion 'that howsoever the Soveraignty of Kings was absolute in general, yet in particular the Kings of England were restrained by their Oath and Priviledges of the People', although he conceded that 'the most strictly religious' wished that James had been 'more spareing in...comparing the Deity with Princes Soveraignty'. James issued a proclamation suppressing *The Interpreter* on 25 March 1610.[19]

The Commons also addressed the issue of whether the king could levy impositions without the consent of parliament and proceeded to appoint a committee to determine if the precedents applied by the judges in Bate's Case were sound. James was furious, and sent a message via the Speaker on 11 May ordering the Commons not to engage in 'any disputation touching the prerogative...in the case of impositions', since that had been 'determined by judgment in the proper court'. Thomas Wentworth, the son of the Elizabethan parliamentarian Peter Wentworth, protested that they were not trying to reverse the judgment in Bate's Case, but insisted that no other man in England was 'bound by that judgment' and that the Commons had the right to examine the legality of impositions; they might conclude that they were lawful, but if they were not allowed to 'dispute the prerogative', then they might as well 'be sold for slaves'.[20] James summoned both Houses to Whitehall on 21 May and warned them it was 'not lawful... to dispute what a king may do'. Parliament could complain about particular inconveniences or irregularities, he said, but not 'go to the root and dispute my prerogative'; all kings, he continued, had the power to lay impositions, and it was no argument to say that because a king might abuse his powers his powers should be limited. 'You must not set such laws as make the shadows of kings and dukes of Venice', he proclaimed; only 'papists and puritans were ever of that opinion'. If they had 'a good king', they were 'to thank God'; if 'an ill king', he was sent as 'a curse to the people', but prayers and tears were their only weapons: 'If a king be resolute to be a tyrant, all you can do will not hinder him. You may pray to God that he may be good and thank God if he be.'[21]

It was a powerful speech, which showed James at the height of his oratorical powers. Yet it had alarming implications, since James seemed to be arguing that there were no safeguards against an abuse of power by the king. Chamberlain reported that the speech 'bred generally much discomfort; to see our monarchical powre and regall prerogative strained so high'.[22] Wentworth said the speech left him 'exceeding sad and heavy'. Sir John Fortescue, the greatly revered medieval English jurist and constitutional theorist, Wentworth continued, had held that 'the difference between England and France' was 'that by the law of England no imposition can be made without assent of parliament', and if it were 'sedition to dispute what a king may do', then all the law books of England were seditious, 'for they have ever done it'. Nicholas Fuller said that although the king was 'very wise', he was 'a stranger to this government', did not know the English precedents, and had got his English history wrong.[23] The Commons drew up a remonstrance, which was read to the king at Greenwich on the 25th, saying they held it 'an ancient... and undoubted Right of Parliament, to debate freely, all Matters which do properly concern the Subject', and if this 'Freedom of Debate' were 'once foreclosed, the Essence of the Liberty of Parliament' would be 'dissolved'.[24] James took time to consider his reply, but later that day told a delegation of MPs that their position was based on a 'mistaking' and 'a jealous interpretation' of what he had said, insisting that he would not meddle with their property rights nor 'impose upon lands and goods, but only upon merchandize imported and exported and that only in parliament', and that 'he never meant to take away any of [the Commons'] liberties', which he hoped they 'would not abuse'.[25]

The issues at stake were too important for the Commons to be fobbed off so easily, and the House spent two weeks discussing impositions in late June and early July. Fuller kicked off the debate on 23 June by listing various statutes placing legal limitations on the crown and insisting that the king had to follow the law and could not take any part of his subjects' lands and goods without the consent of parliament.[26] In a lengthy speech delivered on 28 June, Thomas Hedley contended that the laws of the kingdom protected the goods and lands of subjects 'against the absolute power and prerogative of the king', that the king could alter neither the law nor property, and that 'all new impositions, taxes, and charges upon the people' were 'to be set only in parliament'. Hedley then proceeded to argue that England's happiness lay in 'the right composition and mixture' of the 'liberty of the subjects' and 'the sovereignty of the king'. England enjoyed 'the blessings and benefits of an absolute monarchy and of a free estate', he continued, citing Tacitus, the great classical theorist of republicanism. Liberty and sovereignty were not incompatible: 'this ancient liberty of the subject in England' had always upheld 'the sovereignty of the king' and made him 'able to stand of himself without the aid of any neighbor princes or states and so to be an absolute King which dependeth immediately upon God'. Security in their goods made the English people wealthy and gave them the courage to defend their liberty and their monarch, whereas without this security they would grow poor and base-minded like peasants in other countries and not be fit to be soldiers. It was for this reason that it had always 'been the ancient policy of this kingdom to keep the commons in wealth and courage in time of peace, to be able to supply the king with men and money in time of war'. Hedley concluded by proclaiming that 'this absolute power of imposing' was 'contrary to...Magna Carta' and 'the common law of England'.[27]

William Hakewill said he had originally accepted the ruling in Bate's Case, but having been appointed by parliament to search the Exchequer records, he found that the precedents applied were not strong enough 'to maintain the Judgement given'. Hakewill did not dispute the king's absolute power; indeed, he acknowledged that the king did have an absolute power to *restrain* trade, 'upon special reasons'—for example, to prohibit trade that might serve to enrich an enemy or to stop exports that might rob England of 'such a Commodity' as might 'not be spared'. But he denied that the king might lay impositions by this absolute power. The king had to protect merchants in trade, by clearing the sea of pirates and other enemies and by maintaining ambassadors to treat with foreign nations, and so it was reasonable that he should impose customs in order to meet 'this publique charge'. Yet the duty of customs given by common law was 'a sum certain', and was 'not to be increased at the King's pleasure by way of Imposition'. In the 480 years—and twenty-two reigns—since the Conquest, impositions had been laid only six times: they were all during times of 'great and apparent necessitie' brought about by war, they were moderate, and they were to endure only for a year or two. They were nevertheless unlawful and they were taken away 'upon complaint'. The present impositions were laid during peace time, and were 'to come to his Majestie, his Heires and Successors for ever'. Impositions, in Hakewill's mind, were illegal at common law and prohibited by various statutes dating back to Magna Carta. The ruling in Bate's Case, he feared, opened the door to more general taxation without parliamentary consent. 'In all other Nations of the world, where the Merchant is subject to impositions at the King's pleasure, the Landlord, the Farmer, the Artificer, the very Plowman, and all others are in like sort subject to Taxes and burdens, when the King pleaseth.' In short, arguments in defence of impositions were not only weak, they were of 'dangerous consequence': 'For by the same reasons, Taxes within the Land', imposed at the pleasure of the king without the consent of parliament, 'may be as well proved to be lawfull'.[28]

Sir Francis Bacon, now Solicitor General, denied that impositions were a tax and insisted that the king's power to levy them on both exports and imports was upheld by 'the fundamental laws of this kingdom'.[29] Sir Robert Hitcham went so far as to maintain that 'upon occasion of a sudden and unexpected war', the king might 'not only lay impositions, but levy a tax within the Realme, without assent of Parliament'—a position which Hakewill was quick to condemn as likely 'to bring us into bondage'.[30] But those who defended the king's position lost the debate. A bill unanimously passed the House 'that by the laws of England no impositions could be lawfully laid by the King upon the subjects' goods but by consent in parliament'.[31]

Whether James could afford to forgo impositions would depend on what other sources of income might be forthcoming from Salisbury's proposed Great Contract. Salisbury had offered ten royal concessions, including the abolition of purveyance, in exchange for an annual grant of £200,000. The Commons, however, also wanted wardship abolished, which was not on the original list. Although Salisbury initially pressed for additional compensation if wardship were to be included, an agreement was eventually struck before the start of the summer recess in July that the Commons would make an annual grant of £200,000 in return for the abolition of purveyance, wardship, and other prerogative revenues. However, James would only promise to assent to a bill not to levy any *new* impositions unless sanctioned by parliament. The Commons remained unsatisfied and voted just one subsidy and one fifteenth, worth around £107,000— nowhere near the £600,000 Salisbury had asked for to clear the royal debts.[32]

Although no vote had been taken on the Great Contract, the lower house was known to be deeply divided, with perhaps only a small majority in favour. During the summer recess, therefore, MPs were encouraged to sound out the views of their constituents, who appeared to be strongly opposed to an annual levy of taxation. When parliament reconvened in October, many peers and MPs delayed their return or simply stayed away, unwilling to be associated with the Great Contract; in the Commons less than 100 of the 497 members were present. As the Commons dragged their feet, James chastised them for their dilatoriness, reminding them that he still needed another £500,000 to cover his debts in addition to the annual grant of £200,000. Some wanted impositions included as part of the Contract, but James said he would need an equivalent revenue by way of compensation. With the mood of the lower house having shifted from scepticism to outright hostility, the Commons decided to inform James on 9 November they would proceed no further with the Great Contract.[33] A frustrated James complained to his Latin secretary Sir Thomas Lake on 20 November that MPs had made themselves 'a confederacy and bulwarke for the protection of all extravagant humors and conceipts among the people', that his 'dignity' and 'souveraynty' had 'been so tossed, questioned [and] censured', and 'himself...so disgraced as seldome had been offred to any Monarch', and that he could only surmise they were motivated by a desire 'to lay the foundations of a popular state'.[34] James sent a letter to the Commons repeating his offer to pass a bill restraining him or his successors from levying any new impositions in the future, but making it clear that he would not give up those that already existed.[35] This was too little for the Commons, and when they resumed the debate on supply on 23 November there was little enthusiasm. James's patience was now exhausted. He told Lake that even if parliament were at its next meeting to vote him a large supply, if it came with 'such taunts and disgraces' as had been 'uttered of him' of late—which were 'so scandalous reproachfull and intollerable', in his mind, as to reach 'very neere to the point of treason'—he would never accept it.[36] James prorogued parliament on 6 December, but it was never to meet again. He formally dissolved it on 9 February 1611. With the dissolution, the bill against impositions was lost.[37]

The Addled Parliament of 1614

James was left frustrated by his dealings with his first parliament. It would be wrong, however, to see the parliament of 1604–10 as a failure. The 1604 session saw the passage of seventy-two Acts, that of 1606 a further fifty-six, and the total legislative achievement of the parliament of 1604–10 was second only to that of the Reformation Parliament of 1529–36 which inaugurated the great break with Rome. Much constructive work had been done on the regulation of alehouses, the draining of fenland, and the reformation of corporations. Such evidence hardly suggests that the crown and parliament were finding it more difficult to work together following the accession of the new dynasty.[38] Yet tensions there had been—over ecclesiastical policy, finances, and the prerogative—and James had at times expressed views about monarchical authority that alarmed MPs. James himself was bitterly disappointed by the failure of the Union and the loss of the Great Contract, and by late 1610 had fallen out of love with English parliaments, complaining how the Commons had 'perilled and annoyed our health, wounded our reputation, emboldened all ill natured people, encroached upon many of our privileges and plagued our purse with their delays'.[39] During the 1610s he did his best to avoid calling parliament: between 1610 and 1621 parliament sat for just nine weeks, in 1614, although because it passed no legislation it was deemed, in fact, not to have been a parliament.

The 1610s were characterized by increasing factionalism at court, especially following the death of Salisbury in 1612, who had done much to keep such factionalism in check. There were two broad interests: the Howard faction, led by the earls of Northampton and of Suffolk, who tended to be against calling parliament and in favour of a pacific foreign policy in alliance with Spain; and a looser group centring around the earl of Pembroke and Archbishop Abbot, who were in favour of a militant Protestant foreign policy and thus keen for the king to deal with parliament. The royal favourite of the time, Robert Carr (Viscount Rochester from 1611 and earl of Somerset from 1613), was at first part of neither group, having been advised by his friend Sir Thomas Overbury to maintain his independence by playing the factions off against each other. However Carr then fell in love with Suffolk's daughter Frances Howard, the wife of Robert Devereux, 3rd earl of Essex. Frances sought a divorce from Essex, on the grounds of non-consummation. Overbury tried to prevent the marriage, but James appointed him ambassador to Russia to get him out of the way; when Overbury refused to accept the assignment, James had him dispatched to the Tower, where he was to die of what were said to be 'natural causes' in September 1613. Carr was able to marry Frances in December 1613, thereby bringing Carr firmly into the Howard camp.[40]

If James was going to avoid calling parliament he needed money. One project devised for the raising of revenues was the creation of the new title of baronet in 1611, to be sold for £1,095 each, the estimated cost of keeping thirty foot soldiers in Ireland for three years. Open to Catholics as well as Protestants—many with strong recusant connections did acquire the title—baronetcies thus served the additional function of implicitly tying their purchasers to the Protestant imperial enterprise in Ireland. By 1614 baronetcies had generated over £90,000, although James ignored his promise to issue a fixed number, leading inevitably to devaluation; by 1622 the price had fallen to a mere £220.[41] Nevertheless, the government was still struggling to make ends meet. At the time of Salisbury's death, the accounts showed an annual deficit of £160,000, and by 1613 the crown debt was again more than £500,000.[42]

What James needed was a lump sum that could help eradicate a significant chunk of the debt, and the most promising source seemed to be a dowry for the marriage of Henry, Prince of Wales, the heir to the throne. It would need to be a large dowry, however, something which only the wealthier dynasties of Europe could afford, and they were all Catholic. James had, in fact, been approached by Spain back in 1604 about the prospect of a match, although at the time none of the king's children was of marriageable age. Yet by 1612 Henry was turning eighteen and James's daughter Elizabeth sixteen, and it was time to find both of them partners. Royal marriages at this time were an important part of international diplomacy, and James came to feel that if he negotiated suitable matches he could advance his foreign policy objective of helping to promote peace in Europe, as well as gain a sizeable cash windfall for marrying his son.

Although there was no shortage of suitors for Elizabeth, in the end she was betrothed to a Protestant prince: Frederick V, Count Palatine of the Rhine and Elector of the Holy Roman Empire, as part of a diplomatic alliance concluded in the spring of 1612 with the Protestant Union, an association of German princes and free cities under the leadership of the Palatinate. At the same time James was hoping to build a closer understanding with the Catholic powers of Europe through a Catholic match for Henry. The duke of Savoy was prepared to offer 700,000 crowns (£210,000) if Henry were to marry his daughter; France was said to be willing to top that with 800,000 crowns (£240,000) for a marriage with the six-year-old Princess Christine, the second daughter of Henri IV. The Prince of Wales himself would have preferred to marry a Protestant. In the end, plans were scuppered by the sudden death of Henry of typhoid fever in November 1612. In the meantime the match between Elizabeth and Frederick went ahead as planned: the couple were formally betrothed on 27 December and the wedding took place at the chapel at Whitehall on 14 February 1613, accompanied by widespread celebrations at court and in the City, including a spectacular fireworks display and other entertainments and a series of tournaments styled by one observer as 'Britaine's great Olympick games'.[43]

Marrying daughters costs money, so James's financial predicament was now more pressing than ever. He thus continued to pursue a French match, offering now his younger son Charles, who although only twelve was arguably a more suitable match because nearer the French princess's age. The majority of James's privy councillors were worried that a match with France, Scotland's old ally, would strengthen the Scottish presence at court. The Howard faction would have preferred a Spanish match, although relations with Spain had soured of late as a result of disputes over Virginia. The last thing Spain wanted, however, was to see England allied with France and the Protestant princes of Germany, and quickly dispatched Don Diego Sarmiento (better known by his later title, count of Gondomar) as ambassador to England. Those who wanted to defeat the French match had to convince James that he did not need France's money, and this required finding an alternative source of revenue. There were two possibilities: parliament, or Spain.

Some had been pressing James to call another parliament for a while. As early as the autumn of 1611 the Berkshire gentleman Sir Henry Neville had offered to 'undertake' to manage the Commons on James's behalf in return for being made Secretary of State. Neville put forward more detailed proposals to James in the summer of 1612, promising that if the king were to offer a certain number of concessions or 'graces' he (Neville) could guarantee to secure a supply. Yet although Neville offered to manage parliament, there is no evidence to suggest that he ever offered to manage the elections. Similarly, from May 1612 Bacon (who would finally achieve his long-term ambition of becoming Attorney General in 1613) had been urging the King to call parliament in order to raise supply and 'for the better knitting of the hearts of your subjects unto your Majesty', boasting that his credit with the lower house would enable him to carry the king's business. Bacon opposed Neville's scheme of offering concessions, but instead hoped through the use of patronage and electoral influence to create a court party in the Commons, insisting that the opposition that was present in the 1610 session was now dissolved. James stalled, but renewed outbreak of civil unrest in France in effect left James with no option. Ironically, it was Suffolk in the end who persuaded James to call parliament. Suffolk was no friend to parliaments, but as one of the commissioners of the Treasury he recognized how desperate the crown's financial situation had become. He also had other agendas: the calling of parliament would put on hold negotiations for a French match, while by spreading rumours of undertaking he hoped to ensure that the parliament would not be a success.[44] James finally issued writs of election on 19 February 1614, although rumours had already begun to fly: five days earlier the dean of St Paul's, John Donne, could report how it was 'taken ill, though it be but mistaken that certain men (whom they call undertakers) should presume either to understand the house before it sit, or to incline it then'.[45]

James did not follow Neville's undertaking scheme. The court, however, did do quite a lot to prepare for the session. Bacon schooled James on how he should present himself to parliament: he should begin his opening speech by talking about his daughter's marriage before raising the issue of money, make it clear that he did not intend to play the part of a merchant as in the last parliament (an allusion to the Great Contract scheme), and emphasize his love for parliaments.[46]

The council prepared certain bills of grace to be offered as concessions to try to induce the Commons to be supportive, following closely Neville's suggestions—although Neville never attended any council meetings and the council did not recommend him for the vacant secretaryship, which instead went to Sir Ralph Winwood. However, hearing that the counties were not well disposed to returning the king's servants, James panicked and urged privy councillors to use their influence to get 'men of credit' elected, leading to widespread suspicion of 'packing'. Overall, some 106 court officials were returned. Thomas Parry, Chancellor of the Duchy of Lancaster, returned fourteen courtiers and servants.[47]

Parliament opened on 5 April. Although in his speech from the throne James drew heavily on Bacon's suggestions, his opening gambit was very much his own. He decided to play the anti-popery card, bemoaning the recent 'great increase of Poperie', which he blamed on the fact that the laws were not being strictly enforced, alleging that in some counties JPs and other local officials actively sympathized with Catholics or were even church papists themselves. James was worried about the threat to royal authority such recalcitrance implied; there were added concerns about the Catholic threat following the assassination of Henri IV of France in May 1610 and the publication in 1613 of a book by the Jesuit Francisco Suarez insisting that kings ruled not by divine right but derived their power from the people and that tyrannical and heretical rulers could be overthrown by their subjects. Yet James's speech was also a sweetener, an attempt to warm MPs to his agenda by giving a sop to anti-Catholic sentiment in the House; James was to use the same tactic in Scotland to powerful effect during the same decade. With the Spanish ambassador, whom James had invited to attend, listening at the back, James insisted that he did not want 'any newe or more rigorouse lawes' against the Catholics and reiterated his opposition to religious persecution: no 'relygione or heresye', he said, 'was evere extirpated by violence or the swoarde', nor was persecution, in his opinion, 'a way of plantyng truthe'. He reported how, following the death of Prince Henry, he had married his daughter Elizabeth to a Protestant prince in order to guarantee the security of the Protestant succession, in case anything should happen to his younger son Charles in the future. But the marriage had been expensive, while there were ongoing security concerns in Ireland, and so he needed money. James then proclaimed that he would not bargain with parliament 'like a marchante'; he would 'expect loving contribushone for loving retribushone'. He was, however, willing to offer bills of grace, the details of which he would outline at a subsequent meeting.[48]

This meeting took place at the Banqueting House on 9 April, where James reiterated the points he had made four days earlier and emphasized that he wanted to make this 'a parleament of love', acknowledging that the last parliament had begun and ended 'with discorde' and that there had been 'misunderstandinge on bothe sydes'. He then had Lord Chancellor Ellesmere read a list of eleven proposed bills of grace plus three other reforms not yet drafted as legislation, although they addressed only minor grievances: Chamberlain described them as 'of no great moment'; the courtier MP Sir John Holles said that 'being lean and ill larded, [they] rather irk than please our appetites'.[49]

MPs were alarmed by the rumours that the court had 'undertaken' to influence the House and were far from reassured by James's insistence 'that if something of this sort had happened, it had not been under his commands'.[50] On the very first day of business they questioned whether Bacon should be allowed to take his seat, insisting it was unprecedented for the king's Attorney General to sit in the Commons; the only one ever to have done so was already a sitting member before being given the job. The House had to concede, however, that Bacon's election had been valid and agreed to let him to sit as a personal favour to the king, although they passed a resolution stipulating that in future no Attorney General would be allowed to serve as a member.[51] The Commons also set up a committee to look into the charges of undertaking: extensive investigations uncovered no firm evidence, save for Sir Thomas Parry at the election for Stockbridge (Hants), who was expelled from the House.[52]

Although Secretary Winwood moved for a subsidy early in the session (12 April), the Commons opted to postpone the debate until after it had had the chance to redress grievances. The main bone of contention proved once more to be impositions, and the House immediately revived its bill from 1610 that no impositions were to be laid without the authority of parliament. 'If the King may impose by his absolute power,' Christopher Brooke proclaimed in the debate following the second reading of the bill on 18 April, 'no man [could be] certain what he has, for it shall be subject to the King's pleasure.' Various members insisted that the judgment in Bate's Case had been 'erroneous' and had opened the floodgates to further impositions— over 1,300 according to Sandys's estimate.[53] James grew frustrated that the debate on impositions was distracting them from the main task at hand. In a speech before the House on 4 May he urged them 'to hasten my relief', remaining adamant that he would not relinquish impositions: it was 'absurd', he said, for them to think of taking away some of his existing revenue, when he was coming to them to ask for more funds. When he came to the English throne, he pointed out, he had kept the same counsellors and judges as Elizabeth, and they had told him that he had the 'right' to lay impositions; he promised he would never lay impositions 'upon homebred commodities, spent within the land', but 'to bar me from my right, to rob my crown of so regal a prerogative', he insisted, was 'mere obstinacy'.[54]

The fact that James was now claiming impositions as a 'right' set further alarm bells ringing for the Commons. 'Some other princes had imposed but never claimed any right', Sandys pronounced the next day, and had done so 'but for a few months', backing down 'at the prayer of the Commons'. However now impositions were 'made perpetual'. 'This liberty of imposing' in effect made the English 'bondmen', Sandys proclaimed, since it 'gives use but no propriety', and 'by the same reasons', the king might 'make laws without parliament'.[55] Members began to debate whether any other kings in Christendom had the right to impose. Several insisted that none did. Others claimed that it depended upon whether one was talking about hereditary or elective monarchies, although this in turn only opened a debate about the origins of kingly power and what constituted tyranny. On 21 May Sandys said that even in hereditary kingdoms the king had at first been elected, and came in 'by consent of people and with reciprocal conditions between king and people'; indeed, even 'a king by conquest' might be expelled by his subjects. The fact that 'the King of France may impose' did not mean 'the King of England may'. Besides, Sandys argued, the French king had usurped the power of imposing from the French estates, and this had resulted in a dramatic proliferation of impositions in France: 'the King of France and the rest of the imposing princes' did 'also make laws that will in short time bring all to a tyrannical course'—another contemporary account of the speech has Sandys saying 'so do our impositions daily increase in England as it is come to be almost a tyrannical government in England'—and 'the last great imposing prince' (i.e. Henri IV of France) had been assassinated.[56] Wentworth said that for laying impositions 'the French King was killed like a calf'.[57]

The Commons pressed for a conference with the Lords, believing that they needed the support of the upper house if they were to stand any chance of getting the king to listen. The Lords were not keen. Bishop Neile of Lincoln did not help matters by proclaiming that 'the matter of impositions' was 'a *noli me tangere*' ('touch me not') and that anyone who had 'taken the oath of supremacy and allegiance' could not 'with a safe conscience argue or dispute the King's prerogative' to lay them. A few days later Neile protested he was against having a conference with the Commons because he knew 'their spirits' and feared 'there will pass from them undutiful and seditious speeches not fit for us to hear'.[58] When MPs learned what Neile had said, they were outraged. Francis Ashley proclaimed there could be 'no greater offense...than to tax our loyalty and discretion'. Sir Dudley Digges agreed: if Neile said this sort of thing in public, he pondered, what did he say when he was alone with the king? John Hoskins recalled that Scotland and Germany had 'swept away greater miters than his', and urged the House 'to pass a bill to seize his bishopric for 7 years for his Majesty's supply'. Edward Duncombe and Roger Owen thought Neile's remarks were treasonous: it was 'Treason to kill any judge', but this was 'greater (if true) to rob us of our opinion of our loyalty'.[59] The Commons were all the more alarmed given that Neile was an anti-Calvinist and ceremonialist. It was 'unworthy' that such a man should have 'the King's ear too much', Fuller protested: 'in his diocese he had dealt hardly with all his clergy' and warned ministers that they would not get preferment if they preached twice on the Sabbath. Others confirmed how Neile had boasted that he never went to two sermons on a Sunday without sleeping during one of them. Neile had also 'raised great taxes on his clergy', imposing a benevolence on them when bishop of Lichfield and now again on his promotion to Lincoln. This made Neile guilty of popery, in Fuller's eyes, since 'he takes this papal authority to himself'.[60]

Neile at first tried to insist that his words had been misconstrued, and that he had said '*noli me tangere*' about himself. Nevertheless, the upper house eventually persuaded Neile to make an apology in the Lords at the end of the month, where he tearfully protested that he never intended his words to cause the Commons, 'whom he did highly esteem, any manner of offense'.[61] It hardly proved acceptable to the lower house. Owen complained that the words were 'not denied, only his intention excused', and moved for a subcommittee to consider how to proceed further against the bishop. Sir Thomas Roe thought Neile not only 'unfit for the King's ear' but even for 'the society of reasonable men'. Sir Walter Chute said he was willing 'to thrust himself into the mouth of the lion' in the service of the king, but 'he would never yield to give the King anything till we were righted in this'. He then delivered a rant against government financial corruption, warned that those who had tried to persuade the king not to call parliament in the first place 'would also labour to dissolve it', and urged the House 'to move the King not to dissolve the parliament till these offenses of the commonwealth were redressed', and only then would they seek 'to relieve his estate'.[62]

Chute's fears were soon confirmed. On 3 June the Speaker delivered a message from the king that unless the House 'forthwith proceed to treat of his supply' he would dissolve parliament. Members were stunned. Roe thought this 'a dissolution...of all parliaments'. Nicholas Hyde argued that if they gave money now it would be out of fear, whereas this was supposed to be 'a parliament of love'. Christopher Neville said that he was astonished by James's message and wanted to know what the king had done to deserve a supply: 'His bills of grace' were 'but mere titles and nothing else'. 'Would the King', he wondered, 'take from us the cedars of freedom and liberty under which the subjects of England were shadowed, and shroud us with these shrubs of bills of grace, O tempora! O mores! O miserable times when we see the commonwealth to groan under more grievous taxations than ever were.' Hoskins—perhaps at the prompting of the pro-Spanish Howard faction, who wanted to sabotage the session—insisted on the need to suppress impositions and take better care of crown lands and then had a go at the Scots, stressing 'that wise princes put away strangers', and reminded members 'of Vesperae Sicilianae'—Sicilian Vespers—an allusion to a rebellion in Sicily in 1282 against their foreign king, Charles of Anjou.[63]

Although a few were in favour of granting supply in order to save the session, most were not. At about 3 p.m. on 7 June the Chancellor summoned the Commons to attend the Lords and read the commission for dissolving parliament. Since the assembly had not passed one piece of legislation, the commission declared it not to have been a parliament, to allow certain statutes that otherwise would have lapsed to remain in force.[64] It had been an unruly session. James complained to the Spanish ambassador that the House of Commons was a body with 'no head' which 'voted without order, nothing being heard but cries, shouts and confusion', and that he was 'astonished' that his 'predecessors had consented to such a thing', though James added that having 'come to England as a stranger' and finding it 'thus when he came...he could not do without it'.[65] Yet although the Addled Parliament passed no legislation, it was not for the want to trying. A total of 116 bills were introduced, 104 of them in the Commons (forty-one of which received a second reading), with seven ultimately passing both Houses (though without receiving the royal assent)—not a bad work rate for just forty-three official days of business.[66]

The Addled Parliament failed in part because the court did not provide strong enough leadership. There were only four privy councillors in the Commons, while newly appointed Secretary Winwood was inexperienced. Courtiers tended to blame unruly spirits in the Commons for the failure: Sir Edward Waldegrave wrote that 'the breaking of this parliament was caused by some few burgesses who desired more to show their wits, and had more regard of their private ends than of the public good and welfare'.[67] James had Chute, Hoskins, Christopher Neville, and Wentworth sent to the Tower. Sandys, Owen, and several others were examined by the council and released on bond; a number of MPs, including Owen, were struck off the commissions of the peace. Yet it is also clear that elements close to the court—particularly Suffolk and Somerset—were out to disrupt the session. The failure of the Addled Parliament haunted James. He made those who had taken part in the conference on impositions produce their notes, which were then destroyed, while a couple of days after the dissolution James himself tore up all the bills and papers relating to the parliamentary session publicly in the banqueting chamber at Whitehall.[68] In a meeting with his privy council on 24 September 1615, he asked them to consider 'whether there were any means to provide for his...subsistence without a Parliament', for although 'he would not avoid a Parliament if he might see likelihood of comfort by it, knowing it to be anciently the way of his progenitors... he would rather suffer any extremity than have another meeting with his people and take an affront'.[69]

Politics without Parliament

The failure of the parliament left the crown in desperate financial straits: by May 1614 the royal debt stood at £680,000. With the winding up of Convocation the bishops decided to offer the king a voluntary gift of their best plate, or money in lieu, hoping their example would encourage wealthy laymen to do the same. Abbot gave £140, the bishop of London £120, the bishop of Winchester a cup of gold containing £100. Privy councillors followed the lead, with Secretary Winwood and Chancellor Ellesmere each giving £100. Soon £5,000 in money and plate had come in. Winwood approached the City of London for a loan of £100,000; the City refused, but instead gave a gift of £10,000. Abbot, who took credit for the initiative, thought such generosity proved 'our people generally love and honour the king, though perhaps his money seem not unto them so well employed sometimes as they desire'. In fact the bishops were not particularly generous, giving less than one quarter of their subsidy; in contrast, it was said that many rich laymen gave the equivalent of more than two subsidies.[70]

In July the court decided to extend the scheme nationwide. Bacon urged that they avoid any show of compulsion or 'pressing it by authority' and 'that the meaner and poorer sort of people be not at all touched or dealt with'.[71] The privy council sent out letters to every shire requesting a voluntary relief, yet despite the pretence that no man was to be pressed against his will, a list of contributors was sent to the king and if gifts were not forthcoming follow-up letters were sent to ask why.[72] Sometimes threats were made. In October 1614 the council wrote to the influential Bedfordshire peer and Lord Lieutenant of Huntingdonshire Oliver St John, Baron St John of Bletso, expressing concern about his 'coldnes' in promoting the benevolence and about the fact that his name was absent from 'the list of those free givers', warning him to be more 'watchfull' over himself, and urging him to take care 'to preserve his Majestie's gracious opinion' by speedily resuming 'the care of his busines'.[73] When the clergy of the diocese of Lincoln were less 'liberall' in their contributions than expected, Neile retaliated by informing them that they were no longer to enjoy exemption from providing arms for the county militias.[74] Another Oliver St John, this one from Marlborough in Wiltshire, penned an open letter to his local mayor—copies of which were widely circulated—insisting that the benevolence was 'against law, reason and religion': against medieval legislation stipulating that no aids or free grants were to be taken 'but by assent of all the Realme'; against reason, to expect people to relieve the king's wants when they did not know what they were or how much was needed; and against religion, because by imposing this benevolence the king violated the oath he took at his coronation 'for the mayntayning of the Lawes, Liberties, and Customes of his noble Realme'.[75] St John was tried in Star Chamber for slandering the king, the laws, parliament, and those who had paid the benevolence, fined £5,000, and sentenced to life imprisonment.[76] Yet despite such practices, the total sum raised was disappointing: only £66,100, less than one lay subsidy.[77]

The failure of the Addled Parliament saw the rise to dominance of the Howard faction at court. In July James made Suffolk Lord

Treasurer and his son-in-law Somerset Lord Chamberlain (to replace the recently deceased Northampton). Suffolk set on foot various projects to raise new sources of revenue for the crown. One involved levying fines on all new buildings within seven miles of London in violation of a proclamation of 1603. The greatest project of them all, however, was Alderman Cockayne's scheme to promote the finishing of woollen cloth in England for exportation to the Continent. Hitherto the English had exported unfinished cloth to the Netherlands, where it was finished and sold on at greatly enhanced prices; if granted a monopoly to export finished cloths, Cockayne calculated he could enrich the crown by £47,500 per year from increased customs. James duly issued a proclamation prohibiting the export of unfinished cloth, and when the Merchant Adventurers' Company, who controlled the trade, protested, he revoked their charter. The project backfired disastrously, however. English clothiers and dyers found they could not possibly finish as much cloth as had previously been exported in white, while the Dutch placed an embargo on the importation of all English cloth; although James modified the scheme to permit the export of some unfinished cloth, English trade and industry was badly dislocated, causing widespread hardship and provoking riots in the weaving centres of Wiltshire and Gloucestershire in 1616. In the summer of 1617 James allowed the Merchant Adventurers to redeem their former privileges at a price of £80,000 (he appears ultimately to have settled for £50,000), but the English cloth industry would remain in recession for many years to come.[78]

In the meantime the Howard family had been rocked by scandal. In the summer of 1615 James learned that Sir Thomas Overbury had almost certainly been poisoned and in the autumn Frances Howard was implicated in his murder. Further investigations led to the arrest and trial of both Frances and her new husband Somerset; both were found guilty in May 1616, and although James issued a pardon, both remained in the Tower until January 1622 and were never to return to court.[79] For the time being Suffolk survived the scandal, even though suspected by James of assisting his son-in-law Somerset in trying to suppress the initial investigations into Overbury's murder. Yet by now James's attentions were coming increasingly to be focused on an attractive newcomer at court, George Villiers, the son of a minor Leicestershire gentleman, who had first come to James's attention during the summer progress of 1614. Abbot and Pembroke saw in Villiers an opportunity to break the dominance of the Suffolk–Somerset duumvirate, and with the help of the queen managed in

April 1615 secure for the twenty-two-year-old the post of gentleman of the bedchamber, a knighthood, and an annual pension of £1000. As Somerset's position crumbled, Villiers rapidly emerged as the new royal favourite, becoming Master of the Horse in January 1616, Viscount Villiers in August of that year, earl of Buckingham in January 1617 and a privy councillor the following month, marquess of Buckingham in January 1618, and then Lord Admiral a year later. Buckingham became James's main companion and confidant, and the king made no secret of his feelings for him. In September 1617 James declared before the privy council that 'he loved the Earl of Buckingham more than any other man', and that as 'Christ had his John' so 'he had his George'. Yet Buckingham was never in a position to dominate the king's counsels: he never rose to the position of favourite minister and James kept all policy decisions to himself; and although Buckingham came to have an enormous influence over the distribution of patronage, which became a source of concern for contemporaries, it was probably never as great as it appeared, since James sometimes let the young earl take credit for what had been his own decision in order to enhance Buckingham's prestige at court.[80]

James continued to hope that his financial problems would be eased by securing a dowry for the marriage of Prince Charles. The French, however, were stalling, refusing now to offer more than 750,000 crowns, and so James began to consider the possibility of a match with Spain, who were ready to offer a larger dowry, although for the time being James remained suspicious that this was merely a ploy to scupper talks with France. With the marriage negotiations going nowhere fast, it looked likely that James would have to call another parliament in 1616. He was saved from this eventuality by the Dutch offer of £250,000 to buy back the Cautionary Towns of Brill and Flushing, which had been handed to England as security for debts incurred during the Elizabethan war with Spain; the sale also saved the crown £26,000 per year in garrison costs.[81]

Such was James's desperation for money that in March 1616 he bowed to pressure from the anti-Spanish faction to liberate Sir Walter Ralegh from the Tower to permit him to undertake a voyage to the Orinoco (in modern-day Venezuela) in search of the fabled gold of El Dorado. After several false starts, Ralegh's expedition finally set sail in August 1617, but proved a disaster: Ralegh himself fell seriously ill, his men seized the Spanish outpost at San Tomé (in direct violation of the commission by which they sailed) but found neither gold nor silver, and most of his fleet eventually deserted. Ralegh returned to England with the remnant of his force, was immediately placed under arrest and, under pressure from Spain, eventually executed in the Old Palace Yard at Westminster 29 October in accordance with the sentence originally meted out in November 1603. When he saw the executioner's axe, Ralegh jested with the sheriff that here was 'a sharp Medicine...a Physitian for all Diseases'.[82]

By now James had come to put all his hopes in a Spanish match. In March 1617 Sarmiento, now count of Gondomar, informed James that Spain's theologians had approved formal negotiations for a marriage treaty, and so James immediately sent Sir John Digby to Madrid to ask for a dowry of £600,000, and to settle for no less than £500,000. Yet James's reluctance to call a parliament meant that he was negotiating from a position of weakness. Aware that James had no other sources of money, in January 1618 Philip III of Spain eventually offered to pay the full sum of £600,000, but only if James revoked the penal laws against Catholics.[83]

The crown's financial situation continued to deteriorate: between the beginning of October 1617 and the end of September 1618 the royal debt rose from £726,320 to £900,000. Determined to avoid calling parliament, but with still no prospect of a dowry, James had no option but to cut expenditure. The man who was to emerge as the key player in the campaign for retrenchment was Lionel Cranfield, a London merchant and financier who had become chief surveyor of the customs in 1613 after having convinced the government that higher rents could be charged for the lease of the great customs farm. Although initially a client of the earl of Northampton, Northampton's death in 1614 did nothing to halt Cranfield's rise in court circles. By 1615 he enjoyed Villiers' support, and the following year he secured his first court office as Master of Requests and in 1618 he became Master of the Wardrobe. Following Suffolk's fall from grace in 1618–19 (Suffolk was suspended from the treasuryship in July 1618 and convicted by Star Chamber of corruption in November of the following year), James placed the treasury in commission and made Cranfield one of the commissioners. Cranfield introduced a number of economies: he reduced expenditure on the royal household, which had risen from nearly £50,000 per annum at the end of Elizabeth's reign to £77,000 under James, by £18,000; cut waste and extravagance in the navy and the ordnance office; and was able to run the wardrobe for £20,000 per annum, compared to an average of £28,000 per annum in the period 1606–12. He also secured an agreement to levy a duty on tobacco imported from Virginia, which had emerged as an increasingly lucrative trade. In the process he upset those who had previously benefited from court extravagance and Sir Edwin Sandys and the Virginia Company, but he was at last bringing government spending under control. By October 1619 there was a surplus on the ordinary accounts of nearly £45,000, while by March 1620 he had reduced the royal debt to £712,206.[84] By now, however, events were rapidly being overtaken by developments on the Continent.

6

....

A True Love Knot Knit Fast

'The English, Scots, and Irish true, | Of three are now combin'd in one,' rhymed an anonymous poet in 1603; 'Their hartes a true love knot fast knit, | All former malice now is gone.'[1] James VI and I was the first king to reign over all the constituent kingdoms of the British Isles; whether or not the 'former malice' between the respective inhabitants of these three realms had dissipated to any significant degree (and there is no doubt that our poet was indulging in wishful thinking), ruling such different kingdoms posed unique challenges. As king of Scotland, James had been busy trying to rebuild the authority of the Scottish monarchy after two revolutions in the 1560s and an extended royal minority. Had he done enough, how much more needed to be done, and could his rebuilt Scottish monarchy survive an absentee kingship? Ireland, when James inherited the English and Irish thrones, was still technically at war with England—a revolt that had erupted in 1593, and came to be led by the earl of Tyrone from 1595—although it was a war that had essentially been won prior to Elizabeth's death. James thus faced the challenge of state building—making sure his rule extended effectively over all parts of his kingdoms; of security—ensuring that both his satellite kingdoms remained loyal and that absentee kingship would not open up a space for disgruntled subjects in the peripheries to rebel against his rule; and of finance—how to pay for it all. Yet the most daunting challenge related to the Church: Scotland and England had different ecclesiastical establishments from each other, while in Ireland the vast majority of his subjects were not even of the same religion as their king.

James's approach to managing this problematic multiple-kingdom inheritance has been described as 'pioneering and impressive', especially given the entrenched structural difficulties he faced.[2] There is much to be said for this view. The challenges James faced were significant, and they needed tackling, but the solutions he devised possessed their own logic and he demonstrated considerable political craft and skill in his pursuit of them. Although he did not achieve all his objectives, he made significant headway in both Ireland and Scotland and left both kingdoms in peace. Nevertheless, James did not solve any of the underlying problems; indeed, the policies he pursued arguably made the situation in both Ireland and Scotland worse in the long run. In Ireland, through his policy of plantation, he laid the basis for a politics of resentment that was to destabilize the kingdom for much of the seventeenth century (one might even say the next 400 years). In Scotland, his religious policies proved bitterly divisive, alienating significant sections of the Scottish population. When the Scots and Irish were to rebel on the eve of the Civil War, Scottish and Irish grievances had their roots in policy initiatives that had begun under James.

A: 'That Infortunate Country of Irelande'[3]

It was an 'old Proverbe', recalled an anonymous pamphleteer in 1642, that 'He that will England win, with Ireland must begin'; 'If our enemies had the command of that back-doore', he forewarned, 'we should not long want them here'.[4] James I did, in a sense, win in Ireland. At the very beginning of his reign the rebel Irish leader Hugh O'Neill, earl of Tyrone, submitted to the English government, bringing to an end the Nine Years War. The English conquest of Ireland was at last complete. Yet keeping Ireland secure was going to be no straightforward task. Ireland was not only a Catholic country ruled by a Protestant minority but one that had been subject to alternate waves of English colonization, first Catholic and then Protestant. Thus there were three competing interests in Ireland: the English Protestants who ran the government in Dublin, or 'servitors', as they were known (councillors of state and those who had served the crown in the long wars in Ireland); the Old English, who had remained Catholic at the Reformation and who still had considerable political power, some of whom had intermarried with the Gaelic Irish and adopted Irish customs and manners, but most of whom still strongly identified with the English crown and the interests of the English state in Ireland; and the Gaelic or native Irish, also Catholic, the original conquered people of Ireland, the most intransigent opponents of English imperial interests in Ireland.

The English took the view that the best way to keep Ireland secure was through a policy of Anglicization: establish a national system of jurisdiction, as existed in England; introduce fixed units of landholding; promote arable farming; and adopt English common law and follow English law with regard to the ownership and inheritance of property.[5] This theory of legal and cultural imperialism was spelled out most fully by Sir John Davies, James's Solicitor General and then Attorney General for Ireland, in a tract first published in 1612. There were two main reasons, Davies felt, why Ireland had not been entirely subdued prior to James's accession: a failure by the English, until very recently, to use sufficient military force, and the fact that 'the Crown of England did not from the beginning give Laws to the Irishry'. Denied either the benefit or protection of English law, it was hardly surprising, Davies thought, that the Irish never accepted English rule:

> For, as long as they were out of the protection of the Law; so as every English-man might oppress, spoil, and kill them without countroulment, how was it possible they should be other than Out-laws and Enemies to the Crown of England? If the King would not admit them to the condition of Subjects, how could they learn to acknowledge and obey him as their Soveraign?

The Norman conqueror did not cast the English out as aliens and enemies to the crown, Davies reminded his readers; nor did Edward I or Henry VIII treat the Welsh in this way when they reduced Wales.[6] Giving the Irish the benefits of English law would help not just to make them loyal but also to civilize them. 'If we consider the Nature of the Irish Customs', Davies observed, 'we shall find that the people, which doth use them, must of necessity be Rebels to all good Government... and bring Barbarisme and desolation upon the richest and most fruitful Land of the World.' English law would give the Irish security of their persons and property, by punishing murder, manslaughter, rape, robbery, and theft with death, where the Brehon Law of the Irish allowed only for a fine. It would protect the weaker from 'Oppression' by the stronger. It would allow the Irish to purchase freehold estates which they could then pass on to their children, undermining the Irish customs of tanistry (whereby the property of a clan chief passed to one of the male members of the clan or sept—the tanist—by a system of election) and gavelkind (whereby the land of inferior tenancies was divided among all the males of the sept). Outlawing this 'uncertainty of estates' would in turn encourage improvement, Davies believed, for who 'wou'd plant or improve, or build upon that Land, which a stranger, whom he knew not, should possess after his death'.[7]

The English also hoped to extend the Protestant reformation in Ireland—it was after all a major responsibility of a king to promote the true religion in his kingdoms—but here there was disagreement over how to proceed. Davies seems to have believed that reformations could be imposed from above. 'The multitude was ever made conformable by edicts and proclamations', he wrote to Salisbury in December 1605, pointing to successes in this regard of the Protestant Edward VI (1547–53), who inherited a kingdom that was half Catholic, and of the Catholic Mary (1553–8), who inherited a kingdom that was half Protestant. If particular individuals were targeted for exemplary punishment and compelled to conform, Davies felt, the rest of the country would follow. The royal administration in England, however, tended to take the view that when a religion was so deeply rooted and widespread, an alteration was not 'suddenly to be obtained by forcing against the current, but gaining by little and little'. Reformation was to be achieved through education, persuasion, and the planting of a godly ministry across the kingdom.[8]

Regardless of the theory, in practice the crown's policy towards Ireland was marked by inconsistency. Moreover, inadequate oversight from the crown—a function in part of distance and in part of other preoccupations—gave those who served the crown at the local level greater freedom to define policy for themselves and to pursue measures that they thought were in the best interest of Church and state but which did not necessarily have royal sanction.

* * *

Although Tyrone's rebellion had started in Ulster, victory over the English at the battle of Yellow Ford in 1598 saw the revolt spread to the whole of the country. Munster rose, bringing about the collapse of the recent English plantation there, as English colonists fled for their lives. With the Ulster Lords having offered the Spanish king the crown of Ireland in return for his support, there was now the prospect that Ireland would become a satellite of Spain if it fell. Elizabeth realized that the rebellion had to be crushed at all costs and was willing to commit the necessary resources to pay and equip an army which, at its height, numbered some 21,000 men. The total cost to the English government was just under £1.85 million. The key turning point in the war was the siege of Kinsale of September–December 1601, when the English repulsed a Spanish invasion force of 4,000 men and defeated an Irish army that had come to relieve the town. Yet although Tyrone's chief ally among the Ulster Lords, Rory

O'Donnell, Lord of Tyrconnell, surrendered in December 1602, Tyrone continued to hold out, seemingly waiting for James VI of Scotland, with whom he had been in correspondence during the 1590s, to succeed Elizabeth. Desperate to bring the war to an end before James became king, the Lord Deputy, Charles Blount, 8th Baron Mountjoy, was willing to offer Tyrone generous terms. In fact Tyrone signed the Treaty of Mellifont ending the war on 30 March, six days after the queen had died, but the news had been kept from him and he made his submission to Elizabeth; Tyrone reputedly wept when he learned of the deception. Yet there were to be no widespread confiscations as there had been when earlier rebellions in Ireland had been put down. In return for Tyrone promising to abjure all dependency on foreign potentates and to assist the abolition of all 'barbarous customs contrary to the laws', the government allowed Tyrone to retain his title and most of his lands. O'Donnell was likewise allowed to keep his lands and was created earl of Tyrconnell. With the peace, the government issued an Act of Oblivion (February 1604) pardoning all offences committed in Ireland during the war.[9]

The English might have won the war, but much needed to be done if they were to win the peace. The war had been enormously destructive. Whole counties had been left devastated, cattle slaughtered, crops burnt, and churches and estates laid waste: Tyrone later claimed that 60,000 people perished as a result of Mountjoy's scorched earth policy.[10] No sooner had the war ended than the country was hit by plague. Rebellion may have been quelled, but brigandage remained endemic. The crown's finances were in a chaotic state. The Protestant Church was weak, whereas by contrast the Roman Catholic clergy were numerous and appeared zealous and efficient. The process of Anglicization had made limited progress. Although most members of the upper classes had adopted English ways and dress, there were to be some members of the Irish parliament of 1613–15 who could speak no English, while the vast majority of the native Gaelic population still spoke only Irish and adhered to Irish traditions.[11] Would such a country remain loyal in the event of a future international crisis?

The Catholics of Ireland, in fact, held out high hopes for James. The Gaelic Irish took comfort from his Scottish ancestry: kings of Scotland traced their descent back to the mythical Fergus mac Ferquhard, who had supposedly come to Scotland from Ireland in 330 BC, making James in theory of ancient Irish stock.[12] The Old English hoped that James, as the son of the Catholic Mary Stewart, would show himself sympathetic to their plight and grant toleration to the Catholic faith. Some of them tried to pre-empt the issue. Upon learning the news of the death of Elizabeth, the Old English in the towns of Munster and a number of towns in Leinster took possession of the churches, brought back the old Catholic images, and restored the mass, driving the Protestant ministers away and burning their bibles and common prayer books. The Catholics were later to claim they had received 'intelligence' that if James were to succeed 'he would permit to Irishmen a free exercise of the Catholicke Religion'.[13] However, several towns in these areas had in fact stalled when they first received notification to proclaim James, questioning the news of the queen's death and worried about proclaiming a foreigner king, especially when the commissions of those telling them to do so had expired upon the death of Elizabeth and not yet been renewed. In Waterford the citizens forcibly prevented the Chief Justice of Common Pleas, Sir Nicholas Walsh, from proclaiming James and a Catholic priest gave a public sermon rejoicing that 'now Jesabell was dead' and thanking God that 'every man might freely enjoy the fruits of his own reward'. Likewise in Cork the citizens, recalling Dublin's mistake in proclaiming the pretender Perkin Warbeck in 1495, initially refused to proclaim James and pledged 'to spend their lives in defence of their profession', while a priest preached that James 'was no King, till the Pope confirmed him'.[14]

Mountjoy quickly gathered an army, marched into Munster, and managed to restore order before the end of May. Yet having forced the townsmen to back down and to swear an oath of allegiance to James, he opted not to pursue further recriminations. For the time being Catholics remained free to practise their faith in the privacy of their own homes until such time as the king opted to regulate matters otherwise.[15] Mountjoy then returned to England, where he was honoured by being elevated to the earldom of Devonshire. He still hoped to retain a supervisory role over Irish affairs, since his replacement as Lord Deputy was his close friend Sir George Carey. However, Carey decided to step down in February 1604, and he in turn was replaced by Sir Arthur Chichester, a former soldier who disagreed with Mountjoy's conciliatory approach. The hardliners now found themselves in control of the Dublin administration.[16]

With the conquest of Ireland finally complete, the English crown set about trying to ensure that English law and English justice extended through the whole of the island. Ulster was divided into nine counties—six new counties of Donegal, Coleraine, Tyrone,

Armagh, Fermanagh, and Monaghan were added to the existing ones of Antrim and Down and to that of Cavan (hitherto regarded as part of Connacht); sheriffs, justices of the peace, coroners, and constables were appointed; and assizes began to be held (the first circuit in Donegal was in 1603). The sees of Derry, Raphoe, and Clogher were temporarily united and given a Protestant bishop in 1605; for the first time all the dioceses in Ireland had a bishop appointed by the monarch. The plantation lands scattered through the counties of Waterford, Cork, Limerick, and Kerry in the province of Munster were resettled and assize circuits resumed for both Munster and Connacht. The Irish customs of tanistry and gavelkind were declared utterly void and extinguished in a series of resolutions by the judges between 1606 and 1608 and English property law and the principle of primogeniture introduced.[17] A whole range of Gaelic taxes, tributes, and exactions were also abolished by act of state. On 11 March 1605 the Irish council issued a proclamation affirming that all inhabitants of Ireland were free, natural, and immediate subjects of the king and not subject to any local lord or chief, and pardoning all offences committed prior to 24 March 1603 (the day of James's accession) on condition of taking an oath of fealty to the king. To give the Irish an opportunity to secure firm titles, a commission for remedying defective titles was set up in 1606.[18] The commission was also exploited by English settlers: Richard Boyle, earl of Cork, for example, was able to secure the title to lands he had acquired in dubious ways in the 1590s and in the process even improved the tenure by which he held such land from the crown.[19] The desire to extend English law throughout Ireland was accompanied by a determination to ensure that the law was interpreted by English Protestant lawyers. Until the end of the Nine Years War, the Irish judiciary had been dominated by Old English lawyers. Following the recusant revolt of 1603, taking the oath of supremacy was made a prerequisite for practising at the Irish bar. Several judges were forced to resign, while the number of judges was increased from seven to nine in 1607 and then to sixteen six years later, to allow for the intrusion of suitable newcomers. By 1613 only two of the judges—Dominic Sarsfield and John Eliott—had been born in Ireland, and both of those were Protestants; the rest were English-born Protestants and practising members of the English bar.[20]

The crown's chronic shortage of money meant that peace saw a dramatic reduction in the size of the military establishment in Ireland, to a mere 880 foot and 234 horse by 1606 (although this had to be rapidly expanded to 2,100 in 1608 to meet the threat of O'Doherty's rebellion before being cut back to 1,450 foot and 212 horse in 1611).[21] However, an extensive network of garrisons and forts was maintained across the kingdom: in Ulster alone there was a series of eighteen forts and the province was divided into ten military districts, each grouped around one or more of these forts and headed by a military governor or governors.[22] Martial law continued to be deployed to meet potential security threats in the immediate aftermath of war. To deal with banditry in the area around Limerick, for example, the English soldier-colonist Captain John Downing received a commission to seek out and kill such as had borne arms in the late war and who had not sought and received a royal pardon, and also to execute by martial law 'masterless men' and 'vagabonds'. Likewise the constable of Maryborough Fort, Queen's County (now County Laois) in Leinster was empowered to punish pre-emptively all suspect groups by martial law, 'as well by death as by losse of members, limbs, whipping, etc.'. Although upon becoming Lord Deputy Chichester issued a proclamation revoking commissions of martial law, in practice he withdrew only those old commissions that had fallen into abeyance but confirmed the power of martial law to dozens of crown officials in every province and in almost every county. Indeed, in the years 1605–7 he was responsible for the setting up of a new official in Ireland, the county provost martial, whose chief task it was to impose martial law in the shires. Local sheriffs were also responsible for imposing martial law.[23]

The Mandates Policy

The Protestants in Ireland wanted firmer action against recusants. The President of Munster, Sir Henry Brouncker, issued a proclamation in August 1604 ordering all Jesuits and seminary priests to leave the province and followed this up with a rigorous search for recusant clergy.[24] James eventually issued a public statement on recusancy on 4 July 1605: Jesuits and seminary priests were to leave the country, and attendance at church was to be strictly enforced, 'upon the pains and penalties' prescribed by law.[25] However, the penalty prescribed by the Irish Act of Uniformity of 1560—Ireland did not have the equivalent of the English recusancy statute of 1581—was a fine of just one shilling for every Sunday or holy day one was absent, a sufficient inducement to conformity for 'the common inhabitants' perhaps, but hardly much of a deterrent for the wealthier sort.[26] Davies complained that the proclamation had 'little effect' and the bishop of Meath that the law continued to be widely 'contemned and resisted' with 'resolute obstinacy'.[27] After first trying to persuade the Catholic aldermen and leading Catholic citizens of Dublin of the importance of performing their duty in coming to church, to no effect, in November Chichester decided to issue mandates in the king's name requiring them to attend Protestant services, under pain of prosecution before the prerogative Court of Castle Chamber (the Irish equivalent of Star Chamber), where steeper punishments could be imposed.[28] The Old English of Dublin were hardly a security risk—they had remained resolutely loyal to the crown during the rebellion of the 1590s—but the council believed it was essential to make Dublin comply: being the principal city and seat of state, 'all the eyes of the kingdom were turned upon it', and 'the people of other parts', it was thought, 'would be much led one way or the other by example of that place'. With the Catholics insisting 'it was against their conscience' to attend Protestant services, Chichester felt he had no option but to act. On 22 November Castle Chamber imposed fines of £100 each on six aldermen and £50 each on the other three citizens, and committed eight of them to imprisonment in Dublin Castle at the Lord Deputy's pleasure. (The other, an Englishman by birth, was ordered to return to England.) Five days later the court was taking action against five more Dublin recusants.[29]

Old English lawyers questioned whether English statutes could be applied in Ireland without ratification by an Irish parliament, but Davies provided medieval precedents to show that they could.[30] The nobility and gentry of the English Pale, led by Viscount Gormanston and Sir Patrick Barnewall, presented Chichester with a petition signed by 217 hands expressing their resentment at the 'fowle and reproachful imputation' that they were 'alienated in [their] affections' and urging the Lord Deputy to suspend the execution of the proclamation until the king could be 'more rightlie informed' of their 'innocency'.[31] Still with no reply a couple of days later, Gormanston and a few others chose to visit Chichester in person and press him for an answer.[32] The timing could not have been worse, since news had just reached Dublin of the Gunpowder Plot in England. Chichester had the ringleaders fined by Castle Chamber, stripped of all their offices, and either imprisoned or placed under house arrest, informing the privy council in England that he found it suspicious that they had decided 'to putt a foote this theyre seditious practice' at the time of the

Gunpowder treason.[33] Gormanston petitioned Salisbury to intervene to 'moderate these extremities', protesting that the proceedings were a clear violation of the king's proclamation (which had called only for the enforcement of penalties prescribed by law), and complaining how in the process of collecting the fines recusants had had 'their houses and doors...broken open', leaving 'their wives and poor children distressed and terrified'.[34] The English privy council, recalling how recently the Catholics in Ireland had lapsed into general revolt, wrote to Chichester early in the new year (seemingly before Gormanston's petition had arrived), urging him to pursue a more temperate course, to release the prisoners (with the exception of Barnewall, who was to be sent to England), and to use 'admonition, persuasion and instruction' rather than 'severity of law and justice', so as not to startle 'the multitude by any general or rigorous compulsion'. Only those 'noted for boasted disobedience and contempt' should be targeted for punishment, so that by 'well and seasonably chosen' example, 'the rest may be kept in awe'. Chichester released the prisoners on bond but seems to have thought his course was 'temperate', grumbling that 'the least punishment in this case' was accounted by 'this people the greatest severity',[35] and continued to pursue select recusants up until July 1606. The mandates policy was extended to Galway and Munster, where even Chichester was prepared to admit that Brouncker took 'somewhat a more violent course'. To the Catholics of Munster, Brouncker was an 'emissary of Antichrist'.[36]

The mandates policy was put on hold in the summer to allow the crown time to review the precedents. Barnewall, who had arrived in London in the spring, was released on bond following a brief stint in the Tower upon condition that he acknowledge his offences and subsequently allowed to return to Ireland, and the English judges gave a definitive ruling at the end of 1606 that the proceedings in Castle Chamber had been legal. Yet although the hounding of recusants temporarily resumed, in April 1607 the crown, worried that too rigorous a course was more likely to provoke a rebellion rather than prevent one, sent instructions to Chichester and Brouncker to abandon the pursuit of conformity.[37] James had made sure he won the legal point, but having done so, he backed down.

The anti-recusant drive soured relationships between the Dublin administration and the Irish Catholics. Catholic clergy complained of 'the fury of this persecution' and 'the cruelty of our tyrants' during these 'Neronian times'. Over the course of just a couple of years, thousands of recusants were either fined, imprisoned, had their property confiscated, or suffered brutality at the hands of local troops. In August 1607 it was estimated that the fines imposed in Munster alone totalled £7,000 (although many of these were subsequently reduced or remitted). Many recusants were 'reduced to such poverty' that they were 'forced to leave their homes and live in obscurity' in other parts of the country, while others were 'driven into exile'. Under the pretence of searching for priests, soldiers would 'break open doors at night, and rob the inhabitants'. Although the campaign against recusants started with the towns, it soon spread to the countryside. Writing in November 1606, one Catholic cleric complained how in Munster 'the villages and country districts' were 'harassed beyond description' and were likely to 'become deserts', since 'the miserable and abandoned Catholics' were so oppressed that they dared not even cultivate the land.[38]

Sometimes the Protestant authorities could be cruelly vindictive. At Drogheda during Lent of 1607, Chichester used soldiers literally 'to drag the townspeople to the Protestant temples'. On one occasion he urged a well-respected local Catholic—a man named Barnewell (presumably of the same Old English family)—'to accompany him to church and hear the sermon'; out of politeness Barnewell agreed to go as far as the church door, but when he refused to go inside Chichester thwacked him on the head with his stick while Chichester's macebearer attacked Barnewell 'so savagely that he fell to the ground like a dead man'. Chichester's men then dragged Barnewell into the church, 'where he lay insensible and gasping all the time of the sermon'; he died of his injuries two hours later. In May 1606, the government issued a proclamation empowering soldiers to hunt out priests and hang them, by martial law, from the nearest tree. Mere suspicion of being a priest was often enough: a few weeks later, it was reported that soldiers had taken three Catholics, only one of whom was a priest, and immediately hanged them all. What the Protestant authorities wanted, however, was not martyrs but compliance. A Salamanca-trained priest named Thady Dimiran, taken by Protestant troops in Ulster in the spring of 1607, was offered a bishopric to induce him to conform. When Dimiran informed his captors that 'he would not abandon the faith for all the bishoprics and goods in the world, and would rather suffer a thousand deaths', they told him that that could be arranged. The soldiers formed themselves into a long file facing towards a wall, and made the priest run between them and the wall as they fired their guns at him. Such was the inaccuracy of early seventeenth-century firearms that none of their bullets hit

Dimiran, although before he got halfway the priest collapsed breath-
less with smoke inhalation and was left with temporary hearing loss.
When subsequent promises and threats failed to persuade Dimiran to
convert, the soldiers tied him to a post, brutally flogged him—on two
successive days—and finally threw him half dead into a dungeon;
according to one report, in order to secure him to the post, 'they
bored holes in his arms and legs, through which they passed the
cords', causing 'excruciating pain'. With such violence seemingly
sanctioned by the authorities, it is hardly surprising to find examples
of Protestant civilian brutality towards Catholic clerics. In Drogheda
in 1607 a poor friar was stopped by a passer-by and asked for money
and badly beaten up when it was found that he had none. Four young
men, hearing the noise, came rushing to his rescue, but when they
saw he was a friar they jumped on him and beat him up even more.
It was the type of vigilante activity which Chichester did not want:
two of the young men were brought to Dublin, fined and imprisoned
for their crime.[39]

In the face of such persecution, the Catholics adopted a variety of
survival strategies. Most tried to remain faithful to their beliefs, as
the intensity and duration of the anti-recusant drive in itself testifies.
It was said that Catholic clergy took oaths from the people not to go
to the Protestant churches, in the hope that the king would eventually
have to face up to reality and if not grant a formal toleration then at
least tolerate 'by connivance, as heretofore'.[40] Occasionally Catholics
tried to assert their right to exercise their religion by force. On Christmas Day 1605 and Easter Sunday 1606, the Catholics of New Ross
in County Wexford, led by the town sovereign, turned up to church
en masse—some 200 of them in total—and with 'an extraordinary
noise and tumult' proceeded 'to make a superstitious offering at the
place where the high altar stood', thereby preventing the minister
from saying his sermon and interrupting the celebration of communion. In November 1606, some 200 Old English from Balrothery in
County Dublin, led by one James Barnewell, rioted against the
attempt by the local Protestant minister Thomas Meredith to bury
Barnewell's mother, Barnewell and his associates 'having beforehand...resolved to burie the said Corps after a superstitious and
Idolatrous fashion', against the king's injunctions. They not only
attacked Meredith, pulling 'away a great part of his beard', and 'buf-
feted him on the face, that his mouth and nose gused [sic] out with
bloud', but also struck 'the booke of common prayer out of his hand',
which they trod 'under their feete' in a 'most scornfull...manner',

and 'beate the...vicar's wife', throwing her to the ground, she 'being great with Child'. At the Wexford assizes in November 1606 a man was condemned to death for burning the Protestant vicar's house, although it was said that this had been done 'rather out of malice to his person than to religion or profession'.[41]

More typically, Catholics tended to engage in various forms of passive resistance. At Cashel in November 1606 the chief magistrate and the citizens refused to publish a proclamation banishing priests. The Protestant archbishop of Cashel therefore decided that he would publish it himself in the market place, dressed up 'in full pontificals', with his servants, and preceded by a herald and drummer; however, he found the market place totally deserted, the townspeople having deliberately opted to stay at home, closing their doors and windows, so they could deny having heard it read. The archbishop posted the proclamation up on the market cross, but the 'boys and girls' tore it down at night; other reports said that they 'besmeared' it 'with cow-dung'. Not that such action had much practical effect: fifteen of the principal inhabitants were summoned to Cork, where they were fined and imprisoned.[42]

Inevitably the poorer sort found it more difficult to sustain the burden of persecution than more well-to-do Catholics, and sometimes opted to go to church rather than to face continual fines. This led some in the Dublin administration to question their strategy: as Sir John Davies put it, they had initially thought that if they compelled 'the better sort' to come to church, 'they of the meaner condition would come for fear', but he now began to wonder 'if the general multitude were drawn to conformity...persons of quality for the most part would come for shame'.[43] Yet 'the better sort' had ways of keeping the lower orders in line. When Brouncker in Munster 'forced a crowd of peasants to the Protestant temple', their landlord refused to continue them as tenants 'until they were reconciled to the Church': they were made 'to undertake a long pilgrimage...on foot, clad in white linen, with crucifixes in their hands' and to tell everyone they met on the way 'they were doing this, in order to atone for the crime committed in going to the Protestant house against their conscience'.[44] When hauled before the courts, recusants tried to avail themselves of any possible legal challenges they could to ward off prosecution. When nigh on 100 citizens and burgesses appeared at the assizes at Cork in the spring of 1606 to answer for not coming to church, they demanded to see copies of their indictments, so that 'they might put their traverses thereunto'. Davies told them he would agree only if they entered bonds to come to church the following Sunday, since this was obviously a wilful delaying tactic. They submitted, and paid the fines.[45] When recusants at Dublin had tried a similar strategy the previous February, the presiding judge refused to let them have copies of their indictments, but he did order the deputy clerk of the court to read them out, to allay any suspicions that they were being denied a fair trial.[46] In general, however, Catholics felt there was no point in going to law to seek to redress, since there was 'no chance of fair play'.[47]

Davies believed the crackdown was having the desired effect. When he toured through Meath, Westmeath, Longford, and King's and Queen's Counties in the summer of 1607, he observed that it was 'almost a miracle to see the quiet and conformity of these people'. Even Catholic leaders acknowledged that people were beginning to bow under pressure. The Catholic archbishop of Cashel noted in the summer of 1606 that 'the hearts of the southerns [were] broken with persecutions', while another Catholic source noted in the spring of 1607 that the inhabitants of Drogheda, 'a populous town...hitherto so tenacious of the Faith, all went to the Protestant churches last Lent'. However, such success was only temporary. As soon as the pressure from above was eased, Chichester noted in October 1607, many who 'had formerly conformed' once more began to withdraw themselves from church.[48]

The Plantation of Ulster

Chichester and the servitors resented the generous terms granted to Tyrone in 1603, having expected to be rewarded for their services with grants of land confiscated from the Irish rebels. One former military leader, Sir John Harington, grumbled how he had 'lived to see that damnable rebel Tir-Owen broughte to Englande, honourede, and well likede', when he had 'adventurede perils by sea and lande, endured toil, was near starvinge', and had been forced to 'eat horse fleshe at Munster; and all to quell that man, who nowe smilethe in peace at those that did hazarde their lives to destroy him'.[49] Chichester, who had fought in Ulster in the last four years of the war, harboured a deep grudge against Tyrone for the part the earl had played in the killing and beheading of Chichester's elder brother, Sir John, the governor of Carrickfergus, in 1597. Back in England, Devonshire, worried about provoking disorder, operated as a check on Chichester's aggression, but years of heavy smoking finally took their toll and he died of a respiratory infection ('Putrefaction of his Lungs') in April 1606 at the age of forty-three.[50] This gave Chichester and the servitors their chance, and they set about trying to make life unbearable for Tyrone and Tyrconnell. They sought to identify 'concealed lands' within the lordships of Tyrone and Tyrconnell that might be claimed for the crown, sanctioning the use of intimidatory tactics by troops stationed in Ulster. Local troops, embittered by their experiences of the war, sometimes sought to impose their own form of retribution on the local inhabitants, committing acts of theft, extortion, and rape. In Donegal local garrisons, acting on orders from Dublin Castle and empowered by martial law, can be found seizing lands belonging to Tyrconnell at sword point, stripping the earl's servants and tenants of their clothes, and stealing his cows, sheep, and pigs. In one particularly distasteful incident in the spring of 1606, one Captain Ellis raped an eleven-year-old girl in County Donegal, ordering two of his soldiers to hold her by the hands and legs when she tried to resist. Although Tyrconnell got Chichester to promise, before witnesses, that Ellis would never receive a royal pardon for his crime, so that Ellis could be indicted at the next Donegal assizes, the pardon came nevertheless. Tyrone suffered less military aggression than Tyrconnell, but also found himself powerless to prevent garrison detachments passing through his lands, stealing his livestock, and molesting, even killing, his kinsmen and tenants. Attempts to obtain justice through proper legal channels proved futile: the violence was invariably sanctioned by the commissions of martial law, which allowed for pre-emptive strikes against 'suspect' groups. It was becoming all too apparent to both Tyrconnell and Tyrone that they were no longer able to fulfil one of the essential functions of lordship, namely to protect those under their charge.[51]

The Dublin administration further sought to undermine the position of the earls by encouraging lesser Gaelic lords in Ulster to stake their own claims against their overlords. A key test case arose when Donal O'Cahan, Tyrone's estranged son-in-law, decided to mount a legal challenge in the Dublin courts to Tyrone's claim to superiority over him; if successful, O'Cahan's case would set a legal precedent for establishing the independent property rights of many of the lesser lords and open up an avenue for the eventual dismemberment of the Tyrone lordship. Tyrone petitioned James for support, and the king decided to hear the case personally, summoning both Tyrone and O'Cahan to London in August 1607. Finding it difficult to manage what remained of his estates in the present economic crisis, and upset (he later said) about the pressures put on him to abandon his religion, Tyrconnell contemplated fleeing to Spain to seek the protection of Philip III. When reports emerged over the course of 1607 first of a conspiracy among disaffected from the Irish Pale (the original conquered area of Ireland centring around Dublin) to seize Dublin Castle and then of a wider conspiracy involving the northern earls and Spanish intervention, Tyrone sensed entrapment and feared he would be arrested if he went to London. In September 1607 both Tyrone and Tyrconnell opted to flee to the Continent, taking about ninety of their servants and followers with them, where they ended up not in Spain, as initially planned (Philip III was eager not to do anything to offend James), but at Rome.[52]

The Flight of the Earls was treated as a confession of treason and their lands were forfeited to the crown.[53] When Sir Cahir O'Doherty rose in rebellion in April 1608 and seized lands in Culmore and Derry—an ill-fated venture that was suppressed within two months—the government had the excuse to seize the property of the lesser Gaelic lords.[54] At the summer assizes of 1608 an official survey adjudged almost all the land of six of the province's counties—Armagh, Cavan, Coleraine, Donegal, Fermanagh, and Tyrone—escheated to the crown and thus open to plantation.[55] Under the scheme for plantation agreed in 1609, three main groups were to receive land in Ulster: English and Scottish 'undertakers' (all of whom were required to take the oath of supremacy to attest to their Protestantism), who undertook to build defensible buildings on their property and replace the existing tenants of their lands with English or Scottish Protestants and who were forbidden to accept Irish tenants or alienate land to the Irish (in 1622 Irish were permitted to become tenants on one quarter of the undertakers' proportions); servitors, who were mainly English, and who were encouraged though not obliged to settle their lands with English or Scottish tenants; and natives who could lay claim to previous freehold possessions in Ulster and who were considered deserving by the crown, who were allowed to have native tenants but required to use tillage and husbandry after the manner of the English Pale. The need to tap into the wealth of the City of London to rebuild the towns of Derry and Coleraine led the government in 1610 to grant the London merchant companies the whole of the county of Coleraine, together with one barony of County Tyrone and nine townlands of County Antrim—a territory which was renamed County Londonderry. James himself was an enthusiastic supporter of the plantation scheme, anticipating that 'a mixt Conversation of different Nations one amongst an other' would help 'induce obedience, civilitie, and Christian policie into these partes' and in turn redound 'to the welfare and tranquillitie of this whole Realme'.[56]

The plantation of Ulster was a remarkable exercise in social engineering. English undertakers received 81,500 acres, Scottish undertakers 81,000 (between them more than one third of the land available), servitors 54,632 acres, Irish grantees 94,013 acres, and the London companies 45,520. An additional 74,852 acres went to the Church, 12,400 to Trinity College Dublin, and 12,548 acres for the use of forts and corporations.[57] By 1622 some 6,902 adult British males had settled in the six escheated counties of Ulster alone, 3,740 of them Scots. Assuming there were three women for every four British men, the total adult British population by 1622 would have been 12,079. This marked a movement of approximately 1,000 adults per year since the plantation had begun. A further 7,000 adult Scots moved to Counties Antrim and Down during this time, not part of the territory confiscated in 1607. By 1630 there were perhaps 15,000 adult British males in Ulster, or 26,000 British adults and a total British population perhaps as high as 37,000. On top of this, many English people migrated to Munster and Leinster to the new plantations being opened up there. Adding all together, the total migration to Ireland in the 1610s greatly exceeded the 20,000 or so who moved to New England during the 'Great Migration' of the 1630s—especially when we consider that the figure for New England includes not just adults but also children, servants, and apprentices. In the period up to 1641, some 100,000 people migrated from Britain to Ireland, 30,000 of them Scots (who predominantly settled in Ulster), and 70,000 English and Welsh; the population of Ireland as a whole rose from about one million in 1600 to one and a half million by 1641.[58] The biggest losers were the native Irish. Under the plantation scheme, Irish grantees were restored to a mere fifth of the land of Ulster, and although they were not given poorer lands than British settlers they were given smaller units. Thus whereas there were 51 English and 59 Scottish undertakers and 55 servitors, the 94,000 acres made available to the native Irish was divided among 280 grantees, of whom only 26 received grants of more than 1,000 acres. About one third of the land allocated to the native Irish went to one branch or other of the O'Neills.[59]

There were few visible signs of social and cultural tension between Scottish and English immigrants in Ulster. In 1614 the Scottish tenants of the earl of Abercorn in Strabane made an unsuccessful attempt to assassinate Lord Audley, a nearby English settler, for allegedly having made 'some unfit speeches against the Scottish nation in general' (Audley denied the allegation), although this is an isolated example.[60] Nevertheless, the plantation scheme fell short of expectations. Those most eager to acquire plantation land were often trying to stave off declining economic fortunes at home, and thus lacked the funds to invest in their Irish estates. The Reverend Andrew Stewart of Donaghadee in County Down, a Scottish Presbyterian and son of a settler, later observed (albeit with some hyperbole) that those who came over from England and Scotland were 'generally the scum of both nations, who for debt, or breaking and fleeing from justice, or seeking shelter' hoped 'to be without fear of man's justice where was nothing, or but little, as yet, of the fear of God'.[61] Many undertakers failed to fulfil the terms of their grants: a survey of 1619 showed that 24 per cent of the settler estates as yet had no principal dwelling, while a lack of settlers from England or Scotland meant that British landowners often had to take Irish tenants.[62]

The Irish Parliament, the Convocation, and the Irish Confession of Faith of 1615

The need for statutory confirmation of the confiscations in Ulster meant that a parliament had to be called in Ireland. In the autumn of 1610 Chichester announced that parliament would meet the following year, and in accordance with the provisions of Poynings' Law a legislative programme was drawn up and dispatched to London for approval in February 1611. In the past, government officials in Dublin had worked on the assumption that there would be a Catholic majority in parliament and had limited their ambitions accordingly. But the last time a parliament had met in Ireland had been 1585–6, and things had changed considerably since then. James questioned the very assumption that Catholic opinion needed to be deferred to. If he was going to call a parliament in Ireland, he wanted one that would serve his turn, and from his point of view this meant making sure it was dominated by English Protestants loyal to the crown. The House of Lords was a safe bet, since the presence of twenty bishops ensured a Protestant majority. Catholics, however, had dominated the House of Commons under Elizabeth and even with the re-shiring and resettlement of Ulster it seemed unlikely that the situation would be much changed in 1611.

The government therefore decided to delay the meeting of parliament, to allow it time to engineer a Protestant majority. As a prelude, it stepped up the campaign against recusants. On 13 July 1611 the Irish council reissued the proclamation of July 1605 calling for the enforcement of the recusancy laws and for Jesuits and seminary priests to leave the country.[63] Chichester began using Castle Chamber to prosecute Catholics who harboured 'popish priests' and local jurors who refused to present those who did not come to church. Following orders from the king, he instructed town corporations to impose the oath of uniformity to ensure that only persons 'conformable in religion' could hold office or vote in the upcoming elections. The climax of the campaign against recusants was reached in February 1612 when two Catholic priests from Ulster—Conor O'Devany, the octogenarian bishop of Down and Connor, and Patrick O'Loughran, the former chaplain to the earl of Tyrone—were executed in Dublin on trumped up charges of treason. If such measures were intended to cow the Catholic community into submission, they backfired, since they served only to escalate tensions. Huge crowds gathered to witness the executions, including many of the better sort of citizens and 'the best men's wives', 'scriking', 'howling', and 'hallowing, as if Saint Patricke himself had bin going to the gallowes'. After O'Devany's execution many stayed to collect relics, dipping their handkerchiefs in his blood, taking away his garments or pieces of hair from his head, shaving chips off the gallows, even (allegedly) cutting off the toes and fingers from his body after it had been 'dissevered into foure quarters' and making off with his head. In the past the recusants of the Pale (predominantly of Old English heritage) had shown little sympathy towards the Gaelic Irish; disturbingly, the actions of the Dublin administration were helping to forge a common Catholic identity that transcended the ethnic divide.[64]

The crown's most decisive initiative to influence the composition of the upcoming parliament was the creation of forty new borough constituencies between December 1612 and May 1613—eighteen of them in Ulster, nine in Munster, seven in Leinster, and six in Connacht. Clogher (Ulster), whose incorporation was intended but not yet carried out, and Trinity College Dublin were also given representation. Since all constituencies returned two members, this meant the creation of eight-four new seats. Given the recent extension of English control over the whole of Ireland, there was a need for some extension of representation: only thirty-seven boroughs had received writs to one or other of the parliaments of 1560 and 1585–6, since then only four new boroughs had been created (all of them under James), and both Ulster and Connacht had previously been seriously underrepresented. However, this was a blatant exercise in gerrymandering. The great majority of the new boroughs were as yet little more than villages, and in every one the franchise was vested in a corporation comprising a provost and twelve burgesses named in the new charters, all of them Protestants. Confident now of a Protestant majority in parliament, the government could afford a more ambitious legislative programme. In addition to bills for the formal recognition of the king's title, the attainder of Tyrone and Tyrconnell, and a new subsidy, bills were prepared against Jesuits and seminary priests, to prevent the Catholic Irish from sending their children abroad to be educated, and to make English Catholics resident in Ireland subject to the English recusancy laws.[65]

The elections took place in the spring of 1613 and were hotly disputed in a number of constituencies. The city of Dublin had its first election voided and saw a second succumb to a 'sudden affray' before, on the third attempt, the Protestant mayor was able to procure the return of two Protestant candidates, although only after he had moved the election to outside the city walls and invited Protestants who were not freemen to vote. Violence erupted in a couple of other places, and there were widespread reports of abuses and vote rigging, with Protestant sheriffs allegedly trying to stop Catholic freeholders from exercising their right to vote or else simply making fraudulent returns.[66]

When the Irish parliament assembled in May—it met in Dublin Castle for security reasons—Protestants outnumbered Catholics by 132 to 100 in the House of Commons, 84 of those 132 from the newly created borough constituencies. The government majority in the Lords was 11.[67] After failing in a desperate attempt to seat their candidate, Sir John Everard, in the Speaker's chair, in place of the Protestants' choice of Sir John Davies—at one stage the corpulent Davies was reduced to sitting on Everard's lap to assert his superior authority, before a general scrum broke out for possession of the chair—the Catholics decided to walk out.[68] The government had no option but to prorogue parliament while it heard their complaints. Although the Catholics elected to parliament were overwhelmingly Old English, the native Irish of Ulster contributed to collections to send a recusant delegation to England to represent Catholic grievances to the crown—further evidence of the growing sense of Catholic solidarity developing in Ireland. James agreed to set up an inquiry to look into their complaints, but he was angered when the delegates returned to Ireland in too obvious a mood of triumph. He summoned them back to London in April 1614 to hear his formal judgment, where he denounced their petitions as 'full of pride and arrogancy' and their conduct in parliament as 'worthy of severe punishment'[69] and had several delegates imprisoned in the Tower for their insolence when they tried to restate their case. He followed this up in June by instructing Chichester to reissue the 1605 proclamation against Catholic priests and recusants. The need for a grant of taxation from Ireland in the wake of the failure of the Addled Parliament in England, however, forced James to back down. He released the imprisoned delegates one by one and in August issued a revised verdict whereby he agreed to deprive eight boroughs of representation in the present parliament because their charters had not arrived until after the election writs had been sent out, to disenfranchise a further three boroughs completely, and to overturn the results in another two on the grounds that the sheriffs had made false returns. Protestants retained their majority in the Commons, but at 108 to 102 it was sufficiently narrow to cause the government to abandon the proposed new anti-recusant laws. When parliament reconvened in October 1614, business proceeded more smoothly. Four measures passed that autumn, including those for the recognition of the king's title and the attainder of the northern earls. When the subsidy bill came before parliament in the spring of 1615, Catholic MPs tried to seize the opportunity to bargain for concessions on recusancy fines and the right of Catholics to practise law in Ireland. The revelation of a Catholic conspiracy in Ulster, however, ensured that in the end the bill received an easy passage—although the subsidy itself yielded a mere £26,000, which went hardly any way towards clearing the deficit on Irish accounts.[70]

The meeting of the parliament was accompanied by the summoning of a national Convocation of the Church, the first time such a body had met in Ireland. We know very little about the Convocation, apart from its final product, the Irish Confession of Faith of 1615, which was largely the work of James Ussher, a professor of divinity at Trinity College Dublin, and future archbishop of Armagh. Significantly, the Irish Convocation chose not to adopt the English Thirty-Nine Articles, but instead drew up a new confession of 104 Articles. There were two main reasons for this: the need to adapt the English Articles to the very different context of Ireland, and the need to update the English Articles, so as to address concerns that had arisen since their original framing in 1563. Thus the new Irish Articles incorporated the English Articles against Catholicism, but added to them to make them stronger. Most significantly, the Irish Articles sought to address an ambiguity that had become apparent in the 1590s over English Article 17 concerning 'predestination and election' by incorporating the doctrinal statements embodied in the Lambeth Articles of 1595, which had been rejected by James at the Hampton Court Conference in 1604. Why this was allowed to happen is unclear. It may have been simply a question of distance from the monarch giving Church leaders in Ireland greater freedom of manoeuvre: it appears that the Irish Articles were not sent to England for approval and that the king never saw the confession which was approved in his name. The Irish Articles therefore pinned down the doctrine of the Irish Church as unequivocally Calvinist, whereas the English Thirty-Nine Articles still allowed considerable room for interpretation.[71]

Despite its growing theological maturity, the Church of Ireland as an institution remained weak and underdeveloped. The poverty of many livings and of some bishoprics made it difficult to attract well qualified clergy or even simply to repair the church buildings that had been damaged during the war. Although the Church probably served the spiritual needs of its own members reasonably well, it made little effort to engage in a missionary effort to reach out to the mass of the population, which remained steadfastly Catholic.[72] The bishop of Ferns and Leighlin, Thomas Ram, writing in September 1612, claimed that he had tried the gentle arts of persuasion to encourage both rich and poor Catholics alike to come to church and that some of 'the Poorer sort' had even privately admitted to him 'their dislike of popery and of the masse', because they did not understand what was said or done there, and that they would prefer not to have to pay double tithes and offerings (to the Protestant clergy and to the Catholic priests); but they dare not 'forsake the masse', they had informed him, for if they turned Protestant 'no popish merchant wold employ them being sailers, no popish landlord wold let them any lands being husbandmen, nor Lett them houses in tenantry being artificers. And therefore they must either starve or doe as they do.'[73] But the Church was not helped in its efforts by the corruption of some of its officials. In November 1621 Robert Travers, an ecclesiastical official in the diocese of Meath, was fined £300, removed from office, and imprisoned for extorting bribes from Catholics in return for leaving their names out of writs of excommunication or for allowing burials, christenings, and marriages to be conducted by Catholic priests.[74]

A Catholic author writing in 1617 insisted that Protestant ministers in Ireland were 'for the most part...careless, idle, and lassie', and took 'but little paine in teaching, catechising, or instructing any, except a few English protestants' who occasionally went 'to heare their Calvinisticall Service'; most of them were ignorant of the Irish language, and their services and sermons were always in English, which most of the Irish did not understand.'[75]

There was a renewed clampdown on recusants in the wake of the Catholic opposition in the parliament of 1613–15. The oath of supremacy was used to exclude Catholics from practising law or from participating in local government (those who declined the oath could also be fined or imprisoned for refusing to serve), there was an attempt to enforce more rigorously the requirement that minors who became wards of the crown take the oath as a condition of entering into their inheritance, and fines continued to be imposed on those who refused to attend Protestant services. In 1615 selected landowners in Munster and the Pale were even ordered to send their children to England, as hostages for their good behaviour and to receive a Protestant education. As always, however, government policy was marked by inconsistency. Waterford's defiance in electing another Catholic mayor was to cost the city its charter 1618. Yet there was seemingly no effort to enforce a proclamation of 1617 ordering foreign-educated priests to leave the country, while James's pursuit of a marriage alliance with Spain led the government largely to suspend the collection of recusancy fines from 1618 onwards.[76]

The crown was by now convinced that the best way of strengthening the Protestant interest in Ireland was to extend the policy of plantation. The method chosen was to exploit the confused state of Irish land tenure and compel those who could not prove a good title to surrender their lands to the crown. Those who cooperated would, in return for a fee, receive anywhere up to three-quarters of their lands back with secure titles, though to be held by feudal tenure, with the crown retaining a rent in the land and able to collect certain dues such as wardship. The remainder was granted to Protestant undertakers, with the crown again retaining a rent, who agreed to build and settle in the area, and although they were not compelled to take British tenants, Irish tenants were expected to settle in English-style villages. It was anticipated that the Protestant proprietors would be followed by Protestant ministers, thus making it possible for the local population to attend Protestant services rather than have no option but to attend the Catholic mass. Such a scheme had first been approved for Wexford in the south-east in 1611, though it was twice suspended in the face of protests from local landholders and its terms modified in 1614 in an attempt to conciliate opposition before it began to be seriously pushed by the government from 1615 onwards. Protests continued but the government was determined to get its way and ordered Chichester to imprison one of the ringleaders. When a group of petitioners took their complaints to London they were summarily transported to Virginia. By 1620 order had been re-established and the local occupiers and the new undertakers confirmed in their possessions.[77]

From Wexford the policy was extended to the Irish midlands, particularly County Longford, and even to County Leitrim in Connacht. Buckingham was a keen advocate of the scheme and many of his clients were able to get a pick of the lands that became available to newcomers; by the early 1620s this Villiers connection had become firmly established as a landed interest in the heart of Ireland.[78] However, the plantations did not achieve the transformation desired. The new Protestant landlords often did not settle upon their estates, and their Irish tenants showed no desire to build in the English fashion. The plantations brought some increase in royal revenue and extended the area of Protestant landownership, but they did little to extend Protestantism or to make Ireland more English. They did, however, antagonize further the Catholic majority, both Old English and Gaelic Irish.

A Work 'Not Yet Conducted unto Perfection'

What conclusions are we to draw, then, about what was accomplished in Ireland under James? The government in England thought it was making progress. Ireland was 'the last...of the daughters of Europe', Sir Francis Bacon (now Lord Keeper) told Sir William Jones upon his appointment as Lord Chief Justice of Ireland in June 1617, 'which hath come in and been reclaimed from desolation and a desert (in many parts) to population and plantation, and from savage and barbarous custom to humanity and civility'. This work was 'not yet conducted unto perfection', but it was 'in fair advance'.[79] Moreover, the English had a benevolent view of their empire. According to Sir John Davies, whereas the Irish, 'in former times, were left under the tyrannie of their Lords and Chieftains', they had now been received under protection of the crown. The English had established assize circuits in all four provinces, which was 'most welcome to the common people',

who, despite being 'rude and barbarous', nevertheless 'quickly appre-
hended the difference between the Tyrannie and Oppression under
which they lived before, and the just Government and Protection
which we promised unto them for the time to come'. 'Upon these
Visitations of Justice…the common people were taught by the Justices of Assize, that they were free Subjects to the Kings of England,
and not Slaves and Vassals to their pretended Lords'; some Irish
Lords, who found they could no longer live by extortion, had fled the
realm; the kingdom had been cleared of 'Thieves, and other Capital
Offenders'; and 'these Civil Assemblies at Assizes and Sessions' had
'reclaimed the Irish from their Wildness, caused them to cut off their
Glibs and long Hair; to convert their Mantles into Cloaks; to conform themselves to the manner of England in all their behaviour and
outwards forms', and to learn the English language. Thus, whereas
'the neglect of the Law' had once 'made the English degenerate, and
become Irish', now 'the execution of the Law, doth make the Irish
grow civil, and become English'.[80] One Protestant author, writing in
1622, observed how the king had spent a 'Mountaine of money' to

> keepe this Irish nation in…blessed peace…to so loade them with
> plenty, to make them laughe when other their neighbours have wepte,
> to keepe them from invation of forren enemies, and the swords of tray-
> tors and rebels at home, to make them riche in money, cattel and good-
> des, to build them strong Castles and faire houses, to fill the kingdome
> with Courts of iustice giving them upright Judges to sitt therein, and
> lawes and statuts, made without respect of persons, that with equitie
> right and good conscience, the widdowe fatherlesse and poore be pre-
> served from the bloodie hands of crueltie violence and oppression, to
> geve them free traffique and commerce with strangers and forreners,
> with manie other blessings throwne upon them, proceeding from his
> Majestie's especiall grace bountie libralitie and royall disposition.[81]

Such optimism was encouraged by the fact that the policies of the English government for once did not seem to be provoking the native population into open revolt. There had also been a couple of minor
conspiracies—O'Doherty's rebellion of 1608 and whatever was the
truth behind the intended Ulster uprising of 1615; the notion of the supposed Jacobean peace in Ireland is therefore misleading. Yet there was
to be no large-scale rebellion in Ireland between the end of the Nine
Years War in 1603 and the outbreak of the Irish rebellion in 1641.

The reasons for the relative quietism of the Catholics in Ireland are
manifold. Some may have bought into English legal imperialism to a

certain degree and opted to fight their battles in the courts of law, albeit English courts which applied English law. Certainly native Irish began to serve as jurors and even took on offices such as those of sub-sheriff or sheriff's bailiff, and by the 1620s men with native Irish names were even being considered for the magisterial bench (though the records do not survive to allow us to determine how many actually became JPs).[82] Yet we should be cautious before assuming a growing native acceptance of English rule. Resistance must have appeared futile given the military superiority of the state, especially at a time when England was not at war with a major European Catholic power that might be willing to lend the dispossessed in Ireland some support. Since they were going to be governed by English law, what were the native Irish to do other than try to make the system work to their best advantage? The Gaelic poets tended to represent the sufferings that befell the Irish people following the Flight of the Earls in providential terms, as punishment by God for their sins, which served to encourage a passive acceptance of one's plight.[83] For those who could not accept their fate with stoic resignation, there was always the option of emigration. Some gravitated towards the various Irish colleges being founded on the Continent—Paris (1578), Salamanca (1592), Louvain (1607), Bordeaux (1615), and Rome (1625). Others went to fight in the European wars. Some 6,260 Irishmen enlisted in armies on the Continent (mostly in Spanish Flanders) between 1605 and 1621—in theory all of them voluntarily. There was, however, some compulsory migration. In 1609 some prisoners were spared their lives on condition that they enlist to fight in the wars in Sweden; Chichester later boasted that he had been responsible for transporting 6,000 native soldiers out of Ireland to serve in the Swedish army, although in reality the figure was probably nearer 2,000, in part due to desertions en route.[84] Internal exile was attempted only once. Between the autumn of 1606 and the summer of 1609 some 289 families from Queen's County belonging to the 'Seven Septs' of O'More, O'Kelly, O'Lawlor, MacEvoy, O'Doran, O'Dowling, and O'Deevey were forcibly removed across the Shannon to Tarbert in Kerry; many tried to evade the crown's agents, and in the summer of 1610 the local garrison commander carried out a series of mass killings in the territory, according to a Gaelic scribe hanging 'every one he could catch', 'men, women and young people', in order to effect 'the final rout and banishment of the inhabitants of Laoighis [Queen's County]'.[85]

Some well-informed New English commentators were far from optimistic about how things were progressing in Ireland. The ex-soldier and writer Barnaby Rich, who shared in the colonization of Ulster and resided near Dublin, thought Davies's emphasis on the transformative effect of English common law was misguided and that things would not improve in Ireland until the issue of popery was satisfactorily addressed.[86] In a vehemently anti-Catholic piece of 1612, set as a dialogue between an Irish Catholic priest and a student from Trinity College Dublin but published in London (and therefore presumably intended as much for an English readership as an Irish Protestant one), Rich recalled 'the persecutions, the tortures and torments, that from time to time hath bin prosecuted by poplings, against the true professors of the Gospell' and the fact that the pope claimed the power from Christ to 'depose any prince, for tyranny or heresie'. For Rich, papists were 'both blind and out of their wits', and popery a religion 'propped up with such counterfeit stuffe, lyes, fables, dreames, visions, unwritten verities, and impossibilities'—in short, nothing 'but Idolatry, superstition and hypocrisie'.[87] Sir George Carew, Brouncker's predecessor as President of Munster whom James sent back to Ireland in 1611 to report on the progress of the plantation in Ulster, observed in 1614 how the recent 'plantation of new English and Scottish' in Ireland had encouraged 'the mere Irish' and 'the old English' to put behind them centuries of mutual hatred and unite in opposition to the present government, and predicted that as a result 'the next rebellion, whensoever it shall happen', would threaten 'more danger to the State than any that has preceded', because 'the revolt is like to be general'.[88]

The Catholics of Ireland—both the Old English and native Irish— harboured bitter resentments at the way they were being treated. When representatives of the Catholic community were summoned to London in 1613 to represent their concerns over the government's attempt to pack the Irish parliament, they seized the opportunity to deliver a lengthy petition to the crown detailing their grievances against the regime more generally. They began by listing the 'disorders' of the 'martial men' under eleven heads, among them: 'the great extortion of soldiers'; the use of martial law, which allowed 'private men... upon malice and corruption' to 'take away a man's life without trial'; and the taking of free quarter. People dared not make any formal complaint, in part 'for fear of the soldiers', and in part because 'so many captains and commanders of late' had been 'made counsellors of states' that they stood no chance of any redress. Then they proceeded to document 'disorders and abuses in the civil government', under eighteen heads: abuses in the legal system, such as the intimidation of jurors (an allusion to how jurors who refused to present recusants were prosecuted in Castle Chamber); the fact that 'very few of the natives of the kingdom' were 'admitted to any judicial place or ministerial office'; that no judges knew the Irish language and thus could not 'understand the party or witness that speak no English'; that the fines levied for recusancy ended up 'not employed upon the poor, according to the statute'; and that 'the ancient nobility of the kingdom' were 'not only debarred from publick employments' but also '[re]viled', 'set at nought', and 'disgraced by those...newly raised to honour, place, and means'.[89] Although a formal inquiry launched by the English crown exonerated Chichester of any misgovernment in Ireland, it did concede that the soldiers were guilty of 'several kinds of...oppressions towards the people', particularly extorting money 'from the poorer people' and forcibly seizing cattle and household goods if they could not pay; admitted that these 'oppressions' were 'very many'; conceded that people were scared to complain about the soldiers for fear of retribution; and further found it true that 'many sheriffs' were guilty of extortion and corruption.[90]

It was the native Irish who had lost most, particularly in the Ulster plantation, but also in Wexford and in parts of the midlands. Sir Toby Caulfield remarked of the Ulster Irish in June 1610 that there was 'not a more discontented people in Christendom'.[91] Sometimes the native Irish vented their resentment by attacking the Protestants who had displaced them: during the years 1616–19 nearly 300 woodkerne (outlaws or robbers who dwelled in the forests) were either killed by or executed for attacking Protestant settlers in Ireland.[92] Many native Irish were driven to despair and distraction. One account from County Longford from June 1620 described how 'divers of the poore natives or former freeholders of that Countie after the losse of all there possession, or Inheritance there' went either 'Madd' or else 'died instantlie from very grif'; some of them, on their death-beds, entreated their family and friends 'to bringe them out of ther said beds to have abroad the last sight of the hills and filds [*sic*] they lost in the said plantation, every one of them', it was said, 'diinge instantlie after'.[93]

B: Scotland

James had been an energetic and reforming king of Scotland prior to his accession to the English throne. He had done much to strengthen the position of the monarchy and to tame magnate power after the upheavals of the 1560s and his own lengthy royal minority, and he had begun the tasks of extending royal authority to the outer-lying regions of his realm and of reshaping the reformed Kirk so that it was more amenable to royal control. Perhaps the biggest testimony to his success in state building in Scotland was the smoothness of the transition to absentee monarchy. On leaving his homeland, James had promised he would return every three years. In fact he was to return just once—in 1617. Improved postal communications meant that it proved possible to govern by royal dispatches—what James styled government by pen. He opted not to appoint a viceroy—the office would have been inappropriate for an independent kingdom like Scotland, since it implied colonial dependency upon the crown of England—but he did rely on two trusted advisors to head the government north of the border: Alexander Seton, one of the Octavians of 1596, appointed Lord Chancellor in 1604 and created earl of Dunfermline the following year, who was the king's right-hand man from 1603 to 1606 and again from 1611 to 1622; and George Home, Lord Treasurer from 1601 and created earl of Dunbar in 1605, who headed the Edinburgh administration from 1606 until his death in 1611.[94]

After 1603, James continued to build upon the reform initiatives that he had begun prior to acceding to the English crown. In 1605 a joint Anglo-Scottish commission was set up to police the Borders—now the middle shires—with a small, armed police force. Despite some initial problems with funding, it gradually brought more stability to the area. By the time it fell victim to cuts in government spending in 1621, the murderous cross-border raids had ceased and the main problem on the Borders was the relatively minor crime of sheep-stealing. In 1604 the Scottish privy council passed a measure imposing severe penalties on lairds found guilty of feuding, and this was followed by a parliamentary statute in 1609 appointing gentlemen as JPs on the English model to maintain order in the shires, as a counterweight to the hereditary sheriffs.[95] The government also continued its efforts to bring the Highlands and Western Isles to civility. It showed itself prepared and able to take tough military action against troublesome Highland chiefs: there were military expeditions in 1605, 1608, 1614, 1615, and 1625, and further ones planned only to be called off when the offending chiefs agreed to toe the line. Attempts at colonization continued, although the Lewis colony was finally abandoned in 1610, defeated by native resistance. Henceforth the government developed a policy of granting greater support to clan chiefs, such as the Mackenzies (who acquired Lewis in 1610) and the

Campbells (who obtained Islay in 1614), who were willing to collaborate. The significance of the Statutes of Iona of 1609—an agreement reached with the chiefs of the Western Isles by the bishop of Isles, Andrew Knox, to establish parish ministers, reduce the military retinues of the clans, modify certain aspects of Gaelic culture, and improve the living standards of the inhabitants of the area—has arguably been exaggerated. But they did set in motion a development that was to lead to regular meetings between the clan chiefs and the privy council in Edinburgh and result in the Bond of 1616, whereby the chiefs gave caution to obey the law, limit their retinues, adopt Lowland farming methods and use the English language.[96]

The area where James had the greatest degree of unfinished business was with regard to the Kirk. James's handling of ecclesiastical affairs in Scotland prior to his accession to the English crown—his need to make compromises, his apparent flip-flopping between Presbyterianism and episcopacy, and his tendency to conceal his real intentions behind carefully worded diplomatic statements—has made it difficult for historians to determine where James actually stood on Kirk polity, and whether or not he changed his mind, either in the late 1590s or after becoming king of England. This very ambiguity is crucial to understanding the development of Scottish ecclesiastical politics in the seventeenth century. It was possible to point to two very different visions of the Kirk that had been sanctioned during James's early rule in Scotland: one which emphasized the Presbyterian structure of the Kirk and its relative autonomy from royal control, another which allowed some role for bishops and stressed that the Kirk was ultimately subordinate to the civil magistrate. James's skill had been to create a position that left him considerable room for manoeuvre, so that in introducing further reforms he could deny that he was claiming powers over the Kirk that he was not acknowledged to possess, or that he had any intention of altering the Kirk, and could represent those who challenged his policies as seditious. Those who disliked James's policies, however, saw them as dangerous innovations which did indeed threaten to alter the very nature of the Kirk, as they understood it.

As king of Scotland, James had had to tread carefully, adapting to circumstances as what appeared feasible changed over time. He certainly wanted a Kirk he could control, and this was most readily done through bishops, but the fact that he made no episcopal appointments prior to 1600 makes us question whether he was ideologically committed to episcopacy from the outset. In 1590 he had even praised the Scottish Kirk as 'the sincerest . . . in the world', and condemned the English prayer book service as crypto-Catholic. By the later 1590s, however, he had undoubtedly come to see the revival of episcopacy as the best way of managing what he saw as an increasingly fractious Kirk and had developed a marked antipathy towards the more extreme Presbyterians. His accession to the English crown created an entirely new context within which he had to work, opening up new possibilities for moving forward as well as generating new constraints. As an absentee monarch in Scotland, he needed to ensure that his control over the Kirk was stronger than ever, if he did not want to risk it developing once more in a direction independent of the crown. As a Scottish king in England, and especially given his initial plans for union between the two kingdoms, he needed to reassure the English that the English Church would be safe, and that it would not fall victim to any Scotticizing. At the same time, becoming head of the Erastian and episcopalian Church in England considerably strengthened his position against the Scottish Presbyterians, since he now could count on the support of a powerful Church interest in England in any steps he took to tame the Kirk, so long as he was careful to offer the right reassuring noises. According to the earl of Clarendon, James would often say that 'his access to the crown of England was the more valuable to him as it redeemed him from the subjection' to the 'ill manners and insolent practices' of Edinburgh's 'turbulent and seditious ministers', which 'he could never shake off before'.[97] Moreover, he recognized the political reality that, despite the fact that the union of the crowns had been brought about by a Scottish king inheriting the English throne, England would be the dominant partner in the relationship. As he asked rhetorically in 1607, 'when I have two Nations under my government, can you imagine I will respect the lesser, and neglect the greater?'[98]

The altered context after 1603, therefore, pushed James into seeing the solution to managing the Kirk as making the Kirk more like the Church in England. James proceeded in two stages. Initially he concentrated his efforts on Anglicizing the government of the Kirk, by reviving diocesan episcopacy and reinvigorating the royal supremacy. From about 1612 he moved to a policy of trying to bring the liturgy of the Kirk into closer conformity with that of the English Church. Whether or not he had been sincere in professing in 1590 his belief that the Scottish Kirk was better than the English Church, by 1616 he appears to have come to the conclusion, as he declared in a speech in Star Chamber, that the Church in England was the 'most pure, and nearest the Primitive and Apostolicall Church in Doctrine and Discipline...of any Church in Christendome'.[99] James's reforms were to involve manipulation, bullying, and intimidation, and although the changes were sanctioned both by parliament and the General Assembly, it required considerable pressure from the crown to achieve the desired ends.

The Revival of Episcopacy

Given that his priority following his accession to the English crown was to work towards a union of the two kingdoms, James decided that the General Assembly should not be allowed to meet until a scheme for union had been concluded, and so he postponed the meetings intended for 1604 and 1605. On the second occasion about thirty ministers decided they should meet regardless, in defiance of the king, in Aberdeen on 2 July. The king's commissioner for Kirk affairs, Sir Alexander Stratoun of Lauriston, urged them to desist; as a compromise the moderator John Forbes agreed to adjourn the assembly until the last day of September. The council moved quickly to issue proclamations prohibiting the September meeting and condemning those who sought to justify the Aberdeen assembly, and summoned the ringleaders to account for their actions. Fourteen who refused to acknowledge the Aberdeen assembly to be illegal were detained in prison in Blackness. Six of these (Forbes among them) were subsequently found guilty of treason at a trial in Linlithgow on 10 January 1606; declining the opportunity to acknowledge their offence and crave the king's forgiveness, in October they were banished from the king's dominions. The rest were ordered to be confined in either Lewis, Kintyre, or Caithness, 'the most barbarrous pairtis of the realme' in the opinion of James Melville.[100]

It was the parliament that met at Perth in July 1606 which paved the way for the restoration of full diocesan episcopacy. James managed to persuade the assembly to accept royal nominations to the Lords of the Articles, on the grounds that he needed to make sure the committee comprised those best acquainted with the ongoing negotiations for Union, although he promised this would be a one-off. To ensure that the crown of Scotland was politically equal to that of England, parliament passed an Act acknowledging 'his majestie's soverane authoritie, princelie power, royall prerogative and privilege of his crowne over all estaittis, persones and causes quatsumevir' to be 'als absolutlie, amplie and frelie in all respectis and considerationis' as any king of Scotland had ever possessed, annulling and rescinding anything ever done in the past, or intended to be done in the future, that was to the derogation of this sovereign authority. Not only did the measure affirm that the Scottish crown was absolute but it also confirmed the royal supremacy in Scotland. (The principle of royal supremacy itself had been articulated by the Black Acts of 1584 and retained by the Golden Act of 1592.) Having thus supposedly brought the powers of the two crowns in line, the Perth parliament then passed an Act for the Restitution of the Estate of Bishops, which repealed the Act of Annexation of 1587 in so far as it related to episcopal lands and confirmed the bishops' right to sit in parliament. (Their precise ecclesiastical role was left for the General Assembly to establish.)[101] Some twenty presbyteries sent delegates to lobby parliament against the restoration, and submitted a written protest signed by at least forty-two ministers stating the episcopacy was against the Confession of Faith of 1581, although to no avail. James had to reassure the laity by promising confirmations and offering compensation, but since only episcopal temporalities were restored most managed to hold on to much of what they had; James further sweetened the pill by using the abbey lands that remained in his possession to endow new peerages, which had the added advantage of creating a new service nobility as a counter to the old nobility.[102]

In an attempt to bring the Scottish Presbyterians on board, James summoned Andrew and James Melville and six other ministers to Hampton Court in September 1606, purportedly so that he could 'treate' with them concerning the peace of the Kirk. When they arrived they found themselves subjected to a crude ideological browbeating: James quizzed and lectured them about the Aberdeen Assembly and explained 'how happily this Church of England was established under the government of Bishops', and they were compelled to listen to sermons by leading Anglican ecclesiasts defending episcopacy and the royal supremacy and comparing the Presbyterians to the pope for their lack of respect for sovereign authority.[103] Andrew Melville was horrified by the 'hie service' with 'strange musick' he was forced to attend at the royal chapel on 29 September (Michaelmas), during which he saw the king and queen make an offering at an altar bedecked with books, basins, and candlesticks, and he penned a poem in Latin condemning such 'Romish rites'.[104] Summoned later that day to Dunbar's lodgings to be grilled before members of the Scottish council about the Aberdeen Assembly, Andrew told his accusers they were 'betraying and overturning' the 'freedome of the[ir] countrey and the gospell'; his nephew James protested he was 'a free subject of the kingdome of Scotland' and should be dealt with according to Scottish law. As punishment for their noncompliance, all eight were for a time warded in the house of an English bishop, although six were eventually allowed to return to Scotland. James Melville was confined first to Newcastle, then to Berwick. Andrew Melville, in trouble for his Latin verses and for an altercation with Bancroft when he seized the archbishop's sleeves and called them 'Romish rags and the mark of the Beast', was committed to the Tower the following spring. He was released in 1611, but forbidden to return to Scotland and lived out his final days in exile in France.[105]

With many of the likely troublemakers among the clergy either banished, warded, or detained in England, James decided to call a convention of the Kirk to meet at Linlithgow in December 1606. It was a carefully stage-managed affair. James wrote to all the presbyteries in advance, instructing them whom to choose as commissioners, and to his own nominees, telling them to attend whether or not their presbytery gave them a commission. Dunbar distributed 40,000 merks among 'the most neiddey' ministers, to buy either their votes or their neutrality. In an effort to win over the 'more preceisse amongst the ministry', James announced in his letter to the convention that he wanted tougher measures against papists, Jesuits, and seminary priests; it was left to the moderator to explain that the government believed that the rise in the number of Catholics in Scotland was due to the fact that the moderators of the presbyteries were altered too frequently. The convention eventually agreed that bishops or their appointed subordinates should be permanent moderators of presbyteries, although the printed version of the acts did not in fact appear for another a year, giving the court time, it was alleged, to falsify the record and insert stronger language concerning the role of the bishops as moderators. The convention had not been summoned as a General Assembly; yet because some ministers whom James had not called did attend, James subsequently chose to style it such.[106]

In 1609 a parliament which met at Edinburgh passed an Act restoring bishops to their 'former authoritie... and jurisdictiouns', thereby paving the way for the restoration of two courts of High Commission (one for each province), while at the same time confirming the king's ultimate 'supremacie in all causes, ecclesiasticall and civill'.[107] The following year a General Assembly held at Glasgow voted to restore bishops to their traditional diocesan functions of visitations, presentations, and deprivations, affirmed the right of the king to call General Assemblies, declared the Aberdeen Assembly of 1605 void, and established that in future all General Assemblies and synods were to be moderated by bishops. It also passed a measure requiring all clergy, upon admission to the ministry, to swear an oath acknowledging James as 'the only lawfull supreame governour of this realme' in matters 'ecclesiasticall' and 'temporall', thereby compelling them to recognize the royal supremacy in Scotland. Again the Assembly had to be carefully rigged to get the measures through: the king and the bishops wrote to the presbyteries suggesting the names of the people they should send; the crown paid the expenses of well-affected ministers who lived far away from Glasgow to make sure they could afford to attend; and Dunbar had troops in attendance to arrest anyone who opposed the king's designs. In order to restore the apostolic succession to Scotland, in December 1610 the archbishop of Glasgow and the bishops of Brechin and Galloway went to London to be consecrated by the bishops of Bath, Ely, and London. (Neither Canterbury nor York was involved, to avoid any suspicion of subordination to England.) Once consecrated, the three returned to Scotland to consecrate the rest of their brethren. The acts of the Glasgow Assembly were then ratified by parliament in 1612, although under pretence of offering a fuller explanation parliament proceeded to modify the provisions of a number of the acts, including omitting a clause stating that bishops were to be subject to the authority of the General Assembly.[108]

Reform of the Liturgy

From 1612 James began to make moves to reform the liturgy of the Kirk to bring it closer into line with the practices of the English Church. It has been suggested that James's aim was not so much Anglicization as ecclesiastical convergence. According to this view he needed to make the two churches outwardly seem more like each other, so that he could not be accused of sanctioning two very different types of worship within his separate kingdoms; in particular, he wanted to get the Kirk to agree in principle that the liturgical practices of the Church in England were legitimate, even though he had no desire to enforce English liturgical practices too strictly in Scotland. The quid pro quo was the promotion of a preaching ministry in England, an effort to reassure both the Scots and English Puritans that he was serious about promoting the word of God. Such a strategy was designed to make it impossible for Protestants in either kingdom to condemn the Church in the other as being in error, while a laxity in enforcing conformity would mean that it would be possible to sustain the fragile ecclesiastical consensus without forcing too many people into opposition.[109]

Put like that, James's policy seems relatively benign. However, the Scots did not see it as such; in fact, large numbers were deeply alarmed. Nor did they see James's strategy as one of convergence; to them it seemed like Anglicization, and there can be no doubt that the Scots were being asked to make many more—and more significant—concessions to English practices than were the English to Scottish practices. Moreover, it would be wrong to see James's promotion of liturgical innovations in Scotland as merely a tactical gesture; he was serious about reform and wanted his reforms enforced. This begs the question of why James wanted to reform the Scottish liturgy along Anglican lines, given that this was likely to ruffle so many feathers in Scotland. A number of reasons suggest themselves. He may well have felt that a more ceremonialist style of worship in Scotland would induce Scottish Catholics to conform, or at least make it easier for notorious Catholic dissidents like the earl of Huntly to make their peace with the regime and subscribe to the confession of faith. After years in England he might genuinely have become convinced that the English Church was the Church that was closest to the apostolic Church. Perhaps most obviously, his aim of reducing religious tensions in Europe by trying to bring the various Christian Churches closer together through an emphasis on their shared heritage stood a greater chance of success if the Church in England was used as a model rather than the Scottish Kirk.[110]

The first hint of intended change came in 1612, when a new confession of faith was drafted in England and sent up to Scotland, although for the time being the plan was put on hold.[111] Recognizing that any liturgical innovations intended to bring the Kirk closer into line with the English Church ran the risk of being seen by Scottish Calvinists as popish, James decided to introduce his proposed reforms under the guise of taking tougher measures against Catholics. In March 1614 the privy council announced that in order to ensure that everyone could receive communion, and to identify remaining Catholics, ministers were to hold communion on Sunday, 24 April—not in itself an objectionable idea, except for the fact that 24 April 1614 was Easter Sunday and as part of its Reformation the Kirk in Scotland had abandoned the celebration of Easter. The contemporary

Scottish Presbyterian and historian David Calderwood later wrote that the king's true intention was to try 'how the people would bear with alterations and innovations'. Most ministers appear to have obeyed, eager to seize the opportunity to strike at Catholicism. A few were suspicious of the motive, especially in the synod of St Andrews, and refused to hold communion that day; the bishops were told to find out who they were and to suspend or even deprive them. The following year the crown issued a proclamation stating that communion should be celebrated one day every year, namely Easter Sunday.[112]

James was now ready to revive the idea of a new confession of faith and summoned a General Assembly to meet in August 1616 at Aberdeen on the north-east coast of Scotland—Aberdeen in part because of the large number of Catholics in the area and in part because those most likely to be opposed to the idea were in the south and would have more difficulty attending. The blatant attempts at packing seen in 1610 were not repeated, although given that the bishops and their appointees, the moderators of the presbyteries, attended *ex officio* and the lay element was summoned by the king, the crown was left with considerable influence. The archbishop of St Andrews, John Spottiswoode, stepped into the moderator's place, without being elected, contrary to normal practice. James's letter announced that he wanted the Assembly's advice on 'rooting out of Popery', and the first few days of business were taken up with making new laws against Catholics as a time-wasting measure (they were never enforced nor ratified by parliament), so that ministers who came from 'the far South', 'being wearied, might withdraw themselves' before 'the matters chiefly aimed at' were treated. Four days into the session Montrose read a list of further instructions from the king calling (among other things) for a new confession of faith (to be sworn by all office holders and all students), a new liturgy, Easter communions, and the codification of ecclesiastical law in canons drawn from the acts of former assemblies. Several ministers walked out in protest; those who stayed found that debate was stifled by Spottiswoode. The Assembly agreed a new confession of faith, which required subscribers to acknowledge that God had ordained kings to govern the Kirk as well as the Commonwealth; upheld Easter communions; and appointed committees to draw up a new book of common prayer and new canons.[113] Buoyed by this success, James sent north five new articles he wanted inserted alongside the canons, relating to kneeling at communion, private baptism, private communion for the sick or infirm, episcopal confirmation, and the celebration of five holy days (Christ-mas, Good Friday, Easter, Ascension Day, and Whitsunday). When Archbishop Spottiswoode pointed out that this would contravene the agreement that the canons should be drawn up from former acts of General Assemblies, James backed down. The articles could wait until he visited Scotland in person the following summer.[114]

In preparation for James's visit, the Scots started to fix up Edin-burgh Castle and Holyrood Palace, to repair the roads, and to clear the capital of vagrants and other undesirables.[115] For his part, James ordered a total renovation of the chapel at Holyrood, installing two brand new organs (costing £400) and 'a glorious altar' with candles, and commissioning Inigo Jones to decorate the pews and stalls with gilded wooden statues of the twelve disciples and four apostles. Those close to the English court knew the refurbishments were likely to prove controversial: 'how welcome they wilbe thether', John Cham-berlain pondered in a letter to Sir Dudley Carleton, 'God knowes'. As the carpenters set to work, rumours began to circulate that 'images were to be set up in the Chappell' and that 'the organs came first, now the images, and ere long they should have the masse'. The bishop of Galloway, who was the dean of the Chapel, together with Archbishop Spottiswoode and several other bishops wrote to the king informing him that the portraits had provoked great offence and advising the work should stop. Outraged, James wrote back lambasting the ignor-ance of those who 'could not distinguish betwixt Pictures intended for Ornament and decoration, and Images erected for worship and adoration', and lamenting the fact that the Scots could 'endure Lions, Dragons and Devils to be figured in [their] Churches', but not the patriarchs and apostles. Nevertheless he did order the work on the statues to stop—not, he was quick to point out, to alleviate the Scots' concerns, but because it had become apparent that the work was not going to be completed in time.[116]

James began his progress north on 15 March.[117] When he reached the border on 13 May, he got off his horse, lay on the ground, and proclaimed that here was the union of Scotland and England in his own person.[118] He made his formal entry into Edinburgh on 16 May 1617, to be greeted by the civic authorities and feted by the citizens; but although the locals welcomed James with 'greate shouts of joye' there were no pageants, the Scots regarding them 'very Idolatrous thinges, and not fitt to be used in soe reformed a place'. When James arrived at Holyrood, the Clerk Deputy, Sir John Hay, delivered a fawning speech, penned by the great Scottish poet William Drummond of Hawthornden, praising the king's prudence, wisdom, and constancy 'in uniting the disjoynted members of this Commonwealth' following 'the tumultuous dayes' of James's 'more tender yeeres' and his 'great vigilancie and godlie zeale in propagating the Gospell, defacing the monuments of idolatrie, banishing that Romane and Anti-christian hierarchie, and establishing of our Church'.[119] James made no secret of his desire to introduce a more ceremonialist style of worship into the Kirk. Of the three bishops he brought with him from England, two were noted ceremonialists—Lancelot Andrewes of Ely and Richard Neile of Lincoln (promoted to Durham later that month)—while the third—James Montagu of Winchester—although a Calvinist, was a staunch defender of episcopacy and the royal prerogative, and had spoken in favour of ceremonies at the Hampton Court Conference. William Laud, recently promoted to dean of Gloucester and who was to rise to prominence as the leader of the Arminian faction in the Church under Charles I, was also in attendance, as part of Neile's retinue.[120] James attended Holyrood Chapel on 8 June for a Whit Sunday communion service conducted along English lines, with 'the singing of quiristers and the playing of organs'. All the Scottish bishops present received communion kneeling (Galloway excused himself on the grounds of ill health), as did half a dozen newly created peers, although the rest of the nobles and the other ministers in attendance refused.[121]

Parliament opened on 17 June. James gave a provocative speech in which he stated that since the Scots 'imitated England in superfluity of apparel, diet and Tobacco', they should conform 'with England in good lawes, spirituall and civill'. Controversy erupted immediately over the selection of the Lords of the Articles. Following the precedent established in 1606, James tried to impose his own nominees; suspicious of James's designs for the Kirk, the nobles assumed anyone recommended by the king to be suspect and put forward the names of those who, according to Spottiswoode, 'stood worse affected to his Majestie's service'.[122] Furious, James threatened to dissolve parliament; in the end a compromise was reached whereby the king was allowed to veto some of parliament's nominees. James attended every meeting of the Lords of the Articles; if he had to be away for any reason, he prorogued the committee until his return. The ministers of Edinburgh, however, lobbied the bishops 'to conclude nothing in prejudice of the Church, without advice of a generall assembly', and the bishops gave their word. The legislative package agreed by the Lords of the Articles came before parliament on 27 June, the most controversial of which was a proposal that whatever the king decided about matters of Kirk policy in consultation with the bishops should have the force of law. The bishops protested that Scottish tradition and precedent required not just the consent of the bishops but also of the body of the presbyters through a General Assembly. James said he did not agree with the 'detestable old Scottish notion' that the opinion of the presbyters could only be ascertained by General Assemblies, but agreed to the modified wording that whatever the king decided 'with the advice of the Archbishops, Bishops, and a competent number of the Ministry' should have the force of law. The proposed statute nevertheless still threatened to uproot the Presbyterian principle that the Kirk should be ruled by free and regularly elected General Assemblies. The Edinburgh ministers, led by Archibald Simpson and David Calderwood, drew up a protestation against the proposed legislation, signed by fifty-three others, which they presented to Spottiswoode the next day. The archbishop tore it in pieces, but the ministers had presented another copy to the bishops in parliament and James, eager to avoid having the royal prerogative debated, decided not to press the matter and withdrew the proposed bill. Instead, James had the High Commission proceed against the ministers behind the protestation: four repented, but Simpson, Calderwood, and one other remained obdurate and were deprived and imprisoned. Calderwood was subsequently banished.[123]

James was not particularly upset by the failure of the bill, believing that it would have given him nothing more than he already possessed by dint of the royal prerogative. He was reassured by David Lindsay, a member of the High Commission, who in a public defence of his doctoral thesis before the King at St Andrews on 12 July proclaimed that kings could 'make Lawes concerning all things in the worship of God' and that their power was not subordinate to the 'Kingdome of Christ, or to any ministry or ministers thereof, whatsoever'; even a magistrate who forsook the Christian religion, Lindsay added, 'looseth not his authority'.[124] At a conference at St Andrews the following day James asked those clergy present to agree to implement his new five articles of religion. Taken aback, the clergy protested that the articles would have to go before a General Assembly. James yielded to the inevitable. After he returned to England, he summoned a General Assembly to meet at St Andrews in November to consider the articles. To his fury, it rejected them. He wrote an angry letter to the two archbishops warning that 'your Scottish Church' would soon 'find what it is to draw the anger of a King upon them' and ordering them to 'keep Christmas day precisely'. He followed this up in the new year by instructing his privy council to issue a proclamation commanding the observation of all five holy days and warning that the contraveners would be punished 'with all rigour, as rebellious or dissobedient personis'.[125]

James brought the five articles before a specially convened 'National Assembly' which met at Perth on 25–27 August 1618. It was a packed body: the king nominated the lay members and also a number of clerical members, while several clergy who in theory had been elected had actually been returned through the careful management of the bishops. James's letter to the Assembly was read twice on the first day, and again on subsequent days, 'to the end the Assembly might see his earnestnesse about the same matters', or—according to critics of the Articles—'to make a more forcible impression of terror'. After 'the disgrace offered unto Us in that late meeting at S. Andrewes, wherein Our just and godly desires were...neglected', it opened, 'Wee were once fully resolved, never in Our time, to have called any more Assemblies there'. Even though, in response to their pleadings, he had allowed another one to meet, they were not to think that the articles 'may not without such a generall consent be enjoyed by Our authoritie: This were a misknowing of your places', James pronounced, 'a disclayming of that innate power, which We have by Our calling from God...to dispose of things externall in the Church, as We shall thinke them to be convenient, and profitable for advauncing true Religion amongst Our Subjects'. They should therefore yield obediently, since he would not 'be satisfied with refuses, or delayes, or mitigations' but expected 'a simple, and direct acceptation of these Articles in the forme...sent'. Recalling the 'many abuses...offered Us by many of the Ministrie' in Scotland 'before Our happie comming to this Crowne', James said he wished not to be 'further provoked...and slandered by such, as under the cloake of seeming holinesse' joined 'in this their disobedience unto Magistracie, with the upholders of Poperie'. Spottiswoode again assumed the role of moderator, without an election, protesting when challenged that since the Assembly was called within his own diocese 'no man would take his place'. In his sermon delivered at the opening of the Assembly, the archbishop claimed that he did not particularly want the innovations himself, but there was 'nothing impious or unlawfull in them' and 'Our religion' taught us 'to obey superiors in all things...not contrarie to the Word of God'. 'The evil of novations, especially in matters of Rite and Ceremonie', he continued, was 'nothing so great as the evill of disobedience', and since these ceremonies were being urged 'by our Soveraigne Lord and King', we could not in conscience refuse them. As for the fear that these ceremonies were to pave the way for the introduction of the rest of the English ceremonies, Spottiswoode insisted that no more would follow if the Scots accepted these, but that 'the ready way to have the rest imposed' was 'to offend his Majestie by our resistance'.[126]

Considerable intimidation was used to get the five articles accepted. An armed guard was present. The ministers were forced to stand while the bishops, officers of state, and lay members were allowed to sit: the future bishop of Edinburgh, David Lindsay, who wrote in defence of the meeting, acknowledged that this upset those who 'cannot abide to heare of degrees in the Church', but claimed that the seating arrangement conformed to 'the degrees of the old Christian Councels' and that 'Church men must learne... to live orderly'. Spottiswoode warned that anyone who dared oppose the articles would face deprivation or banishment, and although at one stage he suggested that James 'wold be merciful in urgeing obedience', later on, exasperated by the criticism of the articles, he blasted: 'Think not but when the act is made I will get obedience'. Those opposed to the five articles insisted that supporters would have to 'prove them necessary and expedient for our Kirk'; supporters, by contrast, maintained that the other side 'must either prove the Articles to be impious and unlawfull, or else they must prove disobedient to his Majesty'. As to the suggestion that 'the Bishops were bringing in Papistrie', Spottiswoode argued that it was not 'ceremonies' that made the 'separation betwixt us and the Roman Kirk, but their idolatrie, which, if the Romanists wold forsake, they wold meet them midway, and joine with them'. When it came to the vote, nothing was left to chance. Spottiswoode warned that James would be told the names of those who voted against. The nobles and barons in attendance were allowed to vote, even though they were not commissioners. Many of the clergy were promised a benefice or an increased stipend if they voted in favour; others were privately told that if they voted to please the king they would not be required to enforce the articles; some were threatened with removal from the ministry if they voted against. A number of those in favour, it was alleged, were called upon to vote a second time, 'after the interjection of other names'. The Five Articles passed by a vote of eighty-six to forty-one (among the dissentients a majority of parish ministers), with four abstentions.[127]

The privy council ratified the Five Articles of Perth on 21 October as having 'the force and strenth of lawis in all tyme comeing',[128] and the bishops urged ministers to enforce them, especially the Articles concerning the observation of holy days and kneeling for communion. Although there is some evidence to suggest that the Articles were accepted in the north of Scotland, opposition was widespread in the south. Many ministers refused to acknowledge the legitimacy of the Perth Assembly and urged noncompliance. Christmas was poorly observed in 1618, notably in Edinburgh, where conformist ministers complained about 'the rarity of their hearers'. At the synod of St Andrews 'benorth Forth' held in April 1619, thirty-six ministers failed to conform and a further seventeen absented themselves. Hence enforcement met with only limited success. In the summer of 1620 the privy council introduced a scale of fines for laity who failed to kneel—earls £100, lords 100 merks, lairds £40, and craftsmen and husbandmen £10—although nonconformity was so widespread that the fines were not imposed. Yet we should not assume from this that James did not want the Five Articles of Perth enforced. In fact he made repeated calls for their enforcement during the remainder of his reign, being particularly keen to secure compliance to those Articles requiring kneeling at communion and the observation of holy days. Calderwood identified forty-three individuals along with various unnamed 'others' who were summoned before the High Commission between 1618 and the end of the reign for failure to conform to the new style of communion. The most concerted effort to enforce the Articles—and the most persistent opposition to them—was in Edinburgh. In February 1619 the privy council summoned several townspeople to answer for having worked on Christmas Day; that Easter (as in subsequent years) thousands of people deserted the capital to take communion elsewhere in an attempt to avoid getting into trouble for refusing to kneel.[129]

'A Concurrence of So Many Faelicities'

When the Thirty Years War broke out in Europe in 1618, James had been on the throne of England for fifteen years. Reviewing the situation just prior to the outbreak of the war, it was possible to reach a highly positive assessment of James's achievements to date. 'In these few yeeres...of your happie Reigne over us', the Warwickshire-based doctor and translator Philemon Holland rejoiced in a speech delivered before the king at Coventry in 1617, as James progressed south through England on his return from Scotland, 'wee have found a concurrence of so many faelicities, proportioned to your incomparable Wisdome, Justice, Mercy, and other Princely Vertues, seasoned all with true Religion, as in no Age, by any Record, the like'. The people of England, Holland pronounced, had 'seene Peace in Church, and Commonwealth fully established: holesome Lawes, respective to the Times, judiciously enacted; the same with mercie, equitie, and moderation...duly executed. The auncient Catholike Faith [i.e. Protestantism]...constantly defended. The holy Scriptures, with profound judgement newly translated.' They had 'seene the Realme of Ireland, without sword drawne, reduced to Civilitie; and Justice setled in all parts thereof', and the 'wild and Irefull Irishry...subdued' and 'governed as Subjects, by ordinary Lawes, under one Soveraigne, a mightie Monarch'. Holland did not specifically mention Scotland, but he did observe how they had 'seene the insolent outrages repressed of those rude and unruly Borderers of the middle Shires of great Britain: where now in stead of deadly-fude, and mortall enmitie, is entertained the mutuall amitie, in lieu of Hostilitie, Hospitalitie'. Finally, Holland proclaimed, God had given James a gift, rare among other kings, 'not onely to maintaine Peace within your owne Dominions at home, but also to be a blessed Peace-maker betwixt forraine Princes, and States abroad'.[130]

In offering such a ringing endorsement, Holland had an agenda: he was hoping that James might do something for Coventry, which had fallen on hard times of late. Yet exaggerated and hyperbolic though his praise unquestionably was, there were elements of truth to Holland's assessment. There is a case to be made that under James there was greater peace in the Church than had existed during the final decades of Elizabeth's reign. He had done much to pacify the Borders and had managed to remain at peace with his European neighbours. He had embarked on an ambitious policy of reform in both Ireland and Scotland, not without some success. He had extended English rule in Ireland and managed to keep the kingdom at peace, in and of themselves no mean achievements. He had re-established episcopacy in Scotland and made significant progress in bringing the Scottish Kirk into closer conformity with the Church in England. His policies were not welcomed by all and he had aroused opposition. Yet he had achieved much, and in the process had shown himself to be a skilled political operator. In Scotland, for instance, he had played on fears of popery to get his reforms through and he had worked with the

General Assemblies of the Kirk and with the Scottish parliament: opponents of his religious reforms might question the legitimacy of the bodies which had enacted them, alleging that they were packed assemblies or subjected to undue intimidation, but they could not claim that James had side-stepped the traditional governing institutions in Kirk and state north of the border.

The extent to which he had really provided a viable solution to any of the problems he faced within his political inheritance at the time of his succession, however, is far from clear. His policies in Ireland had caused bitter resentments; the kingdom might have been more peaceful than it had been under Elizabeth, but the native Irish and the Old English were beginning to form common cause in opposition to the English government, a development which contemporaries saw as ominous. James might have been tactically astute in the way in which he succeeded in inducing the Assemblies of the Kirk and the Scottish parliament to enact his desired religious reforms, but his policies proved not only bitterly divisive but arguably counterproductive: instead of building towards greater religious consensus he had generated greater discord; he had even managed to undermine his own achievement in getting the Scots to accept episcopacy (itself a controversial enough policy, but which many Scots might have been willing to accept) by then pushing for liturgical reforms which in turn created a backlash against the bishops.[131] In England, he might have held religious tensions in check via his delicate balancing act in the Church, but he had hardly solved any of the underlying problems, he had failed to solve the problem of royal finance, and his relationship with the English parliament had become so strained that he had opted to try to rule without calling one for an extended period, which in turn compromised his financial position and his foreign policy options. Moreover, the success of James's strategy was heavily dependent on his ability, to borrow Holland's words, 'not onely to maintaine Peace within your owne Dominions at home, but also to be a blessed Peace-maker betwixt forraine Princes, and States abroad'. The trouble was the peace of Europe was about to be shattered.

7

The Bohemian Revolt and the Crisis of the Early 1620s

On 18 November 1618 a great comet—estimated to be 1/27th the size of the earth, or nearly twice as large as the moon—was seen in the sky over south-east England. Over the next several weeks it whirled around the earth every twenty-four hours on a gradually declining orbit, passing directly over London on 11 December before hastening northwards towards the Orkney Islands off the far north-eastern tip of Scotland. The contemporary Scottish historian James Balfour, who recorded the motions of the comet in an account penned on 2 October 1648, retrospectively interpreted its appearance as a portent of the troubles to come. 'Since wich tyme', he observed, 'ther begane grate warrs in Germanie' that were ultimately to involve all the major rulers of Europe; 'sundrie attemptes, batells, assaults...betuixe the K[ing] of Grate Brittane and his subiects'; the 'grate and creuell massacker of the Scottes and Englishe protestants, by the inhumane and bloodie Irishe, in Ireland'; and an 'wnnaturall warre, in all the 3 kingdomes', which, when Balfour wrote, still continued 'to this day', without 'aney appirance of peace'.[1] The London Puritan diarist Nehemiah Wallington later recalled how King James had had a discussion with mathematicians at Cambridge University about the comet, and concluded that though 'the body of this great star' was over Germany, and 'denounceth much war and desolation to that nation', the star's tail was over his own dominions and territories; and since the sting was in the tail, it would, James allegedly concluded, 'chiefly centre and have its primary influence upon me, or my children'. Writing as he was in the early 1640s, Wallington observed: 'How true this prophetical presage hath fallen out.'[2] But there was plenty of speculation at the time over the meaning of this celestial omen. In a poem composed when the comet first appeared, King James commented on 'the rash Imaginations' of 'the Curious man', who anticipated 'Famine plague and war', thought 'the match with spaine hath causd this star', and feared that either the Prince of Wales or the country might be forced to change their religion.[3] The king himself was more sceptical, believing the comet was 'nothing else but Venus with a firebrand in her—'.[4]

1618 was the year in which the Protestant estates of Bohemia (the modern-day Czech Republic) rebelled against their Roman Catholic king Ferdinand II, of the House of Habsburg, thereby triggering what is known to history as the Thirty Years War. In August 1619 the Bohemians offered their crown to James's son-in-law, Frederick V, Elector Palatine, who was duly crowned king on 4 November 1619. Ferdinand, now Holy Roman Emperor, struck back in alliance with the Catholic League of Germany and Habsburg Spain. In September 1620 Spain invaded the Palatinate while Imperial forces marched into Bohemia, where Ferdinand decisively defeated Frederick at the Battle of White Mountain, near Prague, on 8 November, forcing Frederick and his family into exile in Holland. The following year the temporary truce between Spain and the Protestant Dutch republic expired, leading to the outbreak of renewed hostilities in the Low Countries. Ultimately most of the countries of Europe were to get caught up in the conflict, which became one of the longest and most destructive wars in European history. With Bohemia falling and then the Palatinate, Protestantism in Europe seemed very much on the retreat; if the United Provinces were to fall, who could be sure that England would not be next? The war was to leave much of the Empire devastated. Prague and those parts of the Elbe valley in Bohemia which saw the heaviest of the fighting lost half of their population. Some towns in the bishopric of Halberstadt lost between 70 and 90 per cent of their inhabitants. In the decade after 1627 the urban population of Brandenburg fell from 113,500 to 34,000, the rural population from 300,000 to 75,000. Overall the German states lost about one third of their population to warfare or disease—perhaps some 8 million in total—and 1618 population levels were in general not reached again until 1710–20, though in parts of the Empire not until the nineteenth century.[5]

The outbreak of war on the Continent created problems for James's entire political strategy. He had sought to be the peacemaker of Europe by pursuing alliances with both Protestant and Catholic powers on the Continent, but how could he continue to pursue a Spanish match for his son when his daughter's husband was at war with the Habsburgs? Would public opinion in England allow him to stay neutral in the European conflict? He had sought to relieve pressure on royal finances by keeping England out of European entanglements and to minimize political conflict at home by avoiding parliament; yet if James did get sucked into the Continental conflict, it would be expensive—even the pursuit of a peaceful solution through diplomacy proved costly—and the only body capable of providing sufficient funds was the English parliament. He had been trying to accommodate a broad spectrum of opinion within the English Church, while at the same time moving the Scottish Kirk closer to the English model. But with the Calvinist clergy the most militant in their anti-popery and most outspoken in their demands that England help Frederick, James's efforts to work towards a diplomatic solution with Spain made it necessary for him to silence godly Protestant critics and turn increasingly towards the Arminians—and this at a time when he was having to hold out the prospect of greater religious freedom to his Catholic subjects and when he was beginning to step up the pressure on Scottish Presbyterians to conform to the Articles of Perth.

The years following the outbreak of the Thirty Years War saw the development of the first crisis of the Stuart monarchy. The crisis was so severe because it was multi-dimensional. It was in part about foreign policy, but it was in part also fiscal, economic (trade depression combined with harvest failure made these desperate times for the country at large), political, religious, and personal. Nor was this just a crisis of high politics. The issues were debated and the political tensions played out within a burgeoning public sphere, as critics of royal policy sought to engage with those out-of-doors via the pulpit, the hustings, and the press. The revolt in Bohemia was to set in motion a train of events that were to highlight how inherently difficult it was to manage the Stuart multiple-kingdom inheritance and also expose the extent to which James, despite all his reforms, had failed to solve many of the basic problems facing his kingship. Yet the way James responded under crisis reveals his skill as a political operator. Although James ruffled more than a few feathers during the final years of his reign, he showed an ability to compromise and a preparedness to back down graciously under pressure which enabled him to restore a more harmonious relationship with the political nation, and particularly parliament, by the end of his reign.

The Palatinate, Public Opinion, and the Meeting of the 1621 Parliament

James turned fifty-two in 1618 and his health had already begun to deteriorate. He suffered from gout, kidney problems, bad circulation, and arthritis. By 1621 his legs had become so weak that he had to be carried to parliament in a chair and his lungs were often affected by bronchitis. His health was not helped by poor habits: he drank too much, ate an unbalanced diet, and bolted down his food unchewed (having by now lost most of his teeth), with the consequence that he suffered from flatulence, haemorrhoids, and frequent insomnia. The combined effects of illness, constant pain, and sleep deprivation left him irritable and prone to bouts of melancholy; it also sapped his energy, which made it increasingly difficult for him to sustain close attention to government business or to keep on top of the routine paperwork. Yet we should not see James as slipping into dotage. Albeit in physical decline, he retained his mental sharpness and political sagacity, and he was still more than capable of asserting himself in politics.[6]

James lost his wife on 2 March 1619, to consumption and dropsy, at the relatively young age of forty-four. Despite not having been close to her for many years, James appears to have been genuinely upset by Anne's death, which triggered in him a bout of illness.[7] He was touched by the letters of condolence he received from the duke of Lorraine, and expressed his grief through poetry:

> Soe did our Queene from hence her court remove,
> and leave the Earth to bee enthroned above;
> then she is changed, not dead, noe good prince dyes,
> but only like the sunne doth sett to rise.[8]

The funeral had to be delayed for lack of money to pay for mourning clothes for the king's or prince's servants,[9] although over the longer term the disbanding of the queen's court at Denmark House did have the effect of introducing some much-needed economies into the royal finances. On the downside, the queen's demise highlighted the extent to which James was becoming increasingly dependent upon his personal favourite, Buckingham.

James was furious with his son-in-law for accepting the crown of Bohemia—in his mind Frederick was complicit with the Bohemians in committing an act of rebellion against their rightful sovereign— and foresaw that it would start a quarrel 'that would never be ended'. Archbishop Abbot, however, had advised Elizabeth that her husband should accept the Bohemian crown, though not tell the king beforehand, believing that James would support his son-in-law if presented with a fait accompli. Abbot saw the conflict in apocalyptic terms, the coming true of John's prediction in Revelation that 'the Kings of the Earth that gave their power unto the Beast...shall now tear the whore, and make her desolate'.[10]

Public opinion in England was decidedly in favour of military intervention to help Elizabeth and Frederick. A combination of Protestant patriotism, wounded national pride, deep-seated anti-popery, and Hispanophobia made it inevitable that it would be. Yet opinion out-of-doors was also heavily influenced by the media, as the public's thirst for news about developments on the Continent was fuelled by sermons, printed pamphlets, corantos (the forerunner of newspapers), the stage, and manuscript newsletters and libels. Much of this material was critical of the government, urging an abandonment of the Spanish match and calling for a declaration of war in support of the Protestant interest in Europe. Many of the printed works were unlicensed: only three of the twenty-four titles relating to Bohemia that were published in 1618–19 were entered in the Stationers' Register. Some were published in the Netherlands (albeit with fake London imprints), to circumvent licensing restrictions.[11]

Some of the most militant voices were heard in the pulpit, ironically a side effect of James's willingness to offer preferment to Calvinist clergy, since it was these very ministers who tended to be the most zealous in their anti-popery and the most reluctant to bite their tongues. In a sermon delivered at St Andrew Holborn in 1618 Dr John Everard, a lecturer at nearby St Martin-in-the-Fields, argued the need for England to arm and go to war in a just cause to 'recover our owne', 'revenge injuries', 'succour the distressed', 'subdue rebels', 'defend our owne land', and (most pointedly) 'maintaine true religion' (albeit that it was not just, Everard qualified, to go to war to propagate the true religion), and heaped scorn on 'this effeminate age' and on how peace had brought forth injustice, prosperity, impiety, plenty, and 'effaeminate wantonnesse'.[12] Over the next few years Everard continued to condemn James's pursuit of the Spanish match, choosing his texts 'on purpose, to shew the unlawfulness, and the great sin of matching with Idolaters'. Over Christmas 1620, for example, he prayed that England might be delivered from a Catholic king. In February 1621 his sermon at St Martin's was so forthright in attacking the intended match that he was immediately dispatched to the Gatehouse for six months, the first of six or seven stints he spent in jail for his efforts.[13]

Several works appeared in 1619–20 justifying the revolt in Bohemia, the decision of the Bohemian Estates to depose Ferdinand and offer the crown to Frederick, and Frederick's agreeing to accept it, which despite adopting a sober, legalistic tone nevertheless evinced a strong commitment to Frederick and Elizabeth as representatives of the Protestant cause in the struggle against the Church of Rome and Catholic imperialism.[14] Pamphlets justifying the deposition of kings were potentially highly subversive, although the emphasis in such works was that Bohemia was different from England because it was an elective rather than hereditary monarchy. Thus in the elective kingdom of Bohemia, just as subjects were 'bound to their Kings in obedience', so were 'theire Kings reciprocally obliged by oath to observe fundamentall Lawes'; if they violated 'the sayd fundamentall Lawes', those 'wronged' conceived themselves to be 'freed from their allegiance'.[15] It was a somewhat uneasy distinction to sustain, given that English kings swore an oath at their coronation to uphold the fundamental laws. Moreover, such pamphlets publicized resistance theory in England, regardless of their authors' protestations that such arguments did not apply to England.

In addition to demands for a more militant foreign policy and justifications of Bohemian resistance, there was also more direct criticism of the court and, by implication, of the king himself. Indeed, the French ambassador commented on 'the hatred in which this king is held, in free speaking, cartoons, defamatory libels'.[16] Several libels circulated condemning the nature of James's relationship with Buckingham. One poet observed how Buckingham made 'Great Jove that swaies the emperiall Scepter [i.e. James I]...drunke with Nectar [i.e. semen]' and James lay with his Ganymede, wasted his 'marrow' (semen or virility), and scourged his lover's arse.[17]

Two works of 1620 stand out for the public stir they caused in criticizing the government's foreign policy. The first, which appeared in June, is Thomas Alured's letter to Buckingham concerning the match with Spain, which was possibly drafted by the Puritan divine John Preston, and which circulated widely in manuscript. (It was not to find its way into print until 1642.) In Alured's view, the proposed match with Spain could 'neither be safe for the King's person, nor good for this Church and Common-wealth', since it would provide 'an in-let to the Romish Locusts, who...may in an instant smite our Gourd, under whose shadow wee sit safe; and then what may we all feare by the heate of persecution'. History afforded no example of a Protestant king marrying 'with a contrary Religion, whose raigne hath bin prosperous', and therefore he begged Buckingham to use his best endeavours to prevent the match: whatever 'the necessities of the Crowne' might be, Alured predicted it would 'find more support by casting it selfe into the Armes of...the two Houses of Parliament, then by seeking to any forraigne fawning foe, or envious enemy'.

Alured had said that he hoped his advice would not 'seeme presumptuous'; the privy council thought that it was, and had Alured thrown in the Fleet prison until he submitted an abject apology.[18]

The second is Thomas Scott's *Vox Populi*, composed while Scott was in Edinburgh in the first half of 1619 but published in the autumn of 1620. (Scott's own identity remains obscure: he may have been the son of a Norfolk cleric, though he may have been Scottish, and appears to have been educated at St Andrews; by the end of 1620 the Thomas Scott who matriculated at St Andrews was rector of St Saviour's, Norwich.[19]) Written as if from the perspective of Spain, supposedly after Gondomar's return home from his diplomatic mission to England in 1618, *Vox Populi* is a scathing attack not only on Jacobean foreign policy but also on James's policies in the Church and on the Jacobean court. It portrays England as being duped by Spain, whose objective was 'to advance the Catholique Romane religion, and the Catholike Spanish dominion togither', and James, 'one of the most accomplisht Princes that ever raign'd', as so desirous of peace that he would 'doe or suffer any thing'. Although 'the English generally loathed the matche', militarily they were no match for the Spanish: 'their bodies' had been 'disabled' by 'long disuse of armes', 'their mindes effeminated by peace and luxury', and their navy, through lack of investment, now lay in ruins. There was the possibility that the calling of a parliament might scupper the whole design; but Gondomar had taken care to create 'such a dislike betwixt the King and the lower house', which the king believed was dominated by 'Puritans', that James would 'never indure parliament againe'. Even if a parliament could not be avoided, it could easily be packed by the court, as it had been in 1614, to secure a body of men ready to 'betray their Countrey and religion'.[20] Scott's Gondomar also saw it in Spain's interest to stir things up between England and Scotland. James desperately wanted 'a perfect union betwixt both the kingdomes' and to bring 'both Churches to uniformitie'. But his trip to Scotland in 1617 had not been as successful as expected, since several of Gondomar's allies in England had 'attended the traine' in order to stir up 'humors and factions'. Although the Scottish Presbyterians appeared to be anti-Spanish, 'their disobedience and example' in fact helped forward Spain's design, which was to destabilize the British polity and compel James to deal with Spain. Besides, it would be easy to discredit critics of the match in England and in Scotland by accusing them of 'pragmaticke Puritanisme'.[21] Scott's work was in such high demand that it ran through seven editions in 1620 alone, while some stationers took to hiring 'younge fellowes' to make manuscript transcriptions for circulation. Scott himself became a wanted man, and prudently opted to go into hiding in the Low Countries.[22]

James was opposed to the idea of war. He lacked the resources for a military intervention; he still hoped to fulfil his self-appointed role as peacemaker of Europe; and he continued to believe that the most likely way to bring long-term peace to Christendom was by uniting the English and Spanish crowns through marriage, which would have the additional benefit of bringing him a much-needed dowry. Yet James recognized that the militancy of the English population could play to his advantage, since if it appeared that the English wanted war this might help him exert pressure on the Habsburgs to seek a diplomatic solution. This in turn meant that he had to be seen to be doing his best to help his son-in-law in the meantime, although he remained reluctant to call a parliament. He ordered Buckingham, now in charge at the Admiralty, to prepare six ships of the royal navy for service, ostensibly to protect English shipping from pirates, which he funded by the old levy of ship money: £40,000 assessed on the City of London, and a further £8,550 on seaport towns.[23] He encouraged the City to lend the Elector £100,000, and in March 1620 he allowed the Elector's agent to collect donations and raise volunteers in England, Scotland, and Ireland for the war effort. At the same time, he instructed the clergy not to represent the conflict as a war of religion in their sermons. The Spanish invasion of the Palatinate in September, however, upped the stakes—although, in James's view, Frederick had been wrong to accept the crown of Bohemia, this did not give the Habsburgs the right to take away his ancestral lands—and when a voluntary benevolence to help Frederick failed to raise much more than £30,000 there was no option left but to call parliament. On 6 November 1620 James issued a summons for parliament to meet the following January, announcing at the same time that he did not want 'discontented persons that cannot but fish in troubled waters' or 'curious and wrangling lawyers' elected. He followed this up with a royal proclamation on 24 December against 'lavish and licentious speech in matters of state' and warned the London clergy not to mention the Spanish match in their sermons.[24] He took comfort from watching an anti-Puritan play staged at court on New Year's Day, in which a Puritan, pleading on behalf of the afflicted Church of God in Bohemia and Germany, was shown wearing donkey's ears, much to the amusement of the audience.[25]

The 1621 elections saw the most intensive court involvement yet, resulting in the return of forty government nominees. Yet the government did less well than it had anticipated, in part because its nominees tended to be outsiders and constituencies preferred local men, and in part because of a generalized suspicion of the court.[26] There were about twenty-four contests, and although most were fought over local issues, fear of popery and hostility to the court also played a part.[27] Within two weeks of the proclamation announcing that parliament would meet, Thomas Gainsford produced a tract which circulated in manuscript criticizing the pretensions of the papacy, the ambitions of the Spanish monarch, and Gondomar's influence at court, and listing all the things that 'A Parliament in England can do' both to scupper the Spaniards' designs and to promote the 'welfare of the Country' (among these calling 'great Officers in question' and suppressing 'all prejudiciall Monopolies'). Other works seemingly appeared which no longer survive. Gainsford complained about how Gondomar persuaded the government to have various items suppressed, including a print showing the king 'holding the Pope's nose to the grindstone with the two Archbishopps turning the same'; yet although 'the plate was cut in pieces, and the publisher imprisoned...it was printed', Gainsford claimed, 'in men's harts'. Gainsford himself was arrested.[28] In the run up to the Suffolk election, the Ipswich Puritan Samuel Ward preached a sermon urging 'heed to be taken of such as were of suspected affection to our religion'.[29] Shortly before the parliament assembled there appeared on the streets of London a stridently anti-Catholic print—published in Amsterdam but the 'invention' of Ward—playing on the memory of England's narrow escape from the Catholic conspiracies of 1588 and 1605. On the left-hand side divine winds blow a single fire ship towards the Spanish Armada, with the legend (in English and in Dutch) 'I blow and scatter'. On the right the eye of God beams down on the basement of the House of Lords, stashed with gunpowder, as Guy Fawkes runs towards it with a dark lantern; the motto in the beam of light reads 'Video Rideo' (I see, I laugh). In between the pope is shown 'in Counsell', seated around a table with a Jesuit, a friar, and a devil, and various other figures, the caption beneath suggesting that they are dreaming up the Gunpowder Plot. One of the figures around the table looks suspiciously like Philip III of Spain; Gondomar thought so, and complained bitterly to James, who had Ward committed to the Fleet prison. Ward admitted responsibility for the print, but claimed he had composed it five years earlier. Even if true, his decision to publish it now was a calculatedly provocative act, and Ward was not to be released until the following year (Plate 9).[30]

Such was the anticipation at the first meeting of parliament in seven years that great crowds thronged to watch the royal procession for the formal opening on 30 January. James himself was observed to be 'very cherefull all the way', as he made the short journey on horse-back from Whitehall to Westminster, stopping frequently to speak 'lovingly to the people' who had turned out in droves to see him—a marked contrast to his former practice, D'Ewes noted, when the king would normally 'bid a p[ox] or plague on such as flocked to see him'. Despite being crippled with arthritis, James still had the intellectual vigour to deliver an opening speech lasting over an hour.[31] He began with a brief lecture on constitutional theory. Parliament, he reminded members, was 'an assembly composed of a head and a body', the monarch being the head, and the body the three estates (lords tempo-ral, lords spiritual, and commons); since kings pre-dated parliaments and created them, it was 'a vain thing for a parliamentman to press to be popular', for without monarchy there would be no parliament. James then explained that the main reason he had called parliament was because he needed money. He had not asked for much since becoming king, but after ten years without parliamentary subsidies it was now time for him to be delivered of his wants. Besides, the crisis in Bohemia had placed extra burdens on the royal coffers. There had been diplomatic expenses, as James tried to work towards a peace-able solution. It was also prudent for England to arm itself in case there should be war. He would try everything 'to obtain a happy peace', James promised, but it was wise 'to be armed against the worse time' and 'to intreat of peace with a sword in my hand'.[32]

As parliament sat, the atmosphere in the capital remained highly charged. Gondomar was deeply unpopular and knew it. His residence had been stormed by angry crowds back in July 1618, after one of his servants had accidentally ridden his horse over a small child and nearly killed the infant. In February 1621 Gondomar took the pre-caution of being out of town on Shrove Tuesday, to avoid the fury of the London apprentices on what had become a notorious day of misrule in the capital.[33] However, trouble erupted on Easter Sunday (1 April), when a group of apprentices, with stones in their hands, approached the Spanish ambassador's horse litter as it was making its way down Fenchurch Street in the heart of the City and began shouting 'There goeth the devil in a dung-cart'. When one of Gon-domar's servants threatened them with Bridewell, back came the reply, 'What, shall we go to Bridewell for such a dog as thou?', where-upon the ambassador's man struck one of the youths round the ear. For their pains, the apprentices were sentenced to be tied to a cart's tail and whipped. It was an over-reaction by the government, to say the least—even though 'the punishment was lightly laide on'—and proved a serious miscalculation, since on the day the sentence was to be carried out a crowd of 'about 300 of all sorts' turned up to rescue the condemned, taking them from the cart and beating 'the marshal's men sore'—although one of those rescued was later to die, not from the severity of the whipping but from injuries sustained to his upper body as the executioner raced the cart through the City. James threat-ened to put a garrison in the City if the lord mayor could not keep better order, and issued a proclamation threatening severe punish-ment against any who expressed any irreverence towards strangers, especially foreign ambassadors.[34]

The first session of the 1621 parliament went reasonably well. There were tensions apparent from the start, to be sure. When the Commons called for a conference with the Lords so that both Houses could petition the king to put the laws in execution against Catholics, James had to remind MPs that, since the Palatinate was 'nowe in the hands of an enemye to our Religion', taking a stricter course against Catholics in England might 'induce him to the like against our Reli-gion there', and urged them to be as concerned about 'the Puritan...as the Papist'.[35] However, the Commons quickly agreed to grant James two subsidies, 'as a present of their loves', worth about £140,000, although they did refrain from granting the customary tenths and fifteenths because they would be a burden on the poor.[36]

Parliament next turned its attention to economic matters. The economy had recently nose-dived, with a dramatic decline of trade brought on by a serious shortage of money. We now know the ulti-mate cause was a currency devaluation in the Baltic, causing silver to fetch a higher price there than in England. At the time, however, MPs blamed England's economic woes on monopolies. Led by the lawyer Sir Edward Coke (the former Lord Chief Justice of King's Bench), parliament set about tackling those who had abused their patents, and in the process revived the medieval process of impeachment (the last impeachment had been in 1459), whereby charges were brought in the Commons and the Lords passed judgment.[37] The first to be charged were Sir Francis Michell and Sir Giles Mompesson, a distant relative by marriage of the marquess of Buckingham, accused of abusing their commissions for enforcing the monopolies for licensing alehouses and the production of gold and silver thread: Mompesson, for example, had prosecuted some 3,320 innkeepers for technical violations of obsolete statutes, some of whom were victims of entrapment. Michell confessed and was fined £1,000, degraded (stripped of his knighthood), and imprisoned during the king's pleasure; Mompesson, who fled before conviction, was fined £10,000, degraded, and sentenced to perpetual banishment.[38] An engraving appeared condemning Mompesson for his pursuit of 'greedie gaine' and praising James for addressing his subjects' concerns and for rendering 'Justice unto great and small', noting that when 'smale ones trippe...great ones downe right fall'—hinting thereby at the need to take action against Buckingham, whose brother and half-brother had been involved with unpopular monopolies (Plate 10).[39] Yet James himself welcomed the attack on the patentees: he had found the numerous suitors for patents 'troublesome' and by appeasing the Commons he could free himself from some of the perpetual pressure he lay under to reward his servants. In a speech to the Lords on 26 March, he expressed his readiness to execute the judgments passed on the convicted patentees, protesting that he would have 'punished them as severely' if their crimes had been brought to his attention before parliament met, 'so precious unto me', he said, 'is the public good'. The Prince of Wales, making his debut in the Lords, sat on the committee appointed to deal with Mompesson, thereby signalling the king's approval of the proceedings.[40]

In addition to the patentees, parliament turned its attention to the 'referees', those who had recommended the patentees in the first place, the most prominent of whom was Lord Chancellor Bacon. Accused of taking bribes, Bacon was impeached but on 30 April submitted a formal written confession to parliament to avoid a trial; on 3 May the Lords found him guilty, imposed a £40,000 fine, and sentenced him to be imprisoned during the king's pleasure, although the fine was never collected and the imprisonment lasted a mere three days.[41] Bacon soon found himself the subject of scurrilous libels, his name lending itself to the predictable pig puns: 'Within this sty heer now doth ly | A hog wel fed with bribery.'[42] Another version of the same rhyme, which was 'caste downe in some parte' of his residence in York House in the Strand, attacked Bacon's known sexual preference for young men: 'Within this sty a hogg doth ly | that must be hang'd for Sodomy'.[43] One poet, alluding to Bacon's failure to have children, observed that 'He should have done his youth less: his Lady more'.[44]

By sacrificing Bacon, James hoped to avoid an attack on Buckingham. For his part, Buckingham tried to ward off criticism by insisting
that if his brothers had been guilty of malpractice, he would not protect them. There was an attempt to strike at Buckingham through his
Irish connections. On 26 April Sir John Jephson, a Munster planter
and a client of the earl of Southampton, raised the issue of misgovernment in Ireland under Viscount Grandison—a client of Buckingham who had replaced Chichester as Lord Deputy in 1616: 'the late
Rebellion there', Jephson warned, had been 'occasioned by Defects in
Government', and Ireland was 'as ready now to shake off the Yoke of
this Kingdom' and has 'as just Cause now, as ever', pointing to 'a
general Defection there to Popery', 'Wrong, Robbery, and Oppression' by those in charge of the country, and the problem of monopolies, which although not as many as in England were nevertheless
'sharp'. The Commons set up a Committee of Irish Affairs, but it was
far from clear the English parliament had any authority to act and in
the face of royal disapproval the investigation was dropped. (James
subsequently set up his own commission of inquiry for Ireland.)[45]
Trouble also threatened when the Lords questioned former Attorney
General Sir Henry Yelverton for the way he had enforced the monopoly for gold and silver thread. Yelverton, as the anti-Buckingham
lobby in the Lords had expected, duly blamed Buckingham's brothers, but he overstepped the line when, in an examination on 30 April,
he went on to compare Buckingham to Edward II's hated favourite
Hugh Despenser. Given that Despenser had been hanged for treason
and Edward II deposed for allowing others to govern to the detriment of Church and people, the Lords could hardly turn a blind eye.
They sentenced Yelverton to a fine of 10,000 marks (c. £6,667) and
imprisonment at the king's pleasure, and also ordered him to pay
5,000 marks to Buckingham in compensation, although Buckingham
immediately remitted the fine. The marquess was left boasting how
he was 'parlement proofe'.[46]

In an extraordinary move, the Commons also brought charges
against an obscure Catholic lawyer named Edward Floyd before the
Lords. Floyd, while in the Fleet prison for calumniating a Welsh judge,
had spoken of his joy at the losses of the king's son-in-law and daughter and expressed his belief that 'Goodman Palsgrave', as he styled
the Elector Palatine, had 'noe more right to the kingdome of Bohemia' than he (Floyd) had 'to be king of Wales'. Floyd was the king's
prisoner, not parliament's, and his words had only come to parliament's
attention because the Commons had launched an investigation into

the conditions in the prisons, but a parliamentary subcommittee recognized the Lords' jurisdictional competence in the matter and on 26 May Floyd was sentenced to a £5,000 fine, a public whipping, a stint in the pillory where he was to be branded on the forehead, and life imprisonment. The Prince of Wales intervened to spare Floyd the whipping, on account of his age (Floyd was over sixty), though the rest of the sentence was carried out. He was not to stay long in prison, however; James had him liberated on 16 July.[47]

The Commons considered various legislative initiatives during the session, including a measure for the stricter observance of the Sabbath, a direct challenge to James's Book of Sports of 1618. In the end, it came to focus its energies on two bills. The first was a bill against monopolies, to stop the problem with patentees recurring in the future, which was pursued with James's approval, and which was eventually to see its passage into law in 1624. The second was a bill for the better discovery and suppression of Catholic recusants. This posed a problem for James. He had called parliament so that England could be ready for war should the attempt to reach a diplomatic solution to the Palatinate crisis fail, but parliament's actions were now undermining any prospect that diplomacy might succeed. Gondomar protested that it was pointless to continue discussions over the Spanish match or the restoration of the Palatinate with England about to start persecuting Catholics. With Lord Digby shortly to depart for Vienna to try to broker a deal with the Emperor Ferdinand II, James decided that it was time for MPs to take a summer break. On 28 May he announced that parliament was to be adjourned on 4 June, citing concerns about how the great concourse of people in London over the summer might 'breed infection' and the need for Lord Lieutenants and JPs to return to their counties to attend to local affairs. Since an adjournment did not put an end to the session, he explained, this would allow them to pick up their legislative business from where they had left off when parliament reconvened.[48]

Many MPs, however, were concerned about returning home to their constituencies having voted subsidies but without having completed their legislative business: they would be less welcome than after the parliament of 1614, one complained, 'for, though that parliament brought forth nothing, yet it parted with nothing'. Sir Edwin Sandys and others urged the two Houses to petition the king to extend the session. James made it clear, however, that he would regard such a petition as 'a derogation of his prerogative', although he did promise to pass any bills forwarded to him in the time remaining. Passions became inflamed in debates over the next few days, as members revealed their concerns over the threat of popery, the fate of the king's daughter and son-in-law, and the state of the economy. Yet the Commons opted not to present any bills for the royal assent at this time, believing it preferable to wait for the opportunity to address the nation's grievances fully rather than committing to an incomplete package of measures and hastily completed bills. On 4 June James announced that parliament was to be adjourned until 14 November. Before departing, MPs unanimously approved a 'Declaration for the Recovery of the Palatinate', wherein they announced that if the king's 'endeavours by treaty' were not successful, they were ready to go to war.[49]

On 16 June James had Sandys arrested and questioned about behind the scenes planning of tactics, his actions in parliament, and his views on foreign policy; although released the following month, he was placed under house arrest until early November. His associate in the Lords, the earl of Southampton, was arrested and confined to the house of Lord Keeper Williams for 'mischievous intrigues with members of the Commons'—Southampton admitted to holding a number of private meetings with some of the more outspoken critics of the government in the lower house, though denied that he had done anything wrong—while the earl of Oxford was briefly imprisoned in the Tower in July for having spoken out against the Spanish match. James was sending out a message he was not to be messed with. On 26 July he reissued his proclamation of the previous December against discussing matters of state. At the same time, he wanted to make clear that he took his responsibility to promote 'the good of the commonwealth' seriously. To that end he published a proclamation on 10 July cancelling eighteen monopolies and promising that seventeen others could be challenged at common law, while the privy council established a commission to look into the depression, consulting with prominent merchants and other expert opinion.[50]

The Scottish Parliament of 1621

The Bohemian crisis led James also to call a parliament in Scotland, albeit as a last resort, after James had failed to raise the necessary funds from conventions of the Scottish nobility that met in November 1620 and January 1621. Originally scheduled to meet on 1 June, its opening was delayed until 23 July to allow the high commissioner—James Hamilton, 2nd marquess of Hamilton—more time to lobby for support of the government's agenda. There were to be two main orders of business: raising money for the Bohemian crisis and ratifying the Five Articles of Perth. In his letter to parliament, James said he wanted a 'trayell of [their] affections', hoping that by straining themselves to their 'wtermost abilities', they would thereby 'giue exemple' to their neighbours 'of grater wealthe, to doe the lyke in ther dew proportione'.[51] It was a self-conscious attempt to play one kingdom off against another.

The government was keen to limit the opportunity for the expression of critical dissent. Those who wanted to bring petitions before parliament had to submit them to the Clerk Register in advance so that they could be vetted by the council. No General Assembly was called, to deny the clergy the opportunity to send commissioners to parliament to represent their concerns. And concerns there certainly were. Some ministers drew up a supplication pleading for 'a full deliverance from...all novations and novelties in Doctrine, Sacraments and Discipline', but the Clerk Register informed them he doubted he would be able to bring it before parliament. Andrew Duncan, who presented the supplication, was sent to Dumbarton Castle, as was Alexander Simpson, who preached a fiery sermon against the Scottish bishops at Greyfriars Kirk on 22 July, the day before the parliament convened. 'Some zealous men of the ministerie' drew up a list of 'Admonitions' concerning the state of the Kirk—warning that 'the sound of the feet of Poperie' was 'at the doores', the discipline of the Kirk 'weell nigh destroyed' and 'turned Antichristian, by the usurpation and tyranny of our Prelates', and 'cursed ceremonies' contrary to the word of God brought back like 'a returning of the dog to the vomit'—together with a 'Protestation' against whatever articles or statutes parliament might pass to the 'prejudice...of the Kirk', which they planned either to present to the Lords of the Articles or affix to the parliament house door or the market cross.[52]

From exile in the Netherlands the Presbyterian minister David Calderwood published a stinging critique of 'the state of the Church of Scotland', in the hope of persuading parliament not to ratify the Articles of Perth. The Five Articles, he protested, were against the king's Confession of Faith of 1581 and the first and second Books of Discipline, and if the Scots violated their promises before God to condemn 'Archbishops, Bishops, Holy dayes, kneeling, Confirmation, private Baptisme', they would face 'the heavie judgement of God'.

Most worrying to Calderwood was where 'this defection' might tend: 'first to perfite conformitie with the English Church, then at last...in full conformitie with the Romane Kirk'. Indeed, 'All the Relicts of Rome', he predicted, 'which are lying like stincking filth in their [the English] Church', would 'be communicated to us', and 'the paterne of their altar, their Service, their Hierarchie...set up in our Church'. He gave the lie to James's supposed plans for ecclesiastical convergence between the Churches of Scotland and England: 'Wee must yeeld all to them', he pointed out, while 'they will not yeeld any thing at all to us'; 'Neither England nor Rome' had even given 'the least token of their comming towards us. Yea wee must play the fooles, and turne our face to them, and take our journey first to England, then to Rome.' There was never a time when it could be right to pursue such a conformity, but it most certainly was not right now, 'When the reformed Churches abroad' were 'in so great hazard' and 'the Antichrist, and all his adherents...hoping wholly to extirpate true Religion out of Europe'. To the possible objection that having bishops and ceremonies were 'not matters of weight, but trifles', Calderwood asked if it was 'a small matter to turne a Minister', who had served many years, 'out of his Office', leaving 'him and his familie...to begge their Bread'? No persecutors in history had ever pronounced the cause for which they persecuted 'to be a trifle', making 'Our persecutors...the worst that ever were'. Two questions, in particular, he directed to parliament: why they suffered the High Commission, 'a court not established by the Statutes of the realme...to tyrannize over the church, over dutifull and loyall Subjects, fyning, confyning, suspending, depriving, warding, and...banish[ing]...Ministers...for not conforming to Popish ceremonies against their conscience'; and why 'acts of pretended and null assemblies', such as 'The Acts of that corrupt, and pretended assemblie at Glasgow' of 1610, had been ratified, confirmed, and even—'under name of explanation'—enlarged by the parliament of 1612. 'Shall the like be done now, for that pretended and null Assemblie holden last at Perth?', he pondered. 'God forbid.'[53]

Responsibility for managing the parliament fell to Hamilton and a 'cabinet counsel' of leading court loyalists. They had a double guard placed both inside and outside the parliament building to make sure that no ministers were admitted unless they had a licence from one of the bishops. In his opening address, Hamilton stressed the king's need for money at this time of foreign crisis and spoke of the Five Articles as 'things indifferent' which 'the Prince...hath lawfull power to command'. Every effort was made to ensure that men 'best affected' to the king's service were elected to the Lords of the Articles, although it in fact proved impossible to find enough barons and burgesses of sufficient social status amenable to the royal agenda, and so the crown did not quite have things all its own way. The Lords of the Articles set about drafting the desired legislation, starting with taxation—a deviation from normal procedure, but the government wanted to get a commitment to a subsidy before addressing the ecclesiastical legislation—and agreed first to a subsidy of £400,000, to be paid in four annual supplements, and eventually, after 'great altercation', to a new tax on annual rents (that is, interest payments and annuities). A bill to ratify the Five Articles of Perth of 1618 was agreed shortly afterwards, although there were four opposing votes. Getting the measures through parliament would be tougher, however. It was traditional for the separate estates to hold their own meetings while parliament was in session, but a nervous government sent spies to infiltrate these meetings and, finding there was considerable opposition to both the Five Articles and the tax on annual rents, ordered a stop to such meetings. In an attempt to catch the dissidents unawares, the cabinet counsel then called the House to sit and vote on the legislation at very short notice. The Act for ratifying the Five Articles was presented first and passed by a majority of seventy-eight to fifty-one, with thirty-one abstentions. The ordinary tax and the annual rents tax were then presented as one measure, thereby forcing those who opposed the latter into the position of having to deny the king the funds to assist the Elector Palatine. With it clear that the government possessed a working majority, few were willing to expose themselves, and the measure passed with less than ten dissentient voices.[54]

The government drew most of its support from areas north of the Tay, where the majority of the population were either conformist Protestants or Catholics, and from the Borders and south-west, where magnate influence remained strong. Those who voted against the Five Articles came mainly from the central lowland belt, an area where Presbyterianism was strong. The voting pattern reveals a marked court–country split. Those who voted with the government either had strong connections with the court already or represented areas that were so dependent upon the crown (such as the royal burghs) that they felt they could not afford to offend the king. Those who opposed the measures were free from court dependence and motivated by a combination of localist, religious, and political concerns—the impact of the new tax on their localities, the ceremonies that the Five Articles imposed on the Kirk, and the government's assault on parliamentary liberties. There is also evidence that the opposition to the court was becoming organized, under the leadership of the earl of Rothes and Lord Balmerino. Indeed, if one looks at those nobles who were present in the parliament of 1621 and still alive when the Scottish troubles broke out in 1638, there is a striking consistency in allegiance over time. The battle lines of 1638 were already beginning to be drawn.[55]

Despite the signs of discontent, James was delighted with the achievement. As he put it in a letter to the Scottish bishops on 12 August, by ratifying the Five Articles parliament had removed 'the greatest matter the Puritans had to object against the Church government', which was that 'their proceedings were warranted by no Law'. It was up to the bishops, now, to enforce the law: 'The sword is now put in your hands,' he exhorted; 'go on therefore to use it, and let it rust no longer, till ye have perfected the service trusted to you.' As for concerns about the Scottish Catholics, James observed that 'As Papistrie is a disease in the minde, so is puritanisme in the brain', and the best remedy for both was 'a grave, settled, uniform, and well ordered Church'.[56]

There continued to be much opposition to the Five Articles, however, particularly in the central lowlands area. With increasing numbers of Presbyterians refusing to take communion, it did indeed become difficult to distinguish 'Puritan' from 'Catholic' nonconformity.[57] In 1622 the minister of Cupar, William Scot—who had been one of those summoned to court along with the Melville brothers in 1606 and disciplined by the government for holding a General Assembly at Aberdeen the previous year in defiance of the crown—published a tract in Amsterdam condemning the new ceremonies and warning how they gave 'great hope to the limbs of Antichrist to settle their tottering kingdome' and an 'easie entrance for the whole body of abhominations'. It was 'a prodigious presage', Scott lamented, that the Five Articles should be enforced 'with greater rigor...against the true servants of God' than all the statutes 'against idolatry and Idolaters, blasphemers and murtherers, and open contemners of the Lord's word'. 'Conformitie', he observed, had come in 'by little and little', and 'Poperie' was 'coming to perfection by Ceremoniousnesse and Ambition'. In Scot's view, not only had the Scots 'cause to fast and pray' that these ceremonies might be 'removed farre from them', but England also.[58]

The Protestation of 1621

In early October James extended the English parliament's adjournment until 8 February 1622.[59] However, the rapidly deteriorating European situation forced him into a rethink. At the end of October Digby returned to England following an unsuccessful attempt to broker a diplomatic solution with Ferdinand II; he had been hoping to persuade the Emperor to leave Frederick his ancestral lands if Frederick relinquished claims to Bohemia, but over the summer the duke of Bavaria had seized the upper Palatinate in the Emperor's name and the Spanish had resumed their offensive in the lower Palatinate. James therefore issued a proclamation stating that due to 'certaine urgent and important occasions' parliament would now meet on 20 November.[60] It was an unexpected move, and MPs were eager to discover what the king needed from them. However, James did not attend the session, ostensibly on the grounds of ill health, but instead remained at Newmarket with Buckingham; the Prince of Wales, sitting in the Lords, served in effect as James's deputy. Thus there was no speech from the throne on the opening day, to explain why parliament had been reconvened.

James appears to have been playing a delicate game of diplomatic bluff. He needed to get Spain back to the negotiating table, and he was prepared to unleash parliament to show that the nation was united in favour of war and willing to fund one. It would not take much to induce MPs to play the role he had allotted for them. It was a risky strategy, and there was always the chance that things might get out of hand, though it was the sort of political intrigue that James relished.[61]

On 21 November, leading ministers of the crown announced at a joint conference of the two Houses that the business of the parliament concerned mainly the Commons because the king needed a supply to recover the Palatinate, making it apparent that this would involve a military engagement though being far from clear on strategy. MPs showed they were somewhat nervous about what was being asked of them when they came to debate the conference on the 22nd. Edward Alford pointed out that the king had recently issued two proclamations stating that no one should meddle with or talk about state affairs, but now MPs were being told that they should meddle with nothing else but the Palatinate; if the king could dictate what business MPs were or were not allowed to discuss, they might 'lose the Privilege of a free parliament'. William Mallory asked why Sir Edwin Sandys had been confined and not taken his seat.[62] The Prince of Wales reported to his father that the House had 'bene a little unrulie', and suggested having 'such seditius fellus' arrested as an example to others, although he acknowledged that they could afford to be patient for a little while longer.[63] On 26 November the Commons began to address the question of finance, and although some MPs voiced their thoughts on what sort of war should be fought and expressed a desire that Charles marry a Protestant, on the 28th the House agreed to vote another subsidy, still unsure of the precise purpose for which it was to be used.

The stakes were upped on the 29th when Sir George Goring, a known client of Buckingham, moved that the Commons should petition the king for war if Spain did not withdraw its troops from the Palatinate or failed to persuade the Emperor to agree to a cessation of arms. A Commons committee brought a draft petition to that effect before the House on Saturday, 1 December, which not only urged James to declare war but also asked that the Prince of Wales marry 'one of our religion'. The councillors present in the lower house realized the explosive potential of the petition and managed to insist that further discussion of it be held over until Monday, 3 December. However, the Prince of Wales was so incensed that he decided to send a copy of the draft petition, together with a strongly worded complaint, straight to his father. On Monday the 3rd, before he had received any formal petition, James penned an angry letter to the Speaker complaining that he had heard that 'some fiery and popular spirits' in the Commons had presumed to debate 'matters far beyond their reach and capacities' and commanding him to instruct the House that no one was to meddle with anything concerning government or speak of the Spanish match.[64]

There has been considerable debate about why Goring proposed his motion and what he was trying to achieve. The Commons, rather than seeking to demand a say on matters regarded as the prerogative of the crown, clearly thought they were responding to a request from the court to offer their opinion on foreign policy. It seems that Buckingham put Goring up to it—although Charles probably knew nothing about it and James might not have done either—perhaps because he felt it would help put pressure on Spain if the political temperature in parliament were raised a little higher (in which case it backfired disastrously), perhaps in an attempt to forestall a possible attack on his Irish interests and clients (if so, it certainly did the trick).[65]

Gondomar was outraged and threatened to break off diplomatic relations; in an effort to reassure him, James promised he would dissolve parliament rather than let matters get out of hand. The Commons, stung by the king's rebuke, drew up a declaration protesting that they had no intent to encroach upon 'the sacred bounds of . . . royal authority', but merely wanted 'to demonstrate these things to your majesty' which otherwise might not have 'come so fully and clearly to [his] knowledge', and asserting their right to free speech, which they presented to James at Newmarket. The king replied that he was 'an old and experienced king, needing no such lessons', accused them of claiming a 'plenipotency . . . in all power upon earth' like the pope and 'the Puritan Ministers in Scotland', and warned that they should 'beware to trench upon the prerogative of the crown' since that might force him 'to retrench them of their privileges'. The Commons replied on 18 December with a Protestation, in which they insisted that the liberties and privileges of parliament were the 'birthright and inheritance of the subjects of England', that 'urgent affairs concerning the King, State, and defence of the realm' were 'proper subjects . . . of counsel and debate in Parliament', and that in the handling of parliamentary business every member 'hath, and of right ought to have, freedom of speech to propound, treat, reason, and bring to a conclusion the same'. James was furious and immediately ordered parliament to adjourn. On 30 December he tore the Protestation out of the Commons Journal with his own hands in front of his privy council.[66] Sir Edward Coke, the lawyer MP who had played a prominent role in helping to frame the Protestation, was dispatched to the Tower, where he was lodged in a room which used to be a kitchen; some wit had written on the door in advance of Sir Edward's arrival 'This room wants a cook'. He was soon followed by Sir Robert Phelips and William Mallory. John Pym, who had criticized the king for his leniency towards Catholics, was placed under house arrest.[67]

On 6 January James dissolved parliament, thereby losing the subsidy, complaining how since Easter MPs had 'misspent a great deale of time . . . inlarging . . . their liberties', culminating with a Protestation which threatened to invade most of the prerogatives of the crown.[68] He followed this with a lengthy declaration justifying his dealings with the parliament, so that 'the truth' might be apparent 'unto all men', blaming the problems on 'some discontented persons . . . endeavouring to clog the good will of the Commons with their owne unreasonable ends'.[69] According to the Venetian ambassador, James told his council that he would 'have no more to do with parliament'.[70]

Retiring to his country retreat at Theobalds in Hertfordshire, the king was later heard to say 'he would govern according to the good of the common weal; but not according to the common will'.[71] The government was decidedly jittery. When the horse-keeper of the Grantchester man and Gray's Inn lawyer Henry Byng spoke out against the dissolution and the arrest of Sir Edward Coke, allegedly predicting 'there would be a rebellion', the government had the poor man—known to be 'a simple fellow'—sent to the Tower and tortured in an effort to get to the root of any possible conspiracy. It was paranoia: Byng had recently been visited by his father-in-law Thomas Clench, the MP for Suffolk, and another (unnamed) MP had also been staying with Byng (who himself had sat for Sudbury in the 1614 parliament), but there was no evidence that they had been conspiring against the government and no charges were ever brought. The government's actions nevertheless added to the climate of fear and tarnished its public image. Rumours were soon flying that Byng's man had died from being racked, or else had already been or was about to be hanged, drawn, and quartered.[72]

James's Strategy Unravels

James's strategy for England was beginning to unravel. He had sought to avoid conflict with parliament, mainly by avoiding calling one; yet by 1621 he had not only been forced to recall parliament but that parliament had proceeded to impeach servants of the crown and to issue a Protestation claiming the right to debate foreign policy. James had needed to balance royal finances, but the Bohemian crisis had added to the expenses of government, and he had not been able to get the funding he needed from parliament to meet those additional expenses. He had hoped to be peacemaker of Europe, but Europe was at war, with his own son-in-law having triggered that war, and the country was demanding English intervention on the Continent. James's plan for a Spanish match was costing him politically, yet having found it necessary to dissolve parliament he had little option but to continue the pursuit, in the hope of the much needed dowry and the prospect of a diplomatic solution over the Palatinate.

The crisis over foreign policy also undermined James's balancing act in the Church. With the Calvinist clergy the most outspoken in their criticism of the Spanish match and issuing calls from the pulpit for England to offer military assistance to Frederick, James found himself increasingly gravitating towards anti-Calvinist or Arminian divines. It would be wrong to give the impression that James all of a sudden radically changed his policy of ecclesiastical preferment. His efforts to incorporate different theological views within the Church meant that Arminians already held seven English bishoprics by 1617, with the leading Arminian of the time, Richard Neile, moving to Durham in that year. Moreover, Calvinists continued to be promoted to leading sees: for example, Thomas Morton to Lichfield and Nicholas Felton to Ely in 1618, George Carleton to Chichester in 1619, and John Williams to Lincoln in 1621, with Williams also being appointed Lord Keeper in that year. William Laud, who was to rise to prominence under Charles I, only acquired the remote Welsh see of St David's in 1621 because the Calvinist incumbent Richard Milbourne was promoted to the vacant see of Carlisle, while when Milbourne died in 1624 he was replaced by another Calvinist, Richard Senhouse.

Nevertheless, Arminian divines were gaining ground at the expense of Calvinists. Archbishop Abbot's influence was on the decline as a result of his support for war to recapture the Palatinate; twice in 1621 he was threatened with house arrest, while his position was further undermined by an unfortunate hunting accident in July of that year when a stray arrow of his struck and killed one of the keepers at Nonsuch Park. When James Montagu of Winchester died in 1618 and John King of London in 1621, both of whom had been influential Calvinist figures at court, they were replaced by Arminians: Lancelot Andrewes at Winchester and George Montaigne at London.[73] When the Calvinist bishop of Norwich John Jegon died in 1618, James decided to place this notoriously Puritan diocese in the hands first of the Arminian John Overall (who had been bishop of Coventry and Lichfield since 1614) and then, upon Overall's death the following year, of the strident anti-Calvinist Samuel Harsnett (bishop of Chichester since 1609). Harsnett immediately signalled his intentions by publishing visitation articles urging churchwardens to crack down on unlicensed lecturers and to enforce strict conformity to the rites and ceremonies prescribed by the Book of Common Prayer (including the wearing of the surplice).[74] With the Arminian bishops came the promotion of more ceremonialist forms of worship. Neile signalled his promotion to Durham in 1617 by having the communion table moved from the middle of the choir to the site of the pre-Reformation altar at the east end. Then in about 1620 his dean, Richard Hunt, threw out the old wooden communion table and had an elaborate marble altar erected at the east end of the Cathedral 'with a carved screen most gloriously painted and guilded' costing over £200, before which the bishop and his chaplain, Dr John Cosin (who became a prebendary of the Cathedral in 1624), would bow frequently; some fifty-three 'glorious Images and pictures' were set up 'over the Bishop's Throne, and about the Quire'; while Cosin even took to commemorating Candlemas by burning some 200 candles in honour of the Virgin Mary.[75] Following Harsnett's translation to Norwich, St Peter's Mancroft saw the installation of images, crucifixes, and a high altar—funds originally raised to repair the church roof were diverted to meet the costs, with Harsnett's approval though against the wishes of the majority of the parishioners—whereas at St Gregory's the churchwardens raised funds to pay not only for the repair of an exterior wall but also for gilded figures on the font and the decorating of the church interior with images of Christ and of the Apostles.[76] By the end of 1621, nine out of twenty-four bishops were Arminians, avant-garde conformists or future supporters of the Laudian reforms; by the end of James's reign twelve of the bishops were.[77] Arminianism was also on the rise at the universities. At the commencement ceremonies at Cambridge in 1622 the University preacher William Lucy, chaplain to the marquess of Buckingham, caused a stir by delivering a sermon 'totally for Arminianism, wonderfully boldly and peremptorily, stiling some passages of the contrary by the name of blasphemy'; considering the time and place was 'so public', it was reckoned he was either incredibly indiscreet, or he 'had some encouragement'.[78]

In an attempt to silence criticism from the pulpit, on 4 August 1622 James issued his *Directions Concerning Preachers* ordering clergy to steer clear of controversial topics. What had caused James finally to lose his tether was a sermon by a young Oxford scholar named John Knight in April of that year in which Knight, in the context of discussing the Palatinate, had suggested that it was lawful for subjects, when harassed on the score of religion, 'to take arms against their Sovereign' in their own defence—an indiscretion that led to Knight's immediate arrest and imprisonment. The *Directions* stipulated that clergymen who were not bishops or deans were not to discuss predestination, election, or universal redemption in their sermons, nor meddle with 'matters of state' or 'fall into bitter invectives, and indecent railing speeches against...either Papists or Puritans', while on Sunday afternoons preachers were to restrict themselves to discussing the catechism, the Creed, Ten Commandments, or the Lord's Prayer; indeed, those preachers were to be most encouraged who spent Sunday afternoons catechizing. Yet although the *Directions* seemed to undermine the Calvinist emphasis on preaching, they cannot be seen as a reflection of a growing Arminian influence in the Church. The idea was James's and the *Directions* were drafted by the Calvinist bishop of Lincoln, John Williams, while publicly, at least, Archbishop Abbot supported the initiative. Responding to the concern raised by 'some few Churchmen, and many of the people' that the restraint on preaching would encourage 'ignorance and superstition'—or, in other words, 'Popery'—Abbot explained in a letter to the archbishop of York that James thought the only way to stop people defecting from the Church was by improving catechetical instruction. This in turn, James hoped, would lead to more, not fewer, sermons. However, as things stood, preachers were touching on 'points of Divinity too deepe for the capacity of the people', when people had not been properly instructed in the principles of the Church of England in the first place, and this was encouraging schism, and allowing 'Anabaptists, Brownists, and Puritans' to poison and infect 'the people of this Kingdome'.[79]

The *Directions* succeeded in quieting the pulpit, without totally silencing critical voices. Some clerics were determined to draw attention to the fact that they were being muzzled. John Everard at St Martin-in-the-Fields announced one Sunday that he would deal with the spiritual implications of his text this week and address the political the following Sunday; as Everard doubtless anticipated, the council had him arrested before he could deliver the second sermon. Another minister ventured forth on a controversial topic and then stopped abruptly, announcing that 'he was not ambitious of lying in prison'.[80] In Norwich Harsnett saw the *Directions* as an excuse to limit the number of sermons full-stop. He reduced the number of civic lectures in St Andrews, Norwich from three per week to just one, and forbade the continuation of all Sunday morning services throughout the city beyond 9.30 a.m., so that the city's inhabitants could be free to attend the sermon in the cathedral; the afternoon they were to spend at catechism classes in their local parish church.[81]

The clampdown on Puritan dissent came at the same time as James was allowing greater freedom to Catholics. Shortly after the dissolution of the 1621 parliament, the king sent instructions to Scotland for Catholics to be treated more leniently and ordered the release of large numbers of Catholic prisoners in England. In the spring of 1622 Buckingham was boasting to Gondomar how English prisons were 'emptied of Priests and Recusants, and filled with zealous Ministers, for preaching against the Match'. Then on 2 August, just two days before issuing his *Directions to Preachers*, James ordered the formal suspension of the penal laws against Catholic recusants, as part of his ongoing negotiations for the Spanish match.[82]

James also took steps to control the press. From October 1621, he employed Francis Cottington, who had spent many years attached to the English embassy in Spain, as government licenser of the press to ensure that no works were published that might upset Spain or undermine the king's diplomacy. Government efforts to enforce the licensing laws more effectively were backed up by a proclamation against disorderly printing in September 1623, complaining of the recent proliferation of 'seditious, schismaticall and scandalous Bookes and Pamphlets' and calling upon the Stationers' Company to search for, seize, and suppress such works. Over the period 1621–4 a number of authors and publishers found themselves in trouble with the government: some were fined and imprisoned and had their presses destroyed; others fled into exile. However, the clampdown was of limited effectiveness. Punishment after the fact was really too late, since the offending works had already entered the public domain. Making examples of a few certainly had a deterrent value: there is some evidence of self-censorship for fear of getting into trouble, while unlicensed works could be seized and destroyed to prevent further circulation. However, a number of authors and printers felt passionately enough about the issues at stake that they were willing to assume the risks.[83]

Thus works critical of the government's foreign policy continued to appear. The anonymous *Tom Tell Troath*, written in the autumn of 1621 and which circulated initially in manuscript before subsequently being published in Holland, warned James just how disaffected his subjects were. Everywhere one went in London, the author alleged, people were 'talking of the wars of Christendome', and in 'the rage and folly of their tongues' spared not the king's 'sacred person'. Some found 'such fault with your Majestie's government', Tom said, 'as they wish Q. Elizabeth were alive againe', since she would 'never have suffered the enemies of her religion to have unballanced Christendome as they have done within these few yeares'. People mocked the king's notion of 'Great Brittaine' and claimed that it was 'a great deale lesse then Little England was wont to be': less in reputation, strength, riches, all manner of virtue, or anything else 'required to make a state great and happy'. Indeed, the economy was in such a mess, Tom warned, that there were 'many thousands' of the king's subjects that lay 'languishing ready to rebell for want of imployment'.[84]

Some of the boldest attacks were made in verse. 'The Common People's Apology to the Queene of Bohemia' lamented the fact that neither England, Scotland, nor Ireland was doing anything to help James's daughter, 'the Cheife glory of this british ile', and predicted that 'our sonnes shall be ashamed to own us'.[85] Another anonymous poet expressed the hope that God would save James from 'Romish druggs', 'the dangerous figg of Spaine', and 'a Ganimede' (an allusion to Buckingham).[86] James hired his own poetasters to respond in kind, in an effort to sway the public to a more favourable view of his foreign policy. One court poet somewhat crudely anticipated how, when Charles was married to the Spanish Infanta, 'our north pole shall bee put in the hole | Of the Southerne Inferior beare'.[87] James even participated himself, penning his own rhyming couplets on the pursuit of the 'golden Fleece'; elsewhere he urged libellers to 'Hold your pratling, spare your penn' and instead 'Bee honest and obedient men'. His very actions betray a man deeply anxious about the perceived impact of anti-government libels on opinion out-of-doors.[88]

Having lost the subsidy, James needed to find other means of raising money to help his son-in-law. He doubled the imposition on wine and levied an extraordinary tax of nine pence in the pound on aliens. He also tried another benevolence, although after a year little more than the value of a single parliamentary subsidy had been collected. Enormous pressure was brought to bear on individuals to contribute. The council summoned 'men of known wealth' and got many of them to give £100, some even £200; Chamberlain thought the sums would have to be lowered otherwise it would 'prove no benevolence, but rather a *volens nolens*' (in other words, compulsory). One London merchant, who had once been a cheesemonger, was 'required' either to give to the king or to go to the Palatinate and supply the army with cheese; he chose the latter option rather than pay, despite being eighty years old and it costing him more money in the long run. Lord Saye refused to collect the benevolence in his capacity as a JP for Oxfordshire, insisting that 'he knew no law, besides by Parliament, to compel men to give away their own goods'; he was summoned before the privy council on four separate occasions between 23 May and 6 June 1622 to explain himself and imprisoned in the Fleet prison for six months.[89] The earl of Oxford was imprisoned again, this time for speaking out against Buckingham's stranglehold on the political patronage system; he was held close prisoner in the Tower for twenty months, and James instructed the Attorney General Sir Thomas Coventry to prepare a Star Chamber prosecution against him.[90]

The government also recognized the need for greater efforts to make Ireland pay its own way. The cost of the Irish civil establishment had almost doubled in the first decade of the reign, to around £18,000 per annum in 1611, partly due to the cost of the expanded judicial system, but mainly due to the number of pensions paid from Irish revenues. And although military expenditure had been reduced significantly since the peace of 1603, the maintenance of a small standing army was costing in the period 1611–21 another £54,000 per annum. The rents from the Ulster plantation brought the crown some additional income, which overall increased from about £20,000 in the early years of the reign to c. £30,000–35,000 in the years after 1612, but this nevertheless left a significant gap that had to be plugged by the English exchequer. Between 1604 and 1619 England paid £708,000 sterling into the Irish treasury (on average c. £47,000 per year), and although this was thereafter reduced to £20,000 (thanks to improved yields from customs and wardships) the annual deficient on the Irish current account for 1619–22 was £18,283 and the accumulated debt to the army £74,854.[91] In 1622 James set up a commission, comprising government officials, politicians, and lawyers based in both Ireland and England, to investigate all aspects of the government of Ireland in Church and state. As an administrative achievement it was a remarkable success, but its findings showed just how little progress had been made with regard to civil and religious reform. About as many views were offered about what had gone wrong in Ireland as were solicited: English servitors, undertakers, reforming officials, English parliamentarians, Old English landowners all had their discrete takes and different axes to grind, a situation further complicated by considerations of self-interest and an individual's clientage relationship with Buckingham. There had been corruption and malfeasance, and those involved were eager to exonerate themselves and shift the blame onto others. Nevertheless, there was broad agreement that things had not worked out as anticipated.[92]

The plantations had not been as successful as they should have been in essence because people had not been observing the rules. This was particularly true in Ulster, where undertakers had preserved Irish tenants on their estates despite having been granted low rents on the explicit condition that they plant British settlers on their lands. Sir Francis Annesley, one of the Secretaries of State in Ireland and a client of Buckingham, whose work on the commission took him to the counties of Cavan and Fermanagh, suggested that the undertakers should be made to pay treble rents if the terms of their original contract were changed, or double rent if they had violated their contract but now conformed; otherwise, the crown should dispossess those who had failed to fulfil the terms of their contracts and give their lands to those who would. Such stringent measures would provide an obvious boost to the revenues of the crown, though Annesley had an ulterior motive and hoped to be a beneficiary himself.[93]

The general account of Ireland which was supposed to be compiled for Buckingham has never surfaced. There does, however, survive a personal report written for Lord Treasurer Middlesex by Richard Hadsor, a Middle Temple lawyer who hailed originally from the Pale and was of Old English stock, albeit a Protestant who had lived in England for thirty-five years, which provides telling insight into the condition of Ireland at this time. Hadsor believed that 'Confusion, disorders and other inormities' had 'Crept in the late plantations by meanes of the under officers there', who had allowed 'the ruder sort of meere Ireish to inhabite their Lands' because they were willing to pay higher rents than the British, thereby frustrating the crown's hope of settling 'industry or Civility'. The undertakers, he alleged, typically had double the portion of land granted to them by patent, since they made up their number of acres out of arable land only, discounting the rich pastures, spacious woods, rivers filled with fish, and mountains rich in mineral deposits. Hadsor was particularly concerned about the plight of the Old English, whom he felt were by instinct 'loyall', but whom he had heard 'lament' that they were 'not truly distinguished from the meere Irish' nor given office under the crown. The mere Irish, by contrast, Hadsor believed, did 'affect the Span-·iard', who in turn distinguished between 'the Irish and the Old English', so it was important that the king bring the Old English into his service to cement their loyalty. It was the king's own servants in Ireland who were letting him down. The subordinate officers ingrossed 'most of the wealth...to themselves', thereby concealing the true worth of the kingdom; as a counterbalance Hadsor thought some of the natives should be employed in office, since the Irish and British would then keep an eye on each other, and the natives would not demand of the king 'soe large annuall fees, and stipends as be now allowed'.[94]

Hadsor also pointed to the sufferings of the Catholics in Ireland: 'Very many' recusants, he said, were 'grievously fyned in the

Starr-Chamber', while he had heard that in Cork some 5,000 recusants were presented in one go and fined 12*d.* per Sunday for not
coming to church, be 'they never soe poore'. And as the sole Irish
speaker on the commission, and thus appointed to receive petitions
that were handed in by the native population, Hadsor was the most
fully aware of the grievances of the Gaelic Irish. The natives of Leinster, he pointed out, complained that whereas under the plantation
scheme they were supposed to lose only a quarter of their land and
the undertakers were supposed to live in the mountains and in territories bordering on the mere Irish, so as 'to plant Civility there', in
practice they (the natives) were removed far away from 'theire owne
fertile soyle' and allowed to keep only a quarter of their former hold-
ings, and 'that only of Barron Mountaines'. Many of English descent
in Connacht had 'sudenly Crept unto great Estates upon very Easy
termes, having purchased...most of their lands from the natives
upon broken titles'; often the natives had delivered their lands to
them as a way of stopping them falling into the king's hands. The
process of Anglicization among the 'Common people' and even the
Irish gentry had made little headway, while in the last twenty years
the mere Irish had 'multiplyed to an incredible number' and devoted
themselves 'wholy...to Idlenes', so that it was to be 'feared that so
great a multitude of beggars' might 'breake forth to some suddaine
mischiefe', unless they were employed 'in publique workes', such as
the repair of the highways, or building bridges, town walls, or churches.
Yet Hadsor remained optimistic that reform was possible. 'The natives
here', he believed, were 'as apt to learne as any nation; as Capable of
discipline...as willing to imbrace good government, Civillity and
industry'; they were known to be excellent soldiers; and 'no people'
were 'more in awe of their soveraigne nor more willing...to obey
when Justice is duely ministered with equality to them, their wronges
redressed, the offenders punished according to their desert'. The implication was clear that Hadsor thought that justice was not being done
and wrongs were not being addressed, and that the government was
storing up a hornets' nest of trouble for itself as a result.[95]

The commission also highlighted problems in the Church. Only
one parish in six possessed a preaching minister.[96] The bishop of Kil-
dare reported in May 1622 that of the seventy-three parishes in his
diocese, thirty-nine had churches that were in a ruinous condition or
serious state of disrepair, while four parishes had no church at all.[97]
Another report identified that 'some of the Clergie' did not 'use such
Rites and Ceremonyes' as proscribed by the canons and Book of

Common Prayer, and that 'neither Provost, Fellowes, or Schollars of the Colledge' wore 'anie surplesse in tyme of divine service in the Chappell'.[98]

It seemed obvious to the Venetian ambassador that James's Irish policy was not working: as he put it in September 1622, Ireland was 'such that it would be better for the king if it did not exist and the sea alone rolled there'.[99] Yet despite the detailed suggestions the commissioners made for how to address the problems, in the end very little in the way of positive reform was achieved. Those most responsible for the failings, many of them clients of Buckingham, lobbied to have the commission's findings disregarded; others who backed change were so shocked by the commission's findings that they had no desire to take on the burden of reform themselves; and the anti-Spanish lobby in England, who had initially called for financial reform in Ireland to fund a militant foreign policy, were worried that the measures it would be necessary to take might further destabilize the kingdom and thus prove counterproductive if England were to get into a war with Spain.[100]

One outcome of the commission, though never explicitly stated, was the decision that in future chief governors of Ireland should come from England, since it had become apparent that those whose primary interest lay in Ireland could not be trusted to run the kingdom in the best interests of the crown. Viscount Grandison was removed as Lord Deputy (he was allowed to resign), to be replaced by Sir Henry Cary, Viscount Falkland (an Englishman with a Scottish title) in September 1622. Falkland was to be succeeded in the 1630s by the Yorkshireman Thomas, Viscount Wentworth (later earl of Strafford).[101] There was an imperative to address the matter of royal finances: by the end of March 1623 the total debt of the crown stood at £87,714 and the deficit on the current account at £22,429. James thought it both a dishonour and a burden that 'a Countrey so fertile and populous' as Ireland 'should not yet after so manie yeares of happie peace and tranquilitie...bee able to defray the ordinarie charge we are at for the generall good and safetie of it'.[102] With effect from 1 April 1623, Lord Treasurer Middlesex pruned the Irish establishment and implemented drastically frugal arrangements for paying off army and pensioners arrears; as a result he reduced the annual supplement paid by England into the Irish treasury to c. £3,333.[103] Royal directions for improving the condition of the Church were drawn up in June 1623 and approved by the privy council in December, while in the autumn of 1623 royal directions were issued banning unmonitored land grants and discouraging new plantation projects. However, a new high-powered commission that was to be sent to Ireland to implement the reforms was at first postponed and then abandoned under pressure from Buckingham, while the fall from grace of treasurer Middlesex in 1624 (again brought about by Buckingham, together with the Prince of Wales), meant that the comprehensive directions on the plantation never came to be implemented.[104]

The Blessed Revolution

James now was pitching all his hopes on the Spanish match. Gondomar had led James to believe that the match would be possible if England granted some degree of informal religious toleration to Catholics; in reality, there was no way that either Spain or the pope would agree to the marriage unless Charles converted. Frustrated with the delays, in February 1623 Charles and Buckingham decided to make a surprise trip to Madrid themselves in an attempt to bring the marriage negotiations to a speedier conclusion. James was against such a risky venture—the couple were to go overland (through France), in disguise (wearing false beards and going by the names of Jack and Tom Smith), with only a couple of attendants—but he agreed to let them go when Buckingham insisted that the Prince would regard it 'as the greatest misfortune and affliction that could befall him' if he denied the request.[105] Murmurings against the match continued across the country. One manuscript libel dated 23 March and nominally addressed to Buckingham warned how 'No good' could 'come from Spain, either to the king, or to the Church'. Henri of Navarre, it continued, had 'allied himself with the Spaniards, but a bullet took him in his own trenches', while his son Henri IV 'was stabbed by Ravaillac'. Queen Elizabeth, on the other hand, had 'refused the King of Spain's suit, and none could touch a hair of her head'. 'Matches with Spain' had 'always been unfortunate. Prince Arthur died without issue, Queen Catharine only reared Queen Mary.' Edward IV and Henry VIII, on the other hand, 'married among their subjects, and the 2 Queens Elizabeth were the issue'. The crown would 'find more support in its necessities', our author predicted, 'by casting itself into the arms of the Parliament, than by any foreign fawning'.[106]

Charles and Buckingham's mission to Spain proved to be a disaster. Once Charles and Buckingham were in Madrid, the Spanish, realizing that Charles was not willing to convert, held out for greater religious concessions, including a full toleration of Catholics in England confirmed by parliamentary statute. Virtually a prisoner in the Spanish capital, Charles in the end agreed to a marriage treaty just so that he could get back to England, leaving Digby, recently raised to the peerage as the earl of Bristol, with his proxy to await the arrival of the papal dispensation allowing the marriage, though making it clear that he was not to give his assent to the marriage.[107]

Charles and Buckingham (who had been made a duke in May) arrived back in England on the evening of 5 October. When they entered London the next day without the Infanta they were greeted with widespread popular rejoicing. The bells rang throughout the capital and there were numerous bonfires: D'Ewes claimed he counted 335 between Whitehall and Temple Bar alone. There were similar displays in the provinces and also in Scotland and Ireland. Cambridge had three nights of bonfires, bells, and fireworks, the townsmen unwilling to be outdone by the colleges. It is true that many of these displays were encouraged from above. For instance, the mayor of Chester 'received orders from the Privy Council to ring the bells and to make bonfires', while in Dublin the Lord Deputy called on the citizens to celebrate the Prince's safe return as he waited 'for letters out of England' to arrive.[108] However, it would be wrong to see the bonfire celebrations simply as 'staged' events; a number of communities, in fact, had put on bonfire displays in late September on hearing false reports that the Prince had already returned.[109] The failure of the Spanish match was commemorated in poems, squibs, sermons, and plays. The aggressively anti-Catholic mood of the capital was further revealed on 26 October, when a garret adjacent to the French ambassador's residence in Blackfriars suddenly collapsed as the Jesuit Robert Drury preached to a crowd of some 300–400 worshippers, killing the preacher and close to a hundred others and injuring many more. Protestants were quick to interpret the event as a providential judgement on the Catholic faith, although what caused particular alarm was the fact that so many English Catholics could openly assemble in the heart of the capital to practise their faith. The noise of the building collapsing quickly drew a huge crowd, and while some rushed to offer first aid and assistance to the survivors, others—'Puritans' according to their critics—gave vent to their outrage at this illicit Catholic conventicle by slinging mud and stones, hurling insults, and even attacking some of the wounded as they were being carried away for treatment.[110]

Once back in England, Charles made it clear he was not prepared to go ahead with the marriage and pressured James into calling another parliament for the specific purpose of funding a war against Spain to recover the Palatinate. Charles and Buckingham set about constructing a 'patriot' coalition, comprising peers and MPs—including Essex, Southampton, Oxford, Pembroke, Saye, Warwick, Coke, Digges, Eliot, Phelips, and Sandys—who had not been particularly sympathetic to either Buckingham or the court but were known for their hostility to Spain. Oxford had to be released from the Tower so that he could take his seat in the Lords. Charles and Buckingham used their electoral patronage to try to ensure that a House of Commons favourable to their design was returned. Far from all of their nominees were returned, although they did manage to establish a considerable power bloc in the Commons, and they were now swimming with the tide of public opinion. Indeed, the mood of the electorate was decidedly hostile to anyone 'inclinable to Popery' or sympathetic to Spain.[111] Charles and Buckingham were planning on uniting with the anti-court faction in parliament and exploiting deepseated anti-popish and Hispanophobic sentiments in the nation at large in order to sabotage James's foreign policy. The king was to be undone by his son and his favourite.

Parliament opened for business on 19 February 1624.[112] The speech from the throne showed a king determined to be conciliatory. 'The Glory of a King stands in the Multitude of his People', James began, and 'the Strength of a Kingdom, stands...in the Hearts of the People', whom he cherished as a husband cherished his wife. Parliaments, he said, were called so that they might 'confer with the King, and give Him their advice in Matters of greatest Weight and Importance', and he had called members together now so that they could give him their advice 'in the greatest Matter that ever could concern any King', namely how to proceed with regard to the Spanish match and the Palatinate, in the aftermath of the Prince's failed mission to Spain. It was a dramatic climb-down from the position he had taken in the second session of the 1621 parliament when he had rebuked MPs for meddling in matters of foreign policy. James took the opportunity to refute suggestions that he had been slack in his care for religion when negotiating with Spain. He had always shown a concern 'for the Weal Public and Cause of Religion'; he had 'only thought good sometimes to wink and connive at the Execution of some Penal Statutes, and not to go on so rigorously as at other Times'. He concluded by urging parliament not to be 'over curious' in 'matters of Privileges, Liberties, and Customs', assuring members that he wanted to maintain their liberties and had no desire to 'alter them in any Thing'.[113] It was a speech that was 'much applauded by the hearers'. A jubilant Thomas Scott asked 'is not this wonderfull?', and thought that these words deserved 'to be lodged in everie Subject's heart'.[114]

With the king looking to put his past disagreements with parliament behind him, business proceeded quite smoothly. Seventy-three statutes were enacted in just over three months, as compared with just two in 1621 and none in 1614, among them the bill against monopolies, revived from the previous parliament, and a couple of Puritan measures against drunkenness and profane swearing. Yet James felt himself being backed into a corner over foreign policy. It was Charles who introduced a motion for war in a speech delivered before both Houses on 28 February, urging the need 'to beginne with Spaine other wise they will beginne with us', which met with widespread applause. He was seconded by Buckingham, who gave a 'long oration' testifying 'his zeal for his country'. The earl of Kellie observed at the beginning of March how many of the men 'that did disturbe the last Parlament' were 'now als mutche for my Lord of Buckinghame as theye war then against him'.[115] 'The roaring boys of London' were soon daily singing Buckingham's praise in the City's taverns: 'Then merry be, my lads, and let us drink his health, | We'll wish him honor and renown, and what he wants of wealth.'[116] James continued to stall as best he could. When a subcommittee of both Houses visited him at Theobalds on 6 March to urge the case for war, he tactfully thanked them for their advice but pointed out that he was short of money, lacked financial support from potential allies overseas, and had always been a peaceful king who wanted 'to avoid the Effusion of Christian Blood'—although he promised that if he went to war he would not meddle with any funds that parliament voted for it.[117] When parliament made a formal remonstrance to the king on 14 March stating their willingness to fund a war, James asked for five subsidies and ten fifteenths for the war and a further subsidy and two fifteenths every year until his debts were paid. Under pressure from Charles and Buckingham, James later dropped the demand to settle his debts and agreed that all six subsidies and twelve fifteenths should go towards the war, but this was a huge sum—roughly £780,000—which many MPs protested the nation could not afford at a time of recession. A compromise was eventually reached whereby the Commons voted three subsidies and three fifteenths (c. £300,000) 'for the present', to be overseen by a council of war accountable to parliament, with the understanding that future funds would be forthcoming when necessary, and on 23 March James announced that he was breaking the treaties with Spain.[118] That evening London celebrated with the ringing of bells and bonfires across the city, although there were ugly scenes outside the Spanish embassy as crowds started hurling insults and throwing stones at some of the Spanish ambassador's servants.[119]

Parliament now wanted the king to take a tougher line against Catholic recusants. In early April the two Houses agreed to a joint petition calling for the deportation of all Jesuits and seminary priests, the strict execution of all laws against Catholic recusants, a prohibition against English subjects attending mass at the houses of foreign ambassadors, and the disarming of all convicted recusants, which they presented to James on 23 April. In his reply the following day James stated that his 'Heart...bled' when he 'heard of the Increase of Popery'; protesting that his opposition to persecution had stemmed solely from his belief that it was counterproductive, and tended rather to fuel religious commitment, he agreed to parliament's demands.[120]

As parliament debated what sort of war they should fund, there remained one potential obstacle, the pro-Spanish Lord Treasurer Lionel Cranfield, now earl of Middlesex, who realized that an open-ended commitment to war would undermine all his recent efforts to reform the royal finances. Charles and Buckingham decided that Middlesex would have to go and had the Commons initiate impeachment proceedings against the Lord Treasurer on trumped-up charges of bribery. James told Buckingham he would 'shortly repent this folly', since he was 'making a rod' with which he would be 'scourged' himself, and warned Charles that he would 'live to have his bellyfull of Parliaments',[121] but Middlesex's retrenchments had made him deeply unpopular and there was little James could do to save his Treasurer. On 13 May Middlesex was sentenced to a £50,000 fine, deprived of office, banished the court, and sent to the Tower.[122] He was not to stay incarcerated long: on 1 June, three days after the end of the parliamentary session, James released him and had him sworn one of the gentlemen of his majesty's bedchamber.[123]

Equally ominously, parliament also began investigating the activities of the English Arminians. On the same day as Middlesex's conviction, the Commons received a petition calling for the suppression of a book recently published by Richard Mountague, the rector of Stanford Rivers (Essex) and also of Petworth (Sussex) and a royal chaplain, called *A New Gagg for an Old Goose*, for upholding the 'dangerous Opinions of Arminius' concerning universal redemption— all the more worrying because such opinions, the petition alleged, had recently begun 'to bee more boldly maintained' by some English divines. The Commons appointed a committee headed by John Pym to investigate the matter, though upon receiving Pym's report the House referred the matter to the archbishop of Canterbury.[124] Of more immediate concern was the complaint brought by the citizens of Norwich accusing Bishop Harsnett of discouraging preaching on Sunday mornings, making all the townspeople come to the Cathedral (which was not even big enough to hold them all), allowing images to be set up in one of Norwich's churches, citing those who would not kneel towards the east, and punishing a minister and others for singing psalms in his own house on the Sabbath. A joint committee of both Houses was established to investigate the accusations, and charges were brought before the Lords on 19 May. In his defence, Harsnett claimed that one of his officials had indeed taken action against some, but only because they refused to kneel at all, that the supposed psalm meeting was in fact the late night conventicle of a sect which maintained 'that the church was no better then...an ale-howse', and that the images had been set up without his knowledge. As for discouraging preaching, he insisted that he was committed to a preaching ministry and had merely responded to a request from 'six or seven of the abler Sort of Ministers in Norwich' to be relieved from having to rush through their services on Sunday mornings to allow time for people to attend the service in the Cathedral.[125]

James had by now had enough and decided to prorogue parliament. In his closing speech on 29 May, he thanked the two Houses for the subsidies, all of which he promised to spend on the restitution of his son-in-law, but warned members that the oath of supremacy forbade them from meddling with 'Church Matters' and expressed his concern about the continued publication of seditious books, 'both popish on the one side, and puritan on the other', which he was determined to suppress.[126]

The 1624 parliament marked the final demise of James's policy for securing peace in Christendom. For the time being, however, Charles and Buckingham were riding the crest of a wave of popularity. Over the course of 1624 a flood of pamphlets appeared backing war against Spain and celebrating both Charles and Buckingham for the stance they were taking. Thomas Scott, previously so outspoken in his criticism of the government's foreign policy, was now writing in praise of 'the gratious Prince of Wales' and 'the illustrious Duke of Buckingham', who together 'with other worthies' had 'in this late time of extreme necessitie stept forth for the rescue of our Lawes, lives, religion, and State from imminent danger'. Elsewhere Scott styled Buckingham 'a Noble, Wise, and Generous Prince, upon whom the King' had 'deservedly conferred his grace' and whose 'faithfull service' had 'gained the generall love of the Common people'.[127] Alexander Leighton, a Scottish-born minister turned medical doctor now resident in London, produced a lengthy tract, published in Amsterdam, justifying a 'holy war' against Spain and Rome, in which he urged Prince Charles to 'Gird on [his] sword': it would be the Prince's 'greatest honour', Leighton predicted, 'to fight God's battles' and 'raze Rome's greatnes'.[128]

The media of 1624 were both Hispanophobic and virulently anti-Catholic, building upon but at the same time serving to reinforce and perpetuate popular fears of popery, thereby cementing an ideological outlook that was to prove highly resilient and deeply influential in English (and Scottish and Protestant Irish) political culture across the seventeenth century. Leighton, for example, wrote of the 'unparalleld inhumanity' of our enemies, pointing to 'the late and fresh bleeding State of Bohemia, and the Palatinate, wherein the Spanyard and Austrian have renued an Indian cruelty; no yeares nor sex, have they had any pitty of'. There were plenty of specific examples to support his allegations. Take the 'monstrous murther' of an elderly Protestant minister when the Spanish had taken Heidelberg: having abused the minister's daughter, the Spaniards 'tyed a small cord' around the minister's head, 'which with truncheons they wreathed about till they squeased out his braines'. Catholics were 'of the bloud of the Whore', Leighton continued:

> Doth not the belluin rage and cruelty, executed upon the Germanes and Bohemians, by woefull experience tell us, what mercilesse and inhumane enemies we contend with; namely, the brats of the bloudy whore. The ripping up of women, the shamefull abusing of them...the torturing of men with new devised torments; the bathing in the bloud of inoffensive children; the cruel murthering of God's Ministers (who by the lawes of God and Nations, have always been sacred).[129]

In Leighton's view 'the Spanyard' was 'like the Irish, who under a perfidious peace doth his adversary more mischiefe then in open war'. Leighton also had strong words to say about the recent suspension of the penal laws in England. The king's job was 'to establish true Religion, and to maintain it', and therefore 'he must extirpate the false'; both the Bible and recent history demonstrated 'the evill ensuyng upon the toleration of any false religion'.[130] Yet to be successful in a just war, 'reformation at home' would be needed to ensure God's continued support. Sin was rife in England: profaning the Sabbath, going to stage plays, 'scoffing precisenesse' [i.e. mocking Puritans], swearing, and usury, and yet for all but the first it was 'counted Puritanism to count them sins'. It was important, therefore, for the English parliament to 'make sure of God's favour' by being zealous for 'his glory', promoting 'the amendment of life', and expelling 'the Canaanites' (i.e. Catholics).[131]

Scott condemned the Spanish as 'false, ambitious, proud, and cruell' and given to 'superstition and Idolatry', and even sought to play the race card by pointing out that they were 'discended of the Moorish race' and 'still infected with Moorish mindes, and...manners'. Their 'crueltie' was 'naturall and inhaerent to [their] Nation': during the recent campaign in the Netherlands, Spanish soldiers had ravished 'young Girles not above eight or ten yeares of age' and turned 'men and women starke naked out of their houses, to shift for themselves in the open fields' during the depths of winter. The English Catholics, according to Scott, not only worked as spies for Spain, but they were 'the only engines and complots of all Treasons, authors of Tumults, and seditions within the Land'. Yet although the Spanish wanted to make themselves 'maisters of great Brittaine', the English had nothing to fear because Spain was 'not so well furnished with men, munition, or money, as the World imagineth'. The English, 'one people of the same Language, Religion, Lawes, Governed by the same Gracious and good King', and 'famous of ould, for her triumphes and many victories over other Nations', should thus not 'care a strawe for the vaine and windy threats of proude Spaine'.[132] John Reynolds published two tracts in 1624 advocating a full-scale war effort, *Vox Coeli* (the voice of heaven) and *Votivae Angliae* (the desires of England). The former, which had been written the previous year, was a criticism of the wisdom of the Spanish match, though the published version contained a new preface calling for the speedy execution of the now intended war against Spain. The latter affirmed that 'all the Subjects of this Kingdome', with the exception of a few Romish and Spanish sympathizers, did 'vehementlie desire Warre with Spayne', and that there was 'not a true Subject, a faythfull and loyall-harted Britton...nor the sonne of an honest man' who was 'not ready...to beare his life on the poynt of his Sword' to reclaim the Palatinate. Reynolds also warned James that the honour of his three kingdoms would suffer if this province was lost and would make himself 'the laughture of all the rest of the Princes of Christendom'.[133]

Similar calls to arms were made from pulpits across the country,[134] while (according to Scott) the Spaniard was also 'derided' in 'verses and unseemely Pictures' and 'in songs and Ballades, sung up and downe the Streetes in many places'.[135] Then there was the London stage. Thomas Middleton's powerful anti-Spanish satire *A Game at Chess*, satirizing Gondomar, was seen by 3,000 people a day during its nine-day run in August 1624 (the longest on the Jacobean stage)— 'old and younge, rich and poore, masters and servants, papists and puritans, wise men, etc. churchmen and statesmen', according to Chamberlain.[136]

With the government now having been won over to the case for war with Spain, there was less need for it to censor the media. Thus anti-Catholic and anti-Spanish writers and preachers were allowed a degree of freedom of expression in 1624 that would have been denied them in 1622–3. Nevertheless, authors had to be careful not to over-step the mark. Reynolds clearly did when he depicted the king as a coward who was terrified of Spain, and was duly imprisoned for his pains. The Spanish ambassador was so offended by Middleton's *Game at Chess* that he urged James to suppress it, which the king eventually did—though he delayed doing so, leaving a long enough time for the play to have its effect.[137]

All Were Equal in Death

To spearhead his campaign to recapture the Palatinate, James secured the services of the German mercenary Ernst, count von Mansfeld, who had fought for the Elector Frederick in 1620–2 and thereby gained something of a reputation in England as a Protestant hero. Over the summer of 1624 James negotiated an agreement with Louis XIII of France whereby Louis promised to pay half of Mansfeld's expenses for six months, allow his troops to land either at Calais or Boulogne, and to provide 3,000 cavalry which would be waiting in northern France. The alliance was to be cemented by the marriage of Prince Charles to Louis's sister Henrietta Maria (whom Charles had met on his way back from Spain the previous year), although Louis held out for religious concessions just as sweeping as those previously demanded by Spain. Under the terms of the marriage treaty, eventually signed at Paris on 10 November 1624 and ratified by James and Charles at Cambridge two days later, Louis was to pay a dowry of £120,000 (in two instalments), while James publicly agreed to allow

Henrietta Maria complete freedom of worship, to have twenty-eight religious attendants who would be allowed to wear their habits in public, and also to have the care of the education of any children of the marriage until they reached the age of thirteen. At the same time, James and Charles signed a private engagement—*Ecrit Particulier*—to release all Catholics imprisoned for their religion and to allow English Catholics to practise their religion in peace.[138] In January 1625 James further agreed to lend Louis XIII seven ships to help put down the rebellion of the prominent Huguenot nobleman the duke of Soubise—a rebellion which initially had been condemned by other French Huguenots.[139]

Mansfeld came to England in early November to raise troops for the joint Anglo-French venture to recapture the Palatinate: 12,000 men were to be recruited in England (mostly by impressment), 10,000 in Scotland, with the earl of Lincoln commanding an additional contingent of cavalry. The venture proved ill-fated from the start. With the parliamentary subsidies yet to come in, there was not enough money to pay or feed the men properly, and the raw recruits—many of whom did not want to serve in the first place—grew disorderly. They 'spoyled' the countryside around Dover 'as yf yt had been in an enemie's countrie'; many tried to desert; others mutinied; while Mansfeld was so concerned that it was said he 'durst not shew himself among them'.[140] Furthermore, James and Louis had different war aims. James was desperate to avoid an open breach with Spain, and so wanted the troops sent directly to the Palatinate; in theory, any Spanish forces that occupied any of Frederick's territories were acting under direction of the Holy Roman Emperor. Louis, by contrast, wanted them to be sent to relieve Breda in the Netherlands, which had been under siege by Spanish forces since August 1624; however, this would involve England intervening on the side of the Dutch in their war of independence against Spain. James objected and instructed Mansfeld to go directly to the Palatinate without passing through any Spanish territory (which would involve a lengthy detour along the French border towards Lorraine, to avoid the Spanish Netherlands); Louis, unhappy at the prospect of having Mansfeld's untrained and ill-disciplined troops marching through north-eastern France, refused to let Mansfeld's army land at Calais. So at the end of January, during the heart of what was an extremely cold winter, the transport ships carrying the men headed off towards the coast of Holland and Zeeland, where the Dutch—whom Buckingham had failed to notify in advance—were totally unprepared to feed them. The results were predictable. Thousands of men died of malnutrition, exposure, and disease. Of those who survived, many deserted. Mansfeld decided to head to Breda, although at first his English colonels, reluctant to disobey their sovereign, refused to join him. It was not until the spring, after James had passed away, that Charles gave Mansfeld permission to take his English troops to relieve Breda. Of the original 12,000 enlisted Englishmen, he now had at most 7,000 men left, of whom half were to die in the next couple of months. When Breda finally surrendered to the Spanish in June, perhaps only 600 Englishmen survived.[141]

Parliament had been due to reassemble on 2 November 1624, but a renewed outbreak of contagious disease in the capital led James to extend the prorogation until 16 February 1625. (Or so, at least, ran the official explanation; James was also nervous about the reaction he might face from parliament to the religious concessions being offered to secure the French match.)[142] On 19 January, James announced that the prorogation would be further extended—'for weighty and important reasons'—until 15 March, and then on the 3 March until 20 April.[143] By now the king's health was in serious decline. In the early spring he fell sick at Theobalds of a 'tertian ague', which developed into a fever. Dr Godfrey Goodman, the newly appointed bishop of Gloucester, who was with James during his final sickness, thought that the king's health problems were brought on by eating too much fruit—grapes, nectarines, strawberries, cherries, and other items imported from abroad—which 'although while he was young did tend to preserve his health, yet now', with the king nearing sixty, 'did a little weaken his body': 'after this eating of fruit in the spring time', Goodman noted, the king 'fell into a great looseness'. James, who normally had an 'averseness to physic and impatience under it', proved 'very orderable' on this occasion, a personality change which contemporaries interpreted as 'a certain prognostic of death'.[144] With his physicians' best efforts coming to naught, the king allowed Buckingham and the duke's mother (who was a Roman Catholic) to apply a 'plaister' which had been prepared by an Essex doctor they knew, although it seemed only to add to the king's torment. Buckingham then gave James a potion that one of his servants had concocted, although the king was too weak to take more than one or two sips. Since the plaister and the potion were administered without the approval of the king's physicians, rumours were soon circulating that the king had been poisoned by the duke as part of a Catholic plot—although Sir James Palmer of the King's Bedchamber, who was also suffering from the ague, said that he had tried both the plaister and the potion on himself first and had been cured. James died just before noon on 27 March 1625, aged fifty-eight years and nine months, in the arms of Palmer and clutching the hand of Buckingham. Prince Charles was waiting outside his father's bedchamber, desperate for any news. When he saw the earl of Holland leave the room, he asked him how his father did, and Holland replied: 'the King was well, God be thanked'. In truth, James was already dead.[145] About three days before, James had suffered a stroke, 'which affected his chin, loosening his jawbone and enlarging his tongue'. In the end, 'a violent dysentry carried him off', so that he died in terrible filth, 'the very bed exuding the excrement'.[146]

Thus the man who aspired to be *rex pacificus* died with his kingdoms still at peace—just. The news of the king's death prompted the usual outpouring of elegies. One described James as 'Christendome's great Champion', 'who love'd peace whilst he liv'd, and did strive | Dying in peace to keepe peace stil alive', adding—somewhat disingenuously in light of the recent fiasco of the Mansfeld expedition— 'No widdowes' curses nor no orphanes' cryes | Shal interrupt thy hallowed obsequies | For their slayne husbands, or their fathers lost | In bloudy wars...'.[147] Other elegists lamented the loss of 'James the peacefull and the just' and suggested that 'the King of Peace' should also be styled 'the blessed King of Unity', for having brought about the 'happy union of great Britanny'.[148] The elegy penned by John Taylor, the 'water poet', offered some criticism of James's pacific foreign policy: 'War I think might well have bin imploy'd | True Britaines wish just warres to entertaine.'[149] Moreover, amidst all the hyperbole, the fact was not lost that this divinely ordained monarch passed away like another other mere mortal, sinking 'silently into a bed of Clay'. There was 'No meteor, no comet, no clap of thunder to alert Christendom'. | All were equal in death. 'Impartiall fates,' one elegist concluded, 'I see that princes then | Though they live like Gods, yet they must dy like men. | And the same passing bell may toul for them | which rang but now the beggars requiem.'[150]

Charles was told that it would take forty days to raise the money for a state funeral and so James was embalmed. In preparing the body, doctors first removed James's organs. They found his heart large but soft, his liver good, one kidney fine but the other with two stones, and his lungs black. His skull was so hard that it had to be opened with a chisel—and so full, that the brains spilled out. The state funeral was on 7 May 1625.[151] It is perhaps fitting that we should leave the last word to Bishop Williams of Lincoln, who preached the funeral sermon. Williams saw James as a latter-day Solomon: never were 'two Kings more fully parallel'd amongst themselves, and better distinguished from all other Kings besides themselves'. To Williams's mind, James was 'the most powerful Speaker, that ever swayed the Sceptre of this Kingdome'. He was 'the most constant Patron of Churches, and Church-men'; the most 'constant, resolute, and settled Protestant in point of Doctrine', who defended 'this Doctrine...with his penne, his Lawes, and his Sword'; an upholder of 'the Discipline of this Church', namely 'the Hierarchie of the Bishops'; and 'as great a Patron of the Maintenance of the Church' as ever known to history. He was known for his 'Justice', for 'his infinite Wisdom', and 'for the managing of a long, and a continued Peace', for which no less was required 'then the Wisedome of Salomon'. As a result, 'all kinde of learning highly improved, manufactures at home daily invented, Trading abroad exceedingly multiplied, the Border of Scotland peaceably governed, the North of Ireland religiously planted', and 'Virginia, New-found-land, and New England peopled'. Moreover, on surveying 'the bounds of his Empire', Williams pronounced, 'King James will prove a King Salomon in this, as being the first King...that raigned here over all this Island, Over all Israel'. Yet just as God had 'made a lively Repraesentation of the Vertues of Salomon, in the Person of King James', Williams reassured mourners, 'So hath he done a like Repraesentation of the Vertues of King James, in the Person of King Charles our Gracious Sovereigne'. Although 'the Father be dead, yet is he, as though hee were not dead, for he hath left One behinde him most like himselfe'.[152]

Charles I

8

················

A Prince 'Bred in Parliaments'[1]

That the King and his people may now, and at all like times, meete in love, consult in wisedome, manage their Counsell with temper...And when their consultation is ended, part in the same love that should ever bring King and People together.

William Laud at the opening of Parliament, 6 February 1626.[2]

Charles I was twenty-four when his father passed away on 27 March 1625. Not since the death of Henry VII in 1509 had a reigning English monarch died leaving a legitimate adult male heir; even then, Henry VIII had been a few months shy of his eighteenth birthday. 1625 saw the smoothest succession in England for well over a hundred years, perhaps since that of Henry V in 1413. Charles was proclaimed 'amid universal applause and rejoicing'.[3] Even 'Children and modest Maids, to all men's thinking', one eulogist rhymed, 'Were drunke with Joy, as others were with drinking', while 'Matrons, that till then, scarce were seene to smile, | To heare King Charles Proclaim'd, laught all the while'.[4] In Cambridge, 'the joy of the people', it was said, 'devoured their mourning': 'all fears and sorrowes...swallowed up in joy of so hopefull a successor'.[5] The Venetian ambassador observed that 'the general rejoicing prevail[ed] over the sorrow of individuals' at the death of King James, for 'the uncertainties of the late rule had wearied all men'.[6] The diarist John Rous believed that Charles's 'coming to the crowne was very joyous to the well-affected'; only 'to Papists' was it 'not very welcome'.[7]

As Prince of Wales, Charles had emerged as a popular patriot hero in the aftermath of the failed Spanish match, he had led the demand for war against Spain and for recapturing the Palatinate for his sister and brother-in-law, and it seemed that he was a better friend to parliament than his father had been; indeed, he was styled a prince 'bred in Parliaments'. However, the honeymoon period did not last long. Tensions soon flared up—over finance, foreign policy, and the Church. Parliament refused to commit to the level of funding necessary to fight the war to which it had committed the crown, it condemned the way the war effort was being managed and sought to impeach the king's leading minister, the duke of Buckingham (who since 1619 had been Lord Admiral), and it was deeply critical of Charles's promotion of Arminian clerics to positions of authority within the Church. As early as 1626 Charles was contemplating pursuing other counsels, and tried to raise funds for the war by means of a Forced Loan. When recalled in 1628 parliament responded by condemning the Forced Loan and other abuses of the prerogative with its Petition of Right and relaunched its attack on Buckingham and Arminianism; Buckingham was saved from parliament's wrath by the king only to fall victim later in the year to an assassin's blade. By 1629 Charles was so sick of parliaments that he decided to try to rule without them. Why, then, did things go wrong so soon? Why did a prince 'bred in Parliaments' find it so difficult to get on with them?

The Personality of Charles I

Charles I has long had a negative press, and most modern-day historians continue to see him as a deeply flawed ruler, who did not have the right intellectual ability or psychological make-up to be an effective king. He was a shy man, lacking in self-confidence, who to cover for his insecurities—so it has been said—was authoritarian, inflexible, and brittle. Self-righteous and arrogant, convinced that he was always right and his critics always wrong, he could—so it has been claimed—be unpredictable, difficult to advise, and frequently duplicitous (and was thus a ruler who did not easily inspire trust).[8] Many of these supposed 'personality traits', however, can only be inferred from how Charles acted as king: they are in effect assessments of his rule and thus interpretations, the validity of which are open to dispute. We should be careful not to begin our consideration of Charles's reign with our judgement clouded by certain preconceptions about his character and attributes derived from how we know things were to work out.

What, then, can we say with confidence about the twenty-four-year-old man who became king in March 1625? Clarendon wrote that he was 'of the most harmless disposition and the most exemplar piety, the greatest example of sobriety, chastity, and mercy, that any prince hath been endued with'.[9] In this regard, he provided a striking contrast with his father. The Venetian ambassador, writing a few weeks after James's death, noted that the new king showed 'signs of being temperate, moderate, and of exchanging all the prodigality of the past for order and profit'.[10] Charles was a deeply religious man. Interestingly, he was raised a Calvinist, his education having been overseen by Thomas Murray, a Scottish Presbyterian who was later to become provost of Eton, though as king he was strongly to favour Arminian divines—more so for their emphasis on ritual in worship and their exaltation of authority and hierarchy in Church government than their views on salvation.[11] James thought that his son had a strong grasp of theology, writing that Charles could 'manage a point in Controversie with the best studied Divine of them all'.[12] Clarendon believed Charles inherited his father's 'zeal for religion', and wanted 'nothing more...than to unite his three kingdoms in one form of God's worship and in a uniformity in their public devotions'.[13] Even the lawyer MP Sir Edward Coke, no great friend to the court in the 1620s, acknowledged in a speech in the Commons in March 1628 that Charles was 'a religious king free from personal vices'.[14]

Charles was Scottish by birth, having been born in Dunfermline Castle on 19 November 1600. The second son and third child of James, he became heir to the throne only when his older brother Henry died in 1612. He was left behind in Scotland when James acceded to the English crown in 1603; he was not to move south for another year, although he became thoroughly Anglicized, and was not to return to Scotland again until 1633. He had rickets in infancy and was slow to walk; indeed, his legs never grew to their full length and as an adult he was no more than five foot four inches tall. Charles was also late to talk and developed a severe stammer, thought at the time to be the result of a deformed tongue: when Charles was about four or five James seriously contemplated having the cord under his son's tongue cut in an attempt to solve the problem.[15] It could have been that Charles's speech impediment reflected underlying psychological problems, although we now know that stammers can be partly genetic. Writing in April 1625, the Venetian ambassador observed that Charles 'expressed himself much more with his heart than his voice, having some difficulty in his speech which prevents him talking easily'.[16] It is not clear that his speech impediment made Charles an ineffective public speaker. His speech before both houses of parliament on 10 March 1624 about the 'affairs of Christendom' went down so well that 'there was clapping of hands for joy'.[17] His stammer clearly bothered him, however. As king Charles invariably delivered very short speeches to parliament, leaving it to his ministers to explain the royal agenda in detail. Addressing his first parliament in 1625, he openly admitted he was 'unfit for much speaking', although MPs— 'wearied with the long orations of King James'—regarded Charles's brevity as refreshing and greeted his speech with 'great applause'.[18] The episode suggests that the speech impediment was a bigger issue for Charles than it was for those who listened to him; at the same time, it betrays the new king's underlying lack of self-confidence.

The extent to which Charles's insecurities were further fuelled by the nature of his relationships with his parents and siblings is difficult to say. Growing up, Charles was teased by his elder brother, but then again many younger brothers are.[19] It has been said that he lacked a close relationship with his mother, who thought him 'a fool' and described him as 'wilful'. The royal chaplain and Caroline apologist Peter Heylyn confirmed that as a young child Charles 'was noted to be very wilful', although he maintained that the queen was always 'a tender and indulgent Mother' to Charles, 'expressing more affection to him then to all the rest of her Children'.[20] In December 1618 the Venetian ambassador described the queen as 'passionately attached' to Charles 'above all her other children'.[21]

Charles had a deeply ambivalent attitude towards his father. James had kept him down, to stop the young prince from becoming the focus of a reversionary interest.[22] This left Charles anxious to please, in an attempt to win his father's affections. Charles once wrote to James that he was studying the divine right of kings and 'how obedience to the king was, after the pursuit of goodness, the greatest wish of Your Majesty's dutiful son'.[23] He appears to have internalized the teachings of *Basilikon Doron*, the study guide for how to be a good king which James had written for Prince Henry, with its emphasis on high moral probity and godliness and its deep suspicion of Puritans.[24] At the same time Charles was disgusted by his father's morality and was determined to set a higher standard himself. Whereas James was given to swearing, 'no execrations' ever 'rashly proceeded from [Charles's] mouth', it was observed, his 'ears abhorring…even the least sordid word'.[25] As he reached adulthood, Charles desperately wanted to be his own man, yet he was also afraid to offend his father by standing up to him. It has been said that developing a close friendship with the duke of Buckingham offered Charles a way out of this impasse: he could please his father by befriending the man his father liked most, but he could also use the favourite to protect him from his father and even—as in the case of the trip to Spain in 1623 and then the formation of the patriot coalition in 1624—to oppose him.[26] Charles appears to have felt in his father's shadow even after James's death, often wondering whether he was living up to his father's expectations. In his early proclamations he presented himself as his father's son; when criticized, he would often retort—as he did to his Scottish privy councillors in February 1626—'you durst not have done so to my father'.[27] Throughout his reign, when defending his policies he would frequently claim that he was doing no more than his father had done before him.

It has been said that Charles lacked his father's shrewdness or ability to understand the views of others,[28] although this is a comparative assessment on which judgement should perhaps be reserved until later. What we can say is that Charles himself appears to have recognized in himself personality traits which historians have seen as limitations. In February 1624, a year before his accession, he told William Laud that he could never have been a lawyer since he could never 'defend a bad, nor yield in a good cause'—although Charles doubtless did not see this as a shortcoming.[29] Yet it would be wrong to suggest that Charles did not have a developed understanding of the arts of kingcraft. He not only imbibed his father's teachings but was also heavily influenced by neo-Stoical moral philosophy (especially Tacitus's analysis of the motivation of politicians and the dissimulation of rulers), he took notes on leading commentators on the art of politics such as Guicciardini and Bacon, and he prided himself on his ability to read other people's motives and to assess their tactics. He embraced the vocabulary of the 'prudential' approach to politics, but unlike the Machiavellian view, which saw politics as operating in a sphere totally separate from that of religion or morality, for Charles prudence had ultimately to be checked by conscience. In short, Charles was no naïve conviction politician. Although he believed that he should not bend from what he knew was right, he recognized that the practical realities of politics meant that a ruler sometimes had to appear to be flexible and ready to compromise in order to achieve his ends. These ends, however, were not personal ones: as a divine-right ruler, Charles believed it his duty to carry out God's will, to promote the true religion and the public good, and to serve the best interests of his subjects—or, more precisely, what he thought God saw as the best interests of his subjects.[30]

Charles was a deeply private man. He barred noblemen from the innermost rooms of the royal palace and installed new triple locks on the doors of his private chambers. He was obsessed with order and virtue. He subjected himself to rigid self-control—drawing up rules dividing his day from his early rising, for prayers, exercises, audiences, business, eating, and sleeping. Right from the beginning of his reign he moved to reverse the informality and moral degeneracy of his father's court. Courtiers were expected to maintain a greater level of propriety. The only man he ever truly got close to was Buckingham—and there was indeed a deep, powerful friendship between the two men. One of the first actions that Charles did as king was to assure the duke that he would continue to enjoy royal favour in the new reign; and Charles was to stand by the man as public criticism of the duke's handling of policy quickly began to pile up. After the duke's assassination in 1628, however, no man was ever again to enjoy the same degree of confidence with the king—not even William Laud.[31]

Initially Charles was not close to his wife Henrietta Maria; she was a mere girl of fifteen when she arrived in England, and Buckingham was said to have been jealous of her and to have done his best to ensure that she 'never had any Credit with the King'.[32] However, Charles and Henrietta Maria's relationship grew stronger from the late 1620s, following the death of Buckingham, and they came to develop a close, loving bond. Their new-found intimacy led to pregnancy, although the child—a boy—was born premature and lived for just two hours in May 1629. The queen was soon pregnant again, however, and produced a healthy son on 29 May 1630, named Charles after his father—the future Charles II. A daughter, Mary, was born on 4 November 1631, and a second son, James, on 14 October 1633. The succession was now secure, though further children followed: Elizabeth in 1635, Anne in 1637, Henry in 1639, and Henrietta in 1644.[33]

'This Heavy Time of Contagion':[34] The Parliament of 1625

When Charles came to the throne in 1625 he had already acquired considerable working knowledge of the English parliament. He had first attended parliament in 1614, when just thirteen; had been active in the House of Lords in 1621; and had shown considerable ability as a party leader in the parliament of 1624. His success in 1624 perhaps gave him a false impression of his ability to manipulate parliament: he had used his position to influence elections, shape the legislative agenda, and to remove his political opponents, but the prime reason why he was able to get parliament to back his political agenda was because he was swimming with the tide of public opinion. The build up to war with Spain meant that on becoming king he urgently needed parliament to vote him a supply, but he initially wanted to continue the 1624 parliament, rather than call fresh elections as was normal at the beginning of a new reign—hinting perhaps at a lack of understanding of, or respect for, parliamentary traditions and even a willingness to contemplate violating procedure if it would serve his interest.[35]

Charles issued election writs on 2 April 1625 for parliament to assemble on 17 May. Delays in finalizing the marriage treaty with France, however, meant that Charles had to postpone the opening of parliament for over a month. It proved the worst possible time to keep the elected members waiting in the capital, for the plague had just hit London and the death toll steadily increased as the warmer weather approached. Parliament finally opened on 18 June, the day that it was announced that the law term was to be adjourned because of the sickness. Over the next two weeks, the number of plague deaths in just twenty-five London parishes rose from 92 to 239. In early July the Cornish MP Sir John Eliot observed that 'no part of the City did stand free' and recorded the horror of seeing people drop dead in the streets. By mid-August 4,500 Londoners were dying each week of the plague, and overall during 1625 the capital may have lost anywhere between one-eighth and one-fifth of its population to the disease.[36] In many churchyards, the playwright Thomas Dekker observed, they were 'compelled to dig Graves like little Cellers', for lack of room, 'piling up forty or fifty in a Pit'.[37]

Preachers and moralists saw the plague as a punishment from God for England's sins. One pamphleteer listed these as 'ignorance', 'contempt of the Gospell', 'Blasphemy', and 'prophanation of the Sabbath' with 'sports and idle pastimes' (a thinly veiled allusion to the Jacobean Book of Sports).[38] William Crashawe, the vicar of St Mary Whitechapel, who lost over 1,100 of his parishioners to the disease, condemned not only 'personal sins'—swearing, excessive drinking, gambling, 'prophaning [God's] Sabbaths', and 'formalitie in Religion'—but also 'the publicke sinnes of our State', such as 'letting our Lawes bee laid a sleepe against Idolatrie and Superstition, whereby much Popish impietie hath not only beene practised in private, but so publickly professed'.[39] The climate of fear and anxiety that gripped the capital gave rise to speculation and rumour over why the meeting of parliament was being delayed. The fact that in order to induce the French to move forward with the marriage treaty Charles was obliged to issue orders on 1 May suspending the laws against Catholic recusants,[40] and the arrival of Henrietta Maria in mid-June with a train of Catholic clergy in tow, further fuelled concerns about the security of the Protestant religion. Charles's decision to postpone his coronation—again because of the plague—led to rumours that the king did not want to be crowned, 'so as to remain more absolute, avoiding the obligation to swear to the laws'. Those elected to serve in the upcoming parliament, it was said, feared that without 'this observance' any laws they passed would be 'at the discretion of the king and not dependent on the general public authority'.[41]

In fact, the government did not have a major legislative agenda for parliament: it merely wanted a vote of supply and confirmation of the right to collect Tonnage and Poundage. James had left debts totalling £1 million, and Charles and Buckingham were committed to launching a joint military and naval campaign against the Spanish mainland, which it was estimated would cost another £1 million per year.[42] Yet Charles was fully aware of the danger posed by the plague and was reluctant to undertake any business that might prolong parliament's sitting. In a short opening speech—Charles announced that because of his speech impediment he was reviving the practice of having the Lord Keeper 'speak for me in most things'—he stressed that he was loath to put MPs at risk by keeping them there long and urged them to act expeditiously to honour the promises made in his father's last parliament about financing the war with Spain. He did, however, feel obliged to respond to recent rumours that he was 'not so true a keeper and maintainer of the true religion', assuring those assembled that 'no man' could ever be 'more desirous to maintain' that religion than he.[43] Insight into where Charles's religious sympathies lay at this time is shed by the fact that he appointed the bishop of St David's, William Laud—a noted ceremonialist and anti-Calvinist—to deliver the court sermon for the opening of parliament on the following day. Yet although Laud reminded his listeners of the commonplace that kings ruled by divine right, the emphasis in his sermon was on a king's duty to maintain and execute justice, to 'all persons and in all causes', and that 'even Kings' had 'need to looke to their waies', since God would 'one day call for an accompt'.[44]

MPs' major concern was the plague and within three days they were proposing an immediate adjournment.[45] When the adjournment was staved off, they moved to discussing the recent suspension of the penal laws and proposals for safeguarding the Protestant religion. Nathaniel Rich even suggested that those Protestant ministers who had been silenced for refusing to subscribe to the Three Articles 'should be allowed preach in all points agreeable to the doctrine and discipline of the Church of England', although his motion failed to generate sufficient support. The House appointed a committee to follow up on the case of the Arminian Richard Mountague and his book *A New Gagg*, which James's last parliament had referred to the archbishop of Canterbury for consideration.[46] The issue of supply was not raised until the last day of the month. The crown made the mistake of not asking for a specific sum, and with MPs suspicious that funds voted in 1624 had been misspent and concerned about the relaxation of the laws against Catholics, the Commons in the end agreed to offer just two subsidies, which would yield a mere £140,000. Sir Robert Phelips thought this a more than adequate testimony of 'the affections of the subjects', given the burdens that had already been laid on the people, the fact that no war had yet been formally declared, and that no account had been given of what had happened to the men and money raised for Mansfeld's failed expedition. Sir Edward Coke said that the king should bear 'Ordinary charges...alone', and reminded the House that 'Ancient parliaments did so limit their gifts, that they might meet again'. At first Charles seems to have been prepared to accept what was on offer, and sent a message to both Houses on 4 July thanking the Commons for its gift.[47] Buckingham was outraged, however. Having first convinced the king of the need to ask for more, he then got his client Sir John Coke to ask the Commons on 8 July either for 'an addition of supply' or to engage to grant one at the next meeting, to provide the necessary credit in the interim to finance the war, otherwise Charles, Coke said, would need to find 'some new way' of raising the money. It was a clumsy move which even Buckingham's own friends and clients opposed. Only one member—Sir William Beecher, a clerk of the council—rose to second the motion, and sensing the hostility of the House the government let the matter drop.[48]

Meanwhile the Commons, recalling how the Tonnage and Poundage Act of 1604 had been used under James to justify extending the number of goods liable to customs,[49] decided to send the proposed Tonnage and Poundage bill to a committee for redrafting. Since to do so properly would take time, and with members eager to leave plague-ravaged London as soon as possible, the committee recommended granting Tonnage and Poundage for just one year (instead of, as usual, for life), so that the matter could be revisited in the near future. Although the council protested that a temporary measure would cause the king to think that his subjects loved him less than his predecessors, the Commons passed the reworded Tonnage and Poundage bill on 8 July and sent it up to the Lords.[50]

The Commons also heard the committee report on Mountague. Parliament had no authority to judge matters of doctrine. Yet Mountague, after getting into trouble with parliament over his *New Gagg* of 1624, had published his *Appello Caesarem* (*Appeal to Caesar*) in early 1625, in defiance of Archbishop Abbot's attempts to stop it, upholding his earlier positions but denying that this made him guilty of popery or Arminianism. Furthermore, when examined by parliament Mountague claimed that his views had the approval of King James. The Commons therefore charged Mountague with dishonouring the memory of the late king, stirring up jealousies between the king and his subjects, and acting in contempt of parliament, and ordered him to be taken into custody. Charles then released a bombshell by announcing on 9 July that Mountague was a royal chaplain and thus his servant and as such had privilege of parliament, and demanded Mountague's immediate enlargement. He was released on £2,000 bail.[51]

With more and more MPs absenting themselves because of the plague, Charles adjourned parliament on 11 July so that it could reconvene at Oxford at the beginning of August. Before adjourning, parliament passed seven bills, including measures confirming the two subsidies granted by the Commons and three granted by the clergy in Convocation, an Act for punishing abuses of the Sabbath, and an Act for the restraint of alehouses. Although Lord Keeper Williams warned Charles that if parliament were to reassemble there would be an attack on Buckingham, Charles seems to have thought that a change of air would make for a more cooperative assembly.[52]

Unfortunately, by the time parliament reassembled the plague had also reached Oxford and MPs were in a tetchy mood. On the first day they expressed their horror at the news that a Jesuit who had been imprisoned in Exeter had received a royal pardon. On the second they asked for Mountague to be brought before the House, only to be informed that he was too sick to travel; when sceptical MPs insisted that he should be made to appear in any case, Solicitor General Heath said that Mountague was a royal servant and that the king would take care of the matter.[53] Given the widespread belief that the only way to avert God's wrath for the visitation of the plague was by spiritual renewal and a stricter upholding of the true religion, the discovery that the king was seemingly protecting those—a Jesuit and an Arminian—who adhered to a false religion was alarming, to say the least. In an effort to get parliament to focus on the business in hand, Charles summoned both Houses to appear before him at Christ Church on 4 August where he made a personal appeal for money to fund the fleet. Yet although the crown's spokesmen presented a united front in making the case for additional supply, MPs launched a scathing attack on the mismanagement of both the crown's finances and of the navy by Buckingham.[54]

Charles tried to appease the Commons by yielding to their petition concerning religion on 9 August, promising a strict enforcement of the laws against Jesuits, seminary priests, and recusants, to allow silenced ministers to preach (if they were 'peaceable, orderly, and conformable to the Church government'), and to do his utmost to restore and establish the 'true religion' in Ireland. Members, though, were further worried about recent developments in France. The ships which James had agreed to lend Louis XIII to put down the rebellion of the duke of Soubise had finally been handed over in late July, after the French had reached a peace settlement with the Huguenots and when it appeared that the ships would never need to be used. However, the peace had broken down after only a couple of weeks and there was now the prospect of English ships being used in war against fellow Protestants. Buckingham gave a lengthy speech before both Houses on 9 August defending his record, insisting that the king needed merely a further £40,000 in order to send out the English fleet against Spain, and promising that the ships loaned to the French would not be used against the Huguenots. The next day Charles himself sent a message asking for immediate supply and promised that parliament would meet again over the winter to consider further reforms.[55] Yet MPs found Buckingham's arrogance offensive, could not understand how the crown's credit had become so poor that the king could not borrow £40,000, and were reluctant to give supply without first having their grievances redressed. Speaking in the Commons on 10 August, John Delbridge recalled that despite their 'hopes and expectations' when they had given previously, 'there was nothing but discouragements, pardons to Jesuits, [and] protection given to papists'; now they heard that ships were going to be sent against the Huguenots of La Rochelle and England's 'own arms...turned against their friends'. Sir Robert Phelips delivered an emotive speech recalling that 'Our ancestors', when 'pressed as we are', had 'taken occasion to look into the state of the commonwealth': under Henry III, for example, the people had refused to grant supply 'unless they might have a confirmation of their liberties'. After offering further examples from the English past and pointing to what had happened in France and Spain when their kings had secured war financing without first redressing grievances, Phelips proclaimed that 'England was the last monarchy that yet retained her liberties' and urged his fellow MPs not to let them 'perish now'.[56] Sir Thomas Wentworth (the future earl of Strafford) insisted that although he was 'not against giving', he was 'against this manner, to put us upon these straits to give or else to adjourn'. Sir Edward Coke gave 'a long discourse of the leak in the King's estate' and 'of the danger to great men if they misled the King', and concluded that he was against giving, 'as a parliament man', because it was 'against precedent', though he would willingly give £1,000 'as a private man'. When the Commons resumed its debate on the 12th, Christopher Sherland suggested that if the king was serious about enforcing the recusancy laws 'there would be money to supply him with far more than is demanded'.[57]

In the end, the Commons decided to draw up a protestation to the king stating that they were comforted by his answer about religion and that they would 'be ready, in convenient time', to discover and reform abuses and to afford all necessary supply.[58] With no immediate prospect of supply on the horizon, there was no point in Charles keeping members sitting in plague-ravaged Oxford, and he immediately dissolved parliament. As a result, the bill to grant the king Tonnage and Poundage for one year was lost.

The 1626 Parliament and the Impeachment of Buckingham

Charles's need for money meant that he was soon contemplating a fresh meeting of parliament. He believed that the difficulties in 1625 had been caused by a handful of troublemakers, and that with more careful management it would be possible to rebuild the patriot coalition of 1624. On 14 August 1625, two days after the dissolution, he acted on the promise he had made in answer to the Commons' petition on religion by issuing a proclamation requiring all Jesuits and Catholic priests to leave the country, and he followed this up on 11 November with further orders calling for the strict enforcement of the laws against Catholic recusants.[59] On 25 September he signed an offensive treaty with the Dutch to send out joint fleets against Spain, Dunkirk, and the Spanish Indies, with the hope of capturing the Spanish treasure fleet; by finally sending out the fleet that had long been in preparation, he hoped not only to convince the nation that he was serious about pursuing the war that they had long been calling for but also to meet his next parliament on the back of a major military victory and a financial windfall. He decided to have six of the more outspoken critics in the 1625 parliament—including Sir Edward Coke, Sir Robert Phelips, and Sir Thomas Wentworth—'pricked' as sheriffs, to prevent them from being eligible to sit in the next parliament.[60] He also dismissed Bishop Williams of Lincoln from the Lord Keepership, replacing him by Sir Thomas Coventry.[61]

By early October 1625 an English fleet of nearly 85 ships with some 10,448 English soldiers and 5,952 seamen under the command of Sir Edward Cecil (raised to the peerage as Viscount Wimbledon the following month) was ready to embark. However, storms caused delays and rendered the vessels barely seaworthy, the ships were poorly supplied, and by the time they reached Spanish waters they were too late to engage the West Indian treasure fleet. Cecil decided to assault the Spanish port of Cadiz, and was able to take the fort guarding the harbour. But the city was more heavily fortified than expected, and Cecil delayed his attack, allowing the Spaniards to bring in further reinforcements. When his forces finally landed, they brought no food or drink with them and Cecil had to let them drink wine from the vats in the local houses. With few if any of his troops remaining sober, Cecil ordered his men to retreat, but 2,000 English soldiers were too drunk even to do that and were put to the sword by the Spanish without a single shot being fired. On its return to England, Cecil's fleet was battered by winter storms, and soldiers and seamen were reduced to eating rotten victuals. Many of them did not make it home alive; in total, more than half of the men were lost. In the meantime, the French alliance was crumbling. In September, the English ships that James had agreed to lend to the French as part of the marriage treaty were sent out to defeat the Huguenot fleet at the Ile d'Oléron and then to blockade the Huguenot stronghold of La Rochelle. When Charles protested to the French, they complained about the enforcement of the penal laws against Catholics. Finally, on 12 December the council decided to equip a fleet to relieve La Rochelle, and four days later issued writs for a new parliament to meet on 6 February. But in late January Louis XIII and the Huguenots agreed to a peace treaty at Fontainebleau, making it now unnecessary to send the fleet and thus leaving Charles without a clear foreign policy when parliament convened.[62]

Charles arranged for his coronation to take place on 2 February 1626, four days before the opening of parliament—although concern about public health in the aftermath of the plague led him to defer his formal royal entry. (In the end, he was never to make one.) The coronation would normally be presided over by the dean of Westminster, but that post was held by the bishop of Lincoln, who was now out of favour, and so Charles appointed Laud to preside instead. The dean of Durham, John Cosin, an Arminian and noted ceremonialist, served as master of the ecclesiastical ceremonies. The coronation oath was slightly modified for the occasion: after making the usual promise to confirm the laws and customs of England, Charles swore to 'be a Protector and Defender of the Bishops, and the Churches under their Government', and to preserve 'all Canonical Privileges'.[63]

Prior to the sitting of parliament, Charles decided to do something about the issue of Mountague. Charles summoned the bishops of London (Montaigne), Durham (Neile), Winchester (Andrewes), Rochester (Buckeridge), and St David's (Laud)—all anti-Calvinists themselves—to attend a conference on 16 and 17 January to advise him on how to proceed; predictably, they reported that Mountague's doctrine was that of the Church of England and that Charles should stand by him. Yet with Charles eager to present himself to parliament as the leader of the Protestant interest, the Calvinists saw the opportunity to mount a counter-attack. Bishop Carleton of Winchester and Archbishop Abbot's chaplain Daniel Featley wrote works denouncing Mountague and the Arminians, while the Calvinist peers Warwick and Saye pressed Buckingham for a conference on doctrine. The upshot was a conference that took place at York House (Buckingham's residence) on 11 and 17 February in the presence of senior privy councillors. The outcome was inconclusive, although the anti-Calvinist spokesmen, despite being in the minority, did avert an outright condemnation of Mountague and defeat a proposal by Warwick and Saye to establish the decrees issued by the Synod of Dort of 1618–19 (which had condemned Arminianism) as authoritative in England.[64]

Laud once more delivered the sermon at the opening of parliament, where he urged the need for unity in both Church and state, reminded his auditory that 'The King's Power [was] God's ordinance' and the subject's duty was to obey, and took a swipe at Presbyterianism, insisting that there was 'not a man that is for Paritie' in the

Church 'but hee is not for Monarchie in the State'. He concluded by expressing his hope that 'the King and his people' might 'meete in love, consult in wisedome' and 'manage their Counsell with temper'.[65] Yet with the government still unsure about its foreign policy objectives, it failed to set a clear agenda: Coventry simply announced that Charles had called parliament to 'advise of provident and good laws, profitable for the public and fitting for the present times and occasions'. It was vague to say the least; all that members knew was that they needed to act quickly, since the king was resolved 'to confine this meeting to a short time'.[66] As the Commons set about dealing with double returns, the king instructed the House to send out writs for a fresh election at Norfolk, since Sir Edward Coke had been returned as one of the knights of the shire even though he had been pricked as sheriff of Buckinghamshire. The most the Commons could do was to keep Coke's seat vacant for him until his term as sheriff had expired, although the parliament was to be dissolved long before then. According to Rous, the business of pricking sheriffs created 'much adoe', causing some to fear 'the utter bringing under of parliament'.[67]

In the absence of a firm lead from the crown, the Commons began to pursue its own grievances. On 10 February Sir John Eliot launched an attack on Buckingham, regarded now as both suspect in religion and responsible for the failure of the Cadiz expedition, and the House set up a grand committee to identify problems and suggest ways forward. Finally on 7 March government spokesmen in the Commons made a request for supply; but although the Commons agreed in principle to grant three subsidies and three fifteenths, worth £300,000, they made the grant conditional upon the redress of their grievances.[68] On 11 March Dr Samuel Turner broadened the attack on Buckingham by alleging that all the problems the kingdom faced were due to the duke's monopoly of power. Subsequent investigations then revealed that Buckingham had administered various medicines to King James in his final days, raising the suspicion that the duke might have poisoned the late king.[69]

Charles demanded that the House leave Buckingham alone and concentrate on the business at hand, but to no avail. On 29 March he summoned both Houses before him at Whitehall to chastise the Commons in front of the Lords for their 'unparliamentary proceedings'. Coventry complained how the king's honour had been offended and his 'regal rights' held in contempt by the Commons' attacking Buckingham, criticizing the Privy Council, and granting an inadequate supply which they made conditional upon the redress of grievances.

The king commanded them to 'cease this unparliamentary inquisition' against Buckingham and return their final answer as to what further supply they would grant, 'without condition', by Saturday, 1 April, or else they would not 'sit longer together'—though Coventry made it clear that Charles recognized there were 'many wise and well tempered men, well affected to the public good and his Majesty's service' in the Commons, and that those who were 'willingly faulty' were 'not many'. It was an astonishing way to address members of the Commons, and to do so in front of the Lords, so that they 'should be witnesses'—as the Lords were told—'of the honor and justice of [Charles's] resolutions'. After Coventry had finished, Charles once more 'took up the strain' and warned members that this was 'not...a way to deal with kings', that parliaments were 'altogether in [his] power for the calling, sitting, and continuance of them', and that he would continue them or not as he found 'the fruits either good or evil'. It was a speech which, the Venetian ambassador noted, 'was considered threatening'.[70]

Charles's desperate need for money meant that he could not afford to carry out his threat. The Commons, meanwhile, aware that their continued sitting was dependent on the expectation that they would grant taxation, spun out the subsidy debates as they continued to address other concerns. On 17 April John Pym, reporting for the committee of religion, brought charges against Mountague for writing against the doctrine of the Church of England, 'setting the King against the people and the people one against another', and discountenancing 'the true profession of the true religion here established' so as 'to draw the people to popery'. Charles assured MPs that he too disliked Mountague's writings, but since they could not judge matters of doctrine he would refer the matter to Convocation, and promised that in future all books would be carefully examined prior to publication to ensure they did not contain 'any matter of sedition'.[71]

The Commons also discussed the possibility of establishing a joint-stock company to fit out a fleet to prey on Spanish ships trading to the Caribbean, thereby effectively funding the war effort through private enterprise. A tentative call for the setting up of an English West India Company had in fact first been put forward in the parliament of 1621 by Sir Nathaniel Rich, cousin to the earl of Warwick and a prominent figure in the Virginia, Somers Islands, and New England Companies, although it met with little response. In April 1625, with England heading for war with Spain, Sir John Coke presented Buckingham with a detailed proposal for an independent English West

India Company, which would have involved sending successive fleets first to destroy Spanish shipping off the coast of Spain and then to the West Indies to intercept the Spanish treasure fleets, the cost of which—estimated to be in excess of £361,000—was to be met by a 'general subscription' across the whole kingdom. Coke hoped thereby to inflict a heavy, perhaps terminal, blow on the Spanish crown's imperial trading system, capture key strategic points on Porto Bello and Panama, establish free trade with Peru and Mexico, and populate newly won colonies with transplanted migrants from Virginia and the Somers Islands (modern-day Bermuda). Coke's plans were put on hold as the government prepared for the forthcoming naval expedition against Spain, and effectively scuppered by the disastrous failure of the assault on Cadiz. It was Sir Dudley Digges, speaking in the Commons on 14 March 1626, who revived the idea of establishing a West India Company as a way of 'financing the war without burdening poor men's purses with subsidies', and the plan came to be outlined in detail by Digges and his associates Rich, Pym, and Sir Benjamin Rudyerd in a Commons debate a month later. The private company, regulated and established by parliament, would raise £200,000 annually to fund a privateering war against the Spanish fleets in the Caribbean; in the event of peace with Spain, the company was to be allowed free trade with the West Indies and to retain whatever lands it had possessed during the war years. As Rudyerd put it, 'the subject will make the warre against the Kinge of Spayne, and his Majestie shall have no more to doe at Sea, but to defend the Coastes'. It was a radical proposal, that would not only have given the company control over the war at sea but also a large amount of say over the conduct of foreign policy, amounting to a significant encroachment on the royal prerogative. As such, it is unlikely that Charles would have given it much consideration.[72]

However, as discussions continued over the next couple of weeks, the plan transformed into a scheme that was potentially more acceptable to the crown. Instead of a private company running the war effort, it would in effect be a nationalized one, with parliament providing £200,000 per year and the crown £120,000, overseen by a committee of both Houses (ten from the Lords and twenty from the Commons) and with 20 per cent of the profits going to the crown. This 'Project for the Defence of the Kingdome', as it was now labelled, involved a mature strategic vision for the whole war, with ships cruising off the Spanish coast and the Azores, blockading Dunkirk and guarding the British mainland as well as in the Caribbean. It would still have taken direction of the war effort out of Buckingham's control, although given his considerable patronage in the Lords it would not have undermined his position completely. It would also have given parliament oversight of how monies voted for war were spent, while offering the crown something in return. Yet the project ultimately failed, as the ongoing investigations into Buckingham's management of the war effort revealed the level of his corruption and incompetence, hardening the minds of MPs towards the duke.[73]

The Commons laid formal charges against Buckingham before the Lords on 8 and 10 May. In his introductory remarks on the 8th, Digges likened the duke 'to a comet'—an omen of ill fortune—'drawn out of the dross of the earth' (another account has 'base and putred matter'); in his concluding remarks on the 10th, Eliot compared Buckingham to Sejanus, the confidant of the tyrannical Roman emperor Tiberius.[74] Charles resented the implications, and on the 11th ordered both Digges and Eliot to be dispatched to the Tower. The Commons, outraged, immediately suspended all business and began preparing a remonstrance against the arrests. In what appears to have been an attempt to cool passions and to forestall hardliners on the privy council, the Vice Chamberlain Sir Dudley Carleton gave a lengthy speech in the House on the 12th in which he reminded members that most kingdoms in Christendom had formerly had parliaments like that in England, but most had seen a change to 'new counsels', for 'when they changed their parliamentary liberty into tumultuary endeavours, it was changed by the sovereign to another form of government'. Carleton insisted that 'His Majesty's love to us' was such that as long as MPs carried themselves 'as fitting dutiful subjects', Charles would 'not take new counsels'; however, his intervention strongly intimates that doing so had been contemplated.[75]

Charles eventually backed down over the arrest of Digges and Eliot, releasing both men a few days later. In the meantime Buckingham remained at liberty, the Lords refusing to agree to the Commons' request that he be sent to the Tower until the duke had been given the opportunity to answer the charges against him. Buckingham gave a detailed rebuttal before the Lords on 8 June, and the next day Charles sent a message to the Commons warning members to turn their attention to supply, otherwise he would be forced 'to take other resolutions'.[76] When the Commons insisted on framing a remonstrance against Buckingham first, Charles dissolved parliament on 15 June, losing in the process the promised subsidies.

On 30 June Charles published a declaration detailing his reasons for dissolving parliament. It was a self-conscious appeal to public opinion and an explicit exercise in damage limitation, and as such reveals a king who sensed he was in trouble. Charles began by professing his 'unspeakable griefe' at the dissolution, and although he was 'not bound to give an account to any' but God for his 'Regall Actions', he nevertheless intended to order 'the great and publike Actions of State concerning the weale of His people', so that they might 'justifie themselves...to His owne people' and indeed 'the whole world'. He wanted to stop 'the mouth of malice'—'the malevolent Report of such' who were 'ill affected to this State, or the true Religion here professed'—and satisfy 'the doubts and feares of His owne good Subjects at home, and of His Friends and Allies abroad'. After explaining that he had called parliament to get money for the war against Spain which parliament itself had advised him to fight, he alleged that his well-meaning intentions had been frustrated 'by the violent and ill advised passions of a few members', who were fixated on 'the prosecution of one of the Peeres of this Realme'. He closed by offering assurances that he would rule 'for the comfort of His good and well affected Subjects', promising he would maintain 'the sinceritie and unitie of the true Religion professed in the Church of England', keep the Church free 'from the open contagion of Popery and secret infection of Schisme', and never expose his subjects 'to the unsatiable desires of the Kinge of Spaine' or 'to the yoke of the Pope of Rome'.[77]

Charles was undoubtedly sincere in his professed desire to uphold the unity of—what he took to be—the true religion against the threat of popery. On 14 June, the day before the dissolution, he issued a proclamation for establishing the peace and quiet of the Church of England. Lamenting the recent controversies over doctrine, which he feared would encourage the Catholics to believe that they might be able to draw English Protestants 'first to Schisme, and after to plaine Popery', he expressed his 'utter dislike' of all those who advocated 'new Opinions' different from the orthodoxy 'established in the Church of England' and declared his resolve not to 'admit of the least innovation', in either the doctrine or discipline of the Church, or in the government of the state. He therefore commanded his subjects not to publish anything that might raise doubts about, 'or maintaine any new inventions or opinions concerning Religion', under pain of prosecution.[78] Ostensibly an attempt to silence the controversies raised by the Mountague affair, without taking sides in the matter, in practice the order tended to be applied (or at least was perceived by contemporaries to have been applied) in a partisan way. Rous commented how it 'was used by some bishops to the suppressing of those that had confuted Montague'. The seventeenth-century historian John Rushworth noted that 'the effects of this Proclamation... became the stopping of the Puritans' mouths, and an uncontrolled liberty to the Tongues and Pens of the Arminian Party'.[79] To demonstrate his sincerity about tackling the threat of popery, on 26 June Charles ordered all the queen's French subjects to depart the realm.[80]

The Forced Loan

Despite his protestations of grief at the dissolution, Charles appears to have been determined not to call another parliament for the time being. According to the Venetian ambassador, he even spoke to the queen's almoner, the bishop of Mende, about 'the means used by the kings of France to rid themselves of parliament'.[81] With the kingdom committed to war, however, he needed other ways of raising money and of putting the nation on a war footing. In early July the privy council issued an order authorizing the continued collection of Tonnage and Poundage, insisting that parliament had intended to confirm it before it had been dissolved, and stipulating that those who refused to pay would be imprisoned. Charles set up a commission to compound with Catholics in the northern province of York for recusancy fines, with the sums collected to pay for ships of war to guard the east coast of England from the Scottish border to the mouth of the Thames. He also levied a charge on the several ports and maritime counties to furnish armed ships to guard the coasts against attempts from Spain or Flanders. When the deputy-lieutenants and JPs of Dorset complained that 'the Case was without President', the privy council replied that 'the defence of the Kingdom in times of extraordinary danger' was 'not to be guided by ordinary Presidents'. The City of London petitioned to have their assessment of twenty ships reduced to ten ships and two pinnaces, pleading 'disability'; the council riposted that the charge was 'moderate', that such petitions tended 'to the danger and prejudice of the Common-wealth' and would not be received, and that precedents were not lacking 'for the punishment of those that disobey his Majestie's commands'. Charles also granted extraordinary commissions to the Lord Lieutenants to muster and arm subjects for the defence of the realm 'against publick

Enemies, Rebels and Traitors' and 'to execute Martial Law, sparing and putting to death according to discretion'.[82]

What the crown needed, however, was a way of in effect collecting the subsidies that had been voted by parliament but lost at the dissolution. At first the government contemplated asking subjects to give the same amount in the form of a benevolence, and ordered JPs to do their best to persuade people thought able to give to do so, though in the face of opposition the scheme was quickly dropped. In August the government introduced a system of Privy Seal loans whereby those who had defied the court would be targeted with crushing loans—anywhere between five and ten times the normal subsidy assessment—as punishment for their opposition, although very little money was collected and the plan was suspended by proclamation on 22 September (those who had already given money were to be repaid without delay). By this time the court had decided upon another method of taxing the subject, through what has become known as the Forced Loan.[83]

The immediate context for the Forced Loan was the news that Imperial forces under Ferdinand II had defeated Charles's uncle Christian IV of Denmark at Lutter, in what is now north-west Germany, leaving some 6,000 Danes dead (with a further 2,500 taken prisoner). Charles felt honour-bound to help Christian, who had entered the war in order to help restore the Palatinate, and promised to send 4,000 troops to Denmark, but when it was suggested that he should call parliament Charles told his council that 'he did abominate the name'. The official rationale offered for the Forced Loan was that since parliament had committed the king to this war but had failed to make a grant of taxation, the king was entitled to an aid by way of a loan; he would request no more than what had been voted by the Commons, people would be assessed as they had been in the last subsidy rolls, and those who had already paid the benevolence would be exempt.[84] To the imposition of the loan was added the burden of billeting the soldiers that had returned from Cadiz, now paid for by local rates after the funds allocated by the central government had run out. According to Rushworth, 'the Companies were scattered here and there in the bowels of the Kingdom, and governed by Martial Law', while the soldiers proved disorderly, committing 'frequent Robberies, Burglaries, Rapes, Rapines, Murthers, and barbarous Cruelties'.[85]

To back its policy the government launched a major PR offensive. On 23 September it issued a detailed set of instructions to the loan commissioners explaining that they were to use 'all possible endeavours' to persuade every one 'willingly and cherefully' to loan the sums assessed, stressing that the king's 'honour', the 'reputation of this nation', the 'true religion', and the 'common safety' were all at stake, and that this course of action, 'enforced by necessitye', would not be used as a precedent; if any were to object that 'this way of raysing money' threatened the existence of parliament, they were to reassure people that 'the suddaynes and importance of the occasions' did not allow for delay but that the king fully intended 'to call a parliament as soone as fittly' and 'as oft as the Common wealth, and State occasions' would require. Those who still refused to pay, however, would incur the king's 'high displeasure'.[86] Laud (now at Bath and Wells) drew up a series of *Instructions* to the bishops, issued in the king's name, on how to direct their clergy to 'exhort the people' to serve both God and the crown at this time of great danger. The current danger stemmed from the 'late blow' suffered by the King of Denmark, opening up the way for Spain to overrun all of western Europe: were that to happen, it would lead to 'the extirpation of true Religion, and the replanting of Romish Superstition in all the neighbouring parts of Christendome'. The clergy were to remind people that the government had not entered upon this war rashly, but had followed the counsel of both Houses of Parliament, and that 'ayde and supply for the defence of the Kingdome, and the like affaires of States', especially as 'advised and assumed by Parliamentary Counsell,' were 'due to the King from his People', by the law 'both of God and men'. The one 'great hinderance' was the 'breach of Unitie', which had of late 'growne too great and common among all sorts of men'. The clergy, therefore, were to lay before their congregations 'what miseries home-divisions have brought upon this and many other Kingdomes', 'to exhort all men to embrace' unity, and to remind people they needed to be thankful to God for His having recently delivered England from the plague.[87]

In financial terms, the Forced Loan proved a considerable success, raising over £243,000 within a year.[88] The political cost, however, was high. The loan was successful because it was forced, and Charles firmly identified himself with the drive for enforcement. On 7 October he issued a declaration stating that he would not let those who spoke against the loan 'goe unpunished'.[89] He tried to bully the judges into subscribing a declaration testifying to the legality of the loan— all that they would agree to say was that they had paid 'as required', out of duty, but 'not for example of others'—and he sacked his Lord Chief Justice of King's Bench, Sir Randolph Crewe, for his refusal to comply.[90] He wrote to each member of the nobility individually warning them that he regarded their willingness to pay as a crucial test of their loyalty; some fifteen or sixteen peers nevertheless refused, amongst them the earls of Essex and Warwick and Lord Saye.[91] Charles was reluctant to take on the peerage—their names were 'put into the black book'—but he sent over one hundred leading gentry to prison for refusal to pay. The common sort who defaulted were threatened with impressment into service overseas, and even—in Essex—with hanging by martial law, as 'an example and terror to others'.[92] Yet although Charles himself was in favour of a hard line, the moderates on the council succeeded in keeping those who favoured coercive measures in check. No one was executed, and there were only two incidents of defaulters being pressed into service; on two other occasions, when the threat had been made, it was withdrawn. The moderates were also against risking a court case which might test the legality of the Loan. As a result, several refusers who were about to face trial found themselves reprieved at the last minute.[93]

In the face of resistance, the crown continued the ideological offensive. Over the course of 1627, a series of sermons was preached before the king, and subsequently published by royal approval, urging the necessity of obedience and pleading the case for unity. All emphasized that monarchs ruled by divine right and could not be resisted, although significantly none explicitly claimed that the king was absolute. Indeed, in many respects they all appealed to commonly held assumptions about the nature of monarchical authority and how it was to be exercised. However, in doing so they stretched the king's power beyond what many took to be hitherto accepted norms.

The first was by Dr Matthew Wren, the Master of Peterhouse, Cambridge, a noted Arminian and ceremonialist, delivered before the king at Whitehall on 17 February. Wren spent much of his time attacking ceremonial nonconformists, the refusal to kneel, bow, or uncover one's head during worship, and the contempt for 'any Beautie of Holines'; he even at one point suggested that people seemed to respect the king more than God, 'For the King's Presence', he claimed, was treated with more 'Reverence and Worship' than 'the Table of the Lord, and the House of the Lord, and the Presence of the Lord'. Wren wanted people to 'Feare God...and the King': given that kings derived their titles from God, and were 'his Deputies and Vicegerents'—as Calvin himself acknowledged, Wren was at pains to point out—how could one who did not fear the king fear God? Even 'the treacherous Jesuite' and 'the factious Schismatick' acknowledged in general terms that 'the King must be feared', although 'when they like not the businesse', Wren continued, they claimed that 'Dutie and Conscience' allowed them to disobey. Having thus tarred the Jesuits and the Puritans with the same brush, Wren concluded by urging his listeners not to meddle 'with them that be Seditious'.[94] The second was by Dr Isaac Bargrave, dean of Canterbury, delivered on 27 March, the anniversary of Charles's accession. Preaching on 1 Samuel 15:23, 'Rebellion is as the sinne of Witch-craft', Bargrave proclaimed that nothing was more likely to provoke God's 'Judgements upon this Land' than our 'disobedience', whether 'against God in heaven' or 'his Deputy on earth'. Bargrave was nevertheless at pains to emphasize the responsibilities of a king in turn to obey God: for 'Though Kings be Gods before men', they were 'but men before God', and just as nothing was 'more hatefull in a subject then rebellion to his King', so nothing was 'more dangerous in a King, then rebellion to God'. The king, therefore, had to promote righteousness and piety, which in turn would prove 'the preservation of the Common-wealth'. Bargrave finished by attacking proponents of resistance and reminded listeners that even Calvin condemned disobedience.[95]

Neither Wren's nor Bargrave's sermons specifically mentioned the Forced Loan, though the implications of their rhetoric were clear for all to see. More forthright was Dr Roger Maynwaring, who preached two sermons before the king in July, the first at Oatlands, in Weybridge (Surrey), on the 4th, the second at Alderton (Gloucestershire) on the 29th. Insisting in his first sermon that the king's power came 'immediately from God' and 'not from any consent or allowance of men', and that therefore 'Regall prehemencie' owed nothing either to the papacy or the people, Maynwaring went on to argue that 'the significations of a Royall pleasure' ought to have the 'force of a Command' and that no one should 'call in question the Judgement of a King'. If a king commanded something that was 'flatly against the Law of God', then people were not to obey, though they were 'to indure with patience' whatever penalty he chose to inflict on them. But if a king commanded something that was not against 'the original Lawes of God, Nature, Nations and the Gospell', even though it might not be 'correspondent in every circumstance, to Lawes National, and Municipall', 'no Subject' could, 'without hazard of his own Damnation...question, or disobey the will and pleasure of his Soveraigne'. Since kings had to defend the faith and protect people in their 'persons, lives, and states', Maynwaring continued, 'nothing' could be denied them that might 'further the supply of the Urgent Necessities', whether 'for the security of their Royall persons', 'the Protection of their Kingdomes', or to 'ayde, and succour...Royall Confederates'. Parliaments existed, Maynwaring asserted, not to grant and approve taxes, but merely 'for the more equall Imposing, and more easie Exacting' of what 'apperteine[d]' to kings 'by Naturall and Originall Law, and Justice'. Thus 'if, upon Necessity...Subsidiary helpes be required', any man who refused to 'satisfie such demaunds' would be guilty of 'resisting the Ordinance of God' and receive 'to himself Damnation'. Refusal to pay, 'Recusancy in Temporalls', was worse than 'disobedience in Spiritualls'; in other words, Protestants who refused to submit to the king's temporal authority were as bad, 'if not worse', than Catholics.[96] In his second sermon, Maynwaring reiterated the need for subjects 'to yeeld all...Obedience to the sacred Mandates of their Soveraignes', castigated 'the Roman Jesuites, and German Puritans' for being the first to deny subjection, and insisted that as 'each person hath a share in the Profits and Honours' of 'every well-ordered Commonwealth' so he ought 'to beare a part in the Taxes and Burthens thereof' and that we should not so 'tie the hands, and clip the wings of sacred Kings' to prevent them from commanding 'that from their Subjects' allowed them by 'the Lawes of God and Nature'.[97] Even Laud thought that Maynwaring's sermons contained 'many things' that would be 'very distasteful to the people' and urged Charles to think twice about publishing them. Charles ignored Laud's advice and insisted they be published bearing the inscription 'by His Majesty's special command'. (They were published jointly as one book.)[98] Maynwaring was later to repeat the same views from his own pulpit of St Giles-in-the-Fields in London on 4 May 1628.

The most controversial sermon relating to the Forced Loan was preached neither at court nor before the king, but at the Northampton Assizes, on 22 February by Dr Robert Sibthorpe, vicar of Brackley, Northamptonshire. Sibthorpe believed that subjects were 'bound in duty' to their princes, 'according to the Lawes and Customes of the Kingdome wherein they live'. The prince, Sibthorpe proclaimed, had the duty not only to command the execution of law and to protect his people but also 'to direct and make lawes': 'Hee doth whatsoever pleaseth him', for 'where the word of the King is, there is power'. Kings were not only to be honoured and obeyed but also maintained, and 'Tribute' was 'due to Princes by a Triple Obligation': by the law of God, the law of nature, and the law of nations. Sibthorpe came close to arguing that royal authority was absolute, insisting that it was the consideration of these things that led the ancient Church

Fathers 'to be absolutely for absolute obedience to Princes in all civill or temporall things'. 'The more moderate moderne Divines', including not just Luther, Melanchthon, or English bishops and other English divines, but also the likes of Calvin, Beza, and 'the Ministers of the Reformed Churches', all acknowledged 'That if a Prince impose an immoderate, yea an unjust Taxe', nevertheless the subject had no right to 'withdraw his obedience and dutie'. 'Let us [not] square our consciences by the Lesbian Rule of Jesuites and Schismatickes', Sibthorpe implored. 'What a difference' there was 'betwixt this happy Throne' and 'the tottering State of those' who governed in a commonwealth 'where the Religion was directed by Bellarmine', and other Jesuits, 'or by Buchanan, Knox...Goodman' and other Protestant resistance theorists: 'The one of which makes the Church above the King, and the Pope above the Church, and so dethrones Princes by his Thunderbolts of Excommunication and Deprivation', and the other of which 'make the Law above the King, and the people above the Law, and so depose Princes, by their Tumults, and Insurrections'.[99]

Charles wanted Archbishop Abbot to license Sibthorpe's sermon for publication, so that it would appear with the apparent backing of the ecclesiastical hierarchy. Abbot refused, protesting that it was not his but his chaplains' job to license books, that King James had never asked him to do such a thing, and that besides the sermon would not support the cause of the Forced Loan since Sibthorpe had argued that subjects were bound to their princes 'according to the Laws and Customs of the Kingdom, wherein they live' and there was 'neither Law nor Custom' for the Loan 'in the Kingdom of England'. In the end, Sibthorpe's sermon was published with a prefatory note saying it had the approval of the Bishop Montaigne of London (one of the Arminians appointed by James), 'as a Sermon learnedly and discreetly preached, and agreeable...to the Doctrine established in the Church of England'. Abbot, for his opposition, was sequestered from his office, and the ecclesiastical jurisdiction of his archiepiscopal see granted in commission to the bishops of London (Montaigne), Durham (Neile), Rochester (Buckeridge), Oxford (Howson), and Bath and Wells (Laud)—all of them Arminians.[100]

Many of those who were keen supporters of the Forced Loan were advocates of tighter measures against Puritans. Sibthorpe, who was also a commissary for the High Commission in Leicester, and his brother-in-law Sir John Lambe, another local ecclesiastical official, complained to their diocesan Bishop Williams of Lincoln that Leicestershire was 'much over-spread' with 'factious Puritans' and asked permission to proceed against them. Williams told them that he already had the duke of Buckingham as his enemy and 'would not draw the Puritans upon him', and pointed out that King James had taken a liberal line with Puritans for political reasons (thereby technically breaching privy council confidentiality). When Sibthorpe and Lambe persisted, Williams somewhat mischievously asked: 'Whether those places, where those Puritans were, did lend money freely upon the Collection of the Loan?' Lambe and Sibthorpe had to admit that they generally did, to which the bishop replied that 'No man of discretion' could say, then, 'that that place is a place for Puritans'. It was a clever put-down but hardly served to convince. Sibthorpe protested that he was 'troubled' to see the Church 'no better regarded' and together with Lambe lodged a complaint against Williams to the privy council for speaking words against the king and government. It resulted in the bishop becoming embroiled in a costly Star Chamber suit for the best part of a decade.[101]

Concerned by rumours that he was denying people justice, Charles finally decided at the beginning of November to allow five knights who had been imprisoned for non-payment to sue for habeas corpus in King's Bench. However, the government did not want this to become a test case over the legality of the Forced Loan, and so in reply to the knights' writ demanding to be told the cause of their imprisonment, the privy council returned simply that the men had been imprisoned '*per speciale mandatum domini regis*'—by the king's special command. The king undoubtedly did have the right to imprison people without showing cause, in certain circumstances—for example, in the case of a treasonous conspiracy against the state, when some, but not all, of the conspirators had been taken into custody and when publicly announcing the cause of their detention might hamper the government's efforts to capture those who had fled justice. The Gunpowder plotters of 1605 had initially been imprisoned by the king's special command, and no one had raised an eyebrow at the time, since the king's discretionary power was accepted in this instance as deployed for the public good. However, it was a different matter to use this power to detain people who had refused to pay a loan which even the judges themselves had refused to confirm was legal. The counsel for the defence argued that the return was insufficient, against Magna Carta and the laws of the land. Serjeant Bramston protested that if this return 'be good', subjects might 'be restrained of their liberties perpetually', without the prospect of remedy at law.[102] Attorney General Heath, however, maintained that the king could imprison without showing cause 'for State-matters': it was not to be presumed that the king did not have a cause, merely that it was 'not ripe' to express it. Heath thus insisted that the five knights should be remitted to custody; their only way to secure their release was by means of 'a Petition of right or of grace' to the king.[103]

In delivering their opinion on 28 November, the judges concluded that the return was sufficient (it was not their job, they protested, to determine 'the truth of the return'), told the five men they could seek justice only from the king, and sent them back to prison.[104] The judges, however, entered an interlocutory order (a temporary order pending further judgment), rather than a final judgment, so as not to be seen to be establishing a legal precedent. The lawyer MP John Selden, who served as counsel for the defence, was later to accuse Heath of falsifying the King's Bench record so as to establish a precedent in favour of the crown's right of arbitrary imprisonment. If true, the implications were alarming, especially if Heath, as suspected, did so at the bidding of the king. The evidence is unclear; it seems unlikely, though, that the crown had any agenda beyond wanting to ensure that the loan defaulters remained in prison while the loan was still being collected.[105]

Although the Forced Loan had been raised to help Christian of Denmark, the funds were diverted to other uses. Over the winter of 1626–7 Anglo-French relations finally collapsed completely. When English warships arrested French ships suspected of carrying prohibited goods from Spain, France's leading minister Cardinal Richelieu retaliated by seizing the English wine fleet at Bordeaux. With the French crown planning a renewed attack on the Huguenot stronghold of La Rochelle, the Huguenot leadership pleaded with the English government for help, and by March Charles and Buckingham were preparing for war with France—thus finding themselves in the disastrous situation of being at war with the two major European Catholic states at the same time. Buckingham put together a fleet of 100 ships with just under 6,000 foot and 1,000 horse which sailed for La Rochelle in June. The mission turned into a tragic comedy of errors. The force was supplied with wheat, but without the means to bake it. Buckingham decided to try to take the Ile de Ré, which guarded the harbour to La Rochelle, but although he effected a successful landing, he was unable to take either of the two fortresses that protected the island. Buckingham's council of war recommended that he try to capture the lesser fortification, Fort de la Prée, but instead the duke went for glory and attempted the citadel of Saint-Martin, which the professional soldiers on his council thought was virtually impregnable. Buckingham did succeed in capturing the town of Saint-Martin, which was inhabited mainly by the wives and children of the French garrison, driving them back into the citadel. But the commander of the citadel refused to surrender, a lengthy siege set in, and when French reinforcements arrived in October Buckingham was left with no option but to withdraw. Before doing so, he decided—against the advice of his council—to attempt a frontal assault on the citadel, in heavy rain, only to find that the ladders they had taken to scale the walls were far too short for the purpose. All told Buckingham lost in the region of 5,000 men or more. A Scottish fleet of 30 ships and 5,000 men had set off in October to reinforce Buckingham, but was broken up in a storm off the coast of Norfolk. The earl of Holland set sail with a relief fleet in November, but this was too late. Simonds D'Ewes wrote in late November that there were not 'five gentlemen in this Kingdome, but have lost a Freind or a Kinsman' in this expedition, adding: 'We may plainly see that God is against us'. Buckingham was widely blamed for the disaster. 'Three things have lost our honour (men surmise)', one poetaster rhymed, namely Buckingham's 'Treachery, Neglect, and Cowardise'. 'Are there no Mayds in Court, to stay thee? Must | Thy hate to France and Spayne exceed thy lust', our rhymester continued, ending: 'Most Graceles Duke wee thanke thy Charity. | And wish the Fleet such speed, as to loose thee: | And wee shall think't an happy Victory'.[106]

Charles was determined to mount another expedition to the Ile de Ré, although the cost would be prohibitive: one estimate suggested that £600,000 was needed to re-equip the fleet. Laud urged the need to maintain the crown's right to tax without consent, following the logic of the arguments put forward by Maynwaring and Sibthorpe.[107] The moderates on the council, however, managed to persuade Charles that he should call parliament, both to raise the necessary funds and also to heal the damage done by the Forced Loan. Early in the new year the government released all those who had been imprisoned for failure to pay the Loan and issued writs for parliament to meet on 17 March 1628. The elections went badly for the court and many critics of the king's policies were returned, including twenty-seven of the Loan refusers recently released from prison.[108] Just before parliament was to sit the government contemplated imposing ship money to pay the navy's debts in anticipation of subsidies expected from parliament. In the past the crown had occasionally demanded aid from merchants and coastal towns in the form of ship money to help supply the navy in times of emergency, the aid normally coming in the provision of actual ships to be used for military purposes: Charles, however, wanted the aid to be in the form of a subsidy, and he intended to impose it on the entire country (including inland areas). In the end, the government decided to cancel the scheme.[109]

'The Crisis of Parliaments': The Parliament of 1628 and the Petition of Right

In his opening speech to both Houses on 17 March, Charles announced that these were times 'for action' and that it was the duty of members 'to maintain this church and commonwealth'. He had called parliament because he judged it 'the ancient, speediest, and best way...in this time of common danger' to give the supply necessary for 'the defense of ourselves and our allies'; but if they failed to do their duty, he would have to take 'other courses'. It was a blatant threat; Charles hardly made it any better by insisting that MPs were not to take it as such, since he scorned 'to threaten any but [his] equals'.[110]

MPs were not to be that easily cowed. Speaking on the 22nd, Sir Francis Seymour urged those assembled not to be 'possessed with fear or with flattery', and proceeded to raise the issues of the Forced Loan and the billeting of troops. Wentworth, who had himself been imprisoned for refusing to pay the Loan, said that he did not blame the king but 'projectors' who had 'extended the prerogative of the King' and raised concern about arbitrary imprisonment, impressment for service overseas, levies made without the consent of parliament, and the billeting of troops.[111] Members were aware, however, that there was the prospect of no further parliaments if they did not deliver. Sir Benjamin Rudyerd, a client of the moderate privy councillor the earl of Pembroke, warned that 'This is the crisis of Parliaments. We shall know by this if parliaments live or die...If the King draws one way and the people another, we must all sink.' Sir Edward Coke said that he was 'absolutely' in favour of giving 'supply to his Majesty' in this juncture, but thought it was essential to redress the grievance of forced loans, for 'who will give subsidies if the King may impose what he will'.[112]

As things were to transpire, the moderate councillors, through their spokesmen in the Commons (men like Rudyerd and Secretary Sir John Coke), did a reasonably good job at keeping MPs on task, steering them away from attacking Buckingham and instead encouraging them to concentrate on redressing grievances resulting from the Forced Loan in return for granting a supply. On 3 April the Commons drew up a series of resolutions concerning the liberty of the subject and on the following day agreed to grant the crown an unprecedented total of five subsidies, worth £300,000.[113] Charles was ecstatic, telling Secretary Coke that having at first 'liked parliaments', but then 'grown to a distaste of them', he now loved them once again and would 'rejoice to meet with [his] people often'.[114] The Commons, however, decided to delay the completion of the subsidy bill until the heads of a bill to preserve the liberties of the subject had been agreed. By the end of the month, Charles's patience was running out. On 28 April he informed the Commons, via Lord Keeper Coventry, that he held Magna Carta and other statutes relating to the liberty of the subject 'to be all in force' and would 'govern according to the laws and statutes of this realm', and urged MPs to 'proceed speedily and unanimously to the business' in hand. He had Secretary Coke repeat his assurances on 2 May, adding that parliament would not sit beyond Tuesday, 13 May at the latest. On 5 May Coventry further announced that the king would be happy for MPs to draw up a bill for the confirmation of Magna Carta and other statutes relating to the subjects' liberty, 'without additions, paraphrases, or explanations', so they could 'be secured from [their] needless fears', but warned them that if they sought 'to tie the King by new . . . bonds', they would be accountable to God and the country 'for the ill success of that meeting', which was due to end in a week's time. In a debate on the following day, MPs made it clear that a confirmation of existing law, without additions or explanations, would not serve their purpose. As William Coryton (or Currington) put it, 'We desire an explanation, that ambiguities may be taken away'. Sir Edward Coke insisted that the question was 'what is the law of the land', and suggested proceeding by way of 'a petition of right to the King for our particular grievances'. This had the advantage of being quicker: whereas a bill would require the Commons to set down in detail the rights and liberties of the subject, a petition of right would merely need to explain what existing law was and invite the king to indicate his assent. It would nevertheless still have the binding force of legislation; indeed, in ancient times there had been no other way of making laws but by petition of the Commons, although it was a course that had not been used much over the last two hundred years. The Commons had a draft of its petition ready to send up to the Lords on 8 May. By the 9th it had an agreed text, focusing on four main issues: the Forced Loan, imprisonment without cause shown, the billeting of troops, and the imposition of martial law.[115]

Charles was ready to accept that the Forced Loan, the billeting of troops, and the imposition of martial law had been illegal, but refused to give up the crown's discretionary right to imprison without showing cause. In a letter to the Lords on 12 May he insisted that in 'matters of state' it was sometimes essential to conceal the cause of imprisonment, and if 'this power' were 'impeached' it would amount to an 'overthrow of sovereignty'; nevertheless he promised that he would never in the future commit anyone to prison for refusing to lend him money, 'or for any other cause' which, in his conscience, did 'not concern the state, the public good, and safety of us and our people'. The Lords suggested that the Commons should modify its petition accordingly, but Sir Edward Coke said this was an unparliamentary way of proceeding and the Lords would have to come up with specific suggestions. A further foreign policy reversal meant that Charles had to back down from his threat to prorogue parliament—another fleet sent to La Rochelle, this one under the command of the earl of Denbigh, had failed to breach the harbour defences and returned to England—and so Charles wrote to all the peers personally to urge them to do what they could to safeguard the prerogative. The Lords proposed inserting a clause into the petition stating that it left 'entire that sovereign power' with which the king was 'trusted for the protection, safety, and happiness of [his] people'. The Commons protested that this would undermine the whole intent of the petition, which was to protect the subject against an abuse of sovereign power. In the end, a majority of peers decided to join with the Commons in rejecting the amendment.[116]

The Petition of Right was presented to the king at the Banqueting House at 3 o'clock in the afternoon of 28 May 1628, with both Houses in attendance.[117] It was a carefully worded document, which sought to clarify existing ambiguities in the law by re-stating the law and making it clear that recent actions by the crown had been illegal. It pronounced that according to legislation dating back to the reigns of Edward I and Edward III no taxes were to be levied without the consent of parliament and that no person could 'be compelled to make any Loanes to the King against his will', and thus the recent requirement to lend the king certain sums of money was 'against the Lawes and free Customes of the Realme'; that the imprisonment of subjects 'without any cause shewed' was against Magna Carta, which provided that 'no Freeman' could be imprisoned, outlawed or exiled 'but by the lawfull Judgment of his Peeres or by the Law of the Land'; that the billeting of troops on 'inhabitants against their wills' was 'against the Lawes and Customes of this Realme'; and that the recent commissions for martial law violated Magna Carta and other laws and statutes which established that 'no man ought to be adjudged to death but by the Lawes established in this...Realme'.[118]

Parliament was looking for a form of royal assent that would give the Petition of Right the force of law. There were two forms of royal assent typically given, in Law French, to parliamentary bills: *le Roy le veult* (the king wills it) was the language used for government sponsored bills, while *soit droit fait comme est desire* (let right be done as is desired) was that for legislation initiated by private members. After consulting with the judges, Charles delivered his reply on 2 June, stating, in English, via his Lord Keeper, that it was the king's will 'that Right be done according to the laws and customs of the realm', and 'that the statutes be put in due execution' so that 'the subject may have no just cause of complaint of any wrong or oppression'.[119] It was a clumsy attempt to evade the implications of the Petition, which the king's answer did not even mention, especially given that the Commons had already made it clear that it would not be sufficient merely to confirm existing laws. Outraged, MPs returned to the pursuit of other grievances, drawing up articles of impeachment against Maynwaring for his sermons on the Forced Loan and a remonstrance against Buckingham. Faced with the prospect of losing the promised subsidies, Charles backed down and on 7 June gave the answer MPs wanted—'Soit droit fait comme il est desire par le petition'—although he insisted that this granted 'no more' than his first answer. Sir Edward Coke said he was 'half dead with joy' that they now had an answer 'as will admit no exception'. The news quickly spread through the capital, Londoners celebrating the news with the ringing of bells and 'bonefires at every doore, such as were never seene but upon his Majesty's returne from Spayne'.[120] On 10 June the king sent a message to the Commons agreeing that the Petition of Right should be entered in the statute roll and printed, and in return the Commons passed the subsidy bill on the 12th and sent it up to the Lords. In the meantime the Lords proceeded to try Maynwaring. On the 14th they sentenced him to imprisonment during the pleasure of the House, ordered him to pay a £1,000 fine and make an acknowledgement of his offences in writing, suspended him from the ministry for three years and barred him from preaching at court, and ordered his sermons to be called in and burnt.[121]

On the 14th the Commons finalized their remonstrance against Buckingham. It was a long catalogue of what MPs took to be the dangers and perils threatening the kingdom. It began by alleging there was 'a general fear' among the people 'of secret working...to introduce into this kingdom innovation and change of our holy religion', pointing to the large number of Catholics at court, the staying of legal proceedings against popish recusants, the increase in the number of papists, the rise of Arminianism ('but a cunning way to bring in popery', since Arminians were 'Protestants in show but Jesuits in opinion'), the fact that the Arminians had friends among the clergy close to the king (notably Neile and Laud) and were allowed to publish their works whereas books written against them were suppressed, and the 'miserable condition' of Ireland, where 'the popish religion' was 'openly professed and practiced in every part'. Such developments were all the more to be feared given that England had already felt 'the strokes' of God's 'divine justice' with the recent visitation of the plague. People also feared 'innovation and change of government', the remonstrance continued. While they had been 'much comforted' by the king's answer to the Petition of Right, there were still armed troops being amassed in coastal areas, many of whom were neither 'natives' nor Protestants; there had of late been 'often breaches of parliament'; Tonnage and Poundage had been collected without parliamentary approval; 'faithful and sufficient officers and ministers' had been removed from the judiciary and other positions of authority; and there had been disastrous expeditions to Cadiz and Ré. Pointing to 'the poverty, weakness, and misery' the kingdom was 'now grown unto by decay of trade and destruction and loss of ships and mariners within these three years', the remonstrance asserted that 'the principal cause' of these 'evils and dangers' was 'the excessive power of the Duke of Buckingham', and his abuse of that power, and asked that Buckingham be removed from office and from the king's presence. When MPs presented the remonstrance to the king on 17 June, Charles said that they clearly did not understand what belonged to either Church or commonwealth 'so well as he had thought' and that he would give their grievances the consideration they deserved. After the remonstrance was read, Buckingham fell to his knees and begged Charles to be allowed to answer for himself; the king refused, but instead gave the duke his hand to kiss. Charles gave no further response to the remonstrance; although Laud drafted a reply, Charles decided not to print it.[122]

Charles hoped that parliament would get round to putting Tonnage and Poundage on a statutory footing before the last day of the

session, set for 26 June. Yet there was simply insufficient time to prepare a bill before the summer recess, and so on the 25th the Commons drew up a remonstrance explaining it needed longer and
pointing out that if Charles continued to collect Tonnage and Poundage he would be in violation of the Petition of Right. Charles was
furious. In order to avoid being presented with the remonstrance, he
summoned the Commons to the Lords early the following morning
and announced an immediate prorogation until 20 October, complaining that the Commons were already beginning to make 'false
constructions' of his answer to their Petition of Right, that he had
'granted no new, but only confirmed...ancient liberties', and insisting that he could not be without Tonnage and Poundage, which he
described as 'a flower of my crown'.[123]

Following the prorogation, Charles began to backtrack. Although
the Petition of Right had initially been printed containing only his
second answer, on 29 June he ordered Attorney General Heath to call
in all existing copies and commissioned a second printing, containing
his first answer, a series of qualifications to his second answer, and the
speech he had delivered at the prorogation of parliament. He also
ordered the statute number originally assigned to the Petition of
Right to be effaced with a pumice stone, so as to cast doubt on its
status as a statute.[124] On 8 July he issued an order pardoning Maynwaring, and ten days later he presented Maynwaring to the rectory of
Stanford Rivers, Essex, subsequently issuing a dispensation allowing
him to hold it *in commendam* with St Giles-in-the-Fields.[125] Blatantly
ignoring the concerns voiced by MPs in their remonstrance against
Buckingham, Charles proceeded to promote a number of Arminians
to prominent positions in the Church. In the month of July alone,
Laud was installed as bishop of London (Laud had in fact been chosen back in June 1627); John Howson, bishop of Oxford, moved to
Durham to replace Neile, who had recently moved to Winchester;
George Mountaigne of London was elected to the archbishopric of
York; and Richard Mountague was elected to the bishopric of Chich-
ester. Mountaigne was to die in October on the day of his enthrone-
ment, and so Charles appointed Samuel Harsnett of Norwich as his
replacement in December. The vacant see of Norwich in turn went to
Francis White, bishop of Carlisle, who had formally defended
Mountague's orthodoxy at the York House conference in 1626. With
Buckeridge having already moved from Rochester to Ely in March
1628, by the beginning of 1629 many of the key sees in England were
in the hands of Arminians.[126]

The Assassination of Buckingham and the Parliamentary Session of 1629

The political landscape was suddenly and dramatically transformed by events that unfolded at the Greyhound Inn in Portsmouth towards the end of August. A disgruntled former soldier named John Felton, who had been wounded on the ill-fated expedition to the Ile de Ré, had made his way to the town to confront Buckingham, who was getting ready for another expedition to La Rochelle. Felton had personal grievances: he believed the duke responsible for twice blocking his promotion to captain and for withholding about £80 of back pay, and he had engaged a London scrivener named George Willoughby to draw up petitions to various privy councillors pleading his case. However, when visiting Willoughby's shop Felton chanced to see a copy of the Commons' remonstrance against Buckingham and became convinced that his own sufferings were related to those of the nation. He bought an ordinary knife from a cutler for about a shilling, travelled down to Portsmouth, and on the morning of Saturday the 23rd, as Buckingham was leaving his lodgings just after breakfast, Felton jumped him from behind, striking him 'over his shoulder upon the Breast' and piercing his heart. Amazingly, amidst the crowd of clients, diplomats, military men, and other hangers-on who were in attendance upon the duke, no one saw exactly what happened and Felton managed to slip away; all that was found was the assassin's hat, which had a paper inside containing four or five lines from the Commons' remonstrance. Because Buckingham had been in a heated discussion with the duke of Soubise and other Huguenot gentlemen about the timing of the departure of the fleet, onlookers assumed that one of the French must have committed the crime and started shouting 'A Frenchman', at which Felton—perhaps thinking they were calling his name—revealed himself and proclaimed 'I am the one'. Another account states that Felton was outed because he was the only man seen without a hat. Either way, Felton clearly had never expected to make it out alive. Inside his hatband he had stitched two signed papers explaining why he had done the deed: one read, 'That Man is cowardly-base, and deserves not the name of a Gentleman nor souldier, that is unwilling to sacrifice his life for his God, his King, and his Country'; the other, 'Let no man commend mee for doing of it: but rather discommend themselves, as the cause therof'. Although some of the onlookers wanted to avenge the murder there and then, calmer minds prevailed and Felton was arrested and taken to London for examination. The government at first thought that Felton must have been part of a wider conspiracy, perhaps involving the Puritans, but Felton insisted that 'no Person whatsoever knew any Thing of his Intentions'. Laud threatened him with the rack if he did not reveal his accomplices, but Felton replied that he did not know whom he might name 'in the extremity of torture', perhaps even Laud himself, and after being told by the judges that torture would not be legal in this case, Charles refused to sanction it. Tried before King's Bench on 27 November, Felton confessed his crime and said that he had done it 'for the good of his country' in order 'to rid the Commonwealth of a monster and to free his country from that misery that he saw it was like to fall into by his misgovernment'. He was hanged at Tyburn two days later.[127]

Charles was deeply distressed, both by the loss of his favourite and—as Clarendon put it—by 'the horrid manner in which he had been deprived of him'. He put on a brave face in public, and appeared 'unmoved' when initially informed; but when he escaped to the privacy of his chamber, he collapsed on his bed in tears, continuing 'in this melancholic and discomposure of mind many days'. In addition to removing the man who had monopolized political power for so long, Buckingham's assassination changed the dynamic of court politics in several ways. Taking Charles's initial composure to be a sign that the king was not unhappy to be rid of his favourite, many began speaking openly about the duke, 'dissecting all his infirmities', thinking they would not incur the king's displeasure; Charles was not one to forgive such indiscretions, and was reluctant ever again to trust any 'who had ever discovered themselves to be enemies to the duke'. According to Sir Dudley Carleton, recently raised to the peerage as Viscount Dorchester, it was now that Charles resolved to take the 'total directory' of affairs into his own hands.[128]

With Buckingham gone, Charles drew closer to his wife Henrietta Maria, who helped him through the period of mourning and henceforth became his constant companion. Instead of paving the way for a better understanding between the king and his subjects, the assassination made Charles more suspicious of them than ever—not simply for the knowledge that one of them could do such a terrible thing, but because so many seemed to applaud it. The news that Buckingham had been killed was greeted with overt rejoicing, toasts to Felton were drunk in alehouses across the country, and the duke's funeral had to be held at night for fear of angry crowds.[129] John Viccars, the rector of St Mary's, Stamford, in Lincolnshire, prayed before his congregation on two successive Fridays that 'the king rejoyce in the death of that wicked Achan'.[130] A slew of satirical epitaphs circulated in manuscript. 'Here Lies Leachery, Treachery, Pride', read one.[131] Another has Charles tell Buckingham he must go 'To Land at Stixe | From whence you had your strategems and tricks'. Others had Felton proclaim that he had done 'a Publick good' and with 'with one stroke' set king and kingdom 'att libertye'.[132] Bishop Wren, by contrast, used the occasion of Buckingham's assassination to deliver a sermon lambasting the Puritans as that 'most pernicious sect, and dangerous to a monarch; as bad as Jesuits in their opinions', since they 'held the same tenet, that their head fellow Felton doth', namely that it was 'lawful to kill any man that is opposite to their party', and that 'their whole doctrine and practice' tended towards 'anarchy'.[133]

The death of Buckingham led to a series of ministerial adjustments giving greater prominence to the pro-Spanish faction at court. The decidedly Hispanophile Richard Weston, who had been appointed Lord Treasurer in mid-July, effectively became first minister—although he enjoyed a much less prominent position than the duke. Weston effected a reconciliation between Charles and the pro-Spanish earl of Arundel, who was restored to the privy council in October, and secured the appointment of Sir Francis Cottington, another Hispanophile, to the council in November and to the chancellorship of the Exchequer in December. Most significantly, Weston managed to recruit for court service the Yorkshire MP Sir Thomas Wentworth, who had been imprisoned in 1627 for opposing the Forced Loan and had been an outspoken critic of the court in the parliaments of 1625 and 1628. Wentworth, who like Weston favoured peace with Spain, was made first a baron in July and then a viscount in December and that same month appointed Lord President of the North. Not that the court became monopolized by one voice: those courtiers who survived into the post-Buckingham era included Pembroke and Dorchester, who were anti-Spanish, pro-Dutch (and also pro-French), and strongly Calvinist and anti-Armininian.[134]

Following the June prorogation, some merchants refused to pay Tonnage and Poundage on the grounds that it had not yet been sanctioned by parliament. The privy council responded by having their goods seized, but in early September some thirty merchants broke into a customs warehouse in London and took back the confiscated merchandise. With resistance escalating, the council had some of the refusers imprisoned. When the Levant merchant Richard Chambers

IACOBVS 6 D·G·R
SCOTORVM
ÆTA·29·
1595

PLATE 1 James VI at age 29, in his prime as King of Scotland. By the court portrait painter Adrian Vanson.

PLATE 2 James VI and I as King of England in 1621. Although only in his mid-50s, he looks an old man. By Daniel Mytens.

PLATE 3 James's Ganymede and Charles's favourite, George Villiers, 1st Duke of Buckingham. Painted here by Gerrit van Honthorst in 1628, shortly before Buckingham's assassination.

PLATE 4 Charles I with his wife Henrietta Maria and their two young children, Prince Charles and Princess Mary. This was Anthony van Dyck's first commission following his appointment as court painter to Charles I in 1632.

PLATE 5 Charles I at the Hunt, also by van Dyck, *c.*1635. Charles was a small man, but even the horse bows his head before divine majesty.

PLATE 7 The cleric James I claimed had a 'restless spirit' and who loved 'to toss and change and bring things to a pitch of reformation floating in his own brain': Archbishop William Laud, painted by van Dyck in 1636.

PLATE 6 (*opposite*) A landscape by Peter Paul Rubens dating from the start of the personal rule, showing Charles I as St.George rescuing Henrietta Maria after he has slain the dragon—and more broadly as a deliverer who will establish peace and harmony and secure Christ's victory over Satan.

PLATE 8 The Forced Loan refuser who went over to the court in 1628 and became Lord Lieutenant of Ireland in 1632: Thomas Wentworth, Earl of Strafford, painted here by van Dyck, c.1639.

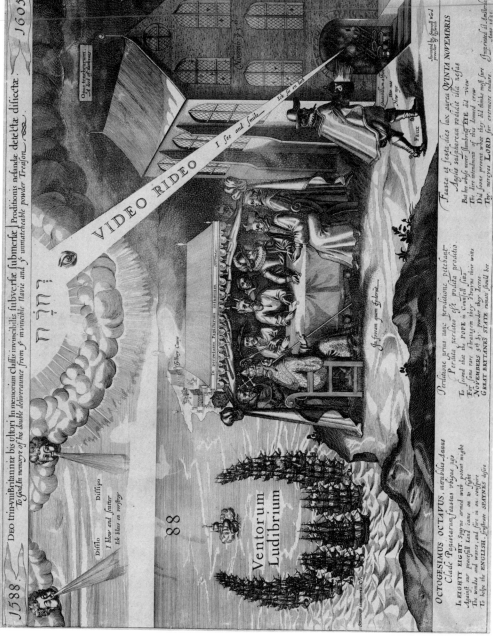

PLATE 9

England's double deliverance from the Spanish Armada of 1588 and the Gunpowder Plot of 1605 by the Ipswich Puritan preacher Samuel Ward, purportedly showing Philip III of Spain seated in the company of the devil, the pope, a Jesuit, and various other Catholic clergy. The engraving appeared just before the meeting of the 1621 parliament, though Ward claimed it dated from five years earlier.

PLATE 10 An engraving celebrating the downfall of the hated monopolist Giles Mompesson, impeached by parliament in 1621.

PLATE 11 Peterhouse College Chapel, Cambridge, which was refurbished in Laudian style in the 1630s, with an east window depicting Christ's crucifixion, a railed altar (fixed at the east end on an ascent of polished marble), candlesticks, and crucifixes.

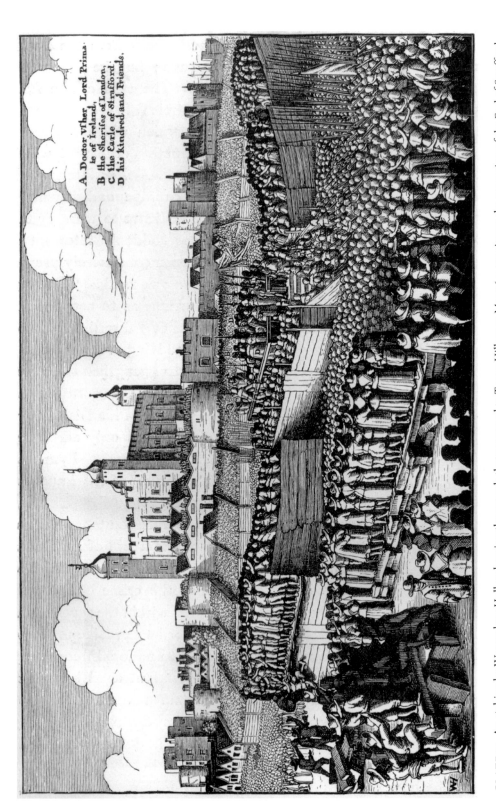

A. Doctor Vſher, Lord Prima-
  te of Ireland,
B the Sherifes of London,
C the Earle of Strafford,
D his kindred and Friends.

PLATE 12 An etching by Wenceslaus Hollar showing the crowds that swarmed to Tower Hill on 12 May 1641 to witness the execution of the Earl of Strafford.

PLATES 15 & 16 These two woodcuts come from an anti-Laudian playlet of 1641. The first depicts Laud dining off the ears of Burton, Bastwick, and Prynne, alluding to the cruel punishments meted out by Charles I's court of Star Chamber. The second shows the lower sort getting their revenge, as a carpenter holds Laud's nose to the grindstone. From *A New Play Called Canterburie his Change of Diot* (1641).

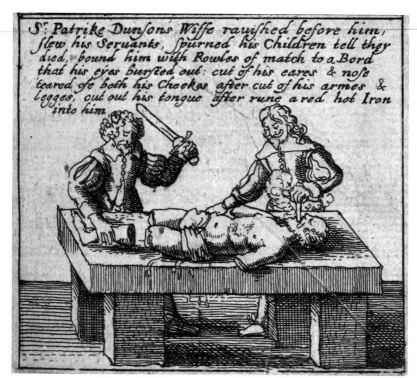

St: Patrike Dunsons Wiffe rauished before him,
slew his Seruants, spurned his Children tell they
died, bound him with Rowles of match to a Bord
that his eyes bursted out: cut of his eares & nose
teared ofe both his Cheekes after cut of his armes &
legges, cut out his tongue after rune a red hot Iron
into him

Companyes of the Rebells meeting
with the English flyinge for their liues,
falling downe before them cryinge for
mercy, thrust theire Pichforkes into
their Childrens bellyes & threw them
into the water,

PLATES 17 & 18 Two images from James Cranford's *Teares of Ireland* (1642) depicting alleged atrocities committed by Catholics on Protestants at the time of the Irish rebellion of 1641. The first shows the supposed murder of Sir Patrick Dunson in Armagh on 22 November 1641, the second Irish rebels brutally murdering young infants.

PLATE 19 (*above*)

A print by Wenceslaus Hollar dating from 1642 showing Colonel Thomas Lunsford supposedly assaulting Londoners at Westminster Hall in December 1641. Those who support the King are labelled 'Cavaleires'.

PLATE 20

The title page of a pamphlet by the royalist water-poet John Taylor from 1641 showing the enemies of true religion—the separatists and the papists—tossing a Bible in a blanket.

was examined before the council in late September for his refusal to pay, he angrily protested that in 'noe parte of the world' were merchants 'soe screwed and wrong [wrung] as in England'—even in Turkey they had more encouragement—and was promptly committed to the Marshalsea prison. Chambers sued for habeas corpus and on 23 October the judges released him on bail in accordance with the provisions of the Petition of Right (the council's warrant for Chambers' detention had merely stated that Chambers had been imprisoned for 'insolent and contemptious words', without specifying what they were); Charles retaliated by having Chambers prosecuted before Star Chamber, where in May 1629 he was found guilty, fined £2,000, and dispatched to the Fleet prison for six years. One of those in trouble was the MP John Rolle, another Levant merchant who had goods to the value of £1,517 confiscated in November; Rolle tried to sue for the return of his goods, but the Court of Exchequer determined that their seizure was justified and subsequently issued him with a subpoena to appear before Star Chamber (though the Attorney General later conceded that this had been done in error).[135]

Charles and his council realized they would need a better strategy for managing the upcoming session of parliament. It was decided that the government should have a Tonnage and Poundage bill ready to go, legitimizing its collection from the first day of the reign (which would in turn end the dispute regarding those merchants who had had their goods distrained for refusing to pay); if parliament proved uncooperative, then Charles was to deliver a speech in person distancing himself from his previous stance and insisting that he had no desire to claim Tonnage and Poundage 'otherwise but by Grant in Parliament'.[136] Recognizing the need to do something to alleviate concerns over the growth of popery and the rise of Arminianism, Charles announced to his council that he intended to turn all papists out of office and that he would have those bishops who were in the London area examine the opinions of the Arminians and condemn any which did not conform with the Thirty-Nine Articles. The earl of Pembroke was quick to point out that it hardly helped to trust 'the consideration of Arminianism ... to the bishops about the town, because most of them were Arminians', and thought the matter should be referred to Convocation. Furthermore, Charles immediately exempted two Catholic lords—the earls of Rutland and of Worcester—from being removed from their lord lieutenancies, because 'he held them to be very good subjects'. Charles nevertheless did order the judges and the bishops to enforce the laws against recusants.[137]

In November Charles also published a new edition of the Thirty-Nine Articles, to which he affixed a declaration affirming that the Articles contained 'the true doctrine of the Church of England' and prohibiting any disputations over them, whether in print or from the pulpit. He claimed that he was simply trying to fulfil his kingly duty of promoting 'the unitie of true Religion' by tying everyone to articles which had 'been allowed and authorized heretofore' and to which the clergy 'generally' had subscribed. Yet in practice the declaration—which was drawn up by Laud—was promoting a partisan agenda under the guise of upholding a presumed consensus. Not all the clergy were convinced that the Thirty-Nine Articles did contain the 'true doctrine' of the Church—that was why Calvinists had for long been seeking to modify them by incorporating the position on predestination upheld by the Lambeth Articles of 1595. The declaration also confirmed that the settlement of questions of doctrine and discipline of the Church of England was to be left to the bishops and clergy in Convocation, which in the light of the recent ecclesiastical preferments meant that matters would be resolved by Arminians. In his own diocese of London, Laud exploited the ban on disputation to stop Calvinist clergy from preaching on predestination.[138] By contrast, the government appeared to go easy on Arminian clerics who became involved in controversy. When the dean of Durham, John Cosin, was brought before Star Chamber accused of denying the royal supremacy and saying that the king hath no more power of excommunication than 'the groom that rubbes his horse heeles', Charles decided the prosecution was malicious and ordered it to be dropped.[139] It is true that Mountague was eventually persuaded to submit a written submission to the archbishop of Canterbury on 12 December, rejecting the five tenets of Arminianism and subscribing to the Council of Dort. And on 17 January, three days before parliament was due to reassemble, Charles issued a proclamation calling in the *Appello* and announcing that there should be no further 'reading, preaching, or making Bookes, either *pro* and *contra*' these 'needlesse Controversies'. However, it was observed that the calling in of Mountague's book was done 'sleigthly'—no search for copies was made, and the book was still being sold as parliament sat—while the proclamation was used to justify the suppression of all writing and preaching that was critical of Mountague's work.[140]

When parliament reassembled on 20 January 1629, the Commons immediately went on the offensive, and launched an inquiry into the ways in which the Petition of Right had been violated since the end of the last session. Speaking on the 21st, Eliot and Selden complained that the first printing of the Petition of Right had been suppressed and another printed containing the king's first answer and that some people had been imprisoned contrary to the Petition of Right. The next day Rolle complained that he had had his goods seized for refusing to pay Tonnage and Poundage; Eliot and Selden were to go on to insist that parliamentary privilege should have protected Rolle's possessions from arrest, as well as his person. In an attempt to cool passions, Charles spoke to both Houses at the Banqueting House on the 24th and (as agreed in advance) insisted that it had not been his intention to claim Tonnage and Poundage as a right but only by grant of parliament; he was merely continuing to collect it, out of necessity, until the Commons passed the Tonnage and Poundage bill, which it had promised to do. 'Let us not be jealous one of another's actions', he implored, so that the session might 'end in a perfect, good understanding between us'.[141]

When Secretary Coke moved to have the Tonnage and Poundage bill read on the 26th, the Commons refused and instead turned its attention to religious grievances. Francis Rous condemned Arminianism as 'this Trojan horse...ready to open the gates to Romish tyranny and Spanish monarchy'; to Rous, 'an Arminian' was 'the spawn of a Papist': 'you shall see an Arminian reaching out his hand to a Papist, a Papist to a Jesuit, a Jesuit gives one hand to the Pope and the other to the King of Spain'. Edward Kirton said it was apparent to all, that 'new opinions' had been 'brought in by some of our Churchmen', with the ultimate intention of bringing in 'the Romish religion'. Christopher Sherland complained of the growth of Arminianism and how 'a new faction' had put the king 'upon designs that stand not with public liberty', encouraging Charles to believe 'he may command what he listeth and do as he pleaseth with goods, lives, and Religion', and stigmatizing those 'good true-hearted Englishmen and Christians' who opposed them 'under the name of Puritans'.[142]

The Commons spent the next two weeks discussing religion. It launched an investigation into the pardons given to Mountague, Cosin, Sibthorpe, and Maynwaring and the suppression of anti-Arminian and anti-Catholic publications. Members also discussed ways of ensuring that the Thirty-Nine Articles would be given an unequivocal Calvinist reading, by giving statutory authority to the Lambeth Articles of 1595, the Irish Articles of 1615, and the resolutions of the Synod of Dort of 1618–19, although there were disagreements over which of these sources should be used and in the end the

House got distracted into an examination of Arminian evil counsellors. Members resumed discussion of Tonnage and Poundage from 11 February, but became preoccupied with the question of how to hold accountable those customs officials who had collected the duties illegally. The officials had been acting under royal warrant, but rather than enter into a confrontation with the crown the Commons came up with the fiction that the officials had seized goods for their own benefit and thus exceeded their own warrant. It would have been one way out of the impasse, to allow servants of the crown to take the rap for wrong that had been done in the name of the crown. Instead, Charles instructed Secretary Coke to tell the lower house on 23 February that he felt it was a matter of honour and justice to inform them 'that what they did was either by his own direct order and command, or by order of the Council-board'.[143]

On 24 February the subcommittee for religion agreed a series of 'Heads and Articles' which it intended to present to the lower house the following day. Although taking pains to exonerate Charles from any blame—thanking God for 'setting a King over us, of whose constancy, in the profession and practice of the true Religion here established' MPs claimed to be 'fully assured'—the Articles were nevertheless a swingeing indictment of religious developments over the last few years. Highlighting the dangers that threatened 'all the Protestant Churches in Christendom'—both on the Continent and in Scotland and Ireland—they proceeded to lament the 'extraordinary growth of Popery' in England and 'the subtile and pernicious spreading of the Arminian faction' and enumerate the causes: negligence in executing the laws against popery; 'defending of points of Popery in sermons and books'; introducing 'new ceremonies...without authority, in conformity to the Church of Rome', such as moving the communion table altar-wise and adorning it with candlesticks; the 'counterfeit conformity of Papists' to evade the law and 'obtain places of trust'; and allowing the publication of books and preaching of sermons contrary to 'orthodox doctrine' while suppressing books written in defence of it. Finally they condemned the favour recently shown to those who had 'published and maintained such Popish, Arminian, and superstitious opinions and practices'—naming Mountague, White, Buckeridge, and Howson ('a long suspected Papist'), Cosin, and Wren—and the fact that 'some prelates, near the King'—they named Neile and Laud—had 'gotten the chief administration of ecclesiastical affairs under his Majesty' and hindered the preferment of those who were orthodox and favoured 'such as are contrary'.[144]

Outraged, Charles sent a message to both Houses on the morning of the 25th commanding them to adjourn until Monday, 2 March. When, after prayers on the morning of the 2nd, the Speaker Sir John Finch rose to deliver a message from the king saying that parliament was to be further adjourned until Tuesday, 10 March, all hell broke loose. Complaining that the Commons' proceedings had been misrepresented to the king, Eliot moved to have read a short declaration of the House's intentions, 'which he flung downe upon the floore'. Sir William Fleetwood picked it up and brought it to the Speaker's chair, and as the Speaker tried to vacate his seat, two of Eliot's allies—Denzel Holles and Benjamin Valentine –'plucked him back by force' and 'held him in his chaire', while Sir Miles Hobart locked the door and pocketed the key to stop anyone from leaving. The Commons continued for some two hours addressing their grievances, and although the king sent several messengers one after the other, they were forcibly kept out; some of the 'patriot' MPs, the Venetian ambassador noted, threw punches at the 'royalists' (*Realisti*), who retaliated by threatening to draw their swords. In the end, the House passed a protestation declaring anyone who had sought to 'bring in innovation in Religion... or introduce Popery or Arminianism', or advised collecting or voluntarily paid Tonnage and Poundage, to be capital enemies of the kingdom and commonwealth, before finally adjourning.[145]

Charles immediately issued a proclamation announcing parliament's dissolution, claiming that his 'Regall authority' had been 'highly contemned' and blaming 'the malevolent dispositions of some ill affected persons of the House of Commons', and had Eliot, Holles, Valentine, and six other ringleaders arrested and dispatched to the Tower. He went to the House of Lords in person on 10 March—many members of the Commons also being present—for the formal dissolution. Men might wonder, he told those assembled, why he did not 'do this by Commission, it being a generall Maxime of Kings, to leave harsh commands to their Ministers, themselves onely executing pleasing things'. But justice, he continued, involved praising virtue as much as it did in punishing vice, and he wanted 'all the world' to know that 'it was merely the undutifull and seditious carriage in the lower House' that caused him to dissolve parliament, that he took 'much comfort' from the 'dutifull demeanours' of the Lords, and that he did not adjudge all the lower house 'alike guilty', which he knew contained many 'dutifull Subjects... it being some few Vipers amongst them, that did cast this mist of undutifulnesse over most of their eyes'.[146]

A few days later, Charles published a lengthy declaration explaining why he had dissolved the parliament, together with the speech he had given at the dissolution. He did not write it himself—it was probably penned by Dorchester—though it clearly reflected Charles's views.[147] After first reminding readers that princes were 'bound to give accompt of their actions but to God alone', Charles stated that he nevertheless wanted to satisfy 'the mindes and affections' of his 'loving Subjects', so that 'the world' might see 'the truth and sincerity' of his actions and not believe how he was represented 'to the publike viewe' by 'some turbulent and ill affected Spirits'. It was another self-conscious exercise in the politics of spin. The Declaration proceeded to represent Charles as a king who had gone beyond the call of duty in trying to alleviate the concerns of MPs. He had called parliament because he needed money to fight a war which parliament had committed him to, and when during the first session some members had stirred up 'causeles jealousies', he had permitted many of his 'high Prerogatives', which had never been questioned under his predecessors, to be debated 'without punishment, or sharpe reproofe'. Prior to the reassembling of parliament in January, he had done what he could to remove any 'ill understanding' between him and his people: he had called in Mountague's *Appello Caesarem*, reprinted the Elizabethan Thirty-Nine Articles and restrained 'all opinions to the sense of those Articles', issued a proclamation calling for the execution of the laws against Catholic priests and recusants, and been careful not to do anything to infringe 'the just and ancient Liberties of Our Subjects', as secured to them by his 'gracious Answere' to their Petition of Right. Yet as soon as parliament sat down, 'these ill affected men began to sowe and disperse their jealousies' and sought to misrepresent 'our proceeding, before the Parliament, about matters of Religion', in order 'to deprave our government'. When they finally got around to discussing Tonnage and Poundage, these men insisted 'we should disclaime any right therein, but by Grant in Parliament', even though all previous kings had received it before they were granted it by parliament. When he declared that he did not claim it by right but took it by necessity, the Commons nevertheless laid the Tonnage and Poundage bill aside and started investigating the complaints of those who had had their goods distrained for 'refusall to pay'. Charles then alleged that the lower house had 'of late yeeres endeavoured to extend their Priviledges, by setting up generall Committees for Religion, for Courts of Justice, for Trade, and the like'; they had sent messengers to examine the Attorney General and the judges; and they had even

tried 'to create a new priviledge...That a Parliament man hath priviledge for his goods against the King'. This was something he could
'never admit', for the result would be 'that he may not be constrained
to pay any duties to the King, during the time of priviledge of Parliament'. While Buckingham still lived, it was the duke who had been
the focus of 'all the distempers and ill events of former Parliaments'.
But now the duke was dead, 'no alteration was found amongst those
envenomed spirits', and so it was clear that these men did not aim at
Buckingham alone, but had 'more secret designes', which were 'to
cast Our affaires into a desperate condition, to abate the powers of
Our Crowne, and to bring Our government into obloquie' so that in
the end 'all things' might be 'overwhelmed with anarchie and
confusion'.[148]

It was a bleak, conspiratorial view of politics, but Charles once
more made it clear that he did 'not impute these disasters to the whole
House of Commons', which contained 'many religious, grave, and
well minded men', but to the 'provocations of evill men'. Moreover,
Charles insisted that nothing had changed his 'good intentions'
towards his subjects, and concluded by professing that he would
'maintaine the true Religion, and doctrine established in the Church
of England, without admitting or conniving at any back-sliding,
either to Popery or Schisme' and 'maintain the ancient and just Rights,
and liberties of Our Subjects'. 'Yet', came the final warning, no man
should 'abuse that liberty, turning it to licentiousnes, nor misinterpret
the Petition, by perverting it to a lawlesse libertie...to resist lawfull
and necessary authoritie'. For as he would maintain his subjects 'in
their just liberties', so Charles expected them to 'yeeld as much submission and duetie to Our Royall Prerogatives, and as ready obedience to Our authoritie and commandments, as hath been performed
to the greatest of our Predecessors'.[149]

Whether Charles's declaration helped assuage public anxieties is
difficult to say. People were talking, and some clearly remained
alarmed at the way the Commons had been treated. MPs returning to
their constituencies began to spread reports that the king 'was for
destroying the liberties of the people, by taking Tonnage and Poundage without consent of parliament; that Trade was quite ruined and
gone; and Religion in danger'.[150] Charles himself was definitely concerned about what he termed 'false and pernicious Rumours' touching the parliament. On 27 March he felt compelled to issue a
proclamation refuting the notion that the Commons' remonstrance of
2 March had been the vote of the whole House, insisting that this

'scandalous and seditious proposition' had been 'decried' by 'the wisest and best affected' at the time and that it had since been 'disavowed...by such as were suspected to have consented there-unto'. Any who raised or nourished 'such false reports', the procla-mation warned, would be 'severely punished'. Noting that, 'for severall ill ends', people were already talking about 'the calling againe of a parliament', Charles announced that having, by 'the late abuse', been driven 'unwittingly' from his intended course of 'frequent meet-ing with [his] People', he would 'account it presumption, for any to prescribe any time unto Us for Parliaments'. He would be 'more inclineable to meete in Parliament againe', he concluded, 'when Our People shall see more cleerely into our Intents and Actions, when such as have bred this interruption shall have received their condigne punishment', and when 'those who are misled by them...shall come to a better understanding of Us and themselves'.[151] The Personal Rule had begun.

9

Halcyon Days or Perilous Times?

On 30 May 1629 an Essex woman named Ann Carter and three male associates were hanged at Witham for orchestrating a food riot at the Essex port of Maldon. This was the second such disturbance in Maldon within the space of three months. In March a crowd of more than a hundred women and children—Ann prominent among them—had boarded a ship that was being loaded with grain for export to the Low Countries and carried away its cargo in their aprons and caps. Then on 22 May a crowd of some three hundred, many of them impoverished clothworkers from the neighbouring towns of Bocking, Braintree, and Witham, once again looted grain from ships bound for Europe. Ann had visited the depressed clothworking towns to recruit reinforcements among the weavers, who had recently petitioned the local justices complaining of their 'extreme necessity' and inability 'to maintain...themselves and their families', and she now set herself up as the 'captain' of the crowd, rallying them to the cry of 'Come my brave lads of Maulden I wilbe your leader for we wil not starve'. The riot occasioned no loss of life; indeed, the participants largely conformed to the pattern of ritualized behaviour typically seen in food riots, where violence was constrained and the goal simply to prevent the exportation of grain at times of shortage. It was the government's pursuit of the death penalty that was untypical. Fearing a general insurrection, the privy council decided that 'an exemplary punishment' should be 'inflicted upon the principall offenders' to deter others from committing 'the like hereafter'. As a result, Ann and her associates have the dubious honour of being the only food rioters to be executed in the seventeenth century.[1]

Ann's fate provides powerful testimony to the jitteriness of the regime and the very real atmosphere of crisis that gripped the country at this time. Dearth and economic recession had provoked rioting not just in Maldon, but also in Colchester, London, and the West

Country. The government's concerns were heightened by the fact that the disturbances occurred in areas and featured occupational groups known to be sympathetic to a hotter form of Protestantism, or Puritanism. The Caroline regime may have overreacted in the case of Ann Carter. Nevertheless it was correct in recognizing that swift and decisive action was needed to address the very real problems England faced.

A few weeks prior to Ann's execution a libellous attack on Charles and his government had been posted on St Paul's Cross, in the heart of the nation's capital. Addressed 'O king or rather no king', it alleged that Charles had 'lost the hearts' of his subjects and was 'therefore noe king, nor they any longer thy subjects', since 'that relation now ceaseth, violated on thy part'. Charles's faults had been to wink at idolatry, undermine the Protestant cause and the true religion, and betray parliament, 'breaking one parliament after another, yea imprisoning and punishing them' who had only sought 'to purge and reforme the commonwealth of Idolatrie', having done all this with the help of 'false, flattering, wicked and pernicious counsellors'. In short, our anonymous author concluded, 'all the world' could 'now see a plaine and popish plot to overthrow the whole church of God'. This was but one of a number of libels posted in London at the beginning of the personal rule. In February one had been left at the house of John Donne, dean of St Paul's, accusing Bishop Laud of being 'the fountain of all wickedness' whom 'neither God nor the world' would 'endure to live', while in mid-April another had been posted at the Exchange attacking the bishops as 'Treazonous evill workers for the Popish Infidells churches cause' who were in league with the pope 'to have the English Protestants more and more impoverished, weakned and disabled'. Such extreme statements should not be taken as representative of the mood of the capital. They might even be dismissed as the views of the lunatic fringe; indeed, when the author of the mid-April anti-episcopal rant was found, he was promptly sent to Bedlam, London's asylum for the insane. Nevertheless, such highly public condemnations of the Caroline government in the heart of the teeming metropolis were a cause for concern, and serve to remind us how highly charged the political atmosphere was at the beginning of the personal rule.[2]

Charles was to rule without calling a parliament again in England until the spring of 1640. What, then, are we to make of this lengthy experiment with personal rule? What was Charles trying to achieve and why did the experiment fail? Earlier assessments tended to be highly negative, depicting the personal rule as an 'eleven years tyranny' which saw the imposition of supposedly illegal taxes (such as ship money), the implementation of highly unpopular religious innovations, and the severe punishment of political and religious opponents of the regime through the prerogative courts of Star Chamber and High Commission. It started off badly and ended in revolution—a high road to civil war. Modern accounts, however, have emphasized that there was nothing unconstitutional about extended periods of rule without parliament and that Charles never technically acted in violation of the law; even in the area of religious reform, some would claim, the government was working very much within the traditions of the Elizabethan and Jacobean Church. A picture has emerged of a reforming government energetically attempting to solve problems, with the personal rule seeing a marked decline in the political temperature when compared to the heated 1620s. Some historians even see the 1630s as halcyon days of peace and prosperity, until the Scottish rebellion of 1638–40—an external and contingent factor—plunged the regime into crisis.[3]

Because we know that the personal rule did fail there has been a tendency to assume that it was bound to do so. Charles, of course, thought he was doing what was needed to right a system that had not been working well. Any assessment of the 1630s, therefore, must seek to do justice to the logic behind Charles's agenda, why Charles thought what he was doing was in the best interests of the kingdom, why reform was deemed necessary, and what the government managed to achieve. We should certainly eschew any notion that Charles I's decision to embark on a period of rule without parliament inevitably set the country on a path to civil war. The problem with the bolder attempts to rehabilitate the personal rule, however, is that they make it difficult to understand why the regime fell apart so quickly in the late 1630s, and why England was to slip into revolution in the 1640s. How healthy could the state of affairs really have been in England, if the Caroline regime of the 1630s could be so easily toppled by a rebellion in the much smaller and poorer satellite kingdom of Scotland? And if England really was such an unrevolutionary place in the 1630s, why did it prove to be such a revolutionary one only a few years later?

This chapter will look in turn at the secular and the religious policies pursued by the government during the 1630s; the following chapter will examine how the regime sought to deal with its critics during the years of the personal rule. We shall see that this was a reforming regime, with Charles making a genuine effort to address the very real problems that the country was facing. He did so in a way that was designed to strengthen the position and authority of both the crown and the Church. However, it would be misleading to infer that Charles was trying to construct a new type of monarchy in England. In many respects his regime should be seen as operating within a traditionalist framework. For example, Charles did not set out to establish a new system of government finance suitable for the modern era; rather he sought to exploit the ancient rights of the crown in order to achieve greater financial independence from parliament. Instead of creating a modern military establishment, as some European monarchs were beginning to do, he sought to reform the existing system of county militias. His welfare programme, while welcome, in essence followed Elizabethan precedents. More generally, Charles saw himself as continuing his father's agenda in Church and state, and trying to live up to the traditional responsibilities of the king, especially with regard to promoting (what he took to be) the true religion. Arguably he always acted within the law, although arguably is the word, because the law always has to be argued: there were many people in the 1630s who thought that what Charles was doing was indeed in violation of the law and/or against normal constitutional practice, even if those who were in control of the law in the 1630s were able to insist that the government's actions were legally justifiable.

Yet for all his efforts at reform, Charles never actually solved any of the problems he was seeking to address; indeed, by addressing them in the ways that he did, he often made the problems worse. We see this in particular with regard to his policies towards the Church, but it was also true about his fiscal policy. Moreover, he never managed to develop a satisfactory system of financing government in the long term in the absence of parliaments; yet by refusing to work with parliament he not only significantly curtailed his foreign policy options but he also made it impossible to get the sort of subsidies he needed when eventually he was forced, by a crisis in Scotland, to call a parliament in England once more. In the pursuit of reform, Charles upset many people and generated much critical dissent. Although an argument can be made that, in objective terms, Charles's regime was not that repressive, whether or not a regime is repressive is a subjective judgement, and there is no doubt that he created a repressive atmosphere and that many people came to feel oppressed.

Personal Monarchy

Charles had been flirting with the idea of ruling without parliament—pursuing 'new counsels'—since 1626. It was the frustrations of the 1629 session, however, that finally persuaded him that he could more readily fulfil his divinely ordained responsibility of ruling for the public good if he avoided calling parliaments.[4] As he was to put it in 1640, the proceedings of the Commons had made him 'averse to those ancient and accustomed wayes of calling his people together, when in stead of dutifull expression towards his Person and Government, they vented their own malice and disaffection to the State'.[5] In May 1629 Charles was said to have declared that anyone who spoke to him about parliament would be 'his enemy'; in 1631 he proclaimed that 'on no account' would he ever call parliament again; and by 1637 it was said that he could not even 'suffer the mention of parliament, much less its assembling'.[6] Charles was arguably within his rights not to call a parliament for eleven years. Certainly it was an acknowledged prerogative of the crown to determine the summoning, proroguing, and dissolving of parliament, and although statutes had been passed in the fourteenth century requiring regular parliaments they had never been observed. (The irony here is that Charles, as we shall see, was at times quite happy to demand that other laws which had long since fallen into abeyance should be enforced.) Nevertheless, the frequency with which Charles had to repeat his opposition to a meeting of the English parliament, and the fact that there are numerous examples of people expressing their hope in the 1630s that the king might be moved to call one, suggests that his failure to do so for so long ran counter to expectations.

The decision to rule without parliament meant that England could not afford to remain at war. Peace with France was concluded in April 1629. Charles's compunction about abandoning his sister Elizabeth and her husband meant that peace with Spain took longer to achieve; it finally came in November 1630 after Philip IV had made an empty promise to do what he could to help Frederick get the Palatinate back.[7] It is true that there was some talk in the 1630s of summoning a parliament in England, most seriously in late 1631, when Charles seemed on the verge of committing to a foreign policy alliance with Spain to restore Frederick and Elizabeth to the Palatinate. However, in a council debate of 21 December Charles showed himself vehemently opposed to the idea, stating that he was offended 'by the discourses... concerning a parliament' and adding 'that he would never be urged by necessity or against his will to summon one'.[8]

There is no doubt that it was Charles who was in charge during the 1630s. He took his duties as king seriously and was extremely attentive to the day-to-day business of government. He regularly attended meetings of the privy council, he expected his ministers to discuss business directly with him, and he made most of the key decisions in both foreign and domestic affairs himself. No other individual rose to take the place of Buckingham as royal favourite, and following the duke's assassination Charles himself was the major influence in ministerial appointments, although he tended to defer to William Laud with regard to posts in the Church. It is in this sense, then, that the eleven years without parliament was a period of personal rule.

Yet Charles was no autocrat. He listened to advice, and not only from those predisposed to agree with him—although it is true that he was less easily persuaded when the advice ran counter to his own inclinations. He promoted men who had opposed him in the 1620s, most famously Sir Thomas Wentworth, who became Lord President of the North at the end of 1628 and Lord Deputy of Ireland in 1632, but also Sir Dudley Digges, who became Master of the Rolls in 1636, and William Noy, one of the counsel for the defence in the Five Knights' Case and an ardent champion of the Petition of Right, who became Attorney General in 1631. Charles's privy council, which comprised some forty-two members—many appointments were honorific and only a dozen or so attended regularly—reflected a broad range of opinions. Contemporaries spoke of Spanish, Dutch, and French factions, although this was an oversimplification. There were those who opposed calling another parliament and favoured pursuing cordial relations with Spain, and others who advocated intervention on behalf of the Protestant cause in Europe, which would have required recalling parliament. Yet it would be wrong to give the impression that there was an even balance. The Protestant constitutionalists on the privy council were a dwindling force as the 1630s progressed, following the deaths of key figures such as the 3rd earl of Pembroke in 1630, Viscount Dorchester in 1632, and Archbishop Abbot in 1633. A number of those who favoured Spain, by contrast, not only rose to prominence in the royal administration, but appear to have been crypto-Catholics themselves. Richard Weston, 1st earl of Portland, who served as Lord Treasurer from 1628, formally converted to Rome before his death in 1635. Weston's protégé Francis Cottington, Chancellor of the Exchequer from 1629 to 1641 and

Master of the Court of Wards from 1635, had spent so much time as a diplomat in Spain that he was thought of as 'almost a naturalized Spaniard' and was at heart a Catholic, even though he nominally conformed, and likewise died in the old faith. Sir Francis Windebank, Secretary of State from 1632 to 1640, was a great protector of Catholic priests, and although probably an Arminian in the 1630s nevertheless was a 'professed papist' by the time of his death in 1646. Then there were the clerical Arminians on the inner ring of the privy council: Laud and Neile, the two leading ecclesiasts in the land, and William Juxon, who replaced Laud as bishop of London in 1633 and who became Lord Treasurer in 1636 upon Portland's death (the first churchman to hold the post since 1470). There were thus several crypto-Catholics close to the centre of power in the 1630s, as well as Arminians such as Laud whose own particular brand of Protestantism seemed to Puritans, and even many mainstream Calvinists, infected with 'popery'.[9]

There were also a number of actual Catholics at court, most of whom were close to the French queen Henrietta Maria—men such as Wat Montagu, Henry Jermyn, Sir Toby Matthew, Endymion Porter, and George Gage (although Montagu and Jermyn did not convert until 1636). Henrietta Maria herself had her own Catholic entourage of French attendants, confessors, and ladies in waiting. Suspicion of the sort of counsel offered by those who had closest access to the king was bound to be heightened at a time when there were no parliaments to speak for the mood of the nation, and suspicion of a foreign, Catholic queen was inevitable given that the whole point of a royal diplomatic marriage was to give the partners to the match some diplomatic clout. Henrietta Maria was supposed to put the case for France at the English court. However, her loyalties had become divided when her mother Marie de Medici lost her place in the French government in November 1630 and was forced into exile in Brussels, as a guest of the Habsburg court. The worry was that this would force Henrietta Maria to lean towards Spain, but in fact the queen hated the leading spokesman of the pro-Spanish faction at court, Lord Treasurer Weston, who she felt kept her on a short financial tether. Henrietta Maria thus became involved with a group of court Protestants (including the earls of Northumberland and Holland, who were to side with parliament in the civil war) who favoured a militant foreign policy to try to recapture the Palatinate. For a time in the period 1635–7 it looked like this might be pursued in alliance with France, who had recently renewed its hostilities with Spain.[10]

Nevertheless, Henrietta Maria came to be a despised figure, resented for what was presumed to be a pernicious influence on the king and at court. This was partly due to the fact that following the death of Buckingham the king and the queen grew particularly close and found it increasingly difficult to be apart. It was also due to the fact that Henrietta Maria, as the most prominent Catholic in the land, personified the Catholic presence at the heart of the English government. In 1632 Inigo Jones commenced work on a splendid new Catholic chapel in the grounds of the queen's residence at Somerset House: over one hundred feet long, it finally opened in December 1635 and became a major centre for Catholic worship in the capital. Overly optimistic reports from English Catholics suggesting that it might prove possible to convert the king himself led Pope Urban VIII to send a series of papal agents to England—the Oratorian priest Gregori Panzani from 1634 and then the Scot George Con from 1636—whose presence at court only served to exacerbate public anxiety. Con did his utmost to help English and Irish Catholics win relief from the penal laws; his private chapel, which on feast days would hold as many as nine masses, became another place where English Catholics might worship unmolested. (Although foreign Catholic residents were allowed chapels for their own private use and the use of their entourage, they were not supposed to make them open to the public.) And not content with ministering to the London-based Catholic community, Con began an active proselytizing campaign, with the hope of gaining further converts. When Henrietta Maria's rapprochement with France finally broke down in 1637, he set out to construct a pro-Spanish party of Catholics and crypto-Catholics at court, centred on the queen. Henrietta Maria was to complete her political transformation following the arrival at court of her mother Marie de Medici, together with some 600 exiled Frenchmen, in the autumn of 1638.[11]

How, then, did this regime seek to represent itself? In ideological terms, it was not an aggressively absolutist one. It is true that the years immediately following the Petition of Right saw a flurry of works written in defence of royal absolutism, among them Sir Robert Filmer's 'Patriarcha' (c.1628), Sir Francis Kynaston's 'True Representation of Fore-Past Parliaments' (c.1629), and John Cusacke's 'Ireland's Comfort' (1629).[12] Filmer maintained that kings possessed 'absolute power', that 'Regal authority' was 'not subject to Positive Laws', and that the king was 'the author and interpreter and corrector of the common laws'.[13] Kynaston held that the king was 'absolute sole Judge of his owne Law' and that he 'alone makes Lawes', and suggested that if the king could 'be supplied with Money...without a Parliament or Subsidies' he would have no need to call parliament.[14] It is significant, however, that Charles refused to allow these works to be published, and it is not clear how widely they circulated in manuscript. Instead, the emphasis in the 1630s tended to be on Charles's obligations to uphold religion and the law and to protect the people. Laud, preaching at St Paul's Cross on 27 March 1631 (the anniversary of Charles's accession), told his auditors that they had a king who was 'constant in religion', kept 'his Lawes in his life' and who planted 'his Judges so, as they may equally distribute his judgement, and justice to his people'. But although Laud saw the king as made by God, he emphasized the king's duties to God: 'For Kings are ordained of God for the good of the people', he proclaimed, and the king had to 'study to preserve the people committed to his charge', 'not in wealth only, and in peace, but in Godlinesse too'; 'he must take care for the souls, as wel as for the body and goods of his people', for if justice were laid aside or anything done to 'debase, and sinck the honour of God, and the sincerity of Religion...there must, ther will come a failing upon all such kingdomes'.[15]

Charles's vision of kingship can perhaps best be discerned from court culture. His most dramatic statement was the ceiling of the Banqueting House at Whitehall, painted by Peter Paul Rubens and devised by Inigo Jones in consultation with Charles himself, which was installed between 1635 and 1637. The ceiling depicts the apotheosis of James I and was intended to highlight the harmonizing and civilizing power of divinely ordained monarchy. One panel shows James as Solomon uniting his two kingdoms of England and Scotland into the new empire of Great Britain. Another is based on the Last Judgement and portrays James as Christ, drawing to himself the blessed on his left side while at the same time vanquishing the hydra-dragon of the papacy. As James ascends into heaven, he leaves behind the gift of peace. Similar themes were emphasized in the paintings of Charles's official court painter, the Flemish artist Sir Anthony Van Dyck. Van Dyck's 'Charles I at the Hunt' (c.1635), now in the Louvre, shows Charles standing before his horse, who bows before the king in a gesture that recalls nativity scenes of beasts paying homage to the baby Jesus (Plate 5). Two famous equestrian portraits—'Charles I with Monsieur de St Antoine, his riding master' (c.1633), still in the royal collection, and 'Charles I on Horseback' (c.1637), now in the National Gallery—portray Charles as an emperor clad in armour ruling over a

British state, the armour intended to depict not a warlike king—the scenes are peaceful—but a chivalrous knight fighting evil on behalf of virtue. Perhaps one of the most revealing insights into Charles's outlook as he embarked on his personal rule, however, is provided by a painting by Rubens in 1629, which represents Charles as St George rescuing a princess (Henrietta Maria) after he has slain the dragon, against a backdrop that shows England in fear and disorder. Charles is thus the deliverer who will establish a reign of peace and harmony, the slaying of the dragon also symbolic of Christ's victory over Satan (Plate 6).[16] The same point—the king and queen imposing order and peace over chaos and fury—was a central theme of the court masques produced by Inigo Jones and staged each year between 1631 and 1640.[17]

Devices to Maintain the State

Writing after civil war had broken out in England, the great contemporary royalist historian Edward Hyde (the future earl of Clarendon), although not uncritical of the policies of the personal rule, could look back on the 1630s as a time when England enjoyed 'the greatest calm and the fullest measure of felicity that any people in any age' had 'been blessed with, to the wonder and envy of all parts of Christendom'. It was a view coloured not just by knowledge of the miseries that were to befall England during the 1640s but also by an awareness of the horrors that faced those countries of Europe caught up in the Thirty Years War.[18] Indeed, a number of commentators during the 1630s spoke of 'halcyon days' under a peaceable government, when 'all Christendom' was threatened with 'universal combustion'. 'When were our days more halcyon', pondered the earl of Dorset in 1634, 'when did the people of this land sing a more secure Quietus', while court poets commonly contrasted peace at home with the chaos that afflicted Europe.[19] When Charles was eventually forced to recall parliament in 1640, he could boast how 'all his people' had 'lived in such peace and felicitie' under 'his gracious government', when 'all the neighbouring Kingdoms and States were in troubles and combustions'.[20]

It is not clear, however, that such a positive view was widely shared. Many saw the times as quite worrisome. The country had sunk into a recession, with high unemployment especially in the textile industry between 1629 and 1631. Although there had been three good harvests in a row between 1626 and 1628, that of 1629 was only average and that of 1630 disastrous: the price of wheat rose from just over 26 shillings per quarter in 1626 to just over 38 shillings in 1629 to nearly 54 shillings in 1630. The 1630s saw only one good harvest—that of 1639.[21] There were also renewed outbreaks of the plague and smallpox epidemics. The plague of 1625–6 caused the national death rate to rise by 43 per cent, while a combination of plague and other infectious diseases led it to rise by 35.1 per cent in 1638–9. National trends are deceptive, though, since the impact of plague was greatest in towns. Chester, Lincoln, and York saw mortality rise by 100 per cent in 1631, as did London and Newcastle in 1636, Norwich in 1636–8, and Leicester in 1638–9.[22] There was no shortage of explanations for why things were going wrong. Puritans blamed the idolatrous innovations in the Church for causing God to forsake England. Writing in 1636, William Prynne expressed his view that there would be no abatement from the plague until 'these purgations [were] rectified, superstition and idolatry removed', the 'preaching of God's word restored', and 'the Romish Prelates and Inquisitors' (i.e. Laudian clerics) 'deservedly punished for these their notorious impieties'.[23] The Caroline establishment tended to blame factious and seditious Puritans for unsettling the peace and quiet of the commonwealth. Either way, it was scarcely the case that people thought all was well. Indeed, the very aggressiveness with which the government set about its reforming agenda shows that it was well aware that all was not well. In 1635 the anti-Puritan Shropshire cleric Peter Studley painted a picture of an England living in 'Perillous times', caused by 'high and overweening spirits' who had 'pestered and disquieted' the 'English Church' and who refused to be subject 'to lawfull Authority', and predicted anarchy would break out if the king did not take appropriate preventative measures.[24] The Laudian divine Samuel Hoard, preaching in March 1637, spoke of 'this licentious age', in which 'the spirit of contention' reigned.[25] Those out of sympathy with the government's preventative measures were equally alarmed. The godly cleric and scholar Thomas Gataker saw the 1630s as those 'troublesom times under the Prelates'.[26] The Puritan lawyer and diarist Robert Woodford records meeting with friends in Dunstable in November 1638 where they 'discoursed of the badnesse of the times', and begged 'Lord amend them for the Lord's sake'.[27]

Given the problems of recession, harvest failure, disease, and social unrest that were gripping the country, one of the most pressing tasks facing the government from the start of the personal rule related to social welfare. Under pressure to act from the localities, in May 1629 the government published a proclamation ordering the execution of the laws for setting the poor on work. More ambitiously, between April 1630 and January 1631 it issued three books of orders (the third is normally thought of as the Book of Orders proper) intended to relieve poverty, punish vagrancy, close down illegal alehouses, set people to work, and combat the problems of famine and pestilence. Although packaging the measures together in this way was novel, as was the requirement that JPs meet monthly in petty sessions to enforce the orders and to draw up quarterly performance reports to be forwarded to the assize judges and the privy council, the books of orders did little more than draw together various aspects of social policy as it had developed over the last half century—and in that sense were quite traditional. They were accompanied by a series of other conciliar directives on social policy, including orders against new building and the subdivision of houses in London, letters to certain Midland counties aimed at stopping enclosures that drove people off the land, a commission for the relief of debtors, and a proclamation enjoining the keeping of fish days, Lent, and Friday fasts.[28]

The new demands added to the pressures on local government, which came to be more keenly felt over time, and the system did not work as smoothly as anticipated. Some resented the central government's interference in the local economy; certainly those landowners who were fined for engaging in enclosure had cause for resentment (fines imposed on those engaged in depopulating enclosure raised £35,600 between 1636 and 1640[29]), while Puritans objected to the imposition of fast and fish days which they saw as part of the pre-Reformation ecclesiastical calendar. We might also question whether the government was ambitious enough in its efforts to get to grips with the problem of poverty and economic dislocation: poor relief under the republican regimes of the 1650s was to be three times higher than during the personal rule. Nevertheless the social policies of the 1630s show Charles taking his responsibilities to promote the welfare of his subjects seriously, building upon although also amplifying the policies of his predecessors, and his strategy commanded broad assent.

Another pressing problem concerned the state of the county militias. The wars with Spain and France had shown the local trained bands to be seriously deficient—poorly trained, ill-equipped, undermanned, and hard to discipline. In 1629 the privy council issued orders for the training and equipping of the county militias, stipulating that all officers and soldiers should be able and sufficient, take the oaths of allegiance and supremacy, and once enrolled be unable to avoid service. Further orders to improve the military capacity of the country followed over the next couple of years, relating in particular to the provision and inspection of arms. The reform initiatives, on the surface, appear to have met with success. Local records suggest that arms were being inspected and maintained and that professional training was being undertaken on a regular basis in most counties. Deputy lieutenants also regularly examined local regiments, to ensure that government standards were being met. Most soldiers served for extended periods and appear to have been happy to do so; indeed, service in the militia brought a certain amount of prestige. Moreover, the financial implications of these reforms were minimal and seen to be a cost worth bearing. Of course, it is one thing to boast of a 'perfect militia' during times of peace; the ultimate test would come when the militia needed to be deployed in war, and that was not to be until 1639–40.[30]

The most challenging problem for the government in the absence of parliaments was finance. Parliaments did not normally grant subsidies to cover peacetime expenditures, so arguably the decision not to call parliament merely limited the crown's foreign policy options. But there were deeper-lying structural problems that meant that it had become increasingly difficult for the crown to live of its own in times of peace. The alienation of crown lands over the generations and the erosion of the value of rents during an age of inflation had seriously depleted royal revenues. Charles sold a further £640,000 of crown lands during the first ten years of his reign, after which there was not much left to sell. It had been recognized with the Great Contract of 1610 that the ultimate solution was a deal with parliament, although nothing could be worked out under James and now Charles had closed that option off—and at a time when the royal debt stood at a massive £2 million.[31]

Peace did bring some immediate benefits, leading to a revival of trade and hence an improvement in the yield from customs. Seizing the opportunity to obtain more from an improving economy, in 1635 Charles issued a new book of rates raising the duties on a number of commodities; as a result, the yield from customs rose from about £270,000 per annum in the early 1630s to over £482,000 by 1641. The problem was that although customs were a traditional source of ordinary revenue for the crown, they nevertheless needed to be approved first by parliament and the Commons had voted Tonnage and Poundage for only one year back in 1625 (and even then the bill had not passed). Charles continued to collect it, simply choosing to ignore the 1629 parliament's objection that this was against 'the liberties of England'.[32]

To supplement government revenues, Charles sought to exploit the remaining feudal rights of the crown to the full. One such was distraint of knighthood. In theory, wealthy landowners were supposed to present themselves to be knighted at the king's coronation or else pay a fine— the original rationale being that under feudalism tenants-in-chief owed the crown knight service, and so if they were not going to make themselves available to serve they would need to give the king monetary compensation so that he could hire a substitute. But wars had long since ceased to be fought with feudal levies and the custom had fallen into abeyance: Elizabeth had regarded it as obsolete, no attempt had been made to levy knighthood fines at James I's coronation, and Charles himself had acknowledged in 1625 that there were already more knights than necessary. Nevertheless, Charles opted to revive the fines in 1627, using the wealth test of £40 which had been set back in Henry VII's reign, even though there had been over 400 per cent inflation since then and landowners worth only £40 hardly possessed the appropriate social and economic status for knighthood. In January 1630 the privy council appointed special commissioners for each county to compound with offenders according to their wealth, making distraint of knighthood in effect a form of non-parliamentary taxation. Some 9,000 landowners suffered as a result, with fines ranging from £10 to as high as £80, generating revenue of £173,537 by Easter 1635. Although accepted as legal, distraint of knighthood caused considerable grumbling. People naturally resented being fined for an oversight they had committed several years earlier. Some objected to the amounts of the fine (in a few cases the amount exceeded the value of the land in question). Others protested they had been wrongly fined—that they were under age at the time of the coronation, or else out of the country, or did not possess the requisite amount of land—although the burden was on them to prove they should be exempt.[33]

Charles also decided to exploit his rights over royal forests for revenue purposes. Forests were areas that had been set aside as game reserves for the crown, but over the centuries they had shrunk in size. James had sold off woodland in order to raise income, and the demands of war had led Charles to continue this strategy in the early years of his reign. Such disafforestation was followed by enclosure and a concomitant loss of common rights for the poor, sparking widespread anti-enclosure riots over the period 1626–32, notably in Gillingham Forest in Wiltshire and the Forest of Dean in Gloucestershire. One of the individuals involved in enclosure in the Forest of Dean was Giles Mompesson, the hated monopolist impeached by parliament in 1621 who, despite his sentence of perpetual banishment, was back in England in late 1630 and the object of anti-enclosure rioters' ire in the spring of 1631.[34] In 1634, however, Charles decided to revive the old forest law and to fine people who encroached upon the royal forest, while a government inquiry set the boundaries of the forests to the maximum they had attained in the Middle Ages. As a result, many came to be accused of violations of the forest law who had never been aware that they had done anything wrong, and recent beneficiaries of disafforestation now found themselves facing an uphill struggle to defend their acquisitions. In total, the fines imposed raised a little over £80,000.[35]

Although these sums were useful, raising money in this way was never going to be a long-term solution: as the Venetian ambassador pointed out, such fines were 'good for once only, and states are not maintained by such devices'.[36] Other feudal incidents held out the prospect of more regular income. Purveyance was worth between £40,000 and £50,000 per year to the crown in the 1630s. The yield from wardship was increased, through more assiduous management, from £45,000 at the beginning of the personal rule to £84,000 by 1640. Yet both purveyance and wardship had long been resented, and both had been slated for abolition under the terms of the Great Contract of 1610. Charles's decision to milk his rights to the full caused much bitterness. Local communities complained about the unfair burden of purveyance, and resistance to payment was widespread; moreover, the practice whereby some counties would raise a rate to cover the difference between the market price and the king's price, so that the royal household could use the money thus raised to subsidize purchases, gave purveyance the appearance of a tax. Wardship, to many, seemed an abuse whereby 'young children without parents may be bought and sold'.[37]

The government also sought to generate income by selling licences, patents, and monopolies—getting around the Act against monopolies of 1624, which had forbidden grants to individuals, by granting them to corporations. There were monopolies for the selling of wine, for the making of playing cards and dice, spectacles, hatbands, beaver hats, tobacco-pipes, for transporting sheepskins, even for gauging butter casks.[38] Such practices hit those traders and manufacturers who were excluded by a monopoly or found themselves forced to pay for trading privileges and were much resented. For example, in 1632 a syndicate with strong Roman Catholic affiliations received a monopoly to manufacture a new soap, in return for which they agreed to pay the crown a royalty of £4 per ton, to the detriment of the independent soap manufacturers. The London washerwomen complained that the 'Papist soap' washed 'not so white nor so sweete' nor went 'soe farr in extent of washing as the old Sope', and that it burned the linen and 'fretteth the hands of those that wash therewith'. Apparently they had a point: in his diary the judge Sir Richard Hutton described the soap as 'so bad that it could not be useful'. So in December 1633 the government staged a public trial, which found that the new soap 'did with a very small difference, lather much better' than the old soap, and that clothes washed with it were 'as white and sweeter'. One man who petitioned the lord mayor against the new soap was committed to Newgate, where he lingered over Christmas and until at least the end of January. Attorney General Noy brought an action in Star Chamber against sixteen London manufacturers which resulted in fines ranging from £500 to £1,500 each being levied against them. However, complaints persisted and in 1637 the old soapmakers were able to challenge the new company for control of the manufacture by paying the crown £43,000 in order to be incorporated themselves and agreeing to double the royalty to the crown to £8 per ton. As a result of a combination of payments, royalties, and fines, soap came to be worth about £30,000 per annum to the crown.[39]

To be fair, many of the projects launched in the 1630s were intended to help boost the economy. The soap monopoly, for example, was to encourage the production of a soap that could be made with domestic materials, rather than imported potash, and thus retail at a lower price, while there were schemes for setting up copper mines in Cornwall, for promoting more efficient ways of growing carrots, and for making salt from seawater, to name but a few. One of the most ambitious was the project to drain the eastern fenlands in order to make them suitable for agriculture. Begun in 1626, when Charles commissioned the Dutch engineer Cornelius Vermuyden to drain Hatfield Chase in the Isle of Axholme, Lincolnshire, further schemes were developed during the 1630s for draining the marshlands of Yorkshire, Nottinghamshire, Lincolnshire, Norfolk, and Cambridgeshire. They nevertheless proved controversial, since they involved denying to the poor rights of common on the marshland that were essential for basic subsistence, although technically many of the people who inhabited these areas were 'squatters' and had no legal rights of common in the first place. The legal issues were complicated, and although the government was willing to offer compensation, the cost of lawsuits threatened to outweigh the benefits to be accrued from the reclaimed land. Disputes between the drainers and the local inhabitants persisted throughout the decade, often erupting in violence as people levelled ditches and sought to obstruct the work. Refusal to pay the rates levied to cover the costs of the drainage was widespread. Progress was therefore slow and delays frequent, although significant advances had been made by the end of the 1630s. The political cost, however, was high. Opposition to fen drainage was a major reason why so many people from the affected parts of the country opposed Charles and sided with parliament in 1640.[40]

The most controversial of Charles's fiscal expedients was ship money.[41] In 1634 the government issued a writ to all maritime counties ordering them to provide a ship for the service of the king and requiring sheriffs to impose a levy on their respective counties in order to raise the funds to pay for the cost of such a ship. The following year ship money was extended to inland counties as well, and continued to be levied each year for the remainder of the personal rule. There were clear precedents, dating back to the reigns of the first three Edwards, of port towns being commanded to provide ships and men for the king's service, at their own charge.[42] In more recent times, Elizabeth had impounded the merchant fleet in 1588 to meet the threat of the Spanish Armada, while James had levied £48,555 in ship money in 1619. Charles himself had issued demands for ship money in 1628, although he had withdrawn the initiative in the face of local hostility at a time when the Forced Loan was still being collected.[43] However, levying ship money year in year out, when there was no emergency, and imposing it on inland counties, which had no shorelines to defend from attack by sea, was a stretch. Moreover, the levy hit further down the social scale than a parliamentary subsidy. Although there was some confusion as to who exactly was supposed to be assessed, most sheriffs appear to have taken personal (moveable) property into account, thus guaranteeing that those below the level of freeholders would become liable. In Essex, where 3,200 names were on the subsidy roll in 1640, 14,500 individuals were assessed for ship money.[44]

Charles had taken legal advice before imposing the levy and again before extending it inland, but such was his desire to be seen to be acting within the law that he wrote to the twelve judges in February 1637 to obtain a formal clarification. Although Justices Croke and Hutton expressed some doubts, all twelve judges affirmed that the king could levy ship money 'when the good and safetie of the king-dome in generall is concerned, and the whole kingdome in danger', and that the king was 'the sole Judge both of the danger and how the same is to bee prevented'.[45] The levy caused a few rumblings when it was first introduced in 1634. New Romney, for example—one of the Cinque Ports—refused to pay.[46] In London the lord mayor and alder-men were told by the lawyers they consulted 'that money could not reasonably be obtained from the people without infraction of the laws, by any way but the ordinary one of parliament', but the lord mayor was promptly summoned before the privy council and advised that the king had taken 'the gravest offence'; departing 'full of fear', he persuaded the City to make an immediate payment of £36,000. The Venetian ambassador observed that many thought the king was acting 'contrary to the laws of the realm', and 'certainly repugnant to the uses and forms observed by the people up to the present time'.[47] More complaints were heard when the tax was extended inland the following year, and protests increased in 1636 once it became appar-ent that ship money was to be permanent.[48] The earl of Warwick aired his misgivings to the king in person in January 1637, brazenly protesting that his tenants 'were all old and accustomed to the mild rule of Queen Elizabeth and King James' and unwilling to end their lives 'under the stigma of having…signed away the liberties of the realm', and urged the king 'to summon parliament'.[49]

Charles had initially been hoping to avoid a court case over ship money, but he subsequently changed his mind, opting to take on the Buckinghamshire squire John Hampden in 1637 for defaulting on a demand for £1 11s. 6d. at Great Kimble. The case was heard at the Court of Exchequer Chamber before all twelve judges in late 1637, with the final judgment coming in June 1638. Hampden's counsel argued that funds for the defence of the realm, in times of peace and in a non-emergency situation, required the consent of parliament, a position that was 'much applauded and hummed' by the spectators in court.[50] The presiding judge Sir Robert Berkeley, however, dismissed the idea that ship money was a subsidy (since the ultimate aim was to provide ships, which remained the property of the contributors, and not money), and maintained that there was sufficient danger on the high seas to warrant the king's action, even though the kingdom was not at war. More provocatively, he insisted that the defence counsel were mistaken in suggesting that the king could have nothing from his subjects 'but upon a common consent in parliament'. 'The law knows no such king-yoking policy', Berkeley proclaimed: no one could meddle with the king's prerogatives, which included the making of war and peace and requiring his subjects to make 'provision...for the defence of the commonwealth' in times of necessity. Lord Chief Justice Finch similarly insisted that the law gave the king the 'power to charge his subjects for the necessary defence and good' of the realm, and as the king was 'bound to defend', so were subjects 'bound to obey'.[51] The judges were divided, however, and decided for the crown by the narrow margin of seven to five. Justices Bramston and Davenport insisted that the king could demand only a service (provision of ships), not money, whereas Hampden was being prosecuted for a debt. Lord Chief Justice Hutton held that ship money was 'contrary to the lawes of the Realme' and launched into a vindication of the rights of parliament, which met 'with much applause of the people' in the courtroom. Citing the statutes enacted under Edward III stipulating that there should be annual parliaments, he wondered how it had come about 'that this kingdom which hath thus flourished by parliaments, should now forget her frequent kind of government by parliament'.[52] Clarendon, writing from the vantage of hindsight, thought the test case had been a mistake. Prior to the ruling, he observed, many had been willing to pay the levy, as 'a testimony of their affection' for the king; yet once a court of law had judged ship money to be 'a right', and upon such grounds as everyone knew 'was not law', the case was no longer that of one man but 'the case of the kingdom', and some now thought themselves 'bound in conscience... not to submit'.[53]

Despite all the concerns, ship money was paid. Between 1634 and 1638 some 90 per cent of the assessments came in, better than for any other contemporary levy. For 1635, the year that ship money was extended to inland counties, the final yield was £218,500, almost as much as parliament's five subsidies had realized in 1628–9. The collection of the tax broke down only in 1639–40, when Charles imposed an additional levy of coat and conduct money to clothe and equip the troops raised to put down the Scottish rebellion, thus placing an unrealistic administrative and economic burden on the country. Although the likes of Warwick and Hampden had tried to force the constitutional issue, most complaints about ship money centred around rating disputes—whether an individual had been fairly assessed, or whether he had to pay twice if he owned property in more than one county.[54] Yet there was a fear factor at work here: it was much safer to hide behind the technicality of a rating dispute than to accuse Charles of acting unconstitutionally. There is plenty of evidence to suggest that many doubted the constitutionality of ship money. Sir Simonds D'Ewes loyally fulfilled his duties as a ship money sheriff in Suffolk, but in the privacy of his own journal agreed with the view of Justice Croke in the Hampden case that 'this taxation was absolutely against law, and an utter oppression of the subjects' liberty'.[55] The Puritan lawyer Robert Woodford, shortly before the judgment in *Rex* v. *Hampden*, pleaded with God 'to ease us of this great and heavy taxe...and graunt us yet to see parliaments'.[56] Recording the reaction in Kent to the judges' statement on ship money of February 1637, Sir Roger Twysden noted that although 'some' accepted the government's position, believing that 'more could not be hoped for from a prince then in causes of weight to proceed by the advice of his judges', and 'all' agreed that 'if a kingdom were in jeopardy it ought not be lost for want of money if it were within it', 'others' thought that there was no emergency, that the precedents allowed for ship money to be imposed only on coastal towns, and that the matter could be decided only 'in a parlyament'; some even feared, Twysden observed, that if the king's counsel 'could make this good by law', Charles would be 'more absolute then eyther France or the great duke of Tuscany'.[57]

The high rate of the returns should be read as testimony to the government's determination to collect the levy rather than as public acceptance of its legitimacy.[58] Returns were, in fact, slow to come in, and there was widespread foot-dragging. The government had to bring pressure to bear on the sheriffs to ensure that the amounts demanded were paid, and the sheriffs in turn sometimes found it necessary to employ their own staff to collect the levy since local officials could not be relied upon. Collecting officers could distrain the goods of those who refused to pay, but in a display of solidarity neighbours often refused to buy the goods distrained, thus frustrating the government's attempt to collect revenue, while the defaulters themselves frequently retaliated by bringing lawsuits for illegal distraint.[59] There was much grumbling across the country. The Oxford don Thomas Crosfield recorded how rumours began to spread that on top of ship money the government was going to require 'that every woman wearing a greene apron must pay 4d, every one wearing a ring [blank] to the King'—a joke which nevertheless betrays a bitterness towards the government (and which Crosfield himself certainly did not find amusing).[60] In March 1638 a Gloucestershire woman named Elizabeth Mace complained that what for ship money and 'the many other payments that come dayly on, one upon another, she thought she would not be able to live'; when a neighbour said that 'the King must be served', Elizabeth's son Thomas riposted: 'If it be so, that the King must have all, I would the King were dead.'[61] That summer William Walker, chief constable of Kingsthorpe, Northamptonshire, allegedly voiced his opinion 'that the Shipmonie was an intolerable Exaction, Burden, and Oppression', that 'The Kinge was under a Law, as much as anie Subject', and that 'the Best, and most Honest' judges had not agreed with the judgment that ship money was legal, and predicted 'that the Shipmonie here in England, woulde cause the like stirres, that were now in Scotland, before it were longe'.[62] There was also active resistance to the collection of the levy. When officials came to distrain goods on two defaulters in Litchborough, Northamptonshire, in 1637, the householders disappeared while their wives locked the doors, armed themselves with prongs and clubs, and held the officials at bay until a crowd of 'women and boys' arrived to drive them away empty-handed.[63] The Venetian ambassador's secretary reported in July 1638 how the Hampden verdict was 'received with incredible bitterness and maledictions against the judges, as influenced more by authority than justice, with talk against the laws sufficient to cause a revolt among the people', and voiced his fear that 'following the example of the Scots, there was a disposition to revolution in England also, to force the king to observe the laws'.[64]

Ceremony-Mongers and Cathedralists

Charles's fiscal policy was, in a sense, working. By the end of the personal rule the crown's overall income was almost £900,000 per year, which even allowing for inflation was more than double the income James had enjoyed when he came to the English throne in 1603, and more than sufficient for the expenses of peacetime government.[65] Nevertheless, there had been a high political price, with Charles's initiatives generating discontent among considerable cross-sections of the population. It is perhaps true that had it not been for the Scottish crisis that developed at the end of the 1630s, and the English government's need to fight two costly campaigns against the Scots, Charles might have been under no fiscal imperative to call another parliament. Yet this is surely missing the point. Governments have to be able to respond to the unexpected, and Charles had not managed to put the finances of his kingdom on a sure enough footing so that it was in a position to respond to the Scottish crisis in an effective enough a manner—a point to which we shall return.

The most controversial policies Charles pursued in the 1630s related to the Church. By promoting the Arminian faction, led by William Laud, who became archbishop of Canterbury in 1633, it is normally argued, Charles ruptured the loose Calvinist consensus of the Jacobean Church and undermined the precarious balancing act whereby his father had been able to sustain relative peace in ecclesiastical affairs.[66] The Arminians were anti-Calvinists and particularly strident in their opposition to anything that smacked of Puritanism; they were also ardent ceremonialists and promoted a style of church worship which to many conventional Protestants smacked of popery. One distinguished Church historian has seen Laud as 'the greatest calamity ever visited upon the English Church'.[67] Laud has had his defenders,[68] although it is difficult to deny that the religious initiatives pursued in the 1630s proved both divisive and destabilizing. This was clearly not Laud's intention, nor Charles's in promoting him. What, then, were they trying to achieve? What was the logic behind their vision of Church reform, and why did they think that what they were doing was in the best interests not just of Church and state but also of the commonwealth?

As we have seen, the Arminians did not suddenly appear on the scene out of nowhere under Charles.[69] Avant-garde conformists—those whose devotional style emphasized ritual over preaching and who challenged the Calvinist doctrine of predestination—had been on the rise since the end of Elizabeth's reign and there were always anti-evangelical elements within the Jacobean Church. James himself had promoted a number of Arminians to bishoprics; indeed by the end of his reign the episcopal bench was already fairly evenly split between Calvinists and Arminians. James also harboured a deep suspicion of Puritans, openly embraced the language of anti-Puritanism himself on occasion, and had been happy to let court preachers fulminate against the supposed Puritan threat. Furthermore, James's strategy of striving for balance in the Church was already showing signs of failing prior to the end of his reign, as the controversy provoked by the proposed Spanish match forced him to silence Puritan preachers and to promote anti-Calvinists.[70] Charles had reason to believe he was following his father in his anti-Puritanism—after all, James in his *Basilikon Doron* had advised his heir to 'represse the vaine Puritane'. Moreover, as Charles was coming of age, it would have seemed to him that his father saw the future as lying with the Arminians. Certainly, with regard to ceremonies, Charles saw himself as following what was laid out in the canons of 1604.

Thus Charles did not regard himself as abandoning his father's vision for the Church. Nevertheless, by building on it and taking it to the next level, he did move the Church in a markedly different direction. It was under Charles that the Arminians secured control of the most important sees. Moreover, Charles promoted Arminians despite the fact that parliament in the late 1620s had specifically pleaded with him not to do so. In 1628, in spite of recent denunciations of Arminianism by the House of Commons, Charles opted to give promotions to Neile (Winchester), Laud (London), Buckeridge (Ely), Montaigne (York), Harsnett (York, to succeed Montaigne who died suddenly), Howson (Durham), and White (Norwich)—all of whom had received their first bishoprics under James—and to appoint to a bishopric for the first time the outspoken anti-Calvinist Richard Mountague (Chichester). Even though in 1629 parliament had cited Neile and Laud as enemies to the state, Charles proceeded to make Neile archbishop of York in 1632 and Laud archbishop of Canterbury in 1633: in other words, at the earliest possible opportunity Charles promoted the pair to preside over the two provinces of the English Church—which if not a deliberately provocative gesture, nevertheless reveals a king disinclined to try to build bridges. Charles also appointed Arminians to deaneries and headships of Oxford and Cambridge colleges, often a stepping stone on a career trajectory towards a bishopric. For example, Charles made Matthew Wren, one of the most notorious Arminians of the age, first Master of Peterhouse, Cambridge, in July 1625 (a post he held until 1634), then dean of Windsor in 1628, bishop of Hereford in 1634, of Norwich in 1635, and of Ely in 1638. When Wren made the last move, Charles translated Mountague from Chichester to Norwich to replace him. By contrast, Charles appointed just two Calvinists to bishoprics between 1625 and 1640: Joseph Hall, an eirenicist who held that the Roman Catholic Church remained a true visible Church, whom he made bishop of Exeter in 1627, and Barnaby Potter, who became bishop of Carlisle in 1629. Of the Calvinist bishops he inherited from his father, the only one to whom he showed any favour was Thomas Morton, the author of James's Book of Sports, and a defender of ceremonies, whom Charles promoted from Coventry and Lichfield to Durham in 1632.[71]

We have been using the label 'Arminians' because it is the one that contemporary critics used to describe the anti-Calvinist ceremonial-ists who rose to prominence in the Caroline Church—the implication here being that such ceremonialists supposedly agreed with the teachings of the Dutch Protestant theologian Jacobus Arminius (1560–1609), who was critical of Calvinist teachings on predestin-ation and believed that Christ's grace was potentially available to all penitent, true believers. To Calvinists, this seemed no different from the Roman Catholic Church's doctrine of universal redemption. Some would question, however, whether Arminian is really the right term. Laud tended to be reticent about his own doctrinal views, although at his trial in 1644 he denied that he was an Arminian; Neile, lampooned by his enemies for his anti-intellectualism, claimed not to have read three lines of Arminius's writings; and Mountague explicitly disavowed 'the name and Title of Arminian' in print.[72] Laudianism is an alternative, but also problematic, since it implies that Laud was the inventor of this style of churchmanship; yet there were Laudians before Laud and there were some clerics who outdid Laud in their Laudianism. There has also been debate as to whether the agenda being pursued was really Laud's or Charles's, although clearly Charles and Laud were working in harmony: Charles put Laud in charge because Laud had a vision for reform in the Church with which Charles concurred. Yet whether or not Laud was a fol-lower of Arminius, he was certainly an anti-Calvinist, believing that the Calvinist doctrine of predestination encouraged the view that the 'elect' could sin and still attain salvation and was thus tanta-mount to antinomianism. Nor should we take the Arminians' deni-als that they were Arminians at face value, since for tactical reasons they found it desirable to deflect the charge: the style of worship they encouraged, their emphasis on the beauty of holiness, and their exaltation of the clerical estate and of the importance of sacraments as channels of grace requiring clergy to administer (turning 'minis-ters' into 'priests') could all be squared with Arminian theology. Arminian remains a useful descriptive label, therefore. Furthermore, when we consider that Laud used his considerable ecclesiastical patronage to ensure that committed supporters were appointed as royal chaplains (a pool from which future bishops were recruited) and to the hundreds of parish livings in the gift of the crown, the term Laudianism conveys an essential truth.[73] Contemporary critics also referred to the Laudian clergy as 'ceremony-mongers' and 'cathedralists'.[74]

Charles and Laud between them saw it as their task to strengthen the Church in England by rebuilding the power and wealth of the clergy, promoting uniformity and decent order in worship, and clamping down on nonconformist activity that seemed to threaten schism and sedition. Although opponents of their religious reforms accused them of promoting innovations, the Arminians saw themselves as restoring the Church 'to the rules of its first reformation'.[75] To their mind, it was the Puritans who might 'more truly by termed *Innovators* in this Church'.[76]

There were many things that needed fixing with the Church. Rampant inflation over the course of the sixteenth and early seventeenth century had hit revenues, but most Church lands (what was left of them after the Reformation) had been leased at low rents for three lives (a hangover from the deflationary era of the late Middle Ages). In 1629, 1633, and 1634 the crown issued letters commanding all bishops, if not required at court, to reside in their sees so that they could look after their estates; those of 1634 added the stipulation that new leases should be for twenty-one years, renewable after seven to ten—not so much to allow rents to be adjusted more frequently to keep pace with market conditions (in practice it often proved difficult to increase rents on Church lands), but to guarantee a more steady stream of income from the fines paid when a lease was renewed. Such was the dire state of episcopal finances in Chichester that Mountague looked for technical faults in leases so that he could renew on different terms, an attack on existing property rights that could involve expensive litigation, often brought little noticeable economic benefit, and did little to win friends. Yet there were other motives behind such reforms. Laud thought shorter leases would require the gentry and yeomanry to treat the Church and churchmen with greater respect, if 'they must depend upon them from time to time for renewing their said estates'. On occasion Laud could prove personally vindictive. For example, he found a technical reason to challenge the lease of Whalley rectory that had been granted to the Ashton family in the 1620s because he thought their Puritanism made them unworthy tenants.[77]

There was a desperate need to improve the income of the lower clergy—something which the Puritans had been campaigning for since the beginning of James's reign. Over half the benefices (some 4,543) were worth less than £10 per year, and the vast majority (some 8,659) less than the £40 per year needed for a tolerable standard of living. Part of the problem stemmed from lay impropriations—the ownership of Church lands and tithes by the laity, which gave the laity not only the right to appoint to a living but also to set the stipend. Charles and Laud would have liked to restore all Church lands, although in practice there was little they could do. They did try to encourage lay patrons and local inhabitants to pay their clergy their due, allowing clerics to sue for tithes in the courts. In 1633 they dissolved the feoffees for impropriations—a group of clergy and laity with Puritan leanings who had been buying up parish livings to fund urban lectureships—using the funds thus confiscated for the maintenance of parish incumbents. There was also a political agenda behind these reforms: Charles and Laud wanted to curtail lay control over clerical appointments, and in particular to prevent Puritans from having the right to present to Church livings or lectureships.[78]

The Laudian desire to improve the estate of the Church was accompanied by an exalted view of episcopacy and of the clerical estate more generally. Many Arminians believed that not just monarchs but also bishops ruled by divine right, which to others seemed to undermine the Erastian principle upon which the English Reformation had been founded. Furthermore, both Charles and Laud felt that the clergy had a vital role to play in secular as well as ecclesiastical government, hence Charles's readiness to promote clerics to positions on the privy council and the magisterial bench. The trend in this regard had started under James, so Charles was once again doing no more than his father had done before him. Indeed, the major expansion in the number of clerical JPs had occurred in the latter part of James's reign, and the proportion was never high, reaching a peak of 7.6 per cent in 1626 and declining thereafter. But James's policy of ecclesiastical preferment had been more balanced; under Charles, giving the clergy jobs in central or local government meant giving those jobs mainly to Arminians and ceremonialists.[79]

The churches themselves also needed to be fixed. Many were in a highly dilapidated state, and some on the verge of imminent collapse. The rebuilding of the churches had begun under James, although it was accelerated under his son. In October 1629 Charles, at Laud's request, ordered the bishops to report on the condition of their churches, leaving it to parishes to raise rates to meet the costs of repairs. To give an idea of the scale of the undertaking, some 65 per cent of churches and chapels in the province of York were ordered to make repairs during Neile's tenure as archbishop.[80] Yet Laud did not just want to fix leaking roofs. He also wanted to beautify the parish churches, installing sumptuously decorated altars and elaborate stained-glass windows depicting scenes from Scripture, to replace those removed or destroyed at the Reformation. Again, these developments were not new; avant-garde conformists had in some areas already begun to beautify church interiors as a way of enhancing their ceremonialist style of worship. But the trend accelerated in the 1630s. When the church of St Katherine Cree in the heart of London was substantially rebuilt in 1628–31, at great expense, it was fitted with a railed-in communion table or altar at the east end, above which was an elaborate stained-glass window depicting Abraham sacrificing his son Isaac, the Old Testament prefiguration of God's later sacrifice of his own Son for the sins of the world—symbolism which could not help but convey a powerful visual message to communicants about the efficacy of sacramental grace (with its obvious Laudian resonance). St Giles-in-the-Fields, rebuilt in 1623–5 but then shut by Laud upon his becoming bishop of London until he reconsecrated it in 1631, was lavishly refurbished under its Laudian rector Dr Roger Maynwaring: the chancel, now reserved territory for 'the priests and subdeacons', was separated from the nave by a large screen on which there were winged cherubim and statues of Peter, Paul, and Barnabas; the sanctuary was richly adorned with carpets and painted cloths; and there were at least eighteen stained-glass windows depicting not just Old Testament patriarchs, prophets, kings, and apostles but also the Virgin and Child and Mary Magdalene, while over the south-west door there was a representation of Christ with two angels and clouds full of cherubim. There were similar developments in the provinces. Viscount Scudamore's new parish church at Abbey Dore in Herefordshire, rebuilt between 1632 and 1635 from the ruins of an old Cistercian abbey that his family had acquired following the dissolution of the monasteries under Henry VIII, had a marble altar set at the east end and railed off—the original abbey altar, which for years had been used for making cheese and salting meat, was cleaned up and reconsecrated—an altar cloth and silver-gilt plate to adorn the altar, walls painted with biblical texts and the Ten Commandments, an impressive carved screen, and extensive stained-glass, with the east window showing the Ascension of Christ, with eleven of the apostles, John the Baptist, and Moses.[81] As the last example indicates, some of this rebuilding and refurbishing was the result of lay initiative. However, some of the laity's past efforts at interior church design came under attack. For example, Laud and Neile insisted that the elaborate high pews erected by wealthy parishioners in many parishes be demolished, on the grounds that it was wrong for parishioners to be seated higher than the communion table and thus 'above God Almighty in his owne house'. They further demanded that existing pews be turned to face east, and that pews which blocked the view of the communion table from the aisle be removed.[82]

Charles and Laud also revived the project to rebuild St Paul's Cathedral, abandoned by James towards the end of his reign for lack of funds. In 1631 Charles established a commission to elicit contributions, supposedly 'voluntary', although in reality threats and intimidation were often used to elicit donations, while in 1637 Laud persuaded Charles to donate all the fines levied by High Commission. Inigo Jones designed the west front in the grand Palladian style, with a portico supported by Corinthian pillars—the Puritan medical doctor John Bastwick said it looked like he was 'making a seat for a priest's arse to sit in'—and adorned by statues of Charles and James. Work was still ongoing when the personal rule came to an end in 1640.[83]

Charles and Laud further wanted to restore order and decorum in church services by insisting on adherence to practices prescribed by the Book of Common Prayer and the Canons of 1604, with the clergy wearing the appropriate ecclesiastical vestments and enforcing ceremonies such as kneeling for communion, bowing at the name of Jesus, and using the sign of the cross in baptism. To the godly, such ceremonies had no Scriptural foundation and were thus popish inventions that should have been eradicated at the Reformation, but for generations their scruples had been accommodated by the indulgence of varying degrees of nonconformity. There had been some attempt to enforce ceremonial conformity under James, but it had been patchy, and much depended on the priorities and energies of the local bishop and clergy. As a result, in some communities some parishioners might receive the communion kneeling, while others took it standing. Sometimes it could be the minister who took the lead in encouraging nonconformist practices, leaving parishioners who wanted to worship in strict conformity to the prayer book little option but to seek their spiritual edification in neighbouring parishes. The situation was a mess, and there seems to have been some pressure for reform from below. For example, in November 1629 forty-one Essex clergymen, claiming to be 'the Conformable part of the Cleargie'—Essex was a divided county, with a strong Puritan presence—petitioned Laud, then bishop of London, urging him to force 'the Irregulars to Conforme' with 'the lawfull Ceremonies of our Church', that there 'may effectually bee wrought a general Uniformitie'.[84]

Particularly controversial was Laud's stance on the communion table. The Elizabethan injunctions of 1559 had required that communion tables be kept at the east end but brought into the chancel for the celebration of communion. The Book of Common Prayer, however, seemed to imply that the tables should stand permanently in the body of the church and stipulated that they should point east–west, rather than north–south or 'altar-wise'. Most parishes had adopted the latter practice, to avoid the hassle of carting the table back and forth for communion services, although this had the disadvantage of leaving the table exposed to all and sundry who might happen to come into the church during the week. Laud noted incidents of parishioners doing their business on communion tables, boys leaving their hats, satchels, and books upon them, glaziers knocking them full of nail-holes, and even of dogs urinating against them.[85] According to an anonymous Essex libel of c.1636, the minister of St Nicholas, Colchester, Theophilus Reynolds, pressed his parish to build a rail around 'About the Tabell...because the doges Against it should not pise'.[86] At Tadlow in Cambridgeshire on Christmas Day 1638 a dog was able to come into the church during the sermon and take the loaf of bread that had been prepared for the holy sacrament; although parishioners rescued the loaf from the dog, the minister thought it not fit to be consecrated, meaning that Christmas communion had to be forgone that year.[87] Laud wanted the communion table situated permanently at the east end of the church, placed altar-wise, and railed in to protect it. To the godly, this savoured of magical territory reserved for the priest and made holy communion seem more like the medieval mass. According to one Suffolk man, railing in the communion table was 'but a dance before Popery', part of a longer-term project to make us all of the queen's religion, which, he believed, was 'the thing the Bishops aime at'.[88] The ceremonialists also encouraged bowing before the altar, which even to many mainstream Protestants (those who might not have harboured Puritan sympathies) savoured of idolatry.[89]

Placing communion tables permanently at the east end was not strictly speaking a Laudian innovation of the 1630s. It had long been the practice in royal chapels (although there were no altar rails in royal chapels until the mid-1620s), while some parish churches had kept their communion tables at the east end and even railed in. The Laudian claim that it had also been the tradition in the cathedrals, however, cannot be taken at face value. When Laud moved the communion table to the east end of Gloucester Cathedral in January 1617, he alleged that this was the use 'in all or the moste part of the cathedrall churches of the realme', yet in fact only one other cathedral is known for certain to have had an east-end table at this time, namely St Paul's in London, and then the table had only been moved to the east end for safety reasons following the collapse of the steeple in the fire of 1561. Neile at Durham followed Laud's lead later in relocating the communion table to the east end in 1617, although altar rails were not to be erected at Durham until c.1626. Matthew Wren's subsequent claim that Norwich Cathedral had altar rails since 'Time out of Mind' was also a misrepresentation.[90] There is thus no doubting that the scale and intensity of the drive that occurred under Charles to make parish churches turn their communion tables altarwise was innovatory. The process began piecemeal from about 1627–8. It became a national policy after 1633, following Charles's ruling in the case of the London church of St Gregory's by St Paul's, which stipulated that parishes should follow 'the cathedral mother church'.[91] There was also a trend towards replacing the old wooden tables with stone altars, while across the country the railed-in altars increasingly came to be adorned by candlesticks, crucifixes, and communion plate (in the eyes of Puritans another sign of a return to pre-Reformation practices). With the Laudian takeover of the universities, several college chapels were refurbished and 'dressed up after a new fashion'. At St John's, Cambridge the Master, William Beale, installed a new altar frontal with an image of Christ on the cross, a large crucifix on the back of the altar, a large canopy above the altar painted with angels, and around the walls large gilt-framed pictures depicting the life of Christ. At Peterhouse, under the Mastership of Neile's former chaplain John Cosin, there was an elaborate silver and gilt altar full of crucifixes and relics and 'much adoration given at the naming of the bare name of Jesus, with hat and knee', while in most college chapels one could hear thanks being offered to God 'for saints departed' and for the Virgin Mary (Plate 11).[92]

The Laudian clergy, then, sought to invoke an elaborate system of 'gestural display', in order to relocate sacredness within the church as the house of God, and salvation in the sacraments at the altar rather than in the pulpit.[93] When Laud re-consecrated the London church of St Katherine Cree in January 1631 after its extensive rebuilding, immediately upon entering the building he fell down 'upon his Knees, with his Eyes lifted up, and his Arms spread abroad', uttering the words 'This Place is holy, this Ground is holy, In the name of the Father, Son and Holy-Ghost I pronounce it holy'. He then approached the railed-in altar and 'bowed towards it several times'; he 'pronounced Curses upon those that should afterwards prophane that Holy Place'; and then following a sermon consecrated the sacrament, making 'several lowly Bowings' in turn towards the altar, the bread, and the wine. It was an incident later to be used by parliament as evidence of Laud's 'inclination to introduce Popery'.[94]

Laudian ceremonialism was accompanied by a greater emphasis on Church music, with organs and choirs. Again, this was not an entirely new development: the early Protestant hostility to liturgical music had softened by the later sixteenth and early seventeenth centuries, with music defended as having the potential to draw more people to church and even to stir the minds of hearers to the worship of God. But the Laudians extended previous practice: in most English cathedrals, for example, spending on Church music in the period 1625–40 reached a level not seen since Mary Tudor's reign (1553–8), while some Laudians began to condemn the psalm-singing by the congregations as not only the tuneless babbling of the ignorant but as irreligious.[95] There was also a concomitant de-emphasis on preaching—motivated again, in part, by a suspicion of the Puritans. In 1629 the crown issued injunctions ordering that catechizing should replace Sunday afternoon sermons and that lecturers read the common prayer book before service, as a way of trying to eradicate Puritan nonconformity. Once more, however, Charles might point to the fact that his father had issued similar orders back in 1622.[96]

What made the Laudian reforms so controversial was the rigour with which they were enforced at the local level. The government encouraged bishops to send in regular reports from their dioceses and to take tougher action on nonconformist practices.[97] Laudian enthusiasts such as Mountague in Chichester and Wren in Norwich drew up lengthy visitation articles designed to enforce ceremonial conformism, stamp out nonconformist practices, and ensure the upkeep of church buildings. Wren's visitation articles of 1636, for example, comprised nine chapters broken down into 142 sections and containing in total 897 questions. Mountague circumvented the local churchwardens, who had a tendency to be economical with the truth, by sending out his own visitors to discover the true state of affairs in the parishes in his diocese.[98] Neile conducted a metropolitical visitation of his northern province of York in 1633–4 and Laud of his southern province of Canterbury 1634 and 1637 to try to ensure the reforms were more widely enforced.[99]

Not only Puritans but also many conventionally pious Protestants saw the Laudians as promoting popish superstitions and even turning the Church back towards Rome. A few Arminians may indeed have been crypto-Catholics: the Caroline divines John Pocklington and John Normanton, for example, converted to Rome before the end of their lives.[100] Most were not. Indeed, a need to distance themselves from suspicions of popery led many Laudians to launch strong attacks on the errors of the Church of Rome. Yet the fact that such moves were at times strategic did not necessarily mean they were insincere. Laud himself had defended the Church against Rome in a conference with the Jesuit John Fisher in May 1622, publishing his views in expanded form in 1639, and he was outspoken in his criticism of the attendance of English Catholics at the queen's private chapel. The personal rule in fact saw a stricter enforcement of the laws against Catholic recusants, not least because of the crown's shortage of money: by the mid-1630s recusancy fines were yielding over £20,000, more than three times as much as they had averaged in the previous decade.[101] Stricter enforcement, however, merely served to convince the godly that recusancy was on the increase: in 1636, for example, a petition from the citizens of Norwich charged that Bishop Wren's actions were encouraging popery, citing as proof the fivefold increase in the presentments of recusants at quarter sessions.[102]

The Laudians protested that their ceremonies were different from those of the Catholics, though outwardly similar, since they meant different things: popery was not using the sign of the cross, but worshipping the cross; kneeling in the service of Baal was idolatry, but 'when used to God' it was not.[103] Indeed, Laudian divines frequently had recourse to conventional conformist defences of Church ceremonies. All Churches had to observe some ceremonies in the worship of God, and it was left to the Christian prince to determine what those ceremonies should be. Thus refusing to observe the ceremonies, which in themselves were things indifferent (that is, neither essential for nor prejudicial to salvation), was disobedience to the king. Giles Widdowes, the rector of St Giles, Oxford, believed that the lawless, kneeless, schismatical Puritans 'should be better Subjects to God, and to his Immediate Vicegerent in these Churches, the King, than to be Prime defenders of Breaking the peace of Orthodoxe Reformed Religion'.[104] The Shropshire cleric Peter Studley complained that the Puritans violated 'their loyalty to their Prince, by renting the unity of the Churches peace', and that such 'Non-subjection to lawfull Authority' could not be tolerated: 'Every Kingdome divided against it self', the gospel of Matthew had pronounced, would 'be brought to desolation', and if the prince were not vigilant in his efforts to stop the 'Gangraine' of 'division and schisme' that had 'lately crept into the heart of the Church', 'Anarchy and confusion' would 'breake in upon us'.[105] Elizabethan and Jacobean conformists had defended Church ceremonies following much the same logic; indeed the classic defence of ceremonies under James had been made by the Calvinist Thomas Morton.[106]

It is possible, therefore, to see Laudianism as the outgrowth of a particular conformist (one might even say 'Anglican') tradition within the Elizabethan and Jacobean Church. It is certainly probable that this was how Laud and Charles saw it. However, a number of qualifications need to be made. There was a distinctive Laudian twist to the defence of ceremonies. The Laudians also tended to see them as rooted in the traditions of the Church, not just as established under Elizabeth and James, but dating back to biblical times, and thus sanctioned by apostolic and ecclesiastical traditions and customs.[107] According to Pocklington, just as 'Christ was Christ before he was born of the blessed Virgin...so were Christians, and Christian Sacraments, and Christian Ceremonies, before Christ was borne or the Jewes either'.[108] As William Quelch, the rector of East Horsley, Sussex, put it in a sermon preached at the metropolitical visitation of Archbishop Laud at Kingston-upon-Thames in July 1635: 'seeing the word is silent concerning ceremonies, and speakes nothing of them in explicite termes, where may we looke for certain direction and resolution in that case, but from the power of the Church, and from the authority of her pastors?' If anyone sought to challenge the legitimacy of our ceremonies, he continued, we should follow the teachings of St Paul: 'let the custome prevaile in the name of God, and let no man presume to speake against it.'[109] Samuel Hoard, preaching at Laud's metropolitical visitation at Chelmsford in March 1637, set out 'to justifie the authority of our Church, in requiring an uniforme subjection' to the 'good orders therein established' and to 'her just authority in these things'. By Church, he made it clear he meant its 'Pilots', namely the 'Bishops', and claimed that the 'heads of the Church' had the power to ordain, change, abolish, or even add ceremonies and rites 'for the begetting of an honourable respect to God's ordinances, or the stirring up of our dead devotions in his service'. Hoard clarified that 'our Rulers', who were the 'judges in these matters', comprised both the king, who was 'supreme', and the 'Prelates of the Church', who were 'subordinate'. Yet there was, to say the least, a tension here: if ceremonies ultimately were sanctioned by apostolic and ecclesiastical tradition, and by the authority of the Church, then to what extent could they be said to rest on the authority of the monarch? Laudian divines may well not have perceived a contradiction; to their critics, however, they seemed to be undermining the royal supremacy. For instance Hoard, like all ceremonial conformists, insisted that 'obedience...to these smaller things of the law', to ceremonies that were things indifferent, was in itself 'no... indifferent thing', since St Paul had taught that every individual, 'without exception', was obliged 'to yeeld obedience' to those that ruled over them. Yet Hoard went on to claim that the persons meant in this context were 'Bishops and Prelates of the Church', explaining that there was 'a twofold seate' of authority in the state, 'a seate of civill government, belonging to Kings and Judges', and 'a seate of doctrine and spirituall Jurisdiction, proper to the priests and heads of the Church'.[110]

Although most Laudians would have professed to oppose popery, the attitude of Laud and his followers towards the papacy and the Church of Rome differed from that of conventional Calvinists under Elizabeth and James. Thus the Arminians, while accepting that the pope was an anti-Christ, tended to deny that he was *the* anti-Christ. 'The markes of the great Antichrist', Mountague had written in 1625, 'fit the Turkish Tyrannie every way, as well as the Papacy', while Laud similarly thought 'the Pope and the Turke' were 'our two great Enemies'. Furthermore, the Laudians were ready to accept the Church of Rome as 'a true Church', albeit 'not a sound Church of Christ', and thus as 'part of the Catholick, though not the Catholick Church'.[111] Laud believed that by being appropriately conciliatory he could win English Catholics over to the established Church.[112] Hence his desire to promote order and unity and to encourage a style of worship which Roman Catholics would not have found too alien. Laud observed in his own polemical work against the Jesuit Fisher that 'no One thing' had 'made Conscientious men more wavering in their owne mindes, or more apt...to be drawne aside from the sincerity of Religion professed in the Church of England, then the Want of Uniforme and Decent Order in too many Churches of the Kingdome'.[113] The Regius Professor of Divinity and Provost of King's College, Cambridge, Dr Samuel Collins, preached in June 1635 'that we should meet the Papists half way, both in preaching and in practice'.[114]

The style of worship promoted during the 1630s may indeed have tempted a few Catholics to conform to the established Church: Laud was to boast at his trial in 1644 that he had personally converted twenty-one.[115] However, many English Catholics, instead of thinking that the time had come to turn Protestant, thought that the English Church was coming back to them.[116] The Catholic John Southcot welcomed Laud's elevation to Canterbury in 1633, predicting that the times would 'every day grow better and better for Catholickes'; he was soon convinced that Laud's de-puritanization of the English Church would encourage the spread of Catholicism and make it easier to convert people to the Roman faith. Nor was it only English Catholics who believed that the Caroline Church was tending Romewards. The pope himself thought so, and twice offered Laud a cardinal's cap.[117] One Catholic priest, writing from Madrid in 1639, observed how the 'protestant heretics' in England were 'making more and more reforms every day in religious matters', encouraging 'auricular confession', exalting 'the cult of the holy virgin and of the saints', decking out 'their temples with images', and adorning 'their altars with wax candles and other ornaments', while their preachers and ministers 'vest themselves as we do, and use ceremonies not very different from ours'—all of which was 'approved by the archbishop of Canterbury and other prelates'.[118]

The Laudians seemed to many to be more concerned about the threat of Puritanism than they were about the dangers of popery. They were especially concerned about what they took to be the inherently subversive nature of Puritanism. In a sermon preached at Whitehall on 21 January 1638, Heylyn warned that the Church faced 'dangers...alike on both sides', from the Church of Rome and from 'a more close and secret enemy', namely those Protestants who resisted the 'unity and uniformity' of the English Church: both aimed 'at the same mark, the subjugating of the Church, and the chief Sovereignty of the State'. This latter group had 'introduced into the Church', Heylyn claimed, 'the ancient Heresies of the Novations, Donatists, Aerians, Priscillianists, and the Apostolic', 'not to say any thing of those dangerous principles which they are known to hold among them against peace and government', and thus it was 'High Time assuredly both for Prince and Prelate to have an eye upon them'.[119] What made the situation all the more troubling was that Puritanism seemed to be on the rise. Studley not only accused the well-to-do in town and country of patronizing the Puritans but even alleged that the Puritan gentry and tradesmen threatened and bullied their tenants and dependants into complying 'with them in their vaine opinions'.[120] Puritanism appeared to be on the rise in part because the

Caroline regime had a particularly broad definition of Puritanism. Writing in 1631, Giles Widdowes claimed that there were 'ten severall Puritanieties', each of which 'distinctly differs from an other': the Perfectionist, the factious Sermonist, the Separatist, the Anabaptist, the Brownist, the Familist, the Precisionist, the Sabbatarian, the Antidisciplinarian, the presuming Predestinatist.[121] In 1641 the parliamentarian propagandist Henry Parker complained how 'broad the devil's net' had become under Laud 'in the vast application of this word'; whereas 'Puritans...were at first Ecclesiasticall only, so called because they did not like a pompous or ceremonious kinde of discipline in the Church like unto the Romish', now 'by a new enlargement of the name', the world was 'full of nothing else but Puritans, for besides the Puritan in Church policie, there are now added Puritans in Religion, Puritans in State, and Puritans in morality'.[122]

Some Laudian divines seemed to acknowledge in their sermons that they were setting new standards for conformity and reclassifying as 'contentious' people who were practising their religion as they had long practised it. Thus Quelch, preaching before Neile at his primary visitation at Kingston-upon-Thames in 1628, observed how 'the customes of the Church' had 'through the stubborne humours of contentious men...growne so obsolete and out of custome in most places'. Yet to Quelch's mind, 'upon the issue of this Skirmish' between 'Contentions and customes' hung 'all the peace and liberty of the Church'; for if 'Contention' should 'win the day...then farewell the Church and all her customes'. Against those who thought contention over 'a bare ceremony' was a small matter, Quelch urged his auditors to consider 'what mischief may grow upon the Church by the least quarrel once begun'. Besides, he continued, 'obedience or disobedience in a small matter was not to be counted a small matter'; 'be the thing commanded never so small', he intoned, 'it cannot excuse the disobedience'. Using what was a common metaphor of the age, Quelch insisted that 'this Cockatrice's egge'—i.e. contention—'must be cracked in the shell, that it may not bring forth a flying serpent'.[123]

To their critics, the Laudians were encouraging not just a false religion but also a propensity to sin. Especially controversial in this regard was Charles's Book of Sports of 1633, which allowed for certain lawful recreations after service on Sundays and other holy days, such as dancing (by either men or women), archery and other sports, May games, Whitsun ales, morris dancing, and the setting up of maypoles. Puritans were outraged, believing the Sabbath should be spent in godly contemplation. The Book of Sports was a royal initiative, not a Laudian one. Moreover, Charles simply reissued his father's Book of Sports, first published in Lancashire in 1617 and then extended nationally the following year. Once again, therefore, one might argue that Charles was doing no more than continuing James's policy. The crucial difference was that the Jacobean Book of Sports had never been strictly enforced: in many areas local magistrates, fearing the disorders that might accompany popular pastimes—anything from drunkenness, to illicit sex, acts of violence, and fatal mishaps—continued to suppress Sunday games and revels.

Charles certainly had no desire to license disorder or to encourage the profaning of the Sabbath, and he upheld the prohibition on illegal sports such as bear- and bull-baitings, interludes, and bowling. But he was concerned that if people were denied their lawful recreations on the one day of the week they were free to exercise they would grow discontented, become so unfit as to be no use in time of war, and might idle away their free time in alehouses or at conventicles. It was a local controversy that prompted Charles to take action. In 1632, in response to complaints from local JPs, the judges at the Somerset assizes had issued an order banning church ales and revels, which they required ministers to read once a year in their parish church. Laud was upset that ministers had been required to publish the order without the consent of their bishop, and reported the matter to the king, who demanded the order be revoked. Charles's position was that if disorders sometimes arose at church ales, they should be dealt with by the local JPs; the solution was not to ban church ales outright. The issue ultimately centred on who had the right to decide whether or not a ban should be imposed, and both Charles and Laud had cause to feel concerned that their authority was being usurped. Hence Charles responded by confirming his father's stance on this issue, insisting that he wanted the laws observed not just in Somerset but in the whole of the kingdom—nothing too unreasonable here, one might think. Since Charles's Book of Sports was simply a republication of his father's, it republished James's charge that it was 'the Puritanes and Precisians' who were the trouble-makers. Charles also required the bishops to ensure that the Book of Sports was published in all parishes in their respective dioceses, thus firmly identifying the Caroline episcopate with the indulgence of Sunday pastimes—though we should not forget that it had been a Jacobean bishop, Thomas Morton, who had drafted the Book of Sports in the first place. What distinguished Charles's from his father's policy was that under Charles the bishops were more determined to enforce the Book of Sports.

The issue did not neatly divide Arminians and Calvinists: some Calvinists supported the Book of Sports, while some Arminians enforced it less strictly than others. However, the policy was to alienate more than just Puritans. Clergy who were far from being strict sabbatarians but who nevertheless had qualms about appearing publicly to endorse mixed-dancing on the Lord's Day were forced into having to decide between their conscience and being disobedient to authority. As the seventeenth-century historian John Rushworth observed, 'it proved a snare to many Ministers very Conformable to the Church of England'.[124] Some tried to side-step the issue by refusing to read the Book themselves but having a clerk or churchwarden do so; some bishops connived at such practices (including Laud himself), while others did not. A spate of suspensions for refusal to read the Book followed. The net effect was to make some appear disloyal who had no desire to be so. And by stigmatizing the opponents of Sunday recreations as 'Puritans and Precisians', the government made many appear to be Puritans who were not.[125] The Puritans themselves, predictably, saw Laudian ceremonialism and the defence of Sunday sports as part and parcel of the same disturbing trend to undermine the true religion. For example, in November 1635 the Ipswich minister Samuel Ward preached a sermon 'against the common Bowing at the Name of Jesus, and against the King's Book of Sports', alleging 'that the Church of *England* was ready to ring Changes in Religion, and the Gospel stood on tip-toe, as ready to be gone'. He was hauled before the High Commission, suspended, and when he refused to give a public recantation, thrown into prison.[126]

The Reception of Laudianism

There was a logic to what Laud and Charles were doing. The Church did need reform, and their reforms were arguably in tune with the spirit of the Elizabethan settlement, or at least with their reading of that settlement. Some effort needed to be made to reach out to the English Catholics, especially at a time of confessional conflict in Europe, lest there remain a disgruntled fifth column within England should the country become embroiled once more in a serious conflict with one of the major European Catholic powers. Recent European history had also revealed the dangers of allowing divisions within the Church at home, and shown how nonconformity and schism, if not checked, could undermine the state. Moreover, it was undoubtedly the case that the Puritans had, in some areas, been a disruptive force. Puritans were critical of what they took to be the sins of their less than godly neighbours, and when in power at the local level they had a tendency to embark on moral crusades to try to reform popular culture. In short, Puritans were antagonistic, confrontational, and often bitterly disliked. Laud not only felt that his reforms were necessary and in the best interests of the country, he also had cause to believe that they would be popular.[127]

Our impression of the reception of Laudianism has been distorted by the fact that hostility to official policy tends to be more visible to the historian than quiet acceptance of it. We should be careful not to read the complaints and actions of a noisy and discontented minority as indicative of the mood of the nation at large. We must also recognize that opposition to one element of the Laudian programme should not necessarily be read as antagonism towards all of it.[128] The Laudian support for Sunday pastimes and traditional festive culture, for example, was welcome to many in certain parts of the country: church ales, revels, maypoles, morris dancing, and village sports, for instance, underwent something of a revival in the West Country in the 1630s.[129] It is likewise probable that a ritualized and ceremonial style of worship that emphasized the beauty of holiness, taught the lessons of Scripture through images on stained-glass windows, and held out the prospect of salvation for all, would have held some appeal to a predominantly agricultural society where illiteracy remained widespread in many parts, and would have been more appealing than a religion of the Word that emphasized the reading of the Bible in private and high moral accountability, and taught that both the damned and the saved were predestined from birth. Indeed, one of the reasons why Puritans were so alarmed by Arminian ceremonies was because they thought too many of the 'simple people' were 'inveigled and begiled' by them.[130] But such ceremonies appealed not just to simple rustics. In England's second city, Norwich, some had become accustomed to a decorous altar-centred style of worship since first introduced under Harsnett and thus were not opposed to Wren's reforms; they nevertheless served to heighten religious tensions in what was already a religiously divided city. Likewise in other cities and towns, such as Bristol, Gloucester, Chester, and Leominster, tensions between the godly and their opponents meant that the Laudians were able to find a lay constituency. Even in London, where the enforcement of Laudian ceremonialism undoubtedly proved highly contentious, there is evidence of some degree of support for communion rails, placing the table altar-wise, and the beautification of churches.[131]

It seems likely that the attack on Puritans resonated with popular sensibilities to a certain degree. Quite a few anti-Puritan ballads circulated during this period, suggesting (perhaps) that latent anti-Puritanism continued to be prevalent, and on occasion the government found itself having to prosecute individuals guilty of disturbing the peace by contriving and spreading anti-Puritan libels.[132] One manuscript libel from this decade rehearsed the by now highly familiar contours of the anti-Puritan stereotype at great length. 'A Purytan is an imperfect kynde of a Christian', it opened; indeed, 'some will have him an Uncircumcized Jewe...For hee affects much the Jewish Religion'. 'Hyppocresye is his best Tutor,' it continued, 'which hath soe well Trayned him upp in the Noble Scyence of Offences, that nowe hee scornes, eyther to yield unto Truthe, Sence, or Reason, His greatest Adversarye, whome hee prosecutes, with deadlye hatred, is all Conformitye to good Orders, which hee onelye Trembles att, not For Feare, butt For wante of Conscyence.' His religion 'he makes wholie to Consiste in longe prayers to little sences, longe Sermons, to little profit, longe wynded exercises, to little Judgment, long graces to small purpose, And longe Journyes, to sanctifye his Saboath, Butt it must bee to...a Man after his owne humor, a pryme Man, in the Congregation of his Presbyterye'. Furthermore, there were several types of Puritan, our author averred: the 'Lyon Purytan', who lives 'Machiavell's Aphorismes' and takes 'Libertye in Rayleinge against Bishopps'; the 'Bull Beiffe Puritan', who 'loves not to worcke' unless on the Sabbath; the 'Goate Puritan', who will 'wayte on his Holye Sister' and retire with her 'into the most secret places', except in the summer, when a 'convenyent Haycocke' serves just as well. Other types included the 'Sheepe Puritan', 'peacocke Puritan', 'Turkye Puritan', 'your lappwinge or Bastard plover Puritan', the 'Cuckowe Puritan', 'Crockodyle Puritan', 'Serpentyne Puritan', and 'goose Puritan'. 'From all Puritans therefore delyver us, gratious Saviour', our anonymous satirist concluded, 'For of that Trybe there are more Jewes, then Hebrewes, or Christians'.[133] The Puritans themselves seemed to believe they were unpopular. Back in 1617, the Suffolk Puritan and future governor of Massachusetts Bay, John Winthrop, had observed in his spiritual diary how 'in this way there is least companie', since those who embraced it were 'despised, pointed at, hated of the world, made a byworde, reviled, called Puritans, nice fooles, hipocrites, hairbrainde fellowes, rashe, indiscreet, vainglorious, all that naught is'.[134]

Often when Puritan clerics ran into trouble with the authorities it was because local parishioners had reported them. When an unlicensed preacher named Walker fell foul of the High Commission for delivering a sermon deemed to contain scandalous and offensive reflections upon the Church and state in St Leonard's Eastcheap in February 1634, the curate of St Leonard's, Henry Roborough, complained to his parishioners how 'some come to Church to catch and insnare the poore Minister and to bring him before Corrupt men or corrupt Judges in theis corrupt tymes'.[135]

In those areas where Puritans had a powerful presence at the level of local government, they could be responsible for orchestrating an aggressive campaign of moral reform and social regulation that was equally as divisive as Laudian attempts at reform. The Puritan elite of Dorchester initiated an impressive campaign of social and moral reform in the aftermath of the great fire which destroyed the town in 1613, which they saw as punishment from God for the community's sins. Puritan townsmen, constables, and churchwardens, inspired by the godly preaching and activism of the rector of Holy Trinity, John White, clamped down on swearing, drunkenness, fornication, and Sabbath breaking; on the positive side, they significantly increased the funds available for poor relief and promoted a fund-raising drive to endow a local hospital, new almshouses, and a municipal brewhouse to control the local drink trade and also to help finance Dorchester's other charitable institutions. Although the drive came from the town elite and the more prosperous middling sort, it could not have been as successful as it was without the support of some humbler types, who served in the lowlier parish offices, as beadles or nightwatchmen, while among the poorest sorts there was clearly some appreciation of the efforts that were being made to alleviate their plight. But there was also considerable resentment towards prying and snooping constables. In 1637 some young wits composed a satirical 'Song of the Constables', which soon became a popular refrain around the town, poking fun at each constable in turn who was known to be overly strict on the sins of the poor. Others felt that the town's reformers were fining the poor for trivial offences such as drunkenness merely to line their own pockets. One enterprising town rebel took it upon himself to rescue people from the stocks whom he felt were being unfairly punished.[136]

Measuring the degree of support for the Laudian initiatives is thus no easy task. Clearly there was some, and perhaps much more than usually recognized. If there had been limited support, the Laudian reforms would not have been so successfully implemented, and thus not have proved as divisive as they did. Local research has shown that although resentment at the Laudian ceremonies could run high in some communities, in others they aroused little opposition. In Staffordshire and north Shropshire, for example, despite some grumblings and foot-dragging, the Laudian reforms were often implemented without recorded problems. But they heightened tensions where tensions already existed, especially in areas where there was a strong Puritan tradition.[137] It is also likely that the rise of Laudianism—the knowledge that various forms of Puritan nonconformity were now deeply out of favour with the regime—afforded greater opportunity for anti-Puritans in the parishes to come forward to denounce Puritans in their midst. In other words, Laudianism might have proved so destabilizing not because it was extremely unpopular, but because it did have a certain popular appeal.

Having said this, many people—not just Puritans and the hotter sort of Protestants, but also conventional parish Anglicans, the lukewarm in religion, and even rabid anti-Puritans—often had some reason for disliking certain aspects of Laudianism. The economic implications of the Laudian reforms hit people's pockets. Repairing the church fabric and installing altar rails could be expensive. In 1635 alone over £1,300 was spent on repairing churches in the East Riding of Yorkshire; for the more populous West Riding the figure was £4,000. Many parishes across the land found themselves paying on average three times as much per year on church repairs in the 1630s as in the 1620s. The levelling of high pews or removal of seats from the chancel upset those who had invested in them. Moving over from long-term to short-term leases so as to make it easier to keep rents in line with inflation upset tenants on Church land. Moreover, the rigour and inflexibility with which some of the Laudian reforms were introduced showed an insensitivity to local needs and customs. Metropolitan or diocesan interference with the way parishes had always run their affairs was seen as a threat to local autonomy, to the ability of those on the ground to negotiate disagreement and conflict in a way that could most realistically preserve local harmony.[138]

The Laudian innovations in the Church, therefore, might antagonize people for a whole range of practical reasons, not all of which we would necessarily describe as being 'religious'. Yet those who criticized the Laudians tended to do so in the main because they held them responsible for promoting religious error and popery. One Colchester churchwarden thought that 'turneing communion tables into Altars, and placeing them altarwise' was 'a popish practise and backslideing to popery'.[139] The curate of Lilbourne in Northampton-shire thought his diocesan, Bishop Francis Dee of Peterborough, was 'a superstitious bishop, for that he bows to the altar and at the name of Jesus'.[140] The Puritan diarist Nehemiah Wallington complained how 'our lordly bishops and prelates' had 'endeavoured to corrupt the Church with errors', how they had 'troubled the whole land . . . with falsehoods' and 'moved troubles by their establishing of Popish cere-monies, by binding the consciences of men to the observation of them, as setting up of altars, images, and crucifixes, bowings, cring-ings, and the like'.[141] The bitterest venom was reserved for Laud. One libel pinned to the south gate of St Paul's Cathedral in the summer of 1637 charged that the devil had let out the church 'to the Archbishop for service, etc., to damne the soules of men'; another, affixed to Cheapside Cross in the heart of London, accused 'the Arch-Wolf of Cant.' of 'persecuting the saints'.[142] Some people undoubtedly thought that Laud really was a Catholic. In May 1634 London apprentice Richard Beaumont alleged that Laud 'had a crucifix in his howse and many other pictures, and mayntayned poperie'.[143]

* * *

Charles and Laud had not created the religious tensions that existed in Caroline England. Yet by seeking to address them in the way that they did they had succeeded in creating further antagonisms. In the past, religious difference had been accommodated by tolerating a diversity of practices, turning a blind eye to various forms of noncon-formity, allowing local communities to negotiate religious pluralism in the way that they saw fit. It was a strategy that had hardly suc-ceeded in creating consensus. Yet the strategy pursued in the 1630s merely served to inflame matters further.

Some Arminian clerics could be quite confrontational towards those members of their congregation who would not worship in the desired way. At Durham in the mid to late 1620s the dean, John Cosin, would allegedly hector worshippers 'like a mad man', scolding parishioners who did not pray facing east, thrusting them out of the church 'by their head and shoulders', and calling them 'pagans' for not observing 'the Ceremonies of our Church'. On one occasion he screamed at some 'Gentlewomen of the best rank' who remained seated for the Nicene Creed, 'Can ye not stand you lazie sows', call-ing them 'durty whores', and 'taking them by the armes, and tearing their sleeves to raise them up'.[144] At Rickmansworth in Hertfordshire in 1638 the newly appointed churchwarden, Mr Olden, boasted that 'he would make the Puritans to come up the middle alley on their knees unto the rails'; those who refused, we are told, 'were persecuted'.[145] At Radwinter in Essex the minister, Richard Drake, refused to let over a hundred parishioners take Easter communion in 1640 'because they would not come up to the Rail', even though 'they all presented themselves kneeling in the Chancel'. Drake's parishioners had been giving him a hard time. One came to receive communion 'now kneeling on one knee, now on another, now on neither, in a very scornfull and uncomely manner'; perhaps understandably, Drake lost his cool, shouting 'Your Knavish tricks will do you no good'.[146] Those opposed to the Laudian initiatives could be equally confrontational. For example, in Essex, although some parishioners were prepared to bow to the altar or receive at the rails, others showed their disapproval of the Laudian style of worship by keeping their hats on and remaining seated when they were supposed to stand.[147] Such evidence hardly suggests an age of peace and felicity. Worrisome times indeed.

10

···············

Contumacious Troublers and Disquieters of the Peace

During the 1630s, Charles embarked upon an ambitious policy of reform in both Church and state and many of the initiatives he pursued proved highly controversial. The personal rule flouted contemporary expectations of how things were normally done: Charles funded the government in an unconventional way, he promoted a style of worship in the Church that ran counter to the way many people had been used to worshipping, and although he arguably never acted unconstitutionally or exceeded his legal powers, the path he pursued was certainly perceived by many to have worrisome implications for the constitution and the rule of law. His initiatives thus caused resentment (in some quarters) and provoked opposition. Yet any government intent on reform is bound to ruffle some feathers, and in Charles's defence it could be argued that he pursued policies that he genuinely believed were in the best interests of his country, that many of his policies were designed to advance the welfare (both secular and spiritual) of his subjects, and that some of his policies had a certain popular appeal. How, then, did Charles deal with critics of his policies? To what extent was this a repressive regime?

Earlier Whig historians saw Charles I as a king who rode rough-shod over public opinion, imposed strict censorship over the press to prevent the articulation of critical dissent, and ruthlessly pursued those who disagreed with his reforms through the prerogative courts of High Commission and Star Chamber—note here the draconian punishments (heavy fines, corporal punishment, mutilation, and per-petual imprisonment) meted out to the likes of Henry Burton, John Bastwick, and William Prynne for publishing works critical of the Laudian bishops. No one would accept such a crude image of Caroline tyranny any more. When punishing dissidents, Charles saw himself as merely seeking to stamp out sedition, which any government in any age would reasonably be expected to do. If Charles failed to carry the public with him, it might be argued, it was because he did not do a good enough job in selling his policies to his people—a political failing, perhaps, but hardly evidence of a desire to tyrannize over his subjects. Yet even this view of a king who was insensitive to his public image or to the need to cultivate public opinion has been challenged by recent research. A number of questions, therefore, need to be addressed. How did Charles I seek to manage public opinion? How strict was censorship? And what was the fate of those who dissented from his policies?

Censorship and the Public Sphere

The first myth to be dispelled is that Charles was a king who was reluctant to engage with the public sphere, or that he did not know how to do so. As seen already, there is plenty of evidence of Charles in the 1620s seeking to court opinion out-of-doors. He may have thought that as a divinely ordained monarch he was under no obligation to account for his actions to his subjects. He nevertheless did so: note the proclamations he issued in the late 1620s explaining why he had acted the way he had with regard to his parliaments. It is true that in the 1630s the government tried to clamp down on the public sphere. Yet this is hardly surprising. Engagements with the public sphere throughout the Tudor–Stuart period were always sporadic. The preference for all regimes in this time period was to try to limit public controversy; if this could not be achieved, the government might seek to engage with the public sphere temporarily in an attempt to rally public opinion, but once the need had passed it would seek to close it down again. Charles II pursued such a strategy with brilliant success towards the end of his reign. Government Whigs in the early eighteenth century were to do the same.[1] Charles I was willing to appeal to public opinion at the time of the Scottish crisis of 1638–40, and again on the eve of the Civil War in 1641–2.[2] Even the notion that Charles withdrew from his people during the personal rule is misleading. Charles did make a number of royal progresses during this time, most notably in 1633 when he went to Scotland to be crowned; he also touched for the King's Evil on numerous occasions; and government spokesmen did engage in religious controversy in print in an effort to explain and justify certain of the Caroline religious initiatives.[3] The question is thus less whether or not Charles was willing to engage with the public sphere but rather whether the way he sought to manage public opinion was effective.

The key from Charles's point of view, as it was for all monarchs in the early modern period, was to try to control the viewpoints to which his subjects would be exposed, in order to prevent the sort of speculation that might lead to the development of subversive ideas. Hence Charles's directives to preachers in 1628 urging them to steer clear of controversial subjects, on the grounds—as one clerical defender of them put it—that the raising of 'deep, needlesse and end-lesse questions, too hard for the people's capacitie', tended rather to encourage 'strife then edification'.[4] On the surface it might seem a sensible and reasonably benign position, and both Charles and Laud professed a desire to see all controversial preaching stopped and Cal-vinists and Arminians 'proceeded with indifferently'.[5] Yet the govern-ment's policy was not quite as innocent as such self-representations would suggest, since in practice Charles's directives tended to be enforced in a partisan manner—to silence Calvinists rather than Arminians.[6]

When works appeared critical of Caroline ecclesiastical policy, the government did not shy away from responding in kind and exploit-ing the media in order to get its position across. During the mid-1630s the government engaged a number of Laudian divines—among them Christopher Dow, John Pocklington, Bishop Francis White of Ely, and most notably the canon of Westminster and royal chaplain Peter Heylyn—to produce pamphlets vindicating the Book of Sports, the altar policy, and the measures taken against Puritan extremists. The mid-1630s also saw a surge in the publication of visitation ser-mons supporting Laud's vision of reform in the Church and extolling the beauty of holiness. Yet if the government was prepared at times to engage in a debate in the media over the merits of its policies, its ultimate objective—quite naturally—was to get its views across and discredit or suppress those of their opponents; it was not in the busi-ness of promoting a fair and open debate. Take the altar controversy, for example. Heylyn and others became involved in an extended debate in print with Bishop Williams of Lincoln over moving com-munion tables to the east end and railing them in, with both sides employing a combination of reasoned arguments and inflammatory polemic in their efforts to sway public opinion. But ultimately what determined the outcome of the battle was not who made the most compelling arguments in print. Williams was preparing his latest response to Heylyn in 1637 when a pending case in Star Chamber

(Williams had been accused earlier in the decade of revealing state secrets and then trying to suborn the king's witnesses against him) finally caught up with him, leading to the seizure of all his books and imprisonment in the Tower.[7]

This brings us to the question of censorship. If the government was having to engage propagandists to combat criticism in print, we might wonder how tight control over the press could have been. Any notion that the Laudians sought to silence the godly appears to be belied by the fact that numerous godly books continued to be published throughout the 1630s on what were accounted controversial topics. Indeed, some historians have doubted whether Charles did indeed seek to impose tighter control over the press, pointing out that he worked within existing law and that his government was concerned just to censor particularly egregious works that threatened to undermine the public order.[8]

So how was the press controlled at this time? There were basically two ways. The first was through the system of pre-publication licensing, whereby books had to be approved in advance by ecclesiastical commissioners and/or privy councillors, with the Stationers' Company accountable to the privy council for the works they produced. The other was by the laws of treason and seditious libel, whereby authors, publishers, and printers could be held accountable after a work had been published. Although such offences could be prosecuted at common law, since Elizabeth's time it had largely become the task of High Commission and Star Chamber to seek out and punish those who produced illicit works or works that were regarded as religiously or political dangerous. Both Elizabeth and James had sought to control the press, and neither had been coy about punishing those who had overstepped the line. In 1579 John Stubbs had had his right hand cut off for writing a book criticizing Elizabeth's proposed marriage to the duke of Anjou, while in 1590 John Udall was sentenced to death for writing against the bishops, and although eventually reprieved he was to die in prison.[9]

Charles may have worked within existing law, but English law is based on precedent, and thus constantly open to transformation on the basis of judicial interpretation. The 1630s saw both High Commission and Star Chamber expand their authority over seditious writing and define a greater range of books as religiously or politically objectionable through the creative redefinition of older precedents and practices. The Elizabethan High Commission had primarily concerned itself with Catholics and Protestant separatists attacking the Church of England. Charles's High Commission, by contrast, took action against authors who were clergy in the Church of England. A similar expansion of traditional practice can be seen with regard to Star Chamber's handling of sedition. Previously certain crimes might have been regarded as seditious—a seditious libel, for example—but during the personal rule sedition itself became the crime, or stirring up the people to discontent as if there were just cause to rebel. The difference is subtle but significant, since it enabled the government to proceed against not only those who specifically advocated rebellion but also against those who merely opposed liturgical changes in the Church of England, because on the government's reading such opposition was intrinsically disloyal. Thus although Charles used the same means of controlling the press as had his predecessors and worked within existing law, he nevertheless did things that his predecessors had not done. As a result, the 1630s did see a rise in censorship. Indeed, the most recent historian of the Caroline press has calculated that Charles imposed censorship five times more often than James and ten times more than Elizabeth.[10]

Yet there were limitations to what the government was able to achieve—hence the continued publication and licensing of godly works. There were a number of reasons for this. First, it was still possible to find sympathetic licensers: prior to the death of Archbishop Abbot in 1633, Abbot's chaplains had served as ecclesiastical licensers and were happy to authorize Calvinist works. The work which first got Prynne into trouble with the authorities—his *Histrio-Mastix* of late 1632 attacking stage plays—had in fact been licensed for publication (although the chaplain who did so claimed he had never been shown the whole text and what he had seen had been altered before going to press).[11] When Laud was translated to Canterbury his own chaplains introduced more restrictive licensing criteria; however, Laud's successor at London, William Juxon, was more indulgent and allowed his chaplain to license a wider range of materials. Secondly, many of the godly works printed in the 1630s were in fact reprints of earlier publications; since the printer already owned the title, there was little the government could do to prevent republication, until the issue was eventually addressed by a Star Chamber decree of July 1637 stipulating that books already licensed were not to be reprinted unless their licence was renewed. (One of the first books to fall foul of this provision was Foxe's *Acts and Monuments*.)[12] Thirdly, even though the Laudians were stricter about new godly works, they did not seek total suppression. Rather than stop moderate Calvinists from going into print, they preferred to massage Calvinist texts to make them compatible with the Laudian outlook, either by purging the text of passages deemed objectionable or by inserting a Laudian preface. It was much better to have notable Calvinist divines appear to endorse the Laudian position than to turn them into martyrs for opposing it. Rather than allow themselves to be compromised in such a way, some Calvinist authors chose self-censorship and opted not to go into print at this time.[13]

Thus Caroline censorship worked in complex ways, but there is no doubt the press was being more tightly controlled than it had been for a long time. However, the control was far from complete. Those who were determined to get their views into print in unadulterated form could always opt to have their works printed in Scotland or the Low Countries, and smuggled into England, as an increasing number did. Moreover, the government was unwilling to embrace more repressive forms of censorship, such as raiding bookshops or destroying presses, not least because of its commitment to working within existing law.

High Commission

A similarly complex view emerges when we look at how the government responded to religious nonconformity and political dissent. Again attention has focused on the way Charles used the prerogative courts of High Commission and Star Chamber to discipline both ecclesiastical and political dissidents, thereby circumventing normal common law procedures. High Commission had the right to tender the hated *ex officio* oath, whereby the accused were made to give evidence against themselves, and to impose not just ecclesiastical censures, such as penance and excommunication, but also fines and imprisonment. Star Chamber was made up of privy councillors as well as common law judges, its proceedings were held in private, with no indictments, no right of appeal, no juries, and no witnesses, and although the court could not impose the death penalty it could impose various forms of corporal punishment, including mutilation. Both courts ended up being so widely hated that they were abolished in 1641. Let us, then, consider them in turn.

It would be wrong to characterize High Commission as an instrument in the hands of the state for the repression of Puritans. In the first place, High Commission was not solely concerned with the godly opponents of Laudian reform. In April 1632 Joseph Harrison, vicar of Shustoke, Warwickshire, appeared before the court charged with frequenting alehouses, keeping company with beggars, being drunk during divine service, christening illegitimate children, conducting clandestine marriages, speaking opprobrious words against the bishop of Coventry and Lichfield, and being 'a professor of the Art of Magick and in particular charmeing of piggs'. Harrison's punishment was severe: he was deprived, degraded (i.e. unfrocked), imprisoned, excommunicated, fined £500, and ordered to pay costs, yet few would disagree with the bishop of Rochester's contention at the trial that 'this was a bad cause'. In May 1632 a case was brought against one Mr Barker for printing a defective bible: not only was it printed on very poor quality paper, but Exodus 20:14 read 'Thou shalt commit Adultery' and Deuteronomy 5:24 'the Lord hath shewed us his glory and his great asse'.[14] Secondly, the majority of prosecutions were not initiated from above: some 80 per cent of the cases that came before the High Commission in the period 1611 to 1640 were brought by local parishioners, not by the government's ecclesiastical agents.[15] Indeed, it may well have been that the Caroline regime's known hostility to Puritan nonconformity served to encourage parish conformists or anti-Puritans in the localities to come forward to denounce those whose behaviour they felt was disruptive of local social harmony. Finally, we need to disabuse ourselves of any notion that this was a regime that adopted a policy of zero tolerance towards dissent. The generally accepted view was that those who erred out of ignorance should be treated leniently. On learning that several ministers in the province of York had failed to read the Book of Sports, for example, Neile told them to read the bishop of Ely's book on the matter and think again.[16] The High Commission certainly did use its powers of search to hunt down conventiclers, including not only out-and-out separatists (of which there were very few in England at this time) but also ministers in Church livings who held conventicles on the side. It also prosecuted clerical nonconformity, such as refusal to comply with the Common Prayer Book or the canons. Nevertheless, the total number of clerical deprivations in the 1630s was quite small—only about thirty ministers. James's subscription campaign of 1604–6, by comparison, had resulted in some eighty deprivations.[17]

Revealing insight into the business of High Commission and the sort of issues the court was being asked to address is provided by the trial of John Viccars, rector of St Mary's, Stamford, Lincolnshire, of November 1631. The case cannot easily be seen as the result of some sort of Laudian or Arminian clampdown from above. Viccars was first in trouble in 1628, when some of his own parishioners reported him to Bishop Williams of Lincoln (himself a critic of Laud), who rebuked Viccars and urged him to mend his ways.[18] When Viccars did not desist, they petitioned the crown. Charles passed on the petition to his privy council, who in turn referred the case to the High Commission, at a time when the archbishop of Canterbury was still George Abbot (a Calvinist who was supposedly soft on Puritan dissent). Although Laud was present at Viccars's High Commission trial in his capacity as bishop of London, Abbot was as hostile towards Viccars as anyone. Viccars did hold strange views. One of the doctrines he allegedly preached was 'That if a man knowe his wife after her Conception with Childe, or when shee is past Childe bearinge, it is both murther, and adulterie', since 'hee spent his seede in Vaine'; it was also adultery 'if a man laie with his Wife in her Monethlie tearmes' or '3 daies before the sacrament' or '3 daies after'.[19] He also supposedly said that those who did not preach twice every Sabbath would 'frie in hell' and those who did 'not heare two sermons everie Sabbath' were 'in the Estate of Reprobation'; he taught that the common prayers were not sufficient to salvation; kept conventicles; was known to single out individual members of his congregation for attack in his services in church, calling them dogs or devils; and held that 'if any temporall Magistrate did prove naught and wicked, hee was to bee put out of his Office' (an attack on the aldermen of Stamford).

The prosecution represented Viccars as a disruptive force in the local community, claiming that Stamford had 'been in peace for a longe tyme' before Viccars came to St Mary's, but now, 'by this man's manifoulde miscarriages, and false doctrines, their peace was disturbed'. Yet Viccars clearly had a local following. When summoned to appear to answer for his views, he appointed two fasts and gave a number of sermons, one of which went on for six or seven hours, attended allegedly by 'a great Company' that had come 'thither out of the Countrey'. A number of witnesses came forward at his trial to testify that Viccars was 'a man of good life, and Conversation, and of good fame and Reputation, and well esteemed of amonge the more sober and honest sort of people'; the witnesses against Viccars, they alleged, were 'Capitall Enemies and adversaries' of Viccars, or relatives of 'the said Enemies', and many were 'great swearers, and...Common frequenters of Tavernes, and Alehouses' who were at 'tymes distempered with drinke'. It was a charge, as one might expect, that was vigorously denied by the prosecution: 'Wee have 2 or 3 Knights, 6 or

7 Gentlemen, and diverse preachers, Parsons of other Parishes, diverse Aldermen', they protested, and while 'some [were] his Enemies' others were 'indifferent men'.

Viccars was found guilty, deprived and degraded from the ministry, fined £100, and imprisoned. The fact that he was a man of honest life and conversation just made him more dangerous in the eyes of those who sat in judgement: it was not drunkards who were able to spread such damnable and seditious doctrines, the civil lawyer and judge Sir Henry Marten pointed out at the trial; heretics were always of austere life. (Marten was a moderate, who opposed the Laudian altar policy and who as dean of the Arches had shown himself sympathetic to Puritan nonconformity.[20]) The commissioners' condemnation of Viccars highlighted certain aspects of the anti-Puritan stereotype prevalent in early Stuart England. For example, in giving his judgment Marten said: 'It appears by your Carriage there lies at your hearte notable pride…noe matter with you for breakinge the peace of the Church, noe matter for the doctrine of the Church…Here is your pride to prefer your opinion to the Judgment of the Whole-Church.' The bishop of Rochester, John Bowle (a champion of altar rails), said that Viccars's views about how magistrates who drew the sword against the godly might be opposed were the views of Mariana the Jesuit. The bishop of St David's, Theophilus Field, complained how Viccars had turned 'God's Oratorie the Pulpit into a place to vent his Malice upon the poore people of Stamford'. And although all the high commissioners were equally outraged at Viccars's behaviour and views, some did think he might be reformable. For example, Bishop White of Norwich (a notorious Arminian who was later—following his translation to Ely—to write in defence of the Book of Sports) thought that Viccars should not be deprived but merely suspended from the ministry for seven years, that he should use that time to read the canons of the Church, the Book of Common Prayer, and the learned works of Hooker and Whitgift, and if at the end of that time he showed himself to be 'reformed', he should be free to exercise his gifts again. Field thought that Viccars should be barred from the pulpit for just three years and that if he repented should be allowed to resume his ministry, albeit not in Stamford, where he had already caused too much division. Indeed, at first the commissioners were evenly split on whether or not Viccars should be deprived or merely suspended; one subsequently changed his mind to tip the balance in favour of deprivation.

The closeness of the call highlights the fact that the High Commission was no kangaroo court. The commissioners on the whole might have been unsympathetic to Viccars's style of Puritanism, but (accepting their preconceptions and prejudices) they seem to have been determined nevertheless to give Viccars's a fair trial.[21] At the same time, the closeness of the call demonstrates that simply counting deprivations is a somewhat crude measure for assessing how oppressive this regime might have seemed to contemporaries. Although the number of outright deprivations was relatively small, there were many more suspensions and excommunications. There were many who were intimidated or harassed but who ended up escaping formal punishment. Hundreds of godly ministers were hauled before the High Commission and other ecclesiastical courts for relatively minor offences, such as omitting aspects of ceremonial dress or practice: for example, some 115 ministers from the diocese of York alone found themselves in trouble with the Church courts between 1632 and 1640.[22] Moreover, the leaders of the Church in the 1630s created an oppressive atmosphere, in which many of the parish clergy, not just the more extreme Puritans but also those who regarded themselves as conformable, felt under the threat of persecution. The intensity with which the Laudian bishops sought to stamp out nonconformist practices varied from diocese to diocese, meaning the godly were more vulnerable in some areas than others, but also leaving those clergy whose local bishop for the time being proved more indulgent unsure about when the screws might be turned. The Laudian hierarchy preferred to use threats and other forms of harassment, rather than the ultimate sanction of deprivation, fearing that too harsh a drive to stamp out nonconformist practices would alienate public opinion. Yet many clergy were left in no doubt what the authorities could do to them if they did not toe the line. For example, one newsletter writer reported in February 1637 that whereas it had been claimed that Wren had deprived sixty ministers in the diocese of Norwich, it was now being said that they had been restored by the king.[23] Such accounts might suggest a reasonably indulgent king, or at least a king struggling to keep Arminian zealots under control. But they also point to the degree to which many clergy lived under constant fear, unsure of what might be their fate.

Numerous clergy found themselves grappling with their consciences over whether they could comply with the Laudian ceremonies without falling into idolatry. Many in the end opted for a reluctant compliance, out of a deeply ingrained sense of obligation to remain obedient to authority and not to risk disturbing the peace of the Church, or a sense of loyalty to their flock, or even a fear of losing their livelihood and being unable to support their families. By definition, such types were not schismatics and many would never have thought of themselves as Puritans. It was in this sense that many ministers came to feel that they were living in 'the dayes of persecution'.[24] Significantly, the Laudian clergy themselves acknowledged that those who were disciplined by the ecclesiastical authorities felt they were victims of persecution: hence their eagerness to defend themselves from the charge. Christopher Dow insisted that 'those that refused to obey Authority' were 'justly punished, and their punishment no cruelty or unjust persecution'.[25] It was wrong 'to brand' the punishments meted out to 'unruly ministers' with 'the disgraceful name of persecutions', Samuel Hoard protested in his visitation sermon of March 1637; his plea to 'leave off…these scandalous criminations', and 'not to make justice odious with such nick-names of tyranny and persecution' nevertheless reveals how some people were choosing to style this regime.[26]

Moreover, clergy were being hauled before the authorities for doing things that they had always done. Take the High Commission proceedings against Henry Roborough, curate of St Leonard's Eastcheap in London, in 1634—Roborough was summoned to appear before the court on three occasions between April and June. Apparently it had been observed by 'many intelligent persons' who had heard Roborough preach that he taught 'that Christ maketh intercession for the elect and for the elect only'; condemned as 'false' the opinion 'that Christ dyed for the Synnes of the whole world'; 'declaimed much against the corruption of the tyme…wherein Heresie and superstition doth abound'; complained of 'the persecution of the Saints in theis tymes'; 'omitted to preach…Christ crucified, faith, repentance and good works'; and digressed from his texts to spend most of his time 'in bitter invectives against the Church and State Ecclesiasticall and the doctrine and Discipline of the Church of England…thereby endeavouring to drawe the people to dislike and contempt therefore' and 'into Schisme and faction'. Roborough denied the charges, claiming that his words had been taken out of context and misunderstood. If Roborough's answers to the charges can be taken at face value, then it does seem to be the case that people were getting the wrong end of the stick, or latching on to particular expressions that Roborough used and immediately taking such offence that they failed to take in his qualifications and contextualizations. Tellingly, Roborough saw himself as a conformist, one who had subscribed according to the canons and who had always prayed for the continuance of the existing government in Church and state as by law established. He also protested in his defence that he had served as curate of St Leonard's Eastcheap for seventeen years and no one before had ever called him into question 'for publishing or defending anything contrary to doctrine of the Church of England'. In the end the case against Roborough was not pursued, although he remained under suspicion of being 'inconformable' for the remainder of the personal rule. Yet his experience is illustrative both of the way that clergy who believed themselves conformable suddenly found themselves being hounded in the 1630s and of an altered atmosphere whereby those who felt alienated or offended by Roborough's particular brand of Calvinism felt empowered to take action to try to silence such a man.[27]

Those who preached against the Caroline vision for the Church ran the risk of provoking the ire of the authorities. Take the example of Richard Spinks, fellow of St John's, Cambridge, brought before the High Commission for a sermon he had preached in his college chapel in May 1632. Spinks had begun his sermon by attacking images: the only image in the church, he intoned, should be the minister, 'who if hee bee paynefull and religious is...a liveinge Image of God by whose exemplary carriage the people should learne to frame and fashion their lives'. He had condemned those who were 'mechanically striveinge to Convert tables of wood, into Altars of stone': recalling how the Swiss of Basel had pulled 'their Images out of their Churches' and 'brought them into the publick market place there to bee devided for fuell amonge the poore people', he had said it would be 'a happie thinge for this Church and Common wealth if all those Reliques of superstition were burnt together, rather then such Combustions, such hartburneings should bee fomented and maynetayned amonge us'. This was fairly indiscreet, to say the least. Reflecting on the Caroline (and indeed early Stuart) tendency to employ clergymen in civil office, Spinks had then averred that 'To conferre a place of Civill Government...upon a preist were to reconcile thinges in their owne nature incompettible [sic], to Joyne those together whom god himselfe hath put asunder'. He had also claimed that 'all ministers' were 'successors to the Apostles', thereby seeming 'to take away all distinction' among the clergy 'and to make a paritie between the degrees of Byshopps and Presbiters'.[28] The authorities did not want to make Spinks a martyr, however; they wanted a recantation, an admission from him that he was in error. It was their way of reclaiming Spinks for the fold, one might even say of helping to make him better informed. Yet it was also a way of making an outspoken critic of the regime acknowledge that the regime's policies were legitimate. Spinks was forced into a humiliating climbdown. He apologized for implying there was a parity between bishops and presbyters and renounced any such meaning; agreed that it was false to suggest that the clergy served 'by divine institution' since this was 'derogatory to the power of King and Church and State'; confessed that he had misinterpreted his sources when arguing that it was unlawful for men in holy orders 'to medle with secular Authoritie'; and admitted that he had 'prophanely termed the beautifull Ceremonies of the holy Church Reliques of Superstition' and 'wished them all burnt rather then the obstinate spirits should bee reduced to the obedience of the Church'. Nevertheless, Spinks clearly resented being forced to recant, as his initial examination revealed, claiming that what he had preached had been said in a college chapel, which he thought had the privilege of a sanctuary, and besides the 'informers' against him were so 'carefull and vigilant...for the good of the Church' that, 'according to their usuall custome', they had been absent 'that morning from Chappell', so that he was 'rather accused of their owne dreames'.[29]

Outspoken critics of Caroline religious policy could land themselves in serious trouble. When Peter Smart preached against innovations at Durham in 1628, he was brought before the High Commission in both the northern and southern provinces, forced to answer articles against himself on oath, deprived of his living, degraded, fined, and imprisoned.[30] Nathaniel Barnard of Emmanuel College, Cambridge was hauled before the High Commission for giving a sermon at Great St Mary's in May 1632 in which he accused those who endeavoured to bring 'the superstitions of the Church of Rome into our worship of God'—such as 'high altars, Crucifixes, and boweing to them'—of being 'enemies' and 'traitors' to the nation; against all such traitors, he urged, 'let us take up armes', pausing for a while before explaining that he meant 'the armes of our church, our prayers'. Barnard was suspended, excommunicated, fined £1,000, and imprisoned. He was to die in jail.[31]

Nor should we create the impression that it was only the godly clergy who experienced a sense of persecution. The laity suffered as well. In Puritan Colchester, for example, where there were a number of zealous clerical supporters of the Laudian drive for ceremonial conformity (a reflection of the near-monopoly of clerical patronage of the gentry who did not share the religious preferences of the corporation), parishioners found themselves hauled before various ecclesiastical courts for failing to pay the parish rate or contribute to the construction of altar rails, refusing to kneel, or absenting themselves from church or failing to take communion (on conscientious grounds, because they disapproved of the Laudian ceremonies). Ultimately the town clerk opted to flee to the Netherlands, while the town's lecturer escaped to New England. An anonymous libeller accused one local minister, Theophilus Roberts of St Nicholas, of having 'turnd to be a persiecutor' like Bonner, the bishop of London responsible for the drive against Protestant heretics under Mary Tudor.[32]

By its strategy for policing the Church, then, the High Commission was fomenting division. It is true that many prosecutions were initiated from below, although this was in part because the regime created a climate in which it was easier for those who disliked what they thought of as 'Puritan' practices to come forward and denounce the Puritans in their midst. It is not that there were no religious tensions in the localities in the first place; there clearly were. However, the government's way of tackling them served to enflame them further.

Star Chamber

The most serious political offenders were brought before the court of Star Chamber. Star Chamber had emerged in the later Middle Ages essentially as a court of equity, intended to ensure the fair enforcement of the law when justice could not be had at common law, and it had been established to make sure that powerful men, whom the common law courts might be too afraid to convict, would still be held accountable. Over time its functions and role had evolved, and it was the Tudors who first used it as a weapon against political opponents of the crown, a practice continued under James. Charles's Star Chamber was arguably no more brutal than his father's. In February 1624 Star Chamber had found a London-based Catholic lawyer guilty of saying that 'K. Henry 8 did pisse the Protestant religion out of his codpiece' and that Queen Elizabeth was a 'bastard' and in hell with her father, and ordered that he have both his ears cut off, his nose slit, his forehead marked with B for blasphemy, be whipped about London, and fined £10,000—a censure, it was said, which Protestants approved of as 'just'.[33] Nor did Charles's Star Chamber merely deal with Puritan critics of the crown. In May 1638 one Mr Pickering, a Catholic, was sentenced to be fined £1,000, whipped at the pillory in both Westminster and London, have his ears cropped, and imprisoned during the king's pleasure for saying: 'the King was a papist in his hart as wel as hee and that Protestants were damned heretickes and…it would have bin a brave sight to have seene 200 or 300 of them in there red gownes flyinge in the ayer…at the time of the Gunpowder Treason'.[34]

Star Chamber continued to function as a court of equity under Charles, helping to provide justice on behalf of the poor and oppressed. In Michaelmas term 1628, for example, it fined Sir John Rous and Sir Thomas Jenkinson, two justices of the peace for Suffolk, £200 each for wrongfully condemning two women to be imprisoned and whipped. It fined Jenkinson an additional £200 for using the power he had with the bench to have witnesses for the defence suppressed. The court wanted to award damages to the women, who were poor and had lost 'all their Creditt' by having their reputations destroyed, although it was not clear that technically the women were entitled to damages because they were not parties to the suit, just relators—the case against Rous and Jenkinson had been prosecuted by information. However, the Lord President went over the legal precedents and concluded that in such a case the relators were deemed sufficient parties as to be entitled to damages, and so the court awarded the two women £200 each.[35] In Michaelmas term 1631, Star Chamber prosecuted William Archer of Southchurch, Essex, for not bringing his corn to market the previous spring and thereby forcing an increase in the price. The judges concluded that such forestalling had contributed to the previous year's famine and that Archer—as Laud put it at the trial—was 'guilty of a most foule offence…grynding the faces of the poore', and recommended that Archer be fined 100 marks and pay £10 to the poor.[36] In a tract published in 1634, the common lawyer Robert Powell praised Charles for his efforts to prevent 'the dearth of corne and victuall' and 'his just and speedy proceedings in his high Court of Star-chamber against Fore-stallers and Ingrossers, the common Catterpillers of our Kingdome'.[37]

Although Star Chamber was a prerogative court, and therefore operated outside of the common law, that does not mean its proceedings were arbitrary or that it was not tied to rules or procedures. In fact a number of treatises were produced in the late Elizabethan and early Stuart period, and reissued at the beginning of Charles's reign, outlining exactly how Star Chamber was supposed to function, what sorts of cases it was supposed to hear and what punishments it was allowed to inflict.[38] Like any other court in a regime that could legitimately claim to be functioning according to the principles of law and upholding the rule of law, Star Chamber judged each case on its merits, according to the evidence, and cases would be dismissed if the evidence was not there to convict. Some accused of subversive activity were let off. For example, in the 1620s a case came before Star Chamber in which one Philip Hayne of Exeter accused local JP Ignatius Jordan (or Jurdain) of setting himself up as the president of a 'schismatical consistory' of 'nonconforming ministers', which convicted Hayne of adultery and sentenced him to be whipped and sent to the house of correction. The prosecution argued that Jordan had acted 'in derogation of the ecclesiastical law' by erecting a consistory to proceed in a judicial manner against adulterers, and accused Jordan of being a schismatic and a Puritan. But Star Chamber was presented with a commendation saying that Jordan and the other ministers were conformable to the rites and discipline of the Church, that Jordan himself was one of the most diligent justices in the city and extremely charitable towards the poor, and that there was no evidence of a consistory but that Jordan, as a local JP, had inflicted punishments on a known adulterer that were in accordance with the customs of the city. Star Chamber therefore fined Hayne £40 for 'false clamour' and in addition ordered him to pay £40 damages to Jordan.[39]

Having said all this, undoubtedly Star Chamber was intended to be an instrument of terror. As contemporary legal opinion acknowledged, it was to be used when the common law did not allow harsh enough penalties. Its punishments were designed to be exemplary rather than penal. No one expected those convicted ever to be able to pay the heavy fines the court imposed; the point was to terrify the general population and to discourage others from committing similar offences.[40] Moreover, Charles's Star Chamber was different from his father's. Procedures were changed, bent or laid aside, so as to favour the crown and disadvantage defendants: for example, the interrogation of the king's witnesses was prohibited, on the grounds that they were the king's witnesses and should not be questioned. James had discussed reforming Star Chamber in 1616, but had never done so. Charles modelled his court on what he thought his father wanted Star Chamber to be, another example of his pursuing innovation by following in his father's footsteps.[41]

Charles's Star Chamber is best remembered for a number of high-profile cases resulting in the severe punishment of those who had criticized royal policy in print. These may have been exceptional cases, but the point is they were high profile, and thus coloured public perceptions of the regime. In June 1630 the Scottish-born minister turned medical doctor Alexander Leighton was charged before Star Chamber with publishing *An Appeal to the Parliament* in which he accused the bishops of being persecuting 'men of blood' and corruptors of the king, alleged that episcopacy was 'antichristian and satanical', called the canons of 1604 'nonsense canons', denounced kneeling at communion, attacked the queen, condemned the king's foreign policy, and denied the royal supremacy over the Church. It was an outrageous attack, and Leighton confessed to having written the book; his defence was simply that he had no 'ill intention'. He could have been tried for treason; it was said that it was due to the king's 'exceeding great mercy and goodness' that Leighton was tried before Star Chamber. Yet although Leighton escaped the death penalty, he was hardly treated mercifully. He was ordered to pay a fine of £10,000, degraded, sentenced to stand in the pillory at both Westminster and Cheapside, where he was to be whipped, have his ears cut off and nose slit, and branded on the cheeks with a double SS for 'Sower of Sedition', and then committed to life in prison. 'Many people', it was alleged, pitied Leighton, 'he being a person well known both for learning, and other abilities'. More damagingly, his 'persecution' made many people seek out his book, 'whereby they were informed of many things they knew not before'.[42]

The English lawyer William Prynne likewise fell victim to Star Chamber's predilection for mutilation in 1634 when he was condemned for publishing his *Histrio-mastix* of late 1632 (published with the date 1633 on its title page), a libellous attack on court masques and dances (and by implication an attack on the queen), stage-plays, and many other recreations, such as hunting, public festivals, bonfires, maypoles, and the observation of Christmas. Prynne's work was clearly seditious: he even went so far as to blame magistrates and those in government for provoking God into sending the visitation of the plague, and quoted approvingly from Leighton and the Jesuit Mariana, a well-known advocate of resistance theory. (Not that Prynne quoted any passages from either author that might be construed as seditious; the government was worried that Prynne's readers would be encouraged to go away and read Leighton and Mariana for themselves.) In giving his judgment Francis Cottington, now Chancellor of the Exchequer, said that if there was 'any thing in the world, worse then the devil, Prynne was'. Prynne's punishment, while severe, was not out of the ordinary given the nature of his crimes: he was fined £5,000 and sentenced to life imprisonment, after first being set in the pillory in Westminster and Cheapside, where his ears were cropped and copies of his book burned before him. It was said that he almost died of smoke inhalation.[43]

Prynne was back before Star Chamber in 1637, this time charged along with the physician Dr John Bastwick and the London clergyman Henry Burton with writing and publishing various 'seditious, schismatical and libellous books' against the bishops, accusing them of bringing innovations into the Church, invading the royal prerogative, advancing popery, superstition, idolatry, and profaneness, and oppressing the king's subjects. What was worrying to the authorities was the evidence they uncovered of an underground distribution network to disperse such works among the godly. A great bundle of Prynne's *Newes from Ipswich* of 1636 (one of the libellous books mentioned in the indictment, which Prynne had written in jail) was found in the house of a silenced minister in Coleman Street in London; a further hundred were sent down to a clothier in Gloucestershire, 'a verie precise man', who was to disperse them about the county for 8*d.* each and send the money back to Burton in London.[44] Burton, Bastwick, and Prynne were condemned to lose their ears in the pillory—Prynne was to have the remainder of his ears removed and stigmatized in the cheeks with two letters, S and L, for Seditious Libeller—to be fined £5,000 each, and to perpetual imprisonment in three remote parts of the kingdom.[45]

When the three were brought to the pillory on 30 June 1637, Londoners lined the road from the Gatehouse 'with flowers and herbs' as a gesture of sympathy. Speaking from the pillory, Bastwick protested that he was in trouble merely for writing 'a book against Antichrist the Pope' and that 'if the presse were open to us wee could scatter this kingdome about his eares', adding that if had he 'as much blood as would swell the Thames' he would shed 'every drop in this cause'. Prynne lectured the crowd on the law, saying that under Queens Mary and Elizabeth the punishment for libel was a maximum fine of £2,000 (and then only if the libel was against the king or queen) plus one month's imprisonment (with the convicted to be set free once the fine was paid), and no corporal punishment (unless the convicted refused to pay the fine), and urged the crowd to see 'the desparitye of our tymes' when they were punished so heavily for allegedly 'libelling against a prelate' and denying that the bishops' calling was *jure divino*. Indeed, the book for which he had suffered before was in fact 'twice licensed by publique Authoritye'. It was for 'your goods and your libertyes', Prynne told the crowd, 'that wee have now engaged our owne', urging those within hearing distance to maintain 'thine own lawful liberty', 'stand firm...for the cause of God and His true Religion', and not deliver themselves and their posterity 'into perpetual bondage and slavery'. When the executioner came to do the branding, Prynne proclaimed somewhat melodramatically: 'I have chosen rather to feare the fyre of hell then the fire on Earth; come burne me, scorch me, I beare in my body the Marke of the Lord Jesus'. Burton claimed he was in trouble not for having said something against the king, queen, or council, or even against religion, but merely for 'discharging [his] Conscience in [his] ministerial function' and fulfilling his obligation to 'strengthen [his] Flocke against Popery, Superstition and Innovations'. What is striking is the depth of sympathy for the trio shown by the crowd. A parson approached Bastwick on the pillory and offered to 'heave upp the board a little higher, supposeing it would be an Ease for his Necke'; Bastwick politely declined, saying 'all places are alike to mee'. When the executioner accidentally cut a vein in Burton's ear, onlookers dipped their handkerchiefs in his blood 'as a thing most precious' as it streamed down the pillory. 'The people', it was said, made a 'great shewe' and gave 'evident testimonye of their love...asking him how he did', to which he answered 'I good Cheere'. The three were initially dispatched as prisoners to the castles of Caernarvon in north-west Wales, Launceston in Cornwall, and Lancaster in north-west England. They were feted all along the way. In short, the trial and punishment were a public relations disaster. Thomas Wentworth, writing from Ireland, observed that 'a Prince that loseth the Force and Example of his Punishments, loseth withal the greatest Part of his Dominion'. In August it was decided that the three should not remain in mainland Britain: Bastwick was removed to the Scilly Isles, Burton to Guernsey, and Prynne to Jersey. They were to remain in custody there until released by the Long Parliament.[46]

In 1638 the future Leveller leader John Lilburne and his associate John Wharton were charged at Star Chamber with importing and dispersing libellous and seditious books from Holland. Both refused to swear an oath to answer truthfully any questions put to them, on the grounds that they could not legally be compelled to incriminate themselves. Both were found guilty of contempt, fined £500 each, and remanded in custody until they obeyed the court's orders, while Lilburne suffered the further punishment of whipping and a stint in the pillory. He too remained in prison until released by the Long Parliament.[47]

The Great Migration

Some people grew so disillusioned with life in England during the 1630s that they chose to emigrate, many opting to settle in New England. Known to New England historians as 'the Great Migration', sometimes even as 'the Puritan hegira', this movement of people across the Atlantic needs to be set in perspective. Over the period 1630–1700 about 540,000 people emigrated from England. Of these 162,400 went to Ireland or Europe, and the remaining 377,600 to the New World, of which 222,500 ended up in the Caribbean, 116,100 in the Chesapeake, and just 39,000 in New England. The emigration to New England was heavily concentrated in the period 1628–40, although within that there were two distinct phases: the first, from 1628 to 1633, often referred to as 'the Winthrop migration', saw about 2,500 individuals go over; the second phase, from 1634 to 1640, sometimes called 'the Laudian migration', somewhere between 15,000 and 20,000. Given that the population of England and Wales in the 1630s was *c.* 5 million, that means that less than half a per cent of the total population opted to emigrate to New England between 1628 and 1640. It was only a great migration when seen from the New England perspective. And because people tended to go over in family units, with husbands and wives taking their children and servants, over half of those who ended up in New England had not personally chosen to go there in the first place. In short, only a tiny proportion of the English population decided to flee England because of the problems of the personal rule.[48]

The emigrants left England for a complex combination of personal, economic, and ideological (political, religious) reasons. A sizeable proportion came from the West Country and East Anglia: both were areas where Puritanism was strong, but both were also areas of depressed manufacturing industry (especially textiles). Most were drawn from the middling ranks of society. One analysis of those who went over in the years 1635–8 has shown that 51 per cent were artisans (21 per cent in textiles), while 20 per cent were husbandmen. There were very few gentry or yeomen and very few labouring poor: those who were prospering in England at this time tended not to go (although there were exceptions), while those who were doing really badly could not afford to. Thus it tended to be people who had the means to emigrate but who were not doing particularly well who made the journey, perhaps suggesting an economic motive, although it should be remembered that Puritanism appears to have been strongest among the middling sort, especially in the towns. Economic factors were likely a powerful trigger. One contemporary diarist noted that in the year that wheat prices rose 50 per cent many left England for America. Others fled to escape debt. Yet many undoubtedly went for religious reasons. Henry Dade, a minor ecclesiastical official in Suffolk, informed Laud in February 1634 that those who left his part of East Anglia were 'either indebted persons or...discontented with the government of our Church'—although he particularly blamed the preaching of the Ipswich Puritan Samuel Ward against the Book of Common Prayer and his raising 'a feare of altering our religione' for having caused this 'guiddienes'.[49] Some were both in debt and religiously disaffected, and unsure themselves whether worldly or godly motives swayed most in their decision to emigrate. Only 76 of those who went to New England at this time were clergymen, of whom some 47 had clashed with their ecclesiastical superiors; of these a mere 22 had, in fact, been suspended or removed from their post, although a further 16 had resigned or left when cited to appear before the High Commission, thereby not giving the authorities the chance to suspend them. Given that there were approximately 10,000 parishes in England at this time, this means that less than 1 per cent of the clergy fled. Of the 76 clerical emigrants, 35 came from Emmanuel College, Cambridge.[50]

Clearly people did not feel so oppressed during the 1630s that they were compelled to leave their homeland in droves to try to build a New Jerusalem on the other side of the Atlantic. On the other hand, it is significant that such a high proportion of those who opted to leave England for New England over the course of the seventeenth century went during the 1630s, suggesting that what was happening during the time of the personal rule was a significant push factor. In the diocese of Norwich the largest exodus was in 1637, the year after Wren's visitation. Once the personal rule was over, the migration went into reverse, with far more people in the 1640s and 1650s opting to leave New England than to go there. Moreover, it is questionable whether emigration, by itself, is a particularly helpful index of public alienation. In addition to looking at who left, we should consider those who might have wanted to leave if they could, but did not have the opportunity or means (and how much will we ever know about these?), and those who were tempted to leave but ultimately chose not to. Many Puritan ministers, suffering under Laudianism, thought that it would be cowardly for them to run away, that they would be abandoning their flock when they most needed them. The Essex clergyman Daniel Rogers, who was suspended by Laud for nonconformity in 1629, for instance, saw emigration as an abdication of one's spiritual duties and a cowardly evasion of God's trials. He thus continued to perform his pastoral duties, to organize fasts and prayer meetings, to lead excursions to hear other ministers preach, and to take students into his household.[51] Viscount Saye, Lord Brooke, and the earl of Warwick all contemplated emigration, although eventually chose not to leave, as did possibly John Hampden and John Pym.[52] So too did Oliver Cromwell, a Huntingdonshire farmer and Puritan who had fallen heavily into debt by the early 1630s. In the end, the death of a childless and widowed uncle in January 1636, from whom Oliver inherited leases on tithe lands belonging to the dean and chapter of Ely, provided a boost to his fortunes and helped persuade him to stay.[53]

Ireland and Scotland under Charles I

Subjects are easily lost…but once lost are hardly regained. Affections are like unto Christiall glases, which being once broken, noe art can sim-mond [cement] them again.

Supposed speech of the duke of Lennox to the English privy council concerning the prospect of war with Scotland, 8 July 1638.[1]

On 20 August 1640 an army of some 18,000 Scottish Covenanters crossed the Tweed and marched into England towards the northern port city of Newcastle upon Tyne. Charles had declared war on his Scottish subjects the previous year in an attempt to put down a national revolt against the crown's recent ecclesiastical reforms in Scotland and against the institution of episcopacy north of the border. After a phoney first Bishops' War in the spring of 1639 and a subsequent failed attempt to reach a compromise, the Scots decided to make a pre-emptive strike in the late summer of 1640, claiming to have been invited into England by members of the English nobility.[2] As they marched into England they were said to have been welcomed by the local inhabitants. At a gathering of over twenty local divines at the Swan Inn, Kettering, in the notoriously Puritan county of Northamptonshire, the parson of Brockhall reported that he had a letter from the Scottish army explaining that when the Scots moved into England they had been 'relieved by the English'; indeed, 'the English Soldiers imbraced them, and offered to be on there [*sic*] side', although the Scots told them there was no need for that, since they 'came not to fight', only to 'goe to the King and have some abuses reformed', naming the archbishop of Canterbury and the Lord Lieu-tenant of Ireland as 'the greivances which they came about'.[3] The second Bishops' War was over almost as quickly as it had started. On Friday, 28 August the Scots defeated the English at the Battle of Newburn (the first time the Scots had defeated the English since the

Battle of Bannockburn in 1314), crossed the Tyne the next day, and occupied Newcastle on the Sunday, thereby strangling London's coal supply. When news reached London of the Scottish victory on 1 September, Covenanter sympathizers in the capital celebrated with 'feasts', while there was 'much ringing' of church bells that night as the citizens rejoiced at the king's defeat.[4]

The Scottish crisis brought to an end Charles's experiment with personal rule in England. Charles had turned to parliament for assistance in his dealings with the Scots in April 1640, but criticism of his policies in England was so intense that he dissolved it after just three weeks. Defeat at Newburn and the subsequent occupation of the north of England by the Scots, however, left Charles with no option but to call another parliament and to negotiate with it. Under the terms of the Treaty of Ripon, concluded between Charles and the Scots on 26 October 1640, Charles agreed to pay the Scots £850 per day (over £25,000 per month) and to allow them to keep control of Northumberland and County Durham until a final resolution was reached. The Long Parliament, as it has come to be known, convened in November 1640 and proceeded to enact a series of reforms aimed at undoing the initiatives of the previous decade and designed to make a future period of prolonged rule without parliament impossible. It also passed an Act stating that it could not be dissolved without its own consent, thereby depriving Charles of the means whereby reigning monarchs had traditionally dealt with troublesome parliaments, through recourse to the prerogative power of dissolution.

In October 1641 the Catholics of Ireland, smarting under a host of grievances that had been building up for decades, rose in rebellion: after all, the Scots had shown that resistance could bring results. The Irish rebellion provoked a debate in England over who was to control the army needed to suppress it and, in the end, both crown and parliament raised their own armies and used them against each other. Hence the start of the English Civil War. It is in this sense that the prior revolts in Scotland and Ireland might be said to have *caused* the English Civil War, or at least to have been the *immediate* causes of it: the Scottish revolt by forcing Charles to call a parliament which he could then not get rid of, and the Irish revolt by triggering the crisis that was to lead directly to war.

Why, then, did things go so dramatically wrong in Scotland and Ireland under Charles? As we have seen, James had embarked upon an ambitious policy of reform in both Scotland and Ireland, and although his policies had proved controversial and stored up resentments, he had nevertheless managed to introduce quite far-reaching changes and had left both kingdoms in peace. What did Charles do which so upset the Scots and Irish, and were the Scots and Irish merely reacting to initiatives begun by Charles or did their grievances have deeper roots? In fact, Charles saw himself as building upon and seeking to fulfil his father's agenda, although in doing so he inevitably went further than his father had done, and therein lay the roots of his problems. Charles seriously mishandled the situation in both Scotland and Ireland, the responsibility for which must lie ultimately at his doorstep. But he did so pursuing a strategy for managing his multiple kingdom inheritance that had been laid out under James, pointing to flaws with the strategy itself.

A: Ireland

James had restored relative stability to Ireland following Tyrone's rebellion in the 1590s and maintained a delicate equilibrium as he pushed ahead with reform. 'Delicate' is the appropriate word, however. The plantation of Ulster and the policy of surrender and regrant in other parts of Ireland, plus the intermittent campaigns against Catholic recusancy, had provoked discontent among both the Gaelic Irish and Old English without really advancing very far the hoped-for objective of Anglicization and Protestantization. Indeed, it is impossible to understand why things went wrong for Charles in Ireland without realizing that the Catholics in Ireland already had grievances as a result of policies pursued under James, grievances that Charles found himself being asked to redress.

What threatened to destabilize the situation for Charles immediately upon his accession was the war with Spain, which broke out in 1625. There was a need for increased security, given that the majority of the population of Ireland was Catholic and Spain had backed the Catholic rebellion in Ireland at the end of Elizabeth's reign. The question was, where was the money going to come from? The Old English, keen to show their loyalty, offered to raise trained bands after the English fashion for defence of the country. Charles provisionally approved of the idea, but had to back down in the face of opposition from the New English, who were horrified at the prospect of entrusting the policing of a largely Catholic country to Catholics at a time of war with a Catholic European power.

In the autumn of 1626, with fear of a Spanish invasion running high, Lord Deputy Falkland put forward the suggestion that the country should fund an army of 5,000 foot and 500 horse in return for certain concessions—'matters of grace and bounty'—from the crown. The proposals on the table covered a wide range of grievances and included far-reaching concessions to the Catholics of Ireland, such as suspending the collection of recusancy fines; abolishing the religious test for inheritance of property, appointment to office, and admission to legal practice; and restoring security of Irish land tenure by providing that sixty years of possession would confer a valid title against the crown. In the face of opposition from the Protestant interest in Ireland, the proposal to suspend recusancy fines was dropped, but a deal was eventually struck in May 1628 whereby the king agreed to fifty-one Graces in return for three annual subsidies of £40,000 each. This still left a deficit on the budget of £10,000 per year, while the Irish debt had by now risen to £60,000, but it went a significant way to addressing the problem.[5]

Under the plan a parliament was to meet in November 1628 to confirm the Graces, and Lord Deputy Falkland duly issued writs for elections. However, Falkland failed to submit the proposed legislation to the king and council in London first for approval, as required under Poynings' Law, and being advised by the judges in England that if the parliament met it would be invalid, he suspended the elections in September. Falkland fell from power the following year and a parliament was never called. However, in the meantime the subsidies had begun to be collected. Half of the £120,000 had been paid by the end of September 1629, by which time peace negotiations with Spain were well under way, allowing Charles to cut the size of the military establishment in Ireland dramatically and close the gap between income and expenditure. Although the government agreed to extend the period over which the remainder of the subsidy was to be collected, there was no longer the same fiscal imperative for Charles to offer concessions to Irish Catholics. Charles did not completely renege on his side of the bargain: he granted some of the Graces by dint of the royal prerogative. What the Catholics lacked, however, was any legal guarantee that the Graces would be honoured.

Following the fall of Falkland, Charles placed the government of Ireland temporarily in the hands of two Lords Justices: Richard Boyle, 1st earl of Cork, and Adam, Viscount Loftus. They immediately began a crackdown on Catholic worship in the Irish capital. There had been a period of Catholic resurgence from 1618, when the Roman Catholic hierarchy had resumed residence in Ireland, and the government had been reluctant to do anything to provoke the Catholic community in Ireland while at war with Spain and France in the late 1620s. By 1628 it was said that there were fourteen Catholic chapels in the Irish capital, 'their altars adorned with images and other idolatrous popish Trash'.[6] However, the peace with France in 1629 and the negotiations for peace with Spain meant that there was no longer the need for the government to tread so carefully. Encouraged by the crown, towards the end of 1629 Cork and Loftus warned Catholics in Dublin not to open schools or provide buildings where mass might be held. Acting under orders from the Lords Justices, on the day after Christmas (St Stephen's Day) the Protestant archbishop of Dublin, together with the mayor and recorder and a small band of soldiers, raided the Franciscan chapel on Cook Street in the heart of the City, pulling down the pulpit, defacing and destroying pictures, and seizing various vestments and chalices. As they tried to arrest the friar holding mass, however, the congregation fought them off, throwing stones and clubs, forcing the archbishop and his associates to take shelter in a neighbouring property. Two or three of the soldiers were seriously injured. One anxious member of the Irish privy council wrote that the riot revealed 'the true danger this state is come to by the Conniveing at Papists these 25 yeares past' and predicted that 'wee', the Irish Protestants, could expect 'to perish in our Plantations by Fyre and Sword if ever they take Armes'. The confrontation gave the authorities the excuse to shut down a total of ten Catholic chapels in Dublin: some were converted into places of business or houses of correction; others were just boarded up; one was demolished. William St Leger, President of Munster, followed suit by shutting down Catholic chapels in Cork, while there were similar clampdowns in Limerick and Galway. However, the drive was not sustained; the Irish mission simply went underground until the storm had passed, and congregations continued to meet for worship, often still in the very same houses that had recently been boarded up (simply gaining access via a side door instead of the front entrance).[7]

The government by Lords Justices was only ever intended as a temporary solution. In July 1631 Charles decided to appoint Sir Thomas Wentworth, Lord President of the North, as Lord Deputy, although the decision was not made public until six months later, and Wentworth was not to leave England for Ireland until July 1633 (after Charles had been to Scotland for his coronation). Wentworth had three main objectives: to make Ireland financially self-sufficient, to bring the Irish Church into closer line with that of England, and to continue the process of trying to civilize the Gaelic Irish, all with the ultimate goal of enhancing the authority of the crown. As Wentworth put it in 1634, Charles was to be 'as absolute here, as any Prince in the whole World can be'.[8]

Wentworth's immediate task was to address the financial situation. In 1632, at the time of his appointment, the Irish debt stood at £76,000, expenditure exceeded revenue by £20,000, and there was only £10,000 of the subsidies voted in 1628 that remained to be collected. One option, favoured by Cork, was to make good this shortfall by imposing fines on recusants. Wentworth preferred an alternative policy of a new farm of the customs at an increased rate, although this would take some time to yield benefits. For the time being, he managed to persuade all parties in Ireland to continue paying the subsidy for one more year, holding out the threat of the enforcement of recusancy fines to persuade the Catholic gentry to agree. Following his arrival in the country in the summer of 1633, however, Wentworth reached the conclusion that parliament would have to be called to raise further taxes. Charles took some persuading, realizing that parliament would push for a confirmation of the Graces, but Wentworth assured him he could control the meeting by getting parliament to settle the revenue first, in the summer session, and by delaying the redress of grievances until the winter, when the king would be free to choose which Graces to confirm without any prejudice to his own interest.[9] A spate of new creations to the Irish peerage—since 1615 the number of Irish peers had been increased from 25 to 99—meant that Protestants would predominate over Catholics in the House of Lords, while the elections produced a lower house in which Protestants outnumbered Catholics by 142 to 112. The government interest was strong, with 50 of the Protestant MPs being office holders. By contrast, only 18 MPs bore native Irish names, and a mere 8 of them represented areas of native Irish influence.[10]

The Irish parliament assembled on 14 July 1634 and voted unanimously to grant six subsidies over four years, the last two of which were set at £45,000 instead of the usual £40,000, with an additional £9,000 from the nobility and clergy. The Old English expected that in return for their support the Graces would be confirmed by statute during the second session, and Wentworth allowed them to prepare legislation to that effect. When parliament reconvened in November, however, Wentworth refused to confirm the crucial Graces regarding security of land tenure, on the grounds that they were prejudicial to the crown. The Old English MPs felt betrayed and did their best to obstruct further government business, though Wentworth managed to rally the Protestant majority and was eventually able to regain control of the House. The meeting had been stormier than anticipated but Wentworth had achieved his ends and, well aware that Charles did not like to hear when things had not gone according to plan, gave the king the impression that everything had been smooth sailing.[11]

Wentworth also pursued reform in the Church. There is no doubt that reform was needed. James Ussher, now archbishop of Armagh and primate of all Ireland, had noted in his letters to Laud in 1629-30 'the miserable conditions of the Bishoprickes and dioceses in Ireland' and also 'the scandalous life of many unworthy ministers' (with 'the Vice of Drunkenness especially' being 'common among them').[12] Upon taking up the Lord Deputyship, Wentworth likewise found the Irish Church—as he put it to Laud—in 'many ways distempered': 'an unlearned Clergy', 'the Churches unbuilt', 'Non-Residency', 'the Possessions of the Church, to a great Proportion in Lay-hands', and 'the Rites and Ceremonies of the Church run over without all Decency of Habit, Order or Gravity'. Charles particularly wanted Wentworth to bring Ireland into 'a Conformity in Religion with the Church of England'.[13] The Irish Articles of Faith of 1615 had left the Irish Church more rigorously Calvinist and more hostile to ceremony than its Jacobean English counterpart, and considerably at odds with the style of worship Laud was promoting in England in the 1630s. The disparity was a problem politically, since it allowed Puritan critics of the Church of England to point to Ireland to show that predestinarian views and less ceremonialist styles of worship were deemed legitimate in other of the Stuart kingdoms.[14] The idea of reform of the Church in Ireland had been on the agenda since the beginning of Charles's reign, and bills had been introduced into parliament in England in 1626 and 1628 to give statutory authority to the English Thirty-Nine Articles, although they had come to nothing. The degree of centralized power in Ireland that Wentworth amassed following his appointment as Lord Deputy meant that he felt he was in a strong enough position to take on the challenge. To assist him in this task he brought with him from England as his chaplain John Bramhall, a fellow Yorkshireman, 'known to be a Man able for Learning' and 'very Active in Businesses of the Church' (as Ussher put it)—though Bramhall was soon to cause a few raised eyebrows by preaching in Dublin that 'the Church of Rome' was 'only schismaticall' and that the pope was 'a Patriarch'.[15] Bramhall was rapidly promoted to the archdeaconry of Meath in October 1633 and then the bishopric of Derry in May 1634.[16] He was shocked by what he learned during a fact-finding mission in the north towards the end of the year: in the united dioceses of Down and Connor, for example, he found 'almost the whole resident clergy absolute irregulars, the very ebullition of Scotland', with 'Conformists very rare', there being not 'twelve Common Prayer Books in all their churches', and no altars; instead, they had a 'table ten yards long, where they sit and receive the Sacrament together like good fellows'.[17]

Wentworth and Bramhall wanted to impose the Thirty-Nine Articles and the English canons of 1604 on Ireland: 'as we live all under one king', Bramhall told Laud, so we should 'both in doctrine and discipline observe an uniformity'.[18] The proposals came before the Irish Convocation in 1634 and proved deeply controversial. Archbishop Ussher sought to have the Irish Articles confirmed along with the English, and Wentworth had to have recourse to a combination of manipulation and intimidation—threatening at one point that the English Articles could be imposed 'by the King's immediate pleasure' without the consent of Convocation—in order to get the English Articles approved. The canons proved even more difficult. A select committee of the lower house raised many objections, partly on the grounds that some of the English canons were inappropriate for the very different conditions in Ireland (for example, canon 41 against pluralism), but mainly because they wanted the Irish Church to retain its relaxed attitude towards conformity. Wentworth believed the members of Convocation had acted most 'unlike Clergymen', who, he thought, ought to demonstrate 'Canonical Obedience to their Superiors', and accused them of evincing 'a Spirit of Brownism' in their deliberations. Yet Ussher himself was against accepting the English canons verbatim and threatened to resign. Laud and Bramhall were not averse to the idea of drafting new Irish canons, however, since they wanted to improve on the English ones, and in the spring of 1635 a compromise was reached in which 141 English canons became 100 Irish ones. The new Irish canons introduced auricular confession, stipulated that communion tables be moved to the east end, and required the use of the ornaments and ceremonies of the English Book of Common Prayer. They also made it a duty for an Irish minister to declare the king's supremacy four times a year and established the penalty of excommunication for anyone who preached or said anything against the Book of Common Prayer. However, the provisions in the English canons for cathedral clergy to wear copes when administering communion, for using the sign of the cross in baptism, for bowing at the name of Jesus, and for kneeling at communion were dropped, Wentworth informing Laud in reference to the last that the Irish Protestants had 'noe more joints in their knee for that than an Elephant'.[19]

There was considerable passive resistance to the reforms. Ussher advocated a policy of minimal compliance, and he and several other bishops urged newly admitted clergy to subscribe not just to the Thirty-Nine Articles but also to the Irish Articles. Opposition was particularly widespread in Ulster, with its large number of Scottish settlers. To enforce obedience, Wentworth revived the Irish Court of High Commission, which at Laud's insistence was subject to the supervisory oversight of the English High Commission. Since the records of the court are largely missing, it is impossible to assess accurately how it conducted itself, although the slim evidence we do possess suggests that it proceeded by making salutary examples of a few rather than systematically proceeding against all nonconformists. But Bramhall and Bishop Leslie of Down and Connor were determined to break the evangelical circle led by the Scottish Presbyterian immigrants John Livingstone and Robert Blair in County Down. Livingstone and Blair, who had been in trouble with the ecclesiastical authorities in the past, were both deprived and ordered to refrain from preaching for refusing to subscribe to the new canons. A further five ministers were likewise subsequently deprived, after first being made to participate in a public disputation during which Leslie sought to refute their objections. In the face of persecution, Livingstone, Blair, and their followers opted to take ship for New England, but they were driven back by bad weather (which they took to be a sign from God), and re-settled in Scotland. By mid-June Bramhall could write optimistically to Laud that 'this Church will quickly purge herself from such peccant humours if there be not a supplie from thence [Scotland]'.[20]

In addition to reforming the liturgy, Wentworth wanted to improve both the quality of the clergy and the financial position of the Church. He used the patronage at his disposal to promote clergy who were sympathetic to his programme of reform. (Although technically episcopal appointments were in the gift of the crown, Charles tended to follow Laud's suggestions, and with regard to Ireland Laud was happy to recommend those whom the Lord Deputy proposed.) Wentworth's ideal would have been to have appointed the 'ablest and hopefullest' of the clergy of England to serve in the Irish Church, but recruitment did not always prove easy, especially for the highest positions. Wentworth was able to make fourteen episcopal appointments during his Lord Deputyship, meaning that roughly half of the bishops who were to sit in the Irish House of Lords in the parliament of 1640 were new men. Although many of those promoted were either Laudians or enthusiasts for Wentworth's vision of reconstruction in the Church—for example, George Webb, the Wiltshire-born and Oxford-educated Laudian and erstwhile chaplain to Charles I, became bishop of Limerick in 1634, while Henry Leslie, the Oxford-trained Scottish Arminian, was created bishop of Down and Connor in 1635—some compromises were necessary. Thus, George Andrews, a staunch defender of the Irish Articles in the Convocation of 1635, found himself promoted to the bishopric of Ferns and Leighlin in May 1635, in part because of the absence of a suitable alternative, and in part to appease Ussher after the government had got its way over the English Articles. All but two of the men advanced to bishoprics under Wentworth had had previous Irish careers. But Wentworth was able to make more extensive changes at the decanal level: there were thirty-three deaneries in Ireland, and appointments were in the gift of the Lord Deputy. Wentworth was able to appoint thirty-four deans—some places saw multiple turnovers (Waterford, for example, got through five deans), while only nine deaneries saw no change under Wentworth—importing like-thinking men to run the Church after his fashion, and to be in line for eventual promotion to their own see. Wentworth and Laud also transformed Trinity College Dublin, once a centre of Puritan teaching which had been modelled at its foundation on Emmanuel College, Cambridge: Laud, who became Chancellor, rewrote the statutes and procured a new charter, with the idea of ensuring that it produced clergy suitable for the type of Church which he wanted to see prosper in Ireland.[21]

To strengthen the economic position of the Church, Wentworth wanted to recover lost Church lands and to increase the revenues from rents and tithes. An Act for the Preservation of the Inheritance of 1634 made all leases and alienations of Church lands by ecclesiastical persons void as of 1 June of that year; henceforth only twenty-one-year leases would be permitted (although a separate Act made allowance for sixty-year leases in the newly settled province of Ulster). Another Act made it easier for lay owners to restore appropriations to the Church. The bishops then took the initiative, making sure not to renew leases without a fair increase in rent, and doing their best to reclaim Church lands where they could, though Wentworth also had recourse to both High Commission and the Court of Castle Chamber to recover Church assets that had fallen into the hands of the laity. The strategy met with most success in the archdiocese of Armagh, where rents had increased by £14,261 by 1639, although this was the province which already had the best-endowed sees and thus where reform was least needed. Moreover, Armagh was in the poorer north and covered the area that had the greatest concentration of Scottish Presbyterians, meaning that the burden of episcopacy was felt most in that part of Ireland that could least afford it and was least sympathetic towards it. In total, the other three archiepiscopal provinces of Dublin, Cashel, and Tuam saw increases of a little over £6,000. Nevertheless, there were some striking gains, even here. The energetic reconstructionist Edward King, bishop of Elphin, improved the value of his Connacht see from 200 marks to £1,000 and transformed the town of Elphin itself from a settlement of chimneyless Irish cabins to a handsome English-style village. John Atherton, bishop of Waterford and Lismore, raised the income of his see from £50 to £1,000 within just one year of taking office.[22]

In his drive for reform, Wentworth was not coy about confronting established Protestant interests across the country. Take his treatment of Richard Boyle, earl of Cork, one of the most powerful and wealthiest men in Ireland at the time of Wentworth's appointment as Lord Deputy. Cork had amassed a fortune in land towards the end of Elizabeth's reign, arguably defrauding the crown in the process during his stint as deputy-escheator in the 1590s, although he had taken out patents to secure his properties under the terms of the commission for defective titles of 1606. Wentworth clearly thought the crown had been cheated and wanted to teach the earl a lesson. In 1634 he made Cork dismantle the enormous funeral monument he had erected for his wife at the east end of St Patrick's Cathedral, Dublin—it stood 32 feet high and had cost £1,000 to build—on the grounds that it stood where the high altar should stand, and place it instead on the south side. Although Wentworth could not challenge Cork's titles to his secular estates, he did pursue Cork for having illegally acquired Church property; in the end a bargain was struck whereby Cork paid a total of £15,000 in three instalments and was allowed to keep some of his lands.[23]

Cork's main rival on the Irish council at the time of Wentworth's appointment had been the vice-treasurer Francis Annesley, Viscount Mountnorris, in whom Wentworth initially found an ally. However,

Wentworth was soon to fall out with Mountnorris over the customs. A revised book of rates combined with improved collection had seen revenues from Irish customs increase dramatically in the years 1632–5, but because the customs were farmed at a fixed fee, it was the farmers who benefited rather than the crown. Wentworth wanted Mountnorris to step down from the vice-treasury and from the customs farm, so that he could introduce a new system whereby a significant proportion of the profits from the farm would go to the king (and some to the Lord Deputy himself). The opportunity for Wentworth to strike was provided in the spring of 1635 when Mountnorris joked over dinner about how a relative of his had dropped a stool on Wentworth's gouty foot in retaliation for the way Wentworth, in his capacity as general of the Irish army, had reproved Mountnorris's brother for alleged insubordination during a cavalry exercise; somewhat disturbingly, Mountnorris had proceeded to add that he had 'a brother that would not take such a Revenge'. Mountnorris later protested that he had meant that 'the said brother would [rather] dye' before giving the Deputy such offence, but the words were capable of a more sinister construction, and the fact that Mountnorris himself held a commission as a captain in the Irish army gave Wentworth cause to have him court martialled. On 12 December a council of war found Mountnorris guilty of calumniating his commanding officer and inciting others to mutiny and sentenced him to be stripped of all his offices and executed (although the death sentence was never carried out).[24]

The government in London even decided to take on the new imperial interest in Ulster, although here Wentworth must be absolved from responsibility. Having grown increasingly frustrated by 'the ill behaviour of the Londoners' in not conforming to the rules of the plantation, in the summer of 1631 it decided to refer the matter to Star Chamber and set up a commission of inquiry.[25] In 1635 Star Chamber condemned the City of London to pay a fine of £70,000 (subsequently reduced to £12,000) and to surrender their patent to Londonderry, ostensibly for their failure to replace the native population with British settlers as under the terms of the original agreement. There was a strong financial motive: the city of Londonderry, Coleraine, and over 40,000 acres of land belonging to the City of London reverted to the crown. Wentworth urged the king to farm the property, and offered to lease it himself. In the end, Charles appointed a commission to manage the property directly, resulting in 1639 in a revision of the terms of tenancy and the unscrupulous rack-renting of large and small tenants alike. It was an incredibly impolitic move at the time of the Scottish crisis, and a pointless one since the new rents could not be collected.[26]

While the government was pursuing measures that struck at the interests of Protestants in Ireland, Wentworth was prepared to allow *de facto* religious toleration to Catholics, opposing the reintroduction of recusancy fines and restraining the ecclesiastical courts from proceeding against Catholic baptisms, marriages, and burials. John Roche, the titular bishop of Ferns (a diocese roughly coterminous with the county of Wexford), noted in late 1633 how the viceroy allowed Catholics to 'live in peace, in private exercise of our religion and of our ministry'.[27] In many parts of Ireland, as a result, the Catholic Church underwent something of a revival, enjoying a more visible and public presence. In the archdiocese of Tuam in the west of Ireland, for example, the number of Catholic priests rose from thirty-four to fifty-seven in the period 1630–7. County Wexford in the south-east bucked the national trend and saw a decline in the number of secular clergy in the same period, but this was more than compensated for by the rise in the religious (Jesuits, Franciscans, and Cistercians).[28]

Wentworth was no friend to Catholicism; he merely did not want to risk upsetting Catholics further while he was pursuing other reforms. His longer-term aim was to convert the Old English, whom he felt were impeding the civilizing process by patronizing friars and Jesuits. This could be achieved, he believed, by reviving and extending the policy of plantation, which would have the additional advantage of boosting revenues for the crown and against which there was no legal bar following his refusal to confirm the provision in the Graces for the security of Irish land tenure.

Wentworth's primary scheme of plantation focused on the lands west of the River Shannon in the province of Connacht, where much of the land was in the possession of Catholics who could not produce valid titles at law. Such occupants were to surrender their land to the crown and then receive three-quarters of it back with a secure title but on the tenure of knight service, which involved the payment of dues to the king in lieu of military service. This would also allow the crown to stipulate that such land could not be inherited unless the heir took the oath of supremacy; in theory, within a generation most landowners in the province would be forced to turn Protestant. The remaining quarter of the land which the crown seized could then be granted to Protestant settlers. With the landowning elite Protestant and no powerful men left to protect Catholic clergy, conversions among the peasantry were expected to follow suit, while the influx of settlers from England was thought likely to lead to civil improvement. Wentworth appears to have believed that the scheme would also be beneficial to the Connacht landowners who would have to surrender some of their lands, on the grounds that the 'three parts remaining...after this settlement' would 'be better and more valuable to them than the former four parts' both in regards of 'the benefit they shall have by the plantation as of the security and settlement they shall gain in their estates'.[29]

The thinking was similar to that which lay behind the policy of plantation pursued under James. Indeed, the idea for the plantation of Connacht, excluding the Old English county of Galway, had first been mooted towards the end of James's reign, and Cork had tried to revive it following the conclusion of peace with Spain in 1630. What was new with Wentworth's scheme, however, was that it included Galway, and threatened the property rights of powerful Old English interests in the area. Although a commission of inquiry was set up to take evidence from local juries, Wentworth insisted that the king's title was incontestable. Little trouble was encountered in Mayo, Roscommon, or Sligo. Galway—where the dominant landowner was Richard Burke, 4th earl of Clanricarde, and earl of St Albans in the English peerage—was a different matter, however. When the commission began its proceedings in Clanricarde's Portumna residence in August 1635, the Galway jury found against the king. The jurors in turn were prosecuted in Castle Chamber for finding against the evidence, fined £4,000 each and imprisoned; the sheriff who had impanelled them suffered a similar fate and was to die in jail. The Clanricarde interest sent a delegation to England to lobby the court in England, but Clanricarde himself died in November (his death supposedly hastened by his despair at the prospect of the loss of his Connacht lands), and although the 5th earl tried to continue the fight, he was so heavily in debt that he had to give up the struggle. The Galway gentry capitulated, and the jury was released before the end of December 1636.[30]

Wentworth did not intend to limit plantations to Connacht. He hoped ultimately to resettle all land in Ireland that remained in Catholic hands, causing alarm among the Old English in the Pale and in Leinster. The opposition in Galway, however, had succeeded in slowing down the implementation of the Connacht scheme. The royal title to Galway was not to be discovered until March 1637, and no action had yet been taken when Wentworth's attention was diverted by the crisis that was developing in Scotland.

* * *

There is a sense in which Ireland appeared to be flourishing in the 1630s. The population was rising, reaching a peak of about one and a half million in 1641, and the economy seemingly prospering. The annual revenue from Irish customs rose from c. £11,000 per annum in 1630 to just under £40,000 in 1635 and £60,000 in 1637, in part a reflection of the increased efficiency of collection under Wentworth but in large measure due to an increase in trade: English imports of Irish hides increased twentyfold between the 1580s and 1639, of Irish wool by more than thirtyfold in the same period; a new trade in processed agricultural products such as butter and barrelled beef opened up; imports of livestock also increased dramatically (from fewer than 7,000 cattle in 1616–17 to over 30,000 by 1626 and more than 45,000 by 1640–1, and from fewer than 7,000 sheep in 1626 to nearly 35,000 by 1640–1); while the non-agricultural sector saw the development of an Irish iron-smelting industry, albeit short-lived, and other forms of manufacturing such as linen, woollen, cloth and glass (by the early 1620s the earl of Cork had already established a substantial enterprise for producing window glass in south County Waterford). An expansion of trade led to growing urbanization: Dublin, with its 10,000 inhabitants in 1600, had more than doubled in size by the early 1640s; Galway, Waterford, and Limerick were also expanding as regional export centres; the population of Cork rose from 2,400 to 5,500 from 1600 to 1641; the smaller towns of Youghal and Kinsale (the former already responsible by 1626 for more than half the exports of Irish sheep) grew even more rapidly. As a result, instead of England's subsidizing Ireland, in 1638 £10,441 passed from the Irish treasury to England, while the following year Wentworth claimed a surplus in the Irish treasury of £100,000.[31] Moreover, it was not only Protestant colonists who were doing well; some Old English were able to develop their estates and take advantage of the economic upturn, and perhaps even a few native Irish landowners.[32] The situation overall for Catholics in Ireland had arguably improved: there was a considerable degree of *de facto* toleration, Catholic priests and bishops were allowed to tend to their pastoral duties without fear of legal reprisal, and Catholic lawyers were allowed to plead before the Irish bar. Wentworth was even willing to allow Catholics to serve as officers in the army which he was to assemble in order to meet the Scottish crisis. And even though there remained the threat of further plantation in the west, for the time being Wentworth's plans had stalled, and there remained the hope that in the long term Wentworth could be persuaded to change his mind.[33]

Such developments are crucial to helping us understand why many Catholics in Ireland would continue to see themselves as loyal to the crown as events unfolded in the late 1630s and early 1640s. If they had had no stake at all in the new Ireland that was emerging under the early Stuarts, then not only would the politics of Catholic discontent in Ireland have been significantly different but so too would the politics of Protestant discontent—since in the face of a generally alienated Catholic population the minority Protestant interest would likely have been much more nervous about expressing criticism of crown policy. Yet it is difficult to argue that Ireland was really in a much healthier position by the late 1630s. Wentworth's reforms had antagonized many interests: Protestant as well as Catholic; English as well as Irish; New as well as Old. He had upset the Protestants of the established Church, the Presbyterians and nonconformists in Ulster, the new planters in Londonderry. As a result it is hardly surprising that the Protestant interest in Ireland came to lead the attack on the former Lord Deputy as he faced impeachment proceedings in 1640–1. He had left the Old English feeling a sense of betrayal for his refusal to confirm the Graces. He had also left both the native Irish and the Old English with the fear of further plantation hanging over their heads.

B: Scotland

In Scotland the most parte hate cleane lynnen
'Piggs Corantoe', satirizing the Scottish
opposition to 'the authority of white
sleeves', i.e. bishops, in 1639.[34]

Charles I was the first king of Scotland to be an absentee monarch from the start of his reign. Although James VI and I had returned to his homeland only once after his accession to the English throne, in the eyes of the Scottish ruling elite he remained a Scottish monarch. By contrast Charles, despite being born in Scotland, had been raised in England since the age of three and a half and appeared to the Scots very much an Englishman. Just three months after his accession the

Venetian ambassador commented upon the increasing 'jealousy between the two nations' and the Scots' concern at their loss of influence with the crown 'since the death of the late king'. When the Scots had asked if they might have their own secretary near the king, Charles simply told them 'that he was born a Scot and would bear for Scotland the same affection as his father'. It was an answer they found far from reassuring.[35]

Many Presbyterians hoped that Charles would not continue his father's policy in the Kirk, but instead listen to their grievances, particularly concerning the Five Articles of Perth.[36] Charles soon disabused them of this notion, issuing a proclamation on 3 July 1625 stating that he so admired 'the government of the Kirk now happilie established that, if the same had not already bene determined', he would, 'with all his care haif advanceit the same', and calling for the execution of the laws against all nonconformists. Particularly galling was that the Presbyterians found themselves 'ranked in with Papists', since Charles's proclamation styled all 'restles and unquiet spiritis' as 'Popishlie disposed'. A proclamation 'of this straine', one prominent Scottish Presbyterian later recalled, led 'many honest people to have harder thoughts of the King than they had before'.[37]

Scottish anxieties were further exacerbated by the prospect of imminent involvement in the Thirty Years War. Charles expected Scotland to contribute to the cost, emphasizing that British interests were at stake; the Scots, however, were allowed no meaningful influence over shaping what was essentially an English foreign policy. A Convention of Estates which met on 27 October 1625 agreed to an award of £400,000 Scots (£33,333 sterling) annual taxation and an extraordinary tax on annual rents (exacted as 5 per cent on free income), both of which were to run concurrently for four years. However, the Estates summarily rejected an alternative proposal from Charles that instead of taxation they vote a sum sufficient to maintain and supply 20 ships, 2,000 soldiers, and 800 sailors to defend the country from foreign invasion for three years, fearing that by establishing the precedent they might 'make themselves subject to it for ever'.[38]

Charles's first controversial initiative was his Revocation of 1625. It was a well-established practice in Scotland that a king, upon reaching the age of majority, might revoke grants made during his minority deemed prejudicial to the crown's interest, as long as he did so before he turned twenty-five. James VI had issued three revocations—in 1581, 1584, and 1587—none of which had caused much controversy.

However, Charles was not a minor when he came to the throne and he had to rush the scheme through at great haste before he turned twenty-five on 19 November, consulting with only a few London-based Scottish courtiers. When the Revocation was read to the Scottish council that November, this was the first they had heard of it. Moreover, Charles's scheme went further than anything attempted in the past. Claiming that he was entitled to revoke what his predecessors had done and that this had been acknowledged by parliament at the time of his father's revocation, Charles proposed to revoke all grants of crown lands since 1540. He further asserted that the legislation regulating his father's revocation had incorporated teinds (tithes) as well as Kirk lands, affording him the pretext to annex alienated properties and revenues belonging to the pre-Reformation Church.[39]

Charles's aim was not just to boost the revenues of the crown. Teind reform was intended to improve the ministry by augmenting the stipends of parish ministers, to increase educational provision by providing salaries for masters of grammar schools, and to generate more funding for poor relief. Charles also hoped to free the gentry and their tenants from dependence upon—and oppression by—the nobility, by extinguishing heritable jurisdictions and certain feudal superiorities and reforming abuses in the teind system. In this respect, Charles saw himself as addressing problems identified in the Revocation of 1587 and in James's *Basilikon Doron* of 1598. The political cost of Charles's Revocation, however, was enormous. One contemporary described it as 'the ground stone of all the mischeiffe that folloued after'.[40] Previous revocations had always been devised and agreed to by parliament. Charles was determined to impose his purely on the basis of his royal prerogative, and although repeatedly pressed by the Scots to call a parliament in Scotland, he protested that he had more important business to attend to in England.[41] The nobles were naturally alarmed by the attack on their privileges. Moreover, Charles did such a bad job of explaining his intentions that even those who stood to benefit—such as the clergy and lesser landowners—remained suspicious. He soon realized that he would need to moderate his demands, although the damage had already been done. In July 1626 he announced that those who surrendered their rights would receive compensation. In February of the next year he set up a Commission of Surrenders and Teinds to proceed by way of negotiation and surrender. Meeting sporadically until 1637, it made little headway, not least because the crown could not afford to pay compensation. Its major achievement was to settle the teind question and boost the standard of living of Scottish ministers, although this was resented by those who felt their vested interests were threatened.[42]

Charles had initially been planning on going to Scotland to be crowned and to meet with his Scottish parliament in the summer of 1628, although political difficulties in England, the foreign policy situation, and periodic outbreaks of the plague led him repeatedly to postpone his plans. He finally went in the spring of 1633. Setting off from London on 11 May, he made a slow progress north, staying with various members of the landed elite on his way and using the opportunity to present an appropriate display of royal majesty to his English subjects. At York on 27 May, for example, he touched for the King's Evil, went to a horse race, dined with the archbishop, and knighted the archbishop's son. At Richmond two days later he gave a gift of £4 to a woman who had recently given birth to quadruplets. He also made it clear that Puritans were decidedly out of favour with his regime. One Catholic newsletter writer noted how the king 'discountenanced the puritans exceedingly in this his journey, and refused to heare puritan ministers preach in severall places'. In Lincolnshire, he caused 'certaine boies to be whipt' who presented him with a petition 'in the name of a puritan minister' who was too afraid to deliver it himself. When Charles reached Durham, he had John Cosin—one of the Arminians denounced by parliament in 1629—sworn in as a royal chaplain. The symbolic significance was not lost on contemporaries: Cosin, as our Catholic source notes, was the man responsible 'for dressing up his church and altar after the Catholick manner contrary to the use of...the bishop there', the Calvinist Thomas Morton (who had been translated to Durham in 1632).[43]

Having crossed the Scottish border on 12 June, Charles finally entered Edinburgh on the 15th to an elaborate and carefully staged civic entertainment. At the entrance to the city was a triumphal arch, representing 'Religion' and 'Justice' overcoming 'Superstition' and 'Oppression', where Charles was presented with the keys of the city and told of the citizens' joy at his 'happy returne' to his 'native country'. As the king processed through the streets, onlookers drank his health, throwing their glasses into the air and crying 'welcome Kinge Charles'.[44] There is no reason to doubt that the inhabitants of Edinburgh were genuinely excited about the royal visit and the opportunity at last to catch a glimpse of their monarch in the flesh. Yet many Scots were soon given reason to doubt whether Charles had come to promote religion and justice. If it was not bad enough that Charles had waited eight years before coming to Scotland to be crowned, the nature of his coronation ceremony proved deeply offensive to Scottish sensibilities. It took place at the abbey kirk of Holyrood which had been reordered for the occasion in Laudian fashion, with a railed-in communion table at the east end, 'in the manner of an altar', decked with candles, and behind it a rich tapestry 'wherein the crucifix was curiously wrought'. Charles's first act, on entering the church, was to kneel ceremoniously before ascending the coronation dais, in full view of the audience—signalling with this one dramatic gesture his commitment to the Five Articles of Perth. Laud himself was present on the coronation dais as dean of the English Chapel Royal, and the six Scottish bishops who participated in the ceremony wore surplices and rochets like Anglican bishops, and bowed their knee to the crucifix when they passed the altar. (The rest of the Scottish bishops sat in the body of the kirk in their black gowns.) The service was conducted according to the English Book of Common Prayer, while the coronation oath, whereby the king swore to uphold the true religion, to rule according to law, and to preserve the privileges of the crown, included an additional promise to preserve the clergy's 'canonical prewilidges' and to defend the 'Bischopes, and the churches wnder their gouerniment'. The contemporary historian John Spalding, himself a committed royalist and episcopalian, conceded that the service 'bred great fear of inbringing of popery'. Nevertheless, following the formalities of the ceremony, bonfires were lit in celebration throughout the Scottish capital.[45]

The fact that Charles called a parliament to meet in Scotland is a further reminder that the personal rule was only a period of rule without parliaments in England. However, it was a short session (as Scottish parliaments tended to be), lasting 18–28 June. The elections were carefully managed to ensure the return of as many royal nominees as possible. Nobles refusing to attend were pressed into placing their proxies in the hands of the court, while five Englishmen with Scottish titles were summoned even though they lacked Scottish estates, thereby violating the constitutional tradition that lords of parliament had to have a territorial qualification in Scotland. Considerable effort was made to control the legislative agenda. As his father had done in 1617 and 1621, Charles ordered that those with business to bring before parliament had to submit it in advance to the Clerk Register; in 1633 this was Sir John Hay, described by one contemporary as 'a slave to the bischopes and courte'. A group of Presbyterian clergy, led by Thomas Hogg, a deposed minister from Fife, presented Hay with a lengthy petition detailing their concerns about the usurped authority of the Scottish bishops, the Five Articles of Perth, and the eclipse of General Assemblies, but got short shrift. Hogg therefore opted to present the petition directly to the king himself at Dalkeith Castle, just prior to Charles's entry into Edinburgh. Although Charles was said to have read the petition 'at lenth', it was never brought before either the Lords of the Articles or parliament. The legislative programme was further vetted by the Lords of the Articles, whose meetings Charles attended on a regular basis. Charles also prohibited separate meetings of individual estates during the parliamentary session, contrary to tradition (in 1621 they had at first been allowed before order came that they should be forborn). Communication between the estates was banned, and a supplication subscribed by members of the nobility, barons, and burgesses was suppressed.[46]

The Lords of the Articles finished their proceedings on 27 June and came up with 168 public and private measures, which were presented for approval the next day. The proposed public legislation included measures for ratifying the Revocation of 1625, introducing higher levels of taxation, and ratifying all previous legislation concerning religion enacted since the accession of James VI (including, therefore, the measures relating to episcopacy and the Five Articles of Perth). Debate was stifled and members had to vote simply yes or no, without giving their reasons, and with the king looking on, noting the names of those who voted no with his own hand. Charles behaved in a blatantly intimidating manner, giving vent 'now and then' to 'a grate deall of spleene': on one occasion he took a list of members out of his pocket and proclaimed, 'Gentleman, I'll know who will doe me service, and who will not, this day'. Members had been tapped up in advance: some were offered titles in return for voting yes, while considerable pressure was brought to bear on those who were thought likely to dissent. Many later admitted they voted yes 'for fear of the King's displeasure'. Officers of state were allowed to vote twice, in their respective capacities as both noblemen and government officials. Even so, the vote was close enough for the disaffected to claim that the legislation was approved only because Hay had miscounted the votes.[47] According to Clarendon, 'what had passed . . . left bitter inclinations and unruly spirits in many of the most popular nobility'.[48] Moreover, Charles's reliance on the bishops to secure control of the Articles, to vet the composite legislative agenda, and to collude in the voting practices encouraged the disaffected to see the source of the problem as being 'the Episcopall and courte faction'.[49]

Following the dissolution of the parliament on 28 June, Charles stayed in Edinburgh for the weekend before going on progress in early July, doing his best to avoid those who were unhappy with recent proceedings. A former crown solicitor William Haig drew up a supplication to the king explaining in detail why the disaffected element in the 1633 parliament had voted against the new legislation. Signed by thirty-five nobles—more than half of the sixty-five votes cast on behalf of that estate in the coronation parliament—it not only expressed concern about the way business had been conducted but was also deeply critical of the new public legislation, particularly that concerning religion. Alleging that the Five Articles of Perth had done nothing but trouble 'the peace of this Kirk', the supplication explained that there was 'now a generall feare of some innovation intended in essentiall poynts of religion', and expressed the hope that Charles would not introduce anything that was incompatible with the Kirk's freedom. Although the supplicants professed their 'ingenious affection' to the king, it was explosive stuff. Charles refused to receive it. A few copies began to circulate privately. John Elphinstone, Lord Balmerino, one of the leading disaffected nobles, showed a copy to a lawyer; the lawyer made an unauthorized copy which he gave to a friend, who brought it to the attention of Archbishop Spottiswoode, who in turn showed it to the king. Charles had no option now but to act. Haig quickly fled to the Low Countries to avoid arrest, but Balmerino was taken, accused of publishing and distributing, or at least concealing, a scandalous and seditious libel. He was eventually found guilty of treason in March 1635 after the jury split down the middle and the casting vote was given by the chancellor of the assize, the earl of Traquair. The verdict caused a public outcry. The disaffected nobles blamed the trial on the bishops. Traquair himself advised Charles not to carry out the sentence. Yet although Balmerino did subsequently receive a pardon, the damage had been done. The Restoration cleric and historian Gilbert Burnet, himself a Scot, later recalled how his father had told him 'that the ruin of the king's affairs in Scotland was in a great measure owing to that prosecution'.[50]

Before departing Scotland, Charles decided to make Edinburgh an episcopal see. Hitherto the burgh had come under the jurisdiction of the archbishopric of St Andrews, although the town's preachers, since the Reformation, had been chosen by the citizens, and had demonstrated a steadfast spirit of independence: Clarendon called them 'the most turbulent and seditious ministers of confusion that could be found in the kingdom'. Endowing the new bishopric with lands he had purchased on the cheap from the duke of Lennox, Charles made St Giles kirk the cathedral and appointed William Forbes, an ardent proponent of the Articles of Perth and of kneeling at communion, the first bishop. Charles was hoping thereby 'the better to prepare the people of that place' for further reforms in the Kirk, and 'at least to discountenance, if not suppress, the factious spirit of Presbytery which had so long ruled there'. At best it was naïve; to many Scots it was a provocative gesture: even Clarendon admitted that 'the people generally thought that they had too many bishops before, and so increasing the number was not like to be very grateful to them'. Charles also decided to appoint the archbishop of St Andrews Chancellor of Scotland and five other bishops to the Scottish privy council, in an attempt to boost the respect for episcopacy north of the border. It was another move that backfired, provoking the resentment of the Scottish nobility who thought that such offices should be reserved for them.[51]

After leaving Scotland, Charles pushed ahead with plans to bring the Kirk in line with the Church of England. In October 1633 a Scottish edition of the English Book of Common Prayer was published and Charles ordered it to be used in bishops' chapels and the Chapel Royal. The Scottish bishops, however, managed to convince Charles and Laud that the English prayer book could not simply be imposed on the Scots, and so in October 1634 the decision was taken to compile a new service book and a new set of canons for the Scottish Kirk. Both had in fact been called for by the General Assembly that had met at Aberdeen in 1616, and Charles was subsequently to insist that he was doing no more than bringing to fruition a project begun under his father.[52] However, James had not pursued this initiative, recognizing that it was too controversial. Moreover, Charles's new liturgy was not to be based on the Jacobean draft but to follow the English prayer book as closely as possible. The Scottish prayer book was largely the work of the Scottish bishops Maxwell and Wedderburn, the latter a client of Laud, and took two years to complete. Charles took a close interest and made frequent recommendations for modifications. In drawing up the prayer book efforts were made to appease Scottish sensibilities, although the final version brought the Kirk closer in line with English practice than ever before. Indeed, in the eyes of the Scots the new prayer book was 'more Popish' than its English counterpart, since several words in the English prayer book which seemed to oppose the real presence were left out and 'severall most Popish expressions' were included; Laud himself acknowledged that these variations were taken from the first prayer book of Edward VI (the still quasi-Catholic one of 1549) and 'some ancient [i.e. pre-Reformation] liturgies'. One Presbyterian critic styled it 'This Popish-Inglish-Scotish-Masse-Service Booke'. At no time during the process did Charles contemplate calling a General Assembly to discuss either the new prayer book or the new canons; they would be imposed simply by dint of his royal authority. As he explained in the preface to the Scottish liturgy, 'It were to be wished that the whole church of Christ were one, as well in form of public worship as in doctrine', but since this could not 'be hoped for in the whole Catholic Christian church', then 'at least in the churches... under the protection of one sovereign prince the same ought to be endeavoured'.[53]

The canons appeared in January 1636. Making no mention of presbyteries or the General Assembly, they reaffirmed the Five Articles of Perth, prohibited extempore prayer, ordered communion tables to be placed at the east end of the chancel, and commanded acceptance of the forthcoming liturgy, under pain of excommunication.[54] The new prayer book was not to be introduced for another eighteen months. It first had to be printed, and although the council proclaimed that all parishes should have two copies by Easter 1637, there were delays in the print run, and it was expensive. Some ministers could not get the book, others could not afford it, while others clearly did not want to have it, as various Presbyterian synods began to complain that it was full of 'popish errors'. Some bishops thought it prudent to give their ministers until the autumn to decide if they would accept the book. Yet if those in authority in Scotland were anticipating trouble, no one told Charles, fearing royal displeasure. Charles was impatient, and had the bishop of Edinburgh issue an edict on 16 July 1637 stipulating that the new prayer book was to be used in all churches in and around Edinburgh the following Sunday.[55]

'A very great auditory of all sorts of people' attended morning service at St Giles Cathedral on 23 July, including many members of the Scottish privy council, the two archbishops and many other bishops, the lords of the session, and the city magistrates. When the dean opened the prayer book to read the Collects, 'all the commone people, especiallie the women', started shouting, cursing, and clapping their hands, crying out 'Woe, woe', 'they are bringand in Poperie among us', and throwing their stools at the dean. The bishop of Edinburgh stepped into the pulpit to try to appease the crowd, only to have a stool thrown at him. When the archbishop of St Andrews tried to calm people down, he was met with 'bitter curses and imprecations'.

The provost and bailiffs ejected the troublemakers but they just started 'rapping at the Church doores' and 'throwing... stones at the church Windowes', so the bailiffs had to leave their seats once more to try to silence them. Somehow the service was completed over all the din, but as the bishop left the church he was surrounded by an angry crowd, who cursed him and accused him of 'bringing in Poperie'. There was a similar tumult when the service book was read in the church next to St Giles, although 'the furie was not as great'. When the minister read the service book at Greyfriars kirk, however, 'he was so cursed and exclaimed against' that he eventually had to give up. After such incidents, the minister of the College kirk, although he approved of the book, decided not to read it. The council, provost, and bailiffs did their best to ensure that there was no trouble in St Giles or other churches when the prayer book was read again that afternoon, but angry crowds continued to gather in the streets to voice their discontent. When the earl of Roxburgh left St Giles with the bishop of Edinburgh, his coach was 'so pelted with stones, and hooted at with execrations' that he and his footmen had to fight the protesters off with their swords. The bishop was so terrified, it was said, that never before had he 'got such a laxative purgation'.[56]

The protest against the introduction of the prayer book was no spontaneous outburst. The planning had begun in April, and there had been several meetings over the following months, where it was decided that the women should lead the protest and the men would take over afterwards. Although official accounts blamed the disturbances on the 'meaner sort', 'a base multitude', 'the scum and froth of the people', and especially 'rascally serving-women' and 'masterless boyes', such reports should not be taken at face value. Jenny Geddes, who according to legend started the stool throwing at St Giles, is probably a mythical figure. The women who coordinated the outburst at St Giles were matrons of the Edinburgh mercantile community, devout Presbyterians associated with conventicling in the city. There are no grounds for believing the rumour that the women were Edinburgh apprentices in disguise.[57]

The authorities were uncertain how best to respond. On 29 July, following the advice of the bishops, the Scottish council suspended the use of the prayer book until the king's pleasure was known. Charles, however, wanted the prayer book enforced and reminded the council that it was their responsibility to guarantee the safety of those using it. The council duly took action to that effect on 9 August, while the next day the bishops issued an edict requiring presbyteries to enforce the earlier order that ministers acquire two copies of the prayer book. The presbyteries of Irvine and Glasgow promptly petitioned for the suspension of the bishops' edict. On the 25th the council decided to delay any further attempts at enforcement until 20 September and wrote to the king the next day informing him that discontent was much more widespread than they had imagined and seeking his advice, adding ominously there was no knowing 'quherwnto the samen may tend'.[58]

Back in England, Laud was against making any concessions to the Scots, fearing that this would encourage the English Puritans in their own nonconformity. Charles agreed, and sent instructions that the use of the prayer book should be promptly enforced. The four-week delay, however, had merely served to give opponents more time to coordinate their opposition. On 20 September one third of the Scottish nobility, together with a considerable number of gentry and clergy, assembled in Edinburgh with sixty-eight petitions from burghs, parishes, and presbyteries against the prayer book. These were then turned into a national petition and presented to the council. There were further violent demonstrations in Edinburgh on 18 October, when the disaffected forced the council to accept their national supplication; in November opponents of the prayer book formed a committee, known as the Tables council, to coordinate their actions; and further petitions followed in December. Charles remained unwilling to compromise. On 19 February 1638 he issued a proclamation saying that he had overseen and approved the prayer book, that he believed it 'a readie meane to mainteane the trew religion', and that those who continued in their opposition would be proceeded against as traitors.[59]

By raising the stakes and declaring all opposition treasonous, Charles forced opponents of the prayer book into a different course of action. They decided to commission a 'band' of mutual association, which was duly published as the National Covenant on 28 February 1638. Drawn up by the dissenting clergyman Alexander Henderson and the young lawyer Archibald Johnston of Wariston, and revised with the assistance of Balmerino, among others, the National Covenant is a long and somewhat convoluted document, couched in conservative language but embedding a revolutionary ideology. Under its terms the signatories pledged to maintain the 'True Religion' according to James VI's Confession of Faith of 1581, the so-called Negative Confession. After first reaffirming the Negative Confession's abhorrence of 'all kind of Papistry', the Covenant proceeds to recount a long list of parliamentary acts aimed at extirpating popery, to recall the oath all kings swore at their coronation to uphold the true religion, and to condemn the recent 'manifold Innovations and Evils' in the Kirk. Although the document professes a desire to defend the king's 'Person and Authority', the Covenanters nevertheless state their resolve to defend the 'true Religion' and to forbear 'the practice of all Novations, already introduced' until 'they be tried and allowed in free Assemblies, and in Parliaments', and affirm that they will 'resist all these contrary Errours and Corruptions' to the utmost of their power. They further add that they did not 'fear the foul Aspersions of Rebellion', since what they did arose 'from an unfeigned desire to maintain the True Worship of God, the Majesty of Our King, and the Peace of the Kingdom', and that they would use 'all lawful means...to further and promote' their agenda.[60]

The Covenant said nothing specifically about the bishops, although Presbyterians had always assumed the Negative Confession's condemnation of the pope's 'wicked hierarchie' to have included bishops,[61] while its reference to 'free' General Assemblies hinted at the fact that bishops had been restored under James VI by General Assemblies which the Presbyterians did not regard as having been free. As the crisis unfolded, however, the Covenanters made it explicit that their grievances over the canons and the prayer book could not be remedied without addressing the problem of episcopacy. In July 1638 Wariston published a *Short Relation* of the religious problems in Scotland in which he traced the origins of the troubles back to the restoration of episcopacy under James VI and complained of the bishops' usurpation, cruelty, and oppressions 'against Law', for which they 'all deserved exemplare punishment'.[62]

Subscription to the Covenant began on 28 February 1638 and continued over the next several weeks. Eventually, most of the adult male population outside the episcopalian strongholds of Aberdeen and St Andrews and the Catholic areas of the Highlands signed. The Covenant merely confirmed Charles in his belief that the Covenanters were rebels, and that if he did not forcibly bring them to heel he would have no more power in Scotland than a doge of Venice. Scottish Catholics such as Con and Robert Maxwell, first earl of Nithsdale urged military intervention, as did some of the English privy council. James Hamilton, 3rd marquess of Hamilton, Charles's chief advisor on Scottish affairs, feared war would be disastrous and tried to persuade Charles to compromise, hoping to divide the Covenanter movement in the process and build up support for the king. Charles replied that he would rather die than yield to their 'impertinent and damnable Demands', as Hamilton had styled them ('rightly' so in Charles's opinion), but he did see the value in playing for time, since it would not be feasible to launch a military expedition that year; Charles thus urged Hamilton 'to flatter them with what hopes [he] please[d], so you engage me not against my Grounds (and in particular that you consent neither to the calling of Parliament nor General Assembly, until the Covenant be disavowed and given up)', so as 'to win time... untill I be ready to suppress them'. Hamilton eventually persuaded Charles to offer a number of concessions in September: he would withdraw the prayer book, canons, and High Commission, suspend the Five Articles of Perth until parliament passed an Act revoking them, refer the power of the bishops to a General Assembly, and authorize a fresh subscription to the Negative Confession of 1581 in his name (thereby replacing the National Covenant with one of his own). There was general resistance to Charles's Covenant, which the Covenanters saw as a trap, since the king had made it clear that he intended the Confession to be sworn 'for the maintenance of religion, as it is already or presently professed', which would create an obligation to maintain both the Articles of Perth and episcopacy. Charles had clearly been negotiating in bad faith. When a General Assembly met at Glasgow on 21 November, he refused to allow it to discuss episcopacy or to concede the principle that future General Assembles should be allowed to make decisions on liturgy and canons. With the Assembly dominated by a well-organized Presbyterian majority, however, Hamilton had no hope of controlling it. When he tried to dissolve it, it carried on meeting without him.[63]

In early December the Glasgow Assembly instituted what was in effect a revolution in the Kirk. It declared the six General Assemblies that had met between 1606 and 1618 to be 'unfree, unlawfull, and null', condemned the new canons and the prayer book as popish, revoked the Five Articles of Perth, denounced the High Commission as illegal, abolished episcopacy (voting that the institution had been 'abjured' by the Negative Confession), and passed Acts affirming the right of the Kirk to summon yearly general assemblies. Hamilton informed Charles that there was now no alternative to war.[64]

12

············

The British Crisis

The Scottish crisis became a British crisis. This was in part because Charles made it so. Not only had he provoked the Scottish revolt by his policy of trying to bring the Churches in his three kingdoms into closer line with each other, but he also sought to tap into resources in England and Ireland in order to suppress discontent in Scotland. It was also in part because the Covenanters sought to make it so. They realized that their only chance of success was if they could win support in England for their cause, they actively cultivated the support of the disaffected in England, and they wanted to try to bring enough pressure to bear on Charles so that he would be forced to recall parliament in England. They also expected the Scots in Ulster to join with them.

In theory it should have been relatively easy for Charles to put down a rebellion in his northern kingdom. England was both much more populous and much wealthier than Scotland, while Charles could also look to Ireland for support. Why, then, did Charles fail to defeat the Scots? There were tactical mistakes made during the campaigns: if different choices had been made at crucial moments, things might have turned out differently. But there were deeper, underlying problems. The Scottish crisis highlighted the failings of the personal rule in England. The government could not raise sufficient funds to finance the war, which was in turn related to Charles's failure to build a working relationship with his English parliament or to establish an effective enough system of government finance in the absence of parliament; it could not recruit an effective enough army; and there was administrative overload which meant that the machinery of local government in England began to break down. Moreover, too many people had become disaffected as a result of the policies pursued by the government during the 1630s, and Charles was also losing the battle for public opinion. In consequence, Charles faced obstruction all around, as many people across all levels of society refused, were reluctant, or found it impossible to come to his assistance at this time of crisis. Yet it is important to stress that the crisis provoked in England as a result of the Covenanter rebellion in Scotland opened up a space for the discontented in England to express their own dissatisfaction with Charles's rule in England. Thus although a sizeable number of the discontented in England came to sympathize with the Scots and even to identify with their struggle, the English had their own grievances, which were primarily related to developments that had been going on in England.

The Bishops' Wars

Charles's strategy for the first Bishops' War involved a three-pronged assault from the west, east, and south. The Catholic earl of Antrim would provide 5,000 foot and 200 horse from Ireland to invade the Western Isles, while Wentworth was to send an Irish force to Dumbarton; Hamilton would lead an amphibious attack on the east coast of Scotland with eight warships and some 5,000 men, landing at Aberdeen, which for the time being remained a royalist stronghold, and hoping to link up with Highland troops under the command of the marquess of Huntly; and Charles would raise a field army of 24,000 foot and 6,000 horse to rendezvous at York and then march to the Scottish border. However, the forces from Ireland never materialized, while Huntly's troops were dispersed by the Covenanters when they captured Aberdeen, forcing Hamilton to divert to the Firth of Forth, which he found impossible to assault. Charles managed to recruit only 15,000 men, most of these being conscripts who were poorly equipped and inadequately trained. One satirist observed that 'instead of Souldiers there goe babies and Sucklings'.[1] Charles appreciated the need for professional and experienced soldiers, and had asked Spain to provide a body of regular troops from the Netherlands in return for allowing Spain to recruit soldiers in Ireland, although Spain declined. A request for Dutch help was quickly turned down by the Prince of Orange.[2]

The Covenanters, by contrast, were able to assemble what seemed a sizeable army, led by professional soldiers who had fought for the Swedes in the Thirty Years War. In fact, the Covenanter army in 1639 probably numbered no more than 15,000 infantry and 1,500 horse, and the Covenanters were beset by their own logistical and financial problems. But they outwitted the English. When a forward English

force under the command of the earl of Holland spotted the Covenanters around the Scottish border town of Kelso on 4 June, the Scottish commander Alexander Leslie drew up his infantry in shallow
formation with extra sets of colours to make it appear that they were
much more numerous than they really were. Fooled, Holland ordered
a retreat. The next day Leslie lined his men up on the heights of Dun's
Law on the Scottish side of the Tweed, within sight of the king's
camp, again giving the impression of a formidable force. Reports
were soon circulating that the Scots had an army totalling 45,000 men,
some 15,000 of whom were already at the English border. Charles
lost his nerve and opted to sign a truce with the Scots at Berwick on
18 June, hoping in the meantime to raise and equip a better army for
a campaign the following year.[3]

Under the terms of the Pacification of Berwick both sides agreed to
disband their troops while Charles would call a General Assembly
and a parliament in Scotland to settle matters in Kirk and state. When
the General Assembly met in Edinburgh in August 1639 it re-enacted
the measures passed at Glasgow the previous year and prevailed upon
the council to pass an Act imposing subscription to the Covenant
with an express extension against episcopacy and the Five Articles.[4]
However, when the Scottish parliament assembled at the end of the
month, Traquair in his capacity as high commissioner prorogued it
until 2 June 1640. Parliament protested that the prorogation was
illegal (on the grounds that Traquair's commission had expired), and
appointed several members of each estate to continue to sit in Edinburgh to draw up the desired reforming legislation.[5] Parliament duly
reassembled on 2 June, without royal sanction, and proceeded to
institute what was in effect a constitutional revolution. In addition to
ratifying the Acts of the Edinburgh General Assembly, it abolished
the clerical estate in parliament, made subscription to the National
Covenant compulsory for all office holders, passed a Triennial Act
requiring that parliaments be held every three years, and rescinded all
legislation in favour of episcopacy.[6] By this time Charles had already
decided he would once more attempt to solve the Scottish crisis
militarily.

Charles's strategy for the second Bishops' War was similar to the
first: a proposed three-pronged attack from the west, east, and south.
Again, the Irish attack was postponed and an intended amphibious
attack on Edinburgh was aborted, while Charles failed to raise an
army that was any larger than the last. In the meantime the Scots
made a pre-emptive strike, marching over the border on 20 August.

The immediate reason why the English lost the second Bishops' War was that they tried to defend an indefensible position. With the Scots having seized the initiative, Charles and his commanders decided that the best option was to fight the Scots as they tried to cross the Tyne. Leslie led his troops to the ford at Newburn and set up his artillery on the higher ground on the north bank of the Tyne, whence they could fire down on the English occupying the low-lying meadows on the south bank from well-entrenched positions. Even the best of English armies would have had no chance of winning.[7]

Military history provides fertile ground for counterfactual speculation.[8] What might have happened if, instead of losing their nerve, the English had opted to strike against the Scots in early June 1639: could they have inflicted a decisive defeat? What might have happened, for that matter, if the English had chosen a better line of defence in 1640? Or even if they had just managed to hold on to Newcastle for a few more days? (It was said by returning English prisoners of war that had the English 'kept Newcastle 3 days longer', the Scots army 'must have been disbanded for want of food'.[9]) What we can say is that the crown's military indecisiveness in 1639 and its failure to deal with the Scottish attack in 1640 were both related to the fact that Charles was unable to put together the sort of military expedition which he deemed was necessary to defeat the Scots. This was due in turn to the fact that he was short of funds, could not raise sufficient troops of high enough calibre, and that public opinion was turning against him in England. In short, the Bishops' Wars highlighted what was going wrong with Charles's regime in England.

Charles had boxed himself into a corner with regard to state finance. His failure to build a working relationship with his English parliament, and his determination not to call another parliament in England if at all possible, led him to go to war without the backing of the institution that was normally responsible for funding wars. The last English monarch to declare a significant war without parliamentary assistance had been Edward II in 1323, hardly a propitious precedent, since Edward II not long after found himself deposed. To pay for his army, Charles intended to rely on a combination of voluntary contributions, loans, and the sale of lands, offices, patents, and monopolies. He would also use his feudal prerogatives to the full. He issued a quasi-feudal summons for the nobility to meet him at York with horses and troops, he enforced scutage (a medieval levy that allowed a knight to buy out of military service), and he demanded that tenants in the northern counties perform feudal obligations of border service. There were many problems with this strategy. Charles found it difficult to secure the level of voluntary funding or loans that were necessary, in part because existing royal fiscal exactions were burdensome enough, and in part because Charles's political capital was low. Crucially, the Common Council of London refused to give any money towards the cost of the war, 'in regard'—it was said—'of the many taxes imposed on them, and the loss of their lands at Londonderry'.[10] Enforcing obsolete feudal obligations was hardly the way to provide an efficient fighting force suitable to the modern era. The nobility had long since become a civilized and peace-loving class, and even when willing lacked the necessary experience or equipment to help the king. Although only seventeen of the 115 peers who received the call tried to get out of their obligation, few were able to offer horses. A further blow came when Charles decided that all those assembled at York should take an oath of allegiance: Viscount Saye and Lord Brooke—whose sympathies lay with the Scots and who may already have been in contact with the Covenanter leadership—refused, on the grounds that the king could not impose a new oath without the consent of parliament.[11] Charles's best hope lay in mobilizing the militia; his recent reform of the militia had, after all, seemingly gone quite well and this would be a test of how efficient a fighting force had been created. The privy council therefore ordered the thirteen northernmost counties to mobilize their militias and place them under the command of royal officers, and in addition ordered Midland and southern counties to furnish a certain number of men from their trained bands. A county militia, however, was supposed to defend its own county; and, nervous about forcing local trained bands to be deployed out of their area, the council decided to allow militiamen from the Midlands and south who preferred not to serve to provide a substitute. This right of substitution was widely invoked, with the result that most of the recruits were pressed men who had not had any previous experience in the militia. The end product was a hopelessly inadequate force: inexperienced, ill-trained, and poorly equipped. No wonder Charles opted for a truce to buy more time to try to get together a better army.[12] Londoner Thomas Davis, 'a poore adged man', holding forth in a pub in Newgate in the last week of June 1639, thought Charles had 'yielded to the Scotts both basely and scurvely', but was not surprised, given that the king had taken with him men who were 'more fitter to use such weapons as thies', Davis said, pointing to his testicles, than they were 'weapons of warr'.[13]

The Irish Parliament, the Short Parliament, and the Convocation

Being advised that the cost of a subsequent campaign against the Scots would be in excess of £1,000,000, Charles finally agreed to call a parliament. To try to ensure that parliament would not be able to exploit the crown's financial weakness, he continued to try to raise money by other means. To help fund the war, Wentworth negotiated a loan of £300,000 from Spain in return for England's helping the Spanish against the Dutch and allowing Spain to recruit 3,000 men for their armies from Ireland. The members of the privy council pledged a loan of £300,000, two-thirds of which had come in by Christmas.[14] What Charles really needed was to tap into the wealth of the City of London, but the City dragged its feet.[15] Meanwhile, other forms of crown revenue were drying up. Ship money collection broke down almost completely, in part because the system was cracking under the strain, and in part because people assumed that if parliament was going to be called the logic behind this emergency levy no longer applied. It also proved difficult to collect coat and conduct money, a prerogative tax levied to clothe and equip new recruits.[16]

The decision to call parliament in England was taken in early December 1639. Charles and his advisors knew it was a risky strategy. Laud, although he went along with the idea, feared he would 'be destroyed the verie first daye of their sitting', to judge from the numerous libels 'to that purpose' that were 'cast in his house'. Charles therefore decided to delay the meeting of the English parliament until the middle of April 1640, to allow a parliament to meet in Ireland first.[17] It was a deliberate attempt to play the two kingdoms off against each other: Charles hoped that taxes raised in Ireland would decrease his dependence on the English parliament, while an appropriate show of loyalty from the Irish parliament might help cajole the English into compliance with his demands.

As we have seen, all was not well in Ireland, and the Scottish revolt threatened to undermine what Wentworth had achieved. Most worrisome was Ulster, with its sizeable Scottish Presbyterian population, and where Wentworth had been busy trying to eradicate Protestant nonconformity. The Covenanting movement gave the Ulster Scots cause for encouragement. Writing in February 1638, Bramhall complained to Laud of the 'desperate example' which 'the contumatious non conformists in Scotland' had given to Ireland, and how 'this contagion' had 'lately spread it self over the Face of the whole counties of Downe and Conner, and some adjacent places', including his own diocese.[18] In September the bishop of Down and Connor informed Wentworth that 'All the Puritans' in his diocese were 'confident that the Arms raised against the King in Scotland' would 'procure them a Liberty to set up their own Discipline here', and that 'many' who had recently been 'brought to some Measure of Conformity' were once again refusing to conform.[19] The nervousness of the government is revealed by the savage sentence the court of Castle Chamber in Dublin imposed on a Scottish gentleman in early 1639 for having allegedly said the queen was intending to 'joyne with the French, when the Kinge was gone to the north against the Scotch': the man was sentenced to be fined £10,000, to stand in the pillory and have both his ears cut off and his tongue bored through, and to be imprisoned during royal pleasure, although the queen herself interceded to have the corporal punishment remitted.[20] Concerned about the allegiance of the Ulster Scots, in April 1639 Wentworth stage-managed a petition from 'divers of the Scottish nation inhabiting Ireland' stating their disapproval of the Covenant and asking the Lord Deputy to prescribe an oath whereby they could testify their loyalty. An oath of loyalty—known by its opponents as 'the black oath'—was duly drawn up and required of all Scots over the age of sixteen living in Ireland, as well as Scots living in and about London. Initially most complied, though resistance began to mount after the Pacification of Berwick, while many dissidents opted to leave Ulster and return to Scotland, with predictable adverse effects on the economy.[21] In February 1640 the bishop of Killala, Archibald Adair, himself a Scot, was deprived and fined £2,000 for chastising John Corbet for leaving his living in Scotland rather than take the Covenant; Adair allegedly said that if he had been in Corbet's shoes he would have taken the Covenant, that Leslie had 'greate, and brave armyes in the field', and that if it were true that 'the Bishopps were the cause' of the misunderstanding between the King and his Scottish subjects 'he wisht they [the bishops] were in hell'.[22]

Apart from 'some unruly Scotts inhabiteinge the North', however, the rest of Ireland seemed in a peaceful and prosperous condition, as one Dublin correspondent observed in January 1640, which augured well for the forthcoming parliament.[23] Considerable pressure was used to get government candidates returned and this, combined with the fact that eight boroughs under the control of Old English Catholics had recently been disenfranchised, meant that Catholic representation in the Commons was a mere 74 in a House of 235. Wentworth (promoted to Lord Lieutenant and raised to the English peerage as earl of Strafford in January 1640) pursued the same strategy as in 1634: demanding supply first and postponing grievances to a later session. Despite being frustrated over the Graces, for the time being the Catholics were more concerned about the prospect of the fiercely anti-Catholic Covenanters emerging victorious. Thus the first session, which opened on 16 March, went remarkably smoothly. In return for a promise to redress their grievances, the Irish parliament unanimously voted four subsidies worth £45,000 each to fund an Irish army of 9,000 men to help suppress the Scots.[24] The Irish House of Commons published a declaration testifying Ireland's 'happinesse' at being 'governed by the best of Kings' and promising further supply in future if needed. The Irish privy council likewise wrote to Charles thanking him for requiring 'Aid of his Subjects in a Parliamentary Way', when there existed precedents for raising money in Ireland by dint of the royal prerogative alone to meet the expenses of an expedition against the Scots. In addition, the Irish clergy voted six subsidies to be paid over the next three years—these on top of the three subsidies that still remained to be paid from last time. Strafford left Ireland in early April in triumphant mood—though not in the best of health—telling Charles things had gone as well as could be wished.[25]

In England, in the build up to the parliamentary elections, the regime was feeling jittery. On 13 February 1640 Lord Keeper Finch gave a rousing speech to all the judges just before they went out on circuit, briefing them on their obligations to administer justice and to serve the king and alerting them to some of the problems the government was facing. 'Courage, stoutnes and Magnanimitie', he began, 'best becomes a Judge', but 'severitie too', for 'yt is your partes to break the Insolencie of the Vulgar before yt approacheth two [sic] nigh the royall throne'. It was impossible for the king 'to knowe all', and so he was dependent on his judges as 'the great Surveyors of the Kingdom'. Finch then warned them about some of the problems the government was experiencing with local officers of law enforcement. There were some JPs of a 'petulant humor' who thought it 'too much to serve the Kinge'; the judges were to find out their names so that they might be punished for their recalcitrance. They were to see that the law was duly executed, since execution was 'the life of the Lawe', though of late 'Sheriffs and under officers' could 'hardly bee got to execute any process at all'. Finch then turned to the problems in collecting ship money, protesting that there was 'not that chearefull obedience given to the Kinge's Writts as his gratious and Fatherly Care doeth deserve'. It was 'a base and unworthy thought', and 'contrarie to that Allegiance…wee owe', to suggest 'that his Majestie would charge his Subjects in vaine and to noe purpose': the king needed ship money so that he could fulfil his duty of safeguarding the narrow seas, its legality had already been determined in Westminster Hall, and the judges were to make sure those who refused to pay were brought to account, 'that they may see what yt is to disobey the Kinge's Writt'. It was also the king's command that they take 'care to preserve Religion' and enforce the laws against Catholic recusants and Protestant separatists: 'The Lawe must bringe men to God's house', Finch proclaimed, 'and there they may Learne to obey the Lawe for Conscience sacke and not for feare'.[26]

The parliamentary elections that spring proved to be 'very tumultary'.[27] There were sixty-two electoral contests, more than ever before. Although the government electoral machinery went into overdrive in an attempt to secure the return of suitable candidates, those associated with the court did badly. The Duchy of Cornwall, for example, nominated seventeen candidates for Cornish boroughs, but only three were chosen. Nationwide, the court nominated thirty-eight candidates, twenty-seven of whom were rejected. In contrast, opposition peers such as Warwick, Essex, Saye, Brooke, and others met with considerable success in placing their candidates: a group of some thirteen 'reform' peers between them nominated thirty-five candidates, of whom only three failed to get elected.[28] In some constituencies political passions ran high. When Laud's secretary campaigned at Canterbury, the citizens cried 'no Images, no Papists, no Arch-bishop's Secretary'.[29] In Lincolnshire a paper was circulated urging voters to choose no 'Court Atheist', 'Church Papist', 'fenn-drainer', 'Shipp Shrieve', or 'lawne sleeve'. Several counties and boroughs presented their members with petitions outlining their grievances. That from Essex complained of 'Innovations in matters of Religion', impositions, monopolies, foresting large parts of the county, and ship money ('a burden unknowne to our fathers, insupportably grievous to ourselves, and exceedingly prejudiciall to the Liberties, and Immunities of his Majestye's Subjects'), and called for annual sessions of parliament in accordance with the laws enacted during the reign of Edward III. The Hertfordshire electorate bemoaned how they had 'bene unusually overcharged, and insupportably burdend in their Consciences, Persons, Estates and Freedomes', citing innovations in religion, abuses of purveyors, monopolies, and 'the paiment of Shipp-money', the legality of which they requested might be re-examined.[30] The 'comons' of Newcastle petitioned the mayor and corporation asking them to instruct their recently elected MPs to 'be carefull...to maintain the Orthodox faith of our Church and wholy to oppose all innovations both in doctrine and discipline', 'to stand for the libertyes and freedome of the subjects' (which they described as being 'principally in the maintenance of magna Charta and the other fundamentall perliamentore lawes'), while local merchants petitioned the MPs directly against the soap monopoly, system of tobacco patents, various impositions, and 'the Taxes and Cessements for Shipmoney and other intolerable', which if they were not laid aside would, they predicted, in a 'short time utterly begger this Corporation, noe part of the Kingdome being burthened in that Proportion'.[31] In Yorkshire the freeholders instructed one of their knights of the shire, Sir William Savile, to make sure that the 'grievance of the shipp money' was 'taken away'.[32]

As with the Irish parliaments of 1634 and 1640, Charles wanted to defer a consideration of grievances until after supply had been voted. Given that Charles had not met with parliament since 1629, and given the circumstances under which this one was called, one might have expected an extended speech from the throne. Instead, Charles merely stated that a 'greate and weighty cause' had caused him to 'call his people together' and left it to Lord Keeper Finch to outline the government's agenda. Finch urged MPs to 'lay aside all other debates' for the time being, so that they could confirm Tonnage and Poundage and vote funds for the war against the Scots.[33] The Commons, however, refused to grant supply before the redress of grievances. Although Charles showed himself willing to offer some concessions, success for him could mean only one thing: obtaining the funds necessary to defeat the Scots and re-impose episcopacy in Scotland by force. There was an influential group of dissident peers and MPs—which included the likes of Bedford, Warwick, Essex, Saye, Mandeville, and Brooke in the Lords, and John Pym, John Hampden, and Oliver St John in the Commons—who knew that outright defeat for the Covenanters would scupper any chance of political and ecclesiastical reform in England. Although the evidence is obscure, this group might have been in active collusion with the Scots and planning to lobby parliament in support of the Covenanters to bring pressure on the king to reach a peaceful reconciliation with his Scottish subjects. However, there was also a sizeable group of MPs who would have been willing to support the king's efforts against the Scots in return for constitutional reform; in 1642 most of these men were to be royalists, though in 1640 Charles was unable to make common cause with them.[34]

Pym set the agenda in the Commons on 17 April with a powerful speech lasting two hours in which he listed some three dozen grievances relating to the liberties of parliament, innovations in religion, and the property of goods—among them Tonnage and Poundage, distraint of knighthood, monopolies, forest fines, ship money, and the intermission of parliaments (Pym arguing that parliaments were supposed to be kept once per year).[35] In response to such demands, Charles promised he would tell the bishops there should be no more innovations in the Church, offered to abandon ship money if parliament would provide some other means of funding the navy, and urged MPs to trust him to remedy their grievances in the future if they voted him money now. The trouble was, the sum needed was large: twelve subsidies, nearly twice the amount voted in 1624 for the recapture of the Palatinate. With the Commons refusing to trust the king, Charles appealed to the Lords not to join with them in demanding redress of grievances before supply. Although the majority of peers rallied behind the crown, twenty-one entered their dissents, among them Saye and Brooke.[36]

Facing an impasse, Charles dissolved what has become known at the Short Parliament on 5 May, after just three weeks. In his declaration explaining the dissolution (probably penned by Lord Keeper Finch), Charles criticized the Commons for departing from the traditional practice of parliaments aiding and assisting the king 'with free and fitting supply towards the maintenance of their Wars' and introducing a way 'of bargaining and contracting', although he blamed the 'misunderstanding' on 'some few sediciously-affected men' and said that if his subjects truly did have any grievances they could petition him for redress 'out of Parliament'.[37] The day following the dissolution Charles sent agents to search the lodgings of Warwick, Saye, Brooke, Pym, Hampden, and Sir Walter Erle for evidence of treasonable dealings with the Scots. Rumours were soon flying that some of 'the best men of the Kingdome' had been 'imprisoned by the King', although nothing distinctly treasonable was uncovered, and Warwick and his fellow suspects remained at liberty.[38]

The dissolution of parliament should have brought to an end the meeting of Convocation, the deliberative body of the Church. Breaking with tradition, however, Charles allowed Convocation to continue to meet, so that it could finalize seventeen new canons intended to put a seal on the ecclesiastical initiatives of the reign and at the same time make a powerful ideological statement in defence of the monarchy. Canon one required clergy to affirm four times a year from the pulpit 'the most High and Sacred order of Kings' to be 'of Divine Right'; that 'the power to call and dissolve Councels both national and provincial' lay with the king, and that anyone who tried to set up, in any of the king's realms, 'any independent Coactive power' was guilty of treason; that 'for subjects to bear Arms against the King...upon any pretence whatsoever', even if merely defensive, was resisting the ordinance of God; and that it was 'the dutie of the subjects to supply their king' for 'the publicke defence'. While canon three enjoined all clergy to do everything in their power to 'reduce all such...who are misled into Popish superstition', canon five urged the same with regard to sectaries, who 'no lesse than Papists' sought to subvert 'the Doctrine and Discipline of the Church of England'. Canon seven required that communion tables be placed at the east end of the church, claiming that this was in conformity with the Elizabethan injunctions and that doing so did not imply it was an altar, and that the table should be railed in. Most controversial was canon six, which required all clergy to swear an oath by 2 November saying they approved 'the Doctrine and Discipline...established in the Church of England, as containing all things necessary to salvation' and that they would never 'consent to alter the Government of this Church, by Arch-bishops, Bishops, Deanes, and Archdeacons, etc. as it stands now established, and as by right it ought to stand'.[39]

The canons were an affront to Puritan sensibilities. The London Puritan Nehemiah Wallington described them as 'cursed' and 'hatched in Hell';[40] ominously, he copied into his diary extracts from a recent book, published anonymously with an Amsterdam imprint, which argued that resistance was justified 'if a king maintain a faction...which go about to oppress his whole kingdom and people in their law and liberties, and most of all in the true religion'.[41] Yet the canons also upset many conventional Anglicans, especially canon six with its ambiguous 'etc.' clause. Several tracts appeared questioning the legitimacy of the clause, while groups of clergy from various parts of the country drew up lengthy statements articulating their concerns about the new oath. One concern was why the clergy should have to acknowledge that not only the doctrine but also the discipline of the Church of England contained all things necessary to salvation, since the doctrine of the Church of England was that scripture contained everything necessary to salvation and that any part of its discipline that was not commanded by scripture could, in fact, be changed. Another was that the new oath undermined the royal supremacy and left clerics 'not at Liberty, to obey the King and his lawes, in case any be made to alter it'.[42] Some of the clergy held meetings to discuss how to respond to the oath. Some twenty-seven ministers from across the south-east Midlands (Northamptonshire, Leicestershire, Rutland)—many of them Puritans—met at the Swan Inn in Kettering on 25 August and concluded 'never...to take the Oath, but rather to loose their liveings', on the grounds that to yield would be to set a dangerous precedent 'for such other Oathes, thereafter' and that the oath was 'alltogether Illegal' and 'against the King's Supremacie'.[43]

The Battle for Public Opinion

The sudden dissolution of parliament and the new canons added to public discontent. Libels began to circulate in the capital in early May summoning the apprentices to meet in St George's Fields on the next holiday to make an attack on the archbishop's residence in Lambeth. At about 12 o'clock on the night of 11 May, Whit Monday, several hundred youths—one report put the figure as high as 1,200—armed with clubs and marching to the beat of drums, stormed Lambeth Palace in search of Laud, though the archbishop had prudently taken a boat to Whitehall about an hour before and, unable to find their man, the apprentices eventually dispersed, promising that by hook or crook they would speak to Laud sooner or later. Some of the ringleaders were arrested and thrown into Southwark prison, but this in turn prompted further unrest on the 13th as a group of apprentices stormed the jail in an effort to free their associates. The government had one of the apprentices racked, because he refused to confess—the last instance of judicial torture in England. Another was hanged, drawn, and quartered for treason.[44] Edward Neale from the parish of Shelley in Essex, informing his fellow parishioners of the attack, predicted 'they would shortly rise in the Countrie', there being 'no lawes now', and that 'the first houses they would pull downe should be the houses of those that tooke part with the Bishopps'. (Neale was thinking in particular of his local parson, Mr Greene.)[45]

The dissolution of the Short Parliament denied Charles the money he desperately needed to fund his army. He decided to push ahead with recruitment nevertheless, with the inevitable result that those recruited were poorly paid and ill-equipped. There was also widespread obstruction of the government's efforts. Some refused to serve. One Essex man was indicted—and acquitted—at the summer assizes for saying that if he were 'prest for a souldier the Kinge should be the first that [he] would ayme att'.[46] Parish officers and local constables were often reluctant to find suitable conscripts, while the widespread abuse of the substitution clause meant many undesirables—even vagrants—were pressed. Many were resentful at being forced into service. Some were even mutinous. There were reports of riots by troops from over twenty counties.[47] In mid-June Dorset recruits on their way to York murdered their commander, Lieutenant William Mohun, when they got to Faringdon in Berkshire (now Oxfordshire), beating him to death with cudgels; Mohun was not only a notoriously cruel taskmaster but also a reputed papist. Three weeks later Lieutenant Compton Evers, another suspected papist, was beaten to death by Devon conscripts stationed at Wellington in Somerset. In several places soldiers attacked local churches, pulling down altar rails and breaking images and stained-glass windows. In April 1640 Essex soldiers recruited to fight against the Scots stormed Radwinter church, destroyed the rails, and tore down the images, which they tied to a tree and whipped before carrying them five miles to Saffron Walden to be burned. When they could not find the minister, Richard Drake, they seized a duck and ripped off its head, which they hurled into the church, promising they would 'sarve the Drake so if they could catch him'. When recruits at Ashford, Kent, learned one of their number had the surname Bishop, they dressed him up 'like a Bishope with a Gowne, white sleeves and a flat Cape' and tried him before a mock court of justice, where they found him guilty of causing 'the troubles that were come on the Church and Commonwealth' and sentenced him to death—even going so far as to hang him 'in jest'.[48]

We should not exaggerate the ideological sophistication of the mutinous troops. Although some were doubtless giving vent to their anger at the recent Laudian innovations in the Church, others were swayed by a cruder form of anti-Catholic bigotry, a more generalized hostility towards the government, and a resentment against the way they were being treated in the army. Certainly it would be naïve to read such acts of iconoclasm as necessarily indicative of a strong identification with the Puritan cause. Essex man John Ayly, who was involved in pulling down altar rails in his local parish church of Kelvedon in September 1640, after the Scots had occupied the north of England, had in the past been in trouble for a range of offences, from not going to church to fornication, and had been excommunicated.[49]

But that, of course, is the point. It was not only the Puritans who were alienated; many who would not necessarily have thought of themselves as having much sympathy with the Puritans were now deeply disaffected. Nevertheless, such disaffection was coming to be expressed in religious terms, not least because the Laudian innovations had become symbolic of the regime they had come to despise.

A further reason why Charles failed to defeat the Scots in the Bishops' Wars, therefore, was that he had lost the battle for public opinion. As the conflict unfolded, both sides engaged in a war of words to try to win support for their respective positions. The Covenanters had to appeal to several different audiences. They needed to cement support within Scotland, to make sure that their cause truly did become a national one; thus some of their writings were aimed at rebuking the position of the episcopalian academics at Aberdeen who remained loyal to Charles and who produced works criticizing the Covenanters. But they also sought to appeal to opinion outside Scotland, particularly in England but also in Ireland and on the Continent, and they had to respond to the charges against them put out in the counter-propaganda sponsored by the government. Covenanter publications started pouring into England from the very beginning of the crisis, as did manuscript separates or newsletters justifying the Covenanters' stance, which were in turn copied for further distribution, either in print or manuscript. Some works were published in Glasgow or Edinburgh and either smuggled across the border, via Carlisle or Newcastle, or sent through the mail. Others were published in the Low Countries and came in through London. Covenanter propaganda was widely distributed and potentially reached a wide audience. Print runs could be quite high; the Scot Thomas Crawford commissioned 10,000 copies in English and 3,000 in Flemish of one particular Covenanter tract. The Covenanters appear to have tapped into established Puritan networks in England to disseminate their message. Works reached not just London but also provincial centres, and were found scattered around in city streets and even left at sporting events where large crowds were expected to gather, and were read out loud in local inns and other meeting places. When the clergy of the south-east Midlands met at the Swan Inn in Kettering to discuss their response to the etcetera oath on 25 August 1640, for example, they also had 'a new booke out of Scotland', outlining the Scots' grievances, 'read amongst them'. Most disturbingly, perhaps, some pamphlets reached troops in the king's army.[50]

How did the Covenanters seek to justify their actions? They were, after all, engaging in active resistance to their divinely ordained sovereign, which was treason. They were also hoping to persuade the English to support them in what was a war against England and ended up being a Scottish invasion of England. There was, of course, a native tradition of resistance theory to which the Scots could appeal: for example, Buchanan's *De Jure Regni Apud Scotos*, justifying the revolution against Mary Queen of Scots, was reprinted in 1638 to remind Scots of how they were entitled to respond to royal tyranny.[51] In their own writings, however, the Covenanters tended to be more cautious. They repeatedly denied that they were seeking to challenge royal authority, instead representing themselves as acting defensively against dangerous popish innovations illegally imposed upon their Kirk. *An Information to all Good Christians* of 1639 insisted that 'Religion' was 'the only subject, conscience the motive, and reformation the aime', and that they never had 'the least intention to call off our duetifull obedience unto his Majestie's most lawfull authoritie' nor 'harboured any thought against our gracious Soveraigne', whom they acknowledged to be 'the Lord's Vicegerent'; they had merely proceeded by humbly 'petitioning his Majestie for legall redresse' against innovations 'pressed upon the whole Church here, without order or consent'.[52] A Covenanter *Remonstrance* of that year denied that the Covenanters aimed at 'the overthrowing of regall power', because 'the pillars of true regall power' were 'religion and righteousnesse', which it was the Covenanters' aim to establish. Agreeing with James VI and I's contention that kings were parents of their people, the Covenanters merely insisted that kings 'ought to be common parents' and 'not make themselves a party', adding that it was their 'delight to obey his Majestie's just commands', and that they had no intention of protesting 'mutinously' against the king's 'unjust' commands: they intended only to protest in a fair and legal way 'for preservation of right, and preventing of evil'.[53]

Within the conservative rhetoric, however, was embedded a revolutionary ideology. The *Remonstrance* of 1639 attacked absentee kingship and embraced contract theory. Insisting that a distinction needed to be made between a resident monarch who 'by opening his ears to both parties' might be 'rightly informed', and 'the King farre from us in another kingdome, hearing the one partie, and misinformed by our adversaries', it alleged that there was a 'mutuall contract betwixt the King and the people', as confirmed by the coronation oath, various Acts of parliament, scripture, and the law of nature, and that 'when our immediate Superiours' went 'out of their line and order', the 'inferiour Magistrats, Judges, Councellors, nobles, Peeres of the land, Parliament men, Barrons, Burgesses and the whole bodie of the Kingdome' were entitled to stand 'to their own defence'.[54] Henderson developed similar arguments about absentee kingship and the right of inferior magistrates to resist in self-defence in his 'Instructions for Defensive Arms' of 1639, which was widely circulated in manuscript before finally being published in 1642. God 'hath ordained Magistrates to be his Ministers for the good of his people' and 'the safety and good of the people' was 'the supream Law', Henderson insisted; it followed that 'the people maketh the Magistrate', and 'the same Law and Order that biddeth us defend the Supream Magistrate against the unjust invasion of his Deputy and Inferiours' also commanded us 'to defend God's right and to preserve the people's peace against the unjust invasions of the Supream Magistrate'.[55]

The Covenanters also represented themselves as having a common cause with the English, whom they styled their 'brethren and neighbours': they both faced a popish plot to subvert the reformed religion and their enemies were the same, namely Laud and the Arminians and evil counsellors such as Wentworth. 'In joyning both kingdoms in a bloody war' and 'by weakning both', the *Remonstrance* alleged, they intended Rome to 'be built in the midst of us, and the Pope...set over all': we were 'all under one roof, in one and the same ship, and members of one body', it continued; 'the cause' is 'the same...Our salvation is common.' The Covenanters further pledged their support for the calling of a parliament in England to resolve the crisis. 'We earnestly entreat all in England', the *Remonstrance* implored, 'to supplicate his Majestie for calling a Parliament there, that this mysterie of iniquity...may be discovered, and the prime agents therein...tried and punished.'[56] An *Information to all Good Christians* predicted that if the 'Parliament of England were convened, and the whole progresse of this businesse faithfully represented to them', they would 'bee moved to become petitioners to his sacred Majestie on our behalfe'.[57] After the meeting of the Short Parliament the Covenanters stated how they were encouraged by the fact that the English parliament's 'grievances and desires' were 'so homogeneall and sibbe to ours'.[58] At first the Covenanters insisted that they would go to war with England only in self-defence and if provoked by English action, it having never been the intention 'to offer the least act of hostilitie to our neighbour Kingdome, except in so farre as we shall bee necessitat in our own defence'.[59] 'We take armes not for invasion, not for alteration of the civill government, not for wronging any man's person, or to possesse what belongeth to any man', the *Remonstrance* clarified, 'but for the defence of our religion, liberties and lives': a 'necessary prevention', which had been 'the practise of France, of Holland, of Germanie, and of our own nation' in the past.[60] When the Covenanters opted to make a pre-emptive strike in August 1640, they protested that by invading England they were acting defensively, that they intended no harm against the English but sought only their 'own peace and preservation' and that they would lay down their weapons as soon as they obtained 'a sure peace', and expressed their hope that their going into England would actually 'link the two nations together in straiter and stronger bonds both of civill and Christian love, then ever before'.[61]

Charles was somewhat slower in getting off the mark in the propaganda war. During 1638 the only major replies to the Covenanters, apart from what Charles said in royal proclamations, came from the Aberdeen doctors.[62] But by 1639 he had come to see the need to engage more wholeheartedly in the battle for public opinion. He commissioned the dean of Rochester, Walter Balcanquhall—a transplanted Scot who had been an observer at the Glasgow Assembly in November and December 1638—to produce a detailed history of the Scottish troubles, written in the king's name, justifying Charles's policies in Scotland and exposing the treasonous nature of the Covenanters' actions, which was published as *A Large Declaration Concerning the Late Tumults in Scotland* in the spring of 1639. Secretary Windebank produced a sequel a year later, taking the story from the Pacification of Berwick up to the meeting of the Short Parliament.[63] The king's printer John Legatt set up at Newcastle upon Tyne in 1639 in order to print royal proclamations and pamphlets stating the government's position. The bishop of Durham, Thomas Morton—a Calvinist who had been an outspoken opponent of Arminianism in the 1620s—preached against the Scots at Durham Cathedral and his sermon was subsequently printed by the king's special command.[64] There were a number of other clerical propagandists: the Church of Scotland minister John Corbet, who had fled to Ireland following his refusal to take the Covenant, the bishop of Down and Connor Henry Leslie (himself Scottish by birth)—both Corbet and Leslie were clients of Wentworth—and the French Huguenot turned Church of England cleric Peter du Moulin.[65] The choice is revealing. The government opted not to draw on the services of the Laudian divines it had used in its propaganda campaign of the mid-1630s (although

Heylyn and Pocklington did deliver sermons at court on the Scottish crisis that were not published); in the context, this would have been counterproductive. Instead the case for the government was made by Scottish-born divines, by one of the few remaining Calvinists on the English episcopal bench, and by someone from the reformed tradition in France.[66] This was a regime that was thinking quite self-consciously about how best to pitch its case. One may wonder how wide an audience government propaganda reached. The *Large Declaration* was large indeed: at 430 pages long, it was expensive and hardly likely to be accessible to those on the margins of literacy. Balcanquhall's work, and Windebank's sequel, were clearly aimed at the political elite; that by Windebank, for instance, was timed to appear just before the meeting of the Short Parliament in the hope of convincing MPs of the need for voting money to suppress the Scots' rebellion.[67] Yet government propagandists saw themselves as furnishing loyalists with arguments which they in turn could use to convince others. Corbet explained that his aim in publishing an anti-Covenanter work of 1639 was to provide 'all our Orthodoxe Divines' with the information and arguments necessary 'to stop the mouth of the Gain-sayers'.[68]

Government propaganda represented the Covenanters as rebels who were challenging the king's authority. It predictably rehearsed traditional arguments concerning irresistible, divine-right monarchy. The Aberdeen doctors, for example, quoting James VI and I's *Trew Law of Free Monarchies*, insisted that the king was God's lieutenant upon earth and was to be judged only by God; even if the king did act wickedly, subjects could do nothing but suffer patiently, 'with Prayers and Teares to God', or else flee the realm.[69] Similarly Morton, preaching at Durham Cathedral on 5 May 1639, took as his text Romans 13:1, 'Let every soul be subject to the higher Powers', reminding listeners and readers that resisting the king was resisting the ordinance of God, and that the Covenanters condemned themselves by representing their resistance as being 'for defence of Religion', since arms were 'not to be taken up by Subjects, for defence of Religion'.[70] Yet government propagandists tended to deny that the Covenanters could possibly be acting in defence of religion, insisting instead that religion had nothing to do with the matter. As a royal proclamation of 27 February 1639 put it, the aim of the Covenanters was 'not Religion' but 'to shake off all Monarchicall government, and to vilifie Our Regall power'.[71] Balcanquhall, ventriloquizing for King Charles, claimed that the Covenanters' 'tumultuous and rebellious courses' demonstrated 'their wearinesse of being governed by Us and Our Lawes'. The question was not, 'whether there shall be a Service Booke, Booke of Canons, high Commission, nay, nor whether there shall be no lay-Elders in Assemblies, or no Episcopall government'; rather, it was 'Whether We [Charles] and Our Successours shall be any more Kings of that Kingdome'.[72] Royal chaplain Henry King (who succeeded Balcanquall as dean of Rochester), preaching at St Paul's Cross on 27 March 1640, the anniversary of Charles's accession, opined that 'what ever else occasions the difference' between Scotland and England, '*Religion* cannot be the Cause'.[73] The charges against Charles, the king's defenders claimed, were simply unfair. As Corbet put it, Charles was 'far from thinking of any innovation of religion' but was instead 'resolved constantly to maintaine the same, as it is established by law in ... Scotland', and all along he had shown himself receptive to his subjects' grievances and been willing to make compromises.[74] Discussing the Covenanter demand that episcopacy should be abolished, Balcanquhall reminded readers that episcopacy was established by Acts of parliament and bishops were one of the three estates of parliament and that Charles could not permit his subjects acting 'out of Parliament, or in Parliament without Our consent' to 'abolish any Act of Parliament', since this 'destroyeth the very foundation of government and justice in all Monarchies', nor to 'destroy any of the three Estates of Parliament'.[75] Corbet insisted that Charles remained determined 'to proceed according to the Laws' and also defended 'the lawfull and laudable calling of Episcopacy'; by contrast, the Covenanters showed contempt for both the king 'and his Lawes', and sought to make themselves judges in their own cause.[76]

Government propagandists even endeavoured to exploit popular fears of popery by arguing that the Covenanters, by resisting the king, were acting on popish principles. Thus Balcanquhall argued that the Covenanters' maxims were 'the same with the Jesuites', while Corbet accused the Covenanters of borrowing their intellectual armoury from 'the Papists' and asked: 'Is your doctrine so Jesuiticall and rebellious, to thinke that the King's authority is of humane institution by positive lawes, and not from God?'[77] Morton maintained that although those of 'the Romish' Church and the Covenanters 'do dissent in Religion', nevertheless they agreed 'in this one Conclusion of professing violent Resistance, for defence of Religion'. It was as if the Covenanters 'meant to be the disciples of Papists'.[78] Du Moulin thought that 'when God revealeth the secrets of the hearts, Some fierce Covenanters shall be found Jesuites, whose purpose was to make the King lose one way or other, that supremacie which the Pope challengeth'.[79]

The government, in its official propaganda, steered clear of invoking crude anti-Scottish stereotypes or attacking the Scots as a people; after all, Charles was also king of Scotland, and so government polemic was careful to target only those Scots who were rebels—the Covenanters—rather than the Scottish people as a whole. Nevertheless, efforts were made to tap into latent Scotophobic sentiments in the recruitment campaigns. The Laudian clergy were observed to rail against the Scots from the pulpit and at local musters. The London-based Puritan diarist Nehemiah Wallington noted how in 1640 the Scots were mocked, scoffed at, and called rebels, observing 'what bookes were made of them and Ballets Songe (of them) by every Rascole at the Corners of our Streets'.[80]

The effect of the rival propaganda campaigns was to polarize opinion in England. Some English people were eager to see the Scots get their come-uppance.[81] Wallington records the story of one common soldier recruited to fight in the first Bishops' War who boasted that 'he would not return till his hand...had plucked out the heart's blood of a Scot'. (Wallington took it as a sign of God's providence that the soldier was subsequently struck lame in his arm.) Captain Thomas Windebank alleged that the English troops sent to Berwick in June 1639 kept their spirits up 'with the hopes of rubbing, fubbing, and scrubbing those scurvy, filthy, durty, nasty, lousie, ytchy, scabby, shitten, stinking, slovenly, snotty-nos'd, logger-headed, foolish, insolent, proud, beggerly, impertinent, absurd, grout-headed, vilainous, barbarous, bestiall, false, lying, rogueish, divelish, long-ear'd, short-hair'd, damnable, Atheisticall, puritanical Crue of the Scotch Covenant'.[82] Others expressed their loyalty to the crown by informing on those they suspected of harbouring pro-Scottish sympathies and reporting those who spoke words in support of the Scots. When Northamptonshire man John Shatchwell told Nicholas Darton, vicar of Kilsby, that he thought 'the king must yield unto...the Scotts', Darton was quick to report the words as being 'full of disloyaltie'. However, in this case we might wonder whether this particular vicar in this notoriously Puritan county was in tune with the sentiments of his parishioners. On another occasion, when speaking with some neighbours about his hope that the king would soon quell the Scots, Darton provoked the response that it was 'the will of god that England's pride should have a fall'. He also reported a number of other parishioners at the same time for urging non-payment of ship money and of the tax levied for fighting the war against the Scots.[83]

The Scottish rebellion forced some to reconsider their loyalty to Charles. During Easter 1639 a local minister named John Girtam alias Haydon climbed into a pulpit in Stockport in the north-west of England and announced that if Prince Henry (Charles's older brother) had lived 'he would never have suffered such popery and idolatry as now is in England', 'never have suffered such massacres in Germany', and 'there had been no rebellion in Scotland'—indeed 'neither durst the Scots so much as have opened their mouths against him'. The last remark suggests that Girtam was not necessarily a huge fan of the Scots, though the implication of his speech is clearly that he wished Charles had never become king.[84] Alarming for the government, however, was the fact that many people in England did seem to be siding with the Scots. There were reports from the beginning of the conflict of how many of the 'nobilyty, gentry, and commonalty' of England were 'well Wishers' to the Scots, and 'hartely...wisht' their cause to succeed.[85] We have noted already support for the Scots among members of the political elite, the circle around Warwick which included the likes of Bedford, Saye, and Pym, but sympathy was more widespread than this. As early as July 1638 John Alured, who hailed from an influential Puritan family in Hull and was to sit for Hedon in Yorkshire in both the Short and the Long Parliaments, was allegedly predicting that if the Scots invaded England 'the Kinge would gett nobody to fight against them, for they were our owne nation and our owne blood'.[86] In May 1639 the Venetian ambassador observed that the plan to send troops against the Scots did 'not coincide with the sympathies of the generality' and that opinion in London was 'entirely favourable to the constancy and interests of the Scots'.[87] In some areas the Puritan clergy took a role in stirring up support for the Scots. In Manchester in March 1639 Thomas Case, the rector of Erpingham, Norfolk, who had relocated to the north-west in the face of Wren's anti-Puritan drive in East Anglia, supposedly preached 'very boldly against the Discipline of the Church of England' and ended his sermon with prayers 'for the good success of the Scotch Rebels'.[88] There was even support for the Scots in the far north of England, an area traditionally noted for its intense Scotophobia because of the long history of Anglo-Scottish tensions on the borderlands.[89] In mid-December 1638 a Newcastle merchant named Raiphe Fewler, having drunk quite a bit of wine, allegedly said that 'the Scottish Covenanters weare noe way to be accused, for they did nothing but in defence of theire owne right and maintenance of the Gospell, and did but defend them selves against those that would have brought in Popery and Idolatrie amongst them'. Pressed by one of his drinking companions whether he would refuse to fight if commanded by the king, Fewler supposedly added that 'if he thought in his owne conscience the Scotts weare in the right, he would not feight against them for all the Kings in the world'.[90] English sympathy for the Scots sometimes went beyond the mere articulation of words of support. In the spring of 1639 government officials in the north of England seized various munitions of war that were intended for Scottish use against the English—'Iron flales with sharpe pegs in them and Iron Harrowes for our horses', 'Scythes which had a most keene Edge', likewise intended 'to kill our Horses', and a 'multitude of Sharpe broade knives' for stabbing people. Upon investigation, it was found that these weapons had been made in Sheffield![91]

The most common reason people gave for sympathizing with the Scots was opposition to Charles's reform agenda in the Church—a fear of popery and a concern about Laudian innovation. Typical in this regard are the remarks of Southwark man Godfrey Cade in June 1639, who said that he thought 'the Bishopp of Canterberry and the rest of the Bishopps' were 'the Cause of this Mutiny in Scotland', 'that the Bishop of Canterberry was the pope of Lambeth' and that he 'doth plucke the royall Crowne of his Majestie's head and trample it under his foote and did whip his Majestie's Arse with his owne rode'. Given the chance to recant the next morning, after he had sobered up, Cade instead reaffirmed what he had said, adding 'that the Book of Comon prayer was false and that he would mainetayne [prove] it'.[92] Similarly, on the last day of May James Machison, a gentleman from Burnham in Buckinghamshire, said that he 'care[d] not for my Lord of Canterbury', for he was 'the occasion of this strife between the Scotts and us'.[93] An anonymous letter found at Ware in Hertfordshire in March 1639, supposedly from one of the soldiers sent to fight against the Scots, urged Charles to think before he shed 'inosent blood': the real enemies were the Laudians—who had been busy in England 'depriving us of our ministers and god's word' and in setting up 'superstition and idoletrey insteade', and who were now doing all they could to get the king to go against his 'true and loving subjects' north of the border. The letter concluded by stating 'wee your pore subjects are in as much feare as the scots'.[94] One Hertfordshire man, recruited to fight in the second Bishops' War, and who claimed to be captain of 500 soldiers, was heard to say in August

1640 that he and his men would march north in search of the king and rebel Scots, and should the king be fighting the 'Papists, they would fight on his side, and if the Scotts fought against the Papists, they would fight on the Scotts' side'. The fact that he said this after he had led his men in a riot pulling down altar rails in Rickmansworth church suggests that he had already made up his mind whether it was the king or the Scots who were fighting against the papists.[95] The Northamptonshire Puritan lawyer Robert Woodford saw the Scottish revolt as divine judgement upon the nation, recalling 'how justly the Lord may bring upon us the Judgment of the sword' and repeatedly expressing his support for the Scots' efforts to carry out 'the worke of reformation'. On 12 August 1640, eight days before the Scots crossed the Tweed and marched into England to start the second Bishops' War, Woodford wrote: 'great expectations of this great business of Scotland, the Lord hath some great worke to doe...in the behalfe of his church to root out Idolatry and superstition...Lord stand up in thine owne cause, fight for those that stand for thee' and 'bringe destruction' to 'thine enemyes'.[96] Kent Puritan Richard Culmer, who had been suspended from his living for refusing to read the Book of Sports, later recalled how 'the first coming in of the Scots into England' had delivered him from 'the persecuting Arch-bishop', causing him to proclaim 'Garamercy good Scot'.[97]

The Scottish rebellion unquestionably destabilized the situation in England, and was the immediate trigger that served to bring to an end Charles's experiment with personal rule in England. The example of Scottish resistance, and the justifications for it offered by Covenanter propaganda, certainly had an impact on opinion in England, served to heighten the political temperature south of the border, and played a role in inspiring some in England as to how to articulate their grievances against the Caroline regime. For example, in 1638 there appeared an anonymous work in England, probably published in the Netherlands, called *The Beast is Wounded*, the main text of which offered a detailed account of the history of the troubles in Scotland but which had marginal comments, allegedly penned by 'a strict Nonconformist' in England, pointing out how the situation south of the border was just as bad or worse. Thus, regarding the main tract's observation that the 'Lordly Prelates' in Scotland 'admitted sundry scandalous persons to the Ministery', the marginal commentator alleged that the Scottish bishops 'never shewed so much prophanes this way, as ours', giving as an example 'Wren, the Norridge Beast'. With regard to the complaint how various 'Worthies of the Church' in Scotland had been banished in the early seventeenth century, our commentator wondered 'How then would they have taken it, had they seene them whipt in their streetes: stood on Pillaries, burnd-marked like rouges, thrust into Dungeons, etc.'. In England there was more than just 'a feare of innovation', since the English had 'sundry innovations established' already among them. Thus our marginal commentator hoped that England might 'vindicate her Honour shortly this way, and like Scotland...drive away these Locusts [the bishops] from her Coast', and concluded by asking: did not England have 'as much Previledge, to reject the Service-book and Canons, High Commission, and all other such like Idolitries, and to establish and maintaine the true worship of God, as hath Scotland?'[98] From early 1640, an underground press in London, the 'Cloppenburg Press', began producing editions of official Covenanter propaganda as well as printing works of Puritan 'martyrs' such as Burton, Prynne, and Lilburne and of other radical Puritans for the English market.[99] On 1 September 1640, with the Scots now occupying the north of England, the vicar of Hackney, Calybute Downing, ventured to offer a public articulation of resistance theory in a sermon delivered before the Artillery Company in London. Taking as his text Deutoronomy 25:17, the story of the Israelites' 'legall warre' against the Amalekites when the latter opposed the Israelites on their coming out of Egypt, Downing outlined the circumstances in which wars could be lawful, which included when carried out in 'just defence'—even if in the process they might 'be driven into an offensive' war (an obvious allusion to the Scottish case). Warning how the English faced a threat from 'the Jesuites, and the Jesuited faction, with their adherents', Downing then alleged it was they who had not only bred 'ill bloud betwixt the King and his people' but also 'puld so hard to draw a Civill sword to the breaking of the happy Union of these Kingdomes'. He first urged the English to pray that these British Amalekites 'may fall under a Civill sword'. But 'when a party by power breaks the Laws of the Land', he insisted, and forced people either to go along with them or else declared them enemies of the state, then 'the Laws of Nations' kicked in and '*salus populi*' (the welfare of the people) became the supreme law. 'For the good of the person of a Prince', and 'for the safety of the body of the State', Downing insisted, 'Latitudes' were 'allowed for security', when, as Grotius had made clear, the law of non-resistance does not bind. There was 'a reall difference', Downing concluded, between 'Christians suffering with prayers and tears in the Primitive Church, under Heathenish Emperours, when their

Religion was not so much as tolerated, but condemned by the Laws of the Empire, and the sufferings of State, where the Religion is *lex terrae*, settled and protected by the Civil Laws and power' but 'affronted by a schismatical faction' that 'cannot consist, with the standing of the state'. Such was the radicalism of Downing's sermon that he subsequently had to flee London and take refuge in the earl of Warwick's house in Essex.[100]

Yet if the Scottish revolt helped trigger the crisis in England, it is also clear that the regime was not functioning that well in England, which was why it was unable to deal with the Scottish rebellion in the first place. England's failure to defeat the Scots, in other words, was related to things that were going wrong in England during the personal rule. And while many in England did sympathize with the Scots, and some in England came to support elements of the Scottish reforming agenda, the English had grievances of their own against the government of King Charles. For that reason it would be misleading to suggest that they needed the Scots to teach them to be 'radical'; they certainly did not need the Scots to teach them to be discontented. The Scottish rebellion may have afforded the opportunity for those in England who had become disaffected as a result of the policies of the personal rule to put forward their case against the Caroline regime, but the political crisis that ensued was an English one, which ultimately had English roots.[101]

* * *

On dissolving the Short Parliament, Charles had said that his subjects could petition him if they had any genuine grievances. Several communities took him at his word. At the Berkshire assizes on 11 July, the Grand Jury approved a petition complaining of 'the illegall and unsupportable charge of Shippmoney', coat and conduct money, 'the Compelling of free men by Imprisonment', 'the Infinite number of Monopolies', and 'the Rigide Execution of the Forrest Lawes'.[102] The lords and gentry of Yorkshire petitioned against the burden of ship money, of military expenses, and of 'the billetinge And Insolencies of soldiers'.[103] A petition from London, dated 23 September and signed by the majority of householders from every ward, complained of impositions, ship money, monopolies, 'innovations in matters of religion, the canons and the etc. oath', 'the great concourse of papists' in London plotting against the established religion, 'the seldome Callinge and suddayne dissolution of Parliaments without redressing the subjects grievances', recent proceedings in Star Chamber, and the danger the king was in from the present war, and called for a parliament to redress grievances.[104]

The most significant petition was that from a group of twelve peers—Bedford, Essex, Warwick, Saye, Brooke, Howard, Mandeville, Hertford, Exeter, Bolingbroke, Mulgrave, and Rutland—which was presented to the king at York on 3 September. Although the evidence is somewhat obscure, it appears that from the end of June Warwick and his associates had been in correspondence with the Covenanters urging them to march into England before the English were ready, thereby seizing the military initiative and hopefully leaving Charles with no option but to call another parliament. It was a desperate gamble—no less than treason; indeed, the Warwick group may even have been contemplating staging some sort of military coup in England, drawing on disaffected elements within the king's army and the county militias. The sheer speed of the Covenanter invasion caught the English army unawares, and helps explain why they were forced to defend an indefensible line at the Tyne rather than rebuff the Scots at the border. Once the Scots had taken Newcastle, and with it gained the ability to starve London of fuel over the coming winter, Charles realized he would have to negotiate. The petition listed 'the great distempers and dangers now threatening the Church and State' and also the king's 'Royal person': the war with the Scots, which had left the king's revenue 'much wasted' and his subjects 'burdened with coat-and-conduct money, billeting of soldiers, and other military charges'; 'the sundry innovations in matters of religion' and 'the oath and canons lately imposed'; 'the great increase of Popery, and employing of Popish Recusants, and others ill-affected to the religion by law established in places of power and trust'; 'the great mischiefs which may fall upon this kingdom if the intentions...of bringing in Irish and foreign forces, shall take effect'; 'the urging of ship-money' and the prosecution of sheriffs who would not levy it; 'the multitude of monopolies, and other patents'; and 'the great grief of your subjects by the long intermission of Parliaments', as well as 'the late and former dissolving of such as have been called'. The remedy, the petitioners suggested, was for the king 'to summon a parliament within some short and convenient time, whereby the cause of these and other grievances which your people lie under may be taken away', and the authors of them brought to punishment. Charles responded by summoning a Great Council of the peers to meet at York on 24 September, where he proclaimed his 'desire...to be rightly understood by my people' and announced his intention to call a parliament for 3 November.[105]

It was news that the nation had been waiting for. 'I cannot express to [your] lordship', Lady Lettice Goring wrote to her father, the earl of Cork, from London towards the end of September, 'how much the City is joyed at the news of a Parliament.'[106] Most people were optimistic that parliament would somehow be able to solve the nation's ills. In the aftermath of military defeat against the Scots, however, Charles must have regarded its meeting with a certain trepidation. As he remained at York pondering his next move, Charles whiled away the time playing chess with the marquess of Winchester. On one occasion, as the king was thinking about how to play his bishop, Winchester blurted out: 'See, Sir, how troublesome these Bishops are?' Charles said nothing, but 'looked very grim'.[107]

13

············

The Grievances of
the Commonwealth

*Religion, thou most sacred power on Earth
...why should theis warrs | Tearme thee the Author
of our Civill Jarres.*[1]

At six o'clock in the evening of 22 August 1642 a somewhat 'melancholic' Charles I raised his standard at Nottingham, 'with the object', as the Venetian ambassador put it, 'of inducing those...disposed to favour him to take service under the royal colours'. Charles had issued the call to arms ten days earlier. Claiming that 'divers Persons, bearing an inward hatred and Malice against [his] Person and Government', had raised an army against him, he stressed the need to suppress this 'Rebellion' with 'all Alacrity', and identified his cause with the defence of 'the true Protestant Religion, the Laws established, the Property and Liberty of the Subject, and the very Being of Parliaments'. The events of 22 August had an element of bathos about them. Charles had actually arrived in Nottingham on the 19th, but rather than wait around killing time he had decided to make a mad dash to Coventry to try to stop the city falling into the hands of parliament. Although he reached Coventry before any of the parliamentary troops, the citizens shut the gates against him, and a number of his own servants were shot and wounded at the walls. When the mayor and town magistrates made it clear they would not allow the king to enter the city, Charles opted to retreat, returning to Nottingham on the 22nd. At the appointed hour the king, with a small train, rode to the top of Castle Hill, where his knight-marshal erected the standard to the sound of drums and trumpets. Yet, as Clarendon relates, 'there appeared no conflux of men in obedience to the proclamation; the arms and ammunition were not yet come from York, and a general sadness covered the whole town'. Moreover, the 22nd had been an unseasonably 'stormy and tempestuous day', and that night the royal standard was blown down by 'a very strong and unruly wind', and could not be set up again until a couple of days later.[2]

There are a number of things that are noteworthy about this scene. One is that it was Charles who declared war. Another is where Charles was. He was not in London; that he had abandoned to parliament the previous January, following an unsuccessful attempt to arrest some of the ringleaders of the parliamentary opposition and in the face of growing popular disorder in the streets of the capital. He was not in York, which was where Charles had been based prior to his departure for Nottingham, and where much of his ammunition was. In fact, many close to Charles thought that it would have made more sense for the king to have raised his standard at York, but the Yorkshire gentry would not have it, fearing that it would make the country 'the seat of the war'. Clarendon later complained how they 'unskilfully' imagined 'that the war would be nowhere but where the King's army was', but we might read their opposition as evidence of the extent to which even the landed elite in a largely royalist county believed the king to be very much on the defensive by the summer of 1642—that the war would be coming to him rather than he taking it to parliament.[3]

It was less than two years since Charles had announced to a council of peers at York his decision to call what became the Long Parliament, a parliament which it was hoped at the time would solve the political crisis facing the nation. How had things come to such a pass that the king now felt that war was his only option? Why did a peaceful solution prove elusive? How had two sides come into being—two sides that were willing to go to war against each other—and what did those two sides stand for? Were the issues at stake essentially constitutional: who was to be in charge of the country? Or were they in essence religious: what was to be the fate of the Church?

A Strong Expectation of Ensuing Good

There was a mood of great public expectation when the Long Parliament assembled on 3 November 1640. The Yorkshire MP Sir Henry Slingsby anticipated 'a happy parliament where the subject may have a total redress of all his grievances', while others spoke of 'the strong expectation of much Ensuing good'.[4] But amidst the expectation, there was a sense of trepidation. The stakes were high: '3 Crownes, 4 Nations', as one rhymester observed.[5]

England was on edge.[6] It was a time of economic crisis. Trade had been badly hit as a result of the wars in Europe (which led to a recession in the cloth industry) and most recently the Scottish wars, the Scottish occupation of Newcastle had disrupted the coal trade, while the prices of many key commodities had been artificially raised thanks to the practice of selling patents or monopolies in the 1630s. The meeting of the Long Parliament also coincided with a renewed outbreak of contagious disease: the plague and smallpox hit London over the spring and summer of 1641, killing large numbers, including several parliament men—the most famous victim being the opposition peer Francis Russell, 4th earl of Bedford, who died of smallpox on 9 May 1641.[7] Many of the fiscal and religious initiatives of the 1630s had provoked widespread resentment, and the popularity of the government had further nose-dived following the mass mobilization for what proved to be an unsuccessful military campaign against the Scots. Recent months had seen growing popular unrest in the form of tax strikes and rioting.

Throughout the period up until the outbreak of civil war members of the Long Parliament were to be subject to pressure—in the form of riots, demonstrations, and petitions—from those out-of-doors to address their political, religious, and economic concerns. Mass political awareness and engagement was further fuelled by the media—sermons, manuscript libels, and verse, and particularly the press—as censorship controls broke down, leading to an outpouring of printed treatises, pamphlets, and broadsides of varying degrees of intellectual sophistication. Whereas in the 1630s an average of 459 known titles were published each year (the number in fact fluctuated from 211 to 695 over the course of the decade), 848 appeared in 1640, 2,042 in 1641, and 4,008 in 1642.[8] The surge in the book trade was a boon to a depressed economy, 'a meanes to help many a poore man in London these dead times of trading', as one contemporary observed. More particularly, the outpouring of the press served to make the offences of the architects of the personal rule 'apparent to the world', while the bitter and hateful tone of much of the invective was such as to inflame public passions and inspire hatred and a desire for revenge.[9]

There was a series of disturbances across the south and east in the build up to the meeting of the Long Parliament. In early October 'unruly people' broke into a church in Reading during the night, smashed the organ into three pieces, and destroyed the organ pipes and the rails around the communion table, while there were similar attacks on altar rails at Ipswich and Sudbury (Suffolk) and Marlowe (Bucks.). There was trouble throughout the diocese of London when Dr Arthur Duck, the bishop of London's chancellor and Laud's vicar-general, embarked on his visitation to enforce the new canons. In many parishes in Essex and London Duck and his entourage met with jeering crowds shouting 'no oath', and when the High Commission sat on Thursday, 22 October to deal with those who refused to comply, an angry crowd forced its way into St Paul's in search of Duck, who had to climb through a window to escape. The following Sunday 'a Companie of rude Rogues' (as a hostile source described them) entered St Paul's during time of divine service, broke into the office where the High Commission records were kept, and tore them to pieces. Although a commission was set up to try the rioters—it was a capital offence 'to sett upon a Court of Justice'—the jury refused to take action.[10]

The elections to the Long Parliament saw over eighty contests, the highest number yet.[11] Court candidates fared very badly: in total, the court appears to have backed some forty-seven candidates, of whom only twenty-three were returned.[12] Yet the absence of contests in the majority of constituencies should not be read as a sign of political indifference; often it reflected the fact that local sentiment was firmly behind two candidates known to be opposed to the court. Passions ran high in many constituencies. At the Chelmsford election 'the country people' cried out 'they would have noe Bishop nor highe Comission'.[13] Eighteen counties, ranging from Devon to Northumberland, and a significant number of boroughs gave their MPs petitions outlining their grievances.[14] The freeholders of Kent identified their grievances as the increase in papists, new ceremonies in religion (moving the communion table altar-wise, bowing at communion, refusing the sacrament to those who would not come to the rails), coat and conduct money and other military charges, the new canons, 'the heavy taxe of Shipp money', the decay of clothing, customs and impositions, and monopolies.[15] Yet the grievances were much the same across the kingdom. Dorset did not draw up a formal petition, but voters informed their MPs they were concerned about 'the great and intollerable burthen of Ship-money', which they were not satisfied was legal, the abuses in pressing soldiers and raising money for them, 'the multitude of Monopolies', and the new canons.[16] The apprentices of London petitioned the Lord Mayor about 'the great number of Monopolies patents and impositions upon Commodities and manufactories', which were such a burden that 'divers of theire Masters' could not 'mainetayne themselves and theire Families', and 'the multitude of papis [*sic*] Preists and Jesuites' in the City who were drawing those 'weake in Learninge and younge in understandinge' to 'the Romish Religion'.[17]

Charles was apprehensive of the mood of the capital. He did not make a grand royal entry when he returned to Whitehall from the north on 30 October: given the humiliation he had suffered at the hands of the Scots, he could scarcely have returned to London in triumph. Similarly on 3 November, instead of the usual public royal procession to open a parliamentary session, Charles opted to go to the palace of Westminster 'in a more private way then ordinary'—by barge along the Thames, instead of through the streets.[18] The session got off to an uneasy start. In his opening speech, Charles urged members to consider the best way to secure 'the safety and security of this kingdom', which, he explained, involved both chasing the Scottish rebels out of England and satisfying 'just Grievances', and stressed his pressing need for financial support. One contemporary newsletter writer expressed astonishment that neither the king nor the Lord Keeper made one mention of religion, and that the king persisted in calling the Scots rebels. Charles returned to the Lords on the 5th and partially withdrew the charge, referring to the Scots now as his subjects though still insisting that they were rebels as long as they had an army that had invaded England.[19]

There was a broad consensus in both Houses concerning the immediate issues that needed to be addressed: the architects of the personal rule should be punished and its victims released from prison; the Laudian innovations undone and the prerogative courts that had helped enforce them abolished; rule without parliament for an extended period made impossible; and the fiscal expedients (such as ship money) that had enabled the king to rule without parliament declared illegal (though this would require finding the crown an alternative source of revenue). Yet parliament was a conciliar body, a forum for airing grievances, rather than an executive one, and normally followed the leadership provided by the crown or the court. In the absence of such, business tended to drift. Parliament decided to proceed by gathering information from across the country about what had gone wrong, setting up numerous investigative committees in its first few weeks. By the new year there were some sixty-five committees, so many that parliament decided to set up a committee to investigate committees.[20]

Some direction was provided by a reform group in the Lords—Bedford, Essex, Warwick, Saye and Sele, Kimbolton, Brooke, Wharton, and Paget—and their clients in the Commons, the most important of whom were Pym, Hampden, St John, Holles, and Fiennes.[21] Pym once again emerged as a dominant figure in the lower house. In a two-hour speech delivered on Saturday, 7 November, he drew together the various secular and religious grievances and represented them as part of a popish conspiracy to alter the law and religion of the kingdom. There were four aspects to this plot. The first concerned ecclesiastical policy: admitting popish tenets into the Church of England, a plan for a union with Rome promoted by the 'corrupt part of our clergy', and the activities of Spanish and papal agents at court and of self-interested Englishmen who were willing to 'run into popery' to secure promotion and preferment. The second related to secular policy: illegal taxes, the arbitrary proceedings of courts of justice, and promoting conflict between England and Scotland. The third was the breach of parliaments, while the fourth related to the military, notably intruding Catholics into the army and planning to use an Irish army against British Protestants.[22] Pym and Bedford's plan for settlement involved removing the king's evil counsellors and replacing them with more reliable ones. Although they wanted to extend parliamentary control over who was appointed to office under the crown, they were still thinking in terms of government being exercised by the king and his ministers, rather than seeking to create a parliamentary system of government. They also recognized that they would need to settle the king's revenue if they were to do away with the unpopular fiscal expedients of the 1630s.

The first order of business was to free those who had suffered for their opposition to Laud. On the 7th the Commons approved petitions for the release of Bastwick and Burton and two days later for the release of Prynne, Lilburne, and Leighton.[23] Burton and Prynne reached London on 28 November, to be greeted by the ringing of church bells and some 2,000 people on horseback and 'innumerable' people on foot crying out 'Welcome home' and 'god bee thanked for your returne'. Bastwick, who had to come all the way from the Scilly Isles, returned to London on 7 December to a similar reception.[24] The House of Lords released Bishop Williams of Lincoln on 16 November, who promptly took his seat in the upper house.[25]

On Monday, 9 November the Commons ordered all members to take communion at St Margaret's Westminster on the following

Sunday, as a way of outing Catholics, set up a committee to devise a means of ensuring there were no Catholics in the House, and issued an order barring monopolists from serving as MPs.[26] Strafford, who returned to London on the 10th to take his seat in the Lords, knowing he was bound to be targeted, wanted Charles to stage a coup against the parliamentary leadership, using the remnants of the army in the north together with the Irish army to seize control of the Tower and round up those peers and MPs suspected of treasonable correspondence with the Scots. In a pre-emptive strike, the Commons moved to impeach Strafford on the 11th, Pym accusing him of turning the king 'against the Scots', advancing 'the private design of the papists', and of intending to bring Irish forces to subdue England. Committed first to the custody of the Gentleman Usher, Strafford was dispatched to the Tower on the 25th, angry crowds jeering as his coach took him from Westminster to his place of imprisonment on the other side of London.[27] Laud was impeached by the Commons on 18 December, after an impassioned speech by Sir Harbottle Grimston accusing him of being 'the sty of all the pestilential filth that hath infected the State and Government' and the 'broker and Pander of the whore of Babylon', and like Strafford before him committed to the custody of the Gentleman Usher. As he was being escorted away, Laud angrily protested that he had only ever 'sought the honor and prosperity of the King and the decency and Reverence of God's House and Service, which this peevish and slovenly Age could not endure'. He was transferred to the Tower on 1 March.[28] Other key advisors of Charles I during the personal rule—notably Secretary Windebanke and Lord Keeper Finch—fled to the Continent.[29]

With his back against the wall, Charles realized that he would need to make concessions. He mapped out his position in a speech delivered before both Houses at the Banqueting House on Saturday, 23 January 1641. Urging the need for speedy action to pay off the armies in the north and to improve the defences of the kingdom, he said he would agree to reform 'all Innovations in Church and Commonwealth', allow 'all Courts of Justice' to 'be regulated according to Law', and 'reduce all Matters of Religion and Government to what they were in the purest Times of Queen Elizabeth's Days'. He could not, however, consent to any 'Alteration of Government'. Thus he would lay down any part of his revenue 'found illegal or grievous to the Public', allow parliament to examine whether bishops had 'incroached too much upon the Temporal', and even agree to a bill for frequent parliaments. But he was determined to uphold the right of the bishops to sit in parliament, and he would not allow others to call parliament in his name, since that would entrench upon 'that inseparable Right of My Crown'.[30]

Charles's need for money forced him to yield on the latter issue. On 16 February, under pressure from both Houses, Charles approved a bill requiring parliament to meet at least every three years and to sit for a minimum of fifty days, with sheriffs and constables to call one in the king's name if the king failed to do so. Although trimmed down since its initial introduction as a bill for annual parliaments, it was nevertheless a landmark piece of legislation—a direct assault on the prerogative that guaranteed parliament an independent political life. Charles gave the royal assent grudgingly, accusing members of having 'taken the government almost in pieces', which was now 'almost off the hinges': 'a skilful watchmaker', he admonished, 'to make clean his watch, will take it asunder', but he would make sure he put it back together without leaving one pin out. Charles did, however, obtain a much-needed grant of four subsidies. Parliament ordered Londoners to celebrate the passage of the Triennial Act with the ringing of church bells and bonfires. Ominously, at one of the bonfires Londoners celebrated the passage of the bill by burning an effigy of a bishop.[31]

Despite broad agreement in both Houses over the need for certain reforms, divisions soon began to emerge over a number of issues. The first was how to deal with the Scots. Thanks largely to the efforts of the marquess of Hamilton, negotiations with the Covenanter commissioners who had arrived in London in November had been making steady progress. In December Charles agreed to authorize the Acts passed in the Scottish parliament of June 1640. In January and early February details relating to reparations to the Scottish army in the north were sorted out. All that now remained to be determined was how to secure a settled peace between the two kingdoms. On 19 February Charles decided to appoint some of the pro-Scots peers to his privy council—including Bedford, Essex, Saye, and Mandeville—although he later admitted that part of his aim was to induce the new appointees to break with the Scots in their stance on episcopacy. Hoping to tie the new men to their side, the Scottish commissioners published a paper on the 24th demanding the execution of Strafford and the abolition of episcopacy in England. Charles was outraged, and vented his anger to the English commissioners appointed to treat with the Scots. When Edward Hyde (probably at Charles's behest) produced the Scots' paper in the Commons on the 27th, it forced a number of the more committed supporters, as well as opponents, of the Scots to reveal themselves. Pym, Holles, and others tactfully opted for silence.[32] Anti-Scottish sentiment in the House was again revealed in early April in the debates over whether to renew the cessation of arms with the Scots until a settlement could be reached. Renewal had been agreed with little controversy between December and March, but now, with rumours circulating that an impatient Scottish army was threatening to march into Yorkshire, some members suggested that the Scots should be declared enemies if they moved south of the Tees. After a long and heated debate on 9 April lasting until 7 in the evening, the anti-Scottish faction forced a division. Pym won the vote for the renewal, but by only 167 to 128, a majority of 39.[33]

A second source of division concerned the fate of Strafford. The trial of Strafford finally opened on 22 March, over four months after his being dispatched to the Tower. He was charged at the suit of all three kingdoms, not just England, and the twenty-eight articles against him sought to establish that he was guilty of treason for introducing arbitrary and tyrannical government against the law. However, although Strafford might have committed a crime against the government, it was far from clear whether he had committed treason, a crime against the king. Fearful that impeachment would not succeed, the Commons chose instead to proceed by way of attainder, whereby instead of trying Strafford parliament would simply enact that he was guilty of the offences of which he stood accused. In the meantime, a petition began to circulate in London demanding justice against the earl. Although Charles ordered the Lord Mayor to suppress it, some 20,000–30,000 signatures were collected, and the petition was presented to the Commons on 21 April by a great multitude of citizens (perhaps as many as 10,000), the same day as the Commons' vote on the attainder. The attainder was passed by 204 to 59 and sent to the Lords together with the petition, though it was said that potential supporters of Strafford had opted not to attend the vote and others had voted for the attainder 'out of a base fear … of a prevailing party'. A list of those who opposed the attainder was immediately posted at the Exchange, the entrance to parliament, and various other places in London and Westminster, condemning them as 'the betrayers of their country' and suggesting that 'these and all other enemies of the Commonwealth should perish with Strafford'.[34]

Charles now contemplated using the army to rescue Strafford. He seems to have hoped the threat of military intervention would prove deterrent enough—hence why it was important for news about it to leak out—and believed he was offering a compromise that would help calm everything down when he announced on 1 May that he was willing to dismiss Strafford from all his offices though would not agree to his execution. But the tactic seriously backfired, since it served only to escalate tensions. The next day calls for justice were heard from many pulpits across London and rumours were flying that the army was to be used against parliament or the London crowd or to free Strafford from the Tower. That evening it was confirmed that earlier in the day Colonel Billingsley, an officer in the Irish army, had indeed arrived at the Tower with 100 men and a letter from the king demanding admission, although the Lieutenant of the Tower, Sir William Balfour, had denied them entry. A huge crowd lined the entrance to the House of Lords early on the morning of Monday, 3 May—estimates vary from 5,000 to 15,000—crying out for justice against Strafford and all other traitors. There were further demonstrations outside the Lords the following day (Plate 12).[35]

As far as many MPs were concerned, the Army Plot merely served to confirm that there was indeed a Popish Plot underway to undermine the true religion and introduce arbitrary and tyrannical government. On 3 May the Commons proceeded to draw up its Protestation, a declaration containing a pledge to 'maintain and defend' the 'true, reformed Protestant Religion, expressed in the Doctrine of the Church of England, against all Popery and Popish Innovations', the king's 'Royal Person, Honour and Estate', the 'Power and Privilege of Parliament', and the 'lawful Rights and Liberties of the Subject'; significantly, a proposal that it include the proviso to defend also the discipline of the Church of England was defeated. Two days later the Commons ordered the Protestation to be printed, and although the Lords rejected a Commons bill that all adult males take the Protestation by Christmas, a national subscription campaign was nevertheless subsequently launched (beginning in London in late May; extended nationwide the following January).[36] Fearful that Charles was still contemplating a coup, the Commons rushed through a bill against the dissolution of the present parliament without its own consent, which came before the Lords on Friday, 7 May and was approved the next day. The Lords also approved the attainder of Strafford on the 7th, by a vote of 51 to 9 according to one account, although it was said that many peers absented themselves for fear of the London crowd. Charles agonized over the weekend what to do, but was advised that he had to consent 'to appease the enraged people'. Apparently afraid that 'a furious multitude' would attack Whitehall if he saved Strafford, a tearful Charles announced to his privy council at 9 p.m. on Sunday the 9th that if his 'own person only were in danger', he 'would gladly venture it to save Lord Strafford's', but seeing that his wife, children, and all his kingdom were 'concerned in it', he felt 'forced to give way'. Charles chose not to go to parliament on the 10th, seemingly for fear of the crowds, but instead gave the royal assent to the bills for the attainder of Strafford and against the dissolution of the present parliament without its own consent by commission. Strafford was executed at Tower Hill on 12 May, in front of a huge crowd of cheering spectators, and in the evening there were bonfire celebrations across the capital.[37]

By forcing Charles to sacrifice Strafford, the leaders in the Commons hoped he would accept their counsels. But they misjudged the king. Charles could never now bring himself to employ men whom he regarded as Strafford's murderers. Moreover, Strafford's execution raised fears more generally about the peril of giving in to pressure out-of-doors. In the immediate short term, however, it seemed that the removal of Strafford had opened a door for constructive legislative reform. Steps were taken towards settling the king's revenue. In May both Houses approved Pym's scheme for granting a fixed sum (£400,000) to the crown, while in June parliament granted a Poll Tax and passed the Tonnage and Poundage Act which removed the king's right to collect customs without parliament's consent, which in turn opened up the possibility of undoing the fiscal expedients of the personal rule. On 5 July Charles gave his assent to legislation abolishing Star Chamber and High Commission, on 7 August he consented to an Act declaring ship money to be unlawful and voiding the judgment in *Rex* v. *Hampden* and another limiting the royal forests to the bounds that had existed in the twentieth year of King James's reign, and three days later to a measure abolishing fines for distraint of knighthood.[38] Many of these reforms were supported by men who were later to emerge as royalists, among them the likes of Edward Hyde (the future 1st earl of Clarendon), Sir John Culpepper, Viscount Falkland (the son of the former Lord Deputy of Ireland, who had a Scottish title and so sat in the English Commons), and Sir John Strangways.

Reform of the Church

The most divisive issue of all was religion. Many MPs were convinced that Charles had become embroiled in a popish plot to subvert the true religion and undermine Protestant liberties. As Pym's speech of 7 November 1640 had made clear, there was both an international and a domestic aspect to this supposed popish plot: the threat posed by Catholic powers overseas, and the threat of popery from within the Church of England itself. Concerns about the international aspect focused on the presence of Spanish and papal agents at court, and Charles's readiness to contemplate taking a papal subsidy and use Irish Catholic troops to suppress Protestant dissidents in Scotland and Ireland. Arguably the more worrying aspect of the popish plot was the attempt by those whom Pym styled 'the corrupt part of our clergy' to undermine the Protestant Church from within, through the revival of popish ceremonies and practices.

Pressure for reform came from out-of-doors—in the form of petitions, informations against scandalous ministers, pamphlets, sermons, and crowd agitation. Those communities which had suffered most under Laudianism or had been most hostile to the Laudian initiatives came to feel that the problem lay not with individual Laudian clerics but with the entire episcopal order, and called on parliament to abolish it, root and branch. London had a root and branch petition ready to go in early November 1640, signed by some 15,000 citizens, although the leaders of the Long Parliament urged the promoters to have patience and to delay its presentation until after they had completed the charge against Strafford. The citizens' patience did not last long: printed copies were soon in circulation, and London's root and branch petition was carried to the Commons on 11 December by a crowd of some 1,500 'honest citizens', dressed in their finest apparel.[39] Kent and Essex presented their root and branch petitions on 13 January, and by the end of the month another eleven counties had followed suit. There were further petitions over the spring and summer, while the last county to petition for the abolition of bishops was Somerset in December. In total nineteen counties followed London in presenting petitions for root and branch abolition over the course of 1641: Essex, Kent, Hertfordshire, Surrey, and Sussex in the southeast; Cambridgeshire, Norfolk, and Suffolk in East Anglia; Lincolnshire and Nottinghamshire in the east and east Midlands; Lancashire and Cheshire in the north-west; Devon, Gloucestershire, and Somerset in the west; and Bedfordshire, Buckinghamshire, Oxfordshire, and Warwickshire in the southern and central Midlands. There was also a petition from the Protestants of Ulster (delivered in early July 1641), complaining about the performance of the prelates in Ireland— 'their favouring of Popery...their persecuting puritie, and indevouring to bring all to a livelesse formalitie'—and asking that the 'unlawfull

Hierarchicall government' of bishops, 'with all their appendices', might 'bee utterly extirpate'.[40]

London's root and branch petition appears to have been orchestrated by militant Puritans in the City, but it would be wrong to assume that all those nationwide who supported root and branch reform were culturally godly or even ideologically committed to a non-episcopalian form of Church government (they certainly were not necessarily Presbyterians or Congregationalists). MPs who presented root and branch petitions often did so out of a sense of obligation to represent the grievances of their constituents, rather than because they shared those grievances themselves. Sir Edward Dering presented the Kent petition at the pressing of a group of Wealden constituents and the urging of the radical cleric Thomas Wilson. But Dering thought the London petition too extreme; his Kent petition concluded with the somewhat ambiguous request 'that this Hierarchicall power may be totally abrogated, if the wisdome of this Honourable House shall find that it cannot be maintained by God's word and to his glory'. A year later Dering was promoting a petition from Kent in defence of the bishops and was to justify his apparent change of sides by saying that he had never, in fact, professed himself for root and branch.[41]

Furthermore, most of the root and branch petitions included a combination of religious and secular grievances against the bishops. There were many conventionally pious Protestants who would not have thought of themselves as sharing a Puritan reformist agenda who were concerned about the 'lordly' pretensions of the Laudian bishops and their abuse of secular power.[42] The London root and branch petition, for example, began by complaining how the Laudian bishops had 'proved prejudiciall and very dangerous both to the Church and Comon-wealth', in that they had not only acted in ways that were 'Derogatory to his Majestie and his State Royall' but had also violated the laws of the realm and the subjects' liberties, listing monopolies, impositions, and ship money among the 'manifold Evils...and Grievances...occasioned by the Prelates, and their Dependants'.[43] Nottinghamshire's petition not only detailed religious grievances—including promoting idolatrous practices such as 'bowing or praying towards the East, bowing to the Altar...and kneeling to the Rayle for the Sacrament', and 'Drawing neere to the Romish Fabricke of Religion, for Doctrine, Worship, Discipline and Orders'—but began by citing a long list of civil grievances, charging the bishops with 'Endevouring to overthrow the subjects' liberties and proprietie in their goods', 'attributing to the King absolute and unlimited power over all' (and hence 'Ship-money, Monopolyes, &c.'), 'Labouring to overthrow or diminish the power of Parliaments' and 'to evert the whole frame of Civill government and Commonwealth, and reduce it to mere arbitrary power', and 'Occasioning...the late wofull differences, betweene his Majestie and his Subjects of Scotland'.[44]

While the root and branch petitions were coming in, parliament actively sought to encourage people to come forward to present their grievances against the Laudian clergy. On 19 December 1640 it set up a committee to examine the current state of the ministry and to remove 'scandalous Ministers', not only instructing MPs to find out what was going on in their own localities but actively inviting 'all ingenious persons in every County of the Kingdome' to give 'a true information' of what was happening in the parishes.[45] By June 1641 some 900 petitions had come in, documenting a range of abuses, including alleged sexual indiscretions and drunkenness, though the most common charges related to ceremonialism (bowing at the name of Jesus, veneration of the altar), upholding Arminian or popish doctrine, and denying the royal supremacy.[46] About twenty early ones complained about various ministers 'taxing the Counties and Boroughs for making choice of Puritanes to be Parliament men'. The vicar of Rothersthorpe in Northamptonshire, George Preston, was accused not only of being a very disorderly person who had administered the sacrament drunk but also of allegedly saying 'the parliaments in England never did good nor never would', 'that his hogs were fit to make parliament men of, and their sty a place fit for them to sit in' (he supposedly gave ten of his hogs the names of actual sitting MPs), and that those who 'went from sermon to sermon...did go to several churches to commit whoredom'. Preston admitted having let slip 'many inconsiderate speeches', though refused to confess to any one charge in particular.[47] Edward Finch, minister of Christ Church London and brother of the disgraced Lord Keeper, was found guilty of 'practising Innovations in the Church, Non-residence, foul Extortions, Neglect of the Duty of his Function, and Prophaning of the Sacraments', and being 'a Man of Prophane Life, scandalous in his Doctrine and Conversation, and a Hinderer of Preaching'. The profanity and scandal included allegedly 'kissing and offering to groape' a woman in the church and 'drinking up the wine provided for the Communion, whereby he was so intoxicated, that the Parishioners wanted a Sermon and the Cup'.[48] The parishioners of Chigwell in Essex informed parliament that their vicar, Emmanuel Uty, another alleged drunkard, had erected an altar, at which he used 'frequent and offensive bowing and cringing' and did 'constantly read the Prayers in the Divine Service with his face toward the Altar and backe toward the people', so that many could not hear what he said. His parishioners, however, had had no trouble hearing him when he said that the king was 'not Supreame head of the Church' but the bishops were, that there had been 'no true Religion in England these 40 yeares', and that 'he loved the Pope with all his heart'. Even Uty's wife supposedly thought Uty was 'a Papist in heart'.[49] Peter Smart, a former prebendary of Durham Cathedral who had suffered at the hands of the High Commissions of both the northern and southern provinces, renewed his charges against the former dean of Durham, John Cosin (now Master of Peterhouse), for promoting innovations, ceremonialism, and image worship, calling the Reformation a 'Deformation', and for publicly stating that the king was not head of the Church.[50]

Parliament acted swiftly to deprive of their livings those found guilty, assuming to itself a quasi-judicial function that was unprecedented. There were reports that a number of ministers summoned to appear before parliament died of grief, or indignation, before their cases were heard.[51] Not all those charged were guilty, or guilty of everything alleged, and undoubtedly the plaintiffs put a partisan gloss on the activities of those clergy of whom they disapproved. But the revelations were shocking, and so numerous that they could not all be excused on the grounds of individual failings. They led many MPs to conclude that there must be something fundamentally wrong with the system of ecclesiastical government for so many abusive practices to have gone on for so long.[52]

Frustrated by the slow pace of ecclesiastical reform, some people in the localities opted to take the law into their own hands to purge their parish churches of altar rails and other symbols of Laudianism. The precise geographical extent of this renewed wave of iconoclasm—it should perhaps be seen as a continuation of the iconoclasm that had begun the previous summer—is hard to assess, although it appears to have been particularly common in the eastern counties, where Puritanism was strong. One contemporary observed that 'the Rayles about the Holy Table' were 'pulled down in many Churches in Suffolk, Essex, Hartfordshire etc and hanged up, burned etc'. To give just one example, on 11 January 1641—Plough Monday—'some of the Zealots' of Hingham in Norfolk (a notorious Puritan town which had seen a number of its residents emigrate to Massachusetts in the 1630s) pulled down the altar rails in the parish church, proclaiming that they intended 'to rayle about a Common Horse-Pond with them next the high way', locally known as 'the Parson's Pond'. There were similar outbreaks, however, in other parts of the country. In the northeast, it was the Scots who took the lead. At Easington in County Durham '6 Scotch Gentlemen pulled downe a Marble Font' in the parish church 'and broke it in peeces', 'battered downe the Communion Table', took away the chalice and the communion cloth, and burned '2 Service Bookes'.[53] In London, iconoclastic outbursts were accompanied by a rise of Puritan separatism. For example, in St Saviour's parish in Southwark on Sunday, 10 January nearly eighty people met in a private house at the time of divine service, 'praying and preaching'; when brought before the local justices, they protested that the Elizabethan Act of 1593 'for the Administration of Common Prayer in the Church, was no good Law, It being made by Bishops', that 'There is no Church, but where the faithfull are', that 'The King can make no Law because he is not perfect (that is) perfectly regenerate', and that the king was to be obeyed 'only in Civill Matters'. The Lords responded on 16 January by sending out an order to all parishes in London, Westminster, and Southwark 'That the Divine Service be performed as it is appointed by the Acts of Parliament', that anyone who disturbed such services 'be severely punished, according to Law', and that the clergy should 'forbear to introduce any Rites or Ceremonies that may give Offence, otherwise than those which are established by the Laws of the Land'.[54] Nevertheless in St George's Southwark the following day a group described as 'a Company of Anabapt[ist] Brownisticall people' marched up to the minister's desk, seized the service book, 'and carried it (in a kind of Procession) to the Church Doore, and having rent it in peeces, cast it out of doores'.[55]

In some areas there was violence towards persons. At Easington the Scottish iconoclasts put surplices on a couple of men to make them represent Laud and Wren and proceeded to 'beate them...wishing they were the Men themselves'. At Witham in Essex a crowd beat up the local curate 'for crossing a Childe in Baptisme'.[56] On occasion, iconoclasm slipped into attacks on the local Catholics. Near Reading in Berkshire, for example, a crowd, after first pulling up the altar rails in the parish church, raided the house of a Catholic (fortunately for him he was not at home), 'fetched out his wooden gods and crucifixes', tied them together, 'and drew them up and down through the town, and then burned them'. They then went to the house of a 'common whore', who had recently brought a successful prosecution against 'an honest man' for ravishing her, forced the woman to confess that she had made a false accusation, and then took her to a well where Catholics got their holy water and thrust her in, head first, several times, saying: 'now when the papist come fore holy watter instead of holy watter they shall have hores watter'.[57] Ominously, there were signs that some regarded their allegiance to the king as conditional upon his willingness to support ecclesiastical reform. In June 1641 Francis Cornewell or Cornehill, a clerk from the village of Loose, just outside Maidstone in Kent, was indicted for saying 'That if the king enjoined the Book of Common Prayer or any other testimonies or discipline that were not expressly delivered in God's words, we ought not to obey him'.[58]

Popular fury against the Laudian regime was further fuelled by pulpit oratory. Parliament recruited a number of ministers who had been in trouble with the ecclesiastical authorities in the 1630s to preach at Westminster, among them Stephen Marshall, Cornelius Burgess, and Henry Burton. The sermons tended both to celebrate England's deliverance from captivity and to urge the need for fundamental reform, and they were invariably printed for a broader consumption.[59] When Burton preached at St Margaret's Westminster on 20 June 1641 he 'made a most rayling Sermon against Bishops' and 'against the abominable Idoll, the Common Prayer Booke', which, he said, 'was framed and composed by the Devill, and practised and mayntayned by the Devil's Impes or Instruments'. At the parish level, local Puritan preachers seized the opportunity presented to articulate their own case for ecclesiastical reform. In mid-February 1641 one minister, before sermon, prayed for 'the Pope-confounding, Church-reforming, God glorifying Parliament'. At Hingham the minister asked God to forgive them for offending Him 'in wearing the Surplesse, in signing with the Crosse, and using the Ring at Marriage'. Some of the things reported as being uttered by local Puritan preachers were alarming to the religiously more conservative. At St George's, Norwich a minister carried with him into the pulpit 'the Service Booke, and stampt it under his feet, saying, hee came not by any Prelaticall Popish Imposition of hands, but was sent from God'. Elsewhere a minister was reported as thanking God that 'we had now a Parliament, that every one might doe what hee list'.[60]

The fall of Laud himself was celebrated in a host of printed works—prose, verse, and song. The satirical song *Canterburies Conscience*, printed as an illustrated broadside, has a penitent Laud confess his sins from the Tower: 'It was I that lately made a way | For Popish wolves to suck thy blood...It was I that mov'd the King of late, | To take up armes against the Scots'. The second part elaborates how Laud abused the laws, threatened the judges so that he could have his 'will, | Against all reason right and law', 'rul'd the law' in his 'high Inquisition Court', licensed pernicious books that were 'Ladders to climbe to Popery', and forced people to bow at altars, 'The Custome of the Popish rammes'. One of the accompanying illustrations shows Laud set against the backdrop of two cities—Canterbury and Rome—with men on horseback riding over a bridge from the former to the latter.[61] A mock emblem book of 1641 depicts Laud, Wren, and the two ecclesiastical lawyers Dr Arthur Duck and Sir John Lambe—'this Church-consuming band Of Romish vermine'—in a ship named 'High Commission' 'spreading her swelling Sayles O're England's Church, and Common-wealth of England' and being blown by gales 'from the lower darkned world beneath' towards the mouth of hell. At the rear of the ship a cannon discharges the etcetera oath (Plate 13). A later verse alleges that Laud—his 'Popish Grace'—'study'd altera-tion, Uniting Rome to England's thriving Nation', upheld his High Commission in imitation of 'the Spanish Inquisition', owned 'that damned Canon-law' (the like of which had never been seen before), and silenced the preaching ministry.[62] Another satire has a doctor administer Laud an emetic to cure him of his sickness: after taking the potion, the archbishop vomits up the tobacco patent, the Book of Sports, an anti-Puritan sermon, the Star Chamber Order against Bur-ton, Bastwick, and Prynne, presentations and suspensions (whereby benefices were filled with 'tongue tied' clergy and 'long winded min-isters' silenced), and the book of canons. An engraving graphically depicting the scene appeared separately, which showed the attending physician as Dr Burton and contained an accompanying verse stress-ing Laud's cruelties—'Eares from the Pillory', 'Prisonments by your high Inquisition'—and alleged that his 'disease' had been 'bredd by to much Plenitude Of Power, Riches' (Plate 14).[63]

The cruel punishments meted out by Star Chamber were focused on time and again. One pamphlet has the king's sometime jester Archie Armstrong proclaim his fear that if he let his sons become scholars 'the Arch-Bishop would cut off their eares'. An illustrated tract, written as a play, shows Laud dining off the ears of Burton, Bastwick, and Prynne. But the people now had their revenge: in a subsequent scene a carpenter holds Laud's nose to the grindstone in retribution for the punishment of Burton, Bastwick, and Prynne, while later Laud is seen together with a Jesuit confessor imprisoned in a bird cage, being goaded and laughed at by the king's jester

(Plates 15, 16).[64] Indeed, the tone of the anti-Laudian literature in the early months of 1641 was highly optimistic, even triumphalist. The mock emblem book concludes with 'the righteous...delivered out of trouble' and Laud in prison, with the promise of vengeance: 'What thou didst doe, should now be done to thee'.[65] The expectation was that if parliament were allowed to 'sit without disturbance', they would amend the many things that were 'amiss both in the Church and Common-wealth'.[66]

Beyond Laud, there were calls to punish all the 'offending Lordly Bishops'. One tract, which appeared at the time of the meeting of the Long Parliament, charged the bishops with being the 'movers of troubles in the Church, both by their establishing of the Popish Ceremonies; and by their Lordly Government', and also the 'movers of troubles in the States...both with our neighbour nations [i.e. Scotland], and also among our selves'.[67] A number of works appeared attacking images and idolatry.[68] The chronicler and poet John Vicars, not to be confused with the one-time rector of St Mary's, Stamford who had fallen foul of the High Commission in the 1630s, produced a lengthy treatise condemning pictures of Christ, whether used for religious or secular purposes, the depiction of the Holy Ghost as a dove, and the representation of angels (which being spirits were not to be given human form).[69] Robert Baillie denounced the 'Lordly government of the Bishops' for allowing 'Herisies, Prophannesse, Idolatry, and superstition into the Church', accusing the prelates of being 'given to bowings and superstitious seremonies...Altars and Images in the Church', binding 'the consciences of men to men's traditions', giving 'liberty to prophane the holy Sabboth [sic]', and silencing and punishing 'many faithfull painefull Ministers'—in short, of being 'the Ruine and Misery of the Church'—and called for the establishment of Presbyterianism.[70]

Passions over the future of the Church thus ran high. Many MPs who had initially thought that a cleansing exercise in the Church would be sufficient were radicalized as they learned about the extent of the problems and came to perceive the need for more fundamental reform. Others, by contrast, grew alarmed at the rise of radical Puritan activity and saw the need to put a check on reform. Although supporters of root and branch reform could muster a majority in the Commons, the lower house was divided. In the Lords, there was always a strong majority in support of episcopacy. Charles himself, as mentioned already, made clear from the start his determination to stick by the bishops. As he put it in his Banqueting House speech of 23 January, while he would undo innovations in the Church, he was alarmed by the petitions 'against the present established Government of the Church', the threats to reduce the bishops to mere 'Cyphers', and the recent interruptions of church services by radical Puritans. Indeed, he went so far as to defend episcopacy by appeal to the theory of the ancient constitution, claiming that bishops had possessed their votes in parliament since 'before the Conquest', and he was 'bound to maintain' them in it, 'as one of the fundamental Institutions of the Kingdom'.[71]

When London's root and branch petition came before the Commons on 8 February it provoked two days of heated debate: that on the 8th lasted ten hours.[72] The House merely had to decide whether or not to commit the petition, but mistaking the question members began debating the merits of the cause. Sir Benjamin Rudyerd, the first to speak, warned that in striving to 'take away Innovations', they should be careful not to bring in 'the greatest Innovation that ever was in England', namely 'a popular Democraticall Government of the Church' neither 'sutable or acceptable, to a Regall, Monarchicall Government of the State'. Rudyerd agreed that there were many English clergy who thought 'the simplicity of the Gospel, too meane a vocation for them to serve in' and wanted 'a specious, pompous, sumptuous, Religion, with Additionalls of Temporall greatnesse and Authority'. But the solution, he felt, was 'to restraine the Bishops to the duties of their Function' and 'to regulate them according to the usage of Ancient Churches', not to abolish episcopacy outright, and he urged his fellow MPs to recall 'those glorious Martyr-Bishops who were burn'd for our Religion, in the times of Popery, who by their learning, zeale, and constancie, upheld and conveyd it down to us' and to remember that 'we have some good Bishops still'.[73] Lord Digby protested that 'no man within these walls' was 'more sensible of the heavy grievance of Church government' than he and that he was eager to see 'the clipping of those wings of the Prelates, whereby they have mounted to such insolencies', but that it would be wrong to abolish an entire order on account of the abuses committed by particular individuals. The London petition, Digby continued, was 'against the government of the Church of England, established by Acts of Parliaments'; it was 'against the Liturgie...ratified by the same Authority'. Episcopacy dated from the time of the Apostles, 'dignified by the learning and Piety of so many Fathers of the Church, glorified by so many Martydomes in the Primitive times, and some since our own blessed Reformation'; it was a system of government admired 'by the learnedst of the Reformed Churches abroad' and

under which, 'till these late yeares', the Church in England had 'flourished'; he failed to understand how, after 1,640 years, this institution
could 'be found to have such a Close Devill in it' that there was no
option but to abolish it completely. Any other form of government
that might be proposed, Digby believed, would be subject to 'greater
inconveniences', adding—alluding to Presbyterianism—that for
'every Bishop wee put downe in a Diocesse, wee shall set up a Pope
in every Parish'. It would be impossible, he pronounced, to 'put downe
Bishopps totally with safety to Monarchy', for if episcopacy were
abolished 'the Government of Assemblies' would likely succeed it,
which, to be effective, 'must draw to it selfe the supremacy of Ecclesiasticall Jurisdiction' and thus 'the power of Excommunicating Kings
as well as any Brother in Christ'. Digby concluded by urging MPs not
to 'destroy Bishopps' but to make them 'such as they were in the
Primitive times', by retrenching their revenues, abolishing their courts,
and preventing them from 'intermedling in secular affaires'.[74] Falkland acknowledged the oppressions of 'some Bishops and their adherents', even accusing them of labouring 'to bring in an English ... popery'
and of conspiring against Magna Carta (by championing the forced
loan and 'appearing forward for monopolies and ship-mony'), but
insisted it would be wrong to lay the faults of these men 'upon the
order of the Bishops'.[75] Speaking on the 9th, Sir John Strangways
expressed his belief that 'if we made a parity in the Church we must
at last come to a parity in the commonwealth'.[76]

It was Nathaniel Fiennes, the younger brother of Lord Saye, who
put the case for root and branch reform most powerfully. After recalling the abuses of the 1630s, which included in his mind the bishops'
'strict urging of Subscription, and Conformity to the Ceremonies,
and Canons of the Church', he insisted that the bishops' great revenues and dignities were 'the seeds of superstition', because these could
not be maintained 'upon the principles of the reformed religion' but
only upon 'popish principles'. Since the bishops, deans, and chapters
did 'little good themselves by preaching, or otherwise', Fiennes concluded that 'if they were felled, a great deale of good timber might be
cut out of them, for the uses of the Church and Kingdome'.[77]

In the end, the Commons reached a compromise whereby London's
petition was referred to a committee and the issue of episcopacy
reserved for the House. Pym finally brought charges against Laud
before the Lords on 26 February, charging the archbishop with having 'traiterously assumed to himself a Papall and tyrannicall power,
both in Ecclesiasticall and temporal matters, over his Majestie's

subjects...to the disherison of the Crowns, dishonour of his Majesty, and derogation of his supreme authority in ecclesiastical matters'. It was now that the Lords decided to remove Laud to the Tower on 1 March, although parliament did not regard him as dangerous and proceedings against him were not to be resumed until 1644.[78] A bill to exclude bishops from parliament passed the Commons on 1 May and went up to the Lords, while on 27 May the Commons—seemingly as part of a tactic to put pressure on the Lords to accept the bishops exclusion bill—approved by a vote of 139 to 108 a more radical measure to abolish episcopacy entirely. The Lords, however, made it clear they would accept neither exclusion nor root and branch reform, and although debates and arguments continued, nothing had been achieved by August.[79]

In the meantime, the gathering of subscriptions to the Protestation (which began in London in late May), with its pledge to defend the true religion against 'popish innovation', triggered a renewed wave of attacks on parish churches in the metropolitan area. At St Saviour's Southwark in early June eight local men violently tore down the altar rails 'in an insolent and tumultuous Manner'—the Lords ordered that those responsible pay for new rails to be set up, 'as they have been for the Space of Fifty Years last past', though significantly 'not as they were for Four or Five Years past'—while in neighbouring St Olave's four men caused 'a great Tumult and Disorder in the Church...in the Time of the Administration of the Blessed Sacrament' (for which they were fined and imprisoned by the Lords). On both occasions the charges were brought by other inhabitants, pointing to the existence of religious divisions within the two parishes. The reading of the Protestation in the church of St Thomas the Apostle in the heart of the City on 11 June prompted a number of inhabitants to tear down and burn the communion rails, while there were similar disturbances at St Magnus the Martyr and at Isleworth in Middlesex. In other City parishes churchwardens hastened to remove altar rails in a peaceful manner in order to forestall disorder.[80]

To defuse tensions, the Commons issued a declaration on 8 August authorizing churchwardens to remove altar rails set up 'without Warrant of Law', though forbidding anyone from presuming 'to oppose the Discipline or Government of the Church established by Law'.[81] Then on 1 September a committee charged with suppressing innovations in religion recommended the House issue an order stipulating that churchwardens should immediately 'remove the Communion-table from the East End of the Church...into some other convenient Place',

'take away the Rails, and level the Chancels', and remove all crucifixes, scandalous pictures of any one of the Trinity, images of the
Virgin Mary, and candlesticks; that all bowing at the name of Jesus
or towards the communion table be henceforth forborn; and that the
Sabbath be duly observed, 'all Dancing, or other Sports...be forborn', and that 'the Preaching of God's Word be permitted in the
Afternoon'.[82] Committed episcopalians in the House, like Culpepper
and Falkland, were worried that unless accompanied by a declaration against those who vilified or condemned the prayer book, disorders would follow. After a series of tense debates and close divisions,
on 8 September the Commons eventually agreed to publish the order,
without the declaration, and invited the Lords to join with them. The
Lords responded on the 9th by voting to publish its order of 16
January that divine service should be performed 'as appointed by
Acts of Parliament', that those who disturbed divine service should be
severely punished by law, and that all ministers should forbear to use
any ceremonies or rites other than those established by law. Livid, the
Commons voted to disapprove of the Lords' action and drew up its
own declaration against innovations in religion, confirming its order
of the previous day, which it ordered to be published immediately.[83]

The Commons' order met with a mixed reception. In some areas it
was readily embraced, as local parish officials seized the opportunity
to remove the hated images and altar rails. The Venetian ambassador
observed that 'in those parishes where the Puritans prevail, the resolution of the Lower House' was 'gladly adopted; but elsewhere they
have refused to receive it and the people protest roundly that they
will stand fast to the ancient observance without any alteration, as
the Upper House directs'.[84] London was perhaps the city in England
where Puritan influence was strongest, but even here only about one
third of the parishes for which records survive—29 out of 85 in the
London and Westminster area—made some sort of change in response
to the Commons' order: of these, images were defaced or removed in
eighteen, altars and/or communion rails taken down in fifteen, and
crosses (probably crucifixes) taken away in two. In at least four London parishes laity as well as clergy are known to have opposed the
removal of the altar rails. The parishioners of St Giles Cripplegate
petitioned the Commons 'that the Railes about the Communion Table
might not be taken away', insisting they had been in place 'neere
upon fourescore yeeres' and were necessary for the 'more speedy
administration of the sacrament', although their request was rejected.[85]
Likewise in Puritan Norwich there is evidence of some residual

attachment to Laudianism: both St Lawrence's and St Gregory's delayed dismantling their rails until 1643, although all the parishes across the city did remove their Laudian fixtures at some point in the 1640s.[86]

In some areas, over-enthusiastic local iconoclasts went beyond what was sanctioned by the Commons' order. In Herefordshire, for example, the local MP Sir Robert Harley destroyed a stone cross at Wigmore church, where he was patron, causing it 'to be beaten in pieces, even to dust, with a sledge'—the debris was 'laid...in the footpath to be trodden on in the churchyard'—although the Commons' order had stipulated that only crucifixes (crosses sculpted into the figure of the crucified Christ) be demolished.[87] When iconoclasts pulled down Isham Cross in Northamptonshire, claiming they were acting according to parliament's recent order, their opponents tried to prosecute them for riot.[88] Reports soon began to circulate of riotous attacks on parish churches by separatist groups. In September a 'riotous Rout' battered down a stained-glass window in Walbrook church in London said to be worth £700, despite the fact that a local glazier had offered to take it down himself and give them a good price for it.[89] Writing from London on 7 October, one correspondent claimed that 'the Brownists and other sectaries' were making 'havock in our Churches by pulling downe of ancient monuments, Glass windows and Railes' and predicted that pretty soon it would 'bee thought blasphemye...to name Jesus Christ, for it is allready forbidden to bow to his name'.[90] In Essex on 5 November a crowd smashed a stained-glass window in Chelmsford parish church, even though the figure of Christ had already been blotted out in plain glass, claiming to be 'illsatisfied with this partial reformation'. When the rector, Dr John Michelson, a Scot by birth and himself of moderate Puritan leanings, preached against 'popular tumultuous reformations' the following Sunday, a crowd tried to rip the surplice from his back and called him 'Baal's priest and popish priest for wearing the rags of Rome'.[91]

Such outbursts alarmed not only social and religious conservatives but also moderates who initially were sympathetic to the need for reform. One author lamented 'the too foule and irreligious tumults lately committed in the House of God, in too many places of this Kingdome'; even if it were true that the altar rails 'were not lawfully set up', they nevertheless ought 'to be taken down by a more lawfull authority', and 'not by unlawfull assemblies and tumultuous riots'.[92] Yet the Commons' order of September 1641 not only provoked the disorders of those in favour of more radical reform; it also encouraged anti-iconoclastic riots. Thus in Kidderminster in Worcestershire, attempts by the churchwardens to enforce the Commons' order drew 'a Crew of the drunken, riotous Party of the town', as the local Puritan divine Richard Baxter described them, 'poor Journey-men and Servants' who 'took the Allarm' and assembled 'with weapons to defend the Crucifix and the Church Images'.[93]

14

The Irish Rebellion, the Grand Remonstrance, and the Drift to War

By the summer of 1641 a certain amount of progress had been made on constitutional reform: regular meetings of parliament had been guaranteed with the passage of the Triennial Act, the fiscal expedients of the personal rule (ship money, distraint of knighthoods, forest fines) had been undone, and the prerogative courts of High Commission and Star Chamber had been abolished. Yet the biggest problems remained to be solved, notably the question of the king's counsel (the parliamentary leadership had driven certain individuals out, but not got themselves in) and the future of the Church. Charles felt that he had granted sufficient concessions, and many around him—including the queen—were urging him to be more resolute. He had given up on the idea of bringing members of the parliamentary opposition into his government—the last overture in this regard had been the appointments of some of the pro-Scottish peers to his privy council in February—and was now beginning to look to construct a royalist party of his own. He worked closely with Secretary Nicholas to identify a group of eleven lay peers, led by Bristol, who could be relied on to support him, and began to court members in the Commons, such as Edward Hyde, who were opposed to root and branch reform. Henrietta Maria busied herself trying to persuade the papal nuncio to pay Charles a subsidy of £150,000, promising in return greater freedoms for Catholics in both England and Ireland, in order to give the king more freedom of action. Charles himself continued to flirt with the idea of staging a coup to recover his position: in mid-June it emerged that he was allegedly trying to persuade the army to march on London and petition the Commons to restore the king's prerogative.[1]

The quest for a workable solution to the crisis would break down in the last months of 1641 and early 1642. Westminster began to polarize, with some pushing for further reform and others believing that reform had gone far enough. Charles and his supporters felt that the parliamentary leadership kept raising the stakes; those doing the stakes-raising, on the other hand, were finding Charles frustrating to deal with. Charles did not help his own cause: although in general the momentum was swinging towards the crown in this time period, he made a series of critical blunders which served to undermine his position just as it looked like he might be getting on top of the situation. But events were also crucially influenced by developments in Charles's other kingdoms.

Having overseen the enactment of legislation in England addressing some of the key constitutional issues deriving from the personal rule, Charles decided the time was right to journey north to meet with the parliament in Scotland, which had already enacted quite extensive reforming legislation in his absence the previous year. Although Charles did not to depart until the second week of August, he had in fact made the decision to go back in April: encouraged by the divisions that were beginning to appear amongst the Covenanters, with the emergence of a group of nobles around the earl of Montrose concerned about the populist implications of the movement, he felt that if he could tap into latent support north of the border and bring a satisfactory conclusion to the peace negotiations he would be able to break the links between the reformist group in England and the Scots.[2] The parliamentary leadership found alarming the prospect of Charles marching through the north of England, where there were two armies in the field, with one of which he had actively been conspiring against the parliament. In response, the Commons drew up Ten Propositions, agreed to by the Lords on 24 June, wherein they requested (among other things) that Charles delay his trip north until the armies had been disbanded, dismiss all evil counsellors and appoint only such as 'his People and Parliament' had 'Cause to confide in', remove Catholics from court, and appoint 'good Lord-Lieutenants and Deputy-Lieutenants' who might be trusted to be 'careful of the Peace of the Kingdom'.[3] They were rejected by the king.

Fearful that the initiative was slipping to the king, Pym proposed that the Commons draw up a remonstrance detailing how they 'found affairs in Church and state', what they had done by way of reform, and where things now stood upon the king's going to Scotland. There had been some discussions about a remonstrance to the king earlier in the Long Parliament. Pym's idea was different, however: his was to be a declaration to the people. Work began in earnest on 3 August, when the Commons appointed a committee of eight, led by Pym, to draw up the remonstrance, although progress was slow and they were still working on the draft in the autumn.[4] In the meantime Charles continued to try to construct his own following in parliament. Just before his departure for Scotland, Charles made Bristol first gentleman of the bedchamber and brought a number of other loyalists into his privy council. In October, while away in Scotland, he appointed a number of Calvinist divines to bishoprics—including Joseph Hall (translated from Exeter to Norwich), John Prideaux (made bishop of Worcester), and John Williams (translated from Lincoln to York)—in an attempt to convince his critics that the Church he would uphold would be one they would feel comfortable with.[5]

Charles left for Scotland on 10 August, arriving on the 14th, and staying for just over three months. In his efforts to please the Scots he proved remarkably conciliatory. After being reprimanded by Henderson for failing to attend the afternoon sermon on his first full day in Edinburgh, he abandoned his scruples and was henceforth assiduous in attending the Presbyterian services which had neither liturgy nor ceremonies. He allowed Balmerino—the man he had had condemned for treason in 1633—to preside over the parliamentary session, which opened on the 17th. In his opening speech Charles expressed his readiness to ratify the measures enacted in June 1640; when the Covenanting leadership objected, since it would imply that those laws were not yet legally binding, Charles agreed instead to allow those Acts to be published in his name without having touched them with his sceptre, thereby acknowledging the Scottish parliament's right to enact legislation without the royal assent while at the same time giving the crown's endorsement to the legislation abolishing episcopacy north of the border. In addition to ratifying the Treaty of London, establishing the terms of the peace between the English and the Scots, he also agreed to an Act 'for abolishing monumentes of Idolatrie' (first passed by the General Assembly in July 1640) ordaining that 'all idolatrous images, crucifixes, pictures of Christ, and all other idolatrous pictures' be 'demolished and removed' from all churches, colleges, chapels, and public places. He was more reluctant to give up his right to appoint to office, not least because of the precedent it would set for England; yet in the end he agreed to a compromise whereby the Scottish parliament was allowed to advise on appointments, given that the king was not resident in the kingdom and might not be in a position to know who was best qualified.[6]

However, Charles found breaking the link between the Covenanters and the parliamentary leadership in England more difficult than he expected. Pym, in fact, had arranged for a delegation from the English parliament, which included both Hampden and Fiennes, to travel to Edinburgh to renew their contacts with the Covenanter leadership, while it now emerged that Hamilton, the man Charles had once relied so heavily upon in his dealings with the Scots but who had recently lost favour at court, had defected to the Covenanters. Frustrated, Charles gave his backing to an attempted coup against Hamilton and the Covenanter leader the Earl of Argyll on 11 October: in what became known as 'the Incident', Hamilton and Argyll were to be seized and either brought to trial for treason or simply murdered, but the couple were tipped off in advance and fled to Hamilton's estate in the country. Charles was quick to deny any involvement in the plot, but it cost him politically: he was forced not only to launch an investigation into the affair but also to admit leading Covenanters into his privy council.[7]

It was while in Scotland that Charles received news that major unrest had broken out in Ireland. With the vantage of hindsight, it might seem that the grievances of the Catholics of Ireland were such that it was only a matter of time before the kingdom erupted in violent upheaval. Yet when the rebellion did occur, it appeared to contemporaries as a bolt out of the blue. In early September Edward Nicholas, clerk to the English privy council, reported how he had just heard from the Lords Justices of Ireland 'that all in that kingdom' was 'very quiet and in good order', while as late as the beginning of October—just three weeks before the rebellion was to break out—Sir John Temple could inform Nicholas that Ireland 'gives nothing worth your knowledge'.[8]

Ireland may have been 'quiet' for the time being but it was clearly not in 'good order'. The policies of plantation and religious and ethnic discrimination had generated deep-seated resentments; indeed, as early as the 1610s some observers in Ireland had been forewarning of the prospect of the Gaelic Irish and Old English combining in a bloody uprising against English Protestant rule.[9] The policies pursued by Wentworth, Bramhall, and Charles had served to alienate most interests in Ireland: Catholic and Protestant; the ethnically Irish and both the Old and the New English; even the new planter interest in Ulster. Although the Irish parliament which met in March 1640 delivered the much needed grant of subsidies, its apparent loyalty was deceptive. Things went much less well in the subsequent sessions.

In June the Irish Commons set up committees, comprising both Protestants and Catholics, to negotiate an end to discrimination against
Galway proprietors and to re-examine the way that subsidies were
being assessed; it issued writs of summons to those boroughs that
had recently been disenfranchised by the government (a concern primarily of the Old English); launched an investigation into the 'many
grievous Exactions, Pressures, and other vexatious proceedings' of
the clergy (a concern primarily of the Presbyterians of the north); and
took issue with the court of High Commission.[10] The Deputy Lord
Lieutenant, Sir Christopher Wandesford, prorogued the session to
stall these initiatives, but when parliament reassembled in October it
simply picked up from where it had left off. On 7 November 1640 it
unanimously approved its Humble and Just Remonstrance, complaining of the abuses of government in the 1630s, the lack of respect
for law and parliament, and the denial of the Graces, and demanding
that Ireland should be governed according to the 'fundamental Laws
of England' (most notably Magna Carta, 'the great Charter for the
Liberties of England'). In addition, it appointed a committee of thirteen (comprising both Old and New English and even one Irishman)
to go to England to represent their grievances.[11]

Eventually bowing to pressure, on 3 April 1641 Charles wrote to
the Lords Justices in Ireland instructing them to draw up bills confirming the Graces.[12] Under Poynings' Law, only the Irish privy council had the right to draw up legislation to submit for approval by the
English privy council, but the Irish council was against confirming
the Graces, arguing that if the policy of plantation were stopped the
Irish government would not be able to finance itself. The Irish parliament therefore had been seeking an 'explanation' of Poynings' Law
that might give it the power to draw up the necessary legislation,
though Charles was adamantly opposed to this idea.[13] The delays
meant that no bills had been drawn up before the Irish parliament
began its summer recess on 7 August. Towards the beginning of
August, the English House of Lords formally asked Charles to stay
the Graces, while it searched the records and precedents concerning
Ireland's dependency upon the kingdom of England.[14]

Repeatedly frustrated in their efforts to secure redress of their
grievances through peaceful means, discontented elements in Ireland
could not help but notice how the Scots had achieved their objectives
through collective resistance and began to consider this as a model
for emulation. The idea of an uprising was first mooted in February
1641, when Rory O'More (the descendant of a great family from the

Irish Midlands which had lost its hereditary lands) approached Connor, Lord Maguire, 2nd baron of Enniskillen (a heavily indebted Ulster peer from County Fermanagh, whose mother was an O'Neill) in Dublin and suggested that the Scottish troubles provided a good opportunity to recover their estates by force, claiming to have the support of many influential families in Leinster and Connacht. Other Ulster leaders were contacted, including Sir Phelim O'Neill, a prominent landowner regarded as 'the chief of his name', and by May tentative plans had been forged for a rising in October—towards the beginning of winter so that the English would not have time to send over forces before the bad weather set in.

Interest now came to focus on what was to happen to the army of 9,000 that Wentworth had raised in Ireland to help suppress the Scots. In May Charles finally agreed to the English parliament's demand that it be disbanded, but to avoid the disorders that might accompany the unleashing on Ireland of large numbers of unemployed men trained in the arts of violence, he gave permission for the disbanded soldiers to be recruited into the service of the King of Spain. However, when Charles announced towards the beginning of July that he intended to renew efforts to recapture the Palatinate from Spain (a desperate attempt to try to rebuild support in England), both the Irish and English parliaments objected to allowing the Irish soldiers to enter Spanish service and refused to let them leave Ireland.[15] The earl of Antrim was later to claim that Charles wanted to keep an Irish army in the field as a contingency, so that he would have an armed force at his disposal to use against the English parliament if necessary, although there is no firm contemporary evidence to support this allegation. What the Irish conspirators might have learned about Charles's intentions from the officers in the Irish army is likewise impossible to discern, though we do know they talked to each other, since in September 1641 the earl of Ormond, the man who had replaced Strafford as commander-in-chief of the forces in Ireland, ordered the army officers to break off all contacts with the Ulster leaders. It does at least seem to be the case that the fact that Charles was seen to be giving orders to keep an army in the field in Ireland encouraged the Ulster conspirators to believe that what they were planning would not necessarily be unwelcome to the king.[16]

What the conspirators originally had in mind was in fact quite limited. On the evening of Friday, 22 October O'Neill was to seize various strongholds and magazines in Ulster, and then at about

9 o'clock the next morning (St Ignatius Day) Maguire was to take Dublin Castle; the leaders of the uprising simply hoped that by capturing the key fortified positions in Ulster and paralysing the government in Dublin they would then be able to negotiate for a redress of their grievances from a position of strength. Contrary to what was later alleged, no general massacre of Protestants was intended. However, the plan to take Dublin Castle was foiled when Owen O'Connolly, the foster brother of one of the conspirators, revealed the conspiracy to the Lords Justices just after 9 p.m. on the evening of the 22nd—it was O'Connolly who first raised the prospect of a massacre, alleging that 'the Irish had prepared Men in all the Parts of the Kingdom, to destroy all the English Inhabitants there'—and Maguire and others were taken into custody.[17] In Ulster, on the other hand, O'Neill and his associates had already swung into action, and taken Dungannon in County Tyrone and Charlemont Fort in County Armagh. Within two days they were in control of a significant chunk of the central heartland of the province.[18] Immediately the dynamic had been changed: Ulster was in revolt but the Dublin government had not been paralysed, and events rapidly spiralled out of control.

Insight into O'Neill's basic intentions can be gleaned from the statements he released during the early days of the rebellion. At Dungannon on 24 October he published a proclamation announcing that the 'Assembling and Meeting' of the Irish was 'nowayes intended against...the King, nor [to] hurt any of his Subjects either of the English or Scottishe nation; But only for the defence and Libertie of our Selves and the Irishe Natives of this Kingdome'.[19] From Newry on 4 November he issued a declaration to 'all the Catholiques of the, Romish partie both English and Irish within the kingedome of Ireland', wishing them 'Freedom of conscience and victory over the English heretickes' who, he alleged, had 'for a longe time tyranyzed over our bodies, and usurped by extortion our estates'. With it he published a commission supposedly from the king, dated Edinburgh, 1 October, in which Charles relates how he had been forced to take up residence in Scotland because of the 'obstinate and disobedient carriage' of the English parliament and orders the Catholics of Ireland to seize for his use all the forts, castles, and other strongholds in Ireland and 'to arrest and seize the goods, estates and persons, of all the English protestants'.[20] The commission was certainly forged, but it convinced many of those who joined in the rebellion that they were acting in accordance with the wishes of the king—and thus that they were not in rebellion against the crown at all.

Despite O'Neill's protestation that the insurgents intended no harm to the English, violence soon erupted. Protestants were forcibly evicted from their lands, stripped of their clothes, and dispossessed of their property and livestock, and reports began to fly of brutal atrocities being committed upon the settler population—torture, dismemberment, rape, murder, and mass killings. From Ulster the revolt quickly spread to both Connacht and Leinster—there were popular disturbances in Leinster even before the Catholic Old English landowners of the province formally threw in their lot with the Ulster rebels at a meeting at the Hill of Crofty on 3 December—and then finally to Munster. The number of Protestant fatalities was soon being reported as in the thousands—and escalating. Not all Irish Catholics rose; indeed, during the early weeks we find Catholic landowners in some areas desperately trying to protect local Protestants from the fury of the insurgents. However, the blatantly sectarian response of the authorities to the outbreak of the rebellion had the tendency to push those Catholics whose instinct was to remain loyal into making common cause with the rebels. Panicked by the news of the foiled plot on Dublin Castle, the Dublin administration immediately announced that it would be imposing martial law and employing torture to get to 'the bottom of the treason'.[21] In Leinster Sir Charles Coote was said to have murdered a number of Catholics in their beds and had others hanged by martial law without cause, whereas in Munster St Leger killed two hundred Catholics and hanged several prisoners, 'for a greater terror to all such as should adventure afterwards to follow their example', proclaiming that 'in these days *Magna Charta* must not be wholly insisted upon'.[22]

There has been considerable debate as to how best to characterize the Irish rebellion: was it at heart a nationalist uprising; a revolt against English rule; an attempt to overthrow the plantation; an ethnic conflict, fuelled by a hatred of the English as a people; or in essence a religious revolt, of Catholics against Protestants? To varying degrees, it was a mixture of all the above, yet at the same time never quite any one of them. Motivation is not always easy to decipher from the available sources, which often sought to disguise, distort, or even misrepresent. We should clearly be wary of seeking a generalized explanation that can apply to all classes of people who supported or joined in the rebellion across the whole of the kingdom. Whatever the original intentions of the gentry leadership, they failed to maintain control over what quickly became a popular rebellion with a momentum of its own, as the common people rose in large numbers to vent their own resentments against the Protestant planters. Furthermore, the insurgency took on distinctive local colorations, dependent upon factors such as the density of English (and Scottish) settlement in a given area, the precise state of the local economy (and the relative rates of unemployment), or the influence of the Counter-Reformation clergy (who typically sought to constrain violence and to channel grievances along religious lines).

The leaders of the revolt in Ulster were not the dispossessed Irish, but rather the 'deserving Irish'—those who had been allowed to benefit from the plantation scheme. Many of them were quite Anglicized. Connor Maguire was a substantial landowner who had acquired his lands by dint of the fact that his branch of the family had sided with the English during the Nine Years War. He had reputedly spent some time at Magdalen College, Oxford and was fluent in both English and Irish.[23] Sir Phelim O'Neill was the grandson of Sir Henry Oge O'Neill, who had deserted the earl of Tyrone towards the end of the Nine Years War and died in the king's service at the time of the O'Doherty revolt of 1608. Phelim inherited his grandfather's lands, was raised as a royal ward, subsequently spent three years at Lincoln's Inn in London, and was knighted by the crown in 1639. By 1624 he had an estate of some 4,500 acres in County Armagh, and he introduced British tenants onto his lands (because they would pay higher rents) and evicted Irish ones to make room for them.[24] Other rebel leaders were the children and descendants of men who had served on the inquisition juries and emerged from the confiscation with still quite considerable property. The Ulster leaders gave orders initially not to meddle with the Scots (in part a tactical measure, to avoid turning two nations against them at the same time)[25]—who had been as much beneficiaries of the plantation scheme as the English and who, of course, were also Protestant—while they were joined in revolt by the Old English Catholics, who had not been dispossessed, and also by recent Catholic immigrants from England.

However, the Old Irish, especially in Ulster (even the 'deserving' kind), had been finding it difficult to adjust to the new economic situation of the post-plantation era and had been sinking further and further into debt. The deserving Irish landowners did not have the same concerns about security of tenure as did the Old English—having recently acquired their lands they usually had clearer titles; the major form of discrimination they suffered under the terms of the plantation was that they were not allowed to buy lands from the British or for themselves. In other words, many Irish landowners were ready to compete in the new system; what irked them were the political restraints placed on their competitiveness. The lower classes in Ulster, on the other hand, suffered major disadvantages: they struggled in competing for tenancies, being unable to afford the rents which the British were willing to pay, while Irish labourers found they were paid significantly less than their British counterparts.[26] Furthermore, the economy of Ireland, which had been prospering for much of the 1630s, took a significant downturn from 1638, following the outbreak of the Scottish troubles, with the worst-hit area being Ulster. The Old English of Leinster, although they might not have been dispossessed themselves, had ample reason to fear what might be in store for them in the wake of Wentworth's policies of the 1630s. The Catholics of Ireland as a whole had the additional shared anxiety of what might be their plight in the wake of calls by the English parliament for tougher measures against popery.[27]

What, then, did the rebels see themselves as fighting for? In their official pronouncements (as noted above), the rebel leaders claimed to be acting in defence of their 'Religion and liberty', called for religious toleration, and professed their loyalty to King Charles.[28] Owen O'Connolly, in his initial revelation, alleged that the conspirator who tried to recruit him said they 'did this for the Tyrannical Government that was over them, and to imitate *Scotland*, who got a Privilege by that Course'.[29] A manuscript in the archives of the Protestant earl of Cork headed 'Certain considerations which the Rebels proposed amongst themselves', which seems to date from November 1641, lists the rebels' objectives as: 'freedom of religion'; 'the restoration of Church livings to their Ministers'; the 'Irish Parliament to be independent' and 'all officers from Deputy downwards to be Irish'; the 'Plantation lands to be restored' and 'forts to be garrisoned by Irish'; and a proposal that 'the Protestant clergy profits, and the estates of such Protestants as shall be banished, to be taken to supply his Majesty's Wars'.[30] On 5 November the Irish authorities wrote to the English council that the rebels publicly stated 'their purpose' was 'totally to extirpate the English and Protestants' and that they would not 'lay down arms' until 'the Romish Religion be established' in Ireland by an Act of the Irish parliament, 'the Government be settled in the hands of natives, and all the old Irish be restored to the lands of their supposed ancestors'.[31]

Among the rank and file, there was a mixture of religious, economic, and political motives—the precise balance between them varying from locality to locality. Religion was undoubtedly a major concern. Many Irish had come to be gripped by a fear that the English parliament, backed by the Scots, was about to begin a campaign of persecution against Catholics in Ireland; indeed, Jesuits and other Catholic clergy were said to have spread rumours of an imminent massacre of Catholics in Ireland, prompting the Irish to make a pre-emptive strike in self-defence.[32] Yet the native Irish also harboured deep resentments towards both the English and Scottish settlers (the orders not to meddle with the Scots notwithstanding), and many had come to see the plantation as the cause of all their woes. It is revealing that in Ulster the earliest victims of the attacks were those English who had been invited by native proprietors to take leases on property that had previously been reserved for Catholic farmers (including the English tenants Sir Phelim O'Neill had settled on his estates), suggesting that action may first have been directed against those who possessed land which the insurgents thought should rightfully have been theirs.[33] Quickly, however, any Protestant settler came to be seen as fair game. One Protestant victim from County Fermanagh alleged that he had often heard the Irish say that they would not leave any Englishman or Scot alive in the kingdom save a few artificers 'whom they would keep as slaves' and 'that they would never have any other then Irish officers and magistrates to rule over them'. Indeed, it was reported to be the cry of the Irish that 'we have been your Slaves all this tyme, now you shalbe ours'.[34] Hatred of the recent English planters could sometimes slip into a hatred of the English race. One deponent from County Fermanagh in Ulster, for example, said that it was a 'common thing' for the rebels to say 'that the Irish old English of the pale, though they joined with them in this rebellion...deserved to be hanged as well as the other English', that 'they would drive all the English and Scotch out of the kingdom', and that 'both man woman and child that had a Dropp of English or Scottish blood in them they would cut off and destroy utterly'.[35] Within the Pale itself there were occasional reports of rebels attacking English Catholics. For example, Ralph Walmisley, who came from near Birr in King's County (now County Offaly), reported that about the middle of November 1641 he, his wife, and three children were forcibly deprived of their goods and chattels and driven out of their home by the rebels (all of those he identified had Irish names), even though Walmisley and his family 'were all Romish Catholicks': the parties who carried out the attack, Walmisley alleged, were such 'notorious robbers oppressors and pillidgers of the English', that they spared not even those 'of the old Romane Catholicks if they were of the English kind';

indeed, such was 'their enveterate hatred and mallice to the English' that they were resolved to 'root all out of the kingdome, soe as neither roote nor branch of them should be left'.[36] Money-lenders were often targeted, reinforcing the view that indebtedness was a motive for rebellion. The animosity directed against Protestant clergy undoubtedly reflected Irish hostility towards the Protestant religion, but it was also linked to the involvement of Protestant ministers in money-lending. Stripping the English of their clothing, while in part a form of humiliation, was in addition, of course, a form of theft.[37]

The insurgents also engaged in acts of violence against symbolic representations of the English plantation in Ireland. Thus they took to 'demolishing and defacing the buildings and improvements of the English',[38] rooting up 'the very trees' and killing their 'very beasts' while sparing 'the Irish breed'.[39] In County Mayo they even subjected English cattle to mock jury trials, in 'contempt and derision of the English Lawes', offering to spare the beasts only if they could read from a book in English.[40] In some areas insurgents destroyed the leases which gave the settlers the titles to their estates and the bonds that testified to the indebtedness of the displaced Irish.[41] They also attacked symbols of the Protestant religion. At Fethard, County Wexford, at the beginning of December 1641, rebels, after despoiling the English planters and taking possession of the local castle, 'went into the Church and Cutt the Pulpit Cloth and the ministers books in peeces, and strewed them about the Church yard, and caused the Piper to play while they daunced and trampled them under their feete and called the minister dogg and stript him of his Cloths'.[42] Similarly in Ballywalter, County Wexford, the rebels not only dispossessed the English of their possessions and goods, and boasted that 'they wold not suffer english man woman or Child nor beast or dog of English breed, or any thing that was English to remayne alive', but they also 'burnt all the bibles they cold meete with' in front of 'the faces of severall protestants', saying 'what will yow doe now your bibles are all burnt'.[43] The destruction of church bibles and service books was so widespread that it has been described as systematic. Typically they were burnt in a great heap at a local market cross, though sometimes other forms of desacralization were improvised: at Armagh Patrick Carragh O Cullen opened a bible he had found in the town's church and 'pissed upon the same', saying he would 'do worse with it' if he could.[44]

The impact which the news of the outbreak of the rebellion in Ireland had on public opinion in England was dramatic, seeming as it did to provide confirmation of the inhuman barbarity of the native

Irish and of an international Catholic conspiracy to overthrow Protestantism in the Stuart kingdoms. The reports that began to filter back were alarming indeed. On 1 November the English privy council informed the Commons that it had received 'certain intelligences' of a 'general Rebellion, of the Irish Papists in Ireland, and a Design of cutting off all the Protestants in Ireland', while later that day the Lord Keeper informed the Lords of the details of O'Connolly's revelations and the supposed intended massacre of Protestants.[45] On the 4th the earl of Northumberland's secretary, Thomas Smith, was writing to a friend that the plot was 'to cutt the throats of all the Protestants in Ireland', which having now been discovered the Irish were 'murdering, ravishing, burning and taking what they can'.[46] Official reports from the government in Ireland made allegations of atrocity from the very beginning. For example, on 5 November the Lords Justices in Ireland and the Irish privy council wrote to the privy council in England reporting how the Irish had 'seized the houses and estates of almost all the English' across several counties in Ulster and in Leitrim, Longford, and the greater part of County Down, and how 'the rebels most barbarously not only murdered' but also 'hewed... to pieces' 'some of the English gentlemen whose houses they seized'.[47] MPs repeated what they heard. On the 11th Sir Simonds D'Ewes wrote that 'many English and Protestants had been slaine' by 'the Rebels in Ireland' and 'with soe much crueltie as was scarce ever heard offe amongst Christians'.[48] Godly ministers further helped to circulate what was being alleged, adding their own colour. Preaching in St Stephen's Coleman Street in the heart of London on 14 November, John Goodwin claimed that the Irish rebels were 'under a vow, to make as cleere riddance of Protestants and Protestant Religion out of the Kingdome, as their lying Legend reports that their Saint Patrick made of Serpents and Toades', insisting that they had 'already consecrated themselves unto the Devill' by murdering and then 'hewing, and hacking... in pieces' 'many of the servants of God'.[49] What was being said in London seemed only to be confirmed by official accounts out of Ireland. On 22 November, the Lords Justices sent further particulars to England concerning 'the Ulster rebels' barbarous cruelty towards the English', namely that they had 'cut off some men's hands and put out their eyes, and... let them go away naked, destitute of sight to guide them or hands to help them, that they might endure the greater torment during the few hours left of their life'.[50]

English awareness of alleged developments in Ireland was further fuelled by print. Newsbooks—the first domestic news periodical began in late November 1641—provided regular coverage of alleged developments in Ireland, typically reporting information that was being fed to the English parliament from the authorities in Ireland. (Pym, who sat on the Commons Committee on Irish Affairs, appears to have been a key source for some of the information that was leaked to the press.) Then there were news pamphlets purporting to document developments in Ireland. Thirty-two appeared in the last few weeks of 1641 alone, while between January and June 1642 nearly a quarter of the pamphlets collected by the London bookseller George Thomason related to Ireland. Between October 1641 and April 1642, 162 works on the Irish rebellion were published in London, some 22 per cent of England's total printed output for this time period.[51]

The consumers of the English pamphlet press would have read graphic accounts of obscene acts of cruelty. *Bloudy Newes from Ireland* of late 1641, for example, related how (according to one recently arrived Protestant refugee) the Irish in Armagh were 'putting men to the sword, deflowering Women...and cruelly murdering them, and thrusting their Speers through their little Infants before their eyes, and carrying them up and down on Pike-points'.[52] Sometimes the pamphlets fed off what was being reported to parliament. For example, on 14 December a letter, purportedly from a Protestant in Ireland to the MP Sir John Clotworthy, was read before both Houses documenting 'the great and barbarous Cruelties acted upon the Protestants in Ireland', such as 'hanging of them, and pulling their Flesh from their Bones, cutting off the Heads, Hands and Feet, unripping of Women great with Children, and killing the Children'. The *Lords' Journal* merely summarizes the gist of the letter, and so we have no way of knowing precisely what the assembled peers would have heard. However, what purported to be the letter itself soon found its way into print as *Worse and Worse Newes from Ireland*, where listed among the 'exquisite' torments inflicted upon 'the poore Protestants' were 'Cutting off their privie members, eares, fingers, and hands, plucking out their eyes, boyling the heades of little Children before their Mothers' faces, and then ripping open their Mothers' Bowels, stripping women naked...killing the Children as soon as they are borne and ripping up their Mothers' bellies, as soone as they are delivered'; 'driving men, women, and children, by hundreds together upon Bridges', from whence they would be 'cast...downe into Rivers' to drown, shooting those who tried to swim to safety or else bashing 'their braines out with Poles'; and 'ravishing wives before their husbands' faces, and Virgins before their parents'.[53]

Such accounts cannot be taken at face value. Much of the pamphlet literature was not just highly sensationalist but fictionalized, mixing truth (the mass drowning mentioned above refers to a real incident that happened at Portadown) with half-truth and distorted exaggeration with outright fabrication. (The printed newsbooks, by contrast, contained remarkably few reports of outrages or widescale massacres.[54]) Some of the pamphlets were simply made up. In January 1642 two Cambridge undergraduates were arrested for 'composing' sundry news pamphlets, which they sold to various publishers for 2s. 6d. a piece, including the above-cited *Bloudy Newes from Ireland* and another entitled *Good Newes from Ireland*.[55] That same month there appeared in print a supposed 'Letter from Ireland' which alleged that all the printed pamphlets concerning the Irish Rebellion were false, nothing more than the 'forgeries' of 'Hellish braines' intended to fool 'credulous people'; although the Irish did 'pillage Protestants' Houses, and take away all manner of Cattell', the reported 'murdering or ravishing' was 'more than we ever heard of in Ireland', and 'onely one Gentleman'—whose story the pamphlet proceeded to relate—had 'lost his life after this manner'.[56]

Many of the worst atrocities alleged in the pamphlet literature prove impossible to substantiate from the depositions later taken from the victims of the rebellion. *The Bloudy Persecution of the Protestants in Ireland*, for example—a pamphlet purporting to be 'the Contents of severall Letters brought by his Majestie's Post from Ireland' on 21 November 1641—after making vague allegations about how women had 'bin slain in their husbands' armes', and 'the braines of children...daily dash[ed] out' and trampled under foot, proceeds to offer one specific account of how the rebels supposedly treated one Sir Patrick Dunson and his family in the city of Armagh on 22 November. When Dunson refused an offer to join with the rebels, the pamphlet claims, they 'took his wife and ravished her...before his face, slew his servants, spurned his children untill they dyed'. Then they bound Sir Patrick to a board, 'so fast, that his eyes bursted of his head', cut off his ears and his nose and 'seered off both his cheekes', then cut off his arms and legs, though miraculously Sir Patrick was not yet dead, so they 'cut out his tongue' and 'ran a red hot Iron into his bowels' (which finished him off).[57] There is no mention of a 'Dunson' (or Dunston) in any of the surviving depositions, though the testimony given by two gentlemen from Armagh in June 1642 does name one 'Patrick Duncan' of Armagh in a list of people whom the rebels 'alsoe murthered' (with no extra details provided).[58] Another pamphlet told a horrific tale of alleged brutalities committed on Christmas Eve by Irish rebels on the family of one Mr Dabnet, a 'Religious and godly man', in County Cork—the account supposedly being derived from a letter written by a Kinsale merchant named Tristram Whetcombe to his brother in England. After storming the house and killing the guards, the rebels first raped Dabnet's wife 'before her husband's face'; they then affixed the Dabnets' two infant children 'upon a red hot spit', which they 'laid down upon a pair of Racks that stood in the chimney, to roast before the fire', and forced the family's older child 'to turn the spit about' before they also cast this child into the fire, holding him 'down till he was dead'; and then they cut off Dabnet's ears and nose, put out both his eyes, cut off his arms and legs, stripped him naked, and 'laid him along close by the fire to scorch him, where he lay until his flesh did rise up in blisters'. Not quite dead, Dabnet seemingly had the strength and courage to warn his tormenters that 'all these things' would 'rise up at the day of Judgement against them', which so enraged the Irish that they 'cut out his tongue' and ran 'an hot Iron downe his throat', at last killing him. The rebels offered to spare Dabnet's wife if she turned Catholic, but she simply fell to her knees, weeping uncontrollably, and so the Irish 'dragged her out of the house by the haire of the head into the yard', and threw her into the well, where she drowned. Given that the rebels had now killed the last remaining eyewitness, we may wonder how the author of this pamphlet (or his supposed source in Kinsale) was able to discover this level of specific detail.[59] There is no mention of a Dabnet (or Davenant) in the depositions, and although there is a deposition from Tristram Whetcombe—he claimed to have been robbed or despoiled of five and a half thousand pounds worth of his goods and chattels—it makes no mention of this episode.[60]

Yet incredible though such stories are, many English readers were willing to suspend disbelief when it came to believing the worst of the native Irish. The London Puritan Nehemiah Wallington was an avid consumer of the atrocity literature and copied out large chunks into his notebooks (including the supposed treatment of the Dabnet family), Wallington's credulity doubtless reinforced by the fact that his wife's brother's family in County Fermanagh were victims of the rebellion.[61] The Puritan preacher Edmund Calamy thought the atrocity literature coincided with what parliament was finding out: 'I need not relate', he said in his sermon preached before the Commons on 22 December, 'the inhumane, barbarous, Canniballisticall, and super-superlative out-rages, butcheries, and massacres that are there committed by those bloudy Rebels', since 'you have great reason to know it better than my selfe'.[62] Repeating the same atrocity stories over and over again served to implant them firmly the public memory. In 1642 James Cranford produced an anthology of the 'perfidious outrages and barbarous cruelties' committed against Protestants in Ireland since the outbreak of the rebellion, littered with graphic illustrations in case the imagination was lacking (Plates 17, 18).[63]

Given the problematic nature of the source material, it is difficult to work out precisely what went on during the early months of the rebellion. According to Wallington, by the beginning of January 1642 it was being reported to parliament that some 'thirty thousand families in Ireland' had been destroyed, totalling 'a hundred thousand persons'. The Ulster clergyman Robert Maxwell deposed that the rebels themselves had calculated they had killed a staggering 154,000 during the early months of the rebellion.[64] Such figures are way too high. Modern estimates suggest that perhaps 3,000–4,000 Protestant settlers were killed, though thousands were left to die after they had been stripped of their possessions and driven from their habitations in winter. A careful examination of the depositions taken from eyewitnesses by the English authorities, set against other types of source material, does at least allow for a more nuanced reading of the range and types of acts of violence (and symbolic significance thereof) perpetrated against the planter population. Although the confrontations were often brutal, rarely was the violence totally indiscriminate, and the evidence belies the notion that the rebels aimed at the general extirpation of all Protestant settlers. The typical pattern was for an armed group of Irish to descend upon a Protestant family and demand that they hand over their goods and vacate their house and farm. Rape appears to have been rare, while there is no evidence to support the gruesome tales of the torture and butchery of infants. Killings usually only occurred if the Protestants resisted, although torture was frequently applied in an effort to get the settlers to reveal where they had hidden their valuables, and beatings could escalate into killings when local leaders failed to maintain discipline over the rank and file, especially in those 'blackspots' where native resentment against British settlers ran particularly high. Thus in the area around Kinard in Ulster, most of the British families planted by Phelim O'Neill eventually ended up being murdered. There were some mass killings, but often these were the result of the conflicts that emerged when Protestants formed themselves into armed groups in self-defence or tried to take the fight to the Irish. In central Ulster the two most notorious atrocities were carried out when the Irish failed to capture Lisnagar-vey (now part of Lisburn), County Antrim, in three separate attacks in November. At Portadown, County Armagh, rebels rounded up about 100 Protestant men, women, and children, stripped them naked, and forced them onto a bridge over the River Bann, which had been cut in the middle, so that they fell headlong into the river and drowned. (Those who attempted to save themselves were either knocked on the head and forced back under the water or shot.) Certainly Irish defeat at the battle of Lisnagarvey on 28 November, when Protestant horsemen killed 300 Irish, trampling them 'under their feete' and thrusting 'their pykes in their very mowths', seems to have prompted an escalation of violation. The Irish were said to have gone on the rampage in County Antrim and neighbouring County Armagh, murdering all Protestants they came across. At Kilmore, County Armagh, in early 1642 (round about Candlemas) rebels herded 'a great number of Protestants', both English and Scots (some of them locals, many of them strangers who had been brought to the town over the previous twenty-four hours), into a thatched cottage, which they then proceeded to set on fire; two managed to escape through a hole in the wall, but the rest were 'miserably and barbarously burned to death'.[65] In Leinster and Munster the killings of Protestant settlers were reprisals for the murder and summary execution of Catholics authorized by Coote and St Leger in their efforts to put down the rebellion.[66]

The Irish rebellion was also reported as being part of a broader international Catholic conspiracy. In mid-November the Lords Justices informed the English council how 'the rebels give out that they expect money and arms out of Spain and the Low Countries'.[67] Similar accusations that the Irish were to be furnished with arms by either Spain or France were made in the press. There were also attempts to link the Irish uprising with supposed Catholic plots in England.[68] One pamphlet followed an account of an alleged Catholic conspiracy to set fire to the city of Norwich in late November 1641 with the latest news out of Ireland and asked: 'O yee blood-thirsty Papists, what are your intents? Doe you thinke that there is not a just God above, who doth see and behold al your wicked designes?'[69] In late February 1642 a newsbook carried a story that the Catholics in Lancashire were plotting to burn the major towns in the county, as a signal for Catholics across England to rise, while it was subsequently reported that the conspirators were coordinating their activities with Catholics in Ireland who were set to land on the Lancashire coast.[70]

Protestant refugees fleeing to England and Wales from Ireland were sometimes mistaken for Irish Catholics. A Puritan from Bradford reported how one Sunday shortly after the Irish rebellion had broken out someone burst into church to raise the alarm that 'we are all as good as dead men, for the Irish Rebels are coming', provoking utter panic; it proved, however, 'only to be some protestants that were escaping out of Ireland', which news the locals 'received with great joy', spending the night 'in praises and thanksgivings to God'.[71]

Edmund Calamy, preaching before the Commons on 22 December, saw the Irish rebellion as one of a series of warnings from God—following on from the visitations of the smallpox and plague and the sufferings of Protestants on the Continent during the Thirty Years War—for England to mend its ways and 'learn to be righteous'. To avert the wrath of God, Calamy insisted, what was needed was not just personal reformation, but a national reformation, 'not onely in reference to the Common-wealth, but also to the Church'. Complaining how doctrine had been polluted, worship defiled, and 'many illegall innovations...obtruded upon us', Calamy said it would not be enough to 'bring us back...to our first Reformation in King Edward's dayes' but that it was necessary to 'reform the Reformation itself', since England was then 'newly crept out of Popery, and...it was impossible but our garments should smell a little of the Dungeon from whence we came'. In an allusion to the disorders of the sects, Calamy insisted that he spoke 'not of any tumultuous, disorderly, illegall way', but rather 'of an orderly and legall reformation', which he saw as the responsibility of the House of Commons to carry out, as the 'representative Body of this Nation': 'For you are the Nation representatively, virtually, and eminently', he intoned; 'if you stand for God's cause, the whole Nation doth it in you'. This did not mean that Calamy thought that the Commons would be carrying out the people's will, since 'the Bulk of our people are wicked' and 'unreformed themselves' and thus not surprisingly opposed 'to a thorow Reformation'; the Commons therefore needed to place 'a faithfull and painefull Ministry throrowout the Kingdom', for 'those places...where the least Preaching hath been' were 'the greatest enemies to Reformation'. In exploring the reasons why the English had remained unreformed for so long, Calamy offered some revealing insights into the religious and social tensions that were tearing the nation apart: 'The Ministers complain of their people, that they are factious, seditious, covetous, dis-respectfull of the Ministery'; 'The people complain of their Ministers, that they are dumb dogs, greedy dogs, which can never have enough, and that they are superstitious, more for pomp than substance'; 'The rich complain of the poor, that they are lazy, and theevish, The poor of the rich, that they are proud and hard-hearted'; 'The superiours cry out against their inferiours, and the inferiours against the superiours'.[72] Preaching before the Commons on the same day, Stephen Marshall, the minister of Finch-ingfield in Essex, similarly saw the recent sufferings of 'our deare brethren in Ireland' as God's warning to the people of England to reform: in addition to the sin of drunkenness—anyone who went 'to the places of greatest resorts, Market-Townes, populous Cities, and Faires', he said, would immediately see the seriousness of the prob-lem—Marshall focused in particular on the sin of idolatry, bemoan-ing the fact that England had 'not onely abundance of Idolatrous Papists', who were 'proud, insolent and daring', but also 'abundance of Popish idolatrous spirits, superstitiously addicted, willing to embrace any thing that goes that way, onely they will not have it goe under the name of Popery'.[73]

The providential worldview so widely embraced by English Protes-tants at this time, however, also inclined some to the opinion that the Irish Protestants must somehow themselves be to blame for provok-ing God's wrath. Calamy found himself combating this line of rea-soning in a subsequent fast sermon preached before the Commons on 23 February 1642. The fact that God had been kind to England com-pared to Germany and Ireland, having recently freed England from 'many grievous yoakes', and by the 'good way of a Parliament', had made people 'prone to censure Germany and Ireland as horrible sin-ners above others'. But 'Nationall mercies', he insisted, came from 'God's goodnes', not 'man's goodnes', and it would be wrong for the English to think themselves 'more righteous then Ireland', because they were 'not wallowing in blood as Ireland'.[74] Another author observed that it was a 'common beliefe and opinion', and especially 'of severall Sectarists', that there were 'none or very few sincere Chris-tians in Ireland, but men of debaucht life, vile conversation, such as England had spewed out', and that the recent atrocities in Ireland were 'the just Judgement of God, to weed them out', so that Ireland afterwards might 'be planted with such as will bring forth the fruits of the Spirit'. Although this author blamed the rebellion on the fact that both James and Charles had been too 'gentle and indulgent' towards the 'Romanists', 'whose Religion is Rebellion', he also con-demned 'the Brownists, Anabaptists, fanatical Familists, and many other Sects swarming amongst you [the English]', and made a plea for unity if England were to avoid Ireland's fate: ask yourselves, he implored, 'if a City or Kingdome so divided can long stand'; is not 'that State most miserable, where every man makes his owne Religion and Law?'[75]

The Grand Remonstrance and the Drift to War

Parliament's response to the Irish rebellion was swift. By 3 November joint committees of both Houses had agreed to raise an army of 6,000 foot and 2,000 horse to put down the insurrection, to send ships to guard the coasts of Ireland, to raise a loan of £50,000 from the City of London, to make an immediate grant of £20,000 out of monies that were available in ready cash, and to send a magazine of arms and ammunition from Carlisle to Carrickfergus. At the same time, the Commons called for the immediate raising of volunteers for service in Ireland and a bill 'for the Pressing of Men'. With Charles still in Scotland, parliament's actions were technically irregular, since it was raising an army without the king's authorization, although parliament did agree to write to Charles urging him to return to England as soon as possible.[76] On the 5th the Lords received a letter from the Scottish parliament offering whatever assistance the English parliament deemed necessary.[77] The Commons initially intended to ask the Scots for 1,000 men, but, with the situation in Ireland rapidly deteriorating, on 11 November it proposed increasing this to 10,000. The Lords, however, were worried that this would unduly increase the influence of the Scots in Ireland and decided that only 1,000 Scots should be sent over at present, leaving the possibility of asking for 9,000 more if need arose.[78] Such dithering proved disastrous, allowing the insurgency to spread across most of Ireland in the meantime.

Charles remained in Scotland until the end of the session of the Scottish parliament on 17 November. He had gone full of optimism, hoping to broker a deal that would finally enable him to extricate himself from the crisis provoked by the rebellion in his northern kingdom. Instead, he returned having conceded more ground than he would have liked and with another one of his kingdoms in revolt. Moreover, he had failed to break the link between the Covenanters and the English parliamentary leadership, and it was far from clear whether his dealings with the Scots had had the sort of impact on English public opinion that he desired. He had, after all, given his official approval to the Scottish revolution in Church and state. One

Oxfordshire cleric recorded ominously in his diary in September how 'The King with Parliament hath cast out all byshops in Scotland as Antichristian'.[79] Rumours soon began to spread that Charles, upon his return, would also 'alter the forme of the Church Government in England', prompting Charles to write to his English privy council on 18 October denying such reports and stressing that he remained 'constant for the doctrine and discipline of the Church of England as it was Established by Queene Elizabeth and my Father'.[80] Yet if those opposed to root and branch reform in England had been given cause for anxiety, the godly also felt despondent, since the king's absence in Scotland meant that there was still 'no reformation' in England, as Wallington lamented in his diary.[81]

Charles decided to make a ceremonial entry into London upon his return. The idea seems to have come from the City government itself, having first been moved in early November, and pressed on the king by Secretary Nicholas, who saw it as an opportunity to woo the City elite, who were weary, he believed, 'of the insolent carriage of the schismatics', and even to 'gain the affections...of the vulgar'. It was a carefully planned and stage-managed affair. Charles arrived in London shortly after eight o'clock on the morning of 25 November to be greeted at Moorfields, north of the City walls, by the Lord Mayor and aldermen and a party of some 500 horse. Briefed on what to say by Nicholas, Charles expressed his delight at the reception and his confidence that 'the better and main part of the City' remained loyal, offered reassurances of his intentions to uphold the Protestant religion and the rule of law, and promised to restore the City's charter to Londonderry. From there the king's entourage processed through the City to the Guildhall, where Charles was entertained with a lavish feast. After dinner, the City leaders led the royal party in a torch-lit procession to Whitehall. The bells of all 121 parish churches were rung, the conduits ran with wine, and there were bonfires throughout the capital, the people expressing their 'love and loyalty', we are told, 'by their shouts and acclamations'; indeed, such was the excess that the 'water poet' John Taylor later recalled that 'Thousands were sick with healths'.[82] The event has been described as 'a public relations triumph', and undoubtedly it showed that considerable goodwill towards the king still existed in the City.[83] But we might ask what the people were cheering for. The king's safe return from Scotland? A king who had abolished bishops in Scotland as anti-Christian? One who would deal with the threat of radical Puritanism in England? Or one who would hopefully restore Protestant English control over

Ireland? Doubtless a mixture of emotions and expectations energized the crowds who celebrated Charles's return to his English seat of government. We should certainly resist any temptation to read the demonstrations as evidence that Londoners were now united behind a common cause. Taylor, admittedly writing much later, noted the fragility of Charles's apparent new-found popularity in the capital, observing how 'three days after they [Londoners] would cut his throat'.[84]

Parliament had its Grand Remonstrance ready to go by the time of the king's return. The Grand Remonstrance was a lengthy catalogue of the ills that had afflicted the nation and a damning indictment of royal misgovernment under Charles, although the blame, the framers alleged, lay not with the person of the king but with those who had abused his royal authority. It opened by alleging that there had been 'a malignant and pernicious design of subverting the fundamental laws and principles of government; upon which the religion and justice of this kingdom [were] firmly established'. The promoters of this design, it claimed, were first 'the Jesuited Papists', secondly 'the bishops, and the corrupt part of the clergy', who cherished 'formality and superstition' as a means to support 'their own ecclesiastical tyranny and usurpation', and thirdly 'such counsellors and courtiers' who, 'for private ends', had 'engaged themselves to further the interests of some foreign princes or states'. These had sought 'to maintain continual differences and discontents betwixt the king and the people, upon questions of prerogative and liberty'; 'to suppress the purity and power of religion, and such as were best affected to it'; to unite those 'who were most propitious to their own ends' by cherishing 'the Arminian Party in those points wherein they agree with the Papists' and 'to divide those who were most opposite' by multiplying and enlarging 'the differences betwixt the common Protestants and those whom they call Puritans'; to introduce opinions and ceremonies that were 'fittest for an accommodation with Popery'; and 'to disaffect the king to parliaments by slanders and false imputations'. Alleging that this plot dated back to the dissolution of the parliament at Oxford in 1625, the Grand Remonstrance proceeded to rehearse in detail everything that had gone wrong between then and the calling of the Long Parliament, as well as the extent to which the Long Parliament's attempts at reform had been frustrated by this malignant party. The horrors of what this popish plot might mean for England were highlighted by pointing to recent developments across the Irish Sea. For despite the fact that the promoters of this design had been 'continually practising to disturb the peace, and plotting the destruction…of all the King's dominions', their attempts against England and Scotland had been 'discovered and defeated' by 'the vigilancy of those who were well affected…before they were ripe for execution'. In Ireland, by contrast, because it was 'farther off', they 'had time and opportunity to mould and prepare their work': they would have gained control of the whole of that kingdom and 'totally subverted the government of it, routed out religion, and destroyed all the Protestants' had not the plot to seize Dublin Castle been prevented at the very last minute 'by God's wonderful Providence', while in other parts of the country they broke out 'into open rebellion, surprising towns and castles, commit[ing] murders, rapes and other villainies, and shak[ing] off all bonds of obedience to His Majesty and the laws of the realm'. 'Had not God in His great mercy unto this land [England] discovered and confounded their former designs', the Grand Remonstrance continued, 'we had been the prologue to this tragedy in Ireland'. Having identified the problems, the Grand Remonstrance recommended that the king appoint a standing commission, composed of men named by parliament, to investigate the activities of the malignant party; that he take action 'to discover the counterfeit and false conformity of Papists to the church'; that 'all illegal Grievances and Exactions be presented and punished at the sessions and assizes'; that the king employ only 'such counsellors, ambassadors, and other ministers' as 'parliament may have cause to confide in'; and that 'all counsellors of state may be sworn to observe the laws which concern the subject in his liberty'.[85]

The Grand Remonstrance came before the Commons on 22 November and provoked a heated debate, lasting from nine in the morning until about two the following morning. According to Clarendon, who voted against it, many in the House thought it both 'unnecessary and unseasonable': unnecessary, because the grievances enumerated had already been 'fully redressed'; and unseasonable to welcome the king home 'with such a volume of reproaches for what others had done amiss and which he himself had reformed'. Yet what caused particular concern was John Hampden's motion that the Grand Remonstrance be printed. It had never been the custom to publish any determinations of the House which had not first been transmitted to the Lords, and it was unclear that the Commons had the authority to order the printing of anything. Clarendon claimed that he argued at the time that the printing was 'unlawful' and 'would produce mischievous effects'. Dering protested that he 'did not dream we should remonstrate downwards, tell stories to the people, and talk of the king as of a third person'. The Commons passed the Grand Remonstrance by 159 votes to 148, a majority of just 11, though decided (by 124 votes to 101) that it not be printed without particular order of the House.[86] For many Londoners the demands in the Grand Remonstrance did not go far enough. On the last couple of days of November and very beginning of December crowds gathered at Westminster shouting 'Down with the Bishops—Down with Antichrist', calling on members as they passed by to abolish episcopacy and crying out against the prayer book.[87]

A committee of the Commons presented the Grand Remonstrance to the king on 1 December, together with a petition explaining why they had felt it necessary to make this declaration of the state of the kingdom. They insisted that they had no intention 'to lay any blemish' on Charles's 'royal person', but only to represent how his 'royal authority and trust' had been abused by 'a corrupt and ill-affected party', composed of 'Jesuits, and other engineers and factors for Rome' with the support of corrupt bishops and counsellors, who sought 'the alteration of government and religion' and the advancement of 'Popery'. The result had been war between England and Scotland, increasing jealousies between the king and his 'most obedient subjects', 'the violent Distraction and Interruption of this Parliament', and 'the Insurrection of the Papists... in Ireland, and the bloody massacre of your people there'. The petitioners therefore asked that the king 'concur with the humble desires of [his] people in a parliamentary way, for the preserving the peace and safety of the kingdom from the malicious designs of the Popish party'; deprive the bishops of their votes in parliament and abridge 'their immoderate power usurped over the clergy'; remove those 'oppressions and unnecessary ceremonies, by which divers weak consciences have scrupled'; execute 'those good laws... made for securing the liberty of your subjects'; remove all evil counsellors and appoint to office only those that 'parliament may have cause to confide in'; and 'forbear to alienate any of the forfeited and escheated lands in Ireland', which might accrue to the crown as a result of the rebellion, so that the crown might have the means to bear the expenses of the war in Ireland.[88] On 15 December the Commons ordered both the petition and the Grand Remonstrance to be printed and distributed 'with great industry... throughout the kingdom', even though the king, when he had been presented with them, had forbidden the Commons to publish either until he delivered his answer. Charles delivered his answer on

23 December, reprehending the Commons 'for the unparliamentariness of their Remonstrance'.[89]

Charles's political position had been steadily improving over the course of the year. At the time of the calling of the Long Parliament in November 1640 he appears to have had limited support either inside parliament or among the general population. By November 1641 the Commons was fairly evenly split, the king had a majority on most divisions in the Lords, and Charles was even able to draw massive crowds when he made a public entry into London on 25 November. Yet by mid-January Charles had fled his capital and by the spring he was arming for war against his subjects. Why, then, was Charles not able to capitalize on the apparent upturn in his fortunes? How do we explain the drift to war?

Charles made a series of mistakes over the course of December 1641 and early January 1642 which caused him to lose control of his capital. It soon became apparent that, despite the reception he had received on 25 November, there remained widespread support in London for further reform in Church and state. In early December the citizens began collecting signatures to a petition to the Commons expressing their concern over the ongoing conspiracies of papists both in England and Ireland and calling for the City to be put in a posture of defence and for 'the Popish Lords and Bishops' to be removed from the House of Lords. The petition also stressed that it would be wrong to read 'the Citizens' dutifull and loyall entertainment of his Majesty' as a deserting of the Commons, 'the least thought whereof' the petitioners did 'utterly detest and abhor'. Above 20,000 people, it was claimed, signed the petition, although the petitioners did themselves admit that 'some interruption was given them by ill affected persons in London, about subscribing of hands', suggesting that Londoners were far from united around this initiative.[90] Charles, worried about trouble breaking out if such a large crowd of people descended on Westminster to present the petition, sent 200 armed halberdiers on 10 December to guard the Commons and prevent any tumultuous assemblies, and issued a proclamation requiring obedience to the existing laws 'for establishing of the true Religion in this Kingdom', calling for the punishment of 'willful Contemners, and Disturbers of Divine Service', and forbidding clergy from introducing 'any Rite, or Ceremonies other then those which are established by the Laws' (thereby affirming his support of the Lords' orders of 16 January and 9 September in defence of the prayer book services).[91] Charles was staking his position on a defence of the established

Church and the rule of law against those who threatened to disturb the peace—a position which had the potential to prove quite popular. When the proclamation was read at Dover, for example, it 'caused much rejoicing, the People crying out god bless his Majestie Wee shall have our ould religion setled againe'.[92] The decision to send the troops, however, was a tactical mistake; Charles failed to stop the petition and merely aroused suspicion that he was willing to use force against the lower house. The Commons thought the troops were intended as 'rather a Gaurde upon us' and voted 'the Setting of any Guards about this House' without their consent a breach of privilege. The London petition was presented on 11 December in an orderly manner by a huge crowd of 400 aldermen, deputies, merchants, Common Council men, and 'others of great ranke and fashion' and accepted by the Commons, who in turn launched an inquiry into those who had sent the troops.[93]

The mood of the City was further revealed in the Common Council elections of 21 December, which saw a massive swing in favour of men with active parliamentary sympathies, many of them radical Puritans.[94] In a serious miscalculation, Charles chose the next day to replace the current Lieutenant of the Tower, Sir William Balfour, the man who had held out against the first Army Plot, with Colonel Thomas Lunsford, a pardoned outlaw who had been convicted for attempted murder in the 1630s but who had fought against the Scots at Newburn. According to Clarendon, Charles wanted the Tower, which was 'looked upon as bridal upon the city', in 'the hands of such a man upon whom he might rely', given that 'seditious preachers every day prevailed in the city...and corrupted the affections and loyalty of the meaner people towards the government of Church and State'.[95] Londoners were horrified, fearing that the cannon of the Tower might be turned against the City, and with the merchants withdrawing their bullion from the mint within the Tower in panic, the Common Council petitioned the Commons for Lunsford's removal. Pym interpreted Lunsford's appointment as sign of an impending coup, and the Commons quickly voted Lunsford unfit for the position. Libels began to spread depicting Lunsford as a cannibal who ate children and there were rumours that the apprentices were planning to rise after Christmas and 'violently put him out'. Charles dismissed Lunsford on the evening of 26 December, but the news was slow to get out and the next morning huge crowds of citizens and apprentices, some of them armed 'with halberds, swords, and other offensive weapons', descended on parliament demanding an answer to their petition concerning the bishops. Even when they learned that Luns-ford had been removed, the crowd refused to disperse but instead demanded to know the answer to their previous petition, haranguing members of both Houses with cries of 'No Bishops, no popish Lords'. The archbishop of York, John Williams, was jostled and had his gown torn by protestors screaming 'No Bishops! No Bishops!' The crowd was further inflamed by the fact that Lunsford happened to be at Westminster Hall that day, having been sent for examination by the Lords, as were forty of so of his fellow officers (described in one source as 'cavaliers'), who had gone to lobby for arrears of pay, occasioning further violent clashes (Plate 19). There was more violence outside parliament over the next two days. On the 28th crowds tried to pull down the organ and the altar at Westminster Abbey, only to be driven away by Archbishop Williams and his servants, resulting in a number of injuries and at least one fatality.[96]

The previous evening the Lords had asked the Commons to join with them in a declaration to express their dislike 'of the assembling of the People in such Companies and Disorders, about the Houses of Parliament', but Pym urged the Commons not to proceed, 'in any way, to dishearten people to obtain their just desires in such a way'; the Lords reacted by debating a motion that pressure from the crowd meant parliament was no longer free and thus should not continue to sit, although it was voted down.[97] The bishops undoubtedly did feel intimidated and were staying away: only two took their seats in the Lords on the 28th; none did so on the 29th. It was now that Charles made an ill-judged intervention. On the 30th he forwarded to the Lords a petition from Archbishop Williams, in the name of twelve bishops, protesting that since they had been prevented from taking their seats by the crowd all votes and resolutions that had passed the House since the 27th should be null and void. The Lords saw the petition as a breach of privilege and called for a conference with the Commons. Pym took it to be a precursor to a forcible dissolution and the Commons urged that the bishops should be charged with treason. The Lords concurred and later that day dispatched ten of the twelve bishops to the Tower. Commenting on the events of 27 to 30 December, the navy captain Robert Slingsby observed how 'both factions talke very bigge' and thought it 'a wonder there is no more blood yet spilt', adding ominously that there was 'no doubt but if the king' did 'not comply with the commons in all things they desire, a sudden civill war must ensue, which every day wee see approaches nearer'.[98]

Some progress had at last been made over how to respond to the rebellion in Ireland. On 21 December the two Houses finally agreed to send 10,000 troops from both England and Scotland, 'upon such Conditions as shall be agreed upon the Parliament in England'.[99] This paved the way for Charles to issue a proclamation on 1 January 1642 condemning 'the wicked and horrible acts' lately committed by 'divers lewd and wicked persons in Ireland' as 'Acts of high Rebellion and detestable disloyaltie', declaring the perpetrators to be 'Rebels and Traitors against Our Royall Person', and warning that if they did not immediately lay down their arms he had ordered the authorities in Ireland, aided by the 'powerfull succours of Our good Subjects of England and Scotland', to prosecute them 'with fire and sword'.[100]

Charles, however, next made his most disastrous blunder. He instructed his Attorney General, Sir Edward Herbert, to bring treason charges in the Lords on 3 January against five members of the Commons—Pym, Hampden, Hesilrige, Holles, and Strode—and one peer, Edward Montagu, Viscount Mandeville (the future earl of Manchester). At about 3 o'clock in the afternoon of the 4th Charles arrived at Westminster Hall with about 400 armed men only to find that the members, forewarned, had escaped by river and taken refuge in the City. The next day MPs voted that the king had breached the privileges of the House, that it was no longer safe for them to sit at Westminster, and adjourned as a committee to Guildhall, where they were provided with an armed guard by the City. Panic ensued in the City on the night of the 6th as a false alarm spread that 'the Cavaliers were coming to fire the city' for harbouring the five members and that the king himself was at the head; soon the gates were shut and thousands gathered in the streets with whatever arms they could muster ready for their defence. Offers of support for the five members came in from the apprentices of London, the Southwark trained bands, and the mariners and seamen, while in Buckinghamshire the freeholders assembled ready to march on London in defence of their member, John Hampden. Fearing he was losing control of the capital, Charles fled London on 10 January, going first to Hampton Court and then to Windsor. On the 11th parliament reassembled at Westminster and passed a resolution stating that anyone who attempted to arrest or trouble any member did 'thereby break the Privileges of Parliament, violate the Liberty of the Subject' and was 'hereby declared an Enemy of the Commonwealth'. The five members marched back to Westminster from their lodgings in the City that afternoon accompanied by 'many thousands of people...making a great clamour against bishops and popish lords and of the privileges of Parliament'.[101]

Charles's actions had seriously undermined his own support in parliament, even in the House of Lords. On 1 February the Lords agreed to join the Commons in a petition asking Charles to put the militia in the hands of those whom parliament could trust. On the 5th, with increasing numbers of royalist peers now staying away, the Lords approved a bill excluding bishops from the upper house.[102] Charles, bitterly resentful of the fact that whenever he made concessions parliament always asked for more, was now contemplating a more aggressive policy. The plan, which may have come from Henrietta Maria—she was certainly deeply involved in the discussions—was that the queen should head for the Netherlands and purchase weapons by pawning the crown jewels while Charles withdrew to the friendlier territory of Yorkshire, where he could use the garrison town of Hull as a base to recruit a royal army and so ultimately coerce parliament into backing down. But Charles needed to stall for time until Henrietta Maria was able to leave the country and thus he had at least to give the appearance that he was still willing to negotiate. A concession was therefore needed. Charles thought that he should give way over the militia, but Henrietta Maria persuaded him this would be foolish given the bigger plan and that it was safer to sacrifice the bishops. Charles gave his assent to the Bishops Exclusion bill on 14 February. On the 23rd Henrietta Maria departed for the Netherlands, and a few days later Charles headed off towards the north, reaching York on 18 March.[103]

War was now virtually inevitable, but Charles needed time to prepare, while Pym's need to keep much of the political nation behind him meant that he had to be seen to be continuing to explore a peaceful solution. On 16 February the Lords had finally agreed to an amended version of the Commons' Militia Ordinance. Charles responded at the end of the month by announcing that anyone who exercised power over the militia without 'lawfull Authority' would be 'proceeded against according to Law'.[104] Parliament pressed on regardless and on 5 March passed the Ordinance putting their choice of lieutenants in charge of the militia, claiming the need to safeguard 'His Majesty's Person, the Parliament, and Kingdom, in this Time of Imminent Danger' from 'the bloody Counsels of Papists and other ill-affected Persons', who had 'already raised 'a Rebellion in Ireland' and intended 'to stir up the like Rebellion' in England backed 'with Forces from Abroad'. It was a direct assault on the crown prerogative to control the armed forces, and drew a formal protest from sixteen peers. Ten days later parliament declared that, 'in this Case of extreme Danger', the people were bound by the Militia Ordinance even though it had not received the royal assent.[105] On 23 April Charles made a disastrous attempt to seize the magazine at Hull, the parliamentarian governor Sir John Hotham refusing to open the gates when Charles arrived with 300 cavalry demanding admission. Whether Charles ever truly believed it likely that Hotham would let him in is impossible to tell. The rebuff did at least leave Charles persuaded in his conscience that both Hotham and parliament were in rebellion against him. On the other hand, Charles's arrival at Hull, with an armed force, to take possession of the magazine convinced the two Houses of Parliament that the king intended to make war on them.[106]

In June, parliament put Nineteen Propositions to the king, its most radical proposal for a settlement yet. Privy councillors and key officers of state were to be approved by parliament; laws against Catholics were to be strictly enforced; the king was to consent 'that such a reformation be made of the Church-government, and Liturgy, as both Houses of Parliament shall advise', accept the ordering of the militia by the Lords and Commons, and clear the five members; all judges and officers were to hold their posts on good behaviour; and new peers would not be allowed to sit or vote in the Lords unless approved by both Houses.[107] Charles rejected the proposals outright. With parliament stepping up its execution of the Militia Ordinance, on 11 June Charles began issuing Commissions of Array to the Lord Lieutenants empowering them to levy forces in support of the king—a medieval method of raising troops, long obsolete, though sanctioned by legislation that had never been repealed. Two armies were now being drawn up. The outbreak of war was only a matter of time.

15

The Rise of Royalism

It takes two sides to fight a war. There could not have been a civil war in 1640, because Charles did not yet have a side. Where, then, did royalism come from? When did it begin to emerge and what did it stand for? And to what extent was Charles responsible for its creation and for giving the royalist movement ideological definition?

In a sense, everyone was a royalist in 1641. Even those who strongly identified with parliament would have seen themselves as acting to preserve monarchy and to defend what they believed to be the best interests of the crown. Yet certainly by 1642 parliamentarians who professed to be 'as zealously addicted to Monarchy as any man' were calling those who took the king's side against them 'Royallists'.[1] The question we need to answer, then, is how was it that two sides came to emerge that were ultimately willing to go to war with each other, with one side firmly identifying itself with what they perceived to be—and helped define as being—the king's cause? Up until the middle of 1641, it is normally argued, there was a broad degree of consensus around the need to undo the worst excesses of the personal rule. Yet as parliament came to press for more radical reforms in both Church and state, this in turn provoked a conservative reaction, forcing those who were worried about the rise of political and religious radicalism, both in- and out-of-doors, to rally behind the crown. Thus a number of MPs who opposed the personal rule and who at first supported parliament's reform agenda subsequently switched their allegiance. In order to take advantage of this royalist reaction, Charles positioned himself as the champion of the traditional order in Church and state, who would defend both the true Protestant religion and the rule of law from a parliamentary coalition that now threatened to overturn both. As a result, it has been said, constitutional outlook does not easily explain why some people came to support parliament and others the crown in 1642. Those people who formed the mainstay of the royalist party at the time of the outbreak of the Civil War were not un-reconstructed supporters of personal monarchy but rather constitutional royalists—men like Edward Hyde, Sir John Culpepper, Lucius Carey, 2nd Viscount Falkland, and Sir John Strangways—who believed in mixed monarchy and the rule of law. What separated people was where they stood on the Church. The supporters of parliament wanted further reforms, which by now included the abolition of episcopacy; the supporters of the crown, by contrast, were (by and large) non-Laudian Anglicans who defended the traditional Church of prayer book and bishops.[2]

As a basic way of explaining the polarization that would lead to war, this framework has much to recommend it. As with all explanatory models, however, it inevitably oversimplifies in an effort to make sense of a complex reality and a number of qualifications are necessary. First, it is important to recognize that royalism did not emerge out of nowhere in the second half of 1641. The policies pursued in Church and state during the personal rule had not alienated everyone. Some communities were already divided when the Long Parliament met in November 1640, and concern about Puritan extremism in particular was already in evidence in several parts of the country. Secondly, as seen earlier, there was considerable disagreement already in parliament in late 1640 and early 1641, notably over what to do about the Scots, the fate of Strafford, and the future of the Church. Although it proved possible to enact certain key reforming measures in the first half of 1641—measures that many future royalists felt able, at the time, to support—it would be wrong to infer that a genuine political consensus existed. Thirdly, while disagreement over how far to reform the Church proved a major source of polarization, it would be misleading to overemphasize ecclesiastical grievances at the expense of civil ones. Just as parliamentarians were concerned about the exercise of secular as well as ecclesiastical authority, so royalists were worried about a threat to the traditional order in both Church *and* state. Even the desire to defend bishops and prayer book had secular as well as religious motivations. Finally, it is important to avoid a one-dimensional characterization of royalism. A variety of factors led people to embrace Charles's cause. There were some early royalists, even if there were more later converts. Although radicalism in parliament and out-of-doors was a spur to royalism for many, others did not need such a spur—although they perhaps had not had the occasion to give voice to already-existing royalist sentiments until they found themselves needing to define themselves against the activities of the parliamentarian coalition against Charles. For some people, secular considerations outweighed religious; for others, vice versa. Principle could play a role, but so too could self-interest.

Procuring Hands for the Continuing of Episcopal Government

Royalism as a mass movement first began to manifest itself as a petitioning campaign in defence of the Church. Because the campaign for ecclesiastical reform had been taken out-of-doors, with the delivery of petitions calling for the abolition of episcopacy and the disciplining of scandalous ministers, opponents of reform responded in kind by trying to mobilize opinion at the local level in defence of the bishops and prayer book. In fact, the first petition in defence of the Church had preceded the root and branch petitioning movement—that from Hertfordshire, delivered to the Short Parliament on 18 April, complaining about Puritan clergy in the county who 'boldly violated and audaciously attempted many things contrary to the Canons of the Church, the Rubrik, and Book of Common Prayer'.[3] The other pro-Church petitions, however, were drawn up in reaction to the campaign for root and branch reform. The need to stand up and be counted became immediately apparent following London's root and branch petition of December 1640. One newsletter writer, noting that similar petitions were being prepared in other parts of the kingdom, observed how 'the Clergie' were boasting that they could 'procure tenne hands for the continuing of Episcopall Government for everie one hand that subscribes against it'.[4] What the defenders of the Church had to do was to prove it.

Between January 1641 and the summer of 1641 (the sources do not always allow for precise dating) some six petitions in defence of the bishops and/or the Book of Common Prayer were either delivered or drawn up: from Bedfordshire, Cheshire, London and Westminster (together), Devon, and both the universities (separately). The cue for this wave of petitioning activity appears to have been Charles's Banqueting House speech of 23 January 1641 announcing his determination to stand by the bishops and denouncing recent Puritan disruptions of church services.[5] Charles clearly welcomed the initiative: in March, for example, he sent a letter approving the Cheshire petition.[6] The period from the autumn of 1641 to June 1642 saw the formulation of a further twenty-two petitions in defence of the Church: from Essex, Kent, Southwark, and Surrey in the south-east; Huntingdonshire and

Suffolk in East Anglia; Cheshire (again) and Lancashire in the north-west; six counties of North Wales (as one petition); Cornwall, Devon, Dorset, Gloucestershire, and Somerset in the west; Herefordshire, Lincolnshire, Oxfordshire, Nottinghamshire, Rutland, Shropshire, Staffordshire, and Worcestershire across the Midlands; plus another from the 'Colledges and Halls, and others, well-wishers to Piety and Learning, throughout the Kingdom of England'. This second wave was prompted by the Lords' order of 9 September in defence of the traditional liturgy, as subsequently endorsed by the royal proclamation of 10 December, although the later petitions were also a response to the Commons' impeachment of the twelve bishops at the end of December.[7] Some of the petitions could boast large numbers of signatories. The first Cheshire petition (in support of episcopacy) was supposedly signed by over 6,000 people; the second from Cheshire (in support of the Book of Common Prayer) over 9,000; that from Devon 8,000; Nottinghamshire over 6,000; Somerset some 14,350; and from the six counties of North Wales 30,000.[8]

The petitions adopted a calculatedly moderate stance on the central issue of Church government and liturgy, and in that sense espoused a non-Laudian view of the Church. For example, the first Cheshire petition, which was delivered to the Lords on 27 February 1641, recognized the need for reform, to be vigilant against popery, and to suppress innovations, but defended bishops as an ancient order 'instituted in the time of the Apostles' who had proven their worth over the centuries by rescuing 'Christianity from utter extirpation in the Primitive Heathen persecutions' and redeeming 'the purity of the Gospell...from Romish corruption' at the time of the Reformation, and recalled how many bishops had become 'glorious Martyrs' under Mary Tudor.[9] That from Huntingdonshire, presented to the Lords on 8 December 1641, insisted 'that the Forme of Divine Service...contained in the Booke of Common prayer' had been freed 'from all former corruptions and Romish Superstitions' at the time of the Reformation and confirmed by 'Act of Parliament, and Royall Injunctions' and that bishops, who dated from 'the first planting of Christian Religion amongst us', had shown themselves to be 'glorious Lamps of God's Church' and had been responsible for redeeming 'the purity of the Gospell' in England and reforming 'the Religion from Romish corruption'.[10]

Yet non-Laudian is not the same as anti-Laudian. The petitions tended not to point to specific Laudian errors, but at most made only the vaguest of references to recent 'innovations' or 'exorbitances', while many made no allusion to any religious problems at all in the 1630s.[11] Moreover, the language of moderation was dropped when it came to discussing the activities of those pressing for further reform in the Church. The first Cheshire petition condemned 'the tenour' of the root and branch petitions, 'the tenents preached publiquely in Pulpits, and the contents of many printed Pamphlets, swarming amongst us', all of which encouraged 'a disobedience to the established forme of Government', leading the petitioners to conclude that the desire was 'to introduce an absolute Innovation of Presbyterall Government, whereby wee who are now governed by the Canon and Civill Lawes...should become exposed to the mere Arbitrary Government of a numerous Presbitery'.[12] Several of the petitions made it clear that the petitioners were reacting to developments at the local level. For example, the Kent petition from the autumn of 1641 bemoaned how, as a result of 'the sinister practises of some private persons ill affected' to 'the Religion and Government by Law established', churches had been 'prophaned, and in part defaced', ministers 'contemned and despised', ornaments 'abused', the liturgy 'depraved, and neglected', the Lord's Prayer 'vilified', the sacraments 'unduly administred' or even 'omitted', fasts 'appointed by private persons', marriages 'illegally Solemnized', burials 'uncharitably performed', and 'the very Fundamentall of our Religion subverted'.[13] The Huntingdonshire petition of December 1641 complained about 'Schismaticks and Sectaries...separating and sequestering themselves from the publike Assembly at Common Prayers and Divine Service' and 'tumultuously interrupting others in the performance thereof'.[14] The Somerset petition of that same month lamented how 'our Common Prayer hath beene interrupted and despised of some mis-understanding or mis-led people, to the great scandal of the Religion professed in our Church'.[15]

Those who petitioned in defence of the Church, then, were concerned not just about the spiritual welfare of the people of England; they were also worried about the threat to the social order posed by Puritan separatism. Those who championed episcopacy did so as much for secular reasons as they did for religious ones. The Cheshire petitioners of February 1641 insisted that Presbyterianism (the inevitable alternative to episcopacy) was incompatible with the English constitution. The presbyters and their ruling elders would leave England with 'neere forty thousand Church Governours' who, 'with their adherents, must needs beare so great a sway in the Commonwealth'; how would these be 'reducible by Parliament', and 'how consistent with a Monarchy' would such a system prove?[16] Similarly the Rutland petitioners of November 1641 asserted that 'Episcopall Government hath consisted with Monarchy, ever since the English Monarchy was Christian' and questioned whether that could be the case under 'any innovated Government'. Moreover, the abolition of episcopacy would be 'against the liberties of the Clergy, indulged to them by the Magna Charta', which was part of fundamental law, the violation of which would be an 'intrenchment upon the right of the lay Subject' and cause everyone to 'feare lest his Liberties may be next in question'. The petitioners also warned that the introduction of lay elders would 'bring an insupportable burthen to all Parishes', who would have to be maintained 'at the Parish charge', and expressed the concern that 'All Learning' would be 'discountenanced' and perhaps even 'extinguished, upon the demolition of Episcopacy', since the bishops were 'parties for the advancement of Learning'.[17] The University of Oxford stressed the many positive benefits bishops brought to society more generally: they were 'the maine authours or upholders of diverse Schooles, Hospitals, High-wayes, Bridges, and other publique and pious Workes'; they brought 'profit and advantage' to cathedral cities, 'not onely by relieving their poore, and keeping convenient Hospitality, but by occasioning a frequent resort of Strangers from other parts, to the great benefit of all Tradesmen, and Inhabitants in those places'; they were 'the chiefe support of many thousand Families of the Laity who enjoy faire estates from them in a free way'; and they yielded 'a constant and ample revenue to the Crowne'.[18]

The rival petition campaigns show that communities were dividing. Clashes over petitions relating to religion occurred in at least sixteen counties.[19] Of twenty-one counties that petitioned in defence of the Church, thirteen had previously delivered petitions in support of root and branch reform; in the metropolis, London and Westminster (together) and Southwark drew up petitions in support of the Church to counter London's root and branch petition. People were defining themselves against enemies in their midst. The Cheshire root and branch petition had been delivered to the Commons on 19 February by Sir William Brereton, knight of the shire, who had a strong following among the local godly; that in defence of episcopacy was delivered to the Lords just eight days later by Sir Thomas Aston, a courtier and ship-money sheriff who had served the county (alongside Brereton) in the Short Parliament but lost his seat in the elections to the Long Parliament. Aston claimed that Brereton's petition did not have the support of the gentry and was fraudulently purporting to speak for the county. Brereton's group claimed that Aston had obtained signatories by misrepresenting what his petition stood for, and had even affixed the names of madmen, children, papists, people who were at sea, and the deceased, an allegation that Aston vehemently denied. Brereton's group had some following among the gentry, but were unquestionably guilty of engaging in deceptive practices when they published a printed version of their petition claiming exactly twice the number of signatories as Aston's.[20] Allegations that rival petitioners had obtained signatures through deception became commonplace, as both sides sought to discredit the efforts of their opponents and tried to claim that they themselves truly represented the voice of the local community. Defenders of episcopacy in Nottinghamshire were said to have gained hands to their petition by claiming that it was to abolish altar rails and that parliament wanted people to subscribe.[21] The truth of the matter is often difficult to determine. We have to be sceptical, then, of taking the petitions as a straightforward index of public opinion in a given locality. At the same time, however, it would be wrong to dismiss the authenticity of these public articulations of support for the Church. It was difficult to manufacture petitions which did not resonate sufficiently with local opinion. In Essex a group of authoritarian royalists led by Henry Nevill, Lord Maynard, and Sir John Lucas—all supporters of the policies of the personal rule—framed a petition in November 1641 in defence of the prayer book (the petition went through two drafts) which emphasized the disorders caused by those who held the prayer book in contempt. However, they were a minority voice in this strongly Puritan county and their attempt to mobilize support proved unsuccessful: there is no evidence that the petition was ever presented (or even circulated for signature).[22]

Petitions in defence of the Church could be backed both by moderates and hardliners. That from Kent, for example, was promoted by Sir Edward Dering, who in the early days of the Long Parliament had been a supporter of reform, backed the attainder of Strafford, and even presented the petition from Kent against episcopacy. Other petitions—such as those from Cheshire or the abortive one from Essex—were launched by individuals closely associated with the court and who had supported the crown during the personal rule. Even hardliners, however, saw the tactical advantage of trying to position themselves in such a way so as to gain the support of local moderates. Aston's first Cheshire petition, that in support of episcopacy, which was vehemently anti-Presbyterian in tone, alienated the influential Booth/Wilbraham/Grosvenor middle group in the county. His second petition, in defence of the prayer book, which skirted the issue of episcopacy and concentrated on attacking the disorders of the sects, did win the support of the Booth/Wilbraham/Grosvenor group (hence the larger number of signatories).[23] In many areas the clergy took a leading role in promoting public affirmations of support for the Church; indeed, signatories to the petitions were often collected in Church after divine service.[24] However, it would be wrong to exaggerate the role of the clergy. Aston was at pains to point out that the Cheshire petition in defence of the bishops was a gentry initiative, and that 'the Bishop and his Clergy...never knew of it till it was done'.[25]

Royalist Propaganda

Royalism, as a political identity, was further shaped and crystallized by the press. The parliamentarian attempt to court opinion out-of-doors was met in kind by publicists who were determined to persuade people not to support those who sought far-reaching reforms in Church and state. Works condemning Puritan radicalism flooded from the presses, starting in 1640 but becoming particularly numerous from the second half of 1641 in response to the perceived rise of sectarian radicalism. Many of these were printed anonymously, and although we can sometimes hazard an informed guess as to authorship, it is not always possible to identify who was behind them. In so far as we can tell, however, it seems that these authors were mostly working on their own initiative, with little if any direction from the crown. One of the key anti-Puritan polemicists was the 'water poet' John Taylor (who published both anonymously and also under his own name); yet despite the fact that Taylor was a royal waterman, he appears not to have enjoyed court patronage.[26]

Anti-sectarian literature was alarmist and sensationalist, exaggerating and distorting the reality of the separatist challenge in order to frighten people into not supporting parliament or those who wanted root and branch reform.[27] Titles such as *A Discovery of 29 Sects here in London* (1641) and *The Divisions of the Church of England Crept in at XV Several Doores* (1642), documenting the existence not only of Puritans, Brownists, and Anabaptists, but also supposedly Adamites, Familists, Socinians, Saturnians, Panonians, Bacchanalians, and

Heathens, were intended to give the impression not only of large numbers but also of never-ending fragmentation. Taylor warned that 'so many Sects and Schismes' had 'lately sprung up...that they (like to the plagues of AEgypt)' had 'over-run the Land'.[28] Elsewhere he alleged that there were 'Novellists'—by which he meant either 'Thraskites, or Sabbaterians, Banisterians, Brownists, [or] Anabaptists'—'almost in every domesticke Diocesian Parish'.[29]

The sects were condemned, in part, for theological error, for getting their scripture wrong. They were repeatedly denounced as heretics, and thus for being enemies of the true religion.[30] One illustrated tract by John Taylor, for example, showed Anabaptists, Brownists, Papists, Familists, Atheists 'sawcily presuming to tosse Religion'— represented graphically as a bible—'in a Blanquet' (Plate 20).[31] Error in turn stemmed from the fact that the separatists hailed from humble social backgrounds: 'Mechanick persons', shoemakers, cobblers, tinkers, pedlars, weavers, tailors, boxmakers, buttonmakers, and chimney-sweeps by trade, 'ignorant soules' who preferred 'the Discipline of ignorant' to that of learned men'.[32]

Yet the sects were also condemned for a whole host of non-religious reasons: for promoting disorders, being a threat to the rule of law, undermining the social hierarchy, and violating gender norms. In October 1641, shortly after the Commons order for abolishing superstition and innovation, Taylor complained of 'violent outrages, and Sacrilegious disorders Committed in the Church, even in the time of Divine Service', such as 'laying violent hands upon the Minister' and tearing off his hood and surplice, or 'rending the Railes from before the Communion Table, chopping them in peeces, and burning them in the Church Yard', all 'done without authority' and 'in a riotous manner'.[33] The Oxford cleric Thomas Cheshire, in a sermon preached at St Paul's that same month, observed how in one church separatists even 'pulled downe the King's Crowne, because it had a Crosse upon it'. He also complained how ministers of God would be abused as they walked about the streets, meeting cries of 'there goeth a Jesuit, a Baal's priest, an Abbey-lubber, one of Canterburie's-Whelps'. Several clergy, he noted, had 'had the Surplisse torne off their backes' and were lucky 'they scaped with their skins'.[34] One satirical song that dates from the eve of the Civil War observed how the 'Roundheads' sought not only the downfall of the bishops, the destruction of stained-glass windows, and the removal of Rome's 'Trash and Trumpery' from parish churches, but also cried down 'all universities' and indeed all 'good manners':

The name of Lord shalbee abhorred
For every man's a brother
Noe reason why in Church of State
One Man should rule another.[35]

Much of the anti-sectarian literature commented upon how the separatists allowed women to preach, violating St Paul's dictum that women should be silent in church. The visible presence of women in the separatist congregations inevitably led to allegations of sexual impropriety. Edward Harris charged how a company of Brownists, separatists, and nonconformists in Monmouthshire had 'drawne divers honest men's wives in the night times to frequent their Assemblies, and to become of most loose and wicked conversation, and likewise many chast Virgins to become harlots, and the mothers of bastards'.[36]

The sects were also seen as un-English, as alien. In one satire, Taylor lamented 'To see Great Brittaine turn'd to Amsterdam' as a result of the 'mad sects ... Who have Religion all in pieces Rent', and prayed that God would 'send those sects, from whence they came againe'.[37] Elsewhere, Taylor referred to the London separatists as 'these Amsterdam whelpes'.[38] One tract of 1642, set as a dialogue between 'Opinion' and 'Time', has its separatist open by speaking Dutch and admitting that he was born in Amsterdam.[39] The sects were thus an external threat, something from outside that was undermining the health of the body politic. Indeed, they were seen as a disease—a cancer or a gangrene—that had to be removed. Taylor appealed to king and parliament to 'recover this almost gangrean'd Church and Common-weale to its former health'.[40]

Anti-sectarian polemic distorted, misrepresented, and invented, but it was nevertheless based on elements of truth. Protestant reformers and moderate Puritans were equally alarmed about the rise of separatism: the parliamentarian propagandist Henry Parker, in a tract written in defence of the Puritans in 1641, condemned 'these swarmes of conventiclers which now sequester themselves from us' as 'the dregges of the vilest and most ignorant rabble'.[41] The people of Puritan Dorchester, it was reported in July 1641, equally disliked the extremism of the 'pestilent sects and schismatics' who pressed for root and branch reform; they had wanted 'a pious reformation, not confusion in the church'.[42] Yet this was precisely why the anti-sectarian card was such a powerful one for royalist propagandists to play, since it had the potential to appeal to the moderate middle ground and thus dislodge people from their previous support for parliament. The way the anti-sectarian card was played, moreover, served to intimate that there was very little difference between conventional Puritans and separatists. Taylor consistently blurred the distinction, making it clear to readers that to his mind the two were the same.[43] It was a tactic repeated by others. John Harris subtitled his anti-Puritan tract of 1641 *The Anatomie of a Puritane or Seperatist* and wrote of 'these Seperatists alias Puritanes'.[44]

Much of the anti-sectarian literature rehearsed the well-entrenched stereotype of the unlettered, hypocritical, uncharitable, and subversive Puritan that dated back to the late Elizabethan and Jacobean periods.[45] Taylor condemned Puritans as 'Ignorants or Hypocrites', who 'cozzen men devoutly', whose brains were 'stuft with froath and bubbles', who promote discord instead of concord, who loved to 'fish in foule and troubled waters', who would never part with their money 'in charity', and whose 'spirits' were so 'bold' and 'audacious' that they dared to disobey 'King, Church, State, and Lawes'.[46] The bitingly satirical *Resolution of the Round-Heads* of 1641 has the Puritans recall 'the transparency' of their charity, which was 'so invisible that neither the right hand nor the left did ere know it'; 'the multitude' of their 'good works which no man can number'; and their condemnation of 'Learning' (supposedly 'no more necessary to religion, then a publick Church'). Continuing in this vein, the pamphlet has the Puritan 'Round-heads and Prickeares' resolve to have their religion, tenets, and manners maintained 'against all reason, Learning, Divinity, Order, Discipline, Morality, Piety, Humanity whatsoever'; to have 'the Felt-maker and the Cobler' appointed 'Metropolitans of the two Arch Provinces', and to have 'the rest of the Sects preserved [*sic*], according to their imbecilities of spirit, to such Bishopricks and other Livings as will competently serve to procure fat Poultry, for the filling of their insatiate stomacks'.[47] John Harris, writing that same year, claimed that whereas 'A Protestant will deale uprightly, a Puritane will cozen his Father...a Protestant will relieve the poore and fatherlesse, a Puritane will oppresse the fatherlesse and Widdow'. In short, the Puritans were 'proud', 'envious', 'enemies to learning', 'self-wil[le]d', 'selfe-conceited', 'covetous', 'lyers', 'persecutors of the poore, oppressors of the needy', and the majority of their followers were 'Mechanick persons, for the most part unlectured'—'ignorant soules' who 'preferred the Discipline of ignorant men of their owne Society, before the Discipline of learned men, they prefer the drosse before the treasure'.[48]

By representing the Puritans and separatists as posing the real threat to the true Church in England, anti-sectarian polemicists were also able to equate the Puritans with papists. This was not a new charge; similar arguments had been made by conformist Protestants under Elizabeth and James, including James himself, and by those who wrote against the Scottish Covenanters in 1638–40.[49] Yet it became a powerful feature of royalist propaganda on the eve of the Civil War, giving scope to opponents of parliamentarian reform to neutralize or even to invert the parliamentarians' exploitation of the fear of popery and the supposed popish plot.[50] Catalogues of sects listed papists alongside Puritans and separatists as threats to the true Protestant religion.[51] In his *Anatomy of the Separatists*, Taylor alleged not only that 'between the Papists and Separatists the Church strangely suffers' but also that some sects did 'approve of Popery, because Ignorance is the mother of Devotion'.[52] In other writings Taylor equated 'The Papist and the Schismatique' because 'both grieves [*sic*] The Church', which was 'like Christ (Between two Thieves)', and even claimed that 'the Papists and Brownists' had formed 'a strong and perfect league' to 'crosse, as much as in them lay, all good proceedings of the English Parliament'.[53] Aston claimed that the Presbyterians and separatists, by insisting on 'the subjection of Prince and people to the tyranny of their Discipline', agreed with 'the Jesuites'; in his opinion, it was 'zealous separatists' who were 'likest to give fire to that Popish powder, which would blow up…all Kingly Supremacy, or Magisteriall Superioritie over the Independent Hierarchie'.[54] The clergy voiced similar arguments when recruiting subscribers to petitions. When William Clarke, a petty canon of Chester Cathedral, urged his congregation to subscribe Cheshire's petition of late 1641 in defence of the prayer book, he identified 'Papists and Puritans' as the 'two grand Enemyes' who sought to 'affect Noveltyes [and] Alterations' in the Church; it did not matter that papists and Puritans thought of each other as enemies, since 'Herod and Pilate were utter enemyes yet agreed in the Crucifying of Christ'.[55]

It is clear, then, what the anti-sectarians did not like. But what did they stand for, and what does this tell us about the burgeoning royalist identity that this literature played a role in helping to forge? At the very basic level, of course, anti-sectarian polemicists defended what Puritans and sectarians attacked: the Church of bishops and prayer book. Taylor acknowledged that 'some parts of our publike Liturgy' might 'be very well corrected', and this was something the king and parliament were considering; but the separatists went too far, he argued, in demanding that 'all formes of publike worship should be utterly abrogated, and that our booke of Common-Prayer should bee quite abolished' and 'Episcopacy everlastingly extirpated'.[56] Bishops were necessary 'to curbe' the 'execrable insolencies' of the sects.[57]

The lack of respect that the separatists showed for holy places and the threat to order they posed led some explicitly to defend policies associated with Laud in the 1630s. Taylor defended both kneeling and bowing in 1640: 'If either Separatist, or Schismatique, | Or Ana-baptist, Hare-brain'd Heretique', he rhymed, 'From Scripture, Church, or Father could but show | That reverently to God men should not bow, | In triumph then, they might display their Banners, | And shew some reason for their want of manners'; he who was 'so stiffe in th'hams' he could not bend, Taylor urged, 'ought'st (in feare and love) bow downe thy knee | To him, whose Grace and Love came downe to thee'.[58] Thomas Cheshire noted how he saw a woman in St Sepul-chre's Church in London 'dandling and dancing her child upon the Lords holy Table' a little before divine service, and afterwards noticed 'a great deal of Water upon the Table', which he suspected 'were not teares of devotion', and asked 'whether it had not beene meeter for the Lord's Table to have stood raild in, as formerly...then to be so polluted'. Yet invariably opponents of the sects maintained that they defended the traditional Church of Elizabeth and James. Cheshire himself made it clear that altar rails had existed in St Sepulchre's long before Laud rose to prominence in the Church, and indeed in many churches since 'time out of mind'.[59] Although not all ceremonies pre-scribed by the Book of Common Prayer were necessary to salvation, they could be defended on the grounds of tradition: using the sign of the cross in baptism, for example, was 'an ancient, laudable, and decent ceremony of the Church of England'.[60] A pamphlet of 1642 noted how the 'Round-head' 'doth disallow, | At Jesus name, his stur-borne knee to bow | Though God commands it', and bemoaned the 'ignorance', 'obstinacie and spirituall pride' of this 'Hypocrite'.[61] One anonymous pamphleteer commented on how those 'of the meanest condition' took it upon themselves 'to lay hands on, and to deface those ornaments their pious Ancestors had with great paines and care laboured to adorne God's house withall'. His reassuring message, however, was that God would punish those who did. Thus the church-warden who destroyed the stained-glass window in the parish church of Towcester, Northamptonshire, he related, shortly thereafter 'fell extreame mad, raving...howling and making a noise untill he died'; his wife likewise fell into extreme pain and died; while his sister, after she had ripped the Common Prayer Book out of her bible in protest against the liturgy, found that her hands 'began presently in a most strange maner to rot, the flesh flying from the bones', such was 'how it pleased God to deale with this poore silly Creature'.[62]

This was a Church that had not only been established by godly monarchs but also confirmed by parliament. One champion of episcopacy, while agreeing that parliament was right to seek some reform in the Church, complained how the schismatics 'raile against us, because wee will not raile against those things which are enacted by former Parliaments'.[63] As Taylor put it, 'The Booke of Common prayer ... was established by Act of Parliament by the good and godly King Edward the sixth, and after re-established by another Parliament, by that unparaleld and peerlesse princesse Queen Elizabeth, and continued since ... for the service of God these ninetie yeeres'.[64] Elsewhere Taylor praised 'that wonder-working Parliament now assembled' for the actions it had taken against 'the Papists in England'—indeed, Taylor appears to have accepted the Popish Plot theory (or, at least, thought it counterproductive to try to deny it), and wrote of the papists' 'hellish Stratagem' of 1639 to make 'a breach between the English and Scottish Nations'; his main objective, however, was to take a swipe at the sects, warning that when parliament was done with the papists it would turn its attention to 'the Brownists'.[65]

A powerful insight into the political outlook of those who championed the Church of bishops and prayer book was offered by Sir Thomas Aston, in a treatise he published in May 1641.[66] Aston dedicated this work to the king—justifying his presumption in doing so on the grounds that Charles had 'so graciously' approved of the Cheshire petition in defence of episcopacy—thereby taking it upon himself to act as a propagandist for the crown.[67] For Aston, the king was sacred and irresistible, obedience 'a Duty both to God and nature', and he condemned at great length the resistance theory developed in the mid-sixteenth century by Protestants like Goodman, Knox, and Buchanan, which he regarded as popish in origin (and indeed going beyond the views of Jesuits like Bellarmine and Suarez).[68] He also maintained that the king had 'the chiefe Government of all estates Ecclesiasticall and Civill, in all causes within his Dominions'.[69] At first glance this might seem to make him a divine-right, royal absolutist. But Aston refused to offer an opinion on whether or not the king ruled by divine right,[70] and chose not to invoke the language of royal absolutism. Instead, he credited the bishops with having established limited monarchy in England: 'Till Bishops help'd to reduce the unbounded wills of Princes to the limits of Lawes, Kings were Tyrants', but 'Long ha's this Nation flourished in the equall dispensation of Lawes, by Divines, Civilians, and Common Lawyers'.[71] It was the Presbyterians who threatened the rule of law, by denying the royal supremacy and setting up their own system of discipline over and above that of both the existing ecclesiastical and civil authorities. 'Under pretext of Reforming the Church, the true aime of such spirits', Aston intoned, was 'to shake off the yoke of all obedience, either to Ecclesiasticall, Civill, Common, Statute, or the Customarie Lawes of the Kingdome, and to introduce a meere Arbitrary Government'.[72] Not only would the king be undermined—'Presbyterie inconsistent with Monarchy' is the title of one of his sections—but so too would parliament, since under the Presbyterian system of Church government by presbyteries, classes, synods, and National Assemblies what would 'become of our old superintendent power of Parliaments?'[73] 'I hold my selfe as free-borne as any man,' Aston proclaimed, 'and as much disdaine the thought of servile fetters of Romish Tyranny, or an insultant Prelacie, as any he that lives.' But it was the Presbyterians who would 'hoyse up unlimited, unbounded Tyranny': they would 'trample under feet the sacred Crownes of Kings, the power of Parliaments, the seats of Justice, the use of Magistrates, the efficacie of Lawes, and make themselves Chancellours over our lives and conversations, our wives, our children, our servants, our private families, and our estates'.[74]

Aston's vision was elitist and hierarchical, and Aston himself was deeply worried about the threat posed by the lower orders. Discussing the root and branch petitions, he complained how 'Plebeians assume to give judgement, the Parliament must execute, the Nobilitie and Gentrie suffer by it'.[75] He also thought that the Presbyterian clergy and separatist ministers were preaching sedition and, after a passing allusion to John Ball preaching at the time of the Peasants' Revolt of 1381 that 'all the sons of Adam' were 'borne free', observed how 'the emptie name of libertie, blowne into vulgar eares', had 'overturned many States' and was especially dangerous 'when enforced as a religious dutie to disobey authoritie'.[76] Yet the Presbyterians, he claimed, were merely using 'the common people' as 'their factors for this freedome'; what would 'these deluded people have of this dreame of libertie', Aston wondered, if Presbyterianism were to triumph?[77] People would be subjected 'to the Tyrannical yoak' of Presbyterian discipline: they would risk being punished twice for the same offence, under both temporal and ecclesiastical law (unless the temporal juris-diction became extinct), and all sorts of petty crimes not under the jurisdiction of the civil law 'must bee brought to their Tribunall'. Indeed, the Presbyterians 'must have a rod for the women too, in correcting their lascivious, dissolute, or too sumptuous attire, private or publike dancing, May-games, visiting stage-playes, Tavernes, or Tipling-houses'. Where, then, Aston asked, would be this 'promised libertie'?[78]

Significantly, those who wrote in defence of the Church and the crown also claimed to be pro-parliament: they championed the tradi-tional Church as upheld by Acts of parliament, and even professed support for parliament's efforts to undo the innovations of the 1630s and the vital role that parliament played with England's limited mon-archy. There were obvious tactical reasons for this. In the first place, it seemed clear, for the time being, that any solution to the political crisis facing England would have to be worked out by parliament. Moreover, royalist propagandists did not want to risk alienating those very people whose support they were trying to cultivate by openly attacking an institution that was prized by so many. This is not to suggest that the professed support for parliament's true role in the constitution, properly understood, was purely cynical; as we have made clear already, many of those who were to become royalists had supported parliament's reforming legislation of late 1640 and early 1641. Furthermore, as the crisis unfolded, championing parliament could be a way of attacking the position and activities of those who supported more radical reform. The moderate Anglican minister Thomas Warmstry, a non-Laudian who was to side with the crown when civil war broke out, described parliament in late 1641 as 'that great Councell, or Colledge of state Physicians, assembled under his Majesty to consider of publike and extraordinary evills'; but this in turn became a defence of the bishops' right to sit in parliament, since for parliament to be fit for 'the discovery and remedy of...diseases' both in Church and state, it was clearly appropriate that it should 'Consist of both Spirituall, and Civill Members'. Warmstry also vaunted the independence of parliament as a way of condemning the tumultuous crowds that assembled at Westminster to try to influence how MPs voted. The people of England, he wrote, had not commit-ted their cause to the vote of the London crowd, 'but to the Parlia-ment, whom they have made their...proxies for the managing of this great work' of healing the diseases that afflicted England: 'they gave them this power freely', and expected 'it may bee freely exercised by them'. Londoners should therefore stay at home and mind their own business. 'Why doe not you Conceive it better for you to follow your trades and callings which is the busines which God hath sett you about, then to trouble yourselves and others in your unnecessary meetings at Westminster?', Warmstry asked. If it appeared that parliament had bowed to popular 'terrour and violence', this would undermine the 'value of those lawes' which parliament made.[79]

Manuscript libels that circulated at the time, by contrast, suggest that some people, at least, were far from enamoured with the exploits of the present parliament. One that appeared in April 1641, for example, alleged that the earl of Strafford's enemies were 'The Anabaptists, Jews, or Brownists of the Howse of Commons'. A manuscript attack on parliament's Protestation that circulated in September 1641 in the name of 'the gentrye, souldiers and all the true protestants' condemned reformist peers such as Essex, Bedford, and Saye (the last labelled an 'Anababtiste) as 'a packe of half witted lords', together with commoners such as Pym, Hampden, Holles, and others, for having 'conspired together against the King, the crowne and posterity', 'subjected our religion to be merely arbitrary', prostituted the honour of Ingland', 'beggered the nation to inriche the Scottes', 'protected the ignorant and licentious sectaryes and sismatikes to stir up sedition, to bringe in Atheisme', 'discountenanced all reverent ministers', and 'endeavoured to take away the common prayer booke'. Other libels from late 1641 and early 1642 blamed parliament for having spent 'So much to purchase peace with the Scot...While we defend we know not what | And fight against we know not whom'; condemned Pym's pretensions to rule the kingdom—'Is there no king but Pym?'; and queried 'Whether the subjects must rule the King, or the King the subjects'.[80] Pym himself was the target of an assassination attempt by a crude form of germ warfare: on 25 October 1641 he received a letter containing 'the contagious plaster of a Plague Sore', intended 'to have wrought his death'. Predictably, it was immediately suspected that papists were responsible.[81]

Charles I's Appeal to the Public

Royalism as a political identity, then, first began to define itself largely independently from the crown. Certainly it took its cue from public pronouncements by the crown and its supporters in the Lords; people could only rally behind the king if they felt they understood what the king stood for. Yet it was not Charles who (initially) was the architect. He made it clear that he welcomed the petitions in defence of the Church, once they started coming in, but he did not engineer them. And while the anti-sectarian/anti-Puritan writings we have examined, and also the lengthier work of Sir Thomas Aston, were doubtless in tune with his thinking, they were not as such his thinking. However, from late 1641 we see a concerted attempt by the king and his advisors to seize the ideological initiative. They did this in several ways: by inserting Charles's own voice more forcibly into the public domain, making it clear what Charles as king stood for; by taking a more interventionist position in promoting or publishing works that supported the Church and king; and by making greater effort to ensure that those who could influence public opinion at the local level were men sympathetic to the king's position.

Charles's own print propaganda campaign only really began in response to parliament's decision on 15 December to publish its Grand Remonstrance; as Charles himself subsequently confessed, it was now that he 'resolved to do [his] part' to give the 'People' a 'cleare satisfaction of [his] upright Intentions to the publike'.[82] There followed a flood of declarations and proclamations outlining the king's position—some seventy-three items have been identified as issuing from the press he set up at York alone, following his flight north. They appear to have been widely disseminated, with loyal sheriffs and other local officers often taking it upon themselves to distribute these works at the local level.[83] Although issued in the name of the king, they were mostly not his own work; Charles used the services of a skilled group of polemicists which included Hyde, Falkland, and Culpepper, whom he appointed to his council in December 1641. They sought to sell Charles as a constitutional monarch, willing to redress the grievances of his subjects through parliament, and committed to the rule of law, but who was determined to uphold the true Protestant religion and the traditional constitution in both Church and state.

Charles issued two responses to the Grand Remonstrance. The first was his formal answer to the Commons, read to the House on 23 December and subsequently published, which was conciliatory in tone but made it clear where Charles would draw the line. It begins with Charles promising to satisfy 'the desires of Our people, in a Parliamentary way', including their concerns over the alleged 'designes of the Popish partie'. Even the issue of bishops voting in parliament, which Charles insisted was a right 'grounded upon the fundamentall

Law of the Kingdom', he was happy to leave to parliament's determination. He also said he would 'willingly concur in the removall' of 'any illegall Innovations which may have crept in' to the Church. But he stressed his conviction that there was no Church on earth that professed 'the true Religion with more purity of Doctrine' than the Church of England, 'nor where the Government and Discipline' were 'joyntly more beautified, and free from superstition', as they were 'here established by Law', and protested that as long as he lived he would maintain the Church of England 'against all invasions of Popery' and 'the irreverence of...Schismaticks and Separatists'. Indeed, he went on the counter-offensive by demanding parliament's 'timely and active assistance' in suppressing the sects. As for parliament's demand to be able to appoint and dismiss ministers of the crown, Charles insisted that there was 'no man' he would 'not leave to the Justice of the Law', if parliament brought 'a particular charge and sufficient proofs against him'; but to deny him the right to choose his own ministers would be to deny him 'that naturall libertie all Free-men have' and infringe 'the undoubted right of the Crown of England'. He concluded by thanking parliament for its care over the Irish rebellion and agreeing that it was important for the rebellion to be suppressed as speedily as possible.[84]

The second response was a declaration to the people, written by Hyde and published, so it claimed, with the advice of the privy council.[85] It opens with Charles recalling how he had 'not refused to passe any Bill' presented by parliament 'for redresse of those Grievances mentioned in the Remonstrance', since he wanted to free his subjects 'from those pressures which were grievous to them'. As for the suggestion that he favoured papists, he protested that he had been 'brought up in...the religion now established in this Kingdom', which he thought 'the most pure, and agreeable to the Sacred Word of God, of any religion...in the Christian world', and would give his life for it, 'if it pleased God to call Us to that sacrifice'. He said he would readily agree to a law granting a degree of religious toleration to those who scrupled to conform over 'matters indifferent', but this had to be pursued in such a way that 'the peace and quiet of the Kingdom' were not disturbed, nor church services discountenanced, nor 'the pious, sober, and devout actions' of the clergy scandalized and defamed. As for 'Civill Liberties', Charles boasted how he had addressed all 'apprehensions of Arbitrary pressures' by passing the Triennial Act and the Acts for the continuance of the present parliament and abolishing the courts of High Commission and Star

Chamber, and by not retaining in his service anyone against whom parliament had taken exception. He therefore believed that all his 'good Subjects' would acknowledge his part 'to be fully performed'. It was up to the people now, if they wanted 'quiet and prosperity', to do their part 'by yielding all obedience and due reverence to the Law', which was 'the inheritance of every subject, and the onely security' for 'Life, Liberty, or Estate', and which Charles insisted he was determined to observe himself. He hoped thereby to preserve 'a good understanding' with his people, so that he and they could unite to relieve 'that unhappy Kingdome' of Ireland, where 'those barbarous rebels', as he styled them, practised 'such inhumane and unheard of Outrages upon Our miserable people'.[86]

Repeatedly over the next several months Charles sought to cast himself as a constitutional monarch who would uphold the rule of law and the established Church, one who was eager to protect his subjects against those who threatened to undermine the traditional constitution and reduce the king to a mere figurehead. In an open letter to parliament dated 15 March, another work penned by Hyde, Charles condemned parliament's Militia Ordinance, insisting that his subjects could not be compelled to obey any Act or order which had not received the royal assent, and emphasized his own resolve 'to observe the Laws' and 'require Obedience to them from all His Subjects'.[87]

The publication that was to emerge as the classic statement of constitutional royalism was Charles's *Answer* to parliament's Nineteen Propositions of June 1642, a work drafted by Culpepper and Falkland.[88] Charles charged 'the Cabalists' in parliament—he made it clear he did not blame the whole body, but only 'ambitious turbulent Spirits, disaffected to God's true Religion'—with seeking 'to remove a troublesome Rub in their way, The Law': they had assumed 'a new Power...to interpret and declare Laws' without the king's consent, erected 'an upstart Authority...To command the Militia', and broached a 'new Doctrine' that the king was 'obliged to passe all Lawes' that the two Houses put before him. He resented the demand that all officers and ministers of state had to be approved by parliament, especially since he had made it clear that if they brought a particular charge against any minister he would leave them 'to the Justice of the Law', and accused the cabalists of seeking to make him 'a Duke of Venice' and turn the kingdom into a 'Republick'. In seeking to deny the legitimacy of the Nineteen Propositions, Charles recast the English monarchy as a mixed and regulated polity in which the king was just one of the three estates. The king's voice in legislation had to be heard, Charles insisted, because the king was 'a part of the Parliament' and it were 'most unreasonable...that two Estates proposing something to the Third, that Third should be bound to take no advice, whether it were fit to passe, but from those two that did propose it'. There were 'three kinds of Government amongst men', Charles continued: 'Absolute Monarchy, Aristocracy and Democracy', but England's wise ancestors had moulded 'a mixture of these, as to give to this Kingdome...the conveniences of all three, without the inconveniences of any one'. The Nineteen Propositions, however, threatened to upset the balance by removing so much of the king's power that Charles would 'not be able to discharge [his] Trust', and amounted to 'a totall Subversion of the Fundamentall Laws, and that excellent Constitution of this Kingdome'. Moreover, Charles predicted, things would not end with the destruction of the monarchy: 'the second Estate [the Lords] would in all probability follow the Fate of the first', leaving all power 'vested in the House of Commons', and then once 'the Common people' realized that they had been used by the Commons and had gained no positive benefits themselves, they would 'grow weary of Journey-work, and set up for themselves'. What would ensue would be a nightmare world of popular anarchy: the common people would 'call Parity and Independence Libertie...Destroy all Rights and Proprieties, all distinctions of Families and Merit' and thus would England's 'splendid and excellently distinguished Form of Government end in a dark equall Chaos of Confusion; and the long Line of Our many noble Ancestours in a Jack Cade or a Wat Tyler'. Charles's answer to parliament's demands was thus '*Nolumus Leges Angliae mutari*'—'We do not wish the laws of England to be changed'. As for the Church, Charles felt he could do no more than repeat what he had said in his two printed responses to the Grand Remonstrance, that he would maintain the Church of England 'against all Invasions of Popery' and also from 'the Irreverence of...Schismaticks and Separatists'. In conclusion, he demanded that he be allowed his 'just Rights' and his 'Share in the Legislative Power', which, he alleged, 'would be counted in Us...Tyranny and Subversion of Parliaments to deny to you'.[89] It was a bold attempt to seize the middle ground. Yet it involved a redefinition of the theoretical powers of the monarch that even some constitutional royalists found troubling. Hyde, for example, thought that to recast the monarch as one of the three estates—which in his view comprised the lords spiritual, lords temporal, and the commons—was 'prejudicial to the King'.[90]

From the spring of 1642 Charles was actively striving to construct a royalist party that would back him in a military conflict with parliament. When he arrived at York on 18 March, his position was still quite weak. Although afforded an appropriate civic reception, the Deputy Recorder Sir Thomas Widdrington made a bold speech—which onlookers noted was 'not very well liked of' by the king—urging Charles 'to hearken unto, and condescend unto his Peeres and Commons now Assembled in Parliament', on the grounds that 'they would resolve upon nothing, but what should be to the good of His Majestie'.[91] There was no immediate throng to join his court: by the end of March Charles was attended by only thirty-nine gentlemen and seventeen guards.[92] In mid-May he gave his supporters leave of absence from parliament, prompting a steady flow of nobles and gentry to join him in the north. In June a group of loyalist peers pledged to maintain a force of 2,000 cavalry in support of the king and presented Charles with a gift of £100,000. Over the summer he made sweeping changes to the commissions of the peace across the country, removing those known to be sympathetic to parliament's Militia Ordinance and replacing them with individuals believed to be willing to execute his Commissions of Array: between 10 June and 7 August he dismissed 177 men from fourteen county benches, adding 154 new names. Charles also made a series of excursions from York to rally support in person and to stem the tide of counties sliding by default towards parliament. Thus when Charles visited Lincoln on 13 July he was greeted by a vast cheering crowd, while the next day seventy-five of the gentry and clergy subscribed a body of 172 cavalry (which they promised to raise eventually to 400) to secure the peace of the county against the incursions of the parliamentary soldiers at Hull—and this despite the fact that the county had accepted the Militia Ordinance 'with all readiness and alacrity' the previous month. It may be that many in Lincolnshire were not ready to choose sides, but saw themselves as being for both king and parliament. Doubtless for some the teachings about the duty of obedience to authority had been so deeply internalized that they felt obliged to obey orders from wherever they came, while a rise in royalist sentiment might also have been in reaction to the recent outbreak of further rioting against the fen drainage schemes. It is thus conceivable that some who appeared at the parliamentary musters subsequently cheered for the king, though it is impossible to know how many. Yet it is also clear that Lincolnshire was a divided county (like so many English counties) and that rival—and ideologically distinct—positions were being staked out. Parliament had ordered the swift execution of the Militia Ordinance there in the first place in response to reports of disaffection among the gentry, while 'some gallants' had sought to disrupt the parliamentary musters and provoke the trained bands to mutiny by reading out royal proclamations. Following Charles's visit, a group of leading gentry drew up a petition to parliament urging it to abandon Hull to the king, cancel the Militia Ordinance, execute the laws in favour of the established Church government and suppress the disorders of the sects, and adjourn to some place where they might meet with the king to discuss further laws that might settle the peace and stability of the Church, crown, and state.[93]

Over the course of the summer some twenty-four counties made an effort to execute the king's Commission of Array.[94] Insight into what led many in the localities to declare for the king is provided by the anonymous *Resolution of the Countie of Hereford* printed in London in July 1642. It began by acknowledging that the kingdom had for many years 'groaned under Takes of Loanes, Ship-money, and the like dismall effects of an Arbitrary Government', and how it was hoped that parliament would provide the 'wholsome Physicke' necessary 'to clense the Body Politique'. Yet this medicine had not delivered the desired results. The 'Protestant Religion' and 'the Liturgie and decent Ceremonies established by Law' had been assaulted and the Church of England was in danger of being 'overcome with Brownisme and Anabaptisme'; 'the just power of the King' had come under attack and even his person threatened with violence; and 'The Lawes of the Land, and The Libertie of the Subject' had been 'violated'. Conceiving themselves 'obliged by the Law of God, the Law of the Land, by the Dictates of Natures reason to maintaine all these', the petitioners therefore pledged themselves to maintain the king 'in all the Premisses' with their 'Lives and Fortunes'.[95]

The Constitutional Theory of the English Civil War

With Charles desperately trying to recapture the ideological middle ground, how, then, did parliament justify its stance against the king? In the king's eyes, the parliamentarians were guilty of rebellion against a divine-right monarch, they had driven him from the capital, and they had even engaged in armed acts of resistance in refusing to deliver Hull—all of which was tantamount to treason. In seeking to deny the imputation, defenders of parliament made a distinction between the king's person and the king's authority, insisting that in resisting the former they were in fact being obedient to the latter.[96] In the process, they came to articulate a view of the constitution which saw government as a trust to be exercised for the common good, where the king's authority had to be exercised through appropriate legal channels and in which sovereignty lay ultimately vested in parliament.

A Declaration of the Lords and Commons of 25 May 1642, written in response to Charles's declaration concerning Sir John Hotham's refusal to admit him to Hull, for example, set out 'to disabuse the People's minds' of 'the false shewes and pretexts of the Law' made by 'the Malignant Party' in their various declarations. To allege that parliament had denied the king admission to his own town of Hull, as if the king had the same 'title to his Townes and his Magazin' that 'every particular man' had 'to his House, Lands and Goods', was a nonsense. 'This erroneous maxime...infused into Princes that their Kingdoms are their own, and that they may doe with them what they will', the Declaration continued, was 'the Roote of all the Subjects' misery.' Kings were 'only intrusted with their Kingdomes', and 'for the good and safety, and best advantage thereof', a trust that 'ought to be managed by the advise of the Howses of Parliament whom the Kingdome hath trusted for that purpose'. Kings of England were therefore under an 'obligation...to passe such bills' offered them by parliament 'for the good of the whole Kingdome'. Refusing the king admission to Hull, the Declaration continued, had involved no resistance to 'the Sovereigne power', nor to a 'command from his Majesty, and his High Court of Parliament (where the Soveraigne power resides)', nor to 'his Majestie's Authority derived out of any other Court', because the two Houses of Parliament had instructed Hotham not to admit the king, unless by the king's authority as 'signified by both Houses of Parliament'; the king's 'verbal commands...against the order of both Houses of Parliament' had no 'validity', and thus not submitting to them could not be 'resisting...the Soveraigne Authority'. As for the suggestion that Hotham had acted treasonously, the original statute of Edward III stated that treason was 'the leavying of war against [the king's] lawes and authority'—even if there were no war levied 'against his person'—and so the levying of war 'against his personall commands, though accompanied with his presence', if 'not against his Lawes and authority', was 'no leavying of war against the King'. In short, the king had two bodies, his personal and his political: 'Treason which is against the Kingdome, is more against the King then that which is against His person', for treason was 'not Treason, as it is against Him as a man, but as a man that is a King'. The *Declaration* concluded by proclaiming parliament's ultimate objective as being 'the maintenance of the true Protestant Religion, the King's Just Prerogatives, the Lawes and liberties of the Land, and the priviledges of Parliament'.[97]

Parliament further clarified its position in a declaration issued on 6 June, in response to a royal proclamation forbidding subjects to obey the Militia Ordinance. Reiterating its stance that the Militia Ordinance was necessary 'in this Time of extreme and imminent Danger', parliament insisted that although the king was 'the Fountain of Justice and Protection', 'Acts of Justice and Protection' were exercised not 'in His own Person' but 'by His Courts, and by His Ministers, who must do their Duty theirein, though the King in His own Person should forbid them'. Even if they gave judgments 'against the King's Will', nevertheless they were 'the King's Judgements'. 'The High Court of Parliament', the declaration continued, was not only 'a Court of Judicature, enabled by the Lawes to adjudge and determine the Rights and Liberties of the Kingdom, against such Patents and Grants of His Majesty' as were 'prejudicial thereunto'; it was also 'a Council, to provide for the Necessities, prevent the imminent Dangers, and preserve the Public Peace and Safety, of the Kingdom, and to declare the King's Pleasure in those Things as are requisite thereunto', even if the king, 'seduced by evil Counsel', personally opposed the same. Parliament was in effect claiming to be the governing body of the kingdom, although it should be pointed out that by this time most of the king's supporters had deserted Westminster, and the upper chamber in particular was significantly depleted: after May attendance levels rarely rose much above a dozen.[98]

The man who was to emerge as the most important defender of the parliamentarian position against the ideological offensive of the crown was Henry Parker, an Oxford-trained lawyer who had already written against ship money and in defence of the Puritans. In 1642 he wrote in reply to several declarations issued in the king's name, the most important being his *Observations upon Some of His Majesties late Answers and Expresses*, which appeared in early July 1642. It provoked 'an armada of royalist replies', rapidly earning Parker the nickname 'the Observator', and is worth examining in some detail.[99]

Parker began his *Observations* by openly confronting the theory of divine right. God was 'no more the author of Regall' than He was of 'Aristocraticall power'; no more 'of supreme, then of subordinate command'. Power was originally 'inherent in the people', who were 'the fountaine and efficient cause', and 'but secondary and derivative in Princes', and 'the Paramount Law' of 'all Politiques' was '*Salus Populi*'—the welfare or safety of the people. Government was a trust: the king's 'interest in the Crowne' was 'not absolute' but 'condition-ate and fiduciary'. If a general at time of war were to turn his cannons on his own soldiers, they would be '*ipso facto* absolved of all obedi-ence, and all oathes and ties of allegiance whatsoever', being 'bound by a higher dutie, to seeke their owne preservation by resistance and defence'. 'In all well formed monarchies...this must needs be one necessary condition, that the subject shall live both safe and free.' Indeed, the kings of England had been 'expressely by the people lim-ited', by 'the great Charter of England'—i.e. Magna Carta—which English kings had ratified 'by their owne grants and oathes'.[100]

Having articulated a theory of popular sovereignty, Parker then went on to consider the purpose of parliament, which was to ensure 'that the interest of the people might be satisfied' and kings 'the better counsailed'. 'The safetie of the people' was 'to bee valued above any right' of the king, and although the people had 'intrusted their protec-tion into the King's hands' they did not leave that trust without lim-its. To ensure that princes were not 'beyond all limits and Lawes', 'the whole community' could 'convene to do justice', but since this would be too vast a body, they set up a representative body, 'which is now called a Parliament'. Parker then set out to challenge several of the basic assumptions of divine-right, monarchical absolutism. Although princes were called gods, fathers, lords, heads, and so forth, such terms merely illustrated 'some excellency in Princes by way of simili-tude' and should not be applied 'in all things'. Kings were 'Gods to particular men', and were 'sanctified with some of God's royaltie', 'not for themselves' but for 'the prosperitie of God's people'. Yet 'as to themselves', they were 'most unlike God', for 'no created thing' could 'impose any dutie or tie upon God', as subjects could 'upon Princes'. Although the natural head no more depended upon the body than the body did upon the head—'both head and members must live and dye together'—it was 'otherwise with the Head Politicall, for that receives more subsistence from the body than it gives'.[101]

What remedies, then, did the people have against a king who abused his trust? Since princes were bound not to act 'contrarie to the end of government' nor to 'effect evill in stead of good', it followed that 'Treason in Subjects against their Prince' was 'not so horrid in nature, as oppression in the Prince, executed violently upon Subjects'.

Because all rule was 'but fiduciarie', a prince was 'more or lesse absolute' as he was 'more or lesse trusted', and since no trust was 'without an intent of preservation', it was 'no more intended that the People shall be remedilesly oppressed in a Monarchy, than in a Republique'. Which side, then, should the people take in the current dispute between the king and parliament? 'How shall they restraine tyranny?', Parker asked. Certainly not by siding with the king, if MPs 'can doe nothing but what pleases Him, or some Clandestine Councellors' and 'be called Traitors' if they did otherwise. On the other hand, it was impossible, Parker asserted, for 'any Parliament freely elected' ever to 'injure a whole Kingdome, or exercise any tyranny'.[102]

Parker insisted that he did not intend to 'upbraid' Charles; the king had been misled 'by the fraud of such as have incensed him against Parliaments'. In answer to the charge that parliament had already resisted the king over Hull, Parker urged that we should not confound 'all resistance to Princes...under one notion': sometimes it could be 'pious and loyall' and at others 'distructive and impious'. An example of the latter was the recent rebellion in Ireland, where the aim of the rebels was 'to extirpate that Religion which hath indeavored so long to bring them from Idolatory and Atheisme, and to massacre that nation which hath indeavoured so gently to reduce them from poverty and beastiall barbarisme'. The supposed rebels in England, who acted to preserve the safety of the kingdom, by contrast, were misnamed. The imputation that parliament 'leavyed Warre upon the King, and drove him away' from London was false. Although the king was now in York, he could still 'concurre with the advice of his Parliament', since 'the distance of the place need not cause any distance of affection'. 'Levying forces against the personall commands of the King', as at Hull, was 'not levying warre against the King'.[103] The suggestion that, by following old precedents, parliament might claim the right to depose the king was absurd: no 'free Parliament' had ever truly consented 'to the dethroaning of any King of England', since the Act by which Richard II was deposed in 1399 was 'rather the Act of Henry the fourth, and his victorious Army'. Yet when its counsel was 'unjustly rejected, by a King seduced, and abused by private flatterers, to the danger of the Commonwealth', then parliament assumed 'a right to judge of that danger, and to prevent it'—for 'if the Parliament may not save the Kingdome without the King, the King may destroy the kingdome in despight of the Parliament'.[104]

Parker was convinced that the traditional principles upon which the English constitution had been based had been subverted by evil advisors. 'Our Law has a wholesome Maxime, That the King may onely do that which is just,' he observed, 'but Courtiers invert the sense of it, and tell him, That all is just which he may do.' Yet there were some things princes 'ought not to do, though no Law limited them from doing thereof'. To have power 'to do such an evill, or not to do such a good' was 'in truth no reall power'. What could be 'more plain then this', Parker asked, 'That Venetians live more happily under their conditionate Duke, than the Turks do under their most absolute Emperours', while 'our neighbours in the Netherlands' were 'a good instance' that there could be 'no defect at all' in 'popular and mixt government'. Despite holding up the examples of two contemporary republics as ideals, Parker insisted that he was not 'in favour of any alteration in England' and that he was 'zealously addicted to Monarchy'. It was clear what sort of monarchy he had in mind, however, when he praised the situation north of the border. In answer to those who claimed that, as a result of recent events, 'our King' was 'no more King of Scotland, then he is King of France', Parker protested that to his mind 'the Policy of Scotland' was 'more exquisite in poynt of prerogative, then any other in Europe, except ours', and that 'if the splendour, and puissance of a Prince' consisted 'in commanding religious, wise, magnanimous, warlike subjects', then 'the King of Scotland is more to be admired then the King of France'. And Parker was certainly at odds with the traditional view of divine-right, irresistible monarchy. It was true that the king, 'as to His own person', was 'not to be forcibly repelled'. However, 'in all irregular acts where no personall force is, Kings may be disobeyed, their unjust commands may be neglected, not only by communities, but also by single men sometimes'. Therefore 'those men' who maintained 'That all Kings are in all things and commands...to be obeyed, as being like Gods, unlimitable', and not to be questioned, were 'sordid flatterers'; and those who allowed 'no limits...but divine and naturall' and allowed 'subjects a dry right without all remedy' were 'almost as stupid as the former'.[105]

As the war of words unfolded over the spring and early summer of 1642, the two sides became increasingly entrenched in locked positions. Although the various parliamentarian and royalist pronouncements were written as responses to each other, there was no genuine dialogue. Such works were exercises in mutual recrimination, rather than serious efforts to resolve any of the issues at stake. They might not quite yet reveal the existence of two parties that were psychologically prepared for civil war, but they do reveal the existence of two sides neither of which was willing to make any significant concession and thus a mentality that would make war inescapable.[106]

And so we return to Charles's call to arms of 12 August 1642. On the same day that he issued his proclamation calling on his supporters to rally to his standard at Nottingham, Charles published a lengthy declaration to 'All His Loving Subjects' vindicating everything he had done since the calling of the Long Parliament, and condemning the traitorous and rebellious actions of the malevolent faction who opposed him. It was a reply to Parker; yet it also laid out what was in effect the political platform of the royalist party at the outbreak of the Civil War.

In a remarkable rhetorical strategy, Charles not only admitted his errors during the personal rule but in effect confessed to tyranny, only to claim that he had redressed all the 'grievances and pressures' his 'Subjects...suffered under' and that the 'Tyranny' would be 'redoubled' if the faction were not stopped.[107] Thus he states that he decided to call parliament in November 1640 after having recognized 'the inconveniences, and mischiefes, which had growne by the long intermission of Parliaments, and by the parting too much from the knowne rule of the Law, to an Arbitrary power'. He then rehearses at length all the things he had done to satisfy his subjects: agreeing to the impeachment of several persons for high treason, 'whom they looked upon as the chiefe causes of the publike sufferings'; passing the bill for triennial parliaments; abolishing the court of Star Chamber, which he admits 'had in the excesse of Jurisdiction...and severity of punishment, invaded the Lawes of the Land, and Liberty of the Subject, by the exercise of an Arbitrary Power'; abolishing the High Commission court, which 'had proceeded with too much strictnesse in many cases...and had so farre out-growne the power of the Law, that it would not be limited and guided by it; but censured, fined, and imprisoned Our People, for matters unpunishable by the Law'; and agreeing that all proceedings with regard to ship money should be 'adjudged voyde and disanulled', because the 'grounds and reasons' of the ship money judgment in *Rex* v. *Hampden* 'were contrary to...the Lawes, and Statutes of this Realme, the Property and Liberty of the Subjects, and to the Petition of Right'. Yet this did not satisfy the faction, since they were ambitious for offices and places for themselves, and wanted 'to change the Religion, and Law of this Kingdome'.[108]

The bulk of the declaration documents the activities of this faction: their campaign against episcopacy, attempts to make law without the consent of the king or even the Lords, encouragement of religious sectarianism, stirring up the people against the king, encouraging the multitude to intimidate peers and MPs who supported the crown, and even engaging in open acts of treason, including calling on subjects to arm themselves against the king (as in the Militia Ordinance) and refusing to surrender the magazine at Hull. Throughout, Charles seeks to justify his own actions against the false aspersions of his opponents—he explains away the alleged army plots, for example, and defends his attempt to arrest the Five Members. He attacks in particular the House of Commons, whom he accuses of desiring to have 'the Whole Managery of the Kingdome, and the Legislative Power' in their own hands, 'without the consent, either of Us, or Our Nobilitie', and claims that he 'saw the Lawes absolutely trampled under feet, and a Designe laid to ruine the Government of the Kingdome, and to destroy Us and Our Posterity'. The months following the presentation of the Grand Remonstrance saw the faction getting bolder and increasing their demands and the escalation of violence out-of-doors, so much so that Charles had to have a guard for his own safety and was eventually forced to leave the capital. But it was the Militia Ordinance, the Nineteen Propositions, and Sir John Hotham's traitorous activities at Hull that proved to be the last straw. There were certain things he could never agree to, because of his accountability to God. 'We will not now depose Our Self', he said, 'and suffer the People and Kingdom (which God and the Law hath committed to Our government and Protection, and for which We must make an accompt) to be devoured by them.'[109]

Although the declaration did not specifically address Charles's decision to raise his standard at Nottingham, it did outline the platform on which he took his stand. This is described right at the beginning as 'the publike Care of the true Protestant Religion, the Preservation of the Law, and the Liberty of the Subject, and the upholding the whole frame and constitution of this Kingdome, so admirably founded and continued by the blessing of God, and the wisedome of Our Ancestours'. Charles elaborates upon this towards the end of the tract, where he emphasizes his desire to defend 'the true reformed Protestant Religion, sealed by the blood of so many Reverend Martyrs, and established by the Wisdom and Piety of former blessed Parliaments'; 'the Dignity, Priviledge, and Freedom of Parliament (Parliaments whose wisdom and gravity have prepared so many wholesome Laws, and whose freedom distinguishes the Condition of Our Subjects from those of any Monarchy in Europe)'; and 'the

Constitution of the Kingdom', and 'Monarchy it selfe', against those men who aim 'to introduce a parity and confusion of all degrees and conditions'. He ends by making it clear that he does not blame everyone who might have concurred with any of the things done by the faction, accepting that they simply failed 'to discern the Guilt, Malice, Ambition, or subtilty of their Seducers', and emphasizes that his 'Quarrell is not against the Parliament, but against particular men'. Indeed, Charles states that he is well aware 'that Our Selfe and Our two Houses make up the Parliament, and that We are like Hippocrates Twins, We must laugh and cry, live and dye together; that no man can be a friend to the one, and an enemy to the other'; indeed, it is 'the Injustice, Injury, and Violence offered to Parliaments', he claims, 'which We principally complain of'.[110]

Conclusion

It is strange to note how we have insensibly slid into the beginning of a civil war by one unexpected accident after another, as waves of the sea which have brought us thus far and we scarce know how.

Bulstrode Whitelocke, *Memorials of the English Affairs* (1682), 176.

Speaking to his army in September 1642, Charles announced that 'he brought them to fight for their religion, king and lawes against traitorous Brownists Anabaptists and Atheists etc', and besought God's 'blessing and protection to maintayne the true reformed protestant religion established in the church of England', in which he promised he would 'live and dy'.[1] Charles eventually was to die for it, albeit not until 30 January 1649—after two civil wars (1642–6, 1648) in England, numerous failed attempts to reach a negotiated settlement, and a political coup orchestrated by parliament's army which resulted in the thrusting into power of radical political Independents. Yet although what we now think of as the Civil War was not fought in order to remove Charles from the throne or to set up a republic, once war had broken out some people soon began to imagine the death of the king. In late November 1642, for instance, one Thomas Baker was boasting in a shop in Ipswich that he had just come from the battle of Edgehill (23 October) where, by his reckoning, 'Tenne of the kings forces' had been slain for every one parliamentarian soldier, and where he would 'have killed the kinge, if he could, because he was his enemye'.[2] Whatever people might have thought they were going to be fighting for in the summer of 1642, once war had actually broken out things began to change quite rapidly.

Edgehill was the first major pitched battle of the Civil War, although as we have seen the fighting had started much earlier than October 1642. The Puritan divine Richard Baxter, commenting on the breakdown in order that occurred in England in 1641–2, observed that 'the Warre was begun in our streets before the King or Parliament had any Armies'.[3] If we take a British perspective, the fighting started in 1639 with the outbreak of the first Bishops' War. My account has taken the story up to 22 August 1642, when Charles raised his standard at Nottingham—the official start of the English Civil War. It has endeavoured to explain why the crisis had reached such a point that Charles thought that the best way forward—for the monarchy, for the Church, and for the peoples over whom he ruled—was for him to declare war on those in England who, he claimed, bore 'an inward hatred and Malice against [his] Person and Government'.[4] It is a convenient ending-point. Inevitably, however, it stops in the middle of a process. I have been able to explore how the two sides came to position themselves ideologically in the months leading up to the outbreak of the English Civil War. I have stopped short, however, of explaining how people chose to align themselves once civil war had broken out. That is a complicated story, about which there is still no historiographical consensus. Was there a basic religious divide, between (non-Laudian) Anglicans and Puritans? Was there a geographical divide, with the economically more progressive south and east siding with parliament and the more conservative and economically backward north and west siding with the king—and, if so, how much did this have to do with the economies of these regions? Did the geographic divide correspond to a class divide? How far down in English society did divisions permeate? Or was it only a small number of hardliners who had the conviction and passion to be willing to fight to the death, and these mainly from the upper levels of society, who in turn had to press men into service in their respective armies to fight for a cause which was not their own?

Reacting against earlier economic-reductionist explanations of Civil War allegiance, Revisionist historians in the 1970s pointed to how reluctant most people were to commit themselves to one side or the other: people saw themselves as being both for the king and for parliament, not for one against the other, and thus neutralism was a widespread response to the outbreak of the Civil War.[5] Recognizing that, as the war progressed, people were eventually forced to take sides, scholars have tried to account for the pattern of allegiance that eventually did emerge. In the 1980s it was suggested that the explanation lay in underlying cultural patterns, which in turn were related to the ecologies of particular regions, with arable areas more likely to give rise to a culture that was sympathetic to royalism, and wood-pasture areas to one that was sympathetic to parliamentarianism.[6] It was a model that had its merits, and which perhaps worked for the English West Country, but one which ultimately proved to be too simplistic, or perhaps even misconceived.[7] Detailed research by local historians has since demonstrated the complexity of the pattern of allegiances that came to emerge during the Civil War and highlighted the many exceptions to the various explanatory models posited by earlier scholars, doing much to show how a variety of different local and national factors and economic, social, cultural, geographical, political, and religious considerations could shape why some people in certain areas would side with parliament, others with the king.[8] Of late scholars have turned their attention to the question of mobilization, though they have found it necessary to emphasize multiple-mobilizations, with one dynamic explaining the ideological polarization that emerged in the months leading up to the outbreak of the Civil War, for instance, and another why people chose to fight for one side or another (or to remain neutral) after Charles had raised his standard at Nottingham. It was one thing to sign a petition in favour of the bishops in 1641 or early 1642; it was another thing entirely to be prepared to enlist in the king's army after August 1642.[9]

Taking the story forward to explore the process of politicization that occurred once war had broken out would be another project. Explaining how regicide and the establishment of a republic was to be the ultimate end result of a civil war that had not been started with the object of removing Charles I and abolishing the monarchy would require a book in itself.

This present study has had a number of aims. It is first and foremost a study of the reigns of James VI and I and of Charles I (up until 1642) in their own terms. It has explored the rule of these two Stuart kings in all three of their kingdoms, and endeavoured to provide an integrated British and Irish history of the period that also does justice to the Scottish and Irish pasts for their own sakes, not just bringing in Scotland and Ireland when they help to shed light on what was going on in England. It has further sought to set politics in a broader social context. This is not just a view from on high, from the perspective of the monarchs themselves, but effort has also been made to examine what it was like for ordinary people to live under these monarchs, and what impact the early Stuarts' policies had on those they ruled. This book has inevitably spent a great deal of time exploring the problems the early Stuart monarchs faced. It has endeavoured to show the complexity of these problems, the various ways in which James VI and I and Charles I sought to address them, and why they chose to address them in the ways that they did. Why did they believe what they were doing was a sensible way forward? It has sought to highlight the intractable nature of many of their problems and the tough choices they invariably had to make. It has also sought to understand why people responded to royal initiatives in the ways that they did. But it has not been written with eyes fixed on the eventual outcome.

Nevertheless, this book has been the story of a monarchy that ultimately failed. Even though the account offered here has not been structured as an investigation into the origins of the English Civil War, it does stop in 1642 with the outbreak of that civil war and it inevitably seeks to shed light on why civil war broke out at this time. In this conclusion, then, it is necessary to address the larger question of why the Civil War happened. Should we look for long-term or short-term causes? Was there something wrong with the system itself, so that some sort of major rupture was bound to occur at some stage? Or was the system, although troubled, basically sound—or at least workable—so that individual errors, personal failings, are ultimately the key to understanding why things were to go wrong? Writing in the 1980s, the distinguished Cambridge historian John Morrill drew upon the analogy of a plane crash: some planes crash due to metal fatigue or mechanical failure, others because of pilot error.[10] In our post-9/11 world it is all too easy to imagine a third alternative: some planes, however well-maintained and no matter how good the pilot, crash because there are people on board who are determined to bring them down.[11]

Some have argued the roots of the English Civil War can be traced back to the early Tudor period. The eminent Princeton historian Lawrence Stone, for instance, began his account of the causes of the English Revolution in 1529, the year of the meeting of the Reformation Parliament that was to go on to instigate the break with Rome in the 1530s. The distinguished Oxford historian Christopher Hill went back even further, to the discovery of America by Christopher Columbus in 1492.[12] Revisionist historians, however, tended to point to short-term causes: Morrill, for example, argued that it was not until late 1641 that civil war became unavoidable. Part of the disagreement relates to how strict a definition of 'cause' we adopt. Stone stressed the importance of short-term triggers and medium-term precipitants as well as longer-term preconditions: it was the immediate triggers that caused civil war to break out when it did, while the precipitants (what went wrong during the 1630s) explained why the situation had become so explosive. Nevertheless, longer-term factors—such as deep-seated religious divisions, the fiscal weakness of the crown, economic problems, and constitutional tensions—possessed for Stone some causal significance. Those who argue for short-term causes tend to take a stricter definition of what constitutes a cause and attach causal significance only to the triggers themselves, believing that the early Stuart monarchy, despite the many problems it faced, could have gone on indefinitely but for immediate, short-term events or developments which pushed it into the crisis out of which it was unable to extricate itself. According to this way of thinking, the precipitants and preconditions possess no causal significance. At most, they merely provide a longer-term context for understanding why developments were to pan out the way that they did. Yet they might, in fact, be red herrings. It is thus arguable that the supposed precipitants and preconditions have been misrepresented by advocates of longer-term explanations: that the deeper lying religious, economic, and constitutional tensions were not as serious as sometimes alleged, that the Caroline regime of the 1630s was not rushing precipitately into crisis but instead reforming itself out of one, and that there was a fundamental discontinuity between the developments that finally compelled Charles to recall parliament in 1640 and those which led to the outbreak of civil war in 1642—illustrated perhaps most poignantly by the fact that many of those who were to side with Charles in 1642 had in fact been critics of the personal rule and the Laudian reforms in the Church in the 1630s.

In sorting out where we stand over the issue of long-term versus short-term explanations, we have to be clear whether the disagreement is merely semantic or historically substantive. There is something to be said for adopting a strict definition of the term cause, at least if it can free us from semantic quibbles and allow us to concentrate on understanding what historically was actually going on. If pressed on what literally caused the English Civil War to break out when it did, I would reply Charles I's decision to raise his standard of Nottingham in August 1642—though this hardly gets us very far, and goes no way towards explaining why the crisis had come to exist in the first place. Nothing is inevitable until it happens, and it is possible to imagine all sorts of ways in which it might still have proved possible to avoid the crisis developing into a civil war, even very late in the day. What if Charles had won the battle of Newburn in 1640?

What if he had not jeopardized some of the goodwill that was beginning to build for him in the latter part of 1641 by the actions he took in December 1641 and early January 1642? What, for that matter, if he had not fled his capital in January 1642 but instead decided to stay in Westminster and continue to work for a viable solution? It might have been that in the early months of 1642 two sides had come to be formed both of which were preparing for war. But it is certainly plausible (albeit highly unlikely in this particular case) that if the king had announced in the summer of 1642, 'OK, this is not worth fighting for; let us get back to the table', civil war could have been avoided.

There can be a certain value to the counterfactual game. It can be a way of trying to test the significance of any given historical development or occurrence, a way—to return to our earlier analogy—of establishing whether metal fatigue or individual error is to blame. Yet in truth we have no way of establishing how things might have worked out had certain things been different. The simple fact of the matter is that Charles did lose the battle of Newburn; he did make an attempt on the five members; he did flee the capital; he did not opt for a last-minute compromise. The historian's task is to explain why, given what did actually transpire, things developed in the way that they did; why particular events, however 'accidental', should have had the ramifications they did. Such an enterprise involves searching for the appropriate contexts (some of them deep-lying) in which to set the historical developments we are interested in explaining. It may be that something happened because one individual made a mistake—a personal blunder that could easily have been avoided. But why making that mistake had the consequences it did is still something that has to be explained, historically and contextually. It is these historical contexts that I have endeavoured to lay out in this book.

What can be said, with confidence, then, about why the Civil War broke out in 1642, and how far back do we need to go in seeking the appropriate contexts? Most would agree that the English were not looking to orchestrate a revolution, that they were not conspiring long in advance fundamentally to restructure the political set-up in England: they believed not only in monarchy but in divine-right monarchy, and even that the king's authority was absolute, albeit at the same time limited by law. With regard to ecclesiastical affairs, where tensions clearly ran deep, most critics of the Church wanted to reform it rather than re-model it; English Presbyterianism was weak in the early seventeenth century, separatists few and far between, and it was not until reasonably late in the day that Puritan reformers were won over to the necessity of root and branch reform. The demands of the parliamentary opponents of King Charles certainly escalated over the course of 1641—so much so that Charles came to feel (legitimately, one might suggest, from his own perspective) that they were trying to reduce him to a doge of Venice and thus effectively turn England into a republic. Nevertheless, they were still hoping to achieve their objectives peacefully, by reform. They were not conspiring to bring down the monarchy by force (albeit there is some evidence to suggest that some opponents of the crown might have been conspiring with the Scots in 1640 to bring an end to the personal rule by force). Moreover, when outlining their grievances—for example, as in the Grand Remonstrance of 1 December 1641—they tended to focus on developments that had happened under Charles. They did not go back to problems that had existed under James.

However, the case is different for Scotland and Ireland. In both of these kingdoms there were significant interests who were bitterly upset with developments under James and Charles, with the early Stuart polity itself (in both Church and state), and who desired fundamental change. The Scottish Presbyterians were unhappy about developments in the Kirk—the revival of episcopacy, the intrusion of ceremonies, the Five Articles of Perth, the Canons, and the prayer book—and they felt that the freedoms of the General Assemblies and parliaments were being interfered with. In short, whereas (the vast majority of) English critics of the early Stuarts accepted the legitimacy of the system and merely wanted reform, Scottish critics did not accept that the system which the early Stuarts were putting into place was legitimate: they wanted a different system, albeit the one which had previously existed rather than something entirely new. Ireland was being newly modelled by the English state following first the final conquest of the island with the suppression of Tyrone's rebellion in 1603 and then the Flight of the Earls in 1607 and the escheatment to the crown of much of Ulster after O'Doherty's rebellion in 1608. The Catholics in Ireland resented the policy of plantation, their increasing economic and political marginalization, and the disabilities placed on them on account of their religion. It is true that for a long time many Catholics endeavoured to make the best of a bad situation, and were prepared to make certain accommodations to the regime just so that they could live their lives as well as might prove possible. Yet this should not fool us into believing they accepted the legitimacy of the regime; many of them clearly never did. Ultimately both the Scots and the Irish were to have recourse to armed rebellion in an effort to secure redress of their grievances. Both the Scottish Covenanters and Irish insurgents made it clear in their pronounce-ments that their grievances went back to the reign of James VI and I, and did not just derive from Charles I's reign. The Scots, in victory, went on to conclude a revolution in Church and the state. The Irish certainly wanted a revolution, namely the undoing of the English plantation.

It is arguable, then, that for England—albeit only for England—we need to look only to the short term to explain why civil war broke out. Yet even this is not true if our goal is to explain—as it surely must be—why things went wrong: that is, how it came to be that the Stuart monarchy got itself into a crisis out of which it could not extri-cate itself without having recourse to arms. The search for the origins of the Civil War cannot be divorced from an account of the origins of the crisis that had emerged by 1640: without that crisis, civil war would never have happened, even though one might concede that it was not inevitable that civil war would be the outcome of that crisis.

It has been suggested that England would not have succumbed to civil war and revolution but for the prior revolts in Scotland and Ire-land: that there was not enough combustible material in England to ignite civil war, and that it took the interventions of first the Scots and then the Irish and the divisions these created to inject enough heat into English society for it to explode.[13] By such logic, one might even suggest that the Caroline regime in England was brought down by contingent and external factors, not by developments within Eng-land itself. There can be no denying that it was the Covenanter rebel-lion in Scotland which ultimately brought to an end the personal rule in England and forced Charles to deal with his English parliament. And it was the dispute over who was to control the army needed to put down the Irish rebellion that caused the controversy over the militia in England which was ultimately to push two sides into war.

However, we cannot regard the revolts in Scotland and Ireland as external events in quite the same way, say, as the Bohemian revolt of 1618, which caused so many problems for James in his final years. Rather, the Scottish and Irish crises emerged as a direct result of the policies pursued by two monarchs who ruled over three kingdoms and who wanted to bring these kingdoms into closer line with each other. Both James and Charles pursued the objective of making Ire-land British (or maybe just more English). Both James and Charles had a policy of trying to bring the Churches of England and Scotland

(and ultimately Ireland) into closer congruity with each—or, as their Scottish critics saw it, they wanted to Anglicize the Scottish Kirk. Either way, what happened in Scotland and Ireland was the result of policy initiatives pursued by successive kings who ruled three kingdoms and who were pursuing a Britannic vision. The revolts in Scotland and Ireland were external only in the literal geographical sense that they occurred outside England. Politically, they were very much internal to the Stuart polity.

Furthermore, the reason why the English government was unable to put down the Scottish rebellion was because things were already going badly wrong in England. The English regime was fragile, and the reasons for its fragility had deep roots. England's failure to defeat the Scots, in other words, requires an English explanation. It is an explanation that in turn highlights not only the failings of the personal rule but also longer-term, underlying weaknesses of the early Stuart monarchy in England. Likewise, why did an uprising by hated Catholics in Ireland (hated by the English both because they were Catholic and because they were Irish) end up dividing the English rather than unifying them? Why did it not propel them to put their differences to one side and instead rally against the foreign, Catholic, hostile 'other'? The explanation, as this book has made clear, has to be sought in England.[14]

Our task, in short, has to be to explain why this polity, why this multiple monarchy, ultimately did not prove robust enough to withstand the various crises that it faced in the early seventeenth century. In turn we have to trace both the roots of those crises and what it was that caused the Stuart polity to be so fragile that it succumbed to the crises it faced—or, alternatively, why the crises were so severe that even a polity that was not particularly fragile could succumb to them. The search for explanation takes us back into the reign of James VI and I, back even into the sixteenth century.

Of course, James survived whereas Charles did not. Although not everything was smooth sailing for James, he did not face a major rebellion in any one of his kingdoms (O'Doherty's revolt of 1608 was a minor affair) and he was to die peacefully in his bed (albeit not that peacefully, given the terrible 'dysentery' he suffered in his final days). By contrast, all three kingdoms were to rebel in turn against Charles, who was eventually to meet a premature demise, executed by his own subjects for committing treason against them! Does not the fact that James managed to get by show that this multiple monarchy, however problematic, was ultimately manageable? If things subsequently went disastrously wrong under Charles, should Charles himself not bear much of the responsibility? Historians have often pointed to certain character flaws that supposedly made Charles unsuited to managing what was undoubtedly a very challenging multiple-kingdom inheritance. Some would even suggest that Charles was politically inept, although such a characterization has been forthrightly challenged in recent years.[15] Yet everyone has certain flaws and limitations; James certainly did as well. The fact that things went wrong under Charles can lead us to assume that it was Charles's particular personality traits and style of rule that created the problems, whereas James's peculiar foibles and weaknesses were not so politically damaging. At one level, there is a basic truism in this observation. Charles was the man in charge after 1625, and ultimately he proved not to be up to the job. It may be that the problems facing the regime after 1625 were much more intense than they had been before, that a better man than Charles would still have got into serious trouble, or that in other contexts Charles's personality and style could have been seen as signs of strength and proved politically successful, although that does not really affect the basic truism: given the circumstances he was facing, history proves that Charles was not the man who could stop the three Stuart kingdoms plunging into crisis. Yet this is not quite the same as saying that the failings of the Stuart monarchy were personal. Rulers who are not particularly able can be quite successful in certain circumstances; those who are more able can also fail in certain circumstances. Ultimately we come back to needing to understand the contexts which enabled a given ruler, with his particular strengths and limitations, to fare in the particular way that he did. In short, we have to look at what was going on in society more broadly— politically, religiously, economically, culturally. These are the developments and processes we must explore, and they are *processes*, so they have a history, and take us back in time. Focusing on the personality of the man in charge is important, but only one part of the story.

Charles clearly did a number of things that turned out not to produce the result he was hoping for, but does that necessarily mean that it was the wrong decision to try what he did in the first place? This opens up the counterfactual can of worms again and could lead to never-ending speculation and disagreement. Was Charles wrong to go to war with the Scots in 1639? What was he supposed to do, as a divinely ordained monarch, when faced with a rebellion from some of his subjects in one of his kingdoms? Was he wrong to go to war, on the first occasion, without calling parliament? With the vantage of hindsight it might seem that he would have been better off trying to negotiate. Yet why should he have negotiated if there was the chance of nipping the rebellion in the bud and reasserting royal authority? Maybe Charles did not understand the seriousness of the situation facing him in Scotland in 1638–9; perhaps he failed to assess the situation accurately and for that reason did not address the problem in the way that was most likely to produce a successful outcome. Yet if that was the case, Charles himself was not necessarily to blame; clearly his advisors in Scotland were not giving him all the information he needed. What historians need to do is understand why Charles chose to fight the Scots; why it seemed to him the right decision to make; why he was unable to defeat the Scots; and why his failure to defeat the Scots had the ramifications it did. It does not get us very far to accuse him of making a stupid decision in the first place.

There were certainly some things that Charles did which from the vantage of hindsight we might struggle to understand. Why, for example, did he stick by Buckingham for so long, especially given that the wisdom of the age was that if anything ever went wrong, a king should let his ministers take the blame. We might also wonder why, when parliament pleaded so forcefully in 1628 that Charles should rid himself of Laud, Neile, and a number of other Arminian clergymen, Charles chose to respond by promoting these very clerics at the earliest opportunity. Yet sacrificing ministers does not always help. Charles sacrificed Wentworth in 1641, but was that the right thing to do? Even when Buckingham was removed by the hand of an assassin it did little to ease the unfolding political crisis. Charles's obligation to God as a divinely ordained monarch was to promote the true religion, and thus put his Church in the hands of men who he felt would promote the true religion, not appoint men MPs wanted. Again we need to understand the nature of the underlying political and religious problems which meant that there ended up being so much contention about what Buckingham, Wentworth, or Laud and Neile were up to. It becomes a story about government finance, the ability to fight a war with Spain and then France, and how that war was run; about political and religious reform in Ireland, how the Irish government should be funded, the extent to which the policy of plantation should be continued, and whether the Irish Confession of Faith should be changed; and what sort of ecclesiastical reforms should be introduced in England (and Scotland and Ireland), how political and religious dissidents should be kept in check, through prerogative courts such as Star Chamber and High Commission, how government might be funded through expedients such as monopolies or ship money.

This study has sought to dispel some of the cruder stereotypes regarding Charles's supposed lack of political competence or the incompetence of his regime. Whatever his personal limitations, Charles had able people working for him. There might be cause for questioning Buckingham's abilities, but Laud and Wentworth were highly able, as were many others who served the government in various capacities—as ministers, privy councillors, administrators, judges, ecclesiastical officials. The Caroline regime got things done; indeed, one of the reasons why it managed to upset so many people was because it was quite effective in getting its policies implemented. The older view that this regime was naïve about PR, that it not only did not know how to appeal to the public sphere but did not even appreciate the need to do so, is seriously misleading. The Caroline regime showed itself to be quite sophisticated in its approach to the politics of spin. Ultimately the regime proved unable to keep public opinion on its side during the 1630s, but this was not because it did not appreciate the need to try to do so. It was because the policies it was pursuing proved too unpopular—and, once more, understanding why they were not better received involves us exploring deeper social, economic, religious, and political contexts.

If we have to revise our opinion about the inadequacies of Charles I, we are likewise forced to rethink some of our assumptions about James VI and I. The trend in recent historiography has been to paint a relatively positive picture of James, itself a much-needed corrective to an earlier view that had been unduly negative. Modern-day scholars tend to see James as an 'energetic, vigorous, intelligent and flexible' king and a shrewd politician.[16] There is much truth to this, to be sure. Yet James did make mistakes. He could bumble into confrontations and create crises when there did not necessarily seem to be ones brewing—from the disputed Buckinghamshire election and the Apology of 1604 through to the Protestation of 1621. He was indeed a powerful orator and a very clever man—a philosopher king—but he could inflame things by his own overdrawn rhetoric, as we have seen on a number of occasions in his dealings with parliament. Undoubtedly at times he could show himself to be brilliant as a political operator. Take, for example, the way he induced the Scots to accept bishops and ceremonies, working all the while through General Assemblies and parliament (albeit that there was considerable royal manipulation and intimidation), even exploiting the Scots' fears about the threat of popery in an effort to outmanoeuvre those who might seek to create difficulties. In the end he could claim that he did nothing in Scotland that did not have the support of the appropriate Scottish deliberative assemblies. Yet if we can admire the tactical acumen, we might question the strategy. James's ecclesiastical reforms in Scotland did not solve any of the underlying problems. They did, however, create huge resentments, the ramifications of which were to be felt by his son.

Indeed we might wonder whether, for all the initiatives he pursued, James managed to develop a satisfactory solution to any of the problems he faced at his accession. In some respects, the ways in which he chose to address these problems made them worse. This is surely true with regard to his dealings not just with Scotland but also with Ireland, where the policy of plantation was to be the cause of the violent upheaval that was to occur in 1641, a policy that was seen by English Protestants during James's reign as likely to provoke a rebellion that would be more dangerous to the state than any that had preceded it, and which was even recognized by the regime in England to be failing.[17] Yet it is also arguably true for England. To what extent did James manage to ease the religious tensions that he had inherited? Was the Church more or less harmonious towards the end of his reign than it had been at the beginning? Were relations with parliament smoother or frostier? Certainly, in terms of the goals James set himself one could argue that James failed on virtually all accounts: he failed to achieve his much-desired union between England and Scotland, he failed to put the monarchy on a firmer financial footing, he failed to heal his kingdoms' religious divisions, and he failed in his foreign policy ambition to be the peacemaker of Europe. The flaws in his strategy for managing his inheritance—so dependent as it was upon keeping England out of war, so as to avoid undue pressure on royal finances and to sustain a delicate balancing act in the Church— were clearly exposed by the outbreak of the Thirty Years War on the Continent in 1618.

We should also question the assumption that there was a fundamental discontinuity in policy between the reigns of James and Charles. In many respects, Charles saw himself as continuing policies that had been begun by his father. Once more, this is most obviously true with regard to Scotland (bringing the Kirk into greater conformity with the Church in England) and Ireland (Anglicization through plantation). Yet it was also true with regard to reform of the Church in England. It was James who advised the need to take heed of the

Puritans and to preserve against their poison. It was James who first began to introduce Arminians into positions of authority in the Church, with the tide seemingly tipping decidedly in their favour by the early 1620s. In continuing and bringing to fruition what he thought were his father's policies, Charles inevitably went further than his father had done and did things that James might never have done. The discontinuities as well as the continuities need to be acknowledged. Yet it is impossible to understand Charles without recognizing that to a large extent his strategy for managing his multiple-kingdom inheritance was a logical extension of his father's. Again, this highlights yet another longer-term context that needs to be explored if we are to understand why things were eventually to go wrong under Charles. It is not the same thing, however, as alleging that James somehow *caused* the English Civil War by the policies he pursued.

We have noted already James's tactical acumen. It has also been said that although the early James was not a particularly good politician, he improved with time.[18] He learned from his mistakes. Perhaps above all, he knew or learned how to back down graciously, rather than force the issue when things were not going his way: note here how he backed away from his plan to introduce a new confession of faith into Scotland in 1616, or his concessions to his 1624 parliament, once his hand had been forced and war with Spain had become inevitable. By contrast, Charles, it has been claimed, was less tactically astute. He saw no need to obtain the approval of the Scottish General Assembly or the Scottish parliament to his canons of 1636 or his prayer book of 1637. In the face of criticism, he tended to bristle rather than back down; he would chastise his critics, even threaten them—note his reactions to criticism from parliament in 1626, 1628, and 1629. Yet we should caution against allowing this contrast to be too starkly drawn. Although the 1624 parliament opened with James making gracious rhetorical concessions, tensions had flared up once again by the end of the session when we find James berating MPs for violating the royal supremacy by meddling with Church matters. Against this we might point to the brilliant way in which Charles was able to rebuild royalism in late 1641 and early 1642—or at least how those whom Charles allowed to speak for him were able to do so (Charles, as we have seen, was still at this time doing things that undermined his own cause)—subtly recasting what the monarchy stood for, retreating rhetorically from earlier positions the crown had identified with, even admitting to past mistakes, and emphasizing the very real concessions that the crown had indeed made, in order to try to regain the ideological initiative and to rally support for the crown against its parliamentary and Puritan opponents. Charles arguably also became a more skilled politician with time. Ironically, it was the very skill with which he—and those who now advised him—were able to forge a royalist party in 1641–2 which explains why it became possible for him to fight a civil war.[19]

The fact that a royalist party, in this sense, emerged quite late in England, is normally taken as evidence in support of a short-term explanation of the origins of the English Civil War. After all, it takes two sides to fight a civil war, and when the Long Parliament was called in November 1640 there were not yet two sides: those two sides only began to coalesce in late 1641 and early 1642.[20] On the face of it, the logic seems compelling. Yet once again matters are more complicated than they might seem at first glance. It is arguable that most of those who came to side with parliament against Charles were radicalized as a result of the Long Parliament's investigations into the state of the Church: that in the process they came to see the need for root and branch reform (the abolition of episcopacy) and adopted a position which they could not have imagined themselves adopting prior to 1641. Yet it is impossible to understand where royalism came from at this time without appreciating that it sought to appeal to, and build upon, a deeply embedded hostility towards Puritans that already existed in this society (albeit not universally shared), a hostility that had deep roots and which can be traced back to the late Elizabethan and early Jacobean periods. If this latent anti-Puritanism had not already existed in English society, then royalism could not have been forged in the way that it was. Thus understanding how the ideology of anti-Puritanism came to be constructed and embraced, by certain sections of society, in the late sixteenth and early seventeenth centuries, becomes a crucial long-term cultural context for explaining the origins of the English Civil War; yet no one would ever suggest that late Elizabethan or early Jacobean anti-Puritanism *caused* the English Civil War. We could make a similar argument concerning the fear of popery that was such a powerful motivating ideological force for those who chose to side with parliament in the build up to civil war. Once more we see why searching only for the immediate causes of a major cataclysmic event such as the English Civil War does not take us as far as we need to go. In order to understand fully why things happened in the way that they did, we need to explain so much more than the immediate causes. We have to explore the longer-term political, religious, social, economic, and cultural contexts which, even if they do not possess strong *causal* significance, certainly possess great *explanatory* significance.

This mention of anti-Puritanism and anti-popery inevitably invites us to reflect on perhaps the greatest old chestnuts of them all, namely whether or not the English Civil War was a war of religion.[21] The account offered here has certainly highlighted the vital importance of religion and religious factors as sources of tension and causes of conflict in England, Scotland, and Ireland throughout this time period. There is a crucial sense in which the rebellions that were to occur successively in Scotland, Ireland, and then England and which were to bring down the early Stuart monarchy were about religion, and that it was how people defined themselves in terms of their ecclesiastical politics which largely determined what sides they took. Thus in Scotland in 1638–40 the divide was between Scottish Presbyterians and those who wanted to maintain episcopacy in Scotland; in Ireland in 1641 the fundamental cleavage was between Catholics and Protestants; in England in 1642 the split was between those who wanted further reform in the Church after Laudianism had been undone and those who wanted to uphold a Church of bishops and prayer book that had now been stripped of the excesses of Laudianism.

While acknowledging the centrality of religion, however, we also need to appreciate that the troubles in England, Scotland, and Ireland were about more than purely religion. There has been a tendency in the historiography to invoke the war of religion interpretation in order to downplay the significance of other types of grievances, the implication being that there was a broad agreement over the constitution, and so if people fell out it was largely about the Church. Such a view is misleading. As this study has shown, there were major political and constitutional sources of conflict, under both James and Charles—about impositions, about the role of parliament, about ship money, about the use of prerogative courts such as Star Chamber and High Commission, about how ministers of the crown might be held accountable for their actions. In the end king and parliament were to go to war over whether or not parliament could control the militia or the appointment of ministers under the crown, matters which had nothing to do with religion. Even disputes over the Church were not necessarily purely about religion: parliamentary critics of episcopacy disliked bishops for their political tyranny as much as for their teachings about how to attain salvation; supporters of Charles I in 1641–2 defended bishops as bulwarks of the social order against the disorders of the sects.

Likewise the troubles in Scotland and Ireland were about more than just religion: in Scotland the nobility were alienated by how both James and Charles sought to subvert the independence of the Scottish parliament, by Charles's Revocation scheme of 1625, by the conviction of Lord Balmerino of treason in 1633. In Ireland resentments relating to the English plantation and to the failure to enact the Graces (especially the provision concerning the security of land ownership) were of paramount importance.

Great upheavals in the past have complex origins. I realize there is the risk of disappointing the reader by not reaching a definitive conclusion as to why civil war broke out in 1642, who was to blame, or whether it had long-term or short-term causes. What this study has sought to do is highlight the deep-rootedness and intractable nature of many of the problems that the early Stuart multiple-monarchy faced. It has shown the interconnectedness of many of these problems, both within the kingdoms (religion, finances, foreign policy, the relations between crown and parliament) and between the kingdoms. Rather than trying to draw up a balance sheet of relative success or failure for either James or Charles, it has sought to explore how these two monarchs attempted to govern their three kingdoms, why they chose to address their problems in the way that they did, and how their policy initiatives could serve to bring latent tensions and antagonisms to the fore. It has tried to understand things from their perspective. It has also endeavoured to understand the fears, concerns, aspirations, and anxieties of the peoples over which they ruled. It has been the story of a polity that ended up going seriously wrong, a multiple monarchy that came to be constructed in the aftermath of rebellions in Scotland and Ireland and which was eventually to be brought down by rebellions in all three of the kingdoms—rebellions which in turn were to lead to Britain's great revolution of the mid-seventeenth century.

Acts & Proc. Gen. Ass.	*Acts and Proceedings of the General Assemblies of the Kirk of Scotland, 1560–1618* (Maitland Club, Edinburgh, 1839–45)
Acts. Gen. Ass.	*Acts of the General Assembly of the Church of Scotland 1638–1842* (Church Law Society, Edinburgh, 1843)
AgHR	*Agricultural History Review*
Bacon, *Letters and Life*	*The Letters and the Life of Francis Bacon*, ed. James Spedding (7 vols, 1861–74)
Balfour, *Historical Works*	*Historical Works of Sir James Balfour*, ed. J. Haig, 4 vols (Edinburgh, 1825)
BIHR	*Bulletin of the Institute of Historical Research*
Bodl. Lib.	Bodleian Library, Oxford
Calderwood, *True History*	David Calderwood, *The True History of the Church of Scotland From the Beginning of the Reformation Unto the End of the Reign of King James VIth* (1680)
Chamberlain, *Letters*	*The Letters of John Chamberlain*, ed. Norman E. McClure (Philadelphia, 1939)
CJ	*Journal of the House of Commons*
CJ, Ire	*The Journals of the House of Commons of the Kingdom of Ireland* (19 vols, Dublin, 1795–1800)
Clarendon, *History*	Edward Hyde, Earl of Clarendon, *The History of the Rebellion and the Civil Wars in England*, ed. W. Dunn Macray (6 vols, Oxford, 1888)
Commons Debates 1621	*Commons Debates, 1621*, ed. Wallace Notestein, Frances Helen Relf, and Hartley Simpson (7 vols, New Haven, 1935)
Commons Debates 1629	*Commons Debates for 1629*, ed. Wallace Notestein and Frances Helen Relf (Minneapolis, 1921)
CSPD	*Calendar of State Papers, Domestic*
CSPIre	*Calendar of State Papers, Ireland*
CSPVen	*Calendar of State Papers, Venetian*
CUL	Cambridge University Library
Des. Cur. Hib.	*Desiderata Curiosa Hibernica*, compiled by John Lodge (2 vols, Dublin, 1772)

D'Ewes, *Autobiography*	*The Autobiography and Correspondence of Sir Simonds D'Ewes*, ed. James Orchard Halliwell (2 vols, 1845)
'Early Stuart Libels'	'Early Stuart Libels: an Edition of Poetry from Manuscript Sources', ed. Alastair Bellany and Andrew McRae, *Early Modern Literary Studies* Text Series I (2005)
EcHR	*Economic History Review*
EHR	*English Historical Review*
FSL	Folger Shakespeare Library
HJ	*Historical Journal*
HLQ	*Huntington Library Quarterly*
HMC	Historical Manuscripts Commission
House of Commons, 1604–29	*The House of Commons, 1604–1629*, ed. Andrew Thrush (Cambridge, 2010)
HR	*Historical Research*
IHS	*Irish Historical Studies*
JBS	*Journal of British Studies*
JEH	*Journal of Ecclesiastical History*
JMH	*Journal of Modern History*
Larkin and Hughes	James F. Larkin and Paul L. Hughes, eds, *Stuart Royal Proclamations* (2 vols, Oxford, 1973, 1983)
Laud, *Works*	*The Works of the Most Reverent Father in God, William Laud, D.D.*, ed. William Scott and James Bliss (7 vols, Oxford, 1847–60)
LJ	*Journal of the House of Lords*
NHI, III	T. W. Moody, F. X. Martin, and F. J. Byrne, eds, *A New History of Ireland. III: Early Modern Ireland 1534–1691* (3rd impression, 1991)
Nichols, *Progresses*	John Nichols, *The Progresses, Processions, and Magnificent Festivities, of King James the First* (4 vols, 1828)
NLI	National Library of Ireland
ODNB	*Oxford Dictionary of National Biography* (Oxford, 2004)
P&P	*Past and Present*
Parl. Deb. 1610	*Parliamentary Debates in 1610*, ed. S. R. Gardiner (Camden Society, 81, 1862)
Parl. Hist.	*The Parliamentary History of England from the Earliest Period to the Year 1803*, ed. William Cobbett (36 vols, 1806–20)
Proceedings 1610	*Proceedings in Parliament, 1610*, ed. Elizabeth Read Foster (2 vols, New Haven, 1966)

Proceedings 1614	*Proceedings in Parliament 1614 (House of Commons)*, ed. Maija Jansson (Memoirs of the American Philosophical Society, 172, Philadelphia, 1988)
Proceedings 1625	*Proceedings in Parliament 1625*, ed. Maija Jansson and William B. Bidwell (New Haven, 1987)
Proceedings 1626	*Proceedings in Parliament 1626*, ed. William B. Bidwell and Maija Jansson (4 vols, New Haven, 1991–6)
Proceedings 1628	*Commons Debates, 1628*, ed. Robert C. Johnson, Mary Frear Keeler, Maija Jansson Cole, and William B. Bidwell (6 vols, New Haven, 1977–83), volumes 5 and 6 also have title *Proceedings in Parliament, 1628*
Proceedings LP	*Proceedings of the Opening Session of the Long Parliament, House of Commons*, ed. Maija Jansson (7 vols, Woodbridge, 2000–7)
Proceedings SP	*Proceedings of the Short Parliament of 1640*, ed. Esther S. Cope and Willson H. Coates (Camden Society, 4th ser., 19, 1977)
Row, *History*	John Row, *The History of the Kirk of Scotland from the Year 1558 to August 1637*, ed. D. Laing (Edinburgh, 1842)
RPCS	*Register of the Privy Council of Scotland*
RPS	*The Records of the Parliaments of Scotland,* ed. K. M. Brown et al. (St Andrews, 2007–13)
Rushworth	John Rushworth, *Historical Collections* (8 vols, 1721–2)
Russell, *FBM*	Conrad Russell, *The Fall of the British Monarchies* (Oxford, 1991)
Scot, *Apol. Narr.*	William Scot, *An Apologetical Narration of the State and Government of the Kirk of Scotland since the Reformation*, ed. D. Laing (Edinburgh, 1846)
SHR	*Scottish Historical Review*
SP	State Papers
Spottiswoode, *History*	John Spottiswoode, *The History of the Church and State of Scotland* (4th edn, 1677)
SR	*The Statutes of the Realm*, ed. A. Luders, T. E. Tomlins, and J. France (12 vols, 1810–28)
ST	*State Trials*, ed. T. B. Howell (33 vols, 1809–26)
Steele	Robert Steele, *A Bibliography of Royal Proclamations of the Tudor and Stuart Sovereigns and of others Published under Authority 1485–1714* (3 vols in 2, New York, 1967)

Strafford Letters	*The Earl of Strafford's Letters and Despatches*, ed. William Knowler (2 vols, 1739)
TCD	Trinity College Dublin
TNA	The National Archives
TRHS	*Transactions of the Royal Historical Society*
Winwood, *Memorials*	Sir Ralph Winwood, *Memorials of Affairs of State in the Reigns of Q. Elizabeth and K. James I*, ed. Edmund Sawyer (3 vols, 1725)
Woodford's Diary	Robert Woodford's Diary, New College Oxford MS 9502, now published as *The Diary of Robert Woodford, 1637–1641*, ed. John Fielding (Camden Society, 5th ser., 42, 2013)

NOTES

Place of publication is London unless otherwise stated.

PROLOGUE

1. *Correspondence of King James VI of Scotland with Sir Robert Cecil and Others in England*, ed. John Bruce (Camden Society, 78, 1861), 31–2.
2. Conrad Russell, 'James VI and I and Rule over Two Kingdoms: An English View', *HR*, 76 (2003), 152.
3. Godfrey Goodman, *The Court of King James the First*, ed. John S. Brewer (2 vols, 1839), I, 96–7.
4. R. Doleman [i.e. Robert Persons], *A Conference about the Next Succession* ([Antwerp], 1594[/5]), Second Part, 258.
5. *The Autobiography and Diary of Mr James Melvill*, ed. Robert Pitcairn (Edinburgh, 1842), 554.
6. Steve Hindle, *The State and Social Change in Early Modern England, c. 1550–1640* (Basingstoke, 2000), ch. 5; John Walter, 'A "Rising of the People": The Oxfordshire Rising of 1596', *P&P*, 107 (1985), 90–143.
7. Derek Hirst, *The Representative of the People?* (Cambridge, 1975). For parliament's place in the political culture of early Stuart England, see Chris R. Kyle, *Theater of State* (Stanford, 2012).
8. Laurence Ginnell, *The Doubtful Grant of Ireland by Pope Adrian IV* (Dublin, 1899), 14–15.
9. Philip O'Sullivan Beare, 'Briefe Relation of Ireland, c. 1618', TCD MS 580, fols. 95–8. For the degeneration of the Old English, see Sir John Davies, *Historical Relations* (3rd edn, 1666), 137–8, 164–5, 242.
10. Steven G. Ellis, *Ireland in the Age of the Tudors 1447–1603* (1998); Colm Lennon, *Sixteenth-Century Ireland* (Dublin, 1994); Hiram Morgan, *Tyrone's Rebellion* (Woodbridge, 1993).
11. Alan R. MacDonald, 'Deliberative Processes in Parliament c. 1567–1639: Multicameralism and the Lords of the Articles', *SHR*, 81 (2002), 23–51. For the Scottish parliament, see Keith M. Brown and Alastair J. Mann, eds, *Parliament and Politics in Scotland, 1567–1707* (Edinburgh, 2005).
12. Diarmaid MacCulloch, *The Reformation* (2004).
13. Geoffrey Parker, *The Military Revolution* (2nd edn, Cambridge, 1998).
14. Mark Nicholls, *A History of the Modern British Isles 1529–1603: The Two Kingdoms* (Oxford, 1999), 273.
15. Here I follow the figures given in Ian Gentles, *The English Revolution and the Wars of the Three Kingdoms 1638–1652* (Harlow, 2007), 436–7, 439–40. See also: Michael J. Braddick, *God's Fury, England's Fire* (2008), 363, 389–90, 393, 395; Charles Carlton, *Going to the Wars* (1992), 204, 210–11, 214.
16. Tim Harris, 'Did the English have a Script for Revolution in the Seventeenth Century', in Dan Edelstein and Keith Baker, eds, *Scripting Revolutions* (forthcoming).

CHAPTER 1. 'HOW TO REIGNE WELL'

1. Bodl. Lib., MS Eng. hist. *c.* 712, p. 564.
2. Paul D. Halliday, 'Whitley, Roger (1618–1697)', *ODNB*.
3. See, in particular, Glenn Burgess, *The Politics of the Ancient Constitution* (Basingstoke, 1992); Glenn Burgess, *Absolute Monarchy and the Stuart Constitution* (New Haven, 1996).
4. Johann P. Sommerville, *Royalists and Patriots* (1999); Richard Cust and Ann Hughes, eds, *Conflict in Early Stuart England* (1989); Thomas Cogswell, Richard Cust, and Peter Lake, eds, *Politics, Religion and Popularity in Early Stuart Britain* (Cambridge, 2002).
5. James VI and I, *The Trew Law of Free Monarchies*, in Johann P. Sommerville, ed., *King James VI and I: Political Writings* (Cambridge, 1994), 62–84.
6. James I, *The Kings Majesties Speech…the XXI of March. Anno Dom. 1609* [1610], sigs A4v, B.
7. Peter Marshall, *Reformation England, 1480–1642* (2003), 23; 24 Hen. VIII, *c.* 12: *SR*, III, 427.
8. David Owen, *Herod and Pilate Reconciled* ([Cambridge], 1610), 1.
9. *Proceedings 1614,* 27.
10. [Thomas Scott], *Vox Regis* ([Utrecht], [1624]), sig. [(] 2, p. 73.
11. R[obert] P[ricket], *The Lord Coke His Speech and Charge* (1607), sig. C1v. Cf. *Commons Debates 1628*, III, 272, speech of 6 May 1628: 'He is God's lieutenant'.
12. [Alexander Henderson], *Some Special Arguments for the Scottish Subjects Lawfull Defence of their Religion and Liberty* (Amsterdam, 1642), 3. The work originally circulated in manuscript in 1639 under the title 'Instructions for Defensive Arms'.
13. *Proceedings and Debates of the House of Commons, in 1620 and 1621* (2 vols, Oxford, 1766), II, 238.
14. [Richard Mocket], *God and the King* (1615), 37–8. For the rival purposes to which Bracton could be put in the seventeenth century, see Michael J. Sechler and Janelle Greenberg, '"There is Scarce a Pamphlet that Doth not Triumph in Bracton": The Role of *De Legibus et Consuetudinibus Angliae* in Stuart Political Thought', *History of Political Thought*, 33 (2012), 25–54.
15. Thomas Scott, *The High-waies of God and the King* ([Amsterdam?], 1623), 67–8, 69.
16. William Lamont, *Godly Rule* (1969); Richard Cust and Peter Lake, 'Sir Richard Grosvenor and the Rhetoric of Magistracy', *BIHR*, 54 (1981), 42–3.
17. Pauline Croft, *King James* (Basingstoke, 2003), 21; *A Defence of the Honorable Sentence* (1587), sig. F3v.
18. Corinne Comstock Weston and Janelle Greenberg, *Subjects and Sovereigns* (Cambridge, 1981).
19. E. N[isbet], *Caesar's Dialogue* (1601), 3–4.
20. FSL, Z.e.28, fol. 101v.
21. *Certaine Sermons Or Homilies* (1623), 74.
22. Richard Crompton, *A Short Declaration of the Ende of Traytors* (1587[/8]), sig. D4v.
23. [John Maxwell], *Sacro-Sancta Regum Majestas* (1644), 140.
24. Thomas Scot, *Christs Politician and Salomons Puritan, in Two Sermons* (1616), *Salomons Puritan*, 7.

25. William Laud, *A Sermon Preached before His Majestie, On Sunday the XIX of June at White-Hall* (1625), 30.
26. Roy C. Strong, *Tudor and Stuart Monarchy* (3 vols, Woodbridge, 1995–8), III, 194–5.
27. BL, MS Egerton 3376, fols. 13v–14.
28. James VI and I, *Trew Law*, 64–5.
29. James VI and I, *Basilicon Doron*, in Sommerville, ed., *Political Writings*, 20, 33.
30. James I, *Speech...XXI of March 1609*, sigs B3r–v.
31. Different versions of the speech survive. For the contemporary printed version, see: Elizabeth I, *Her Majesties Most Princelie Answere, Delivered...on the Last Day of November 1601* (1601), 4–5. For the version recorded in the Commons' Journal, see: Simonds D'Ewes, *The Journals of all the Parliaments during the Reign of Elizabeth* (1682), 659–60.
32. James VI and I, *Basilicon Doron*, 20; Goodman, *Court of King James*, I, 268; Peter Seaby and P. Frank Purvey, *Standard Catalogue of British Coins,* Volume 2: *Coins of Scotland, Ireland and the Islands* (1984), 58.
33. Charles I, *His Majesties Declaration...of the Causes which Moved Him to Dissolve the Last Parliament* (1640), 46–7.
34. Bodl. Lib., MS Eng. hist. *c.* 712, pp. 455, 562, 569.
35. John Guy, 'The "Imperial Crown" and the Liberty of the Subject: The English Constitution from Magna Carta to the Bill of Rights', in Bonnelyn Young Kunze and Dwight D. Brautigam, eds, *Court, Country and Culture: Essays on Early Modern British History in Honor of Perez Zagorin* (Woodbridge, 1992), 65–87 (esp. 66–7).
36. Sir John Davies, *Jus Imponendi Vectigalia* (1659), 31.
37. G. L. Harriss, 'Medieval Doctrines in the Debates on Supply, 1610–1629', in Kevin Sharpe, ed., *Faction and Parliament* (Oxford, 1978), 73–104.
38. Tim Harris, *Restoration: Charles II and his Kingdoms 1669–1685* (2005), 62–3.
39. *ST*, II, 389.
40. Bodl. Lib., MS Eng. hist. *c.* 712, p. 574.
41. *The Book of Oaths* (1689), 3.
42. Scot, *Christs Politician: Salomons Puritan*, 2, 3, 4–5.
43. James VI and I, *Basilicon Doron*, 43.
44. Laud, *Sermon...XIX of June*, 22.
45. James I, *Speech...XXI of March 1609*, sig. B3.
46. FSL, V.a.251, fol. 22v.
47. *The Diary of John Manningham*, ed. Robert Parker Sorlien (Hanover, NH, 1976), 36.
48. Sechler and Greenberg, 'There is Scarce a Pamphlet That Doth Not Triumph in Bracton', 26.
49. Guy, 'Imperial Crown', 70–1.
50. Guy, 'Imperial Crown', 68.
51. James VI and I, *Trew Law*, 73.
52. James I, *Speech...XXI of March 1609*, sig. B3v.
53. *Book of Oaths*, 2–3.
54. John Corbet, *The Ungirding of the Scottish Armour* (Dublin [i.e. London], 1639), 43–4.
55. *Diary of John Manningham*, 241.

56. *King James His Opinion* (1647), sig. Av.
57. James VI and I, *Trew Law*, 81.
58. Bacon, *Letters and Life*, VII, 358–9.
59. *Book of Oaths*, 6, 120–1; TCD MS 723, p. 60.
60. TCD MS 861, fols. 32v–33.
61. John Knox, *The First Blast of the Trumpet against the Monstrous Regiment of Women* (1558).
62. A. N. McLaren, *Political Culture in the Reign of Elizabeth I* (Cambridge, 1999); Patrick Collinson, 'The Monarchical Republic of Queen Elizabeth I', in his *Elizabethan Essays* (1994); John F. McDiarmid, ed., *The Monarchical Republic of Early Modern England* (Aldershot, 2007); Natalie Mears, *Queenship and Political Discourse in the Elizabethan Realms* (Cambridge, 2005); John Guy, 'The Rhetoric of Counsel in Early Modern England', in Dale Hoak, ed., *Tudor Political Culture* (Cambridge, 1995), 292–310; Guy, 'Tudor Monarchy and its Critiques', in Guy, ed., *The Tudor Monarchy* (1997), 78–109.
63. Alexander Leighton, *Speculum Belli Sacri* (1624), 106–7, 116.
64. Scott, *Vox Regis*, 30–1.
65. TCD MS 532, fols. 90r–v.
66. TCD MS 806, fol. 597.
67. TCD MS 731, fol. 195. For a general discussion of the theory of ministerial responsibility, see Clayton Roberts, *The Growth of Responsible Government in Stuart England* (Cambridge, 1966).
68. Conrad Russell, 'Parliamentary History in Perspective, 1604–1629', *History*, 61 (1976), 1–27. For an important corrective, see Thomas Cogswell, 'A Low Road to Extinction? Supply and Redress of Grievances in the Parliaments of the 1620s', *HJ*, 33 (1990), 283–303.
69. FSL, V.a.251, fol. 22–22v.
70. *House of Commons, 1604–29*, I, 39–40.
71. *Proceedings 1610*, I, 8.
72. J. G. A. Pocock, *The Ancient Constitution and the Feudal Law* (Cambridge, 1957); Pauline Croft, 'The Debate on Annual Parliaments in the Early Seventeenth Century', *Parliaments, Estates and Representation*, 16 (1996), 163–74; Colin G. C. Tite, *Impeachment and Parliamentary Judicature in Early Stuart England* (1974).
73. *Kings' Letters: From the Early Tudors: With the Letters of Henry VIII and Anne Boleyn*, ed. Robert Steele (1904), 220.
74. *CSPVen, 1625–6*, 513, 597.
75. Hirst, *Representative of the People?*, 104–5.
76. *Parl. Hist.*, I, 1176.
77. Bodl. Lib., MS Eng. hist. c. 712, p. 687.
78. John Aylmer, *An Harborowe for Faithfull and Trewe Subjectes* (1559), sig. H3; Sir Thomas Smith, *De Republica Anglorum*, ed. Mary Dewar (Cambridge, 1982), 78.
79. John Selden, *Jani Anglorum Facies Altera* (1610), reprinted in *Tracts Written by John Selden of the Inner-Temple* (1683), 94; John Selden, *Table Talk*, ed. Sir Frederick Pollock (Selden Society, 1927), 64.
80. This and the following paragraph are based on Tim Harris, *London Crowds in the Reign of Charles II* (Cambridge, 1987); Tim Harris, 'Was the Tory Reaction Popular?', *London Journal*, 13 (1988), 106–20; Mark Goldie, 'The Unacknowledged Republic', in Tim Harris, ed., *The Politics of the Excluded, c. 1500–1850* (Basingstoke, 2001), 153–94.

81. E. Anthony Wrigley, 'Urban Growth and Agricultural Change: England and the Continent in the Early Modern Period', *Journal of Interdisciplinary History*, 15 (1984–5), 700.
82. Quoted in Phil Withington, *The Politics of Commonwealth* (Cambridge, 2005), 58. My discussion here draws heavily on Withington, esp. chs 1–3.
83. Thomas Wilson, *The State of England, Anno Dom. 1600*, ed. F. J. Fisher, *Camden Miscellany*, 16 (Camden Society, 3rd ser., 52, 1936), 20.
84. Goldie, 'Unacknowledged Republic'; Markku Peltonen, *Classical Humanism and Republicanism in English Political Thought 1570–1640* (Cambridge, 1995); Markku Peltonen, 'Citizenship and Republicanism in Elizabethan England', in Martin Van Gelderen and Quentin Skinner, eds, *Republicanism: A Shared European Heritage*, Volume 1: *Republicanism and Constitutionalism in Early Modern Europe* (Cambridge, 2002), 85–106.
85. Richard Crompton, *A Short Declaration of the Ende of Traytors* (1587), sig. Bii.
86. Thomas Cogswell, 'The Politics of Propaganda: Charles I and the People in the 1620s', *JBS*, 29 (1990), 192.
87. David Cressy, *Bonfires and Bells* (1989); Kevin Sharpe, *Selling the Tudor Monarchy* (2009) and *Image Wars* (2010); Steven Pincus and Peter Lake, eds, *The Politics of the Public Sphere in Early Modern England* (Manchester, 2007).
88. [Persons], *Conference*, I, 29.
89. BL, Add. MS 34,218, fol. 131.
90. TCD MS 734, fol. 311r–v.
91. FSL, V.a.1, fol. 19.
92. John Everard, *The Arriereban* (1618), 12.
93. Jason C. White, 'Militant Protestants: British Identity in the Jacobean Period, 1603–1625', *History*, 94 (2009), 154–75.
94. Charles Prior, 'Ecclesiology and Political Thought in England, 1580–c.1630', *HJ*, 48 (2005), 862.
95. Thomas Bilson, *True Difference* (1585), 129, 251.
96. Robert Some, *A Godly Treatise… Whereunto One Proposition More is Added* (1588), 6.
97. James I, *By the King. A Proclamation for the Authorizing and Uniformitie of the Booke of Common Prayer to be used throughout the Realme* (1603[/4).
98. John Marshall, *John Locke, Toleration and Early Enlightenment Culture* (Cambridge, 2006).
99. Peter Marshall, *Reformation England, 1480–1642* (2003), ch. 7.
100. Patrick Collinson, *The Elizabethan Puritan Movement* (1967); Joseph Black, ed., *The Martin Marprelate Tracts* (Cambridge, 2008).
101. Kenneth Fincham and Nicholas Tyacke, *Altars Restored* (Oxford, 2007), 74–90.
102. For the Lambeth Articles see Peter Lake, *Moderate Puritans and the Elizabethan Church* (Cambridge, 1982), 218–26; H. C. Porter, *Reformation and Reaction in Tudor Cambridge* (Cambridge, 1958), ch. 16.
103. Michael Watts, *The Dissenters* (Oxford, 1978), 26–40; Stephen A. Chavura, *Tudor Protestant Political Thought, 1547–1603* (Brill, 2011), 217; Patrick Collinson, 'Barrow, Henry (c.1550–1593)', *ODNB*; Michael E. Moody, 'Greenwood, John (c.1560–1593)', *ODNB*; Claire Cross, 'Penry, John (1562/3–1593)', *ODNB*.
104. Conrad Russell, 'Arguments for Religious Unity in England, 1530–1650', in his *Unrevolutionary England, 1603–1642* (1990), 179–204.

105. James I, *An Apologie for the Oath of Allegiance... Together, with a Premonition* (1609), 127.
106. I. H., *The Divell of the Vault* [1606], sig. Bv.
107. Robert Tynley, *Two Learned Sermons* (1609), 19, 24.
108. William Laud, *A Sermon Preached before His Majesty, On Tuesday the Nineteenth of June, at Wansted, Anno Dom 1621* (1621), 17.
109. Bodl. Lib., MS Eng. *c.* 2693, pp. 158–9.
110. TCD MS 582, fol. 135.
111. *Proceedings 1625*, 504–5.
112. [Maxwell], *Sacro-Sancta*, ep ded, p. 2.
113. Felicity Heal, *Reformation in Britain and Ireland* (Oxford, 2003).
114. *Certaine Sermons or Homilies*, 74.
115. Thomas Scott, *The High-waies of God and the King* ([Holland], 1623), 70–1.
116. Quentin Skinner, *The Foundations of Modern Political Thought* (2 vols, Cambridge, 1978), II, 211–12, 221–4, 227–30, 234–8, 339–45.
117. James VI and I, *Trew Law*, 71, 80.
118. Owen, *Herod and Pilate Reconciled*, 43–4.
119. Mocket, *God and the King*, 89–91.
120. Bodl. Lib., MS Eng. hist. *c.* 712, pp. 345, 562.
121. James VI and I, *Trew Law*, 80, 83.
122. FSL, V.a.478, fol. 99.
123. FSL, X.d.29, fols. 30v–31.
124. Charlwood Lawton, *Jacobite Principles Vindicated* (1693), 23.
125. Peter Studley, *The Looking-Glasse of Schism* (2nd edn, 1635), 196.
126. Bodl. Lib., MS Eng. hist. *c.* 712, p. 569.
127. Tony Claydon, *Europe and the Making of England, 1660–1760* (Cambridge, 2007), 257–8, 261.
128. John Walter, *Crowds and Popular Politics* (Manchester, 2007), 197. See also John Walter '"The Pooremans Joy and the Gentlemans Plague": A Lincolnshire Libel and the Politics of Sedition in Early Modern England', *P&P*, 203 (2009), 29–67 (esp. 61–4).
129. Mihoko Suzuki, 'The London Apprentice Riots of the 1590s and the Fiction of Thomas Deloney', *Criticism*, 38 (1996), 186.

CHAPTER 2. JAMES VI OF SCOTLAND, 1567–1603

1. Anthony Weldon, *The Court and Character of King James* (1650), 178–9.
2. Bacon, *Letters and Life*, III, 77.
3. CUL, Add. MS 6862, p. 215.
4. *The Court and Times of James the First*, ed. Thomas Birch (2 vols, 1848), II, 301.
5. *Calendar of State Papers Relating to Scotland 1547–1603*, ed. William K. Boyd (12 vols, Edinburgh, 1903–52), VII, 274; Bodl. Lib., MS Sancroft 76, p. 25; HMC, *Salisbury*, III, 60.
6. *The Journal of Sir Roger Wilbraham*, ed. Harold S. Scott, *Camden Miscellany*, 10 (Camden Society, 3rd ser., 4, 1902), 60.
7. Cited in Charles Carlton, *Charles I* (2nd edn, 1995), 9.
8. William Barlow, *The Summe and Substance of the Conference* (1604), 84.
9. Weldon, *Court and Character*, 186–7.
10. Arthur Wilson, *The History of Great Britain, Being the Life and Reign of King James the First* (1653), 289.

11. A. W. Beasley, 'The Disability of James VI and I', *Seventeenth Century*, 10 (1995), 151–62; Roger Lockyer, *James VI and I* (1998), 200.
12. [William Sanderson], *Aulicus Coquinariae* (1650[/51]), 98; *Diary of John Manningham*, 219; *Calendar of State Papers Relating to Scotland*, VII, 274; Bodl. Lib., MS Sancroft 76, pp. 26–7, which has 'rustic' instead of 'rude', a more literal translation of the original French 'agreste'; HMC, *Salisbury*, III, 60–1.
13. Goodman, *Court of King James*, I, 92. Cf. *A Royalist's Notebook: The Commonplace Book of Sir John Oglander*, ed. Francis Bamford (1936), 196.
14. Weldon, *A Cat May Look Upon a King* (1652), 48.
15. Alan Stewart, *The Cradle King* (2003), 236–7.
16. R. Malcolm Smuts, *Court Culture and the Origins of the Royalist Tradition in Early Stuart England* (Philadelphia, 1987), 28, 45–6. See also R. Malcolm Smuts, 'Public Ceremony and Royal Charisma: The English Royal Entry in London, 1485–1642', in A. L. Beier, David Cannadine, and James M. Rosenheim, eds, *The First Modern Society: Essays in English History in Honour of Lawrence Stone* (Cambridge, 1989), 65–93.
17. *CSPVen, 1603–7*, p. 513.
18. TCD MS 802, fols. 171v–2.
19. FSL, V.a.180, fol. 108. Cf. Wilson, *History of Great Britain*, 3.
20. TNA, PRO, SP 14/90, fol. 119.
21. Diana Newton, *The Making of the Jacobean Regime* (Woodbridge, 2005), 142; Sharpe, *Image Wars*, 104–6; Lockyer, *James VI and I*, 112; Wilson, *History of Great Britain*, 289.
22. *CSPVen, 1603–7*, 513.
23. Weldon, *Court and Character*, 189.
24. Oglander, *Royalist's Notebook*, 193; Pauline Croft, '*Rex Pacificus*, Robert Cecil, and the 1604 Peace with Spain', in Glenn Burgess, Rowland Wymer, and Jason Lawrence, eds, *The Accession of James I* (Basingstoke, 2006), 150.
25. *Hinc Illae Lachrymae* (1692), 19.
26. Keith Thomas, *The Ends of Life* (Oxford, 2009), 76.
27. BL, Add. MS 63,783, fol. 10v.
28. Francis Osborne, *Traditional Memoyres on the Raigne of King James* (1658), 127.
29. Oglander, *Royalist's Notebook*, 196.
30. *The Diary of Sir Simonds D'Ewes (1622–1624)*, ed. Elizabeth Bourcier (Paris, 1974), 92–3; David M. Bergeron, *King James and Letters of Homoerotic Desire* (Iowa City, 1999), 98; Michael B. Young, *James VI and I and the History of Homosexuality* (Basingstoke, 2000), esp. 49–50; Michael B. Young, 'James VI and I: Time for Reconsideration', *JBS*, 51 (2012), 540–67; Lockyer, *James I*, ch. 8.
31. Maureen Meikle and Helen Payne, 'Anne [Anna, Anne of Denmark]', *ODNB*.
32. Oglander, *Royalist's Notebook*, 194.
33. Leeds Barroll, *Anna of Denmark, Queen of England* (Philadelphia, 2001).
34. Croft, *King James*, 10–20; Julian Goodare and Michael Lynch, 'James VI: Universal King?', in Julian Goodare and Michael Lynch, eds, *The Reign of James VI* (East Linton, 2000), 1–2; Jenny Wormald, 'James VI and I (1566–1625)', *ODNB*; Young, *James VI and I and the History of Homosexuality*, 10–12, 39–42.
35. *A Dialogue on the Law of Kingship among the Scots, A Critical Edition and Translation of George Buchanan's De Iure Regni apud Scotos*, ed. and trans. Roger A. Mason and Martin S. Smith (Aldershot, 2004).
36. HMC, *Salisbury*, III, 57.

37. FSL, V.b.41, pp. 252–5.
38. James VI, *Basilicon Doron*, quotes on pp. 21, 24–30, 45.
39. *RPS*, 1581/10/87, 1584/5/32, 1587/7/24.
40. *RPS*, 1598/6/2; Keith Brown, *Bloodfeud in Scotland 1573–1625* (Edinburgh, 2003), 240–3.
41. Brown, *Bloodfeud*, ch. 8; Julian Goodare, 'The Nobility and the Absolutist State in Scotland, 1584–1638', *History*, 78 (1993), esp. 163–70; Julian Goodare, 'Scottish Politics in the Reign of James VI', in Goodare and Lynch, eds, *Reign of James VI*, 38–42; Croft, *King James*, 31–6; Maurice Lee, *Great Britain's Solomon* (Urbana, 1990).
42. Julian Goodare, 'The Admission of Lairds to the Scottish Parliament', *EHR*, 116 (2001), 1103–33; Keith M. Brown and Alastair J. Mann, 'Introduction', in Brown and Mann, eds, *Parliament and Politics in Scotland*, 18–20.
43. Alan R. MacDonald, 'Uncovering the Legislative Process in the Parliaments of James VI', *HR*, 84 (2011), 606–8; Robert S. Rait, *The Parliaments of Scotland* (Glasgow, 1924), 59–60, 371–3.
44. Croft, 'King James', 38–42; Julian Goodare, 'The Debts of James VI of Scotland', *EcHR*, 62 (2009), 926–52; Julian Goodare, 'Thomas Foulis and the Scottish Fiscal Crisis of the 1590s', in W. M. Ormrod, Margaret Bonney, and Richard Bonney, eds, *Crises, Revolutions, and Self-Sustained Growth* (Stanford, 1999), 170–97.
45. Row, *History*, 73–8 (quotes on pp. 75–6); Scot, *Apol. Narr.*, 46–7; *Ane Short and Generall Confession of the Trewe Christian Fayth* (Edinburgh, [1581]).
46. *RPS*, 1584/5/8 (quote), 10, 11, 75; Alan R. MacDonald, 'Ecclesiastical Representation in Parliament in Post-Reformation Scotland: The Two Kingdoms Theory in Practice', *JEH*, 50 (1999), 39–44.
47. Alan R. MacDonald, *The Jacobean Kirk, 1567–1625* (Aldershot, 1998).
48. *Acts & Proc. Gen. Ass.*, 771; Scot, *Apol. Narr.*, 57; Calderwood, *True History*, 256–7; MacDonald, 'Ecclesiastical Convergence', 886. Bancroft's sermon is discussed in Mary Morrissey, *Politics and the Paul's Cross Sermons, 1558–1642* (Oxford, 2011), 208–13.
49. Alan R. MacDonald, 'The Parliament of 1592: A Crisis Averted?', in Brown and Mann, eds, *Parliament and Politics in Scotland*, 57–81. For Adamson's bulimia, see Row, *History*, 116.
50. *The Autobiography and Diary of Mr James Melvill, 1556–1614*, ed. Robert Pitcairn (Edinburgh, 1842), 369–71, 508–17; Scot, *Apol. Narr.*, 68, 71–9, 83–6; Row, *History*, 184–6; Calderwood, *True History*, 329, 336–57, 364–6; MacDonald, 'Ecclesiastical Representation', 39.
51. *Acts & Proc. Gen. Ass.*, 954.
52. *RPS*, A1586/9/2.
53. *RPS*, 1587/7/70.
54. *RPS*, 1597/11/40.
55. Michael Lynch, 'James VI and the Highland Problem', in Goodare and Lynch, eds, *Reign of James VI*, 208–27; Lee, *Great Britain's Solomon*, 197–202; Newton, *Making of the Jacobean Regime*, 8–9; John L. Roberts, *Feuds, Forays and Rebellions* (Edinburgh, 1999), 135–43.
56. *RPS*, 1600/11/12; *Gowreis Conspiracy* (Edinburgh, 1600); Samuel Cowan, *The Gowrie Conspiracy and its Official Narrative* (1902); W. F. Arbuckle, 'The "Gowrie Conspiracy"', *SHR*, 36 (1957), 1–24, 89–110; Richard Cavendish, 'The Gowrie Conspiracy 5th August 1600', *History Today*, 50 (August, 2000), 52–3.

57. Jenny Wormald, 'James VI and I: Two Kings or One', *History*, 68 (1983), 187–209.
58. Scot, *Apol. Narr.*, 124; Melvill, *Diary*, 554.

CHAPTER 3. A STRANGER IN THE LAND

1. Bacon, *Letters and Life*, III, 63.
2. Markku Peltonen, 'Bacon, Francis, Viscount St Alban (1561–1626)', *ODNB*.
3. TNA, PRO, SP 14/2, fol. 239v. For discussions of anti-Scottish sentiment at the time of James's accession, see David Cressy, *Dangerous Talk* (Oxford, 2010), 91–3; Jenny Wormald, 'Gunpowder, Treason, and Scots', *JBS*, 24 (1985), 159–60; Wormald, 'James VI and I: Two Kings or One?', 206.
4. TNA, PRO, SP 14/2, fol. 239.
5. TNA, PRO, SP 14/1, fols. 68, 73.
6. HMC, *Salisbury*, XII, 676; Questier, *Catholicism and Community*, 265.
7. TNA, PRO, SP 14/2, fol. 240.
8. TNA, PRO, SP 14/2, fol. 238v.
9. Manningham, *Diary*, 209; Goodman, *Court of King James*, II, 56–8.
10. FSL, X.d.393, fol. 26v.
11. *CSPVen, 1603–7*, 15.
12. Nichols, *Progresses*, I, 64, 76, 113; Sharpe, *Image Wars*, 89–92.
13. Bacon, *Letters and Life*, III, 74.
14. HMC, *Various Collections*, IV, 166; Nichols, *Progresses*, I, *127; R. W. Hoyle, 'The Masters of Requests and the Small Change of Jacobean Patronage', *EHR*, 126 (2011), 558–9, 564–5.
15. Nichols, *Progresses*, I, *129–30.
16. Charles H. McIlwain, ed., *The Political Works of James I* (Cambridge, MA, 1918), 328.
17. Steele, I, no. 938.
18. *CSPVen, 1603–7*, 17, 33, 41, 139; Pauline Croft, 'Cecil, Robert, First Earl of Salisbury (1563–1612)', *ODNB*; Keith M. Brown, 'The Scottish Aristocracy, Anglicization and the Court, 1603–38', *HJ*, 36 (1993), 552–3; Croft, *King James*, 51; Linda Levy Peck, *Court Patronage and Corruption in Early Stuart England* (1993), *passim*; Neil Cuddy, 'The Revival of the Entourage: The Bedchamber of James I, 1603–1625', in David Starkey, ed., *The English Court from the Wars of the Roses to the Civil War* (1985), 173–225.
19. TCD MS 802, fol. 171.
20. Sharpe, *Image Wars*, 92–3.
21. Thomas Bilson, *A Sermon Preached at Westminster before the King and Queenes Majesties, at their Coronatiouns…the XXV of July 1603* (1604), sigs A3, B5r–v, B6r–v, B8r–v.
22. Michael C. Questier, *Catholicism and Community in Early Modern England* (Cambridge, 2006), 266; Sandeep Kaushik, 'Resistance, Loyalty and Recusant Politics: Sir Thomas Tresham and the Elizabethan State', *Midland History*, 21 (1996), 60–1; HMC, *Various Collections*, III, 117–23.
23. Akrigg, *Letters*, 207.
24. James VI and I, *Basilicon Doron*, 6, 7, 26.
25. Henry Gee and William John Hardy, ed., *Documents Illustrative of English Church History* (New York, 1896), 508–11.
26. TNA, PRO, SP 14/1, fol. 110v.

27. Manningham, *Diary*, 245.
28. HMC, *Various Collections*, IV, 166.
29. Mark Nicholls, *Investigating Gunpowder Plot* (Manchester, 1991), 129–30; Mark Nicholls, 'Sir Walter Ralegh's Treason: A Prosecution Document', *EHR*, 110 (1995), 902–24; Mark Nicholls and Penry Williams, 'Ralegh, Sir Walter (1554–1618)', Mark Nicholls, 'Brooke, Henry, eleventh Baron Cobham (1564–1619)', Mark Nicholls, 'Watson, William (1559?–1603)', *ODNB*; Penry Williams and Mark Nicholls, *Sir Walter Raleigh* (2011).
30. Lee, *Great Britain's Solomon*, 112–13; Larkin and Hughes, I, 70–3; James I, *By the King. A Proclamation Commanding All Roman Catholic Priests to Depart the Kingdom Before the 19th of March* (1604); *CSPVen, 1603–7*, 138.
31. Larkin and Hughes, I, 62; Steele, I, no. 974; Akrigg, *Letters*, 216–17.
32. Winwood, *Memorials*, II, 14; Akrigg, *Letters*, 221.
33. William Barlow, *The Summe and Substance of the Conference* (1604), 79, 82.
34. Frederick Shriver, 'Hampton Court Re-Visited: James I and the Puritans', *JEH*, 33 (1982), 48–71; Patrick Collinson, 'The Jacobean Religious Settlement: The Hampton Court Conference', in Howard Tomlinson, ed., *Before the English Civil War* (1983); Kenneth Fincham and Peter Lake, 'The Ecclesiastical Policy of King James I', *JBS*, 24 (1985), 174; Kenneth Fincham, *Prelate as Pastor* (Oxford, 1990), 213–14; Alan Cromartie, 'King James and the Hampton Court Conference', in Ralph Houlbrooke, ed., *James VI and I* (Ashgate, 2006), 61–80.
35. David Cressy, *Birth, Marriage, and Death* (Oxford, 1997), 121–2.
36. James I, *By the King. A Proclamation for the Authorizing and Uniformitie of the Booke of Common Prayer to be used throughout the Realme* (1603[/4]); Steele, I, no. 982.
37. Jenny Wormald, 'Ecclesiastical Vitriol: The Kirk, the Puritans and the Future King of England', in John Guy, ed., *The Reign of Elizabeth I* (Cambridge, 1995), 189.
38. Lori Anne Ferrell, *The Bible and the People* (New Haven, 2008), 88–92; Adam Nicolson, *When God Spoke English* (2011), esp. 58–9, 75–7.
39. Paul Slack, *The Impact of the Plague in Tudor and Stuart England* (1985), 151. This figure excludes the outparishes.
40. *Parl. Hist.*, I, 967–70; *CSPVen, 1603–7*, 130; Steele, I, no. 979.
41. Sharpe, *Image Wars*, 93–9.
42. *CJ*, I, 142–6; *The Kings Majesties Speech … On Munday the 19 Day of March 1603* (1604).
43. *CJ*, I, 158, 162–4, 166, 939; *Parl. Hist.*, I, 997–1017; Winwood, *Memorials*, II, 18–19; J. H. Hexter, 'Parliament, Liberty and Freedom of Elections', in Hexter, ed., *Parliament and Liberty from the Reign of Elizabeth to the English Civil War* (Stanford, 1992), 21–55; George Yerby, *People and Parliament* (Basingstoke, 2008), 45–6; Wallace Notestein, *The House of Commons, 1604–1610* (New Haven, 1971), 64–78; Linda Peck, 'Goodwin v. Fortescue: The Local Context of Parliamentary Controversy', *Parliamentary History*, 3 (1984), 33–56; Andrew Thrush, 'Commons v. Chancery: The 1604 Buckinghamshire Election Dispute Revisited', *Parliamentary History*, 26 (2007), 301–9; Conrad Russell, *King James VI and I and his English Parliaments* (Oxford, 2011), 28–30.
44. Edward Hawkins, *Medallic Illustrations of the History of Great Britain* (2 vols, 1885), I, 187 (no. 1), 191 (no. 11).
45. Larkin and Hughes, I, 19; Steele, I, no. 949.
46. *LJ*, II, 277; *CJ*, I, 173.

47. *CJ*, I, 177–8.
48. *LJ*, II, 287–8.
49. *CJ*, I, 194.
50. Winwood, *Memorials*, II, 21; *Parl. Hist.*, I, 1018–23, 1027–8; John Thornborough, *A Discourse Plainely Proving the Evident Utility and Urgent Necessity of the Desired Happy Union of England and Scotland* (1604); *CJ*, I, 226; *LJ*, II, 314; Galloway, *Union of England and Scotland*, 18–23; Russell, *James VI and I and his English Parliaments*, 30–8.
51. *Parl. Hist.*, I, 967.
52. The original logic here was that the minor would not be able to serve the king in war and so would need compensation to be able to hire someone else: William Hakewill, *The Libertie of the Subject* (1641), 20.
53. *CJ*, I, 150–1.
54. Nicholas Tyacke, 'Wroth, Cecil and the Parliamentary Session of 1604', *BIHR*, 50 (1977), 120–5.
55. *Parl. Hist.*, I, 1026–7.
56. I Jas. I, *c.* 25, which was a re-enactment of 39 Eliz. I, *c.* 2; *Statutes at Large* (6 vols, 1758), II, 523.
57. *History of Parliament, 1604–29*, I, 23–4; *Parl. Hist.*, I, 1023–6.
58. *CJ*, I, 230, 243; *Parl. Hist.*, I, 1030–42; J. R. Tanner, ed., *Constitutional Documents of the Reign of James I* (Cambridge, 1930), 217–30; TNA, PRO, SP 14/8, fols. 134–40.
59. Notestein, *House of Commons 1604–10*, 125–40; Hexter, 'Parliament, Liberty and Freedom of Elections'; Johann P. Sommerville, 'Parliament, Privilege, and the Liberties of the Subject', in Hexter, ed., *Parliament and Liberty*, 56; Russell, *James VI and I and his English Parliaments*, 22–5. For the more dismissive view, see Geoffrey Elton, 'A High Road to Civil War?', in Elton, ed., *Studies in Tudor and Stuart Politics and Government* (2 vols, Cambridge, 1974), II, 164–82.
60. TNA, PRO, SP 14/8, fol. 187v.
61. James I, *By the King. As Often as We Call to Minde the Most Joyfull and Just Recognition* (1604); Steele, I, no. 1003; Bruce Galloway, *The Union of England and Scotland, 1603–1608* (Edinburgh, 1986), 59–62.
62. TNA, SP 14/1, fol. 253; Larkin and Hughes, I, 30–2.
63. Pauline Croft, 'Rex Pacificus, 140–54; Andrew Thrush, 'The Parliamentary Opposition to Peace with Spain in 1604: A Speech of Sir Edward Hoby', *Parliamentary History*, 23 (2004), 301–15; Roger Lockyer, *The Early Stuarts* (2nd edn, 1999), 153–4; Newton, *Making of the Jacobean Regime*, 49–54; Larkin and Hughes, I, 91; Nicholls, *Investigating Gunpowder Plot*, 134.
64. BL, Add. MS 38,139, fol. 70; Samuel R. Gardiner, *History of England from the Accession of James I to the Outbreak of the Civil War, 1603–1642* (10 vols, 1883–4), I, 214.
65. Louis B. Wright, 'Colonial Developments in the Reign of James I', in A. G. R. Smith, *The Reign of James VI and I* (1973), 128–9; Karen Ordahl Kupperman, *The Jamestown Project* (Cambridge, MA, 2007).
66. *CJ*, I, 304.
67. For the canons see Edward Cardwell, *Synodalia: A Collection of Articles of Religion, Canons, and Proceedings of Convocations, In the Province of Canterbury, from the Year 1547 to the Year 1717* (Oxford, 2 vols, 1842; repr. 1966), I, 245–329.

68. W. J. Sheils, *The Puritans in the Diocese of Peterborough 1558–1610* (Northampton, 1979), 80.
69. Larkin and Hughes, I, 87–90; Steele, I, no. 996.
70. BL, Add. MS 38,139, fols. 103, 181, 194; Winwood, *Memorials*, II, 40; Peter Lake, 'Matthew Hutton—a Puritan Bishop?', *History*, 64 (1979), 182–204.
71. HMC, *Salisbury*, XVI, 363; *CSPVen, 1603–7*, 202; Winwood, *Memorials*, II, 36; B. W. Quintrell, 'The Royal Hunt and the Puritans 1604–5', *JEH*, 31 (1980), 45–6.
72. HMC, *Montagu of Beaulieu*, 45–6; TNA, PRO, SP 14/12, fols. 159, 160, 162, 168, 169–70, 188–93; Chamberlain, *Letters*, I, 203; Sheils, *Puritans in the Diocese of Peterborough*, 86, 110–11; Newton, *Making of the Jacobean Regime*, ch. 4.
73. *Certaine Arguments to Perswade and Provoke the Most Honorable and High Court of Parliament* (1606), 10–11.
74. Gabriel Powell, *A Consideration of the Deprived and Silenced Ministers Arguments* (1606), 40–1, 48.
75. Sheils, *Puritans in the Diocese of Peterborough*, 110.
76. *CSPVen, 1603–7*, 219–20.
77. *CSPVen, 1603–7*, 232.
78. TNA, PRO, SP 14/28, fol. 241; HMC, *Salisbury*, XVII, 73, 76–7, 98–9, 178.
79. *CSPVen, 1603–7*, 227, 231–2; TNA, PRO, SP 14/13, fols. 29v, 63, 73; Sheils, *Puritans in the Diocese of Peterborough*, 111.
80. Sheils, *Puritans in the Diocese of Peterborough*, 84–5.
81. Fincham, *Prelate as Pastor*, 213–16 and Appendix VI; Collinson, 'Jacobean Religious Settlement', 28.
82. Nicholas Tyacke, *Aspects of English Protestantism, c. 1530–1700* (Manchester, 2001), 112–16.
83. Winwood, *Memorials*, II, 195.
84. Newton, *Making of the Jacobean Regime*, 45; John J. LaRocca, '"Who Can't Pray with Me, Can't Love Me": Toleration and the Early Jacobean Recusancy Policy', *JBS*, 23 (1984), 29.
85. Chamberlain, *Letters*, I, 204; Newton, *Making of the Jacobean Regime*, 87–90, 104–5.
86. *CSPVen, 1603–7*, 232.
87. Birch, ed., *Court and Times of James I*, I, 37; Nicholls, *Investigating Gunpowder Plot*, 9–10, 219–20; Wormald, 'Gunpowder, Treason and Scots', 161.
88. Nicholls, *Investigating Gunpowder Plot*, 3; Chamberlain, *Letters*, I, 213.
89. I. H., *The Divell of the Vault* (1606), sigs B2v, C2v; Jason White, *Militant Protestantism and British Identity, 1603–1642* (2012), 26. See also Thomas Dekker, *The Double PP* (1606); William Leigh, *Great Britaines, Great Deliverance* (1606).
90. *Certaine Arguments to Perswade*, 22–3.
91. Oliver Ormerod, *The Picture of a Papist* (1606), sig. A2v, pp. 181–206, and *Pagano-Papismus* (annexed at end).
92. Powel, *Consideration*, 10–11.
93. *LJ*, II, 358.
94. William Barlow, *The Sermon Preached at Paules Crosse, the Tenth Day of November* (1606), sigs C2v, E3v.

95. *Parl. Hist.*, I, 1069–70.

96. *SR*, IV, 1071–7.

97. Michael Questier, 'Loyalty, Religion and State Power in Early Modern England: English Romanism and the Jacobean Oath of Allegiance', *HJ*, 40 (1997), 311–29; Anthony Milton, *Catholic and Reformed* (Cambridge, 1995), 56–7, 253–5; Johann P. Sommerville, 'Papalist Political Thought and the Controversy over the Jacobean Oath of Allegiance', in Ethan Shagan, ed., *Catholics and the 'Protestant Nation': Religious Politics and Identity in Early Modern England* (Manchester, 2005), 162–84; Stefania Tutino: *Empire of Souls: Robert Bellarmine and the Christian Commonwealth* (Oxford), ch. 4; Bernard Bourdin, *The Theological-Political Origins of the Modern State: The Controversy between James I of England and Cardinal Bellarmine*, trans. Susan Pickford (Washington, DC, 2010); William Brown Patterson, *James VI and the Reunion of Christendom* (Cambridge, 1997), ch. 3.

98. James I, *An Apologie for the Oath of Allegiance... Together, with a Premonition* (1609), 9–10.

99. Robert Tynley, *Two Learned Sermons* (1609), 14, 19.

100. John King, *A Sermon Preached at Whitehall the 5 Day of November ann. 1608* (1608), 5, 23, 24.

101. Lancelet Andrewes, *Tortura Torti* (1609); Milton, *Catholic and Reformed*, 251–61.

102. James I, *A Proclamation for the Due Execution of All Former Lawes against Recusants* (1610); Steele, I, no. 1093.

103. John J. LaRocca, 'James I and his Catholic Subjects, 1606–12: Some Financial Implications', *Recusant History*, 18 (1987), 251–62; Questier, 'Loyalty, Religion and State Power', 323–5; Michael C. Questier, *Conversion, Politics and Religion in England, 1580–1625* (Cambridge, 1996), 137; A. W. R. E. Okines, 'Why Was There So Little Government Reaction to the Gunpowder Plot?', *JEH*, 55 (2004), 275–92; Kenneth Fincham, 'Abbot, George (1562–1633)', *ODNB*.

104. G. F. Nuttall, 'The English Martyrs, 1535–1680: A Statistical Review', *JEH*, 22 (1971), 191–7; Wormald, 'Gunpowder, Treason, and Scots', 150; Claire Cross, *Church and People, 1450–1660* (Glasgow, 1976), 166.

105. Russell, *James VI and I and his English Parliaments*, ch. 4.

106. *CJ*, I, 315; *Parl. Hist.*, I, 1071–5.

107. *CJ*, I, 318; Lockyer, *Early Stuarts*, 109–10.

108. Conrad Russell, 'James VI and I and Rule Over Two Kingdoms', *HR*, 76 (2003), 151–63.

109. *CJ*, I, 334–5; *Parl. Hist.*, I, 1081–2. For Fuller, see Stephen Wright, 'Nicholas Fuller and the Liberties of the Subject', *Parliamentary History*, 25 (2006), 176–213 (esp. 184–8 for his views on the Union).

110. *Parl. Hist.*, I, 1096–8; *CJ*, I, 333, 335.

111. Louis A. Knafla, *Law and Politics in Jacobean England* (Cambridge, 1977), 202–53 (quote on p. 205); Christopher W. Brooks, *Law, Politics and Society in Early Modern England* (Cambridge, 2009), 133–5.

112. Steve Hindle, 'Imagining Insurrection in Seventeenth-Century England: Representations of the Midland Rising of 1607', *History Workshop Journal*, 66 (2008), 21–61 (quote on p. 27); Walter, 'Pooremans Joy'.

CHAPTER 4. SETTLING THE AFFAIRS OF RELIGION

1. James I, *By the King. A Proclamation for the Authorizing and Uniformitie of the Booke of Common Prayer to be used throughout the Realme* (1603[/4]).
2. This interpretation is associated with Nicholas Tyacke, 'Puritanism and Arminianism', in Conrad Russell, ed., *The Origins of the English Civil War* (1973), 119–43 and Patrick Collinson, *The Religion of Protestants* (Oxford, 1982), esp. 81–2. The currency of the terms 'Calvinist consensus' and 'Jacobean consensus' has frequently been noted by historians, though often in the context of exposing their limitations. See for example: Anthony Milton, 'The Church of England, Rome, and the True Church: The Demise of a Jacobean Consensus', in Fincham, ed., *Early Stuart Church*, 187–210; Peter Lake, *The Boxmaker's Revenge* (Manchester, 2001), 239–40; Marshall, *Reformation England*, 126–35; Peter Marshall, 'England', in David M. Whitford, ed., *Reformation and Early Modern Europe* (Kirksville, MO, 2008), 260. Conrad Russell has denied that he or Tyacke ever used the term 'Calvinist consensus': Russell, *Causes*, 84. Collinson acknowledged in *The Birthpangs of Protestant England* (Basingstoke, 1988), 140, that in his *Religion of Protestants* he had talked about Calvinist Protestants as being almost 'consensual'.
3. For a discussion of the problematic nature of the term 'Arminian', see p. 302.
4. Fincham, *Prelate as Pastor*, 220–2, 228.
5. For the lack of theological consensus in the Jacobean Church, see also Charles W. A. Prior, *Defining the Jacobean Church* (Cambridge, 2005).
6. Alan Cromartie, *The Constitutionalist Revolution* (Cambridge, 2006), 162–3.
7. Lori Anne Ferrell, *Government by Polemic* (Stanford, 1998), 137.
8. William B. Patterson, *King James VI and the Reunion of Christendom* (Cambridge, 2000).
9. James I, *Apologie for the Oath*, 44.
10. Fincham, *Prelate as Pastor*, 39–40; Lockyer, *James VI and I*, 116; Newton, *Making of the Jacobean Regime*, 120, 132.
11. Fincham and Tyacke, *Altars Restored*, 74–90; J. F. Merritt, 'The Cradle of Laudianism? Westminster Abbey, 1558–1630', *JEH*, 52 (2001), 623–46.
12. Fincham and Lake, 'Ecclesiastical Policy', 187; Fincham, *Prelate as Pastor*, 302; Lockyer, *James I*, 123; Peter Lake, 'Lancelot Andrewes, John Buckeridge, and Avant-garde Conformity at the Court of James I', in Linda Levy Peck, ed., *The Mental World of the Jacobean Court* (Cambridge, 1991), 113–53.
13. The eight in 1619 were: Samuel Harsnett (Chichester), Richard Neile (Durham), Lancelot Andrewes (Ely), George Montaigne (Lincoln), John Overall (Norwich), Thomas Dove (Peterborough), John Buckeridge (Rochester), and John Bridgeman (Chester, a keen promoter of the beautification of churches already in the early 1620s and who was to sympathize with Laud's drive for order and beauty in worship in the 1630s, although arguably a somewhat reluctant Laudian collaborator). I am grateful to Ken Fincham for advice on the theological complexion of the Jacobean bench.
14. Fincham, *Prelate as Pastor*, 46–7.
15. Margo Todd, 'Powell, Gabriel', *ODNB*; Patrick Collinson, *Richard Bancroft and Elizabethan Anti-Puritanism* (Cambridge, 2013).
16. Fincham, *Prelate as Pastor*, 225, 231–8.
17. TNA, PRO, SP 14/94, fol. 116; Chamberlain, *Letters*, II, 121, 140; Jeanne Shami, *John Donne and Conformity in Crisis in the Late Jacobean Pulpit* (Woodbridge,

2003), 38–9; Peter White, *Predestination, Policy and Polemic* (Cambridge, 1992), 177–8.

18. Fincham, *Prelate as Pastor*, 214–19, 228–9, 241–3; Ian Atherton and David Como, 'The Burning of Edward Wightman: Puritanism, Prelacy and the Politics of Heresy in Early Modern England', *EHR*, 120 (2005), 1215–50.

19. James I, *Apologie for the Oath*, 44, 46.

20. *Proceedings 1610*, II, 103. See p. 122.

21. See pp. 68–9.

22. William Covell, *A Modest and Reasonable Examination* (1604), 46, 209–10, 212; Stephen Wright, 'Covell, William (d. 1613)', *ODNB*.

23. William Wilkes, *Obedience or Ecclesiastical Union* (1605), 9, 10, 16, 17, 58, 68.

24. Oliver Ormerod, *The Picture of a Puritane* (2nd edn, 1605), sig. A3v.

25. Ormerod, *The Picture of a Puritane*, 9.

26. Ormerod, *The Picture of a Puritane*, 19.

27. Ormerod, *The Picture of a Puritane*, sig. A4v, p. 8.

28. Ormerod, *The Picture of a Puritane*, 2, 16, 26.

29. Ormerod, *The Picture of a Puritane*, 8–9.

30. Ormerod, *The Picture of a Puritane*, 12, 18, 49.

31. Anthony Maxey, *The Churches Sleepe* (1606), sigs Br–v, B2r–v.

32. Maxey, *The Churches Sleepe*, sigs B4r–B6v, B7v.

33. Peter McCullough, *Sermons at Court* (Cambridge, 1998), 113–15.

34. *Certaine Arguments to Perswade*, 18–19.

35. James I, *A Meditation upon the Lords Prayer* (1619), 5, 6–7, 11–12, 14–15, 18–19. See also Kevin Sharpe, 'The King's Writ', in his *Remapping Early Modern England* (Cambridge, 2000), 137.

36. Fincham and Tyacke, *Altars Restored*, 82–3. For James's approval of images, see p. 178.

37. Andrew Foster, 'Neile, Richard (1562–1640)', *ODNB*.

38. Fincham and Tyacke, *Altars Restored*, 92–110; Andrew Foster, 'Churchwardens' Accounts of Early Modern England and Wales', in Katherine French, Gary Gibbs, and Beat Kumin, eds, *The Parish in English Life 1400–1600* (Manchester, 1997), 87–8; Julia Merritt, 'Puritans, Laudians, and the Phenomenon of Church-Building in Jacobean London', *HJ*, 41 (1998), 935–60.

39. TNA, PRO, SP 14/90, fol. 146; Laud, *Works*, IV, 233–4, VI, 239–41; Brian Taylor, 'William Laud, Dean of Gloucester, 1616–21', *Transactions of the Bristol and Gloucestershire Archaeological Society*, 77 (1958), 85–96.

40. Fincham and Tyacke, *Altars Restored*, 115–19; Ian Atherton, 'Cathedrals, Laudianism, and the British Churches', *HJ*, 53 (2010), 900–2.

41. Lancelot Andrewes, *A Sermon Preached before His Majestie, at Whitehall, on Easter Last, 1614* (1614), sig. A2v; Anthony Maxey, *A Sermon Preached before His Majestie at Bagshot, September 1 Anno Dom 1616* (1634), 24, in Maxey, *Certaine Sermons Preached Before the King* (7th edn, 1636), 'The Ninth Sermon'; John Buckeridge, *A Sermon Preached before His Majestie at Whitehall, March 22 1617* (1618), 6, 8, 12, 17.

42. Norwich Spackman, *A Sermon Before His Majestie at White-hall the First of May 1614* (1614), 73.

43. See pp. 177–8, 180–3.

44. Thomas Morton, *A Defence of the Innocencie of the Three Ceremonies of the Church of England* (1618); John Buckeridge, *A Discourse Concerning Kneeling*

at the Communion, which is appended to his *A Sermon Preached before His Majestie at Whitehall, March 22 1617* (1618).

45. James I, *A Meditation upon the...XXVII Chapter of St Matthew* (1620), 11–12.
46. R. C. Richardson, *Puritanism in North-West England* (Manchester, 1972), 76.
47. Christopher Haigh, *The Plain Man's Pathways to Heaven* (Oxford, 2007), 103, 107, 135, 212.
48. Ronald A. Marchant, *The Puritans and the Church Courts in the Diocese of York, 1560–1642* (1960), 172–3.
49. Foster, 'Neile', *ODNB.*
50. Haigh, *Plain Man's Pathways,* 136, 219.
51. Yerby, *People and Parliament,* 189.
52. King James Bible, Matthew X, vv. 34–5.
53. William Perkins, *The Workes* (3 vols, 1612–13), I, 311.
54. Richardson, *Puritanism,* 48–50.
55. Patrick Collinson, *The Puritan Character* (1989); Patrick Collinson, 'Ben Jonson's *Bartholomew Fair:* The Theatre Constructs Puritanism', in David L. Smith, Richard Strier, and David Bevington, eds, *The Theatrical City: Culture, Theatre, and Politics in London, 1576–1649* (Cambridge, 1995), 157–69; Patrick Collinson, 'Ecclesiastical Vitriol: Religious Satire in the 1590s and the Invention of Puritanism', in John Guy (ed.), *The Reign of Elizabeth I: Court and Culture in the Last Decade* (Cambridge, 1995), 150–70; J. J. Scarisbrick, *The English People and the English Reformation* (Ocford, 1984); Peter Lake and Michael Questier, *The Anti-Christ's Lewd Hat* (New Haven, 2002), sections IV and V; Peter Lake, 'Anti-Puritanism: The Structure of a Prejudice', in Kenneth Fincham and Peter Lake, eds, *Religious Politics in Post-Reformation England: Essays in Honour of Nicholas Tyacke* (Woodbridge, 2006), 80–97; Christopher Haigh, *English Reformations* (Oxford, 1993), 283, 289–90.
56. Haigh, *Plain Man's Pathways,* 122–3.
57. Manningham, *Diary,* 114.
58. Haigh, *Plain Man's Pathways,* 126–7; David Underdown, *Fire from Heaven* (1992), 27–30.
59. FSL, V.a.399, fols. 18–20.
60. FSL, V.a.137, p. 124.
61. Charles J. Sisson, *Lost Plays of Shakespeare's Age* (Cambridge, 1936), 190–1, 194, 201; Haigh, *Plain Man's Pathways,* 66.
62. James Craigie, ed., *Minor Prose Works of King James VI and I* (Edinburgh: Scottish Text Society, 1982), 102–9; James I, *The Kings Majesties Declaration to His Subjects, Concerning Lawfull Sports to bee Used* (1618).
63. HMC, *Buccleuch and Queensbury,* III, 213–14.
64. Kenneth L. Parker, *The English Sabbath* (Cambridge, 1988), ch. 5; Richardson, *Puritanism,* 21, 148–9, 157; Nicholas McDowell, 'The Stigmatizing of Puritans as Jews in Jacobean England', *Renaissance Studies,* 19 (2005), 348–62; John Spurr, *English Puritanism, 1603–1689* (Basingstoke, 1998), 77; James Tait, 'The Declaration of Sports for Lancashire', *EHR,* 32 (1917), 561–8; Neil Rhodes, Jennifer Richards, and Joseph Marshall, l, *King James VI and I: Selected Writings* (Ashgate, 2003).
65. Haigh, *Plain Man's Pathways,* 47.
66. David Cressy, 'Conflict, Consensus, and the Willingness to Wink: The Erosion of Community in Charles I's England', *HLQ,* 61 (2000), 131–50.

CHAPTER 5. ONE GOOD STEWARD WOULD PUT ALL IN ORDER

1. Bodl. Lib., MS Sancroft 53, pp. 47, 57.
2. Lockyer, *Early Stuarts*, 40; Newton, *Making of the Jacobean Regime*, 35; Russell, *James VI and I and His English Parliaments*, 4–8; Roger Schofield, 'Taxation and the Political Limits of the Tudor State', in Claire Cross, David Loades, and J. J. Scarisbrick, eds, *Law and Government under the Tudors* (Cambridge, 1988), 227–56; B. P. Wolffe, *The Royal Demesne in English History* (1971), 219–33; Michael J. Braddick, *Parliamentary Taxation in Seventeenth-Century England* (Woodbridge, 1994), ch. 2; Christopher Durston, *James I* (2002), 26.
3. *CSP Ven, 1603–7*, 285.
4. *The Parliamentary Diary of Robert Bowyer 1606–7*, ed. David Harris Willson (Minneapolis, 1931), App. A, p. 372; Peck, *Court Patronage*, 34; Lockyer, *Early Stuarts*, 31–2, 39, 40; Lockyer, *James VI and I*, 82; Croft, *King James*, 64–5; Pauline Croft, 'Libels, Popular Literacy and Public Opinion in Early Modern England', *HR*, 68 (1995), 277.
5. Daniel W. Hollis, III, 'The Crown Lands and the Financial Dilemma in Stuart England', *Albion*, 26 (1994), 419–42 (esp. 426, 433); Richard Hoyle, 'Introduction', in Hoyle, ed., *The Estates of the English Crown, 1558–1640* (Cambridge, 1992), 16.
6. Lockyer, *Early Stuarts*, 35; Croft, *King James*, 72; Frederick Dietz, *English Public Finance, 1558–1641* (1964), 332–3; A. P. Newton, 'The Establishment of the Great Farm of the English Customs, 1604', *TRHS*, 4th ser., 50 (1919).
7. *CSP Ven, 1603–7*, 285.
8. *Parl. Hist.*, I, 1064–5.
9. Lockyer, *Early Stuarts*, 38.
10. *ST*, II, 387–8. For the background, see Pauline Croft, 'Fresh Light on Bate's Case', *HJ*, 30 (1987), 523–39; Michael J. Braddick, *The Nerves of State* (Manchester, 1996), 133–7; Brooks, *Law, Politics and Society*, 136–8.
11. Sommerville, *Royalists and Patriots*, 141; Lockyer, *James VI and I*, 97; Dietz, *English Public Finance*, 119, 368–72.
12. *Parl. Deb. 1610*, pp. xv, xx; Eric Lindquist, 'The Failure of the Great Contract', *JMH*, 57 (1985), 625; Lockyer, *James VI and I*, 83. For the problems in assessing the data relating to Jacobean finance, see Russell, *James VI and I and his English Parliaments*, ch. 9.
13. *Proceedings 1610*, I, 3–8, 12 (quote on p. 7); II, 9–27, 359 (quote on p. 24).
14. *CJ*, I, 400–1.
15. John Cowell, *The Interpreter* (Cambridge, 1607), quotes on sigs Qq1, Rrr1; *Proceedings 1610*, II, 38–9.
16. *Parl. Hist.*, I, 1122–3; Arthur Wilson, *The History of Great Britain* (1653), 45–6; Pauline Croft, 'Capital Life: Members of Parliament outside the House', in Cogswell, Cust, and Lake, eds, *Politics, Religion and Popularity*, 80–1.
17. *Proceedings 1610*, I, 29, II, 49–50.
18. James I, *Speech...the XXI of March 1609*, quotes on sigs A3v, A4v, Bv–B2v, B4v. The speech is discussed on pp. 13, 16, 19, 20, 21.
19. Winwood, *Memorials*, III, 141–2; Steele, I, no. 1092. My discussion of Cowell draws on Sommerville, *Royalists and Patriots*, 113–19; Michelle O'Callaghan, '"Talking Politics": Tyranny, Parliament, and Christopher Brooke's *The Ghost of Richard the Third (1614)*', *HJ*, 41 (1998), 109; Clive Holmes, 'Liberty,

Taxation and Property', in Hexter, ed., *Parliament and Liberty*, 125; Cyndia S. Clegg, *Press Censorship in Jacobean England* (Cambridge, 2001), 137–43.

20. *Proceedings 1610*, II, 82–3.
21. *Proceedings 1610*, II, 101, 102, 103.
22. Chamberlain, *Letters*, I, 301.
23. *Proceedings 1610*, II, 108–9.
24. *CJ*, I, 431.
25. *Proceedings 1610*, II, 115–16.
26. *Proceedings 1610*, II, 152–65; Stephen Wright, 'Nicholas Fuller and the Liberties of the Subject', *Parliamentary History*, 25 (2005), 207.
27. *Proceedings 1610*, II, 170–97 (quotes on pp. 189, 190, 191, 195, 196, 197).
28. Wiliam Hakewill, *The Libertie of the Subject* (1641), quotes on pp. 3, 9, 13, 35, 36, 99, 130, 133, 141.
29. Bacon, *Letters and Life*, IV, 192.
30. Hakewill, *Libertie of the Subject*, 22.
31. *Proceedings 1610*, II, 165. See also Yerby, *People and Parliament*, 60–75.
32. *Proceedings 1610*, II, 273, 383; *Parl. Deb. 1610*, 123n.; Birch, ed., *Court and Times of James I*, I, 122; *CJ*, I, 448.
33. TNA, PRO, SP 14/58, fol. 27; Lockyer, *Early Stuarts*, 117–24; Croft, *King James*, 75–82; John Cramsie, *Kingship and Crown Finance under James VI and I, 1603–1625* (Woodbridge, 2002), ch. 4; Lindquist, 'Failure of the Great Contract'; Russell, *James VI and I and his English Parliaments*, ch. V.
34. TNA, PRO, SP 14/58, fol. 61.
35. *Proceedings 1610*, II, 340–1; Gardiner, *Parliamentary Debates in 1610*, 138.
36. TNA, PRO, SP 14/58, fols. 76v, 77v.
37. *LJ*, II, 683–4.
38. Derek Hirst, *England in Conflict 1603–1660* (1990), 91.
39. HMC, *Salisbury*, XXI, 266.
40. Winwood, *Memorials*, III, 447, 453; Roger Lockyer, *Buckingham* (1981), 14–15; Alastair Bellany, *The Politics of Court Scandal in Early Modern England* (Cambridge, 2002).
41. Hirst, *England in Conflict*, 92; Okines, 'Government Reaction to Gunpowder Plot', 285; Pauline Croft, 'The Catholic Gentry, the Earl of Salisbury and the Baronets of 1611', in Peter Lake and Michael Questier, eds, *Conformity and Orthodoxy in the English Church, c. 1560–1660* (Woodbridge, 2000), 262–81.
42. Conrad Russell, *The Addled Parliament of 1614* (Reading, 1992), 15–16; 'Journal of Sir Roger Wilbraham', 107.
43. Winwood, *Memorials*, III, 434, 435; Andrew Thrush, 'The French Marriage and the Origins of the 1614 Parliament', in Stephen Clucas and Rosalind Davies, eds, *The Crisis of 1614 and the Addled Parliament* (Aldershot, 2003), 29–30; Andrew Thrush, 'The Personal Rule of James I, 1611–1620', in Cogswell, Cust, and Lake, eds, *Politics, Religion and Popularity in Early Stuart Britain*, 84–102; White, *Militant Protestantism*, 32–3. For Prince Henry, see Catherine MacLeod, with Timothy Wilks, Malcolm Smuts, and Rab MacGibbon, *The Lost Prince: The Life and Death of Henry Stuart* (2012).
44. Clayton Roberts and Owen Dunham, 'The Parliamentary Undertaking of 1614', *EHR*, 93 (1978); Clayton Roberts, *Schemes and Undertakings* (Columbus, 1985), ch. 1; Lisa Jardine and Alan Stewart, *Hostage to Fortune* (1998), 344–5; *House of Commons, 1604–29*, I, 388–1.
45. *The Life and Letters of John Donne*, ed. Edmund Gosse (2 vols, 1899), II, 34.

46. Bacon, *Letters and Life*, V, 24–30.
47. Roberts, *Schemes and Undertakings*, 23–4; Chamberlain, *Letters*, I, 515; *House of Commons, 1604–29*, I, 391–2.
48. *Parl. Hist.*, I, 1149–52. See also *Proceedings 1614*, 13–19, which has a different version of the speech. The book by Francisco Suarez was *De Defensione Fidei Catholicae Adversus Anglicanae Sectae Errores* (1613). It had been burned in England by royal proclamation.
49. *Parl. Hist.*, I, 1153, 1155; *Proceedings 1614*, 43–6; Chamberlain, *Letters*, I, 526; HMC, *Portland*, IX, 28.
50. *Proceedings 1614*, 9.
51. *Proceedings 1614*, 54–8.
52. *Proceedings 1614*, pp. xxvii–xxix, 208–10; Thomas L. Moir, *The Addled Parliament of 1614* (Oxford, 1958), 97–100, 102–7; Roberts, *Schemes and Undertakings*, 26–9.
53. *Proceedings 1614*, 95, 96, 212, 219, 222, 224.
54. *Proceedings 1614*, 141–2.
55. *Proceedings 1614*, 146–7.
56. *Proceedings 1614*, 312, 316.
57. *Proceedings 1614*, 313 n. 19, 316, 317, 340.
58. *Proceedings 1614*, 361, 363; HMC, *Hastings*, IV, 249, 253.
59. *Proceedings 1614*, 341, 342, 344.
60. *Proceedings 1614*, 365, 370.
61. *Proceedings 1614*, 400; *LJ*, II, 713.
62. *Proceedings 1614*, 402, 404, 408.
63. *Proceedings 1614*, 413, 415, 417, 419–20, 422–3 (and n. 33); Chamberlain, *Letters*, I, 538; Linda Levy Peck, 'The Earl of Northampton, Merchant Grievances and the Addled Parliament of 1614', *HJ*, 24 (1981), 544–51.
64. *Proceedings 1614*, 442–3; *LJ*, II, 717.
65. *El Hecho de los Tratados del Matrimonio Pretendido por el Principe de Gales…Narrative of the Spanish Marriage Treaty*, ed. and trans. Samuel R. Gardiner (Camden Society, 101, 1869), 288. Gardiner offers a somewhat looser translation of the original Spanish in his *History of England*, II, 251, though this is the version most frequently cited.
66. *Proceedings 1614*, pp. xvii, 483; Russell, *Addled Parliament*; Russell, *James VI and I and his English Parliaments*, ch. 6.
67. HMC, *Downshire*, IV, 431.
68. Damian X. Powell, *Sir James Whitelocke's Liber Famelicus, 1570–1632* (Bern, 2000), 89; Moir, *Addled Parliament*, 146–7. Northampton died a week later from a tumour in his thigh which turned gangrenous.
69. Bacon, *Letters and Life*, V, 195.
70. TNA, PRO, SP 14/77, fol. 114; HMC, *Downshire*, IV, 428, 429, 431, 458; Goodman, *Court of King James*, II, 157–60.
71. Bacon, *Letters and Life*, V, 81.
72. FSL, G.b.10, fol. 78; *Acts of the Privy Council of England 1613–1614*, ed. E. G. Atkinson (1921), 491–6.
73. TNA, PRO, SP 14/78, fol. 26.
74. TNA, PRO, SP 14/80, fol. 194.
75. TNA, PRO, SP 14/78, fols. 38–9; FSL, V.b. 277, fols. 70–71v; *Letters from George Lord Carew to Sir Thomas Roe*, ed. John MacLean (Camden Society, 76, 1860), 140–3.

76. *ST*, II, 899–912; HMC, *Downshire*, V, 144, 206.

77. Moir, *Addled Parliament*, 151.

78. Menna Prestwich, *Cranfield: Politics and Profits under the Early Stuarts* (Oxford, 1966), 164–70, 172–7; Astrid Friis, *Alderman Cockayne's Project and the Cloth Trade* (Copenhagen, 1917), figure on p. 239; Robert Brenner, *Merchants and Revolution* (Princeton, 1993), 211.

79. Lockyer, *Buckingham*, 22–3; Bellany, *Politics of Court Scandal*; David Lindley, *The Trials of Frances Howard* (1993).

80. Lockyer, *Buckingham*, 18–20, 25–9, 43; Roger Lockyer, 'Villiers, George, First Duke of Buckingham (1592–1628)', *ODNB*; Alexander Courtney, 'Court Politics and the Kingship of James VI and I, c. 1615–c. 1622', unpub. Cambridge PhD thesis (2008), 80–3, 111, 137, 180–6.

81. Thrush, 'Personal Rule', 92–3; Russell, *James VI and I and his English Parliaments*, 100, 159.

82. Mark Nicholls and Penry Williams, *Sir Walter Raleigh in Life and Legend* (2011); Andrew Fleck, '"At the Time of his Death": Manuscript Instability and Walter Ralegh's Performance on the Scaffold', *JBS*, 48 (2009), 4–28.

83. Thrush, 'Personal Rule', 94–5.

84. Thrush, 'Personal Rule', 95–6; Michael J. Braddick, 'Cranfield, Lionel, First Earl of Middlesex (1575–1645)', *ODNB*; Prestwich, *Cranfield*; Cramsie, *Kingship and Crown Finance*.

CHAPTER 6. A TRUE LOVE KNOT KNIT FAST

1. David G. Mullan, *Episcopacy in Scotland* (Edinburgh, 1986), 96; Arthur H. Williamson, 'Scotland, Antichrist and the Invention of Great Britain', in John Dwyer, Roger A. Mason, and Alexander Murdoch, eds, *New Perspectives on the Politics and Culture of Early Modern Scotland* (Edinburgh, 1982), 44.

2. Croft, *King James*, 153–4.

3. Barnabe Rich, *A Catholicke Conference* (1612), sig. A2v.

4. *That Great Expedition for Ireland* (1642), 4–5. The proverb was frequently invoked at this time. See for example Edmund Calamy, *England's Looking Glass* (1642), 16; Wallington, *Historical Notices*, II, 34; [David Lloyd], *Never Faile* (1663), 10.

5. *NHI*, III, 187.

6. Davies, *Historical Relations*, 89, 106, 116–17.

7. Davies, *Historical Relations*, 150–1, 152–3, 154.

8. *CSPIre, 1603–6*, 371–2, 389–90.

9. *CSPIre, 1603–6*, 13–14; Nicholas Canny, *Making Ireland British, 1580–1650* (Oxford, 2001), 165; Beckett, *Making of Modern Ireland*, 23–4. For the war and its legacy, see: Hiram Morgan, ed., *The Battle of Kinsale* (Bray, Co. Wicklow, 2004); Nicholas Canny, 'The Treaty of Mellifont and the Reorganization of Ulster, 1603', *Irish Sword*, 9 (1969–70), 249–62.

10. John McCavitt, 'The Political Background to the Ulster Plantation, 1607–1620', in Brian Mac Cuarta, ed., *Ulster 1641* (Belfast, 1993), 9.

11. J. C. Beckett, *The Making of Modern Ireland, 1603–1923* (1966), ch. 2; Roy F. Foster, *Modern Ireland, 1660–1972* (1988), ch. 1.

12. Michelle O Riordan, 'The Native Ulster *Mentalité* as Revealed in Gaelic Sources, 1600–1650', in Mac Cuarta, ed., *Ulster 1541*, 61–91; Breandán Ó Buachalla,

'James our True King: The Ideology of Irish Royalism in the Seventeenth Century', in G. Boyce, Robert Eccleshall, and Vincent Geoghegan, eds, *Political Thought in Ireland since the Seventeenth Century* (1993), 1–35.

13. [Patrick Comerford], *The Inquisition of a Sermon Preached in the Cathedrall Church of the City of Waterford* (1644), 18, 28, 29.

14. *Calendar of the Carew Manuscripts*, 7–12 (quote on p. 10); NLI, MS 12,813/1, fols. 13–16 (quotes on p. 15).

15. C. Litton Falkiner, 'William Farmer's Chronicles of Ireland. (Continued), *EHR*, 22 (1907), 529–33; Anthony Sheehan, 'The Recusancy Revolt of 1603: A Reinterpretation', *Archivium Hibernicum*, 38 (1983), 3–13.

16. Canny, *Making Ireland British*, 171–2.

17. Hans S. Pawlisch, *Sir John Davies and the Conquest of Ireland* (Cambridge, 1985), esp. 12, 45–6, 60–1, 69–70, 75–81; John McCavitt, '"Good Planets in their Several Spheres": The Establishment of the Assizes Circuits in Early Seventeenth-Century Ireland', *Irish Jurist*, 24 (1989), 248–78; Sean J. Connolly, *Contested Island: Ireland 1460–1630* (Oxford, 2007), 311–15.

18. Steele, II, nos. 180, 186; Raymond Gillespie, *Seventeenth-Century Ireland* (Dublin, 2006), 35; T. W. Moody, *The Londonderry Plantation, 1609–41* (Belfast, 1936), 24–7; Robinson, *Plantation of Ulster*, 7; NHI, III, 193, 205–7; Canny, *Making Ireland British*, 169–70; Brooks, *Law, Politics and Society*, 129; David Edwards, 'The Legacy of Defeat: The Reduction of Gaelic Ireland after Kinsale', in Morgan, ed., *Kinsale*, 282.

19. Nicholas Canny, *The Upstart Earl: A Study of the Social and Mental World of Richard Boyle, First Earl of Cork 1566–1643* (Cambridge, 1982), 5–6; Gillespie, *Seventeenth-Century Ireland*, 36.

20. Pawlisch, *Sir John Davies*, 42.

21. Beckett, *Making of Modern Ireland*, 36; Connolly, *Contested Island*, 316–17.

22. T. W. Moody, *The Londonderry Plantation, 1609–41* (Belfast, 1939), 24; CSPIre, 1606–8, 401–3.

23. Steele, II, no. 178; Edwards, 'Legacy of Defeat'; David Edwards, 'Two Fools and a Martial Law Commissioner: Cultural Conflict at the Limerick Assize of 1606', in David Edwards, ed., *Regions and Rulers in Ireland, 1100–1650* (Dublin, 2004), 244–5.

24. Steele, II, no. 174; Henry Fitzsimon, SJ, *Words of Comfort to Persecuted Catholics*, ed. Edmund Hogan (Dublin, 1881), 112–13.

25. Steele, II, no. 182; CSPIre, 1603–6, 301–3.

26. CSPIre, 1603–6, 467.

27. CSPIre, 1603–6, 334, 354.

28. CSPIre, 1603–6, 346–7.

29. TCD MS 672, fols. 22–3; CSPIre, 1603–6, 348–9, 353–4, 355–8, 370. For the mandates policy, see: John McCavitt, *Sir Arthur Chichester: Lord Deputy of Ireland 1605–1616* (Belfast, 1998), ch. 7; Brendan Fitzpatrick, *Seventeenth-Century Ireland* (Dublin, 1998), 8–17; Canny, *Making Ireland British*, 172–5; Pawlisch, *Sir John Davies*, ch. 6.

30. CSPIre, 1603–6, 350–2.

31. TNA, SP 63/217, fols. 231–4. There are transcription errors concerning the number of signatories in CSPIre, 1603–6, 362–5. Pawlisch, *Sir John Davies*, 110, says signed by 219 gentry and five peers.

32. CSPIre, 1603–6, 367.

33. TCD MS 672, fol. 25v; CSPIre, 1603–6, 358.

34. CSPIre, 1603–6, 365–6.

35. *CSPIre, 1603–6,* 389–90, 414.
36. *CSPIre, 1603–6,* 405, 466, 468; Patrick Moran, *History of the Catholic Arch-bishops of Dublin* (Dublin, 1684), 235; Colm Lennon, 'Civic Life and Religion in Early Seventeenth-Century Dublin', *Archivium Hibernicum,* 38 (1983), 17.
37. *CSPIre, 1606–8,* 137–9; Jon G. Crawford, *A Star Chamber Court in Ireland: The Court of Castle Chamber, 1571–1641* (Dublin, 2005), 290–300; Judy Barry, 'Barnewall, Sir Patrick', *Dictionary of Irish Biography.*
38. Fitzsimon, *Words of Comfort,* 64, 66, 125, 157–8, 170, 173, 174.
39. Fitzsimon, *Words of Comfort,* 134, 163, 167, 171–2.
40. *CSPIre, 1603–6,* 544.
41. TCD MS 852, fol. 96v; Crawford, *Star Chamber,* 145–6, 150, 295, 300–1, 491–2; *CSPIre, 1606–8,* 15.
42. Fitzsimon, *Words of Comfort,* 124, 125, 155.
43. *CSPIre, 1603–6,* 467.
44. Fitzsimon, *Words of Comfort,* 156.
45. *CSPIre, 1603–6,* 469.
46. *CSPIre, 1603–6,* 398.
47. Fitzsimon, *Words of Comfort,* 174.
48. Fitzsimon, *Words of Comfort,* 65, 140, 174, 179.
49. John Harington, *Nugae Antiquae,* ed. Henry Harrington (2 vols, 1804), I, 340.
50. Winwood, *Memorials,* II, 206; Christopher Maginn, 'Blount, Charles, Eighth Baron Mountjoy and Earl of Devonshire (1563–1606)', *ODNB.*
51. David Edwards, 'The Plight of the Earls: Tyrone and Tyrconnell's "Grievances" and Crown Coercion in Ulster, 1603–7', in Thomas O'Connor and Mary Ann Lyons, eds, *The Ulster Earls and Baroque Europe* (Dublin, 2010), 53–76.
52. Pawlisch, *Sir John Davies,* 66–74; Canny, *Making Ireland British,* 179–83; Hiram Morgan, 'Policy and Propaganda in Hugh O'Neill's Connection with Europe', in O'Connor and Lyons, eds, *Ulster Earls,* 45–50; John McCavitt, *The Flight of the Earls* (Dublin, 2002); Connolly, *Contested Island,* 272–5.
53. Steele, II, no. 191.
54. McCavitt, 'Political Background', esp. 11–14.
55. Philip Robinson, *The Plantation of Ulster* (Dublin, 1984), 85–6. For the Armagh survey, see TCD MS 582, fols. 83–92.
56. TCD MS 747, fol. 117; *CSPIre, 16011–14,* 98; Ian Archer, 'The City of London and the Ulster Plantation', in Micheál Ó Siochrú, ed., *The Plantation of Ulster* (Manchester, 2012); Canny, *Making Ireland British,* 187–242; Moody, *London-derry Plantation* (Belfast, 1939).
57. Robinson, *Plantation of Ulster,* appendices 1–9 (pp. 195–211); Canny, *Making Ireland British,* 208–9; Connolly, *Contested Island,* 293–4, 298.
58. Canny, *Making Ireland British,* 211; Robinson, *Plantation of Ulster,* 104, and App. 10:7 (p. 223). See also Michael Perceval-Maxwell, *The Scottish Migration to Ulster in the Reign of James I* (1973); Gillespie, *Colonial Ulster;* Connolly, *Contested Island,* 279, 301–2, 405; Ohlmeyer in Nicholas P. Canny and Alaine Low, *The Oxford History of the British Empire,* Volume 1 (Oxford, 1998), 139–40. For the 'Great Migration' to New England, see pp. 342–4.
59. Connolly, *Contested Island,* 298–9.
60. *CSPIre, 1611–14,* 538–40; Gillespie, *Seventeenth-Century Ireland,* 51–2.
61. Rev. George Hill, *An Historical Account of the Plantation in Ulster* (Belfast, 1877), 447.
62. Gillespie, *Seventeenth-Century Ireland,* 54–5.

63. Steele, II, no. 203.
64. Rich, *Catholicke Conference*, sigs B3–B4 (quote: sig. B3v); Crawford, *Star Chamber*, 301–2; Kieran Devlin, 'The Beautified Martyrs of Ireland (7)', *Irish Theological Quarterly*, 65 (2000), 265–93; McCavitt, *Chichester*, 175–7; Patrick Moran, *Spicilegium Ossoriense* (Dublin, 1874), 123–6.
65. T. W. Moody, 'The Irish Parliament under Elizabeth and James I: A General Survey', *Proceedings of the Royal Irish Academy*, 45, sect. C (1939), 53–4, 72–80; *NHI*, III, 212–14.
66. *CSPIre, 1611–14*, 359–64; *Des. Cur. Hib.*, I, 156–8, 335–512; Stephen Carroll, 'The Dublin Parliamentary Elections, 1613', in Sheehan and Cronin, *Riotous Assemblies*, 50–63; Lennon, 'Civic Life and Religion', 18.
67. Moody, 'Irish Parliament', 54–5; Bríd McGrath, 'The Membership of the House of Commons in Ireland, 1613–15' (unpublished MA thesis, TCD, 1986); Victor Treadwell, 'The House of Lords in the Irish Parliament of 1613–1615', *EHR*, 80 (1965), 92–107.
68. *CSPIre, 1611–14*, 349–50, 351, 359; *Des. Cur. Hib.*, I, 351–5; McCavitt, *Chichester*, 184.
69. *Calendar of the Carew Manuscripts 1603–23*, 288, 291.
70. McCavitt, *Chichester*, chs 10, 11; Connolly, *Contested Island*, 362–4; Beckett, *Making Modern Ireland*, 48–51; *NHI*, III, 210–19. See account of the proceedings in *Calendar of the Carew Manuscripts, 1603–23*, 270–5, 278–85. For the Ulster conspiracy, see TCD MS 672, fols. 61–93; Raymond Gillespie, *Conspiracy: Ulster Plots and Plotters in 1615* (Belfast, 1987).
71. Alan Ford, *James Ussher* (Oxford, 2007), ch. 4.
72. *NHI*, III, 228–9.
73. TCD MS 1066, fols. 135–6.
74. TCD MS 852, fol. 81.
75. [Comerford], *Inquisition*, 207.
76. Connolly, *Contested Island*, 364–6.
77. TNA, PRO, SP 63/235, fol. 215; *CSPIre, 1615–25*, 306; Canny, *Making Ireland British*, 175–80; *NHI*, III, 219–23; Connolly, *Contested Island*, 326–30.
78. Victor Treadwell, *Buckingham and Ireland* (Dublin, 1998), 130–47.
79. *CSPIre, 1615–25*, 167.
80. Davies, *Historical Relations*, 235–6, 238, 240–2.
81. TCD MS 808, fol. 24.
82. Gillespie, 'Negotiating Order in Early Modern Ireland', in Michael J. Braddick and John Walter, eds, *Negotiating Power in Early Modern Society* (Cambridge, 2002), 199–200.
83. O Riordan, 'Native Ulster *Mentalité*', 78–82.
84. Gráinne Henry, 'Ulster Exiles in Europe, 1605–1641', in Mac Cuarta, ed., *Ulster 1641*, 42 (Table 1); Gillespie, *Seventeenth-Century Ireland*, 61; Gráinne Henry, *The Irish Community in Spanish Flanders, 1586–1621* (Dublin, 1992), 28; David Edwards, 'The Legacy of Defeat: The Reduction of Gaelic Ireland after Kinsale', in Morgan, ed., *Kinsale*, 293; Steve Murdoch, 'The Northern Flight: Irish Soldiers in Seventeenth-Century Scandinavia', in O'Connor and Lyons, eds, *Ulster Earls*, 90; Robert D. Fitzsimon, 'Irish Swordsmen in the Imperial Service in the Thirty Years War', *Irish Sword*, 9 (1969–70), 22–3.
85. Edwards, 'Legacy of Defeat', 294.
86. Eugene Flanagan, 'The Anatomy of Jacobean Ireland: Captain Barnaby Rich, Sir John Davies and the Failure of Reform, 1609–22', in Hiram Morgan, ed., *Political Ideology in Ireland, 1541–1641* (Dublin, 1999), 158–80.

87. Rich, *Catholicke Conference*, sigs A3v, B, C2, D3v, E2.
88. *Calendar of the Carew Manuscripts, 1603–23*, 305–7.
89. *Des. Cur. Hib.*, I, 237–50 (quotes on pp. 238, 240, 241, 243, 246, 249).
90. *Des. Cur. Hib.*, I, 362–3, 365, 368.
91. *CSPIre, 1608–10*, 474.
92. *CSPIre, 1615–25*, 262–3; McCavitt, 'Political Background', 21.
93. TCD MS 672, fol. 159.
94. Maurice Lee, *Government by Pen* (Urbana, 1980).
95. *RPCS*, 1st ser., VI, *1599–1604*, 594–6; Brown, *Bloodfeud*, 243–4; S. J. Watts, *From Border to Middle Shire: Northumberland 1586–1625* (Leicester, 1975), esp. chs 7, 9; *RPS*, 1609/4/26.
96. Julian Goodare, 'The Statutes of Iona in Context', *SHR*, 77 (1998), 31–57; Allan Macinnes, *British Confederate: Archibald Campbell, Marquess of Argyll, 1607–1661*(Edinburgh, 2011), 58–9; Roberts, *Feuds, Forays, and Rebellions*, 145–7; Martin MacGregor, 'The Statutes of Iona: Text and Context', *Innes Review*, 57 (2006), 111–81; Alison Cathcart, 'The Statutes of Iona: The Archipelagic Context', *JBS*, 49 (2010), 4–27; Anna Groundwater, 'The Chasm between James VI and I's Vision of the Orderly "Middle Shires" and the "Cikit" Scottish Borderers between 1587 and 1625', *Renaissance and Reformation*, 30, no. 4 (2007), 105–32.
97. Clarendon, *History*, I, 115.
98. David Stevenson, *The Covenanters: The National Covenant and Scotland* (Edinburgh, 1988), 10.
99. Cited in MacDonald, 'Ecclesiastical Convergence', 887. My discussion of James's reforms in the Kirk draws extensively on MacDonald's work, especially his *Jacobean Kirk*. Also useful is Mullan, *Episcopacy in Scotland*.
100. Row, *History*, 227–8; Spottiswoode, *History*, 486–7; Steele, III, nos. 1067, 1068; *RPCS*, 1st ser., VII, *1604–7*, 101–3, 113–15; Melvill, *Diary*, 668–9.
101. *RPS*, 1605/6/30, 31; Calderwood, *True History*, 532. See MacDonald, 'Deliberative Processes in Parliament', 47–8.
102. Calderwood, *True History*, 527–31; Lockyer, *James VI and I*, 182; MacDonald, *Jacobean Kirk*, 120–1.
103. *Original Letters Relating to the Ecclesiastical Affairs of Scotland*, I, 48–50, 59–67 (quote on p. 60); William Barlow, *One of the Foure Sermons…Sept. 21 1606* (1606); John Buckeridge, *A Sermon Preached at Hampton Court…23 September, Anno 1606* (1606), sig. B4r; Lancelot Andrewes, *A Sermon Preached before the King's Majesty at Hampton Court…the 28 of September Anno 1606* (1606); John King, *The Fourth Sermon Preached at Hampton Court…the last of September 1606* (Oxford, 1606).
104. Melville, *Diary*, 664, 682–3; Row, *History*, 234–5.
105. Scot, *Apol. Narr.*, 170–1, 178, 194; Row, *History*, 231–8; Melvill, *Diary*, 653–83; MacDonald, *Jacobean Kirk*, 124–6; James Kirk, 'Melville, Andrew (1545–1622)', *ODNB*; Prior, *Defining the Jacobean Church*, 127–8; Ferrell, *Government by Polemic*, 125–32; Stephen King, '"Your Best and Most Faithfull Subjects": Andrew and James Melville as James VI and I's "Loyal Opposition"', *Renaissance and Reformation*, 24, no. 3 (2000), 17–30.
106. Balfour, *Historical Works*, II, 17–19; Scot, *Apol. Narr.*, 188–93; Row, *History*, 238–42; Andrew Lang, *A History of Scotland from the Roman Occupation* (4 vols, Edinburgh, 1900–1907), II, 492–3; *Acts & Proc. Gen. Ass.*, 1022–38.
107. *RPS*, 1609/4/20; *RPCS*, 1st ser. VIII, *1607–10*, 417–20.

108. *Acts & Proc. Gen. Ass.*, 1085–1108 (quote on p. 1097); *The XXI Parliament of our Most High and Dread Soveraine, James by the Grace of God, King of Scotland, England, France and Ireland* (1612); *RPS*, 1612/10/8; Scot, *Apol. Narr.*, 221–38; *Briefe and Plaine Narration* (1610), sigs A5, B; MacDonald, *Jacobean Kirk*, 144–9; Alan Macdonald, 'James VI and the General Assembly, 1586–1618', in Julian Goodare and Michael Lynch, eds, *The Reign of James VI* (East Lothian, 2000), 181–4; MacDonald, 'Ecclesiastical Convergence', 890.

109. Russell, *Causes*, 49; John Morrill, 'A British Patriarchy? Ecclesiastical Imperialism under the Early Stuarts', in Anthony Fletcher and Peter Roberts, eds, *Religion, Culture and Society in Early Modern England* (Cambridge, 1994), 209–37.

110. MacDonald', 'Ecclesiastical Convergence'; Patterson, *James VI and I and the Reunion of Christendom*.

111. *Original Letters Relating to the Ecclesiastical Affairs of Scotland*, I, 293.

112. Calderwood, *True History*, 649–50; Scot, *Apol. Narr.*, 238; MacDonald, *Jacobean Kirk*, 155–6.

113. Calderwood, *True History*, 656–73; Scot, *Apol. Narr.*, 241–4; *Acts & Proc. Gen. Ass.*, 1116–39.

114. *RPCS*, 1st ser., XI, *1616–19*, p. xlvi; MacDonald, *Jacobean Kirk*, 157.

115. Balfour, *Historical Works*, II, 64, 66–7; *RPCS*, 1st ser., X, *1613–16*, 681–4; Nichols, *Progresses*, III, 309–15; Steele, III, nos. 1266, 1267, 1273.

116. Spottiswoode, *History*, 530; Calderwood, *True History*, 673–4; Chamberlain, *Letters*, II, 42; Scot, *Apol. Narr.*, 246; Row, *History*, 307; *Original Letters Relating to the Ecclesiastical Affairs of Scotland*, II, 497–500.

117. Nichols, *Progresses*, III, 257.

118. Fincham, *Prelate as Pastor*, 39.

119. [Anthony Weldon], *A Discription of Scotland* (4th edn, [Netherlands?], 1626), 5; Nichols, *Progresses*, III, 317–27 (quotes on pp. 320–1).

120. *RPCS*, 1st ser., XI, *1616–19*, p. xxi.

121. Scot, *Apol. Narr.*, 246; Calderwood, *True History*, 674.

122. TNA, PRO, SP 14/92, fol. 185; Spottiswoode, *History*, 531; Calderwood, *True History*, 675; MacDonald, 'Deliberative Processes in Parliament c. 1587–1639', 48.

123. BL, Harl. MS 4931, fol. 29r–30v; *RPCS*, 1st ser., XI, *1616–19*, pp. xlviii–lv; Nichols, *Progresses*, III, 345–8; *Original Letters Relating to the Ecclesiastical Affairs of Scotland*, II, 502–4.

124. *RPCS*, 1st ser., XI, *1616–19*, p. liii; BL, Harl. MS 4931, fol. 30r–v; David Lindsay, *De Potestate Principis Aphorisme* (1617).

125. *RPCS*, 1st ser., XI, *1619–19*, pp. lv–lx; Scot, *Apol. Narr.*, 251–2; Row, *History*, 311; *Original Letters Relating to the Ecclesiastical Affairs of Scotland*, II, 522–4 (quote on p. 524), 540–2 (quote on p. 542); David Lindsay, *A True Narration of all the Passages of the Proceedings in the Generall Assembly…Holden at Perth* (1621), 17–18.

126. Lindsay, *True Narration*, 49–52, 70; Scot, *Apol. Narr.*, 256; *Original Letters Relating to the Ecclesiastical Affairs of Scotland*, II, 568–71; *The Spottiswoode Miscellany*, ed. James Maidment (2 vols, Edinburgh, 1844–5), I, 66, 81, 83.

127. Scot, *Apol. Narr.*, 253, 255–65 (quotes on pp. 259, 260, 264); Lindsay, *True Narration*, 47, 54, 70, 72; *Original Letters Relating to the Ecclesiastical Affairs of Scotland*, II, 573–7; I. B. Cowan, 'The Five Articles of Perth', in Duncan Shaw, ed., *Reformation and Revolution* (Edinburgh, 1967), 160–77.

128. *RPCS*, 1st ser., XI, *1619–19*, 454–6 (quote on p. 455).

129. Scot, *Apol. Narr.*, 267; *Acts & Proc. Gen. Ass.*, 1143–67; *RPCS*, 1st ser., XI, *1616–19*, pp. lxix–lxx, lxxiv, 454–6, 579–81; *RPCS*, 1st ser., XII, *1619–22*, pp. lxi–lxiii; Warriston, *Short Relation*, sigs A4v–B; MacDonald, *Jacobean Kirk*, 162–4; MacDonald, 'Ecclesiastical Convergence', 896–901; Laura Stewart, '"Brothers in Treuth": Propaganda, Public Opinion and the Perth Articles Debate in Scotland', in Ralph Houlbrooke, ed., *James VI and I: Ideas, Authority, and Government* (2006), 151; Laura Stewart, *Urban Politics and the British Civil Wars: Edinburgh, 1617–53* (Leiden, 2006), ch. 5.

130. Philemon Holland, *A Learned, Elegant, and Religious Speech* (1622), 2–4.

131. Stewart, 'Brothers in Treuth'.

CHAPTER 7. THE BOHEMIAN REVOLT AND THE CRISIS OF THE EARLY 1620S

1. Balfour, *Historical Works*, II, 72–5 (quotes on pp. 74–5).

2. Nehemiah Wallington, *Historical Notices of the Events Occurring Chiefly in the Reign of Charles I*, ed. R. Webb (2 vols, 1869), I, 11.

3. James I, 'You men of Britaine, wherefore gaze yee so', in 'Early Stuart Libels', Ni; John Craigie, ed., *The Poems of James VI of Scotland* (2 vols, Edinburgh, 1955–8), II, 172; James Doelman, 'The Comet of 1618 and the British Royal Family', *Notes and Queries*, 54, 1 (March 2007), 30–5.

4. Birch, ed., *Court and Times of James I*, II, 110.

5. Peter H. Wilson, *Europe's Tragedy* (2009), 787–9, 795.

6. Archibald L. Goodall, 'The Health of James the Sixth of Scotland and First of England', *Medical History*, I (1957), 17–27; Croft, *King James*, 101.

7. TNA, PRO, SP 14/107, fol. 7v.

8. Craigie, ed., *Poems of James VI*, II, 174.

9. TNA, PRO, SP14/108, fols. 70, 125.

10. Goodman, *Court of King James*, I, 239–41; Simon Adams, 'Foreign Policy and the Parliaments of 1621 and 1624', in Kevin Sharpe, ed., *Faction and Parliament* (1978), 147; Fincham, 'Abbot', *ODNB*.

11. Clegg, *Press Censorship in Jacobean England*, ch. 5; Jayne E. Boys, *London's News Press and the Thirty Years War* (Woodbridge, 2011).

12. John Everard, *Arriereban* (1618), 16–17, 27, 87.

13. John Everard, *The Gospel Treasury Opened* (1657), sig. A8v; Elizabeth Allen, 'Everard, John (1584?–1640/41)', *ODNB*.

14. Clegg, *Press Censorship in Jacobean England*, 171–3; T. K. Rabb, 'English Readers and the Revolt in Bohemia, 1619–1622', in Moshe Aberbach, ed., *Aharon M. K. Rabinowitz Jubilee Volume* (Jerusalem, 1996), 152–75.

15. FSL, V. b. 207, fol. 2: 'Mirabilia Huius Anni' (*c.*1619). Cf. Bodl. Lib., MS Rawl. D. 924, fol. 89, 'Justification of the States of Bohemia for Deposition of King Ferdinand'.

16. Quoted in Helen Pierce, *Unseemly Pictures* (New Haven, 2008), 29–30; David Cressy, *Dangerous Talk* (Oxford, 2010), 102.

17. 'Early Stuart Libels', L7; James Knowles, '"To Scourge the Arse | Jove's Marrow so had Wasted": Scurrility and the Subversion of Sodomy', in Dermot Cavanagh and Tim Kirk, eds, *Subversion and Scurrility* (Aldershot, 2000), 74–92; Paul Hammond, *Figuring Sex Between Men from Shakespeare to Rochester* (Oxford, 2002), 143–6.

18. Thomas Alured, *The Coppie of a Letter Written to the Duke of Buckingham Concerning the Match with Spaine* (1642), 2–3, 6, 8; Simon Healy, 'Alured, Thomas (*bap.* 1583, *d.* 1638)', *ODNB*.

19. Sean Kelsey, 'Scott, Thomas (*d.* 1626)', *ODNB*.

20. [Thomas Scott], *Vox Populi; Or, Newes from Spayne* (1620), sigs A4v, Bv, B2, B2v, B3, B3v, B4.

21. [Scott], *Vox Populi*, sigs C2, C3. Cf. Peter Lake, 'Thomas Scott and the Spanish Match', *HJ* (1982), 805–25.

22. Clegg, *Press Censorship in Jacobean England*, 178, 186; Kelsey, 'Scott', *ODNB*; Alastair Bellany, 'Libel', in Joad Raymond, ed., *The Oxford History of Popular Print Culture* (Oxford, 2011), 155.

23. Gardiner, *History of England*, III, 288.

24. Steele, I, nos. 1290, 1296; Chamberlain, *Letters*, II, 328, 331; Thrush, 'Personal Rule of James I', 96–7; John K. Gruenfelder, *Influence in Early Stuart Elections, 1604–1640* (Columbus, 1981), 62–3; Fincham and Lake, 'Ecclesiastical Policy', 198–9.

25. Goodman, *Court of King James*, II, 200; Birch, ed., *Court and Times of James I*, II, 227–8.

26. Gruenfelder, *Influence in Early Stuart Elections*, 63, 108–9; Chris Kyle, 'Prince Charles in the Parliaments of 1621 and 1624', *HJ*, 41 (1998), 607–8.

27. Hirst, *Representative of the People?*, 140, 143, 146, and App. IV.

28. [Thomas Gainsford], *Vox Spiritus* (Exeter, 1983), quotes on fols. 7v, 8, 28v. Manuscript copies of the work include: BL, Harl. MS 7187, fols. 2–30; Bodl. Lib., MS Rawl. B. 151, fols. 51–4; TCD MS 862, fols. 232–49. S. L. Adams, 'Captain Thomas Gainsford, the "Vox Spiritus" and the Vox Populi', *BIHR*, 59 (1976), 141–4.

29. Birch, ed., *Court and Times of James I*, II, 232.

30. Samuel Ward, *Deo Trin-Uni Britanniae bis Ultori... To God, In Memorye of His Double Deliverance* (1621); Pierce, *Unseemly Pictures*, 35–47; Alexandra Walsham, *Providence in Early Modern England* (Oxford, 1999), 255–63; J. M. Blatchly, 'Ward, Samuel (1577–1640)', *ODNB*. The print was reprinted in 1680, and again in 1689 (with alterations).

31. D'Ewes, *Autobiography*, I, 170; Chamberlain, *Letters*, II, 338.

32. *Parl. Hist.*, I, 1176–9; *The Diary of Sir Richard Hutton, 1614–1639*, ed. Wilfrid R. Prest (Selden Society, vol. 9, 1991), 27–30. For the 1621 parliament see Robert Zaller, *The Parliament of 1621* (1971); Conrad Russell, *Parliaments and English Politics, 1621–1629* (Oxford, 1979), ch. 2.

33. Birch, ed., *Court and Times of James I*, II, 81–2, 222; Chamberlain, *Letters*, II, 163–4, 165, 343.

34. Birch, ed., *Court and Times of James I*, II, 245–6, 247–8; Chamberlain, *Letters*, II, 360–1, 363; TNA, PRO, SP 14/120, fol. 105v; TNA, PRO, SP 94/24, fol. 160; BL, Harl. MS 383, fol. 12; *CSP Ven*, 1621–3, 31–2; Zaller, *Parliament of 1621*, 88; *London's Looking-Glasse* (1621), 5–6; James I, *A Proclamation for Suppressing Insolent Abuses* (1621); Steele, I, no. 1313.

35. *Commons Debates 1621*, IV, 72, V, 472, 513; Birch, ed., *Court and Times of James I*, II, 230.

36. *Commons Debates 1621*, II, 92; Russell, *Parliaments and English Politics*, 91.

37. Colin G. C. Tite, *Impeachment and Parliamentary Judicature in Early Stuart England* (1974).

38. *Parl. Hist.*, I, 1229–30, 1250.

39. *The Description of Giles Mompesson Late Knight Censured by Parliament* (1621); Pierce, *Unseemly Pictures*, 69–80.
40. *Parl. Hist.*, I, 1224–5; Lady de Villiers, ed., 'The Hastings Journal of the Parliament of 1621', *Camden Miscellany*, 20 (Camden Society, 3rd ser., 83, 1953), 26, 28; *LJ*, III, 68–70; *Commons Debates 1621*, IV, 202–5; Richard Cust, 'Prince Charles and the Second Session of the 1621 Parliament', *EHR*, 122 (2007), 428.
41. *Parl. Hist.*, I, 1244–7, 1249–50; Lisa Jardine and Alan Stewart, *Hostage to Fortune: The Troubled Life of Francis Bacon* (1998), ch. 16.
42. 'Early Stuart Libels', Mii7.
43. BL, Harl. MS 646, fol. 59v.
44. 'Early Stuart Libels', Mii4.
45. *CJ*, I, 593; Treadwell, *Buckingham and Ireland*, 157–9, 165–8.
46. *Parl. Hist.*, I, 1256, 1258; Chamberlain, *Letters*, II, 374; S. R. Gardiner, *Notes of the Debates in the House of Lords…AD 1621* (Camden Society, 103, 1870).
47. Hutton, *Diary*, 36–7; Chamberlain, *Letters*, II, 370, 372, 377, 390; *Parl. Hist.*, I, 1259–62; D. A. Orr, 'Floyd, Edward (fl. 1588–1621)', *ODNB*.
48. *Parl. Hist.*, I, 1262.
49. *Parl. Hist.*, I, 1264–7, 1285, 1292, 1294–5.
50. Steele, I, nos. 1314, 1315; James I, *By the King. A Proclamation declaring His Majesties Grace to His Subjects, Touching Matters Complained of, as Publique Greevances* (1621); Park Honan, 'Wriothesley, Henry, Third Earl of Southampton (1573–1624)', *ODNB*; *House of Commons, 1604–1629*, I, 409–10; Zaller, *Parliament of 1621*, 138.
51. Balfour, *Historical Works*, II, 89–90; *State Papers and Miscellaneous Correspondence of Thomas, Earl of Melros* (2 vols, Edinburgh, 1837), II, 417–20.
52. Scot, *Apol. Narr.*, 282–93; [William Scot], *The Course of Conformitie* ([Amsterdam], 1622), 66–70; Calderwood, *True History*, 759–74.
53. [David Calderwood], *Quaeres Concerning the State of the Church of Scotland* (reprinted [London?], 1638), 6, 7, 8, 9, 12, 13, 14, 15. See also [David Calderwood], *The Altar of Damascus* ([Amsterdam], 1621).
54. Scot, *Apol. Narr.*, 293–7; Row, *History*, 328–30; Calderwood, *True History*, 774–83; *RPS*, 1621/6/13–14; [Scot], *Course of Conformitie*, 72–103; *Melros Papers*, II, 416, 422, 426.
55. Julian Goodare, 'The Scottish Parliament of 1621', *HJ*, 38 (1995), 29–51; Vaughan T. Wells, 'Constitutional Conflict after the Union of the Crowns: Contention and Continuity in the Parliaments of 1612 and 1621', in Brown and Mann, eds, *Parliament and Politics*, 95–100.
56. Calderwood, *True History*, 784–5; Scot, *Apol. Narr.*, 298.
57. MacDonald, *Jacobean Kirk*, 165–6.
58. [Scot], *Course of Conformitie*, sigs A4v, a2v.
59. Steele, I, no. 1318.
60. Steele, I, no. 1322; James I, *By the King. A Proclamation Concerning the Adjournement of the Parliament* (1621).
61. My account follows Richard Cust, 'Prince Charles and the Second Session of the 1621 Parliament', *EHR*, 122 (2007), 427–41 and Glynn Redworth, *The Prince and the Infanta* (2003), ch. 4, rather than Brennan Pursell, 'James I, Gondomar and the Dissolution of the Parliament of 1621', *History*, 85 (2000), 428–45.
62. *Parl. Hist.*, I, 1301–2.
63. Cust, '1621 Parliament', 440.
64. Akrigg, ed., *Letters*, 378; *Parl. Hist.*, I, 1326–7.

65. Treadwell, *Buckingham and Parliament*, 178–85.

66. *Parl. Hist.*, I, 1334–6, 1338–44, 1360–1.

67. Birch, ed., *Court and Times of James I*, II, 281, 283, 284, 285, 288; *Parl. Hist.*, I, 1371. For Coke's influence on the Protestation, see Stephen D. White, *Sir Edward Coke and 'The Grievances of the Commonwealth' 1621–1628* (Chapel Hill, 1979), 177–8.

68. James I, *By the King. A Proclamation Declaring His Majesties Pleasure Concerning the dissolving of the Present Convention of Parliament* (1621/[2]), 2, 4.

69. James I, *His Majesties Declaration Touching his Proceedings in the Late Assemblie and Convention of Parliament* (1621[/2]), 3, 18.

70. *CSPVen, 1621–3*, 207.

71. Birch, ed., *Court and Times of James I*, II, 289.

72. Birch, ed., *Court and Times of James I*, II, 283–5; *House of Commons 1604–1629*, III, 375, 540.

73. Fincham and Lake, 'Ecclesiastical Policy', 201–2; Lambert, 'Richard Montagu, Arminianism and Censorship', 40–2; Fincham, 'Abbot', *ODNB*.

74. Kenneth Fincham, ed., *Visitation Articles and Injunctions of the Early Stuart Church* (2 vols, Woodbridge, 1994–8), I, 216.

75. Peter Smart, *Canterburies Crueltie* (1643), 1–2; Smart, *Vanitie* (1628), 23; Julia Spraggon, *Puritan Iconoclasm during the English Civil War* (Woodbridge, 2003), 26; Graham Parry, *The Arts of the Anglican Counter-Reformation* (Woodbridge, 2006), 1–3; Nicholas Tyacke, *Anti-Calvinists: The Rise of English Arminianism c. 1590–1640* (Oxford, 1987), 116–18; 'Articles…to be exhibited by his Majestie's Heigh Commissioners, against Mr. John Cosin', in *The Correspondence of John Cosin*, ed. G. Ornsby (2 vols, Surtees Society vols 52, 55, 1869–72), I, 165.

76. Matthew Reynolds, *Godly Reformers and their Opponents in Early Modern England* (Woodbridge, 2005), 133–5, 146–9; Spraggon, *Puritan Iconoclasm*, 19–20.

77. The twelve by the end of the reign were: Richard Neile (Durham), Valentine Carey (Ely), George Montaigne (London), Samuel Harsnett (Norwich), John Howson (Oxford), Thomas Dove (Peterborough), John Buckeridge (Rochester), Lancelot Andrewes (Winchester), William Laud (St David's), plus Robert Wright (Bristol) and John Bridgeman (Chester), both of whom were somewhat cautious in their implementation of Laudian reforms in the 1630s, and Godfrey Goodman (Gloucester), a sacramentalist and a supporter of the beauty of holiness widely perceived to be sympathetic to Rome who was even to fall out with Charles I and Laud in the 1630s. I am grateful to Ken Fincham for discussions on this matter.

78. Birch, ed., *Court and Times of James I*, II, 319–20.

79. George Abbot, [*The Coppie of a Letter Sent from the Lord Grace of Canterburie*] (1622), quote on p. 3; *King James His Letter and Directions to the Lord Archbishop of Canterbury Concerning Preaching and Preachers* (1642), quotes on pp. 4, 5–6; Fincham, *Visitation Articles*, I, 211–14; Chamberlain, *Letters*, II, 434; Joseph Marshall, 'Reading and Misreading King James 1622–42: Responses to the *Letter and Directions touching Preaching and Preachers*', in Daniel Fischlin and Mark Fortier, eds, *Royal Subjects: Essays on the Writings of James VI and I* (Detroit, 2002), 476–511.

80. Birch, ed., *Court and Times of James I*, II, 335; Chamberlain, *Letters*, II, 449; Thomas Cogswell, *The Blessed Revolution* (Cambridge, 1989), 33.

81. Reynolds, *Godly Reformers*, 118, 126–7.
82. *Cabala, Sive, Scrinia Sacra* (1663), 242; Redworth, *Prince and Infanta*, 42 (who miscites zealous as jealous); TNA, PRO, SP 14/132, fol. 213.
83. Steele, I, no. 1362; James I, *By the King. A Proclamation against the Disorderly Printing, Uttering, and Dispersing of Bookes, Pamphlets, etc.* (1623); Clegg, *Press Censorship in Jacobean England*, ch. 5; Jayne E. E. Boys, *London's News Press and the Thirty Years War* (Woodbridge, 2011), ch. 7.
84. *Tom Tell Troath* [n.d., Holland?, 1630?], 1, 2, 11. On the dating see Courtney, 'Court Politics', 208.
85. Bodl. Lib., MS Eng. poet c. 50, fol. 21v.
86. 'From Such a Face Whose Excellence', 'Early Stuart Libels', L8.
87. Cogswell, *Blessed Revolution*, 46.
88. Craigie, ed., *Poems of James VI*, II, 190, 192; Bellany, 'Libellous Politics in Early Stuart England', 294, 258–9. For James's late poetry, see: Curtis Perry, '"If Proclamations Will Not Serve": The Late Manuscript Poetry of James I and the Culture of Libel', in Fischlin and Fortier, eds, *Royal Subjects*, 205–32; Jane Rickard, *Authorship and Authority: The Writings of James VI and I* (Manchester, 2007), ch. 5.
89. Chamberlain, *Letters*, II, 421,439; Birch, ed., *Court and Times of James I*, II, 285, 289, 312; David L. Smith, 'Fiennes, William, First Viscount Saye and Sele (1582–1662)', *ODNB*.
90. Victor Stater, 'Vere, Henry de, Eighteenth Earl of Oxford (1593–1625)', *ODNB*.
91. Treadwell, *Buckingham and Ireland*, 216; Connolly, *Contested Island*, 319–22.
92. Canny, *Making Ireland British*, 243–54; Treadwell, *Buckingham and Ireland*, chs 5, 6; Victor Treadwell, *The Irish Commission of 1622: An Investigation of the Irish Administration, 1615–22, and its Consequences, 1623–24* (Dublin, 2006).
93. Canny, *Making Ireland British*, 248.
94. TCD MS 842, quotes on fols. 176v, 177, 180v; George O'Brien, ed., *Advertisements for Ireland* (Dublin, 1923); Victor Treadwell, 'Richard Hadsor and the Authorship of the "Advertisements for Ireland", 1622/3', *IHS*, 30 (1997), 305–36.
95. TCD MS 842, quotes on fols. 181v, 182v, 184v, 198r–v, 205v. Cf. TCD MS 672, fol. 156r–v, for the claim that the natives of County Longford had not left them as much as the fourth part of their former possessions whereas the king had said that they were not to take any more than a fourth part of the lands of the natives.
96. *NHI*, III, 228.
97. NLI, MS 8,013 (9).
98. NLI, MS 8,013 (9).
99. *CSPVen, 1621–3*, 435.
100. Canny, *Making Ireland British*, 244–5.
101. Canny, *Making Ireland British*, 246–7.
102. NLI, MS 8,013 (iii), 'His Majesties directions touching his Revenewe in Ireland, December 1623'.
103. Michael Perceval-Maxwell, *The Outbreak of the Irish Rebellion of 1641* (Montreal, 1994), 32; Dietz, *English Public Finance*, II, 434.
104. Treadwell, *Irish Commission*, pp. xxxvi–xxxvii.
105. Clarendon, *History*, I, 16; Hutton, *Diary*, ed. Prest, 47; Wilson, *History of Great Britain*, 225.

106. NLI, MS 12,813/2, fol. 283.
107. Redworth, *Prince and the Infanta*, chs 6–13.
108. D'Ewes, *Diary*, 162–3; Wallington, *Historical Notices*, I, 4; Bodl. Lib., MS Top. Oxon. C. 378, p. 321; Birch, ed., *Court and Times of James I*, II, 420, 422; Chamberlain, *Letters*, II, 515–16; NLI, MS 12,813/2, fol. 313; Cogswell, *Blessed Revolution*, 6–12; White, *Militant Protestantism*, 54; John Taylor, *Prince Charles his Welcome from Spaine* (1623), 4–9.
109. NLI, MS 12,813/2, fols. 303, 305.
110. Birch, ed., *Court and Times of James I*, II, 426–31; Balfour, *Historical Works*, II, 98; Matthew Rhodes, *The Dismall Day, at the Black-Fryers* (1623); Alexandra Walsham, '"The Fatall Vesper": Providentialism and Anti-Popery in Late Jacobean London', *P&P*, 144 (1994), 36–87.
111. Robert E. Ruigh, *The Parliament of 1624* (Cambridge, MA, 1971), ch. 2; Kyle, 'Prince Charles in the Parliaments of 1621 and 1624'; Cogswell, *Blessed Revolution*, 140–1; Richard Cust and Peter Lake, 'Sir Richard Grosvenor and the Rhetoric of Magistracy', *BIHR*, 54 (1981), 40–53.
112. It had been adjourned for a week from its original intended starting date of 12 February.
113. *LJ*, III, 209–10; *Parl. Hist.*, I, 1373–6.
114. BL, Add. MS 36,447, fol. 68; Scott, *Vox Regis*, 49, 50.
115. HMC, *Mar and Kellie*, 193.
116. NLI, MS 12,813/2, fols. 344–5; Kyle, 'Prince Charles in the Parliaments of 1621 and 1624', 611.
117. *LJ*, III, 250–1; BL, Harl. MS. 1219, fols. 145–6; HMC, *Mar and Kellie*, 195; Cogswell, *Blessed Revolution*, 183.
118. *LJ*, III, 266, 275, 282–3; *Parl. Hist.*, I, 1394–9, 1402–6; Ruigh, *Parliament of 1624*, ch. 4.
119. *CSP Ven*, 1623–5, 261–2; *LJ*, III, 280; Ruigh, *Parliament of 1624*, 232–3.
120. *LJ*, III, 289–90, 317–18; *Parl. Hist.*, I, 1407–11.
121. Clarendon, *History*, I, 28.
122. *LJ*, III, 383; *Parl. Hist.*, I, 1411–77; Prestwich, *Cranfield*, ch. 10; Ruigh, *Parliament of 1624*, ch. 6; Treadwell, *Buckingham and Ireland*, 252–8.
123. *William Whiteway of Dorchester: His Diary 1618 to 1635*, ed. David Underdown (Dorset Record Society, Dorchester, 1991), 63.
124. *CJ*, I, 704; Hillel Schwartz, 'Arminianism and the English Parliament, 1624–1626', *JBS*, 12 (1973), 43–6.
125. *CJ*, I, 699; *LJ*, III, 388–90; Hutton, *Diary*, 51–2; Reynolds, *Godly Reformers*, 131–7.
126. *Parl. Hist.*, I, 1503; *LJ*, III, 424; Birch, ed., *Court and Times of James I*, II, 457.
127. Scott, *Vox Regis*, 1; Thomas Scott, *The Second Part of Vox Populi* (1624), 25.
128. [Alexander Leighton], *Speculum Belli Sacri* ([Amsterdam], 1624), sigs Br–v.
129. Leighton], *Speculum Belli Sacri*, pp. 166, 182.
130. [Leighton], *Speculum Belli Sacri*, pp. 183, 234, 239.
131. [Leighton], *Speculum Belli Sacri*, pp. 266, 267, 269, 307–8.
132. Scott, *Second Part of Vox Populi* (1624), 4, 12, 13, 31, 42, 48, 49, 60.
133. John Reynolds, *Votivae Angliae* (1624), sigs iii, iv, Aiir–v.
134. Cogswell, *Blessed Revolution*, 297–8.
135. Scott, *Second Part of Vox Populi* (1624), 5.
136. TNA, PRO, SP 14/171, fol. 103; Chamberlain, *Letters*, II, 578; Gary Taylor, ed., 'A Game at Chesse: An Early Form' and 'A Game at Chesse: A Later Form', in

Gary Taylor and John Lavagnino, eds, *Thomas Middleton: The Collected Works* (Oxford, 2007), 1173–885; Cogswell, *Blessed Revolution*, 302–3; Margot Heinemann, *Puritanism and Theatre: Thomas Middleton and Opposition Drama under the Early Stuarts* (Cambridge, 1980), ch. 10; Jerzy Limon, *Dangerous Matter: English Drama and Politics in 1623/24* (Cambridge, 1986); Trudi L. Darby, 'The Black Knight's Festival Book? Thomas Middleton's *A Game at Chess*', in Alexander Samson, ed., *The Spanish Match* (Aldershot, 2006); Thomas Cogswell and Peter Lake, 'Buckingham Does the Globe: *Henry VIII* and the Politics of Popularity in the 1620s', *Shakespeare Quarterly*, 60 (2009), 262–3.

137. Cogswell, *Blessed Revolution*, 290, 299, 306–7.

138. Pauline Gregg, *King Charles I* (1981), 105–6; *House of Commons, 1604–29*, I, p. xlviii; Lockyer, *Buckingham*, 198–210.

139. Lockyer, *Buckingham*, 229–30; Thomas Cogswell, 'Foreign Policy and Parliament: The Case of La Rochelle, 1625–1626', *EHR*, 99 (1984), 249–50.

140. Chamberlain, *Letters*, II, 597.

141. Lockyer, *Buckingham*, 222–9; Roger B. Manning, *An Apprenticeship in Arms* (Oxford, 2006), 105–7.

142. James I, *By the King. A Proclamation Concerning the Prorogation of the Parliament* (1624); *LJ*, III, 426.

143. James I, *By the King. A Proclamation Concerning the Prorogation of the Parliament... Given... the Nineteenth Day of January* (1624/[5]); James I, *By the King. A Proclamation Concerning the Prorogation of the Parliament... Given... the Third Day of March* (1624/[5]).

144. Goodman, *Court of King James*, I, 409–10 and n. Cf. Wilson, *History of Great Britain*, 287.

145. FSL, V. a. 402, fols. 68v–70v; *Hinc Illae Lachrymae* (1692), 48.

146. *CSPVen, 1623–5*, p. 627.

147. FSL, V.a.345, p. 155.

148. FSL, V. b.303, p. 261; FSL, E.a.6, fo. 3v; *Musarum Deliciae*, 207 (epitaph 285).

149. John Taylor, 'A Funerall Elegie Upon King James', in *All the Workes of John Taylor* (1630), 323.

150. FSL, V.a.345, p. 155. Various versions of this elegy survive, with minor modifications in wording. See, for example, FSL, V.a.124, fol. 5; FSL, V.a.162, fol. 83v; Hunt. Lib., HM 116, pp. 86–7.

151. Carlton, *Charles I*, 60; Jennifer Woodward, *The Theatre of Death* (Woodbridge, 1997), ch. 10.

152. John Williams, *Great Britains Salomon* (1625), 37, 41, 46, 47, 49, 50, 52, 53, 57, 59, 63, 76.

CHAPTER 8. A PRINCE 'BRED IN PARLIAMENTS'

1. The term was coined by Sir Benjamin Rudyerd in a speech in the Commons on 22 June 1625: *Proceedings 1625*, 219, 503.

2. William Laud, *A Sermon Preached on Munday, the Sixt of February, At Westminster: At the Opening of the Parliament* (1625[/6]), 52.

3. *CSPVen, 1625–6*, 2. For the proclamation, see TNA, PRO, SP 16/521, fol. 1. Cf. Thomas Cogswell, '1625', in Raymond, ed., *Oxford History of Popular Print Culture*, 589.

4. *Mirth in Mourning* (1625).

5. BL, Harl. MS 383, fol. 20.
6. *CSP Ven, 1625–6*, 4.
7. *Diary of John Rous*, ed. Mary A. E. Green (Camden Society, 66, 1856), 1.
8. This conventional view is reflected in what is a splendid recent textbook: David Smith, *A History of the Modern British Isles, 1603–1707* (Oxford, 1998), 67. See also Kishlansky, 'Case of Mistaken Identity', who outlines the conventional view in order to critique it.
9. Clarendon, *History*, I, 95.
10. *CSP Ven, 1625–6*, 11.
11. Mark A. Kishlansky and John Morrill, 'Charles I (1600–1649)', *ODNB*; Austin Woolrych, *Britain in Revolution 1625–1660* (Oxford, 2002), 49–50; Sharpe, *Personal Rule*, 279–81.
12. Peter Heylyn, *Cyprianus Anglicus* (1668), 104.
13. Clarendon, *History*, I, 111.
14. *Proceedings 1628*, II, 64.
15. Charles Carlton, *Charles I* (2nd edn, 1995), 2–3, 5; Pauline Gregg, *King Charles I* (1981), 12.
16. *CSP Ven, 1625–6*, 18.
17. NLI, MS 12,813/2, fol. 344.
18. *Proceedings 1625*, 29, 493.
19. Peter Heylyn, *A Short View of the Life and Reign of King Charles* (1658), 10.
20. Heylyn, *Short View*, 12, 17; Carlton, *Charles I*, 7.
21. *CSP Ven, 1617–19*, 392–3.
22. Heylyn, *Short View*, 14–15.
23. Carlton, *Charles I*, 9.
24. Cust, *Charles I*, 12–13.
25. Sir Henry Wotton, *Reliquiae Wottonianae* (4th edn, 1685), 146.
26. Carlton, *Charles I*, 29.
27. Sharpe, *Image Wars*, 150–1; Cust, *Charles I*, 25.
28. Christopher Durston, *Charles I* (1998), 5.
29. Laud, *Works*, III, 147.
30. Cust, *Charles I*, 16–19; Kevin Sharpe, 'Private Conscience and Public Duty in the Writings of Charles I', *HJ*, 40 (1997), 643–65.
31. Sharpe, *Personal Rule*, 46–50, 209–17; Lockyer, 'Buckingham', *ODNB*.
32. Clarendon, *History*, I, 48.
33. Caroline M. Hibbard, 'Henrietta Maria (1609–1669)', *ODNB*.
34. Thomas Dekker, *A Rod for Run-Awayes* (1625), sig. A2.
35. Charles I, *A Declaration of the True Causes* (1626), 6; Kyle, 'Prince Charles in the Parliaments of 1621 and 1624', 620–2.
36. *Proceedings 1625*, 3, 509; Russell, *Parliaments and English Politics*, 204–5.
37. Dekker, *Rod for Run-Awayes*, sig. C3v.
38. S. P., *Two Precious and Divine Antidotes against the Plague* (1625), 3–4.
39. William Crashaw, *Londons Lamentation for her Sinnes* (1625), sigs Bv, B2; W. H. Kelliher, 'Crashawe, William (*bap.* 1572, *d.* 1625/6)', *ODNB*.
40. *CSPD, 1625–6*, 16.
41. *CSP Ven, 1625–6*, 51.
42. *House of Commons, 1604–29*, I, xlviii; *CSP Ven, 1625–6*, 12.
43. *Proceedings 1625*, 29.
44. William Laud, *A Sermon Preached before His Majestie, On Sunday the XIX of June, at White-Hall* (1625), 16, 22.

45. *Proceedings 1625*, 500–1.
46. *Proceedings 1625*, 247, 268. See pp. 222–3.
47. *Proceedings 1625*, 278–9, 510.
48. *Proceedings 1625*, 350–3, 354–5, 521–2 (quotes on pp. 351, 522).
49. The specific issue here was the government's claim in 1618 that it allowed for the collection of customs on cloth made of wool as well as on wool itself, which the Commons had determined in 1624 had no legal basis.
50. *Proceedings 1625*, 109, 313–14 and n. 8, 317–18, 349, 510–11; *House of Commons, 1604–29*, I, 421; Russell, *Parliaments and English Politics*, 227–9.
51. *Proceedings of 1625*, 336–9, 359, 517–18. For the Mountague affair, see Tyacke, *Anti-Calvinists*, ch. 6.
52. *Proceedings 1625*, 118–19, 525–6; *House of Commons, 1604–29*, 421–2.
53. *Proceedings 1625*, 529–32.
54. *Proceedings 1625*, 132–3, 388–9, 391–408.
55. *Proceedings 1625*, 154–60 (quote on p. 157), 433–9, 442.
56. *Proceedings 1625*, 448–9, 556–7.
57. *Proceedings 1625*, 451, 452, 566.
58. *Proceedings 1625*, 475.
59. Steele, I, no. 1445; *CSPD, 1625–6*, 148.
60. *Proceedings 1626*, I, 3 n. 3.
61. Cogswell, 'Foreign Policy and Parliament'.
62. John Glanville, *The Voyage to Cadiz in 1625*, ed. Rev. Alexander B. Grosart (Camden Society, n.s. 32, 1883); Carlton, *Charles I*, 72–6; Manning, *Apprenticeship in Arms*, 110–14; Cust, *Charles I*, 49–51; Woolrych, *Britain in Revolution*, 54.
63. *Book of Oaths*, 154–5; Rushworth, I, 199–201; TNA, PRO, SP 16/20, fol. 15; Condren, 'Coronation Oaths', 261.
64. BL, Harl. MS 7000, fol. 193; Laud, *Works*, III, 178–9; Cust, *Charles I*, 89–91; Barbara Donagan, 'The Work House Conference Revisited: Laymen, Calvinism and Arminianism', *HR*, 64 (1991), 312–30; Tyacke, *Anti-Calvinists*, 172–80.
65. Laud, *Sermon... the Sixt of February*, 32, 40, 52.
66. *Proceedings 1626*, I, 21.
67. *Proceedings 1626*, II, 12; *Diary of John Rous*, 2.
68. *Proceedings 1626*, II, 381.
69. Alastair Bellany and Thomas Cogswell, *The Murder of James I* (forthcoming).
70. *Proceedings 1626*, II, 391–5; *CSPVen, 1625–6*, 385.
71. *Proceedings 1626*, III, 4, 30.
72. John C. Appleby, 'An Association for the West Indies? English Plans for a West India Company 1621–29', *The Journal of Imperial and Commonwealth History*, 15 (1987), 213–41.
73. Thomas Cogswell, '"The Warre of the Commons for the Honour of King Charles": The Parliament Men and the Reformation of the Lord Admiral in 1626', *HR*, 84 (2011), 618–36.
74. *Proceedings 1626*, I, 409, 462; III, 195, 223; BL, Harl. MS 383, fols. 31v, 32.
75. *Proceedings 1626*, III, 241–2; L. J. Reeve, *Charles I and the Road to Personal Rule* (Cambridge, 1989), 13.
76. *Proceedings 1626*, III, 406.
77. Charles I, *Declaration of the True Causes*, 2–3, 19–20, 26, 27, 28.
78. Charles I, *By the King. A Proclamation for the Establishing of the Peace and Quiet of the Church of England* (1626).

79. *Diary of John Rous*, 6; Rushworth, I, 413.
80. BL, Harl. MS 383, fol. 33.
81. *CSP Ven, 1625–6*, 508.
82. Rushworth, I, 413–16.
83. Rushworth, I, 416; Steele, I, no. 1492; Richard Cust, *The Forced Loan and English Politics 1626–1628* (Oxford, 1987), 36–9.
84. Cust, *Forced Loan*, 42, 46–7; *House of Commons, 1604–29*, I, p. lii.
85. Rushworth, I, 420; Cust, *Forced Loan*, 122–6.
86. TNA, PRO, SP 16/36, fols. 68–73 (quotations at 69r–70v).
87. Charles I, *Instructions Directed from the Kings Most Excellent Majestie* (1626).
88. Cust, *Charles I*, 65; Cust, *Forced Loan*, ch. 2.
89. Charles I, *By the King. A Declaration of His Majesties Cleare Intention, in Requiring the Ayde of His Loving Subjects, in that Way of Loane which is now intended* (1626); Steele, I, no. 1494.
90. Hutton, *Diary*, 65–6; Brooks, *Law, Politics and Society*, 167–8; *ST*, III, 1, n.
91. HMC, *Buccleuch*, I, 264; TNA, PRO, SP 16/41, fol. 4.
92. *The Court and Times of Charles the First*, ed. Thomas Birch (2 vols, 1848), I, 177; Rushworth, I, 422.
93. Cust, *Forced Loan*, 54–62.
94. Matthew Wren, *A Sermon Preached before the Kings Majestie On Sunday the Seventeenth of February last, at White-Hall* (1627), 16, 17, 25, 28, 30, 31.
95. Isaac Bargrave, *A Sermon Preached before King Charles, March 27 1627* (1627), 1, 14, 16–17, 18–19.
96. Roger Maynwaring, *Religion and Alegiance in Two Sermons ... The First Sermon* (1627), 13, 17, 18, 19, 20, 26, 27, 30–1.
97. Maynwaring, *Religion and Alegiance in Two Sermons*, 11, 42, 45, 46.
98. *Proceedings 1628*, V, 642; Cust, *Forced Loan*, 62–3; *ST*, III, 357.
99. Robert Sibthorpe, *Apostolike Obedience* (1627), 6, 10–11, 15–16, 18, 22–3.
100. Sibthorpe, *Apostolike Obedience*, inside front cover; Rushworth, I, 437.
101. Rushworth, I, 420–1; Brian Quintrell, 'Williams, John (1582–1650)', *ODNB*.
102. *ST*, III, 6, 8.
103. *ST*, III, 37, 44–5, 50.
104. *ST*, III, 51, 58–9. See also Rushworth, I, 458–62.
105. John Guy, 'The Origins of the Petition of Right Reconsidered', *HJ*, 25 (1982), 289–312; Mark Kishlansky, 'Tyranny Denied: Charles I, Attorney General Heath, and the Five Knights' Case', *HJ*, 42 (1999), 53–83; Brooks, *Law, Politics and Society*, 169–74; Paul D. Halliday, *Habeas Corpus* (Cambridge, MA, 2010), 137–9, 159–60.
106. BL, Harl. MS 383, fol. 49; Bodl. Lib., MS Rawl. Poet. 26, fol. 80r–v; Manning, *Apprenticeship in Arms*, 114–16; Lockyer, *Buckingham*, 378–404 (the figure of 5,000 is on p. 401).
107. Cust, *Forced Loan*, 75; Cust, *Charles I*, 68–9; Milton, 'Laud, William (1573–1645)', *ODNB*.
108. Smith, *History of the Modern British Isles*, 72.
109. Robin J. S. Swales, 'The Ship Money Levy of 1628', *BIHR*, 50 (1977), 164–76.
110. *Proceedings 1628*, II, 2–3.
111. *Proceedings 1628*, II, 56, 60–1.
112. *Proceedings 1628*, II, 58, 64.

113. *CJ*, I, 879; Cust, *Charles I*, 71.

114. *Proceedings 1628*, II, 325.

115. *Proceedings 1628*, III, 125, 213, 254, 269, 272, 273 n. 38, 339–41; Elizabeth Read Foster, 'Petitions and the Petition of Right', *JBS*, 14 (1974), 21–45.

116. *Proceedings 1628*, III, 372, 452, 563, 565; Cust, *Charles I*, 73–4; Reeve, *Road to Personal Rule*, 41–2.

117. *Proceedings 1628*, IV, 9.

118. *SR*, V, 23–4.

119. *Proceedings 1628*, IV, 52.

120. *Proceedings 1628*, IV, 182, 185; TNA, PRO, SP 16/106, fols. 127–131v; *Diary of John Rous*, 16.

121. *Proceedings 1628*, IV, 220, 280, 309–10.

122. *Proceedings 1628*, IV, 312–17, 352 and n. 41; VI, 52–6. The remonstrance is discussed in Reeve, *Road to Personal Rule*, 24–30.

123. *Proceedings 1628*, IV, 470–1, 480, 482.

124. Smith, *History of the Modern British Isles*, 73; Elizabeth Read Foster, 'The Printing of the Petition of Right', *HLQ*, 38 (1974–5), 81–3; Russell, *Parliaments and English Politics*, 401–2; John Morrill, *The Nature of the English Revolution* (1993), 289.

125. Vivienne Larminie, 'Maynwaring, Roger (1589/90?–1653)', *ODNB*. Maynwaring was to be presented with the additional rectories of Muckleton, Staffordshire in 1630 and Mugginton, Derbyshire, in 1631; installed as dean of Worcester in 1634; and consecrated as bishop of St David's in 1636.

126. These appointments can be tracked through the biographies in the *ODNB*.

127. Bodl. Lib., MS Rawl. Poet. 26, fol. 81v; Bodl. Lib., MS Top. Oxon. C. 378, p. 250; BL, Harl. MS 383, fols. 72, 74; Oglander, *Royalist's Notebook*, 34–42; Clarendon, *History*, I, 33–7; Rushworth, I, 635, 638–9; Alastair Bellany, 'Felton, John (d. 1628)', *ODNB*; Alastair Bellany and Thomas Cogswell, *England's Assassin: John Felton and the Killing of the Duke of Buckingham* (forthcoming).

128. Clarendon, *History*, I, 37–8; TNA, PRO, SP 16/117, fol. 120.

129. Samuel R. Gardiner, *A History of England under the Duke of Buckingham and Charles I* (2 vols, 1975), II, 341–4; Braddick, *God's Fury*, 43–4.

130. TNA, PRO, SP 16/119 fol. 70.

131. BL, Harl. MS 4931, fol. 9; 'Early Stuart Libels', Pi13.

132. Bodl. Lib., MS Rawl. Poet. 26, fols. 14, 33r–v. For anti-Buckingham libels more generally, see Alastair Bellany, '"Raylinge Rymes and Vaunting Verse": Libellous Politics in Early Stuart England', in Kevin Sharpe and Peter Lake, eds, *Culture and Politics in Early Stuart England* (1994), 297–309.

133. Birch, ed., *Court and Times of Charles I*, I, 410.

134. Reeve, *Road to Personal Rule*, 34–5, 39–40; Perez Zagorin, 'Did Strafford Change Sides?', *EHR*, 101 (1986), 149–63.

135. TNA, PRO, SP 16/119, fol. 59; TNA, PRO, SP 16/142, fol. 36; TNA, PRO, PC 2/38, fol. 489; Rushworth, I, 641–2, 670–7; Robert Ashton, 'Chambers, Richard (c.1588–1658)', *ODNB*; W. A. Shaw, 'Rolle, John (1598–1648)', rev. Robert Ashton, *ODNB*; Linda S. Popofsky, 'The Crisis over Tonnage and Poundage in Parliament in 1629', *P&P*, 126 (1990), 44–75; Reeve, *Road to Personal Rule*, 32.

136. Rushworth, I, 642.

137. *Barrington Family Letters, 1628–1632*, ed. Arthur Searle (Camden Society, 4th ser., 28, 1983), 39; Birch, ed., *Court and Times of Charles I*, I, 439; Reeve, *Road to Personal Rule*, 61.

138. *Articles Agreed Upon by the Archbishops and Bishops of both Provinces, and the Whole Cleargie: In the Convocation Holden at London in the Yeere 1562* (1628), 1–2; David Como, 'Predestination and Political Conflict in Laud's London', *HJ*, 46 (2003), 263–94.

139. BL, Harl. MS 383, fol. 73r–v; *Correspondence of John Cosin*, I, 147–50.

140. Steele, I, no. 1568; Charles I, *By the King. A Proclamation, for the Suppressing of a Booke, Intitutled, Appelo Caesarum, or, An Appeale to Caesar* (1628[/9]); BL, Harl. MS 383, fols. 78, 80; A. Ar., *The Practice of Princes* (1630), 15; Rushworth, I, 634–5.

141. *Commons Debates 1629*, 4–5, 7, 10–11.

142. *Commons Debates 1629*, 13, 14, 15–16. Rous's speech was published in 1641, under the title *A Religious and Worthy Speech Spoken by Mr Rowse*.

143. *Commons Debates 1629*, 94.

144. *Commons Debates 1629*, 95–100.

145. *Commons Debates 1629*, 101–6, 239–44; BL, Harl. MS 383, fol. 82; *CSPVen, 1628–9*, 580; Kyle, *Theater of State*, 53–4. For the 1629 session see: Russell, *Parliaments and English Politics*, ch. 7; Christopher Thompson, 'The Divided Leadership of the House of Commons in 1629', in Sharpe, ed., *Faction and Parliament*, 245–84; Reeve, *Road to Personal Rule*, ch. 3.

146. Charles I, *His Majesties Declaration to all His Loving Subjects, Of the Causes which Moved Him to Dissolve the Last Parliament* (1628[/9]), 1–2, 3, 5–6.

147. Cust, *Charles I*, 119.

148. Charles I, *His Majesties Declaration.... Of the Causes which Moved Him to Dissolve the Last Parliament*, quotes on pp. 9–10, 11, 12, 20–1, 23, 25, 26, 27, 29–30, 34, 40–1.

149. Charles I, *His Majesties Declaration.... Of the Causes which Moved Him to Dissolve the Last Parliament*, 41–3.

150. *Parl. Hist.*, II, 524.

151. Charles I, *By the King. A Proclamation for Suppressing of False Rumours touching Parliament* (1629); Steele, I, no. 1578.

CHAPTER 9. HALCYON DAYS OR PERILOUS TIMES?

1. BL, Harl. MS 7000, fol. 259; John Walter, 'Grain Riots and Popular Attitudes to the Law: Maldon and the Crisis of 1629', in John Brewer and John Styles, eds, *An Ungovernable People* (1980), 47–84; John Walter, 'Carter, Ann (*d.* 1629)', *ODNB*; William Hunt, *The Puritan Moment* (Cambridge, MA, 1983), 239–42.

2. TNA, PRO, SP 16/140, fol. 88; TNA, PRO, SP 16/142, fols. 135–6; Como, 'Predestination and Political Conflict', 275–7.

3. For the positive view, see in particular Kevin Sharpe, 'The Personal Rule of Charles I', in Howard Tomlinson, *Before the Civil War* (1984), 53–78; Kevin Sharpe, *The Personal Rule of Charles I* (1992); Julian Davies, *The Caroline Captivity of the Church* (Oxford, 1992); Conrad Russell, *Unrevolutionary England 1603–1642* (1990).

4. Sharpe, *Personal Rule*, 60.

5. Charles I, *His Majesties Declaration: To All His Loving Subjects, Of the Causes which Moved him to Dissolve the Last Parliament* (1640), 3.

6. *CSPVen, 1629–32*, 75; *CSPVen, 1636–9*, 124; Michael B. Young, *Charles I* (Basingstoke, 1997), 73.

7. Reeve, *Road to Personal Rule*, 42–57, 234–56.
8. Cited in Cust, *Charles I*, 127.
9. Cust, *Charles I*, 125–6, 171–8; Reeve, *Road to Personal Rule*, 185; Kishlansky, 'Case of Mistaken Identity'; Woolrych, *Britain in Revolution*, 51, 62–3, 72–5.
10. Malcolm Smuts, 'The Puritan Followers of Henrietta Maria in the 1630s', *EHR*, 93 (1978), 26–45.
11. Caroline Hibbard, *Charles I and the Popish Plot* (Chapel Hill, 1983); Hibbard, 'Henrietta Maria', *ODNB*.
12. Linda Peck, 'Kingship, Counsel and Lw in Early Stuart Britain', in J. G. A. Pocock, ed., *Varieties of British Political Thought* (Cambridge, 1993), 106–13; Linda Peck, 'Beyond the Pale: John Cusacke and the Language of Absolutism in Early Stuart Britain', *HJ*, 41 (1998), 121–49.
13. Robert Filmer, *Patriarcha and other Writings*, ed. Johann P. Sommerville (Cambridge, 1991), 32, 34.
14. FSL, V.b.189, pp. 38, 83. For discussions of Kynaston's work, see Sommerville, *Royalists and Patriots*, 235–8; Burgess, *Absolute Monarchy*, 38–9; Esther Cope, *Politics without Parliaments, 1629–1640* (1987), 27.
15. William Laud, *A Commemoration of King Charles His Inauguration* (1645), 10, 13, 17, 25, 26.
16. Strong, *Tudor and Stuart Monarchy*, 131–48, 173; Eveline Cruickshanks, ed., *The Stuart Courts* (Stroud, 2000), 4; Cust, *Charles I*, 157–61; Smuts, *Court Culture*, 236–7; Roy C. Strong, *Van Dyck: Charles I on Horseback* (1972); Sharpe, *Image Wars*, ch. 6; Julius S. Held, 'Le Roi à la Ciasse', *The Art Bulletin*, 40, no. 2 (June, 1958), 139–49.
17. Kevin Sharpe, *Criticism and Compliment* (Cambridge, 1987), ch. 5; Martin Butler, *The Stuart Court Masque and Political Culture* (Cambridge, 2008), ch. 9.
18. Clarendon, *History*, I, 93.
19. Sharpe, *Personal Rule*, 609–10; Butler, *Stuart Court Masque*, 280; Raymond A. Anselment, 'Clarendon and the Caroline Myth of Peace', *JBS*, 23 (1984), 37–54.
20. Charles I, *His Majesties Declaration: To All His Loving Subjects, Of the Causes which Moved Him to Dissolve the Last Parliament* (1640), 41.
21. W. G. Hoskins, 'Harvest Fluctuations and English Economic History', *AgHR*, 16 (1968), 15–31 (esp. 19–20, 28).
22. Slack, *Impact of the Plague*, 58, 62.
23. [William Prynne], *Newes from Ipswich* (3rd edn, Ipswich [i.e. London?], 1636), sigs. ¶3r–v.
24. Peter Studley, *The Looking-Glasse of Schisme* (1635), 1, 10–11, 238, 243.
25. Samuel Hoard, *The Churches Authority Asserted* (1637), 64–5.
26. Thomas Gataker, *A Discours Apologetical* (1654), 26.
27. Woodford's Diary, 19 November 1638.
28. This and the following paragraph are based on Paul Slack, 'Books of Orders: The Making of English Social Policy, 1577–1631', *TRHS*, 5th ser., 29 (1980), 1–22; B. W. Quintrell, 'The Making of Charles I's Book of Orders', *EHR*, 95 (1980), 553–72; Sharpe, *Personal Rule*, ch. 7; Henrik Langelüddecke, '"Patchy and Spasmodic?": The Response of Justices of the Peace to Charles I's Book of Orders', *EHR* (1998), 1231–48; Lawrence Stone, 'The Bourgeois Revolution of Seventeenth-Century England Revisited', *P&P*, 109 (1985), 44–54.
29. Frederick C. Dietz, *English Public Finance 1558–1641* (1932), 283.
30. Sharpe, *Personal Rule*, 487–500; Henrik Langelüddecke, '"The Chiefest Strength and Glory of this Kingdom"; Arming and Training the "Perfect Militia" in the 1630s', *EHR*, 118 (2003), 1264–1303.

31. Sharpe, *Personal Rule*, 105–7.
32. Smith, *History of the Modern British Isles*, 89; Sharpe, *Personal Rule*, 129.
33. Cope, *Politics without Parliaments*, 135–7; Sharpe, *Personal Rule*, 112–16; Braddick, *Nerves of State*, 76; H. H. Leonard, 'Distraint of Knighthood: The Last Phase, 1625–41', *History*, 63 (1978), 23–37. Brooks, *Law, Politics and Society*, 104–5 points out that the Caroline judges denied that distraint of knighthood was a feudal imposition but instead derived from a duty at common law to compel those who were fit to defend the realm.
34. Buchanan Sharp, *In Contempt of All Authority* (Berkeley, 1980), ch. 4; Pierce, *Unseemly Pictures*, 83; Martin Ingram, 'Ridings, Rough Music and the "Reform of Popular Culture" in Early Modern England', *P&P*, 105 (1984), 91.
35. George Hammersley, 'The Revival of the Forest Laws under Charles I', *History*, 45 (1960), 85–102; Lockyer, *Early Stuarts*, 283–4; Sharpe, *Personal Rule*, 112–20; Daniel C. Beaver, *Hunting and the Politics of Violence before the English Civil War* (Cambridge, 2008), 84–6, 107–17.
36. *CSPVen, 1629–32*, 298.
37. *The Diary of Sir Henry Slingsby*, ed. Rev. Daniel Parsons (1836), 17–18; Sharpe, *Personal Rule*, 108–11; Braddick, *Nerves of State*, 75, 79–82; G. E. Aylmer, 'The Last Years of Purveyance 1610–1660', *EcHR*, 2nd ser., 10 (1957–8), 81–93.
38. Pauline Gregg, *King Charles I* (1981), 216; Carlton, *Charles I*, 190–1.
39. TNA, PRO, SP 16/252, fol. 40; TNA, PRO, SP 16/254, fol. 73r–v; TNA, PRO, SP 16/259, fol. 130; TNA, PRO, SP 16/260, fol. 102; Hutton, *Diary*, 105; *Articles of Accusation, Exhibited by the Commons...against Sir John Bramston* (1641), 2–3; Brooks, *Law, Politics and Society*, 197–8; Capp, *Gossips*, 309; Sharp, *Personal Rule*, 122, 259–61.
40. Keith Lindley, *Fenland Riots and the English Revolution* (1981); Clive Holmes, *Seventeenth-Century Lincolnshire* (Lincoln, 1980).
41. Kenneth R. Andrews, *Ships, Money and Politics* (Cambridge, 1991), ch. 6.
42. TNA, PRO, SP 16/276, fols. 186–90.
43. Woolrych, *Britain in Revolution*, 67. See pp. 193, 261–2.
44. Morrill, *Revolt of the Provinces*, 27.
45. TNA, SP 16/346, fols. 22–5; *CSPD, 1636–7*, 416–19. See also BL, Add. MS 36,913, fol. 40; BL, Harl. MS 7000, fol. 380.
46. Brian P. Levack, *Gender and Witchcraft* (2001), 150; Peter Clark, *English Provincial Society from the Reformation to the Revolution* (Hassocks, 1977), 358–9.
47. *CSPVen, 1632–6*, 314.
48. BL, Add. MS 35,331, fol. 64.
49. *CSPVen, 1636–9*, 124–5.
50. *ST*, III, 859–62, 883, 905; Woodford's Diary, 4 November 1637.
51. *ST*, III, 1098–9, 1226, 1234, 1235.
52. Woodford's Diary, 28 April 1638; *ST*, III, 1196; Wilfrid Prest, 'Ship Money and Mr Justice Hutton', *History Today*, 41 (January, 1991), 42–7; Brooks, *Law, Politics and Society*, 201–8.
53. Clarendon, *History*, I, 86–7.
54. John Morrill, *The Revolt of the Provinces* (Harlow, 1980), 24–30; Sharpe, *Personal Rule*, 567–83; M. D. Gordon, 'The Collection of Ship-Money in the Reign of Charles I', *TRHS*, 3rd ser., 4 (1910), 141–62; Woolrych, *Britain in Revolution*, 67–9 (whose figures I have followed).

55. D'Ewes, *Autobiography*, II, 130; Clive Holmes, 'The County Community in Stuart Historiography', *JBS* (1980), 66; S. P. Salt, 'Sir Simonds D'Ewes and the Levying of Ship Money, 1635–1640', *HJ*, 37 (1994), 253–87.

56. Woodford's Diary, 17 January 1638.

57. Kenneth Fincham, 'The Judges' Decision on Ship Money in February 1637: The Reaction of Kent', *BIHR*, 57 (1984), 230–7.

58. Peter Lake, 'The Collection of Ship Money in Cheshire', *Northern History*, 17 (1981), 44–71.

59. Henrik Langelüddecke, '"I Finde all Men and My Officers All Soe Unwilling": The Collection of Ship Money, 1635–1640', *JBS*, 46 (2007), 509–42.

60. *The Diary of Thomas Crosfield*, ed. F. S. Boas (Oxford, 1935), 86.

61. TNA, PRO, SP 16/387, fol. 114.

62. TNA, PRO, SP 16/395, fol. 74; Bodl. Lib., MS Bankes 42, fol. 137; Adam Fox, 'Rumour, New and Popular Political Opinion in Elizabethan and Early Stuart England', *HJ*, 40 (1997), 619. Walker predictably denied the charge (TNA, PRO, SP 16/399, fol. 74), though the words are so specific as to suggest someone must have said them; someone had certainly thought them.

63. TNA, PRO, SP 16/351, fol. 37; Capp, *Gossips*, 315. For a similar example, see Woodford's Diary, 18 September 1638.

64. *CSPVen, 1636–9*, 429–30.

65. Sharpe, *Personal Rule*, 129–30; Christopher W. Daniels and John Morrill, *Charles I* (Cambridge, 1988), 74, who put Charles I's income by 1637 at over £1m.

66. Tyacke, 'Puritanism, Arminianism, and Counter-Revolution'.

67. Collinson, *Religion of Protestants*, 90.

68. Sharpe, *Personal Rule*, ch. 6; Julian Davies, *The Caroline Captivity of the Church* (Oxford, 1992).

69. Cf. John Fielding, 'Arminianism in the Localities: Peterborough Diocese 1603–1642', in Fincham, ed., *Early Stuart Church*, 93–103.

70. See pp. 208–11.

71. Kenneth Fincham and Peter Lake, 'The Ecclesiastical Policies of James I and Charles I', in Kenneth Fincham, ed., *The Early Stuart Church, 1603–1642* (Basingstoke, 1993), 37–8. I am indebted to Ken Fincham for discussing ecclesiastical preferment under Charles I in detail with me.

72. Richard Mountague, *Appello Caesarem* (1625), 10; Davies, *Caroline Captivity*, ch. 3 (esp. p. 117); Sharpe, *Personal Rule*, 286–8.

73. Foster, 'Church Policies of the 1630s', 214–15; Como, 'Predestination and Political Conflict', 286–7; Kenneth Fincham, 'William Laud and the Exercise of Ecclesiastical Patronage', *JEH*, 51 (2000), 69–94.

74. Peter Smart, *The Vanitie and Downe-Fall of Superstitious Popish Ceremonies* (Edinburgh, 1628), 21; Richard Culmer, *Cathedrall Newes from Canterbury* (1644), 8.

75. Laud, *Works*, VI, part I, p. 42.

76. Christopher Dow, *Innovations Unjustly Charged upon the Present State and Church* (1637), 192.

77. Felicity Heal, 'Archbishop Laud Revisited: Leases and Estate Management at Canterbury and Winchester before the Civil War', in Rosemary O'Day and Felicity Heal, eds, *Princes and Paupers in the English Church 1500–1600* (1981), 129–51 (quote on p. 132); Foster, 'Church Policies of the 1630s', 198–9; Christopher Hill, *Economic Problems of the Church* (Oxford, 1956).

78. Sharpe, *Personal Rule*, 309–15; Marshall, *Reformation England*, 198.
79. Andrew Foster, 'The Clerical Estate Revitalised', in Fincham, ed., *Early Stuart Church*, 139–60; Christopher Haigh and Alison Wall, 'Clergy JPs in England and Wales, 1590–1640', *HJ*, 47 (2004), 233–59.
80. Foster, 'Church Policies of the 1630s', 202; Sharpe, *Personal Rule*, 318–19; Marshall, *Reformation England*, 198.
81. Lake, *Boxmaker's Revenge*, 304, 307; Parry, *Arts of the Anglican Counter-Reformation*, 30–1, 34–5, 37–9.
82. Bodl. Lib., MS Rawlinson A 128, fol. 29v; Samuel R. Gardiner, *Reports of Cases in the Courts of Star Chamber and High Commission* (Camden Society, n.s. 39, 1886), 312–13; Foster, 'Church Policies of the 1630s', 204–5.
83. Sharpe, *Personal Rule*, 322–8; Charles Carlton, *Archbishop William Laud* (1987), 94–5; H. R. Trevor-Roper, *Archbishop Laud, 1573–1645* (1962), 123–6, 346–7, 350–1; Davies, *Caroline Captivity*, 76–9.
84. TNA, PRO, SP 16/152, fol. 4; Tyacke, *Anti-Calvinists*, 188–91.
85. Peter Heylyn, *Cyprianus Anglicus* (1668), 289.
86. John Walter, *Understanding Popular Violence in the English Revolution* (Cambridge, 1999), 171–2.
87. Laud, *Works*, V, part II, p. 367.
88. Walter, *Understanding Popular Violence*, 214.
89. Peter Smart, *A Short Treatise of Altars* (1643), 15.
90. Sharpe, *Personal Rule*, 340; Atherton, 'Cathedrals and Laudianism', 900–1. The situation at York and Lincoln was unclear. See p. 108.
91. Fincham and Tyacke, *Altars Restored*, ch. 5; Fincham, 'Restoration'.
92. Wallington, *Historical Notices*, I, 23–4; Tyacke, *Anti-Calvinists*, 194; Parry, *Arts of the Anglican Counter-Reformation*, chs 4, 5.
93. John Walter, 'Gesturing at Authority: Deciphering the Gestural Code of Early Modern England', *P&P*, 203, suppl. 4 (2009), 111.
94. Rushworth, II, 77; William Prynne, *Canterbury's Doom* (1646), 113–15; Peter Lake, *The Boxmaker's Revenge* (Manchester, 2001), 310–11.
95. Atherton, 'Cathedrals and Laudianism', 912–13.
96. Marshall, *Reformation England*, 198. For James's order, embodied in his *Directions Concerning Preachers*, see pp. 210–11.
97. Andrew Foster, 'The Clerical Estate Revitalized', in Fincham, *Early Stuart Church*, 141, 156–9; Foster, 'Church Policies', 209.
98. *Articles to be Inquired Within the Dioces of Norwich* (1636); Anthony Fletcher, *Sussex 1600–1660* (Chichester, 1980), ch. 4; Webster, Godly Clergy, 207–8; Kenneth Fincham, ed., *Visitation Articles and Injunctions of the Early Stuart Church*, Vol. II (Woodbridge, 1998), 129–49; R. W. Ketton-Cremer, *Norfolk in the Civil War* (Norwich, 1969), 65.
99. Fincham and Tyacke, *Altars Restored*, ch. 5; Fincham, 'Restoration'.
100. Michael Questier, 'Arminianism, Catholicism and Puritanism in England during the 1630s', *HJ*, 49 (2006), 58.
101. Sharpe, *Personal Rule*, 281, 285–6, 303; Milton, *Catholic and Reformed*, 86–90.
102. Walter, *Understanding Popular Violence*, 214.
103. Mountague, *Appello Caesarem*, 278; Anthony Cade, *A Sermon Necessarie for these Times...An Appendix...Concerning the Ceremonies of the Church of England* (Cambridge, 1639), 18.
104. Giles Widdowes, *The Lawlesse Kneelesse Schismaticall Puritan* (1631), 1.

105. Studley, *Looking-Glasse*, 145, 238, 242–3.
106. Morton, *Defence of the Innocencie*; Cromartie, *Constitutionalist Revolution*, 246–7.
107. Lake, 'Laudian Style'; Peter Lake, 'The Laudians and the Argument from Authority', in Kunze and Brautigam, eds, *Court, Country and Culture*, 149–75; Jean-Louis Quantin, *The Church of England and Christian Antiquity* (Oxford, 2009).
108. John Pocklington, *Altare Christianum* (1637), 4.
109. William Quelch, *Church-Customes Vindicated: In Two Sermons* (1636), 40, 50.
110. Samuel Hoard, *The Churches Authority Asserted* (1637), sigs A2r–v, pp. 7, 25, 26, 30, 57–8, 59. Hoard claimed that the king, by dint of the royal supremacy, granted these powers to the bishops of our Church: p. 61.
111. Mountague, *Appello Caesarem*, 113, 139, 140; William Laud, *A Sermon Preached Before His Majesty, On Tuesday the Nineteenth of June, at Wansted, Anno Dom. 1621* (1621), 26; Milton, *Catholic and Reformed*, chs 2, 3.
112. Alexandra Walsham, 'The Parochial Roots of Laudianism Revisited: Catholics, Anti-Calvinists and "Parish Anglicans" in Early Stuart England', *JEH*, 49 (1998), 638–50; Questier, 'Arminianism, Catholicism and Puritanism', 59; Milton, *Catholic and Reformed*, 64–5.
113. William Laud, *A Relation of the Conference betweene William Laud...and Mr. Fisher* (1639), sig. *3.
114. Wallington, *Historical Notices*, I, 23.
115. Laud, *Works*, IV, 62–6.
116. Smart, *Vanitie*, sig *4v.
117. Laud, *Works*, III, 219; Questier, 'Arminianism, Catholicism and Puritanism', 54, 59, 66, 69.
118. Cited in Perceval-Maxwell, *Outbreak*, 109.
119. Peter Heylyn, *The Parable of the Tares* (1659), 55–7.
120. Studley, *Looking-Glasse*, 245–6.
121. Widdowes, *Lawlesse Kneelesse Schismaticall Puritan*, 2; Giles Widdowes, *The Schismatical Puritan* (Oxford, 1631), sig. C3.
122. [Henry Parker], *A Discourse Concerning Puritans* (1641), 12–13.
123. Quelch, *Church-Customes Vindicated*, 1, 2, 11, 12, 26–7.
124. Rushworth, II, 196; Charles I, *The Kings Majesties Declaration to His Subjects, Concerning Lawfull Sports to bee used* (1633).
125. Sharpe, *Personal Rule*, 351–9; Thomas G. Barnes, 'County Politics and a Puritan *Cause Célèbre*: Somerset Churchales, 1633', *TRHS*, 5th ser., 9 (1959), 103–32; Davies, *Caroline Captivity*, ch. 5; Parker, *English Sabbath*.
126. Rushworth, II, 301. Ward had been imprisoned for the anti-Catholic print *Video Rideo* of 1621: see pp. 194–5.
127. Keith Wrightson and David Levine, *Poverty and Piety in an English Village* (Oxford, 1995), 157–62; David Underdown, *Revel, Riot and Rebellion* (Oxford, 1985); Tim Harris, '"A Sainct in Shewe, a Devill in Deede": Moral Panics and Anti-Puritanism in Seventeenth-Century England', in David Lemmings, ed., *Moral Panics, the Press and the Law in Early Modern England* (Palgrave, 2009), 97–116; Patrick Collinson, 'The Cohabitation of the Faithful with the Unfaithful', in Ole Peter Grell, Jonathan I. Israel, and Nicholas Tyacke, eds, *From Persecution to Toleration* (Oxford, 1991), 76; Alexandra Walsham, *Charitable Hatred* (Manchester, 2006), 307; Haigh, *Plain Man's Pathways*, ch. 6.

128. Walsham, 'Parochial Roots', 624.
129. Underdown, *Revel, Riot and Rebellion*, 66–8; Ronald Hutton, *The Rise and Fall of Merry England* (Oxford, 1996), 197–8.
130. Sharpe, *Personal Rule*, 331–3; Walsham, 'Parochial Roots', 620–32; *Correspondence of John Cosin*, I, 165.
131. Reynolds, *Godly Reformers*, chs 9, 12. See also Tyacke, *Anti-Calvinists*, 216–23.
132. Bodl. Lib., MS Rawlinson A 128, fols. 15v–16v; Gardiner, ed., *Reports of Cases*, 149–53; C. H. Firth, 'The Reign of Charles I', *TRHS*, 3rd ser., VI (1912) 33, 35–8.
133. TCD MS 861, fols. 9–16.
134. Frank Bremer, 'The Heritage of John Winthrop: Religion along the Stour Valley, 1548–1630', *The New England Quarterly*, 70 (1997), 540.
135. TCD MS 293, fol. 388v.
136. Underdown, *Fire from Heaven*, chs 4, 5.
137. Sylvia Watts, 'The Impact of Laudianism on the Parish: The Evidence of Staffordshire and North Shropshire', *Midland History*, 33 (2008), 21–42; Haigh, *Plain Man's Pathways*, 214.
138. Foster, 'Church Policies of the 1630s', 215–16; Watts, 'Impact', 40; David Cressy, 'Conflict, Consensus, and the Willingness to Wink: The Erosion of Community in Charles I's England', *HLQ*, 61 (1998), 131–49; Marshall, *Reformation England*, 206–7. Cf. Darren Oldridge, *Religion and Society in Early Stuart England* (Aldershot, 1998), ch. 6, esp. pp. 114–17.
139. John Walter, 'Anti-Popery and the Stour Valley Riots of 1642', in David Chadd, ed., *Religious Dissent in East Anglia* (Norwich, 1996), 129.
140. Haigh, *Plain Man's Pathways*, 211.
141. Wallington, *Historical Notices*, I, 9–10.
142. Laud, *Works*, III, 228–9, VI, 371; Alastair Bellany, 'Libels in Action: Ritual, Subversion and the English Literary Underground, 1603–42', in Harris, ed., *Politics of the Excluded*, 114; Thomas Cogswell, 'Underground Verse and the Transformation of Early Stuart Political Culture', in Susan Amussen and Mark A. Kishlansky, eds, *Political Culture and Cultural Politics in Early Modern England* (Manchester, 1995), 277–8.
143. TNA, PRO, SP 16/267, fol. 192.
144. BL, Harl. MS 1219, fol. 435r–v; Smart, *Vanitie*, sigs *3, *4; Smart, *Short Treatise of Altars*, 14. Cosin was twice indicted at Durham assizes for such violent behaviour.
145. Wallington, *Historical Notices*, I, 70–1.
146. Bodl. Lib., MS Rawl. D. 158, fol. 46v. See also John Walter, '"Affronts and Insolencies": The Voices of Radwinter and Popular Opposition to Laudianism', *EHR*, 122 (2007), 43. Further examples can be found in David Cressy, *Agnes Bowker's Cat: Travesties and Transgressions* (Oxford, 2001), 157.
147. John Walter, 'Confessional Politics in Pre-Civil War Essex: Prayer Books, Profanations, and Petitions', *HJ*, 44 (2001), 683–4.

CHAPTER 10. CONTUMACIOUS TROUBLERS AND DISQUIETERS OF THE PEACE

1. Harris, *Restoration*, chs 4, 5; Brian Cowan, 'The Rise of the Coffeehouse Reconsidered', *HJ*, 47 (2004), 21–46.
2. See pp. 390–3, 473–9.

3. Bodl. Lib., MS Jones 17, fol. 300r; Mark Kishlansky, 'Charles I: A Case of Mistaken Identity?', *P&P*, 189 (2005), 49, 61; Sharpe, *Image Wars*, chs, 5, 7. For the progress to Scotland, see pp. 363–4.
4. Anthony Cade, *A Sermon Necessarie for these Times* (Cambridge, 1639), 33.
5. Bodl. Lib., MS Jones 17, fol. 303r.
6. Como, 'Predestination and Political Conflict', 264–5, 278–94; Sarah Bendall, Christopher Brooke, and Patrick Collinson, *A History of Emmanuel College, Cambridge* (1999), 205; Reynolds, *Godly Reformers*, ch. 8.
7. Anthony Milton, *Laudian and Royalist Polemic in Seventeenth-Century England* (Manchester, 2007), 53–65.
8. Sheila Lambert, 'The Printers and the Government, 1604–1637', in R. Myers and M. Harris, eds, *Aspects of Printing from 1600* (Oxford, 1987), 1–29; Sharpe, *Personal Rule*, 645–54.
9. Sharpe, *Personal Rule*, 646, 681; Natalie Mears, 'Counsel, Public Debate, and Queenship: John Stubbs's *The Discoverie of a Gaping Gulf*, 1569', *HJ*, 44 (2001), 629–50.
10. Cyndia S. Clegg, *Press Censorship in Caroline England* (Cambridge, 2008), ch. 3 (figures on p. 121).
11. TCD MS 542, fols. 7v–11.
12. *A Decree of Starre-Chamber, Concerning Printing* (1637); Rushworth, III, 306–15; David Cressy, *England on Edge* (Oxford, 2006), 283.
13. My account follows Anthony Milton, 'Licensing, Censorship, and Religious Orthodoxy in Early Stuart England', *HJ*, 41 (1998), 625–51; Clegg, *Press Censorship in Caroline England*, ch. 4.
14. Bodl. Lib., MS Rawl. A 128, fols. 27, 35, 38; Gardiner, ed., *Reports of Cases*, 272, 305.
15. Sharpe, *Personal Rule*, 377.
16. Foster, 'Church Policies of the 1630s', 206.
17. Marshall, *Reformation England*, 125, 208. For the subscription campaign, see pp. 81–4.
18. TNA, PRO, SP 16/119, fols. 68–77.
19. For Viccars's High Commission trial, see TCD MS 534 (which offers the fullest account). Another version can be found in BL, Harl. MS 4130, which was published in Gardiner, ed., *Reports of Cases*, 198–238.
20. James S. Hart, Jr, 'Marten, Sir Henry (c.1561–1641)', *ODNB*.
21. Cf. the High Commission's treatment of Stephen Denison of St Katherine Cree, London, in 1634: Lake, *Boxmaker's Revenge*, ch. 11.
22. Foster, 'Church Policies of the 1630s', 206; Marshall, *Reformation England*, 209.
23. BL, Add. MS 35,331, fol. 66v.
24. Webster, *Godly Clergy*, 229–30.
25. Christopher Dow, *Innovations Unjustly Charged upon the Present State and Church* (1637), 105.
26. Hoard, *Churches Authority Asserted*, 48, 50.
27. TCD MS 293, Additional Articles, fol. 392; P. S. Seaver, 'Roborough, Henry (d. 1649)', *ODNB*; Como, 'Predestination and Political Conflict', 288–9; David Como, *Blown by the Spirit* (Stanford, 2004), 412–13; Arnold Hunt, *The Art of Hearing* (Cambridge, 2010), 378–9.
28. TCD MS 232, fols. 5r–v, 6, 9, 36, 39; TNA, PRO, SP 16/216, fol. 118; CUL, MS Com. Ct. I, 18, fols. 58, 69–72v.

29. TCD MS 232, fols. 5–6, 9, 36, 39, 42, 48; TNA, PRO, SP 16/216, fol. 118; TNA, PRO, SP16/232, fols. 206–15; CUL, MS Com. Ct. I, 18, fols. 58, 69–72v.

30. BL, Harl. MS 1219, fols. 436v–437v; Peter Smart, *Canterburies Crueltie* (1643), 1–6.

31. CUL, MS Comm. Ct. I, 18, fols. 59v–66; Bendall et al., *History of Emmanuel College*, 206; Benjamin Brook, *The Lives of the Puritans* (1813), 400–4. See BL, Harl. MS 7019, fol. 91; J. Heywood and T. Wright, eds, *Cambridge University Transactions During the Puritan Controversies of the 16th and 17th Centuries* (2 vols, 1854), 392–403.

32. Walter, *Understanding Popular Violence*, 171–200 (quote on p. 171).

33. BL, MS Egerton 784, fol. 38v; Chamberlain, *Letters*, II, 545; NLI, MS 12,813/2, fol. 341.

34. Bodl. Lib., MS Rawl. D. 720, fol. 49v.

35. BL, MS Lansdowne 620, fols. 60v–61; TCD MS 649, fols. 125v–6.

36. Gardiner, *Reports of Cases*, 43–9.

37. Robert Powell, *The Life of Alfred, or, Alured...1634*, ed. Francis Wilson and Shaun Tyas (Stamford, 1996), 34.

38. [William Hudson, d. 1635], 'A Treatise of the Court of Star Chamber', in Francis Hargrave, ed., *Collecteana Juridica* (2 vols, n.d.); TCD MS 704, fols. 79v–110, 'Treatise on Star Chamber'; TCD MS 721, fols. 338–55, 'Of the Courte of Starr-Chamber'; TCD MS 722, fols. 1–227, 'A Treatise of the high Courte of Starchamber'.

39. BL, MS Lansdowne 620, fols. 47v–48v; TCD MS 649, fols. 105–6v.

40. TCD MS 704, fol. 79v; TCD MS 722, fol. 211; TCD MS 843, p. 399.

41. Clive Holmes, 'Law and Politics in the Reign of Charles I: The Case of John Prigeon', *Journal of Legal History*, 28 (2007), 179–82; Clive Holmes, 'Debate: Charles I: A Case of Mistaken Identity', *P&P*, 205 (2009), 182–3.

42. [Alexander Leighton], *An Appeal to the Parliament; Or, Sion's Plea against Prelacy* [1629]; *ST*, III, 383–8; Row, *History*, 351–2.

43. TCD MS 542, quote on fol. 124v; *ST*, III, 561–86; Milton, *Laudian and Royalist Polemic*, 44–5. For the view that these were standard punishments for such offences, see TCD MS 722, 'A Treatise of the high Courte of Starchamber' [temp. James I], fols. 210v–212. For Prynne, see also Cressy, *Agnes Bowker's Cat*, ch. 13.

44. BL, Harl. MS 7000, fol. 384.

45. *ST*, III, 711–55.

46. TCD MS 541, fols. 123v, 124v–128v, 130, 134; FSL, V.a.248, anno 1637; *ST*, III, 747–9, 754, 770; Wallington, *Historical Notices*, I, 90–111 (esp. 98–9, 109–10); Kneeler, *Strafford Letters*, II, 119; Richardson, *Puritanism*, 182–3.

47. *ST*, III, 1315–42.

48. Robert Charles Anderson, 'A Note on the Changing Pace of the Great Migration', *The New England Quarterly*, 59 (1986), 406–7; David Cressy, *Coming Over* (Cambridge, 1987), ch. 2 (esp. pp. 68–9); Carla Gardina Pestana, *The English Atlantic in an Age of Revolution, 1640–1661* (Cambridge, MA, 2004), 229–32.

49. TNA, PRO, SP 16/260, fol. 34.

50. Cressy, *Coming Over*, ch. 3; Susan Hardman Moore, *Pilgrims: New World Settlers and the Call of Home* (New Haven, 2007), ch. 2 (esp. p. 23); Virginia DeJohn Anderson, *New England's Generation* (Cambridge, 1991); Roger Thompson, *Mobility and Migration* (Amherst, 1994); Underdown, *Fire from Heaven*, 131–8.

51. Webster, *Godly Clergy*, ch. 14; Jason Yiannikkou, 'Rogers, Daniel (1573–1652)', *ODNB*; Reynolds, *Godly Reformers*, ch. 10.

52. John Adamson, *Noble Revolt: The Overthrow of Charles I* (2007), 35–6; Conrad Russell, 'Hampden, John (1595–1643)', *ODNB*; Conrad Russell, 'Pym, John (1584–1643)', *ODNB*.

53. John Morrill, 'Cromwell, Oliver (1599–1658)', *ODNB*.

CHAPTER 11. IRELAND AND SCOTLAND UNDER CHARLES I

1. FSL, V.a.248, fol. 63v. Other versions, with minor variants, are BL, Add. MS 72,432, fol. 85; BL, Harl. MS 1219, fol. 403v; BL, Harl. MS 4931, fol. 35, which claims it was 'a fained thing, made and scattered abroad, An. 1639, when the K. first intended war against Scotland'. See also *CSPD, 1637–8*, 564–5.

2. BL, Add. MS 11,045, fol. 125; CUL, Mm. I. 45, p. 112.

3. TNA, PRO, SP 16/465, fols. 16, 87, 89.

4. Adamson, *Noble Revolt*, 71; *Calendar of the Clarendon State Papers... Vol. V*, ed. F. J. Routledge (Oxford, 1970), 722.

5. Treadwell, *Buckingham and Ireland*, 279–83; Connolly, *Contested Island*, 366–9; Kearney, *Strafford in Ireland*, 33; Aidan Clarke, *The Old English in Ireland, 1625–42* (1966).

6. *CSPIre, 1625–32*, 442.

7. TNA, PRO, SP 63/249, fol. 312; Dublin City Library, Gilbert MS 169, pp. 197–200; Mark Empey, '"We are not Yet Safe, For They Threaten Us with More Violence": A Study of the Cook Street Riot, 1629', in William Sheehan and Maura Cronin, ed., *Riotous Assemblies: Rebels, Riots and Revolts in Ireland* (Cork, 2011), 64–79.

8. *Strafford Letters*, I, 344.

9. *Strafford Letters*, I, 183–7.

10. *NHI*, IIII, 247–8

11. Dublin City Library, Gilbert MS 169, pp. 212–13; *Strafford Letters*, I, 273, 274, 310–28, 338–9, 345, 350; Milton, 'Wentworth and Political Thought', 143–9; Sean J. Connolly, *Divided Kingdom: Ireland, 1630–1800* (Oxford, 2008), 11.

12. Alan Ford, 'Correspondence between Archbishops Ussher and Laud', *Archivium Hibernicum*, 46 (1991/2), 10, 12.

13. *Strafford Letters*, I, 187.

14. Henry Roborough of St Leonard's Eastcheap claimed his views on election were vindicated by the Irish Articles which had been confirmed by King James: TCD MS 293, fol. 395v. See also William Prynne, *Anti-Arminianisime* (1630), esp. pp. 17–21.

15. Ford, 'Correspondence', 16; Dublin City Library, Pearse Street, Gilbert MS 169, Sir James Ware, 'Diary', 211.

16. For Bramhall, see John McCafferty, *The Reconstruction of the Church of Ireland: Bishop Bramhall and the Laudian Reforms, 1633–1641* (Cambridge, 2007); Jack Cunningham, *James Ussher and John Bramhall* (Aldershot, 2007), esp. pp. 175–200.

17. TCD MS 1697, unpaginated, 20 December 1634, Bramhall to Laud.

18. *The Works of the Most Reverend John Bramhall*, ed. A. W. Hadden (5 vols, Oxford 1842–5), I, p. lxxx.

19. TCD MS 1697, Bramhall to Laud, 20 December 1634; *Strafford Letters*, I, 343; McCafferty, 'Irish Convocation of 1634'; McCafferty, *Reconstruction*, 3; Ford, *Ussher*, 184–97; Kearney, *Strafford in Ireland*, 116.

20. TCD MS 1697, Bramhall to Laud, Dublin, 18 June 1637; McCafferty, 'Irish Convocation'; McCafferty, *Reconstruction*, 157–70, 177–92; Connolly, *Divided Kingdom*, 20–1; Kearney, *Strafford in Ireland*, 117–18.

21. McCafferty, *Reconstruction*, ch. 4.

22. McCafferty, *Reconstruction*, 47–51, 127, 147–8. On 5 December 1640 Atherton was hanged for murder, incest, and buggery: Bodl. Lib., MS Top. Oxon. C. 378, p. 313; CUL, MS Mm. 1. 45, p. 33; Aidan Clarke, 'Atherton, John (1598–1640)', *ODNB*.

23. Dublin City Library, Gilbert MS 169, p. 216; NLI, MS 12,813/2, fols. 443, 471–4; HMC, *Various*, VII, 414; Connolly, *Divided Kingdom*, 21–2; Canny, *Upstart Earl*, 12–13; Canny, 'Attempted Anglicization', 171; McCafferty, *Reconstruction*, 140–4; Clodagh Tait, 'Colonising Memory: Manipulations of Death, Burial and Commemoration in the Career of Richard Boyle, the First Earl of Cork (1566–1643)', *Proceedings of the Royal Irish Academy*, vol. 101C, no. 4 (2001), 107–34 (esp. 126–32).

24. TCD MS 808, fols. 114–20; TCD MS 1038, fols. 118–20.

25. NLI, MS 12,813/2, fol. 419.

26. TCD MS 843, pp. 373–91; *NHI*, III, 265–6; Jane Ohlmeyer, 'Strafford, the "Londonderry Business" and the "New British History"', in Julia Merritt, ed., *The Political World of Thomas Wentworth, Earl of Strafford, 1621–1641* (Cambridge, 1996), 209–29; Ian Archer, 'The City of London and the Ulster Plantation', in Éamonn Ó Ciardha and Micheál Ó Siochrú, eds, *The Plantation of Ulster: Ideology and Practice* (Manchester, 2012).

27. Moran, ed., *Spicilegium Ossoriense*, 190; Patrick Moran, *History of the Catholic Archbishops of Dublin Since the Reformation* (Dublin, 1864), 382.

28. Tadhg Ó hAnnracháin, *Catholic Reformation in Ireland* (Oxford, 2002), 57–8; Jason McHugh, '"For Our Owne Defence": Catholic Insurrection in Wexford, 1641–2', in Brian Mac Cuarta, SJ, ed., *Reshaping Ireland 1550–1700* (Dublin, 2011), 221–2.

29. Canny, 'Attempted Anglicization', 173–80 (quote on p. 176); Canny, *Making Ireland British*, 275–98; Hugh F. Kearney, *Strafford in Ireland, 1633–41* (Manchester, 1959); Clarke, *Old English*.

30. Dublin City Library, Gilbert MS 169, p. 216; TCD MS 672, fol. 242r–v; Colm Lennon, 'Burke, Richard, Fourth Earl of Clanricarde and First Earl of St Albans (1572–1635)', *ODNB*; *NHI*, III, 253–4; Brendan Kane, *The Politics of Culture and Honour in Britain and Ireland, 1541–1641* (Cambridge, 2010), 235–45.

31. Perceval-Maxwell, *Outbreak*, 33; Connolly, *Contested Island*, 281–3, 405; Donald Woodward, 'The Anglo-Irish Livestock Trade of the Seventeenth Century', *IHS*, 18 (1973), 489–523.

32. Perceval-Maxwell, *Outbreak*, 30–41.

33. Canny, *Making Ireland British*, 457–8.

34. TCD MS 861, fol. 106v.

35. *CSP Ven, 1625–6*, 89–90.

36. See pp. 177–8, 180–3, 201–3.

37. *RPCS*, 2nd ser., I, *1625–7*, 91–2; Row, *History*, 340.

38. *RPS*, A1625/10/3, 8; *RPCS*, 2nd ser., I, *1625–7*, 151–6; *CSP Ven, 1625–6*, 294.

39. BL, MS Add. 23,110, fol. 1; *RPCS*, 2nd ser., I, *1625–7*, pp. xix–xxi, xli–xlii, 193–4, 227–32. For James VI's Revocations, see p. 53.

40. Balfour, *Historical Works*, II, 128.

41. *CSPVen*, 1625–6, 294, 499–500.

42. Allan I. Macinnes, *Charles I and the Making of the Covenanting Movement* (Edinburgh, 1991), ch. 3; David Stevenson, *The Scottish Revolution 1637–1644* (Newton Abbot, 1973), 35–42; Maurice Lee, *The Road to Revolution* (Urbana and Chicago, 1985), ch. 2; Cust, *Charles I*, 213–17; Julian Goodare, 'Debate: Charles I: A Case of Mistaken Identity', *P&P*, 205 (2009), 189–92.

43. Bodl. Lib., MS Rawl. D. 49, fol. 2; Michael C. Questier, ed., *Newsletters from the Caroline Court, 1631–1638* (Camden Society, 5th ser., 26, Cambridge, 2005), 192.

44. Bodl. Lib., MS Rawl. D. 49, fol. 4; William Drummond, *The Entertainment of the High and Mighty Monarch Charles King of Great Britain, France, and Ireland, into his Auncient and Royall City of Edinburgh* (1633).

45. John Spalding, *The History of the Troubles and Memorable Transactions in Scotland* (2 vols, Aberdeen, 1792), I, 23; Balfour, *Historical Works*, IV, 393; Bodl. Lib., MS Rawl. D. 49, fol. 5; TCD MS 853, fol. 206v; Morrill, *Nature of the English Revolution*, 93–5; John Young, 'Charles I and the 1633 Parliament', in K. M. Brown and A. J. Mann, eds, *The History of the Scottish Parliament, II: Parliament and Politics in Scotland, 1567–1707* (Edinburgh, 2005), 102; Dougal Shaw, 'St. Giles' Church and Charles I's Coronation Visit to Scotland', *HR*, 77 (2004), 481–502.

46. Balfour, *Historical Works*, II, 206–16; Scot, *Apol. Narr.*, 329–36; Row, *History*, 356–64; *RPCS*, 2nd ser., V (1633–5), 81–2.

47. Scot, *Apol. Narr.*, 339; Row, *History*, 366–7; Balfour, *Historical Works*, II, 200; *RPS*, 1633/6/16–46 (for the public legislation); Rushworth, II, 183. My account of the 1633 parliament also draws on: Young, 'Charles I and the 1633 Parliament'; MacDonald, 'Deliberative Processes'; Macinnes, *Making of the Covenanting Movement*, 128–32.

48. Clarendon, *History*, I, 137.

49. Macinnes, *British Confederate*, 90.

50. Balfour, *Historical Works*, II, 216–20; Row, *History*, 375–89 (quotes on pp. 378, 380); Burnet, *Own Times* (1838), 14; Young, 'Charles I and the 1633 Parliament', 128–35; Macinnes, *Making of the Covenanting Movement*, 135–41; John Coffey, 'Elphinstone, John, Second Lord Balmerino (d. 1649)', *ODNB*; *RPCS*, 2nd ser., VI (1635–7), pp. xlvi–xlvii, 334.

51. Clarendon, *History*, I, 115–17; James Cooper, 'Forbes, William (1585–1634)', rev. David George Mullan, *ODNB*.

52. Clarendon, *History*, I, 110–11; [Walter Balcanquhall], *A Large Declaration Concerning the Late Tumults in Scotland* (1639), 16–17.

53. *The Booke of Common Prayer* (Edinburgh, 1637); Row, *History*, 398; Joong-Lak Kim, 'The Scottish-English-Romish Book: The Character of the Scottish Prayer Book of 1637', in Michael J. Braddick and David L. Smith, eds, *The Experience of Revolution in Stuart Britain and Ireland* (Cambridge, 2011), 14–32; Lee, *Road to Revolution*, ch. 6; Goodare, 'Debate: Charles I', 192–7; Gordon Donaldson, *The Making of the Scottish Prayer Book of 1637* (Edinburgh, 1954).

54. *Canons and Constitutions Ecclesiasticall...for the Government of the Church of Scotland* (Aberdeen, 1636); Row, *History*, 392–5.

55. Lee, *Road to Revolution*, 203–5; Macinnes, *Making of the Covenanting Movement*, 147–9, 158–9.

56. Row, *History*, 408–9; Spalding, *History of the Troubles*, I, 57–8; [Balcanquhall], *Large Declaration*, 23–5; *CSP Ven, 1636-1639*, 259; Clarendon, *History*, I, 144–5; John Leslie, Earl of Rothes, *A Relation of Proceedings Concerning the Affairs of the Kirk of Scotland*, ed. David Laing (Edinburgh, 1830), 198–200.

57. [Balcanquhall], *Large Declaration*, 23, 25; Spalding, *History of the Troubles*, I, 57; *RPCS*, 2nd ser., VI (1635–7), 483–4; *Memoirs of Henry Guthry* (1702), 20–1; David Stevenson, 'Geddes, Jenny (*fl.* 1637)', *ODNB*; Stevenson; *Scottish Revolution*, 58–63; Lee, *Road to Revolution*, 208–12; Macinnes, *Making of the Covenanting Movement*, 159–60.

58. *RPCS*, 2nd ser., VI (1635–7), 490, 509, 514–15; Balfour, *Historical Works*, II, 230; Macinnes, *Making of the Covenanting Movement*, 160–1.

59. *RPCS*, 2nd ser., VI (1635–7), 529, 699–716; *RPCS*, 2nd ser., VII (1638–43), 3–4; Balfour, *Historical Works*, II, 238–9; Spalding, *History of the Troubles*, I, 62; Macinnes, *Making of the Covenanting Movement*, 161–72; Stevenson, *Scottish Revolution*, 66–9.

60. Rushworth, II, 734–41 (quotes on pp. 734, 735, 739–41); Macinnes, *Making of the Covenanting Movement*, 173–6; John Morrill, ed., *The Scottish National Covenant in its British Context* (Edinburgh, 1990); Morrill, *Nature of the English Revolution*, ch. 5.

61. See p. 56.

62. Archibald Johnston, Lord Wariston, *A Short Relation of the State of the Kirk* (1638), sig. B3.

63. Gilbert Burnet, *The Memoires of the Lives and Actions of James and William Dukes of Hamilton and Castleherald* (1677), 55–6; [Alexander Henderson], *The Protestation of the Noblemen, Barrons, Gentlemen, Borrowes, Ministers, and Commons...September 9. 1638* ([Edinburgh], 1638), sig. B4v; Bodl. Lib., MS Rawl. D. 720, fols. 1–2; Peter Donald, *An Uncounselled King: Charles I and the Scottish Troubles, 1637–1641* (Cambridge, 1990), ch. 3; Stevenson, *Scottish Revolution*, ch. 3.

64. *Acts. Gen. Ass.*, 1–35; Cust, *Charles I*, 236–7.

CHAPTER 12. THE BRITISH CRISIS

1. TCD MS 861, 'Piggs Corantoe' [n.d.—1639?], fol. 110.

2. Russell, *FBM*, 80; Hibbard, *Charles I and the Popish Plot*, 105–7; Mark Charles Fissel, *The Bishops' Wars* (Cambridge, 1994), 162–6.

3. My account of the first Bishops' War draws on: Ohlmeyer, *Civil War and Restoration*, 82–90; Fissel, *Bishops' Wars*, 3–39; Woolrych, *Britain in Revolution*, 115–22; Cust, *Charles I*, 244–7. 4 *Acts. Gen. Ass.*, 35–43.

5. *RPS*, 1639/8/31/10.

6. *RPS*, 1640/6/5, 27, 33, 37, 38; J. J. Scally, 'Constitutional Revolution, Party and Faction in the Scottish Parliaments of Charles I', *Parliamentary History*, 15 (1996), 59–61; John R. Young, *The Scottish Parliament 1639–1661* (Edinburgh, 1996), 1–29; William Croft Dickinson, Gordon Donaldson, and Isabel A. Milne, eds, *A Source Book of Scottish History* (3 vols, 1952–4), III, 114; Allan I. Macinnes, 'The "Scottish Moment", 1638–45', in John Adamson, ed., *The English Civil War* (Basingstoke, 2009), 132.

7. Russell, *FBM*, 144–5; Fissel, *Bishops' Wars*, 39–61.

8. John Adamson, 'England without Cromwell: What if Charles I had avoided the Civil War', in Niall Ferguson, ed., *Virtual History: Alternatives and Counterfactuals* (2003), 91–124.

9. NLI, MS 12,813/3, fol. 562.

10. NLI, MS 12,813/3, fol. 500.

11. Sharpe, *Personal Rule*, 799, 822; Fissel, *Bishops' Wars*, 153–60.

12. Fissel, *Bishops' Wars, passim.*

13. TNA, PRO, SP 16/426, fol. 12.

14. Fissel, *Bishops' Wars*, 119; Adamson, *Noble Revolt*, 19, 40–2; Woolrych, *Britain in Revolution*, 129.

15. Valerie Pearl, *London and the Outbreak of the Puritan Revolution* (Oxford, 1961), 99–105.

16. Morrill, *Revolt of the Provinces*, 28–9; Fissel, *Bishops' Wars*, 129–37.

17. BL, Add. MS 11,045, fol. 82r–v.

18. TCD MS 1697, unpag., Bramhall to Laud, Dublin 23 February 1637/8; TNA, PRO, SP 63/265, fol. 203v.

19. *Strafford Letters*, II, 219.

20. BL, Add. MS 11,045, fol. 3.

21. BL, Harl. MS 1219, fol. 53; BL, Add. MS 11,045, fols. 25, 29; Dublin City Library, Gilbert MS 169, p. 219; *NHI*, III, 268; Kevin Forkan, '"The Fatal Ingredient of the Covenant": The Place of the Ulster Scottish Colonial Community during the 1640s', in Mac Cuarta, ed., *Reshaping Ireland*, 265; Michael Perceval-Maxwell, 'Strafford, the Ulster Scots and the Covenanters', *IHS*, 18 (1973), 524–51.

22. BL, Add. MS 11,045, fol. 100v; Dublin City Library, Gilbert MS 169, pp. 220, 221; Connolly, *Divided Kingdom*, 27; McCafferty, *Reconstruction*, 168–9.

23. BL, Add. MS 33,936, fol. 206.

24. Connolly, *Divided Kingdom*, 27, 30; Bríd McGrath, 'Parliament Men and the Confederate Association', in Micheal Ó Siochrú, ed., *Kingdoms in Crisis: Ireland in the 1640s* (Dublin, 2001), 92. Cf. Perceval-Maxwell, *Outbreak*, 70, who gives the figure of 76 Catholic MPs in a house of 238.

25. BL, Add. MS 11,045, fols. 107v–8r; Bodl. Lib., MS Rawl. D. 317B, fol. 181v; *Strafford Letters*, II, 397–8, 402.

26. TCD MS 861, fols. 22–7.

27. *Calendar of the Clarendon State Papers... Vol. I*, ed. O. Ogle and W. H. Bliss (Oxford, 1872), 196. My account of the Short Parliament draws on Russell, *FBM*, 90–123 and Kishlansky, 'Charles I and the Short Parliament', though with different emphases.

28. Gruenfelder, *Influence in Early Stuart Elections*, 182, 188, 190–1. The figures are somewhat different if we take *possible* court influence into account: this would show them backing perhaps as many as 61 candidates and getting 30 elected. See also Hirst, *Representative*, App. IV.

29. Culmer, *Cathedrall Newes*, 19.

30. BL, Harl. MS 4931, fols. 8v, 41, 42; *Proceedings SP*, 275–8.

31. TNA, PRO, SP 16/449, fols. 67, 69, 70.

32. Hirst, *Representative of the People?*, 183; Cliffe, *Yorkshire Gentry*, 317.

33. *Proceedings SP*, 115, 120–1; *Parl. Hist*, II, 533.

34. Adamson, *Noble Revolt*, 13–14 and ch. 1; Conrad Russell, 'The Scottish Party in English Parliaments, 1640–2 OR The Myth of the English Revolution', *HR*, 66 (1993), 47–8; Cromartie, *Constitutionalist Revolution*, 252.

35. *Proceedings SP*, 254–60, 300–2; Judith D. Maltby, ed., *The Short Parliament (1640) Diary of Sir Thomas Aston* (Camden Society, 4th ser., 35, 1988), 8–10.

36. *Proceedings SP*, 79–80, 110; *LJ*, IV, 66–7.

37. Charles I, *His Majesties Declaration… Of the Causes which Moved Him to Dissolve the Last Parliament* (1640), 44, 46, 51, 52, 54; Esther S. Cope, 'The King's Declaration concerning the Dissolution of the Short Parliament of 1640: An Unsuccessful Attempt at Public Relations', *HLQ*, 40 (1977), 325–31.

38. Adamson, *Noble Revolt*, 21–4 (quote on p. 22); TNA, PRO, SP 16/458, fol. 212.

39. *Constitutions and Canons Ecclesiasticall* (1640).

40. BL, Add. MS 21,935, fol. 88v.

41. Wallington, *Historical Notices*, I, 29; *England's Complaint to Jesus Christ Against the Bishops' Canons* (Amsterdam, 1640).

42. Bodl. Lib., MS Rawl. D. 353, fol. 146, 163.

43. TNA, PRO, SP 16/465, fol. 16.

44. Bodl. Lib., MS Top. Oxon. C. 378, p. 306; Woodford's Diary, 3, 11, 14, 15, and 16 May 1640; BL, Add. MS 35,331, fol. 77; BL, Add. MS 11,045, fol. 117; BL, Harl. MS 383, fol. 163; *Diary of John Rous*, 90; Cressy, *England on Edge*, ch. 5; Keith Lindley, *Popular Politics and Religion in Civil War London* (Aldershot, 1997), 4–8.

45. TNA, PRO, SP 16/454, fol. 80; TNA, PRO, SP 16/468, fol. 260; Walter, *Understanding Popular Violence*, 124, 161.

46. Walter, *Understanding Popular Violence*, 120.

47. Morrill, *Revolt of the Provinces*, 29.

48. BL, Add. MS 21,935, fols. 88v, 89, 91; BL, Harl. MS 383, fol. 178; Woodford's Diary, no date (entry after 8 July 1640); Bodl. Lib., MS Top. Oxon. C. 378, pp. 308–9; Wallington, *Historical Notices*, I, 122–3, 126; *Diary of John Rous*, 90; Fissel, *Bishops' Wars*, ch. 7. For iconoclasm and hostility to Laudianism on the eve of the Civil War, see: John Walter, 'Popular Iconoclasm and the Politics of the Parish in East England, 1640–1642', *HJ*, 47 (2004), 261–90; John Walter, 'Abolishing Superstition with Sedition? The Politics of Popular Iconoclasm in England 1640–1642', *P&P*, 183 (2004), 79–123; John Walter, '"Affronts and Insolencies": The Voices of Radwinter and Popular Opposition to Laudianism', *EHR*, 122 (February, 2007), 35–60; Cressy, 'Battle of the Altars', in his *Agnes Bowker's Cat*, 203–6.

49. J. A. Sharpe, 'Crime and Delinquency in an Essex Parish in 1600–1640', in J. S. Cockburn, ed., *Crime in England 1550–1800* (1977), 320.

50. TNA, PRO, SP 16/374, fols. 24, 25; TNA, PRO, SP 16/465, fols. 16, 25; Sharpe, *Personal Rule*, 813–15; Joad Raymond, *Pamphlets and Pamphleteering in Early Modern Britain* (Cambridge, 2003), 172–87, 191; Donald, *Uncounselled King*, 188; Sarah Waurechen, 'Covenanter Propaganda and Conceptualizations of the Public During the Bishops' Wars, 1638–1640', *HJ*, 52 (2009), 63–86; David Como, 'Secret Printing, the Crisis of 1640, and the Origins of Civil War Radicalism', *P&P*, 196 (2007), 37–82; David Stevenson, 'A Revolutionary Regime and the Press: The Scottish Covenanters and their Printers', *Library*, 7, 4 (December 2006), 315–37; Joseph Black, '"Pikes and Protestations": Scottish Texts in England, 1639–40', *Publishing History*, 42 (1997); Alastair J. Mann, *The Scottish Book Trade* (East Lothian, 2000), 83–4, 90.

51. Laud, *Works*, VII, 544.

52. *An Information to all Good Christians* (Edinburgh, 1639), 4–5, 7.

53. *The Remonstrance of the Nobility, Barrones, Burgesses, Ministers and Commons within the Kingdome of Scotland* (Edinburgh, 1639), 5–6, 7, 12. For the king being the father of his people, see p. 16.

54. *Remonstrance of the Nobility*, 24–6.

55. [Alexander Henderson], *Some Special Arguments for the Scottish Subjects Lawfull Defence of their Religion and Liberty* [1642], 5; Stevenson, *Scottish Revolution*, 133.

56. *Remonstrance of the Nobility*, 17–18, 26, 28.

57. *Information to All Good Christians*, 11.

58. *The Lawfullnesse of our Expedition into England Manifested* (Edinburgh, 1640), sigs A3r–v.

59. *Information to All Good Christians*, 12.

60. *Remonstrance of the Nobility*, 31–2.

61. *The Lawfullnesse of Our Expedition*, sigs A2v, A3, A3v.

62. [John Forbes], *Duplies of the Ministers and Professors of Aberdene* (London, 1638); John Forbes, *Generall Demands, Concerning the Late Covenant* (Aberdeen, 1638); John Forbes, *A Peaceable Warning* (London, 1638).

63. [Balcanquhall], *Large Declaration*; [Sir Francis Windebanke], *His Majesties Declaration Concerning his Proceedings with his Subjects of Scotland* (1640).

64. John Philipson, 'The King's Printer in Newcastle Upon Tyne in 1639', *Library*, 11 (1989), 1–9; Jason Peacey, *Politicians and Pamphleteers: Propaganda during the English Civil Wars and the Interregnum* (Aldershot, 2004), 43; Thomas Morton, *A Sermon Preached before the King's Most Excellent Majestie in the Cathedrall Church of Durham* (London, 1639).

65. John Callow, 'Corbet, John (1603–1641)', *ODNB*; John Corbet, *The Ungirding of the Scottish Armour* (Dublin [i.e. London], 1639); John Corbet, *The Epistle Congratulatorie of Lysimachus Nicanor* (London, 1640); Henry Leslie, *Full Confutation of the Covenant* (1639); Peter Du Moulin, *A Letter of a French Protestant to a Scottishman of the Covenant* (London, 1640).

66. Milton, *Laudianism and Royalist Polemic*, 66–7.

67. Kishlansky, 'Charles I and the Short Parliament', 24.

68. Corbet, *Ungirding*, sig. A4.

69. [Forbes], *Duplies*, 19–20, 106.

70. Morton, *Sermon Preached…in…Durham*, 1–2. For other sermons emphasizing divine right and non-resistance preached and published at this time, see: Henry Valentine, *God Save the King: A Sermon Preached in St. Pauls Church the 27th of March 1639. Being the Day of His Maiesties happy Inauguration, and of His Northerne Expedition* (1639); Malachi Harris, *Britaines Hallelujah: Or, A Sermon of Thanksgiving For the Happy Pacification in Britain Preached in the English Church at Hamburch* ([Hamburg], 1639); Henry King, *A Sermon Preached at St. Pauls March 27. 1640, Being the Anniversary of His Majesties Happy Inauguration to his Crowne* (1640).

71. Charles I, *By the King. A Proclamation and Declaration to Inform our Loving Subjects of Our Kingdom of England* (London, 1638[/9]).

72. [Balcanquhall], *Large Declaration*, 2, 428.

73. Henry King, *A Sermon Preached at St. Pauls March 27. 1640* (London, 1640), 44.

74. Corbet, *Ungirding*, 15.

75. [Balcanquhall], *Large Declaration*, 424–6.

76. Corbet, *Ungirding*, 12–13, 52.

77. [Balcanquhall], *Large Declaration*, 3; Corbet, *Ungirding*, 22, 29, 38.

78. Morton, *Sermon Preached…in…Durham*, 3–4, 9.

79. Du Moulin, *Letter of a French Protestant*, 49.

80. Culmer, *Cathedrall Newes*, p. 9; BL, Add. MS 21,935, fol. 93.

81. Russell, *FBM*, 85–7, 139–40.
82. TNA, PRO, SP 16/424, fol. 110.
83. TNA PRO, SP 16/438, fol. 166v; Russell, *FBM*, 83–7.
84. David Cressy, *Dangerous Talk: Scandalous, Seditious, and Treasonable Speech in Pre-Modern England* (Oxford, 2010), 183.
85. Russell, *FBM*, 61; D. L., *Scots Scouts Discoveries* (printed for William Sheares, 1642), 42. Cf. Raymond, *Pamphlets*, 185.
86. TNA, PRO, SP 16/395, fol. 56. Alured claimed he had called the Scots 'madd boys' (fol. 58).
87. *CSPVen, 1636–9*, 535–6.
88. Reynolds, *Godly Reformers*, 171–2.
89. TNA, PRO, SP 16/446, fol. 120; TNA, PRO, SP 16/454, fol. 109; TNA, PRO, SP 16/459, fol. 85.
90. TNA, PRO, SP 16/413, fols. 81, 82. Upon examination Fewler denied the charge and said he would be willing to fight against the Scots (fol. 83).
91. Bodl. Lib., MS Ashmole 800, fols. 50v–51.
92. TNA, PRO, SP 16/423, fol. 183.
93. TNA, PRO, SP 16/422, fol. 200.
94. TNA, PRO, SP 16/415, fols. 252v–253r.
95. TNA, PRO, SP 16/466, fols. 67, 69, 71, 73, 75; Fissel, *Bishops' Wars*, 265–6.
96. Woodford's Diary, 2 April 1639, 20 September 1639, 12 August 1640.
97. Richard Culmer, junior, *A Parish Looking-Glasse* (1657), 4.
98. *The Beast is Wounded* [Amsterdam?, 1638], 'To the Reader', 4, 9, 16, 23. The tract is discussed in Raymond, *Pamphlets*, 179; White, *Militant Protestantism*, 104–5.
99. David Como, 'Secret Printing, the Crisis of 1640, and the Origins of Civil War Radicalism', *P&P*, 196 (2007), 37–82.
100. Calybute Downing, *A Sermon Preached to the Renowned Company of Artillery* (1641), 10, 12, 14, 16, 22, 27–8, 36–8. The tract is discussed in Perez Zagorin, *The Court and the Country: The Beginning of the English Revolution* (1969), 144–5 and Adamson, *Noble Revolt*, 67–70.
101. Cf. Como, 'Secret Printing'.
102. BL, Harl. MS 1219, fols. 31–4; BL, Harl. MS 4931, fol. 66; FSL, V.a.492, fols. 9–10; *Diary of John Rous*, 91–2.
103. FSL, V.a.492, fols. 52, 71–2; BL, Add. MS 35,331, fol. 77v.
104. FSL, V.a.492, fol. 74; BL, Add. MS 11,045, fols. 120–1; Wallington, *Historical Notices*, I, 216–17.
105. BL, Harl. MS 4931, fols. 67–8; Bodl. Lib., MS Ashmole 800, fols. 110v–112; FSL, V.a.492, fol. 57; *Parl. Hist.*, II, 585–6, 589–90; Adamson, *Noble Revolt*, pp. 44–50, 55–62.
106. NLI, MS 12,813/3, fol. 560.
107. NLI, MS 12,813/3, fols. 563–4.

CHAPTER 13. THE GRIEVANCES OF THE COMMONWEALTH

1. Bodl. Lib., MS Ashmole 36–7, fol. 76v.
2. *CSPVen, 1642–3*, 134, 139–40, 145; Clarendon, *History*, II, 283, 289–92; *The English Civil War: A Contemporary Account*, ed. Edward and Peter Razzell (5 vols, 1996), II, 273, 277–8, 283; Charles I, *By the King. A Proclamation…Requiring the Aid and Assistance of all His Subjects on the North-side Trent, and Within Twenty Miles Southward Thereof* (1642).

3. Clarendon, *History*, II, 284–5.
4. *The Diary of Sir Henry Slingsby*, ed. Daniel Parsons (1836), 64; TNA, PRO, SP 16/469, fol. 58. Cf. *Diary of John Rous*, 98; Woodford's Diary, 2 December 1640; HMC, *De L'Isle and Dudley*, VI, 337.
5. Bodl. Lib., MS Rawl. Poet. 26, fol. 95.
6. Valuable studies of the crises years 1640–2 are Cressy, *England on Edge*; Adamson, *Noble Revolt*; Anthony Fletcher, *The Outbreak of the English Civil War* (1981); Russell, *FBM*, chs 5–13.
7. Bodl. Lib., MS Top. Oxon. C. 378, pp. 319, 322; Cressy, *England on Edge*, ch. 3; Conrad Russell, 'Russell, Francis, Fourth Earl of Bedford (*bap.* 1587, *d.* 1641)', *ODNB*.
8. Raymond, *Pamphlets*, 163. These figures underestimate, since they are based on surviving titles, but give an indication of the trend.
9. *Sion's Charity* (1641), 4–5.
10. BL, Add. MS 11,045, fols. 125v, 127, 129–31; BL, Harl. MS 383, fol. 186; *Diary of John Rous*, 99; HMC, *De L'Isle and Dudley*, VI, 333; HMC, *Cowper*, II, 262; *CSPVen*, 1640–2, 93; Cressy, *England on Edge*, 158–62.
11. Hirst, *Representative of the People?*, 111, 217–22; Kishlansky, *Parliamentary Selection*, 18, 108–9; Braddick, *God's Fury*, 118 (who puts the figure of contested elections at 86).
12. Gruenfelder, *Influence*, 188–9. Out of twenty-two court nominees, only two were elected.
13. Walter, 'Confessional Politics, 683.
14. Fletcher, *Outbreak*, p. xxvi.
15. FSL, V.a.378, fol. 7; Rushworth, IV, 33.
16. *The Speeches of the Lord Digby in the High Court of Parliament* (1641), 2–3.
17. BL, Harl. MS 1219, fol. 428–31; BL, Add. MS 11,045, fol. 166v.
18. HMC, *De L'Isle and Dudley*, VI, 337, 339; Adamson, *Noble Revolt*, 89–93.
19. *Proceedings LP*, I, 7, 13–14; BL, Add. MS 11,045, fol. 131v; *CSPVen*, 1640–2, 95.
20. Adamson, *Noble Revolt*, 121.
21. Paul Christianson, 'The Peers, the People, and Parliamentary Management in the First Six Months of the Long Parliament', *JMH*, 49 (1977), 576; Adamson, *Noble Revolt*, ch. 5.
22. *Proceedings LP*, I, 35–6; Hibbard, *Charles I and the Popish Plot*, 170–1.
23. *CJ*, II, 22, 24. They were to receive formal pardons in May 1641.
24. Woodford's Diary, 28 November 1640; Bodl. Lib., MS Rawl. D. 141, pp. 8, 10; Bodl. Lib., MS Top. Oxon. C. 378, p. 313; Lindley, *Popular Politics*, 13–14.
25. *LJ*, IV, 92.
26. *CJ*, II, 24.
27. *CJ*, II, 26; *Proceedings LP*, I, 99; HMC, *Cowper*, II, 262; Adamson, *Noble Revolt*, 102–10.
28. *Mr Grymstons Speech in Parliament upon the Accusation and Impeachment of William Laud* (1641); *Proceedings LP*, I, 656, 658–9, 662–3; CUL, Mm. I. 45, p. 35.
29. Bodl. Lib., MS Rawl. D. 141, p. 11.
30. Jansson, *Proceedings LP*, I, 264–5.
31. *Parl. Hist.*, II, 716–17; *Proceedings LP*, II, 463; *SR*, V, 54–7, 58–78; *LJ*, IV, 163–4; Wallington, *Historical Notices*, I, 271–2; Woodford's Diary, 16 February 1640/1; CUL, Mm. I. 45, p. 31; Yerby, *People and Parliament*, ch. 6.

32. Russell, *FBM*, 268–70.
33. *CJ*, II, 118; *Proceedings LP*, III, 477–8, 480–1; Fletcher, *Outbreak*, 20–1.
34. Russell, *FBM*, 291; *CJ*, II, 125; *Proceedings LP*, IV, 36–7, 51, 89–90.
35. Wallington, *Historical Notices*, I, 242; Manning, *English People*, 8–14; Lindley, *Popular Politics*, 19–24.
36. *CJ*, II, 132, 135; David Cressy, 'The Protestation Protested, 1641 and 1642', *HJ*, 45 (2002), 251–79.
37. *LJ*, IV, 238–9, 243; TNA, PRO, SP 16/480, fol. 33v; Fletcher, *Outbreak*, ch. 1; Russell, *FBM*, ch. 7; Manning, *English People*, 17–18; Lindley, *Popular Politics*, 25–6.
38. Braddick, *God's Fury*, 140–1.
39. Manning, *English People*, 4. For the root and branch petitions more generally, see Fletcher, *Outbreak*, ch. 3.
40. *The Humble Petition of the Protestant Inhabitants of the Counties of Antrim, Downe, Tyrone, etc., part of the Province of Ulster* (1641), 2.
41. *To the Honorable Houses of Parliament Now Assembled, The Humble Petition of Many of the Inhabitants within His Majestie's County of Kent* (1641); *A Collection of Speeches made by Sir Edward Dering* (1642), 2–3; Derek Hirst, 'The Defection of Sir Edward Dering 1640–1', *HJ*, 15 (1972), 193–208; Fletcher, *Outbreak*, 96.
42. Cf. Cromartie, *Constitutionalist Revolution*, 256.
43. *The First and Large Petition of the Citie of London and Other Inhabitants Thereabouts* (1641), quotes on pp. 1–2, 3.
44. *A Petition Presented to the Parliament from the Countie of Nottingham* (1641), quotes on pp. 1, 6, 13, 14.
45. *An Order Made to a Select Committee: Chosen By the Whole House of Commons to Receive Petitions Touching Ministers* (1640), sig. A3v.
46. Gryffith Williams, *The Discovery of Mysteries* (1643), 20; Adamson, *Noble Revolt*, 123; Cressy, *England on Edge*, 176–9.
47. BL, Add. MS 11,045, fol. 146; *CJ*, II, 56, 71; *Proceedings LP*, Part I, Vol. II, 245–6.
48. *CJ*, II, 139; CUL, Mm. I. 45, p. 40.
49. *To the Right Honourable the Knights, Citizens and Burgesses of the Commons House of Parliament. The Humble Petition of Some of the Parishioners in the Parish of Chigwell in the County of Essex and Divers Others* (1641); John White, *The First Century of Scandalous, Malignant Priests* (1643), 2–3.
50. BL, Harl. MS 1219, fols. 432–6; Smart, *Canterburies Crueltie*.
51. CUL, Mm. I. 45, p. 40.
52. Morrill, *Nature of the English Revolution*, 78–9.
53. CUL, Mm. I. 45, pp. 37, 38; BL, Add. MS 21,935, fols. 89v–90v; Wallington, *Historical Notices*, I, 124–5; Walter, 'Popular Iconoclasm' Walter, 'Abolishing Superstition'.
54. BL, Harl. MS 6424, fol. 6r–v; *LJ*, IV, 134.
55. CUL, Mm. I. 45, p. 38.
56. CUL, Mm. I. 45, pp. 37–8.
57. Wallington, *Historical Notices*, I, 125–6; BL, Add. MS 21,935, fol. 90v.
58. *Calendar of Assize Records: Kent Indictments*, ed. J. S. Cockburn (1989), no. 2073, p. 438.

59. Cressy, *England on Edge*, 170–1.
60. CUL, Mm. I. 45, p. 29, 31, 32, 38, 39; Henry Burton, *England's Bondage and Hope of Deliverance* (1641).
61. *Canterburies Conscience Convicted* (1641).
62. Thomas Stirry, *A Rot Amongst the Bishops* (1641).
63. *The Bishops Potion* (1641); Pierce, 'Anti-Episcopal Satire', 831; Cogswell, 'Underground Verse', 287–90.
64. *Canterburie His Change of Diot* (1641); *Archy's Dream* (1641), sigs A2–4.
65. Stirry, *Rot Amongst the Bishops*, 7.
66. *Sion's Charity* (1641), 2.
67. *The Jury of Inquisition De Jure Divino* (1640), 2–3.
68. Spraggon, *Puritan Iconoclasm*, ch. 2.
69. John Vicars, *The Sinfulness and Unlawfulness of Making or Having the Picture of Christ's Humanity* (1641).
70. Robert Baillie, *Prelacie is Miserie* (1641), 1–2, 4, 6, 7.
71. *LJ*, IV, 142.
72. *Proceedings LP*, II, 389 n. 12; *Two Diaries of the Long Parliament*, ed. Maija Jansson (Gloucester, 1984), 84.
73. Benjamin Rudyerd, *The Speeches of Sir Benjamin Rudyer in the High Court of Parliament* (1641), 15–20. For Rudyerd, see David L. Smith, 'Sir Benjamin Ruyderd and England's "Wars of Religion"', in Braddick and Smith, eds, *Experience of Revolution*, 52–73 (esp. 62–3).
74. *The Third Speech of the Lord George Digby, To the House of Commons, Concerning Bishops* (1641), 6, 10–11, 12, 16, 17, 18, 19.
75. Lord Falkland, *A Speech made to the House of Commons Concerning Episcopacy* (1641), 3, 7, 8, 10.
76. *Proceedings LP*, II, 398.
77. Nathaniel Fiennes, *A Speech...Concerning Bishops* (1641), 25–7.
78. *LJ*, IV, 172; *The Speech or Declaration of John Pymm...against William Laud* (1641), 6.
79. *CJ*, II, 159; Braddick, *God's Fury*, 131; Adamson, *Noble Revolt*, 179–87.
80. *LJ*, IV, 277, 295; Cressy, 'Protestation Protested', 262–3; Spraggon, *Puritan Iconoclasm*, 138–40; Cressy, 'The Battle of the Altars: Turning the Tables and Breaking the Rails', in *Agnes Bowker's Cat*, 186–9, 207; Lindley, *Popular Politics*, 39–41; William Grant, *The Vindication of the Vicar of Istleworth* (1641), 18; HMC, *4th Report*, 74, 80.
81. *CJ*, II, 246.
82. *CJ*, II, 279.
83. *CJ*, II, 283, 286–7; *LJ*, IV, 395; Steele, I, nos. 1886, 1887; *The Orders from the House of Commons for the Abolishing of Superstition and Innovavation* [sic] *in Church Affaires* (1641); *A Declaration of the Commons in Parliament, made September the 9th, 1641* (1641); Spraggon, *Puritan Iconoclasm*, 64–8.
84. *CSP Ven*, 1640–2, 222.
85. *The Diurnall Occurrences or Dayly Proceedings of Both Houses* (1641), 368; Fincham and Tyacke, *Altars Restored*, 278; Fletcher, *Outbreak*, 118; Spraggon, *Puritan Iconoclasm*, 68–9, 99–101, 129–30, 140–57; Adamson, *Noble Revolt*, 389.
86. Reynolds, *Godly Reformers*, 240–1.
87. Jacqueline Eales, *Puritans and Roundheads: The Harleys of Brampton Bryan and the Outbreak of the English Civil War* (Cambridge, 1990), 115.
88. Cressy, *England on Edge*, 205; Adamson, *Noble Revolt*, 386.

89. CUL, Mm. I. 45, p. 38.
90. TNA, PRO, SP 16/484, fol. 146v.
91. Hunt, *Puritan Moment*, 292–3.
92. I. W., *Certaine Affirmations In Defence of the Pulling Down of Communion Rails, by Divers Rash and Misguided People, Judiciously and Religiously Answered* (1641), sig. A2 and pp. 2, 5.
93. *Reliquiae Baxterianae*, ed. Matthew Sylvester (1696), 40.

CHAPTER 14. THE IRISH REBELLION, THE GRAND REMONSTRANCE, AND THE DRIFT TO WAR

1. Cust, *Charles I*, 292–4, 299–300.
2. Donald, *Uncounselled King*, 243–4, 297.
3. Rushworth, IV, 298–300 (quotes on p. 299).
4. *CJ*, II, 234; Fletcher, *Outbreak*, 81–2.
5. Cust, *Charles I*, 291, 301.
6. *RPS*, 1641/8/6, 21, 25, 32, 46, 55; *Acts. Gen. Ass.*, 44; Young, *Scottish Parliament, 1639–61*, 34–42.
7. Cust, *Charles I*, 303–5; Donald, *Uncounselled King*, 309–17; Russell, *FBM*, 316–29.
8. TNA, PRO, SP 16/484, fol. 3v; Russell, *FBM*, 373.
9. See p. 167.
10. *CJ, Ire*, I, 145–51 (quote on p. 150).
11. *CJ, Ire*, I, 162–3, 164–5.
12. *CJ, Ire*, I, 211–12.
13. *CJ, Ire*, I, 167.
14. *LJ*, IV, 339. My account draws on *NHI*, III, ch. 10; Russell, *FBM*, ch. 10; Perceval-Maxwell, *Outbreak*, chs 3, 5, 6.
15. *CJ, Ire*, I, 276–7; *CJ*, II, 284–5; BL Add. MS 11,045, fol. 140; White, *Militant Protestantism*, p141–9.
16. Perceval-Maxwell, *Outbreak*, chs 8, 9; Russell, *FBM*, 393–6; Jane H. Ohlmeyer, 'Communications: The "Antrim Plot" of 1641—A Myth', *HJ*, 35 (1992), 905–19; Michael Perceval-Maxwell, 'The "Antrim Plot" of 1641—A Myth? A Response', *HJ*, 37 (1994), 421–30.
17. Dublin City Library, Gilbert MS 169, p. 224; HMC, *Ormond*, NS II, 1–2; *LJ*, IV, 415.
18. TCD, MS 1071, 'O'Mellan's Journal', fol. 4v. My discussion of the Irish Rebellion draws on Michael Perceval-Maxwell, 'The Ulster Rising of 1641, and the Depositions', *IHS*, 21 (1978), 149–50; Perceval-Maxwell, *Outbreak*, ch. 10; Canny, *Making Ireland British*, ch. 8.
19. TNA, PRO, SP 63/260, fol. 135.
20. TCD MS 836, fol. 18r–v.
21. HMC, *Ormond*, NS, II, 3.
22. Micheál Ó Siochrú, 'Atrocity, Codes of Conduct and the Irish in the British Civil Wars 1641–1653', *P&P*, 195 (2007), 61; Micheál Ó Siochrú, *God's Executioner* (2008), 25–6; 'The Humble Apology of the Lords, Knights, Gentlemen, and Other Inhabitants of the English Pale of Ireland for Taking Armes, 1641', in *History of the Irish Confederation and War in Ireland*, ed. John T. Gilbert, 7 vols (Dublin, 1882–91), I, 238; Sir John Temple, *The Irish Rebellion* (1646), §2, p. 36 (sig. E e 2v).

23. Brian Mac Cuarta, 'Maguire, Connor, Second Baron of Enniskillen (c.1612–1645)', *ODNB*.

24. Jerrold I. Casway, 'O'Neill, Sir Phelim Roe (1603–1653)', *ODNB*; Perceval-Maxwell, *Outbreak*, 10, 45.

25. Forkan, 'The Ulster Scots Colonial Community', 266–7.

26. Perceval-Maxwell, *Outbreak*, 46–7.

27. Perceval-Maxwell, *Outbreak*, ch. 1; Jason McHugh, '"For Our Owne Defence": Catholic Insurrection in Wexford, 1641–2', in Mac Cuarta, ed., *Reshaping Ireland*, 214–40.

28. Bodl. Lib., MS Rawl. D. 932, fols 69v–70r; Perceval-Maxwell, *Outbreak*, 234.

29. *LJ*, IV, 415.

30. NLI, MS 12,813/3, fol. 588v.

31. HMC, *Ormond*, NS II, 8.

32. Brian Mac Cuarta, 'Religious Violence against Settlers in South Ulster, 1641–2', in David Edwards, Pádraig Lenihan, and Clodagh Tait, eds, *Age of Atrocity* (Dublin, 2007), 154–75.

33. Canny, *Making Ireland British*, 474–5.

34. TCD MS 835, fols. 95r, 201v.

35. TCD MS 835, fol. 210v.

36. TCD, MSS 814, fols. 264r–265r; Canny, *Making Ireland British*, 522; David Edwards, 'A Haven of Popery: English Catholic Migration to Ireland in the Age of Plantations', in Ford, ed., *Origins of Sectarianism*, 124 (who says incidents of Irish rebels attacking English Catholics were rare).

37. Nicholas Canny, 'What Really Happened in Ireland in 1641?', in Jane Ohlmeyer, ed., *Ireland from Independence to Occupation* (1995), 32–3; Mac Cuarta, 'Religious Violence', 160–2.

38. HMC, *Ormond*, NS II, 20.

39. BL, Harl. MS 383, fols. 193v, 195v.

40. TCD MS 831, fols. 169r, 174r–v, 190v–191r; Perceval-Maxwell, *Outbreak*, 232–3.

41. Canny, *Making Ireland British*, 476.

42. TCD MS 818, fol. 88r.

43. TCD MS 818, fol. 124r. In many areas Catholic priests were active in trying to redirect the energies of the insurgents away from attacking Protestants towards attacking symbols of the Protestant religion: Canny, *Making Ireland British*, 489.

44. TCD MS 836, fol. 64r; Mac Cuarta, 'Religious Violence', 170–1.

45. *CJ*, II, 300; *LJ*, IV, 412–18.

46. TNA, PRO, SP 16/485, fols. 145v–146r.

47. HMC, *Ormond*, NS II, 7.

48. *The Journal of Sir Simonds D'Ewes*, ed. Willson H. Coates (1942), 118.

49. John Goodwin, *Irelands Advocate* (1641), 28–9.

50. HMC, *Ormond*, NS II, 18.

51. David O'Hara, 'English Newsbooks and the Outbreaks of the Irish Rebellion of 1641', *Media History*, 9 (2003), 179–93 (esp. 181, 185); David O'Hara, *English Newsbooks and the Irish Rebellion of 1641–1649* (Dublin, 2006), 29; Joseph Cope, 'Fashioning Victims: Dr Henry Jones and the Plight of the Irish Protestants, 1642', *HR*, 74 (2001), 376; Braddick, *God's Fury*, 197; Keith J. Lindley, 'The Impact of the 1641 Rebellion upon England and Wales, 1641–5', *IHS*, 18 (1972), 143–76.

52. James Salmon, *Bloudy Newes from Ireland* (1641), title page.
53. *LJ*, IV, 475; Thomas Partington, *Worse and Worse Newes from Ireland. Being the Copy of A Letter Read in the House of Parliament* (1641), 1–2.
54. O'Hara, *English Newsbooks*, 37–42; O'Hara, 'English Newsbooks', 185.
55. *CJ*, II, 396.
56. *No Pamphlet, But a Detestation of All Such Pamphlets As are Printed Concerning the Irish Rebellion* (1642), sig. A2.
57. *The Bloudy Persecution of the Protestants in Ireland* (1641), sigs A, A2v, A3v.
58. TCD MS 836, fol. 71r.
59. Tristram Whetcombe, *The Rebels Turkish Tyranny* (1641), 1–3.
60. TCD MS 822, fols, 26r–27v.
61. Cope, *England and the 1641 Irish Rebellion*, ch. 4; Wallington, *Historical Notices*, I, 304–7.
62. Edmund Calamy, *England's Looking Glass* (1642), 34.
63. James Cranford, *The Teares of Ireland* (1642), quote on p. 20.
64. Wallington, *Historical Notices*, I, 301; TCD, MS 809, fol. 8v.
65. TCD, MS 836, fols. 2r, 16r–v, 35r–36v, 87r–89v, 92r–93r; Canny, 'What Really Happened in Ireland in 1641?', 34; Canny, *Making Ireland British*, esp. 484–5 (Portadown and Kilmore), 544–5 (rape); Stephen C. Manganiello, *The Concise Encyclopedia of the Revolutions and Wars of England, Scotland and Ireland, 1639–1660* (Oxford, 2004), 317; Pádraig Lenihan, *The Confederate Catholics at War* (Cork, 2001), 31–2.
66. Kenneth Nicholls, 'The Other Massacre: English Killings of Irish, 1641–2', in Edwards et al., eds, *Age of Atrocity*, 176–91.
67. HMC, *Ormond*, NS II, 15.
68. O'Hara, *English Newsbooks*, 29–33; Cope, *England and the 1641 Irish Rebellion*, ch. 5; Ethan Howard Shagan, 'Constructing Discord: Ideology, Propaganda, and English Responses to the Irish Rebellion of 1641', *JBS*, 36 (1997), 1–34 (esp. 23–6).
69. *Bloody Newes from Norwich* (1641), sig. A2.
70. O'Hara, 'English Newsbooks', 183.
71. *The Autobiography of Joseph Lister of Bradford in Yorkshire*, ed. Thomas Wright (1842), 7–8.
72. Calamy, *England's Looking Glass*, quotes on pp. 16, 45, 46–7, 49, 56–7, 59.
73. Stephen Marshall, *Reformation and Desolation* (1642), 45, 48.
74. Edmund Calamy, *God's Free Mercy to England* (1642), 6, 7, 17, 18.
75. *A Warning Peece Shot Off from Ireland to England* (1642), 4, 5, 7.
76. *CJ*, II, 303–5; *LJ*, IV, 420–1.
77. *LJ*, IV, 423; *RPS*, 1641/8/128.
78. *CJ*, II, 306, 312; *LJ*, IV, 435; Bodl. Lib., MS Rawl. D. 932, fol. 8v.
79. Bodl. Lib., MS Top. Oxon. C. 378, p. 322.
80. TNA, PRO, SP 16/485, fol. 5; Bodl. Lib., MS Rawl. D. 317B, fol. 205; *King Charles His Resolution Concerning the Government of the Church of England, Being Contrary to that of Scotland* (1641), 2.
81. Wallington, *Historical Notices*, I, 275.
82. Fletcher, *Outbreak*, 160–3; Adamson, *Noble Revolt*, ch. 15; Sharpe, *Image Wars*, 238–9, 283–4; John Taylor, *Englands Comfort* (1641), 3, 5; John Taylor, *Impartialist Satire* (1652), 8; Bodl. Lib., MS Top. Oxon. C. 378, p. 326; Wallington, *Historical Notices*, I, 275–6; Anna Keay, *The Magnificent Monarch: Charles II and the Ceremonies of Power* (2008), 33–4.
83. Cust, *Charles I*, 314.

84. Taylor, *Impartialist Satyre*, 8.
85. *Parl. Hist.*, II, 946–64.
86. Clarendon, *History*, I, 417–20; *Parl. Hist.*, II, 938; *CJ*, II, 322.
87. Manning, *English People*, 52–4; Lindley, *Popular Politics*, 96–8.
88. *Parl. Hist.*, II, 943–6.
89. *CJ*, II, 344, 354; Clarendon, *History*, I, 436.
90. *The Citizens of London's Humble Petition…Presented the 11 of Decem. 1641* (1641).
91. Steele, I, no. 1903; Charles I, *By the King. A Proclamation for Obedience to the Lawes Ordained for Establishing of the True Religion* (1641).
92. TNA, PRO, SP 16/486, fol. 144.
93. *CJ*, II, 338–9; Bodl. Lib., MS Rawl. D. 932, fols. 68v–69r, 72.
94. Pearl, *London and the Outbreak*, 132–41.
95. Clarendon, *History*, I, 448.
96. TNA, PRO, SP 16/486, fol. 227; Wallington, *Historical Notices*, I, 280–2; *The Scots Loyaltie* (1641); NLI, MS 12,813/3, fols. 595–6; Manning, *English People*, 74–87; Lindley, *Popular Politics*, 103–15; Cressy, *England on Edge*, 388–91; Basil Morgan, 'Lunsford, Sir Thomas (*b.* c.1610, *d.* in or before 1656)', *ODNB*.
97. *LJ*, IV, 493–4; Clarendon, *History*, I, 452.
98. *CJ*, II, 362–4; *LJ*, IV, 496–9; TNA, PRO, SP 16/486, fol. 227v.
99. *LJ*, IV, 486; *CJ*, II, 353.
100. Charles I, *By the King. Whereas Divers Lewd and Wicked Persons Have of Late Risen in Rebellion in…Ireland* (1641[/2]); Steele, I, no. 1915.
101. *CJ*, II, 370; Clarendon, *History*, I, 485, 508; NLI, MS 12,813/3, fol. 597; Lindley, *Popular Politics*, 117–26; Manning, *English People*, 95–8; Cressy, *England on Edge*, 392–5.
102. *LJ*, IV, 558, 564; Russell, *FBM*, 470–1.
103. Cust, *Charles I*, 333–4; Russell, *FBM*, 474–7; William J. Bulman, 'The Practice of Politics: The English Civil War and the "Resolution" of Henrietta Maria and Charles I', *P&P*, 206 (2010), esp. 56–8.
104. *LJ*, IV 587–9; *CJ*, II, 459–60.
105. *LJ*, IV, 625–7, 646; James S. Hart, 'Images of Parliament as Great Council', in Braddick and Smith, eds, *Experience of Revolution*, 87–9; Michael Mendle, 'The Great Council of Parliament and the First Ordinances: The Constitutional Theory of the Civil War', *JBS*, 31 (1992), 133–62.
106. Russell, *FBM*, 503–5; Cust, *Charles I*, 341.
107. *Nineteen Propositions Made by Both Houses of Parliament* (1642).

CHAPTER 15. THE RISE OF ROYALISM

1. Henry Parker, *Observations upon Some of His Majesties Late Answers and Expresses* (1642), 38, 41.
2. Morrill, *Nature of the English Revolution*, chs 3, 4; Russell, *Causes*, ch. 6.
3. Judith Maltby, *Prayer Book and People in Elizabethan and Early Stuart England* (Cambridge, 1998), 108, 238.
4. BL, Add. MS 11,045, fol. 135.
5. *LJ*, IV, 142.
6. Peter Lake, 'Puritans, Popularity and Petitions: Local Politics in National Context, Cheshire, 1641', in Cogswell, Cust, and Lake, eds, *Politics, Religion and Popularity*, 282.

7. Eales, *Puritans and Roundheads*, 130. See pp. 423, 451–2.
8. Maltby, *Prayer Book and People*, App. 1, pp. 238–47.
9. Thomas Aston, *A Collection of Sundry Petitions* (1642), 2.
10. Aston, *Collection*, 10.
11. Anthony Milton, 'Anglicanism and Royalism in the 1640s', in Adamson, ed., *English Civil War*, 68.
12. Aston, *Collection*, 3.
13. Aston, *Collection*, 26.
14. Aston, *Collection*, 12.
15. Aston, *Collection*, 14.
16. Aston, *Collection*, 2–3.
17. Aston, *Collection*, 18, 19, 20.
18. Aston, *Collection*, 5.
19. Fletcher, *Outbreak*, 289.
20. Lake, 'Puritans, Popularity, and Petitions'; Fletcher, *Outbreak*, 289; Thomas Aston, *A Remonstrance against Presbitery* (1641), sigs a–a2v, **–**2.
21. *Journal of Sir Simonds D'Ewes*, ed. Coates, 290.
22. Walter, 'Confessional Politics'; Walter, *Understanding Popular Violence*, 126–7.
23. Lake, 'Puritans, Popularity, and Petitions'.
24. Fletcher, *Outbreak*, 290; Maltby, *Prayer Book and People*, 152–3.
25. Aston, *Remonstrance*, sig. Bv.
26. Bernard Capp, *The World of John Taylor the Water Poet, 1578–1653* (Oxford, 1994), esp. 63, 143–6, 163–70.
27. For a valuable survey, see Cressy, *England on Edge*, ch. 10.
28. John Taylor, *The Brownists Synagogues* (1641), 1. Also in *The Brothers of the Separation* (1641), sig. A2.
29. [John Taylor], *The Brownists Conventicle* (1641), 2.
30. See, for example, Richard Carter, *The Schismatick Stigmatized* (1641).
31. John Taylor, *Religions Enemies* (1641).
32. John Taylor, *A Swarme of Sectaries* (1641), subtitle; John Harris, *The Puritanes Impuritie* [1641], 4; Carter, *Schismatick Stigmatized*, 7, 14.
33. [John Taylor], *The Brownists Synagogue* (1641), 2.
34. Thomas Cheshire, *A True Copy of that Sermon which was Preached at S. Pauls the Tenth of October Last* (1642), 13–14.
35. Bodl. Lib., MS Ashmole 36, 37, fol. 81r–v.
36. Harris, *True Relation of a Company of Brownists*, sig. A2.
37. John Taylor, *Mad Fashions* (1642), sigs A3v–A4.
38. [John Taylor], *The Discovery of a Swarme of Seperatists*, sig. A3.
39. [Peacham], *Square-Caps Turned into Round-Heads* (1642). This theme is developed further in Hillary Taylor, '"An Epidemicall Disease...Raigneth over the Whole Land": Separatist Disorder, Patriotism and the Early Royalist Press, 1640–42', unpub. Brown University honors thesis (2009).
40. [John Taylor], *Tom Nash His Ghost* (1642), 3.
41. Parker, *Discourse Concerning Puritans*, 55.
42. Underdown, *Fire from Heaven*, 194.
43. See, for example, [John Taylor], *The Divisions of the Church of England* (1642), frontispiece.
44. John Harris, *Puritanes Impuritie*, 2.

45. Harris, 'Moral Panics and Anti-Puritanism'. See also pp. 111–12.
46. John Taylor, *Differing Worships* (1640), 13, 17, 18.
47. *The Resolution of the Round-Heads* (1641), sigs A1v–A2v.
48. Harris, *Puritanes Impuritie*, 4, 5.
49. See pp. 96, 101, 103, 392–3.
50. G. E. Aylmer, 'Collective Mentalities in Mid-Seventeenth-Century England: II. Royalist Attitudes', *TRHS*, 5th ser., 37 (1987), 12–13.
51. *A Discovery of 29 Sects Here in London* (1641); [Taylor], *Divisions of the Church of England*.
52. [John Taylor], *The Anatomy of the Separatists* (1642), 1–2. Cf. [Taylor], *Brownists Conventicle*, 3.
53. Taylor, *Mad Fashions*, sig. A4; [John Taylor], *The Hellish Parliament* (1641), 5.
54. Aston, *Remonstrance*, sig. G2v.
55. Maltby, *Prayer Book and People*, 153.
56. [Taylor], *Anatomy*, 4.
57. Cheshire, *True Copy*, 12.
58. Taylor, *Differing Worships*, 5.
59. Cheshire, *True Copy*, 13.
60. John Locke, *A Strange and Lamentable Accident* (1642), sig. A3.
61. *A Puritane Set Forth in his Lively Colours* (1642), 4.
62. *Wonderfull Newes: Or, A True Relation of a Churchwarden in the Town of Toscester* (1642), sigs A2–A3.
63. Richard Carter, *The Schistmatick Stigmatized* (1641), 3.
64. Taylor, *Religions Enemies*, 6.
65. [John Taylor], *The Hellish Parliament, Being a Counter-Parliament to this in England* (1641), 2–3.
66. Aston's tract is discussed in Maltby, *Prayer Book and People*, 156–70 and Charles W. Prior, *A Confusion of Tongues: Britain's Wars of Reformation, 1625–42* (Oxford, 2012), ch. 7, though my emphasis differs from both.
67. Aston, *Remonstrance*, sig. A2.
68. Aston, *Remonstrance*, sig. *v. His condemnation of resistance theory is mainly in Sections 10 and 11.
69. Aston, *Remonstrance*, sig. F3v.
70. Aston, *Remonstrance*, sig. G.
71. Aston, *Remonstrance*, sig. *v.
72. Aston, *Remonstrance*, sig. B3v.
73. Aston, *Remonstrance*, sigs Gv, L4.
74. Aston, *Remonstrance*, sigs E3r–v.
75. Aston, *Remonstrance*, sig. B4.
76. Aston, *Remonstrance*, sigs I4v–K.
77. Aston, *Remonstrance*, sigs K2r–v.
78. Aston, *Remonstrance*, sigs K4r–L2v.
79. Thomas Warmstry, *Pax Vobis* (1641), 17, 21, 23, 29.
80. TNA, PRO, SP 16/479, fol. 149; TNA, PRO, SP 16/483, fol. 215; HMC, *Salisbury*, XXIV, 277; Cressy, *England on Edge*, 338–41.
81. CUL, Mm. I. 45, 36; *A Damnable Treason by a Contagious Plaster of a Plague Sore* (1641), sig. A3.
82. Charles I, *His Majesties Declaration to All His Loving Subjects. Of the 12 of August 1642* (York and Oxford, 1642), 38.

83. Fletcher, *Outbreak*, 296; Laurence Hanson, 'The King's Printer at York and Shrewsbury 1642–3', *The Library*, 4th ser., 23 (1943), 129–31.
84. Charles I, *His Majesties Answer to the Petition which accompanied the Declaration of the House of Commons: Presented to Him at Hampton-Court, the First of December* (1641); *CJ*, II, 354.
85. Clarendon, *History*, I, 493–6; B. H. G. Wormald, *Clarendon: Politics, History and Religion, 1640–1660* (Cambridge, 1951), 30–42; Joan E. Hartman, 'Restyling the King: Clarendon Writes Charles I', in James Holstun, ed., *Pamphlet Wars* (1992), 45–59.
86. Charles I, *His Majesties Declaration, To all His Loving Subjects: Published with the Advice of His Privie Councell* (1641).
87. *LJ*, IV, 647.
88. Smith, *Constitutional Royalism*, 90–1; Michael Mendle, *Dangerous Positions* (University, AL, 1985), ch. 8.
89. Charles I, *His Majesties Answer to the Nineteen Propositions of both House of Parliament* (1642).
90. *The Life of Edward, Earl of Clarendon* (2 vols, Oxford, 1760), I, 102–3.
91. John Strickland, *The Kings Entertainment at Yorke* (1642); *A Letter Written by Master Symon Rodes* (1642). Cf. Sir Nathaniel Rigby, *The Kings Noble Entertainment at York* (1642), which claims the speech was given by the Lord Mayor. All three carry different versions of the speech.
92. Fletcher, *Outbreak*, 231.
93. Braddick, *God's Fury*, 212; Cust, *Charles I*, 344; Holmes, *Seventeenth-Century Lincolnshire*, 145–57.
94. Cust, *Charles I*, 352.
95. *A Declaration, Or Resolution of the Countie of Hereford* (1642).
96. For the medieval roots of this doctrine, see Ernst Kantorowitz, *The King's Two Bodies* (Princeton, 1957).
97. *A Declaration of the Lords and Commons...In Answer to the King's Declaration Concerning Hull. Die Mercurii, 25 Maii 1642* (1642), 2, 4–5, 7, 11, 15, 16, 17, 18, 20.
98. *LJ*, V, 112–13; Hart, 'Images of Parliament as Great Council', 89–91.
99. Michael Mendle, 'Parker, Henry (1604–1652)', *ODNB*. See also Mendle, *Dangerous Positions*; Quentin Skinner, 'Classical Liberty and the Coming of the English Civil War', in Martin Van Gelderen and Quentin Skinner, eds, *Republicanism: A Shared European Heritage*, Vol. 2: *The Values of Republicanism in Early Modern Europe* (Cambridge, 2002), 21–4; Quentin Skinner 'Rethinking Political Liberty', *History Workshop Journal*, 61 (2006), 156–70; Michael Mendle, *Henry Parker and the English Civil War* (Cambridge, 1995), ch. 4.
100. Henry Parker, *Observations upon Some of His Majesties Late Answers and Expresses* (1642), 1, 2, 3, 4, 5.
101. Parker, *Observations upon Some of His Majesties Late Answers and Expresses* (1642), 5, 8, 15, 18, 19.
102. Parker, *Observations*, 19, 20, 21, 22.
103. Parker, *Observations*, 25, 29, 33, 45.
104. Parker, *Observations*, 32, 34, 36.
105. Parker, *Observations*, 39, 40, 41, 42, 44.
106. Russell, *FBM*, 478–87.

107. Charles I, *His Majesties Declaration...12 of August 1642*, 83–4.
108. Charles I, *His Majesties Declaration...12 of August 1642*, 3, 6, 8, 9–10, 13.
109. Charles I, *His Majesties Declaration...12 of August 1642*, 24, 33, 76.
110. Charles I, *His Majesties Declaration...12 of August 1642*, 2, 77, 80, 83, 88–9.

CONCLUSION

1. Bodl. Lib., MS Top. Oxon. C. 378, 351.
2. Bodl. Lib., MS Bankes 52, fol. 61.
3. *Richard Baxter: A Holy Commonwealth*, ed. William Lamont (Cambridge, 1994), 211.
4. Charles I, *Proclamation... Requiring the Aid and Assistance of all His Subjects on the North-side Trent.*
5. Morrill, *Revolt of the Provinces.*
6. Underdown, *Revel, Riot and Rebellion.*
7. John Morrill, *Nature of the English Revolution*, ch. 11.
8. Andy Wood, 'Beyond Post-Revisionism? The Civil War Allegiances of the Miners of the Derbyshire Peak District', *HJ*, 40 (1997), 23–40; Walter, *Understanding Popular Violence.*
9. Michael Braddick, 'Mobilisation, Anxiety and Creativity in England during the 1640s', in John Morrow and John Scott, eds, *Liberty, Authority, Formality: Political Ideas and Culture, 1600–1900* (Exeter, 2008), 175–98.
10. John Morrill, 'The Stuarts (1603–1688)', in Kenneth O. Morgan, ed., *The Oxford History of Britain* (Oxford, 1988), 350.
11. This seems to be the view of Mark A. Kishlansky, 'A Lesson in Loyalty: Charles I and the Short Parliament', in Jason McElligott and David Smith, eds, *Royalists and Royalism during the English Civil War* (Cambridge, 2007), 16-42, who concludes (p. 42): 'Against such men, Charles I never had a chance.'
12. Lawrence Stone, *The Causes of the English Revolution, 1529–1642* (1972); Christopher Hill, *The English Revolution 1640* (1940).
13. David A. Scott, *Politics and War in the Three Kingdoms, 1637–49* (Basingstoke, 2004), 22; Russell, *Causes.*
14. Ethan H. Shagan, 'Constructing Discord: Ideology, Propaganda, and English Responses to the Irish Rebellion of 1641', *JBS*, 36 (1997), 1–34.
15. Kishlansky, 'Case of Mistaken Identity'.
16. Newton, *Making of the Jacobean Regime*, 146; Fincham and Lake, 'Ecclesiastical Policy', 208; Ralph Houlbrooke, 'James's Reputation, 1625–2005', in Ralph Houlbrooke, ed., *James VI and I* (Aldershot, 2006), 169–90.
17. See pp. 167, 214–17.
18. Russell, *James VI and I and his English Parliaments*, 177.
19. Russell, *Causes*, ch. 8.
20. Morrill, *Revolt of the Provinces*, 13.
21. Charles W. A. Prior and Glenn Burgess, eds, *England's Wars of Religion, Revisited* (Farnham, 2011).

GUIDE TO FURTHER READING

The historiography on the early Stuarts and the origins of the Civil War is vast and complex. For the range of secondary literature I have drawn on for this study, the reader is referred to the notes. What is offered here is a brief guide to some of the more important general books and edited volumes that might serve as a useful introduction to the period.

Authors have been debating what caused the English Civil War ever since it happened. A useful entrée into this literature is R. C. Richardson, *The Debate on the English Revolution* (Manchester, 1977, 3rd edn, 1998). There exist a number of excellent modern surveys, either covering the early Stuart period or the seventeenth century as a whole, including: Michael Braddick, *God's Fury, England's Fire: A New History of the English Civil Wars* (2008); Barry Coward, *The Stuart Age: England, 1603–1714* (4th edn, Harlow, 2012); Ann Hughes, *The Causes of the English Civil War* (2nd edn, Basingstoke, 1998); Derek Hirst, *England in Conflict, 1603–1660: Kingdom, Community, Commonwealth* (1999); Mark A. Kishlansky, *A Monarchy Transformed: Britain 1603–1714* (1996); Roger Lockyer, *The Early Stuarts: A Political History of England, 1603–1642* (1999); Conrad Russell, *The Causes of the English Civil War* (Oxford, 1990); David L. Smith, *A History of the Modern British Isles, 1603–1707: The Double Crown* (Oxford, 1998); Austin Woolrych, *Britain in Revolution, 1625–1660* (Oxford, 2002). Important collections of essays addressing some of the larger interpretive issues surrounding early Stuart kingship and the origins of the Civil War are Richard Cust and Ann Hughes, eds, *Conflict in Early Stuart England: Studies in Religion and Politics 1603–1642* (1989); Thomas Cogswell, Richard Cust, and Peter Lake, eds, *Politics, Religion and Popularity in Early Stuart Britain: Essays in Honour of Conrad Russell* (Cambridge, 2002); John Morrill, *The Nature of the English Revolution; Essays* (1993); Conrad Russell, *Unrevolutionary England 1603–1642* (1990); Linda Levy Peck, ed., *The Mental World of the Jacobean Court* (Cambridge, 1991).

The best general studies of the reign of James VI and I are Pauline Croft, *King James* (Basingstoke, 2003) and Roger Lockyer, *James VI and I* (1998). Also important are Diana Newton, *The Making of the Jacobean Regime: James VI and I and the Government of England, 1603–1605* (Woodbridge, 2005); Michael B. Young, *James VI and I and the History of Homosexuality* (Basingstoke, 2000); Leeds Barroll, *Anna of Denmark, Queen of England: A Cultural Biography* (Philadelphia, 2001); Alastair Bellany, *The Politics of Court Scandal in Early Modern England: News Culture and the Overbury Affair, 1603–1660* (Cambridge, 2002); and Thomas Cogswell, *The Blessed Revolution: English Politics and the Coming of War, 1621–1624* (Cambridge, 1989). For Jacobean and early Caroline parliaments, see Conrad Russell, *King James VI and I and his English Parliaments* (Oxford, 2011), *The Addled Parliament of 1614: The Limits of Revision* (Reading, 1992), and *Parliaments and English Politics, 1621–1629* (Oxford, 1979); Chris R. Kyle, *Theater of State: Parliament and Political Culture in Early Stuart England* (Stanford, 2012). For elections and electioneering see Derek Hirst, *The Representative of the People? Voters and Voting in England under the Early Stuarts* (Cambridge, 1975) and Mark A. Kishlansky, *Parliamentary Selection: Social and Political Choice in Early Modern England* (Cambridge, 1986). For Charles I's reign, see: Charles Carlton, *Charles I: The Personal Monarch* (2nd edn, 1995); Richard Cust, *Charles I: A Political Life* (Harlow, 2007); Conrad Russell, *The Fall of the British Monarchies, 1637–1642* (Oxford, 1991); Kevin Sharpe, *The Personal Rule of Charles I* (1992). Sharpe has also provided a fascinating study of how the first two Stuarts (and the succeeding republican regimes) sought to represent themselves to the public: *Image Wars: Promoting Kings and Commonwealths in England, 1603–1660* (2010). Important studies of the crisis years leading up to the outbreak of civil war in 1642 are: John Adamson, *The Noble Revolt: The Overthrow of Charles I* (2007); David Cressy, *England on Edge: Crisis and Revolution 1640–1642* (Oxford, 2006); Anthony Fletcher, *The Outbreak of the English Civil War* (1981).

For political ideology see: Alan Cromartie, *The Constitutionalist Revolution: An Essay on the History of England, 1450–1642* (Cambridge, 2006); Johann P. Sommerville, *Politics and Ideology in England, 1603–1640* (1986; 2nd edn 1999 as *Royalists and Patriots: Politics and Ideology in England, 1603–1640*); Glenn Burgess, *The Politics of the Ancient Constitution: An Introduction to English Political Thought, 1603–1642* (Basingstoke, 1992) and *Absolute Monarchy and the Stuart Constitution* (1996). The issue of press censorship is excellently treated by Cyndia S. Clegg, *Press Censorship in Jacobean England* (Cambridge, 2001) and *Press Censorship in Caroline England* (Cambridge, 2008). For religion and the Church, see in particular: Julian Davies, *The Caroline Captivity of the Church: Charles I and the Remoulding of Anglicanism, 1625–1641* (Oxford, 1992); Kenneth Fincham, *Prelate as Pastor: The Episcopate of James I* (Oxford, 1990); Kenneth Fincham, ed., *The Early Stuart Church, 1603–1642* (Basingstoke, 1993); Lori Anne Ferrell, *Government by Polemic: James I, the King's Preachers, and the Rhetorics of Conformity, 1603–1625* (Stanford, 1998); Kenneth Fincham and Nicholas Tyacke, *Altars Restored: The Changing Face of English Religious Worship, 1547–c.1700* (Oxford, 2007); Christopher Haigh, *The Plain Man's Pathways to Heaven: Kinds of Christianity in Post-Reformation England, 1570–1640* (Oxford, 2007); Anthony Milton, *Catholic and Reformed: The Roman and Protestant Churches in English Protestant Thought, 1600–1640* (Cambridge, 1995) and *Laudian and Royalist Polemic in Seventeenth-Century England: The Career and Writings of Peter Heylyn* (Manchester, 2007); Charles Prior, *Defining the Jacobean Church: The Politics of Religious Controversy, 1603–1625* (Cambridge, 2005) and *A Confusion of Tongues: Britain's Wars of Reformation, 1625–1642* (Oxford, 2012). Much of the best work on popular politics has been in the form of articles and essays, but important books include: Brian Manning, *The English People and the English Revolution* (2nd edn, 1991); David Underdown, *Revel, Riot and Rebellion: Popular Politics and Culture in England 1603–1660* (Oxford, 1985) and *Fire from Heaven: The Life of an English Town in the Seventeenth Century* (1992); John Walter, *Understanding Popular Violence in the English Revolution: The Colchester Plunderers* (Cambridge, 1999).

James's and Charles's Scottish rule can be traced through a trilogy of works by Maurice Lee: *Government by Pen: Scotland under James VI and I* (Urbana, 1980), *Great Britain's Solomon: James VI and I in his Three Kingdoms* (Urbana, 1990), and *The Road to Revolution: Scotland under Charles I, 1625–37* (Urbana, 1985). For religious disputes in Scotland, see in particular Alan R. MacDonald, *The Jacobean Kirk, 1567–1625* (Aldershot, 1998); Allan I. Macinnes, *Charles I and the Making of the Covenanting Movement, 1625–1641* (Edinburgh, 1991); David Stevenson, *The Covenanters: The National Covenant and Scotland* (Edinburgh, 1988). For Ireland, important studies are: Nicholas Canny, *Making Ireland British, 1580–1650* (Oxford,

2001); Sean J. Connolly, *Contested Island: Ireland 1640–1630* (Oxford, 2007) and *Divided Kingdom: Ireland, 1630–1800* (Oxford, 2010); Joseph Cope, *England and the 1641 Irish Rebellion* (Woodbridge, 2009); Alan Ford, *James Ussher: Theology, History, and Politics in Early-Modern Ireland and England* (Oxford, 2007); Raymond Gillespie, *Seventeenth-Century Ireland* (Dublin, 2006); John McCafferty, *The Reconstruction of the Church of Ireland: Bishop Bramhall and the Laudian Reforms, 1633–1641* (Cambridge, 2007); T. W. Moody, F. X. Martin, and F. J. Byrne, eds, *A New History of Ireland*. III:*Early Modern Ireland 1534–1691* (3rd impression, 1991); Jane Ohlmeyer, *Making Ireland English: The Irish Aristocracy in the Seventeenth Century* (2012); Michael Perceval-Maxwell, *The Outbreak of the Irish Rebellion of 1641* (Montreal, 1994).

PICTURE ACKNOWLEDGEMENTS

INDEX

Note: James VI and I is referred to as such in his main entry in the index. Elsewhere in the index he is referred to as either James VI or James I depending on the context.